WITHDRAWN

DEFINING DOCUMENTS
IN AMERICAN HISTORY

The American Economy

DEFINING DOCUMENTS
IN AMERICAN HISTORY

The American Economy

Volume 1

Editor
Michael Shally-Jensen, PhD

SALEM PRESS
A Division of EBSCO Information Services, Inc.
Ipswich, Massachusetts

GREY HOUSE PUBLISHING

Cover: (Photo): iStock and Wikimedia Commons

Copyright © 2021 by EBSCO Information Services, Inc., and Grey House Publishing, Inc.

Defining Documents in American History: The American Economy, published by Grey House Publishing, Inc., Amenia, NY, under exclusive license from EBSCO Information Services, Inc.

All rights reserved. No part of this work may be used or reproduced in any manner whatsoever or transmitted in any form or by any means, electronic or mechanical, including photocopy, recording, or any information storage and retrieval system, without written permission from the copyright owner. For information, contact Grey House Publishing/Salem Press, 4919 Route 22, PO Box 56, Amenia, NY 12501.

∞ The paper used in these volumes conforms to the American National Standard for Permanence of Paper for Printed Library Materials, Z39.48 1992 (R2009).

Publisher's Cataloging-In-Publication Data
(Prepared by The Donohue Group, Inc.)

Names: Shally-Jensen, Michael, editor.
Title: The American economy / editor, Michael Shally-Jensen, PhD.
Other Titles: Defining documents in American history (Salem Press)
Description: Ipswich, Massachusetts : Salem Press, a division of EBSCO Information Services ; Amenia, NY : Grey House Publishing, [2021] | Includes bibliographical references and index.
Identifiers: ISBN 9781642657562 (set) | ISBN 9781642657579 (v. 1) | ISBN 9781642657586 (v. 2) | ISBN 9781642657593 (ebook)
Subjects: LCSH: United States--Economic conditions--History--Sources. | United States--Economic policy--History--Sources. | United States--Politics and government--History--Sources. | Social change--Economic aspects--United States--Sources. | Financial crises--United States--History--Sources. | Business cycles--United States--History--Sources.
Classification: LCC HC103 .A44 2021 (print) | LCC HC103 (ebook) | DDC 330.973--dc23

FIRST PRINTING
PRINTED IN THE UNITED STATES OF AMERICA

Table of Contents
Volume 1

Publisher's Note ix
Editor's Introduction xi
Contributors xvii

COMMERCE & CONTROVERSY IN EARLIER TIMES

"Advice to a Young Tradesman" 3
Adam Smith, from *The Theory of Moral Sentiments* 9
Letter from Robert Morris to Alexander Martin 19
Federalist No. 35 (Concerning the General Power of Taxation) 41
Patent Act of 1790 51
Thomas Jefferson on the Constitutionality of a National Bank 57
Alexander Hamilton on the Constitutionality of a National Bank 67
The Whiskey Tax of 1791 and George Washington's Proclamation Regarding the Whiskey Rebellion . . . 81
McCulloch v. Maryland 93
Henry Clay's Speech on American Industry 105
Gibbons v. Ogden 112
Andrew Jackson's Bank Veto Message 123
Charles River Bridge v. Warren Bridge 129
The Discovery of Gold in California 137
"Cotton Is King" 149
Treaty between the United States and Great Britain for the Suppression of the Slave Trade 161
"The Money Power" 175

BOOMS & BUSTS IN A GROWING ECONOMY

Documents Relating to Black Friday, 1869 181
Observations Regarding the Transcontinental Railroad 188
Cornelius Vanderbilt Cartoon, Map, and Illustration 195
Bell Telephone Patent 202
From *Progress and Poverty* 213
Sharecropping Contract 223
Dawes Severalty Act 228

Andrew Carnegie: "The Gospel of Wealth" 239
Eugene Debs: "What Can We Do for Working People?" 247
Sherman Antitrust Act 253
"Wall Street Owns the Country" 258
Populist Party Platform 262
President Grover Cleveland on Repeal of the Sherman Silver Purchase Act 269
"Political Causes of the Business Depression" 275
"The Absurd Effort to Make the World Over" 288
"Cross of Gold" Speech 295
From *The Theory of the Leisure Class* 305
Theodore Roosevelt on Corporate Trusts 317
Eugene V. Debs: "How I Became a Socialist" 330
Robert La Follette on Amending the National Banking Laws 337
John D. Rockefeller on Standard Oil 345
Remarks on Politics and Business 359
Federal Reserve Act 365
Sixteenth Amendment to the U.S. Constitution 377
Clayton Act 383
A Survey of American War Readiness 399
From *My Life and Work*, by Henry Ford 411

Volume 2

CRASH, BURN AND RECOVERY IN THE GREAT DEPRESSION

President Hoover Responds to the Stock Market Crash 419
President Roosevelt: Fireside Chat on "The Forgotten Man" 425
FDR on Government's Role in the Economy 431
President Roosevelt: Fireside Chat Outlining the New Deal 444
John Maynard Keynes: An Open Letter to President Roosevelt 453
"Share Our Wealth" Address 462
Letter-Report Concerning the Tennessee Valley 469
FDR on Social Security 477

Schechter Poultry Corporation v. United States 485
President Roosevelt: Fireside Chat on the Current Recession 495

Mid-Century Modern

Lend-Lease Act 511
From *Capitalism, Socialism and Democracy* 519
Letter to Robert Oppenheimer regarding a "Special Laboratory" in New Mexico 523
From *The Fountainhead* 531
From *The Road to Serfdom* 539
Youngstown Sheet & Tube Co. v. Sawyer 547
What's Good for General Motors. 554
Eisenhower Message to Congress Regarding a National Highway Program 559
Eisenhower on Science in National Security 567
National Aeronautics and Space Act of 1958 579
Patent Application for "Miniaturized Electronic Circuits" 601
JFK: "We Choose to Go to the Moon" 607
Proposal for a Nationwide War on the Sources of Poverty 615
IBM System 360 Announcement 623

Business and Economics in Recent Decades

"The Social Responsibility of Business Is to Increase Its Profits" 633
The "Powell Memo": Attack on the Free Enterprise System 645
Gerald R. Ford's State of the Union Address, 1975 663
Bill Gates' Letter to Hobbyists 677
Jimmy Carter's Second State of the Union Address 683
The Laffer Curve 691
Ronald Reagan on the Strategic Defense Initiative 696
"Greed Is Good" 703
Lost American Jobs Tied to Unfair French Competition 708
North American Free Trade Agreement 719
Netscape Network Navigator Web Browser Launch 727
Interview with Former Fed Chairman Paul Volcker 735
Sarbanes-Oxley Act 749

Paula Dobriansky: "On Working Together to Build Prosperity" 756
Apple Announces the iPhone 765
Lehman Brothers—Announcement of Bankruptcy 775
Foreclosure in the Nation's Capital: How Unfair and Reckless Lending Undermines Homeownership. . 781
Dodd-Frank Wall Street Reform and Consumer Protection Act—A Synopsis 789
From *Big Business: A Love Letter to an American Anti-Hero* 795
Congressional Leaders on a Second COVID-19 Relief Package 805
New Jersey Adopts "Millionaire's Tax" 819

Appendixes

Chronological List 827
Web Resources 831
Bibliography 833
Index 851

Publisher's Note

Defining Documents in American History series, produced by Salem Press, offers a closer look at important historical documents by pairing primary source documents on a broad range of subjects with essays written especially for the series by expert writers, including historians, professors, researchers, and other authorities in the subject under examination. This established series includes nearly forty titles that present documents selected to illuminate specific eras in American history—including The Vietnam War, Civil Rights, and Postwar 1940s—or to explore significant themes and developments in American society—The Free Press, Business Ethics, Prison Reform, and Slavery.

This set, *Defining Documents in American History: The American Economy*, offers in-depth analysis of eighty-nine documents, including book excerpts, speeches, political debates, testimony, court rulings, legal texts, legislative acts, essays, newspaper and magazine articles, and interviews. These selections trace the role that the economy has played in the history of the United States, from the American Revolution to the effects of the COVID-19 pandemic.

The first volume focuses on commerce, controversy, booms and busts prior to the Great Depression, and includes such topics as:
- Alexander Hamilton on the Constitutionality of a National Bank
- Henry Clay's Speech on American Industry
- The Discovery of Gold in California
- Black Friday 1869
- Excerpt from *The Theory of the Leisure Class*

The second volume is dedicated to the Great Depression through business and economics in recent decades, including:
- Bill Gates' Letter to Hobbyists
- NAFTA
- Apple Announces the iPhone
- Lehman Brothers—Announcement of Bankruptcy
- New Jersey Adopts the "Millionaire's Tax"

These documents, and more, provide an overview of the history and contemporary issues surrounding the American Economy, past and present.

Essay Format

Each Historical Document is supported by a critical essay, written by historians and teachers, that includes a Summary Overview, Defining Moment, About the Author, Document Analysis, and Essential Themes. An important feature of each essay is a close reading of the primary source that develops broader themes, such as the author's rhetorical purpose, social or class position, point of view, and other relevant issues. Each essay also includes a Bibliography and Additional Reading section that provides suggestions for further readings and research.

Appendixes

- **Chronological List** arranges all documents by year.
- **Web Resources** is an annotated list of websites that offer valuable supplemental resources.
- **Bibliography** lists helpful articles and books for further study.

Contributors

Salem Press would like to extend its appreciation to all involved in the development and production of this work. The essays have been written and signed by scholars of history, humanities, and other disciplines related to the essays' topics. Without these expert contributions, a project of this nature would not be possible.

A full list of the contributors to this set with their affiliations appears following the Editor's Introduction.

Editor's Introduction

Historians generally see a nation's "economic development" as consisting of a broad set of social and political changes as well as deliberate changes in economic policy. In U.S. history, these economic changes have included the move from small-scale farming communities to larger towns and cities, the settlement of a vast "frontier" in the West, the great expansion of industrial technology, and an enormous influx of immigrant workers to satisfy labor demands in manufacturing centers. That history also includes, up until the mid-nineteenth century, the use of enslaved persons to perform work, especially in the South.

From the Founding Period through the Civil War

During the colonial period, settlers in the Americas established subsistence farms along the Atlantic seaboard and began developing maritime and shipbuilding industries. The timbers needed for ships and homes were provided by the abundant forests. Wood also was the nation's principal source of fuel; and potash from its ashes went into the making of soap and glass. Off the New England coast lay Georges Bank, which was and remains one of the world's great fishing areas. Whaling, too, was a key industry until its demise in the mid-nineteenth century.

During the first half of the 1700s, Britain's American colonies grew rapidly in population and wealth. Trade and cities flourished, and settlement expanded from the coastal regions into the so-called back-country areas with their divergent modes of living (subsistence farming, hunting/fishing, logging, etc.). Cities like Boston and New York, in the East, and Charlestown and New Orleans, in the South, served as merchant hubs in the emerging economy of North America. (New Orleans, of course, was a French and, briefly, a Spanish possession until 1804.)

British policies sometimes interfered with colonial trade with other nations. The colonists, however, largely escaped the harshest Crown regulations while enjoying the ability to export grain, lumber, livestock, and other goods. With the start of the Revolutionary War, the American economy, such as it was, suffered a serious blow because merchants lost some of the privileges and commercial connections they had had under British rule.

One of the most prominent developments of both the pre- and post-Revolutionary era was the expansion of slavery. Throughout the South, the number of slaves grew exponentially as the region's tobacco plantations became the main source of revenue. In many communities, the slave population outnumbered the white population yet its members were held in check by a brutal system of discipline and control. The plantations also created sharp distinctions in wealth among whites. Yet, with the cotton boom of the early nineteenth century, the slave system spread westward as quickly as the free labor system of the North expanded and spread into new areas. The latter system, too, was marked early on by a growing divergence in wealth between owners and workers.

In the eastern United States, the development of steamboats improved transportation, and the construction of canals permitted access by inland waterways to the Appalachians and the Ohio River. Waterfalls were exploited for the power they provided to mills and factories from the early nineteenth century on, as the Industrial Revolution took hold. Canals were followed by railroads in the opening of the continent's interior, with new cities such as Pittsburgh and Chicago coming into being, and new manufacturing and trading opportunities arising in turn. The use of coal as fuel for railroads and factories increased dramatically. And where iron and coal (in the form of coke) were brought together, as in Pittsburgh, a giant steel industry developed.

Meanwhile, practically all North American Indians east of the Mississippi, or at least those that had survived, were placed on small reservations or forced to move to the Great Plains beyond the Missouri River.

The Rocky Mountain states had long seen small groups of fur traders active in the region, some working for companies such as John Jacob Astor's American Fur Company. By the time of the discovery (1848) of gold in California, trappers and hardscrabble miners had already set the pace for boom-and-bust local economic cycles. After the gold rush of 1848–49, industrial development in the East was stimulated by the arrival of $500 million in gold and silver from the western regions. Not only California but Nevada and the Rocky Mountain region contributed to the influx, later followed (in the 1890s) by Alaska.

In the Central states, transportation lines spread and settlement increased in the nineteenth century. Copper and iron were extracted, complementing a growing agricultural economy. The mechanized plow and harvester were invented to reap the output of the enormous planting fields there.

Political and social changes affected the economy, too. The Civil War ultimately freed the slaves, but increased prices for cotton led to borrowing to hire manual laborers. A collapse of the market (owing to international competition) brought ruin to the old plantation system and led to an era of small farms and the emergence of some small industries. For decades after the war, the South lagged behind much of the rest of the nation economically.

It was often state governments, rather than the federal government, that most contributed to furthering economic growth between 1800 and 1865. In New York and Pennsylvania, for example, state-run canal systems forged the way for commercial expansion and the establishment of new population centers. With the railroads, it was a combination of state and federal land grants, subsidies, and expertise that created the basis for growth, while private investors supplied most of the capital. Equally important to these developmental schemes was government enforcement of property rights (including patented technology) through legislation and the courts, along with the rise of a banking system capable of dealing with entrepreneurs and large-scale enterprises alike. As the legal and financial foundations of economic development solidified, so too did the idea of national markets.

From the Gilded Age through the Great Depression

What is known as the Gilded Age (1870s to 1890s) was a period of rapid economic growth and exploitative capitalism, particularly around railroads, steel, and, later, oil. As industry and markets continued to expand, a mood of optimism infected the investor class, even as widespread suffering was experienced by industrial workers, southern sharecroppers, displaced American Indians, and other groups. The concept of Social Darwinism gained a foothold, causing many to accept the (false) notion of "survival of the fittest": those who stood at the top of the socioeconomic ladder, the theory went, were naturally suited to the competitive human environment, while those who languished near the bottom were lesser human specimens. Fortunately, the theory eventually faded from the scene.

During the Gilded Age ambitious and unscrupulous capitalists ranged the land looking for new opportunities. Business profits turned sharply upward and downward in erratic cycles while the nation's industrial base grew significantly. Factories and mines poured out raw materials and finished goods in service to the railroad system. In 1869 the first transcontinental line was completed, signaling a new era of connectedness. The system grew in tandem with telegraph lines, which were later (in the early twentieth century) replaced by telephone lines.

In the West, cattle ranching became a large-scale enterprise. The industry was based on the use of the open range as pastureland and of key railheads as commercial transport centers. Over time, as homesteading increased, the open range gave way to fenced pastureland and the practice of "dry farming," where soil moisture was preserved by regular plowing. Millions of farmers moved into the high plains, augmented, in 1889, by a second great wave following the Homestead Act (which granted land to settlers). At times, the grain output was so large as to cause a slump in world prices.

By the early 1900s, the national business environment was dominated by a handful of large firms that sold nationwide as well as to the world at large. With great size, however, came large and complex legal and economic issues. In 1887, Congress acted to curb some of the worst excesses of the railroad companies and to ensure that railroad rates remained "reasonable and just." Three years later Congress passed the Sherman Antitrust Act, which declared illegal certain large corporate trusts and other combinations that restrained trade. Meanwhile, the U.S. Supreme Court, favoring the idea of the free market, regularly blocked state and federal efforts to regulate private business. Left relatively unchecked in the process were the so-called robber barons, who exploited the nation's natural resources, amassed immense fortunes, and dominated American economic life.

The changes taking place around the start of the twentieth century came to be known as the Progressive Era. Government corruption in the cities was attacked; urban slums were cleaned up; health and education programs were launched; and politicians were expected, more so than in the past, to be honest brokers. Under Theodore Roosevelt, the federal government expanded the activities of regulatory agencies to oversee business enterprise: the Hepburn Act (1906) strengthened the Interstate Commerce Commission; the Forest Service ensured that lumber companies did not overexploit woodland resources; the Pure Food and Drug Act (1906) aimed to protect consumers from adulterated products and fraudulent labeling. Roosevelt also made use of the Justice Department to mount a renewed campaign against monopoly under the Sherman Antitrust Law. His successor, William Howard Taft, pulled back on most progressive reforms but allowed antitrust cases to proceed. Taft also endorsed the Sixteenth Amendment (ratified 1913), authorizing the income tax amendment. Henceforth, the federal government would not lack for revenues.

That same year Democrat Woodrow Wilson took over the presidency. Questioning corporate power, he succeeded in drawing down prevailing tariffs and establishing a Tariff Commission (1916); creating the Federal Reserve System to organize central banking and the currency; expanding antimonopoly powers under the Clayton Antitrust Act (1914); regulating labor hours in the railroad industry (Adamson Act, 1916); and creating the Federal Trade Commission body to ensure fair and open competition in business.

Among the corporate giants at the time were Standard Oil, U.S. Steel, Armour & Co., and the American Tobacco Company. Changes in technology and production, not to mention consumer demand, also led to the rise of Ford Motor Company and General Motors, as the automobile era came into being. The telephone too was taking off under Bell Telephone and its distribution branch, American Telephone & Telegraph. Some of these large firms organized research divisions designed to develop new technology. Meanwhile marketing and distribution were becoming as important as mass production; business invested heavily in advertising in print and on radio (another growing enterprise). Consumer goods became widely available nationwide for the first time. At the same time, the laboring classes relied more on pressure from their unions to secure reasonable wages and hours from employers than they did on any government regulations. Some of this changed when the nation was put on war footing following Wilson's announcement, in April 1917, that the United States would enter World War I. This led to both massive expenditures and major economic growth related to building the national war apparatus.

The 1920s were known as the Roaring Twenties because of the thriving economy of the time and the cultural dynamism it fueled. Even so, reliance on high tariffs at home (and abroad) tended to slow international trade. Domestically, there was a sizeable group of industries that performed more poorly than the rest—coal mining, textiles, shoes and boots, shipbuilding, and even railroads, as they lost traffic to a growing number of trucking operations. At the end of the decade, moreover, after a rush in security investment, the stock market crashed (October 1929), ushering in a long period of economic decline known as the Great Depression. By 1933, fourteen million Americans faced unemployment, industrial production had slid to one-third its 1929 level, and national income had dropped by more than half. Amid a mood of deep national despair, the Democratic presidential nominee, Franklin D. Roosevelt, easily won election over the incumbent Republican, Herbert Hoover, in the 1932 race. Shortly after FDR's assumption of power, his New Deal program emerged in a flurry of major legislation.

The whole of the program is too vast to summarize here. Suffice it to say that in the "First New Deal" (1933–35) the Roosevelt Administration created government bodies to help, for example, business owners and farmers to cooperate in establishing satisfactory prices instead of competing against one another—a move, nonetheless, that was later declared unconstitutional. In the "Second New Deal" (1935–38)

Roosevelt launched a great relief program called the Works Progress Administration (WPA) to get people back to work and jumpstart consumer spending. Offering to buy gold at $35 an ounce, he induced a flow of the precious metal into the nation's stock and saw its value increase by one-third by 1940. His policies succeeded in turning the economy toward recovery, and were augmented by such measures as managing the money supply; placing stock exchanges under the sights of the Securities and Exchange Commission (SEC); insuring bank deposits under the Federal Deposit Insurance Corporation (FDIC); putting labor relations in key industries under new regulations; and supplying electrical power to entire regions under such agencies as the Tennessee Valley Authority. In addition, the Social Security Act (1938) created provisions for old-age and disability pensions, unemployment insurance, and other assistance to individuals in need. The New Deal also gave citizens confidence that in a time of economic disaster the federal government could step in to ameliorate suffering. Many in the business community, however, remained adamantly opposed to government interference in commercial affairs and the economy more generally.

From the World War II through the Atomic Age

With war erupting in Europe, the U.S. military budget was increased to enable the nation to operate a two-ocean navy along with a powerful combined army and air force. Aid to Britain and later to Russia was extended through the Lend-Lease program as a means of staying the advance of Adolf Hitler and the Nazis. At Pearl Harbor, Hawaii, a Japanese air attack in December 1941 proved a defeat for the United States and brought the country into the war. Now, war mobilization was a top priority, with many industries converting to military production. For manufacturers, laborers, and farmers, the war meant a return to prosperity. Great resources combined to make the United States a military and economic powerhouse. Meanwhile, the Office of Price Administration (OPA) froze prices on hundreds of items to prevent gauging during material shortages.

By April 1945 Nazi Germany was defeated and the Americans concentrated on the war in the Pacific. A large-scale program to develop the world's first atom bomb was already underway, at Los Alamos, New Mexico, and other facilities. The effort was perhaps the first instance of "big science" in the United States, in which the government poured billions of dollars into a research and development program that was not guaranteed success. In this case it did achieve its goal: in August 1945 two cities in Japan were obliterated and, within a week, a cease-fire was agreed to, followed by a peace settlement.

In the postwar years tens of millions of Americans found themselves moving upward into a middle-class way of life. The Cold War, centered on a tense face-off between the Soviet Union and the United States (and its Western allies), served as the dark backdrop against which the United States's rise to world power and economic strength occurred. In 1949 the Soviet government conducted its first successful atom bomb test. Eight years later it launched its first orbiting satellite, Sputnik. The United States responded to these developments, spawning both the nuclear arms race and the race to explore space. Both efforts resulted in the spending of huge sums of money to retool the American economy. Industry and education benefited greatly while contributing, in turn, to an expanding economy. The National Aeronautics and Space Administration (NASA; founded 1958) in many ways embodied the spirit of this new age, fostering a healthy collaboration between public and private enterprise. The mid-twentieth century also came to be known as the age of the automobile, as the Interstate Highway System and the growth of the suburbs gave a massive boost to the auto industry (and to transportation/infrastructure generally).

In 1960 John F. Kennedy was elected president. He sought to use the presidency to advance liberal social and economic reforms even as he understood the need to satisfy his Republican opponents—by, for example, reducing taxes and maintaining a U.S. military presence in Indochina, where North and South Vietnam were at war. Kennedy worked to expand America's influence in the world, based on the country's strong economy, technological sophistication, and vibrant form of government. He instituted the largest tariff cuts in modern history. He set a goal for the space program of landing an astronaut on the moon. Ultimately, however, his accomplishments were not extensive because his time in office was cut short by his assassination in Dallas, Texas, in November 1963. His replacement, Lyndon Johnson, continued to promote reform programs, including unemployment measures, civil rights legislation, and a "war on poverty" that entailed research and remedial efforts. The latter effort did not prove particularly effective. In 1965 Johnson realized a string of legislative successes, including Medicare for the elderly and federal aid to education. Ultimately, however, he was brought down by public opposition to America's growing involvement in the Vietnam War, which was beginning to cost the nation dearly in both blood and treasure. Johnson's successor, Richard Nixon, won election (in 1968) in part by claiming that he would bring the war to a conclusion—which he did only after four more years of sustained conflict.

From the 1970s to Today

The decade of the 1970s has been viewed as a kind of transitional period between the chaos and upheavals of the 1960s, on the one hand, and the conservative revolution of the 1980s, on the other. While some of the social and political trends of the '60s continued into the '70s, the latter saw the rise of a more politically aligned corporate America in the form of a more aggressive U.S. Chamber of Commerce together with right-wing think tanks and lobbying groups such as the Heritage Foundation and the American Legislative Action Council (ALEC). The decade also saw Nixon, toward the end of his first term (1971), taking the surprising steps of taking the nation off the gold standard and imposing a temporary freeze on wages and prices. These measures were meant to address rising inflation. During Nixon's tenure the nation's increasing dependence on petroleum led to the energy crisis of the 1973, which spilled over into subsequent years. For the first time in its history, the United States was using more oil than it generated. When other oil-producing nations raised their prices, it resulted in inflation that affected every American household and business.

In connection with this, the U.S. economy experienced a general slowdown as many manufacturing jobs began to move overseas (where labor costs were lower). Such jobs were replaced by fewer ones in more technologically sophisticated industries and large numbers of service jobs, many of them low paid. By the 1980s, the country had tipped into a recession, with unemployment rising above 10 percent for the first time since the Great Depression.

A movement toward the deregulation of industry and commerce had begun as early as the presidency of Jimmy Carter (1977–81), who neither denounced it nor cultivated it. The movement took flight, however, during the administration of Ronald Reagan (1981–89). Reagan was a strong advocate of the free market and privatization. He instituted major tax cuts in order, he said, to stimulate business growth, and he worked to spin off public functions to private contractors. A number of federal agencies, such as the Civil Aeronautics Board and the Interstate Commerce Commission, were eliminated, and many industries (railroads, trucking, airlines, radio, television, electric power, and telecommunications) were significantly freed of regulation by the government. In stock trading and in the field of business mergers and acquisitions, a willingness on the part of executives to take risks formerly thought wildly imprudent became a national virtue. A kind of second Gilded Age was felt in parts of the economy, even though the federal budget deficit and the national debt soared to new heights (or rather depths) because of the effects of tax cuts paired with a major buildup of military hardware. Moreover, not all communities experienced the benefits of the new financial wizardry; communities of color and many working- and middle-class households remained more or less untouched by it. Reagan's "trickle-down" theory of economic resurgence, that is, did not play out everywhere as expected.

The emergence of the desktop computer in the 1980s and the internet and World Wide Web in the 1990s opened a new era of American economic development. The budding "information age" brought with it a combination of characteristics seen earlier, namely, the rapid growth of a new technology, a mix of large corporations and smaller firms to usher it in, and an expectation of light regulation to allow the free enterprise system to operate optimally. Following a brief recession in the early 1990s, growth accelerated as information technology (IT) helped to increase productivity.

Besides the IT boom, the other major economic news of the 1990s was the North American Free Trade Agreement (NAFTA; 1994), whereby Canada, Mexico, and the United States agreed to function as a single economic zone, somewhat in the manner of the European Union. Businesses in areas like the automobile and textile industries indeed saw a sharp increase in revenues, since they could rely on low-cost labor outside the United States and get materials more efficiently. But workers inside the United States often paid the price, seeing their jobs go abroad and long-established factories in their home towns shut down.

The 2000s, in fact, began with an economic slowdown. Newly elected president George W. Bush urged a $1.6-trillion tax cut, subsequently cut back by Congress to $1.35 trillion. The economy took another hit as a result of the terrorist attacks of September 11, 2001. The most significant growth area then became security operations and military technology, as the budget for U.S. military action in Afghanistan and Iraq ballooned. Ethical lapses and illegalities in the private sector also played a role in dousing promised business growth, with companies like Enron symbolizing corporate greed and the need to re-regulate some areas. Nevertheless, soon the economy improved.

A slowdown in early 2008 caused Bush to sign a $168-billion relief package, but a deeper disorder was already becoming apparent. In the last quarter of 2008, a near collapse of U.S. financial markets—owing to major problems in the home mortgage industry and other areas—precipitated a global financial crisis. The crisis led to widespread recession, sometimes dubbed the Great Recession of 2008–09. When President Barack Obama took over the presidency from Bush in January 2009, one of his first actions was to sign the American Recovery and Reinvestment Act (ARRA). This $787-billion stimulus bill provided tax cuts, expanded unemployment benefits, and increased government spending. Despite the stimulus, however, the U.S. economy continued in recession for most of 2009, and unemployment remained above 8 percent. Even when growth resumed in late 2009, progress was slow and erratic. By 2011, the economy was back on track, save for the unemployment rate, which hovered between 8 and 9 percent. Also, the debt remained high, necessitating some sharp negotiations with Congress. (The president could raise the debt ceiling, but only by making large spending cuts.) Obama's reelection in 2012 was helped by an uptick in economic growth.

With the election of Donald Trump in 2016, the economy remained solid initially but began to falter in some areas (e.g., agriculture) after Trump imposed tariffs on China to punish that nation for its past and present behavior in U.S. markets. Afterward, Trump was obliged to offer subsidies to American farmers. Trump also opened negotiations with Canada and Mexico to remake NAFTA. The final arrangement, called the U.S.-Mexico-Canada Agreement (USMCA; 2018), required two changes related to automobile manufacturing, namely, that a higher proportion of each new car had to be made in North America, and that 40 percent of each car be made by workers making at least $16 an hour. Little else changed.

Like many modern American Republican presidents before him, Trump also saw to it that a large tax cut was enacted during his administration. Under his 2017 tax package, corporations received some $1.25 trillion in benefits, while individual taxpayers received more modest improvements via rate changes. Throughout his presidency Trump touted the rising stock market as proof of the effectiveness of his actions. In early 2020, however, stocks began to dive as a result of the spreading COVID-19 pandemic. Trump deliberately downplayed the deadliness of the virus, even as quarantines and the shuttering of businesses had a devastating impact on the economy. Nor did the lack of action at the federal level in the area of public health inspire optimism. Eventually, the administration, working with Congress, announced a round of relief measures and a plan to aid medical research firms in developing a vaccine. Both actions were widely praised, and a vaccine was approved in late 2020. A second major relief package, however, got stalled in Congress over wrangling between Republicans and Democrats regarding the size and design of the measure. A compromise measure looked possible following the election of Joe Biden to the presidency in November 2020.

—*Michael Shally-Jensen, PhD*

Bibliography and Additional Reading

Greenspan, Alan, and Adrian Wooldridge. *Capitalism in America: A History.* New York: Penguin, 2018.

Lind, Michael. *Land of Promise: An Economic History of the United States.* New York: HarperCollins, 2012.

Lindert, Peter H., and Jeffrey G. Williamson. *Unequal Gains: American Growth and Inequality since 1700.* Princeton, NJ: Princeton University Press, 2016.

Srinivasan, Bhu. *Americana: A 400-Year History of American Capitalism.* New York: Penguin, 2018.

Contributors

Michael P. Auerbach, MA
Marblehead, Massachusetts

Amanda Beyer-Purvis, MA
University of Florida

William E. Burns, PhD
George Washington University

Steven L. Danver, PhD
Walden University

K. P. Dawes, MA
Chicago, Illinois

Amber R. Dickinson, PhD
Washburn University

Tracey DiLascio, JD
Framingham, Massachusetts

Justus Doenecke, PhD
New College of Florida

Gerald Goodwin, PhD
LeMoyne College

Bethany Groff Dorau, MA
Historic New England

Ashleigh Fata, MA
University of California, Los Angeles

Kay Tilden Frost
Washington, DC

Aaron George, PhD
Tarleton State University

G. Mehera Gerardo, PhD
Youngstown State University

Aaron James Gulyas, MA
Mott Community College

Mark S. Joy, PhD
Jamestown University

Nicole Mitchell, PhD
University of Alabama, Birmingham

Michael J. O'Neal, PhD
Independent Scholar

Jonathan Rees, PhD
University of Colorado, Pueblo

Carey M. Roberts, PhD
Liberty University

Carl Rollyson, PhD
Baruch College

Michael Shally-Jensen, PhD
Amherst, MA

Noëlle Sinclair, JD, MLS
University of Iowa Law Library

Robert Surbrug, PhD
Bay Path University

Vanessa Vaughan, MA
Chicago, IL

Anthony Vivian, PhD
University of California, Los Angeles

Donald A. Watt, PhD
Middleton, ID

Commerce & Controversy in Earlier Times

As early as the pre-Revolutionary era, General George Washington already recognized the value of good intelligence concerning one's enemies. In this section, we include a 1755 exchange of letters between Washington and a governor of Pennsylvania regarding enemy movements during the French and Indian War. In the Revolutionary War, too, Washington had a small circle of spies to monitor British movements, starting (informally) with Paul Revere, who in 1775 made his famous "midnight ride" to warn of the coming of the British. Revere participated in a kind of intelligence-gathering ring, which he remembered fondly after the war. Espionage *against* the new United States also took place, most notably by U.S. General Benedict Arnold, who in 1780 revealed military secrets to the British and forever blackened his name as a synonym for a traitor.

We also include here an examination of the Alien and Sedition Acts of 1798, which were passed in anticipation of war with revolutionary France but mostly targeted Republican opposition leaders in the United States. The laws restricted immigration and penalized American citizens for speaking or acting against the government—acts understood to be instances of sedition.

Then there is the encoded letter (1806) of American founding figure and general provocateur Aaron Burr, addressed to the scandal-prone United States. General James Wilkinson. The letter implicated Burr in a plot to occupy westerns lands to set up a state there. Arrested for treason, Burr was ultimately acquitted on the grounds that the letter was a copy and could not be taken as evidence of his plans or intentions.

Jumping ahead to the mid-nineteenth century, we look at a similarly dubious bit of global intrigue conducted by the physician and mercenary William Walker. In 1856, Walker brought a private mercenary force into Nicaragua in order to seize its government for himself. His actions were roundly condemned by supporters of U.S. president Franklin Pierce, who passed an executive order against "filibustering," as it was called at the time.

Also in the mid-nineteenth century, the American Civil War erupted. During that conflict, the Union Army benefitted from the contributions of Allan Pinkerton and his Pinkerton Detective Agency. Pinkerton personally served as a spy on behalf of the Union, and in so doing he laid the groundwork of the modern spy agency.

Similar groundbreaking work was conducted near the end of the century by the chief of the U.S. Secret Service, Elbert Wilkie, against a Spanish spy ring during the 1898 Spanish-American War.

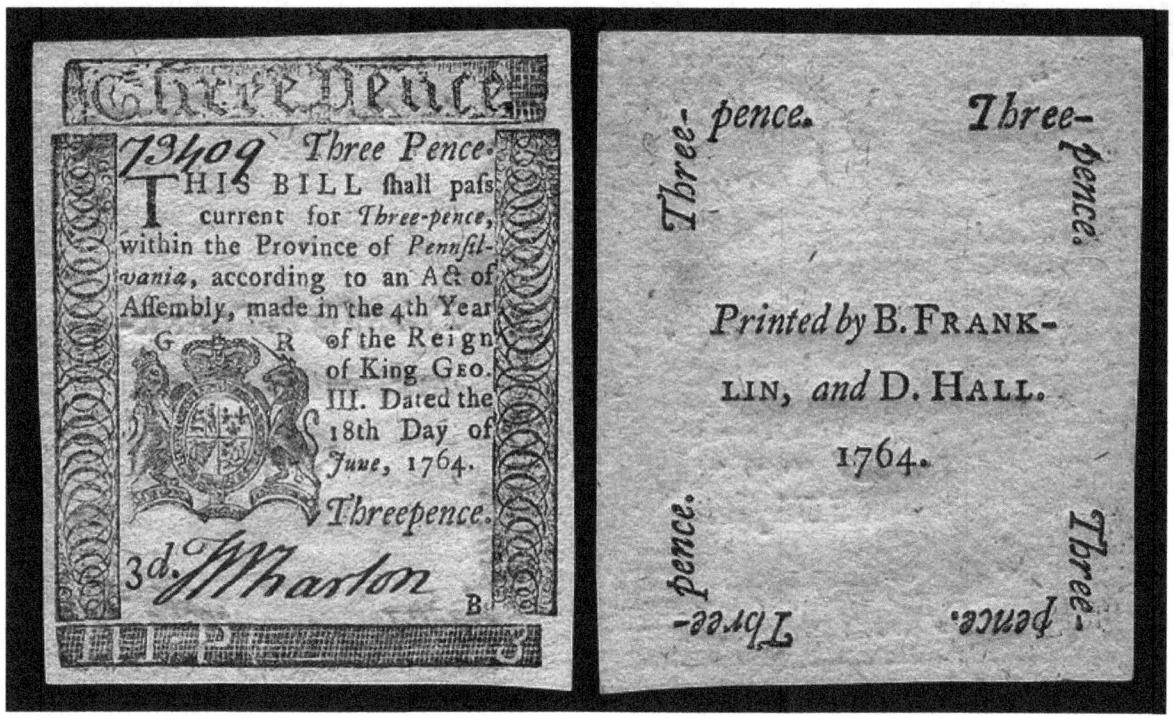

Pennsylvania colonial currency printed by Franklin in 1764.

◼ "Advice to a Young Tradesman"

Date: 1748
Author: Benjamin Franklin
Genre: essay

Summary Overview

Benjamin Franklin's 1748 essay giving "Advice to a Young Tradesman" offers us a glimpse into the financial and occupational world of Britain's American colonies in the mid-eighteenth century. Perhaps surprisingly, much of the financial wisdom Franklin conveys in this brief essay is broadly applicable to modern life (or is, at least, recognizable). In the twenty-first century, financial experts encourage business owners and consumers alike to live within their means, save for the future, and manage credit wisely. Franklin's examples of behaviors that can damage a tradesman's financial reputation are analogous to modern activities that might damage one's credit rating.

Despite these parallels, Franklin's essay shows us an America where communities are smaller—where personal reputations could be damaged and business growth shattered because the wrong person saw you in the tavern at the wrong time of day. At the same time, it helps establish a line of thought that would persist in Colonial America, and ultimately in the United States: namely, that a person's wealth and status are the direct result of individual decisions made and actions taken. Franklin's essay presents an early America where, for the independent tradesman, the possibilities are nearly limitless.

Defining Moment

This essay first appeared in 1748 as part of a book entitled *The American Instructor: or Young Man's Best Companion.* *The American Instructor* was one example of the several handbooks aimed at adolescent and young adult males that served as a guide not only to general business knowledge but also topics such as grammar, writing, mathematics, accounting, and penmanship—all useful subjects to a young man finishing his apprenticeship and beginning a career as a tradesman. This particular book was an Americanized version of *The Instructor,* compiled by George Fisher in Britain. For this American edition, publisher Benjamin Franklin replaced some chapters or essays with ones that spoke directly to issues that men would encounter in the American colonies. Franklin also added a brief discussion and historical account of the colonies as well as his own summary of advice for young men entering a trade.

"Tradesmen," in the context in which Franklin composed his advice, were artisans in a number of fields who had undergone a lengthy apprenticeship and were prepared to enter the workforce on their own. In the British American colonies, these trades ranged from carpenters to dressmakers and from printers (like Franklin had been) to tavern keepers. Thus, any advice directed at tradesmen had to be sufficiently broad as to be applicable to this wide variety of occupations.

Books such as these are one indication of the rapid growth the British colonies in America were experiencing in the mid-eighteenth century. In cities like Franklin's Philadelphia, new arrivals to the colonies and internal migrants moving from rural areas to the city for new opportunities provided plenty of customers and laborers. Franklin's reprinting of a British book demonstrates the close cultural connection between the mother country and the colonies while his Americanization demonstrates the persistent cultural differences between the two lands.

Author Biography

One of the most well-known, multifaceted figures in the history of the United States, Benjamin Franklin has long served as a model for entrepreneurial spirit and civic engagement. Born in Boston in 1706, Franklin never completed a formal education but would nonetheless enter the worlds of publishing, science, politics, and diplomacy. Franklin initially made an impact in the newspaper business; a career that began when he was fifteen years old when he worked as an apprentice for his brother James. James had founded the first independent newspaper in the colonies, the *New-England Courant*.

Benjamin eventually abandoned his apprenticeship and, as a fugitive from the law because of this, moved to Philadelphia at age 17. It was in Philadelphia that he and other young men who sought to learn and improve themselves, established a library for their benefit—this collection of books would evolve into a library that would allow members of the public to purchase membership and, after being incorporated as the Library Company of Philadelphia would be the first library in the American colonies and is an example of the way in which much of Franklin's work blended business management with public benefit.

In 1728, Franklin took charge of the *Pennsylvania Gazette* and began publishing other newspapers, religious books, and pamphlets. He attempted to build a network of newspapers that would stretch across the many British colonies but the project never achieved the success he desired. Despite not achieving these ambitious goals, Franklin published the first monthly news magazine in the Americas, the *General Magazine and Historical Chronicle for All the British Plantations in America*. Franklin also found success as an author, with his *Poor Richard's Almanack* being incredibly popular. He used his skills for promotion to generate publicity for evangelist George Whitefield during the Great Awakening. Franklin's broad experience made him an ideal advisor to young tradesmen.

HISTORICAL DOCUMENT: Benjamin Franklin's "Advice to a Young Tradesman"

Remember that Time is Money. He that can earn Ten Shillings a Day by his Labour, and goes abroad, or sits idle one half of that Day, tho' he spends but Sixpence during his Diversion or Idleness, ought not to reckon That the only Expence; he has really spent or rather thrown away Five Shillings besides.

Remember that Credit is Money. If a Man lets his Money lie in my Hands after it is due, he gives me the Interest, or so much as I can make of it during that Time. This amounts to a considerable Sum where a Man has good and large Credit, and makes good Use of it.

Remember that Money is of a prolific generating Nature. Money can beget Money, and its Offspring can beget more, and so on. Five Shillings turn'd, is *Six:* Turn'd again, 'tis Seven and Three Pence; and so on 'til it becomes an Hundred Pound. The more there is of it, the more it produces every Turning, so that the Profits rise quicker and quicker. He that kills a breeding Sow, destroys all her Offspring to the thousandth Generation. He that murders a Crown, destroys all it might have produc'd, even Scores of Pounds.

> *Remember that Time is Money*

Remember that Six Pounds a Year is but a Groat a Day. For this little Sum (which may be daily wasted either in Time or Expence unperceiv'd) a Man of Credit may on his own Security have the constant Possession and Use of an Hundred Pounds. So much in Stock briskly turn'd by an industrious Man, produces great Advantage.

Remember this Saying, *That the good Paymaster is Lord of another Man's Purse.* He that is known to pay punctually and exactly to the Time he promises, may at any Time, and on any Occasion, raise all the Money his Friends can spare. This is sometimes of great Use: Therefore never keep borrow'd Money an Hour beyond the Time you promis'd, lest a Disappointment shuts up your Friends Purse forever.

The most trifling Actions that affect a Man's Credit, are to be regarded. The Sound of your Hammer at Five in the Morning or Nine at Night, heard by a Creditor, makes him easy Six Months longer. But if he sees you at a Billiard Table, or hears your Voice in a Tavern, when you should be at Work, he sends for his Money the next Day. Finer Cloaths than he or his Wife wears, or greater Expence in any particular than he affords himself, shocks his Pride, and he duns you to humble you. Creditors are a kind of People, that have the sharpest Eyes and Ears, as well as the best Memories of any in the World.

Good-natur'd Creditors (and such one would always chuse to deal with if one could) feel Pain when they are oblig'd to ask for Money. Spare 'em that Pain, and they will love you. When you receive a Sum of Money, divide it among 'em in Proportion to your Debts. Don't be asham'd of paying a small Sum because you owe a greater. Money, more or less, is always welcome; and your Creditor had rather be at the Trouble of receiving Ten Pounds voluntarily brought him, tho' at ten different Times or Payments, than be oblig'd to go ten Times to demand it before he can receive it in a Lump. It shews, besides, that you are mindful of what you owe; it makes you appear a careful as well as an honest Man; and that still encreases your Credit.

Beware of thinking all your own that you possess, and of living accordingly. 'Tis a Mistake that many People who have Credit fall into. To prevent this, keep an exact Account for some Time of both your Expences and your Incomes. If you take the Pains at first to mention Particulars, it will have this good Effect; you will discover how wonderfully small trifling Expences mount up to large Sums, and will discern what might have been, and may for the future be saved, without occasioning any great Inconvenience.

In short, the Way to Wealth, if you desire it, is as plain as the Way to Market. It depends chiefly on two Words, Industry and Frugality; i.e. Waste neither Time nor Money, but make the best Use of both. He that gets all he can honestly, and saves all he gets (necessary Expences excepted) will certainly become Rich; If that Being who governs the World, to whom all should look for a Blessing on their honest Endeavours, doth not in his wise Providence otherwise determine.

GLOSSARY

groat: a small amount of money, usually four pence

stock: in this context, money retained in savings

trifling: seemingly small or insignificant

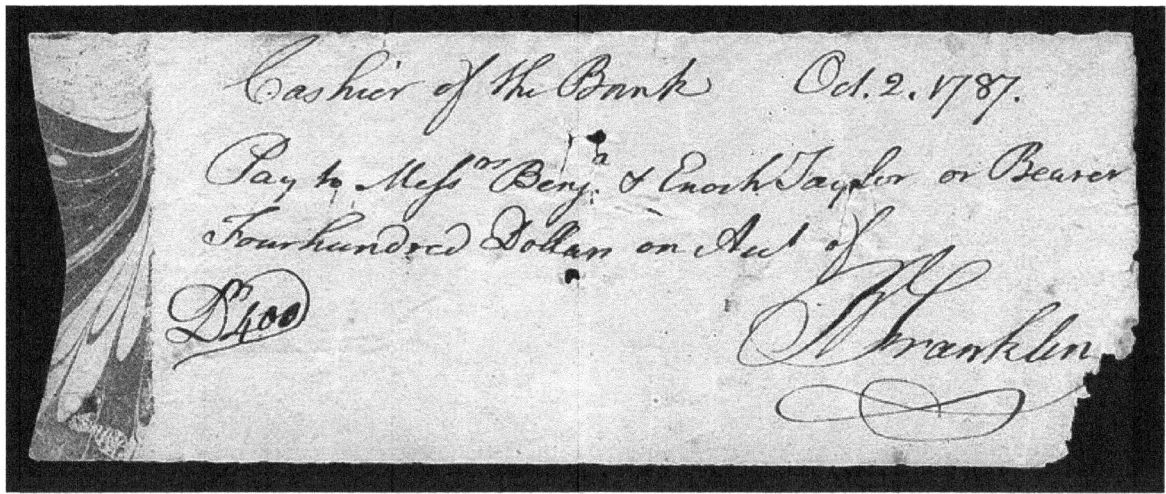
Franklin autograph check signed during his Presidency of Pennsylvania. (National Museum of History)

Document Analysis

Franklin begins his advice with the aphorism "time is money." He expands on this by specific amounts of time and money as an easily understandable object lesson—illustrating that time spent away from profitable work results in more lost money than one might expect. The second piece of advice, rhetorically, echoes the first. Time is money, but credit is money as well. Here, Franklin explains the dangers of credit and interest for the debtor and the benefits to the creditor—the nature and use of credit is a theme on which Franklin will spend a great deal of time in this essay, giving modern readers some indication of the financial arrangements into which young artisans in the American colonies would enter when they launched their careers.

Franklin moves away from the subject of credit for the next two pieces of advice. He discusses the "prolific generating Nature" of money. As he talks about the "turning" of small amounts of money into larger ones, we can understand this in terms both of interest that can be earned on money that is deposited in banks or loaned out but also the benefit that can be gained through the investments in equipment that might be made by artisans and tradesmen who were making an effort to grow their businesses. The illustration of the shortsightedness of killing a breeding sow would very likely resonate with the largely agricultural British American colonies. Next, Franklin breaks down the virtues of saving even a small amount of money on a regular basis. In his example, he points out that a groat a day will total six pounds a year. A groat was—even in 1748—an outdated amount of currency. While it originally was valued at around four pence, more generally it denotes a small amount of money. Regardless of the mathematics of Colonial currency, Franklin's larger point is that small amounts of money, managed carefully, would build to larger amounts over time; the discipline of saving would eventually pay off. With additional careful management of credit, a scrupulous saver could build a great deal of wealth over time.

From here, Franklin moves into an extensive discussion of credit, beginning with the admonition to repay borrowed money on time, if not earlier. Doing so, he explains, will make it more likely that one would be able to borrow money when necessary in the future. Paying late—or not at all—will close off avenues of borrowing. Paying borrowed money back in a timely manner is not the only behavior to follow. Franklin next discusses activities that will set a creditor's mind at ease, and behaviors that will cause concern. The wise borrower, Franklin explains, will be diligent in his work, earning money to repay his debts on time. Unwise borrowers will waste their time—engaging in leisure activities when they should be working. Franklin's examples emphasize that creditors will learn of these activities, and either be satisfied that the borrower is a good bet and that his money is safe or be suspicious that the money lent may be in jeopardy and demand early repayment. In the same way, Franklin warns that those in debt should not spend money more extravagantly than they should—particularly, not more extravagantly than the people to whom they owe money.

Essential Themes

Franklin also recommends making payments on debts on a regular basis, even if one cannot repay the entire amount. Doing so demonstrates good management of income but also mindfulness of what today we might call "debt to income ratio." Following this, Franklin concludes with some more general advice. He emphasizes the importance of living within ones' means and not becoming overly reliant on credit. He closes with a brief discussion of the need for both industry and frugality: working hard at one's trade and managing one's money carefully. Echoing his advice earlier in the essay, he reiterates the importance of careful saving as the foundation of wealth. His final sentence, which he presents almost as a caveat, is that—basically—even the most careful planning can be upset by unexpected disasters, described spiritually here as the determination of God's providence. Throughout, we see the wit and wisdom of this founding figure at work, and can appreciate why he continues to be read as a "popular author" even today.

—*Aaron James Gulyas, MA*

Bibliography and Additional Reading

Isaacson, Walter. *Benjamin Franklin: An American Life.* New York: Simon & Schuster, 2003.

Taylor, Alan. *Colonial America: A Very Short Introduction.* London and New York: Oxford University Press, 2012.

Schultz, Ronald. "The Small-Producer Tradition and the Moral Origins of Artisan Radicalism in Philadelphia 1720–1810." *Past & Present*, no. 127 (1990): 84–116.

Stott, Richard. "Artisans and Capitalist Development." *Journal of the Early Republic* 16, no. 2 (1996): 257–71.

Adam Smith, from *The Theory of Moral Sentiments*

Date: 1759
Author: Adam Smith
Genre: nonfiction book (excerpt)

Summary Overview

Adam Smith's first published book, *The Theory of Moral Sentiments*, elucidates a philosophical framework that would figure prominently in his later and more well-known work, *The Wealth of Nations*, a foundational text in classical economics. In this earlier work, Smith focuses on the origins of morality by analyzing how complex of psychological motives, including self-interest, fomented sociological connections. This was in contrast to previous writers like Bernard Mandeville and Thomas Hobbes, who had pessimistic views about benevolence and believed moral virtues derived primarily from self-interest. In sum, Smith argues that "sympathy," or the ability to identify and reflect others' emotions and consider the causes of them, produces feelings of moral approval or disapproval. A major feature in Smith's moral philosophy is the theory of the "impartial spectator," or an imagined self that humans use to consider the ramification of actions in a larger community. In this selection from the beginning of Part VI of *The Theory of Moral Sentiments*, Smith describes a particular virtue, prudence, and its relation to security (including financial). Smith travels from the individual level to the scope of the state, and ultimately asserts that the standards for assessing prudence should be analogous. That is, if a prudent man lives within his means and endeavors to live in harmony with conditions around him, so too should the leader of a state.

Defining Moment

The eighteenth century was a time of political, economic, and intellectual transformations in Scotland, the home of Adam Smith. The Acts of Union in 1707 officially made Scotland and England one political unit, but the two states had been dynastically linked since at least the seventeenth century when Queen Elizabeth made the reigning Stuarts in Scotland the heirs to her throne in England. Although the dynastic connection did not solve entirely the tumultuous relations between Scotland and England, the Glorious Revolution in 1688 threatened the tenuous political harmony. The Glorious Revolution was the bloodless overthrow of the Catholic James II, the Stuart king, and his infant son in favor of James II's Protestant son-in-law and daughter, William of Orange and Mary. For the Catholics in Scotland, the rejection of the Catholic Stuart line was intolerable.

The Jacobites were a political group that formed in reaction to the overthrow of James II and his son; adherents to the cause came from across the British Isles. In Scotland adherents primarily came from the Catholic minority in the Lowland and various Highland clans. Over time, however, the cause attracted individuals of various backgrounds who clashed with the religious and political status quo in Scotland and, after 1707, in Great Britain. Jacobite uprisings continued to flare until the disastrous Battle of Culloden in Scotland, the final Hanoverian success over the political rebels in 1745. This defeat resulted in a crackdown against all rebels and their supporters: officers were executed,

Jacobite gentry had their lands stripped and sold, and punitive measures against traditional clothing were enacted in an attempt to integrate Scotland more closely with the rest of Britain.

Nonetheless, Scotland reaped the economic benefits of union with England, even if the political situation was often precarious throughout the eighteenth century. The political travails of the seventeenth century and a devastating famine in the 1690s kept the economy of Scotland small, especially in comparison to England. Laboring under these political and environmental complications, Scotland could not hope to compete on the global stage when the dominant European economic system at the time was mercantilism. As an economic theory, mercantilism held that a country should maximize exports, minimize imports (or at least place tariffs on them), and accumulate gold in the treasury. Colonialism aided mercantilist countries greatly. England, for example, implemented policies that restricted trade between English colonies and other nations to benefit the state coffers. Scotland, without any official colonies, could not build its commercial interests in the same way. In the late 1690s, nevertheless, Scotland attempted to enter into this market by establishing a colony called "Caledonia" on the Isthmus of Panama. This colonizing attempt, named the Darien scheme after the Gulf of Darién where the colony was located, suffered from poor planning, disease, and attacks from the Spanish military. A significant portion of circulating Scottish money had backed this venture, and so the collapse of the Darien scheme financially devastated the state. This botched colonizing experiment perhaps compelled Scotland to the Acts of Union in 1707 since closer political ties with England meant closer economic ties. A shared market with England and English colonies did prove fruitful for Scotland, which could now profit officially from trade with the Americas.

Scotland also benefited from a prominent intellectual climate at the same time as the Age of Enlightenment was transforming minds across the European continent. This philosophical movement stressed reason as the source of knowledge, whereas previous thinkers had stressed theological explanations. Although Scotland may have been relatively distant in terms of geography from the continent, the country was not remote from contemporary intellectual currents. In contrast to England's two universities, Oxford and Cambridge, Scotland had four long-standing and intellectually rigorous universities that produced important thinkers like Frances Hutcheson, David Hume, and Adam Smith (St. Andrews, Aberdeen, Glasgow, and Edinburgh). In addition to these universities, there were a number of clubs promoting discussion about reason and philosophy. David Hume and Adam Smith were both members of clubs like the Political Economy Club and The Select Society. These intellectual associations, publications, and universities mutually interacted with each other and fostered dialogue about the tumultuous contemporary developments, both in Scotland and globally.

Author Biography

Adam Smith (1723–1790) was a prominent member of the Scottish Enlightenment whose writings contributed to his reputation as one of the founding fathers of the modern economics. His pioneering philosophy also earned him the moniker "Father of Capitalism." Not much is known about Smith's childhood in Kirkcaldy, Scotland, but his education at the University of Glasgow and Balliol College, Oxford would prove to be formative for his later work. Francis Hutcheson, in particular, was an influential teacher of Smith's in Glasgow: Smith's philosophy reflects Hutcheson's interest in moral sense theory. Smith would not enjoy his time at Oxford as much, and he soon returned to Glasgow with an unfavorable opinion about the quality of English instruction.

Back in Glasgow, Smith began delivering public lectures in 1748 and became a professor in his own right in 1751. During this time Smith established a friendship with another heavyweight of the Scottish Enlightenment, David Hume; this friendship would prove intellectually fruitful for both men. It was in this academic position that Smith also formulated many of the ideas that would garner him respect in his lectures and find publication in *The Theory of Moral Sentiments* (1759).

When he received the opportunity to travel and tutor a Scottish nobleman in 1764, Smith resigned his professorship and took to the road. On this tour Smith met leading figures of the day, including Voltaire, Francois Quesnay, and Benjamin Franklin. Smith's service as professional tutor only lasted two years before he returned to Great Britain. He spent the next decade working on the book *The Wealth of Nations* (1776), which became an instant success upon publication.

This work would be the last of Smith's writings to achieve acclaim or to survive his last bequests. In the remainder of his career, Smith served as commissioner of customs in Scotland starting in 1778 and became a founding member of the Royal Society of Edinburgh, an academic organization, in 1783. He died in 1790 from illness, and left instructions to destroy any writing unsuitable for publication. Although his published works undeniably influenced economic theory, Smith's dearth of writing, combined with a nebulous personal life, has contributed to continued debate about the nature and intent of his philosophical thought.

HISTORICAL DOCUMENT: From *The Theory of Moral Sentiments*

We suffer more, it has already been observed, when we fall from a better to a worse situation, than we ever enjoy when we rise from a worse to a better. Security, therefore, is the first and the principal object of prudence. It is averse to expose our health, our fortune, our rank, or reputation, to any sort of hazard. It is rather cautious than enterprising, and more anxious to preserve the advantages which we already possess, than forward to prompt us to the acquisition of still greater advantages. The methods of improving our fortune, which it principally recommends to us, are those which expose to no loss or hazard; real knowledge and skill in our trade or profession, assiduity and industry in the exercise of it, frugality, and even some degree of parsimony, in all our expences.

The prudent man always studies seriously and earnestly to understand whatever he professes to understand, and not merely to persuade other people that he understands it; and though his talents may not always be very brilliant, they are always perfectly genuine. He neither endeavours to impose upon you by the cunning devices of an artful impostor, nor by the arrogant airs of an assuming pedant, nor by the confident assertions of a superficial and imprudent pretender. He is not ostentatious even of the abilities which he really possesses. His conversation is simple and modest, and he is averse to all the quackish arts by which other people so frequently thrust themselves into public notice and reputation. For reputation in his profession he is naturally disposed to rely a good deal upon the solidity of his knowledge and abilities;

and he does not always think of cultivating the favour of those little clubs and cabals, who, in the superior arts and sciences, so often erect themselves into the supreme judges of merit; and who make it their business to celebrate the talents and virtues of one another, and to decry whatever can come into competition with them. If he ever connects himself with any society of this kind, it is merely in self-defence, not with a view to impose upon the public, but to hinder the public from being imposed upon, to his disadvantage, by the clamours, the whispers, or the intrigues, either of that particular society, or of some other of the same kind.

The prudent man is always sincere, and feels horror at the very thought of exposing himself to the disgrace which attends upon the detection of falsehood. But though always sincere, he is not always frank and open; and though he never tells any thing but the truth, he does not always think himself bound, when not properly called upon, to tell the whole truth. As he is cautious in his actions, so he is reserved in his speech; and never rashly or unnecessarily obtrudes his opinion concerning either things or persons.

The prudent man, though not always distinguished by the most exquisite sensibility, is always very capable of friendship. But his friendship is not that ardent and passionate, but too often transitory affection, which appears so delicious to the generosity of youth and inexperience. It is a sedate, but steady and faithful attachment to a few well-tried and well-chosen companions; in the choice of whom he is not guided by the giddy admiration of shining accomplishments, but by the sober esteem of modesty, discretion, and good conduct. But though capable of friendship, he is not always much disposed to general sociality. He rarely frequents, and more rarely figures in those convivial societies which are distinguished for the jollity and gaiety of their conversation. Their way of life might too often interfere with the regularity of his temperance, might interrupt the steadiness of his industry, or break in upon the strictness of his frugality.

But though his conversation may not always be very sprightly or diverting, it is always perfectly inoffensive. He hates the thought of being guilty of any petulance or rudeness. He never assumes impertinently over any body, and, upon all common occasions, is willing to place himself rather below than above his equals. Both in his conduct and conversation, he is an exact observer of decency, and respects with an almost religious scrupulosity, all the established decorums and ceremonials of society. And, in this respect, he sets a much better example than has frequently been done by men of much more splendid talents and virtues; who, in all ages, from that of Socrates and Aristippus, down to that of Dr. Swift and Voltaire, and from that of Philip and Alexander the Great, down to that of the great Czar Peter of Moscovy, have too often distinguished themselves by the most improper and even insolent contempt of all the ordinary decorums of life and conversation, and who have thereby set the most pernicious example to those who wish to resemble them, and who too often content themselves with imitating their follies, without even attempting to attain their perfections.

In the steadiness of his industry and frugality, in his steadily sacrificing the ease and enjoyment of the present moment for the probable expectation of the still greater ease and enjoyment of a more distant but more lasting period of time, the prudent man is always both supported and rewarded by the entire approbation of the impartial spectator, and of the representative of the impartial spectator, the man within the breast. The impartial spectator does not feel himself worn out by the present labour of those whose conduct he surveys; nor does he feel himself solicited by the importunate calls of their present appetites. To him their present, and what is likely to be their future situation, are very nearly the same: he sees them nearly at the same distance, and is affected by them very nearly in the same manner. He knows, however, that to the persons principally concerned, they are very far from being the same, and that they naturally affect them in a very different manner. He cannot therefore but approve, and even applaud, that proper exertion of self-command, which enables them to act as if their present and their future situation affected them nearly in the same manner in which they affect him.

The man who lives within his income, is naturally contented with his situation, which, by continual, though small accumulations, is growing better and better every day. He is enabled gradually to relax, both in the rigour of his parsimony and in the severity of his application; and he feels with double satisfaction this gradual increase of ease and enjoyment, from having felt before the hardship which attended the want of them. He has no anxiety to change so comfortable a situation, and does not go in quest of new enterprises and adventures, which might endanger, but could not well increase, the secure tranquillity which he actually enjoys. If he enters into any new projects or enterprises, they are likely to be well concerted and well prepared. He can never be hurried or drove into them by any necessity, but has always time and leisure to deliberate soberly and coolly concerning what are likely to be their consequences.

The prudent man is not willing to subject himself to any responsibility which his duty does not impose upon him. He is not a bustler in business where he has no concern; is not a meddler in other people's affairs; is not a professed counsellor or adviser, who obtrudes his advice where nobody is asking it. He confines himself, as much as his duty will permit, to his own affairs, and has no taste for that foolish importance which many people wish to derive from appearing to have some influence in the management of those of other people. He is averse to enter into any party disputes, hates faction, and is not always very forward to listen to the voice even of noble and great ambition. When distinctly called upon, he will not decline the service of his country, but he will not cabal in order to force himself into it; and would be much better pleased that the public business were well managed by some other person, than that he himself should have the trouble, and incur the responsibility, of managing it. In the bottom of his heart he would prefer the undisturbed enjoyment of secure tranquillity, not only to all the vain splendour of successful ambition, but to the real and solid glory of performing the greatest and most magnanimous actions.

Prudence, in short, when directed merely to the care of the health, of the fortune, and of the rank and reputation of the individual, though it is regarded as a most respectable and even, in some degree, as an amiable and agreeable quality, yet it never is considered as one, either of the most endearing, or of the most ennobling of the virtues. It commands a certain cold esteem, but seems not entitled to any very ardent love or admiration.

Wise and judicious conduct, when directed to greater and nobler purposes than the care of the health, the fortune, the rank and reputation of the individual, is frequently and very properly called prudence. We talk of the prudence of the great general, of the great statesman, of the great legislator. Prudence is, in all these cases, combined with many greater and more splendid virtues, with valour, with extensive and strong benevolence, with a sacred regard to the rules of justice, and all these supported by a proper degree of self-command. This superior prudence, when carried to the highest degree of perfection, necessarily supposes the art, the talent, and the habit or disposition of acting with the most perfect propriety in every possible circumstance and situation. It necessarily supposes the utmost perfection of all the intellectual and of all the moral virtues. It is the best head joined to the best heart. It is the most perfect wisdom combined with the most perfect virtue. It constitutes very nearly the character of the Academical or Peripatetic sage, as the inferior prudence does that of the Epicurean.

Mere imprudence, or the mere want of the capacity to take care of one's-self, is, with the generous and humane, the object of compassion; with those of less delicate sentiments, of neglect, or, at worst, of contempt, but never of hatred or indignation. When combined with other vices, however, it aggravates in the highest degree the infamy and disgrace which would otherwise attend them. The artful knave, whose dexterity and address exempt him, though not from strong suspicions, yet from punishment or distinct detection, is too often received in the world with an indulgence which he by no means deserves. The awkward and foolish one, who, for want of this dexterity and address, is convicted and brought to punishment, is the object of universal hatred, contempt, and derision. In countries where great crimes frequently pass unpunished, the most atrocious actions become almost familiar, and cease to impress the people with that horror which is universally felt in countries where an exact administration of justice takes place. The injustice is the same in both countries; but the imprudence is often very different. In the latter, great crimes are evidently great follies. In the former, they are not always considered as such. In Italy, during the greater part of the sixteenth century, assassinations, murders, and even

> *The prudent man always studies seriously and earnestly to understand whatever he professes to understand, and not merely to persuade other people that he understands it*

murders under trust, seem to have been almost familiar among the superior ranks of people. Caesar Borgia invited four of the little princes in his neighbourhood, who all possessed little sovereignties, and commanded little armies of their own, to a friendly conference at Senigaglia, where, as soon as they arrived, he put them all to death. This infamous action, though certainly not approved of even in that age of crimes, seems to have contributed very little to the discredit, and not in the least to the ruin of the perpetrator. That ruin happened a few years after from causes altogether disconnected with this crime. Machiavel, not indeed a man of the nicest morality even for his own times, was resident, as minister from the republic of Florence, at the court of Caesar Borgia when this crime was committed. He gives a very particular account of it, and in that pure, elegant, and simple language which distinguishes all his writings. He talks of it very coolly; is pleased with the address with which Caesar Borgia conducted it; has much contempt for the dupery and weakness of the sufferers; but no compassion for their miserable and untimely death, and no sort of indignation at the cruelty and falsehood of their murderer. The violence and injustice of great conquerors are often regarded with foolish wonder and admiration; those of petty thieves, robbers, and murderers, with contempt, hatred, and even horror upon all occasions. The former, though they are a hundred times more mischievous and destructive, yet when successful, they often pass for deeds of the most heroic magnanimity. The latter are always viewed with hatred and aversion, as the follies, as well as the crimes, of the lowest and most worthless of mankind. The injustice of the former is certainly, at least, as great as that of the latter; but the folly and imprudence are not near so great. A wicked and worthless man of parts often goes through the world with much more credit than he deserves. A wicked and worthless fool appears always, of all mortals, the most hateful, as well as the most contemptible. As prudence combined with other virtues, constitutes the noblest; so imprudence combined with other vices, constitutes the vilest of all characters.

GLOSSARY

bustler: one who moves in an engergetic fashing

quackish: presented falsely as having curative powers

Senigaglia (also spelled Sinigallia/Senigallia): a location in Italy where Cesare Borgia lured would-be conspirators under false promises of security on December 31, 1502; after he had trapped the conspirators with his army, Borgia summarily executed them for disloyalty

Document Analysis

As a complete work, *The Theory of Moral Sentiments* is a wide-ranging examination of human psychology and society. Smith's character analysis of the prudent man, however, valorizes apolitical life at the same time as it shows the pernicious effects political engagement can have. While this is only a small section of a larger work, the attitude to political life in this section reflects Smith's involvement in Enlightenment thought, especially concerning issues of individual liberty, and political trends in Great Britain away from absolute monarchy.

At the beginning of this section on the prudent man, Smith leads the reader to believe that his character analysis will simply concern security and human livelihood. In his first detailed description of this character, however, it becomes clear that Smith has a greater point to make about political involvement. As Smith elaborates, the prudent man "is averse to all the quackish arts by which other people so frequently thrust themselves into public notice and reputation." Namely, the prudent man does not actively seek public recognition. Furthermore, "he does not always think of cultivating the favour of those little clubs and cabals." The link between "public notice" and specialized clubs does not automatically connote political aspirations, but Smith's description of these clubs as leading to competition and attention implies that they are connected to a struggle for power. As Smith continues to describe the conduct of the prudent man, he says that this character "never assumes impertinently over any body, and, upon all common occasions, is willing to place himself rather below than above his equals." By specifically placing this virtuous man as willing to humble himself for the sake of security, Smith associates virtue with lack of political ambition.

Aside from his general statements about the prudent man's behavior, Smith's specific references to historical individuals solidifies the author's antipathy toward politics based on a cult of personality. After Smith describes the prudent man's tendency to humble himself, he explains that this man is a better example than "men of much more splendid talents and virtues; who, in all ages, from that of Socrates and Aristippus, down to that of Dr. Swift and Voltaire, and from that of Philip and Alexander the Great, down to that of the great Czar Peter of Moscovy have too often distinguished themselves by the most improper and even insolent contempt of all the ordinary decorums." Half of the names Smith mentions were not actual political leaders, but they did concern themselves with political issues in their philosophical thoughts or writings. By linking personalities like Socrates with Peter the Great, Smith also generalizes the behavior

Portrait of Smith by John Kay, 1790.

of an absolute monarch with all individuals who interject on political matters. The last paragraph of this selection emphasizes the deleterious effect politics have on the individual in the explication of events at Senigaglia (or Senigallia). While Smith does not approve of Cesare Borgia's duplicitous behavior, he does acknowledge that great power tends to corrupt the ability of individuals to assess whether behavior is just or not. In this distortion between prosaic, quotidian behavior and great matters of state, Smith's sympathy clearly lies with the man who lives a simple, unambitious life.

In this small selection it is possible to see how Adam Smith's antipathy toward overbearing political rulership correlates with his disdain for mercantilism as an economic theory. Since mercantilism relied on strong rulers who could establish strong controls over trade and national spending, it interfered with individual freedom to buy and sell where one pleased. Smith's prioritization of individual liberty in this work would receive more attention in relation to economic theory in his magnum opus, *The Wealth of Nations*, but this earlier work establishes the psychological and political groundwork that made the later work such a success.

Essential Themes

This selection from *The Theory of Moral Sentiments* illustrates Adam Smith's optimism about human behavior and economics. Smith was aware of a pessimistic current in philosophical thought which decried the effect of self-interest in society (such as in Jean-Jacques Rousseau's *Discourse on Inequality*). Equally Smith was aware of the uproar caused by a satirical poem written by Bernard Mandeville, *The Fable of the Bees*. This parable describes a fictitious bee colony that thrived while vice ruled, but the introduction of moral virtue caused the collapse of the bee colony's economy. Mandeville's satire upholds a view of society that financial profit and self-interest could not coexist with higher concerns about human rights. In response Smith conceived of an economic system where human self-interest and financial gain could be mutually beneficial for all involved.

As Smith describes in the character of the prudent man, the self-interested desire to provide oneself with security yields positive social gains. Smith ascribes part of this positive social effect to the assessment of the "impartial spectator," essentially a form of social consciousness. This separate conscience determines human virtues based on which behaviors are most aware and agreeable with community well-being. The "impartial spectator" as described here naturally values the prudent man's desire not to

The first page of The Wealth of Nations, *1776 London edition.*

importune the present at the expense of future pleasure. Smith recognizes, however, that this assessment is not always impartial and often the scale of an action distorts the impartial spectator, as he explains in the case of Cesare Borgia and Machiavelli. Nevertheless, Smith remains convinced that the unintended positive consequences of evil actions, such as Borgia successfully preventing a coup against himself through duplicitous means, does not diminish the cruelty of these behaviors in a universal assessment.

Smith's equivocation on this dichotomy between positive consequences and unjust behavior to others underlies a larger issue with his overall optimistic outlook. Although the idea of the "invisible hand," that is, the unintended social benefits of self-interested behavior, does appear in *The Theory of Moral Sentiments*, it is most often associated with Smith's later work, *The Wealth of Nations*. This later work proposes in general that nations would experience more profit in a free market where human self-interest dictated the flow of goods and division of labor. Although Smith's economic system is of course more complicated, it does presuppose that an abundance of resources would be available; it also presupposes that in most people and in most contexts exists the natural inclination to operate according to this "mutual sympathy," which Smith argues negotiates human behavior toward one another. As the "father of capitalism," Smith also does not seem to account for the role that advanced technology would play in this type of economy. At what point should a more authoritative power like a political government step in to enact restrictions to prevent rising income inequality, or unfair commercial practices? Smith could not have predicted the consequences of his system, both good and bad, as increased profit interacted with more global connections and industrial advancements.

—*Ashleigh Fata, MA*

Bibliography and Additional Reading

Milgate, Murray and Shannon C. Stimson. *After Adam Smith: A Century of Transformation in Politics and Political Economy*. Princeton, NJ: Princeton University Press, 2009.

Muller, Jerry Z. *Adam Smith in His Time and Ours: Designing the Decent Society*. Princeton, NJ: Princeton University Press, 1993.

Norman, Jesse. *Adam Smith: Father of Economics*. New York: Basic Books, 2018.

Rasmussen, Dennis C. *The Infidel and the Professor: David Hume, Adam Smith, and the Friendship That Shaped Modern Thought*. Princeton, NJ: Princeton University Press, 2017.

Smith, Adam. *The Wealth of Nations*. 1776. New York: Bantam Books, 2003.

■ Letter from Robert Morris to Alexander Martin

Date: July 29, 1782
Author: Robert Morris
Genre: correspondence

Summary Overview

Americans' concerns about government debt, spending, and taxation are as old as the nation itself. While nominally a matter of fiscal policy, this 1682 letter from Robert Morris, the Superintendent of Finance for the United States, to Governor Alexander Martin of North Carolina illustrates that in the earliest years of the United States, the question of public debt was also deeply intertwined with concerns about national unity and the limits of national power in the era of the Articles of Confederation. Morris's thoughts on the state of the American economy would be echoed in later years by Alexander Hamilton in his efforts to establish the Bank of the United States. In addition to examining the uses of public credit and debt, in this letter Morris also discusses the necessity of both taxation and the use of credit and the manner in which these things should be done.

Defining Moment

In mid-1782, the American War for Independence was nearing its conclusion. Following the British surrender at the Battle of Yorktown in October of 1781, negotiations to end the war began in earnest. While British troops still occupied several American cities, the greatest looming crisis for the soon-to-be independent United States was financial, not military. The war had been incredibly expensive and there were a number of factors limiting the Americans' ability to raise funds to cover these expenses. The British navy maintained an effective blockade on American port cities, limiting revenue from trade in addition to outright occupying major ports such as New York City and Charleston, South Carolina; the American government under the Articles of Confederation had no authority to levy taxes and relied on voluntary contributions from individual states. In order to fight the war, the United States deferred payments to soldiers in the Continental Army as well as payment for supplies those soldiers needed. In fact, until 1781, when Morris was appointed Superintendent of Finance, there was no single official responsible for managing the fiscal affairs of the new nation. Morris attempted to stabilize the economy by establishing a central bank.

Currency issued by the Continental Congress during the war had drastically decreased in value, leading to inflation. The country had a rapidly increasing debt to its ally, France, as well. The inability of the United States to pay its soldiers in a timely manner led to decreased morale and disciplinary issues.

Individual citizens were also owed money by the national government. In 1782, a group of prominent citizens including Blair McClenachan and Benjamin Rush authored a statement entitled "To the Citizens of American who are Creditors of the United States." The authors expressed concern about the fact that the government had ceased making interest payments on some loans, which caused hardship to those who depended on this money and undermined public trust in the new nation's credit and overall financial strength. They called on Congress and the Superintendent of Finance, Robert Morris, to formulate a plan to remedy the situation. In July, Morris wrote this letter to Alexander Martin, the governor of North Carolina outlining his thoughts on the matter and the wider issues of finance for the new United States.

Author Biography

Robert Morris was born in Liverpool, England, in 1734. Migrating to the British colony of Pennsylvania as a young man, Morris built a career in the shipping industry. After the French and Indian War (1754–63), Morris was among those who believed British tax policy was violating the rights of British colonists in America. He became involved with the American War for Independence, serving in the Continental Congress mostly working to obtain weapons, ammunition, and other supplies for the war effort and served on committees concerned with foreign policy and oversight of the Navy.

Near the end of the war, in 1781, Morris accepted the position of superintendent of finance. In this role, he was not only responsible for overseeing the material needs of the American military but also general supervision of the young nation's financial health. He established the first central bank in the United States, the Bank of North America. Despite these efforts, Morris was convinced that the United States could not overcome its financial difficulties unless the national Congress had the authority to collect taxes and tariffs, which it did not have under the Articles of Confederation. He resigned as superintendent of finance in late 1784 and, later, would be a delegate to the Constitutional Convention where his desire for a national government with the power to tax was fulfilled. Following the ratification of the Constitution, Morris served as a senator from Pennsylvania from 1789 to 1795. He died in 1806.

HISTORICAL DOCUMENT: Letter from Robert Morris to Alexander Martin

Sir:

The reference which Congress were pleased to make of a remonstrance and petition from Blair McClenachan and others has induced me to pray their indulgence while I go somewhat at large into the Subject of that remonstrance. The Propriety and utility of public loans have been subjects of much controversy. Those who find themselves saddled with the debts of a preceding generation naturally exclaim against loans, and it must be confessed that when such debts are accumulated by negligence, folly or profusion, the complaint is well founded. But it would be equally so against Taxes when wasted in the same way. The difference is that the weight of Taxes being more sensible, the waste occasions greater clamor & is, therefore, more speedily remedied, but it will appear that the eventual evils which posterity must sustain from heavy Taxes are greater than from loans. Hence may be deduced this conclusion that in Government liable to a vicious administration it would be better to raise the current by Taxes; but where an honest and wise appropriation of money prevails it is highly advantageous to take the benefit of loans.

> *In every Society ... there must be some Taxes, because the necessity of supporting Government & defending the State always exist.*

Taxation to a certain point is not only proper but useful, because by stimulating the industry of individuals it increases the wealth of the Community. But when Taxes go so far as to intrench on the subsistance of the people they become burthensome and oppressive. The expenditures of money ought in such case to be (if possible) avoided, and if unavoidable, it will be most wise to have recourse to loans. Loans may be of two kinds, either domestic or Foreign. The relative advantages and disadvantages of each, as well as those which are common to both, will deserve attention. Reasonings of this kind (as they depend on rules of Arithmetic) are best understood by numerical positions. For the purposes of elucidation, therefore, it may be supposed that the annual Tax of any particular husbandman were fifteen pounds during a ten year's war, and that his net revenues were but fifteen pounds, so that (the whole being regularly consumed in payment of Taxes) he would be no richer at the end of the War than he was at the beginning. It is at the same time notorious that the profits made by husbandmen on funds which they borrowed were very considerable. In many instances their plantations, as well as the Cattle and farming utensils, have been purchased on credit, and the Bonds given for both have shortly been paid by sales of produce. It is, therefore, no exaggeration to state the profits at 12 per cent. The enormous usury which people in trade have been induced to pay, and which presently be noticed, demonstrates that the profits made by other professions are equal to those of the husbandman.

The instance, therefore, taken from that which is the most numerous class of Citizens will form no improper standard for the whole. Let it then be further supposed, in the case already stated, that the party should annually borrow the sum of Ten pounds at six per cent. to pay part of his Tax of Fifteen pounds. On this Sum he would make a profit of twenty-four shillings, and have to pay an interest of twelve shillings.

The enclosed calculation will show that in ten years he would be indebted one hundred pounds, but his additional Improvements would be worth near one hundred and fifty, and his net revenue be increased near twelve, after deducting the Interest of his debt. Whereas, if he had not borrowed, his revenue (as has been already observed) would have continued the same. This mode of reasoning might be pursued further, but what has been said is sufficient to show that he would have made a considerable advantage from the yearly loan. If it be supposed that every person in the community made such loan a similar advantage would arise to the Community. And lastly, if it be supposed that the Government were to make a loan, and ask so much less in Taxes, the same advantage would be derived. Hence also may be deduced this position that in a Society where the average profits of stocks are double to the interest at which money can be obtained, every public loan for necessary expenditures provides a fund in the aggregate of National wealth, equal to the discharge of its own interest.

Were it possible that a Society should exist in which every member would, of his own accord, industriously pursue the increase of National property without waste or extravagance, the public Wealth would be impaired by every Species of Taxation, but there never was, and unless human nature should change, there never will be such a Society. In any given number of men there will always be some who are idle and some who are extravagant. In every Society also there must be some Taxes, because the necessity of supporting Government & defending the State always exist. To do these on the cheapest Terms is wise, and when it is considered how much men are disposed to indolence and profusion it will appear that (even if those demands did not require the whole of what could be raised) still it would be wise to carry Taxation to a certain amount, and expend what should remain after providing for the support of Government and the National defence in Works of public utility, such as opening of roads and Navigation. For Taxes, operate two ways towards the increase of National Wealth. First they stimulate industry to provide the means of payment, secondly they encourage economy so far as to avoid the purchase of unnecessary things and keep money in readiness for the Tax gatherer. Experience shows that those exertions of Industry and Economy grow by degrees into habit. But in order that taxation may have these good effects the Sums which every man is to pay and the period of payment should be certain and unavoidable. This digression open the way to a comparison between Foreign and Domestic Loans. If the loan be domestic, money must be diverted from these channels in which it would otherwise have flowed, and, therefore, either the public must give better Terms than individuals or there must be money enough to supply the wants of both. In the latter case if the public did not borrow the quantity of money would exceed the demand, and the Interest would be lowered. Borrowing by the public would therefore keep up the rate of interest which brings the latter case within the reason of the former. If the Public outbid individuals, those individuals are deprived of the means of extending their industry. So that no case of a Domestic Loan can well be supposed where some public loss will not arise to counter-balance the public gain except where the creditor spares from his consumption to lend to the Government which operates a National economy. It is, however, an advantage peculiar to Domestic Loans that they give stability to Government by combining together the interests of monied men for its support, & consequently in this Country a Domestic Debt would greatly contribute to that Union which seems not to have been sufficiently attended to, or provided for in forming the National compact.

Domestic Loans are also useful from the further consideration that as taxes fall heavy on the lower orders of a community the relief obtained for them by such loans more than counter-balances the loss sustained by those who would have borrowed Money to extend their Commerce or tillage. Neither is it a refinement to observe that since a plenty of money & consequent ease of obtaining it induce Men to engage in Speculations which are often unprofitable, the check which these receive is not injurious, while the relief obtained for the Poor is highly beneficial. By making Foreign Loans the Community (as such) receive the same extensive benefits which one Individual does in borrowing of another.

This Country was always in the practice of making such Loans. The merchants in Europe trusted those in America. The American merchants trusted the Country Store-Keepers and they the people at large. This advance of credit may be stated at not less than 20 million of dollars, and the want of credit is one principal reason of those usurious contracts mentioned above. These have been checked by the institution of the Bank, but the funds of that corporation not permitting the extensive advances which the views of different people require, the price given for particular accommodations of Money continues to be enormous, and that again shows that to make Domestic Loans would be difficult, if not impracticable. The Merchants not having now that extensive credit in Europe which they formerly had, the obtaining such credit by the Government becomes in some sort necessary. But there remains an objection with many against Foreign Loans which (though it arises from a superficial view of the subject) has no little influence. This is that the interest will form a balance of Trade against us, and drain the Country of the Specie, which is only saying in other words that it would be more convenient to receive Money as a present than as a Loan, for the advantages derived by the loan exist notwithstanding the payment of Interest. To show this more clearly, a case may be stated, which, in this city, is very familiar. An Island in the Delaware overflowed at high Water has, for a given sum, suppose a thousand pounds, been banked in, drained and made to produce by the hay sold from it at Philadelphia a considerable sum annually—for instance, two hundred pounds. If the owner of such an Island had borrowed (in Philadelphia) the thousand pounds to improve it, & given six per cent., he would have gained a nett revenue of one hundred and forty pounds. This certainly would not be a balance of trade against his Island nor the draining it of Specie. He would gain considerably and the City of Philadelphia would also gain by bringing to market an increased quantity of a necessary article.

In like manner, money lent by the City of Amsterdam to clear the forests of America would be beneficial to both. Draining marshes and bringing forests under culture are beneficial to the whole human race, but most so to the proprietor. But at any rate in a Country and in a situation like ours to lighten the weight of present burthens by Loans must be good policy. For as the Governments acquire more stability and the people more wealth, the former will be able to raise and the latter to pay much greater sums than can at present be expected. What has been said on the general nature and benefit of public Loans, as well as their particular utility to this Country, contains more of detail than is necessary for the United States in Congress, tho' perhaps not enough for many of those to whose consideration this subject must be submitted. It may seem superfluous to add that credit is necessary to the obtaining of Loans. But among the many extraordinary conceptions which have been produced during the present Revolution it is neither the least prevalent nor the least pernicious that foreigners will trust us with millions while our own Citizens will not trust us with a shilling. Such an opinion must be unfounded, and will appear to be false at the first glance. Yet men are (on some occasions) so willing to deceive themselves that the most flattering expectations will be formed from the acknowledgement of American Independence by the States General. But surely no reasonable hope can be raised on that circumstance unless something more be done by ourselves. The Loans made to us hitherto have either been by the Court of France or on their credit. The Government of the United Netherlands are so far from being able to lend that they must borrow for themselves.

The most, therefore, that can be asked from them is to become Security for America to their own Subjects, but it cannot be expected that they will do this until they are assured & convinced that we will punctually pay. This follows necessarily from the nature of their Government, and must be clearly seen by the several States, as well as by Congress, if they only consider what conduct they would pursue on a similar occasion. Certainly Congress would not put themselves in a situation which might oblige them to call on the several States for Money to pay the debts of a Foreign Power. Since then no aid is to be looked for from the Dutch Government without giving them sufficient evidence of a Disposition & ability to pay both principal and Interest of what we borrow, and since the same evidence which would convince the Government must convince the Individuals who compose it, asking the aid of Government must either be unnecessary or ineffectual. Ineffectual before the measures are taken to establish our credit and unnecessary afterwards.

We are, therefore, brought back to the necessity of establishing public credit, and this must be done at home before it can be extended abroad. The only Question which can remain is with respect to the means, and here it must be remembered that a free Government, whose natural offspring is public credit, cannot have sustained a Loss of that Credit unless from particular causes, and, therefore, those causes must be investigated & removed before the effects will cease. When the Continental Money was issued a greater confidence was shown by America than any other people ever exhibited. The General promise of a Body not formed into nor claiming to be a Government was accepted as current Coin. And it was not until long after an excess of quantity had forced a depreciation that the validity of these promises was questioned. Even then the public Credit still existed in a degree, nor was it finally lost until March, 1780, when an idea was entertained, that Government had committed injustice. It was useless to enter into the reasons for and against the Resolutions of the Period, they were adopted and are now to be considered only in relation to their effects. These will not be altered by saying that the Resolutions were misunderstood, for in those things which depend on public opinion it is no matter (as far as consequences are concerned) how that opinion is influenced. Under present Circumstances, therefore, it may be considered as an uncontrovertible proposition that all Paper Money ought to be absorbed by Taxation (or otherwise) and destroyed before we can expect our public credit to be fully re-established. For so long as there be any in existence the holder will view it as a monument of National perfidy.

But this will be taking only a small step in the important business of establishing National Credit. There are a great number of individuals in the United States who trusted the Public in the hour of distress, and who are impoverished and even ruined by the confidence they reposed. There are others whose property has been wrested from them by force to support the War and to whom Certificates have been given in lieu of it which are entirely useless. It needed not inspiration to show that Justice establisheth a Nation, neither are the principles of Religion necessary to evince that Political Injustice will receive political chastisement. Religious men will cherish these Maxims in proportion to the additional force they derive from divine revelation. But our own experience will show that from a defect of Justice this Nation is not established, and that her want of honesty is severely punished by her want of credit. To this want of credit must be attributed the weight of taxation for support of the War, and the continuance of that weight by the continuance of War. It is, therefore, with the greatest propriety your Petitioners already mentioned have stated in their Memorial that both policy and Justice require a solid provision for funding the public debts.

It is with pleasure, Sir, I see this numerous, meritorious and oppressed Body of Men who are creditors of the Public beginning to exert themselves for the obtaining of Justice. I hope they may succeed, not only because I wish well to so righteous a pursuit, but because their success will be the great ground work of a Credit, which will carry us safely through the present just, important and necessary War, which will combine us closely together on conclusion of a Peace, which will always give to the Supreme Representative of America a means of acting for the General defence on sudden emergencies and which will of consequence procure the third of those great objects for which we contend—*Peace, Liberty and Safety.*

Such, Sir, are the cogent principles by which we are called on to provide solid funds for the National Debt. Already Congress have adopted a plan for liquidating all past accounts, and if the States shall make the necessary grants of Revenue what remains will be a simple executive operation which will presently be explained. But however powerful the reasons in favor of such grants, over and above those principles of Moral Justice which none, however exalted, can part from with Impunity, still there are men who (influenced by pernicious selfishness) will grumble at the Expence, and who will assert the impossibility of sustaining it. On this occasion the sensations, with respect to borrowing, are reversed. All would be content to relieve themselves by Loan from the weighty Taxes, but many are unwilling to take up as they ought the weight of Debt. Yet this must be done before the other can happen, and it is not so great but that we should find immediate relief by assuming it *even if it were a Foreign Debt*. I say if it were a Foreign Debt because I shall attempt to show first, that being a Domestic Debt will cost the Community nothing, and secondly, that it will produce (on the contrary) a considerable advantage, and as to the first point, one observation will suffice. The expenditure has been made and a part of the Community have sustained it. If the debt were to be paid by a single effort of Taxation, it would only create a transfer of property from one individual to another and the aggregate wealth of the whole community would be precisely the same. But since nothing more is attempted than merely to fund the Debt by providing for the Interest (at 6 per cent.,) the question of ability is resolved to this single point. Whether it is easier for a *part of the people* to pay one hundred Dollars than for *the whole people* to pay six Dollars? It is equally clear, though not equally evident, that a considerable advantage would be produced by funding our Debts over and above what has already been mentioned as the consequence of National Credit. This advantage is threefold.

First, many persons by being creditors of the public are deprived of those funds which are necessary to the full exercise of their skill and industry. Consequently the Community are deprived of the benefits which would result from that exercise. Whereas, if these Debts which are in a manner dead were brought back to existence monied men would purchase them up (tho' perhaps at a considerable discount) and thereby restore to the public many useful members who are now entirely lost, and extend the operations of many more to considerable advantage. For although not one additional shilling would by this means be brought in, yet by distributing property into those hands which would render it most productive, the Revenue would be increased, while the original stock continued the same.

Secondly, many Foreigners who make speculations to this Country would, instead of ordering back remittances, direct much of the proceeds of their Cargoes to be invested in our public funds which, according to principles already established, would produce a clear advantage with this addition, (from peculiar circumstances) that it would supply the want of Credit to the Mercantile part of Society. The last, but not least, advantage is, that in restoring ease, harmony and confidence, not only the

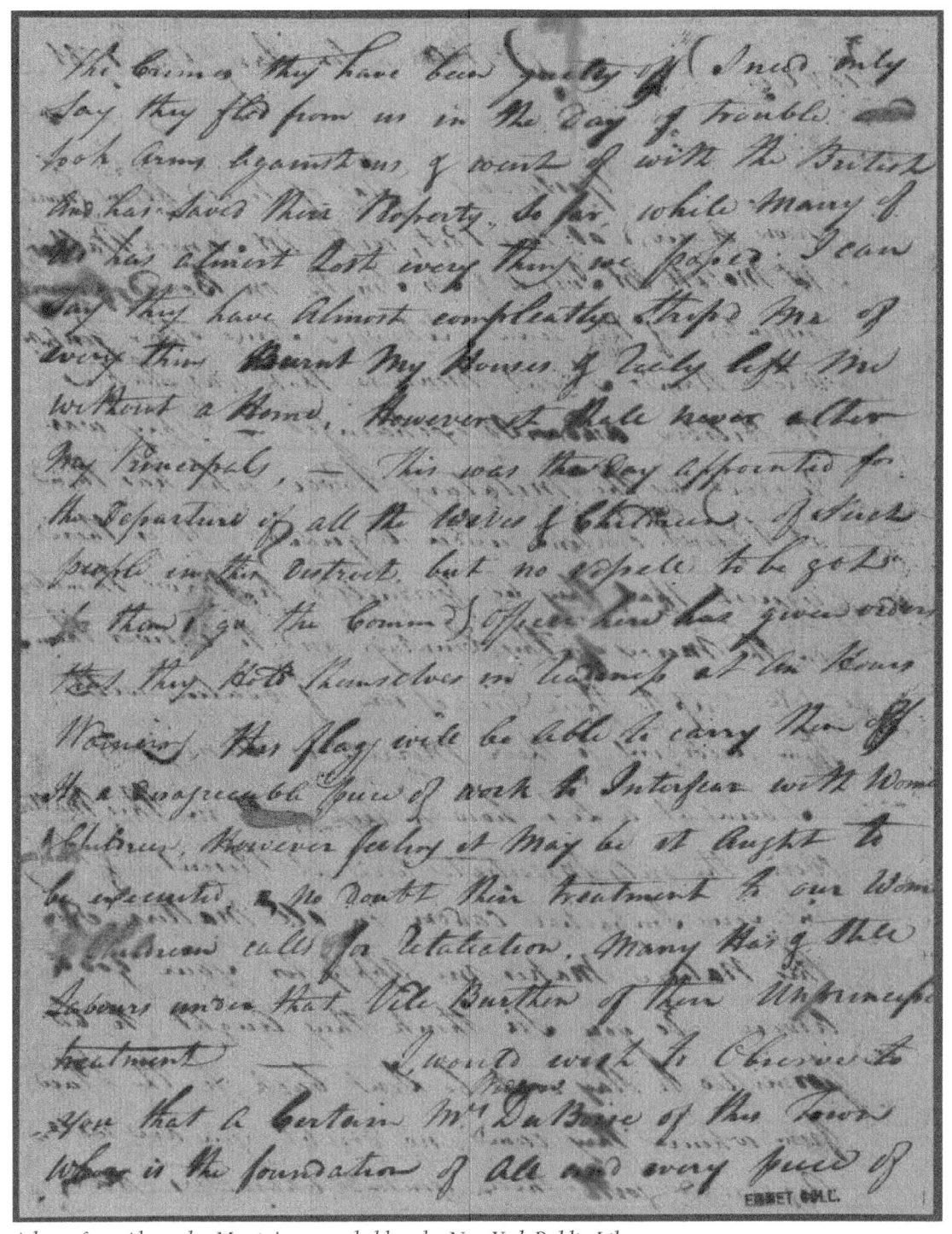

A letter from Alexander Martin's papers, held at the New York Public Library

Government (being more respectable) would be more respected, and consequently better obeyed, but the mutual dealings among men on private credit would be facilitated. The horrors which agitate people's minds from an apprehension of depreciating paper would be done away, the secret hoards would be unlocked. In the same moment the necessity of money would be lessened and the quantity increased. By these means the collection of Taxes would be facilitated, and thus instead of being obliged to give valuable produce for useless Minerals, that produce would purchase the things we stand in need of, and we should obtain a sufficient circulating medium by giving the people what they have already a right to demand—solid assurance in the integrity of their rulers.

The next consideration which offers is the amount of the public Debt, and every good American must lament that confusion in public Affairs which renders an accurate state of it unattainable. But it must continue to be so until all accounts, both at home and abroad, are finally adjusted. The enclosed is an estimate furnished by the Comptroller of the Treasury from which it appears that there is already an acknowledged debt, bearing interest to the amount of more than twelve million of Dollars. On part of this also there is a large arrearage of Interest, and there is a very considerable debt unsettled, the Evidence whereof exists in various Certificates given for property applied to the public service. This (including pay to the Army previous to the present year's service) cannot be estimated at less than between seven and eight millions. Our Debt to his most Christian Majesty is about five millions. The nearest guess, therefore, which can be made at the sum Total is from twenty-five to twenty-seven million of Dollars; and if to this we add what it may be necessary to borrow for the year 1783, the amount will be (with Interest) by the time proper Revenues are obtained considerably above thirty millions.

Of course the interest will be between eighteen hundred thousand and two million Dollars. And here previous to the consideration of proper Revenues it may not be amiss to make a few general observations, the first of which is, that it would be injurious to the United States to obtain money on loan without providing before hand the necessary funds. For if those who are now so deeply engaged to support the War will not grant such funds to procure immediate relief, certainly those who come after them will not do it to pay a former debt. Remote objects dependent on abstract reasoning never influence the mind like immediate sensibility. It is, therefore, the province of wisdom to direct to proper objects that sensibility which is the only motive to action among the mass of Mankind. Should we be able to get money from the Dutch without first providing funds, which is more than doubtful, and should the several States afterward neglect making provision to perform the engagements of Congress, which is more than probable, the Credit of the United States abroad would be ruined forever. Very serious Discussions also might be raised among Foreign Powers. Our Creditors might have recourse to Arms and we might dishonorably be compelled to do what we dishonestly had left undone.

Secondly, the idea which many entertain of soliciting Loans abroad to pay the Interest of Domestic Loans is a measure pregnant with its own destruction. If the States were to grant Revenues sufficient only to pay the Interest of present Debts, we might perhaps obtain new Credit upon a general opinion of our Justice, tho' it is far from being certain. But when we omit paying by Taxes the Interest of Debts already contracted & ask to borrow for the purpose, making the same promises to obtain the Loans which had already been made to obtain the old, we shall surely be disappointed.

Thirdly, it will be necessary not only that Revenues be granted, but that those Revenues be amply sufficient for the purpose because (as will presently appear) a deficiency would be highly pernicious while an excess would be not only unprejudicial but advantageous. To perceive this with all necessary clearness, it must be remembered that the Revenues asked for on this occasion must be appropriated to the purpose for which they were asked. And in like manner the sums required for current expenditures must be appropriated to the Current Service. If then the former be deficient, the latter can not be brought in to supply the deficiencies, and of course the public credit would be impaired. But should there be an excess of Revenue it could be applied in payment of a part of the debt immediately. And in such case if the Credits should have depreciated, they would be raised to par, and if already at par, the offer of payment would induce the creditors to lower the Interest. Thus in either case the means of making new loans on good terms would be extended, and the necessity of asking more Revenues obviated. Lastly, the Revenues ought to be of such a nature as naturally and necessarily to increase, for Creditors will have a greater confidence when they have a clear prospect of being repaid, and the People will always be desirous to see a like prospect of relief from the Taxes. Besides which it will be necessary to incur some considerable expence after the War in making necessary establishments for a permanent naval force. And it will be least objectionable to borrow for that purpose on funds already established.

The requisition of a five per cent. impost made in the 3rd of February, 1781, has not yet been complied with by the State of Rhode Island, but there is reason to believe that their compliance is not far off; this Revenue may be considered as already granted. It will, however, be very inadequate to the purposes intended. If goods be imported and prizes introduced to the amount of twelve millions annually, the five per cent. will be six hundred thousand, from which at least one-sixth must be deducted as well for the cost of collection as for the various defalcations which will necessarily happen, and which it is unnecessary to enumerate. It is not safe, therefore, to estimate this Revenue at more than half a million of Dollars, for tho' it may produce more, yet probably it will not produce so much.

It was in consequence of this that on the 27th of February last I took the liberty to submit the propriety of asking the States for a Land Tax of one Dollar for every hundred Acres of Land, a Poll Tax of one Dollar on all free men and on all male slaves between sixteen and sixty (excepting such as are in the Federal Army, and such as are by wounds or otherwise rendered unfit for service) and an excise of one-eighth of a Dollar per Gallon on all distilled Spirituous Liquors. Each of these may be estimated at half a million, and should the product be equal to the estimation, the sum total of Revenues for funding the public Debts would be equal to two millions.

What has been the fate of these propositions I know not, but I will beg leave on this occasion not only to review them, but also to state some reasons in their favor and answer some objections against them. And first as to a Land Tax the advantages of it are, that it can be reduced to a certainty as to the amount and time, that no extraordinary means are necessary to ascertain it, and that land being the ultimate object of human avarice, and that particular Species of permanent property, which so peculiarly be to a long Country as neither to be removed or concealed, it stands foremost for the object of taxation and ought most particularly to be burthened with those Debts which have been incurred by defending the freedom of its inhabitants.

But besides these general reasons there are some which are in a manner peculiar to this Country. The Lands of America may as to the proprietors be divided into two kinds. That which belongs to the great Land-holders, and that which is owned and occupied by the industrious cultivators. This latter class of Citizens is generally speaking the most numerous, and most valuable part of a community. The artisan may under any Government minister to the luxuries of the rich, and the rich may under Government obtain the luxuries they covet. But the free husbandman is the natural Guardian of his Country's Freedom. A Land Tax will probably at the first mention startle this order of men, but it can only be from the want of reflection or the delusion must be kept up by the artifice of others. To him who cultivates from one to five hundred Acres a dollar per hundred is a trifling object, but to him who owns a hundred thousand it is important.

Yet a large proportion of America is the property of great land-holders. They monopolize it without cultivation, they are (for the most part) at no expence either for money or personal service to defend it, and keeping the price higher by monopoly than otherwise it would be, they impede the settlement and culture of the Country.

A Land Tax, therefore, would have the salutary Operation of an Agrarian Law without iniquity. It would relieve the indigent and aggrandize the State by bringing property into the hands of those who would use it for the benefit of Society. The objections against such a Tax are two-fold; first, that it is unequal, and secondly, that it is too high.

To obviate the inequality, some have proposed an estimate of the value of different kinds of Lands. But this would be improper, because first, it would be attended with great delay, expence and inconvenience; secondly, it would be uncertain, and, therefore, improper, particularly when considered as a fund for public debts; thirdly, there is no reason to believe that any estimate would be just, and even if it were it must be annually varied or else come within the force of the objection as strongly as ever. The former would cost more than the latter and the latter would not afford the remedy asked for. Lastly, such valuations would operate as a Tax upon Industry, and promote that Land monopoly which every wise Government will study to repress.

But farther, the true remedy for the inequality will be obtained in the apportioning other Taxes, of which there will always be enough to equalize this. Besides, the Tax being fixed and permanent, it is considered in the price of Land on every transfer of Property, and that produces a degree of equality which no valuation could possibly arrive at. In a word, if exact numerical proportion be sought after in Taxes, there would be no end to the search. Not only might a Poll Tax be objected to as too heavy on the Poor and too light on the Rich, but when that objection was obviated the Physical differences in the human frame would alone be as endless a source of contention as the different qualities of Land.

The second objection that the Tax is too high is equally futile with the former. Land which is so little worth that the owner will not pay annually one penny per Acre for the defence of it, ought to belong to the Society by whom the expence of defending it is defrayed.

But the truth is that this objection arises from, and is enforced by those men who can very well bear the expence, but who wish to shift it from themselves to others. I shall close this subject by adding that as such a Tax would, besides the benefits to be derived from the object of it, have the farther advantage of encouraging settlements and population, this would rebound, not only to the National good, but even to the particular good of Land-holders.

With respect to the Poll Tax, there are many objections against it, but in some of the States a more considerable Poll Tax already exists without inconvenience.

The objections are principally drawn from Europe by men who do not consider that a difference of circumstances make a material difference in the nature of political operations. In some part of Europe where nine-tenths of the people are exhausted by continual labor to procure bad cloathing and worse food, this Tax would be extremely oppressive, but in America where three days of Labor produce sustenance for a week, it is not unreasonable to ask two days out of a year as a Contribution to the payment of public debts. Such a Tax would, on the Rich, be next to nothing, on the middling rank it will be of little consequence and it cannot affect the Poor because such of them as are unable to Labor will fall within the exception proposed.

In fact, the situation of America differs so widely from that of Europe as to the matter now under consideration that hardly any maxim which applies to one will be alike applicable to the other. Labor is in such demand among us that the Tax will fall on the consumer.

An able bodied man who demands one hundred dollars bounty to go into a Military Service for three years cannot be oppressed by the annual payment of one Dollar while not in that service. This Tax will also have good effect of placing before the eyes of Congress the number of men in the several States an information always important to Government.

The excise proposed is liable to no other objection than what may be made against the mode of collection, but it is conceived that this may be such as can produce no ill consequences. Excise Laws exist and have long existed in the several States. Of all Taxes those on the consumption of articles are most agreeable, because being mingled with the price they are less sensible to the people, and without entering into a discussion with which speculative Men have amused themselves on the advantages and disadvantages of this Species of Taxation, it may be boldly affirmed that no inconvenience can arise from laying a heavy Tax on the use of Ardent Spirits. These have been always equally prejudicial to the Constitution and Morals of the People.

The Tax will be a means of compelling Vice to support the cause of Virtue, and like the Poll Tax will draw from the idle and dissolute that contribution to the public Service which they will not otherwise make.

Having said this much on the propriety of these Taxes, I shall pray leave to assure you of my ready acquiescence in the choice of any others which may be more agreeable to the United States in Congress, praying them nevertheless that as the situation of the respective States is widely different, it will be wise to adopt a variety of Taxes, because by this means the consent of all will be more readily obtained than if such are chosen as will fall heavy only on particular States.

The next object is the collection which, for the most obvious reasons ought to be by authority derived from the United States. The collection of a Land Tax as has been observed above will be very simple, that of the Poll Tax may be equally so, because Certificates of the payments may be annually issued to the Collectors, and they be bound to return the Certificates or the Money and empowered to compel a payment by every man not possessed of a Certificate.

If, in addition to this, those who travel from one State to another be obliged to take out and pay for a new Certificate in each State that would operate an useful regulation of Police, and a slight distinction between those and the Common Certificates would still preserve their Utility in numbering the people.

It is not necessary to dwell on the mode of Collecting these Branches of Revenue, because (in reason) a determination on the propriety of the Taxes should precede it. I will only take the Liberty to drop one Idea, with respect to the Impost already required.

It is conceived that Laws should be so framed as to leave little or nothing to the discretion of those by whom they are executed. That Revenue Laws in particular should be guarded in this respect from Odium being (as they are) sufficiently odious in themselves, and, therefore, that it would have been well to have stipulated the precise sum, payable on different Species of Commodities. The objection is that the List (to be accurate) must be numerous. But this accuracy is unnecessary, the description ought to be very short and general so as to comprize many commodities under one head, and the duty ought to be fixed according to their average value. The objection against this regulation is, that the Tax on fine commodities would be trivial, and on coarse commodities great.

This, indeed, is true, but it is desirable for two reasons. First, that coarse and bulky commodities *could* not be smuggled to evade the heavy *duty*, and that fine commodities *would* not be smuggled to evade the *light* duty.

Secondly, that coarse commodities (generally speaking) minister to the demands of necessity or convenience, and fine commodities to those of Luxury. The heavy duty on the former would operate as encouragement to produce them at home, and by that means a stoppage of our Commerce in time of War would be most felt by the wealthy who have always the most abundant means of procuring relief.

I shall now, Sir, take the Liberty to suppose that the Revenues I have mentioned or some others to the amount of at least two millions net annual produce were asked for and obtained as a pledge to the Public Creditors, to continue until the Principal and Interest of the Debts contracted, or to be contracted should be finally paid. This supposition is made that I may have an opportunity (thus early) to express my sentiments on the mode of appropriation. It would be as follows: Any one of the Revenues being estimated, a Loan should be opened on the Credit of it by subscription to a certain amount, and Public Debts of a particular description (or Specie) be received in payment of the subscriptions. This Funded Debt should be transferable under particular forms, calculated for the prevention of fraudulent and facilitating of honest negotiations.

In like manner on each of these Revenues should subscriptions be opened, proceeding by degrees so as to prevent any sudden revolution in money matters, such revolutions being always more or less injurious.

I should further propose that the surplus of each of these Revenues (and care should be taken that there would be a surplus) should be carried to a Sinking Fund, on the Credit of which, and the general promises of Government, new Loans should be opened when necessary. The interest should be paid half yearly, which would be convenient to the Creditors and to the Government, as well as useful to the people at large, because by this means if four different Loans were opened at different times the Interest would be payable eight times in the year, and thus the money would be paid out of the Treasury as fast as it comes in, which would require fewer Officers to manage the business, keep them in more constant and regular employment, dispence the Interest so as to command the confidence and facilitate the views of the Creditors and return speedily the Wealth obtained by Taxes into the common stock. I know it will be objected that such a mode of Administration would enable speculators to perform their operations. A general answer to this would be that any other mode would be more favorable to them.

But further, I conceive:

First, that it is much beneath the dignity of Government to intermeddle in such considerations.

Secondly, that speculators always do least mischief where they are left most at liberty.

Thirdly, that it is not inhuman prudence to counteract their operations by Laws, whereas, when left alone they invariably counteract each other.

And fourthly, that even were it possible to prevent speculation it is precisely the thing which ought not to be prevented, because he who wants money to commence, pursue or extend his business, is more benefitted by selling stock of any kind (even at a considerble discount) than he would be by the rise of it at a future period, every man being able to judge better of his own business and situation than the Government can for him. So much would not perhaps have been said on the head of this objection if it did not naturally lead to a position which has hitherto been ruinous and might prove fatal.

There are many men (and some of them honest men) whose zeal against speculation leads them to be some times not only unmindful of sound policy, but even of moral Justice. It is not uncommon to hear that those who have bought the public Debts for small sums ought only to be paid their purchase money. The reasons given are, that they have taken advantage of the distressed Creditor and shown a diffidence in the public faith.

As to the first, it must be remembered that in giving the creditor money for his debt, they have at least afforded him some relief which he could not obtain elsewhere, and if they are deprived of the expected benefit they will never afford such relief again.

As to the second, those who buy up the public Debts show at least as much confidence in the public faith as those who sell them. But allowing (for argument's sake) that they have exhibited the diffidence complained of, it would certainly be wiser to remove than to justify it.

The one mode tends to create, establish and secure public Credit, and the other to sap, overturn and destroy it. Policy is, therefore, on this (as I believe it to be on every other occasion) upon the same side of the question with honesty. Honesty tells us that the duty of the public to pay is like the same duty in an individual, having benefitted by the advances they are bound to replace them to the party or to his Representatives. The Debt is a Species of property, and whether disposed of for whole nominal value or the half, for something or for nothing is totally immaterial. The right of receiving and the duty of paying must always continue the same.

In a word that Government which can (through the intervention of its Courts) compel payment of private Debts and performance of private contracts, on the principles of distributive Justice, but refuse to be guided by those principles as to their own contracts and debts merely because they are not amenable to human Laws, show a flagitious contempt of moral obligations which must necessarily weaken as it ought to do their authority over the people.

Before I conclude this long letter it will be unpardonable not to mention a fund which has long since been suggested, and dwells still in the minds of many.

You, doubtless, Sir, anticipate my naming of what are called the Back Lands. The question as to the property of those Lands, I confess myself utterly incompetent to decide, and shall not for that reason presume to enter on it. But it is my duty to mention that the offer of a pledge, the right to which is contested would have ill consequences, and could have no good ones. It could not strengthen our Credit because no one would rely on such a pledge, and the recurrence to it would give unfavorable impressions of our Political Sagacity. But admitting that the right of Congress is clear, we must remember also that it is disputed by some considerable members of the Confederacy. Dissentions might arise from hasty decisions on the subject, and a Government torn by intestine commotions is not likely to acquire and maintain Credit at home or abroad.

I am not, however, the less clear in my opinion that it would be alike useful to the whole Nation and those very constituent parts of it, that the entire disposition of these Lands should be in Congress. Without entering, therefore, into the ligitated points, I am induced to believe, and for that reason to suggest, the proposing this matter to the States as an amicable arrangement. I hope to be pardoned when I add, that considering the situation of South Carolina and Georgia it might be proper to ask their consent to matters of clearest right. But that supposing the right to be doubtful urging a decision in the present moment might have a harsh and ungenerous appearance. But if we suppose this matter to be arranged either in the one mode or in the other so that the right of Congress be rendered indisputable (for that is a previous point of indispensable necessity) the remaining question will be as to the appropriation of that fund. And I confess it does not appear to me that the benefits resulting from it are such as many are led to believe. When the imagination is heated in pursuit of an object, it is generally over-rated. If these lands were now in the hands of Congress and they were willing to mortgage them to their present Creditors, unless this was accompanied with due provision for the Interest, it would bring no relief. If these lands were to be sold for the public Debt they would go for almost nothing. Those who want money could not afford to buy the land. Their Certificates would be bought up for a trifle. Very few Monied men would become possessed of them, because very little money would be vested in so remote a speculation. The small number of purchasers would easily and readily combine. In consequence they would acquire the land for almost nothing, and effectually defeat the Intentions of Government, leaving it still under the necessity of making farther provision after having needlessly squandered an immense property. This reasoning is not new, it has been advanced on similar occasions before, and the experience which all America has had of the sales of Confiscated estates and the like, will now show that it was well founded. The Back Lands then will not answer our purpose without the necessary Revenues. But those Revenues will alone produce the desired effect. The Back Lands may afterwards be formed into a Fund for opening new Loans in Europe on a low Interest, redeemable at a future period (for instance twenty years) with a right reserved to the Creditors of taking portions of those Lands on the non-payment of their Debts at the expiration of that term. Two modes would offer for liquidation of those Debts. First to tender payments during the Term to those who would not consent to alter the nature of the Debt which (if our Credit be well established) would place it on the general footing of National faith. And Secondly, to sell portions of the Land (during the Term) sufficient to discharge the mortgage. I persuade myself that the consent of the reluctant States might be obtained, and that this fund might hereafter be converted to useful purposes. But I hope that in a moment when the joint efforts of all is indispensable no cause of altercation may be mingled unnecessarily in a Question of such infinite Magnitude as the restoration of public Credit. Let me add, Sir, that unless the money of Foreigners be brought in for the purpose, sales of public Lands would only absorb that surplus wealth which might have been exhaled by Taxes. So that in fact no new recourse is produced, and that while (as at present) the demand for money is so great as to raise Interest to five per cent. per month, Public Lands must sell extremely low, were the title ever so clear. What then can be expected when the validity of that title, is one object of the War?

ROBT. MORRIS.

CALCULATIONS TO SHOW THE EFFECTS OF A YEARLY LOAN OF £10 FOR TEN YEARS ON THE SUPPOSITION THAT THE INTEREST OF MONEY BE £6 AND PROFITS £12 PER CENT.
[From Executive Letter Book.]

Dr.					
First year borrowed	£10		First year borrowed	£10	
	10			10	
2nd year interest at 6 per ct.		6	Second year profits at 12 per ct.	1.	2
	10.	6		11.	2
Paid interest		6	Paid		6
	10			10.	6
Borrowed	10		Borrowed	10	
	20			20.	6
Third year interest	1.	2	Third year profits	2	472
	21.	2		23.	072
Paid interest	1.	2	Paid	1.	2
	20			21.	872
Borrowed	10		Borrowed	10	
	30			31.	872
Fourth year interest	1.	8	Fourth year profits	3.	824
	31.	8		35.	696
Paid interest	1.	8	Paid	1.	8
	30.	0		33.	896
Borrowed	10		Borrowed	10	
	40			43.	896
Fifth year interest	2.	4	Fifth year profits	5.	267
	42.	4		49.	163
Paid interest	2.	4	Paid	2	4
	40			46	763
Borrowed	10		Borrowed	10	
	50			56.	763
Sixth year interest	3		Sixth year profits	6.	811
	53			63.	574
Paid interest	3		Paid	3	
	50			60	574
Borrowed	10		Borrowed	10	
	60			70.	574
Seventh year interest	3.	6	Seventh year profits	8.	468
	63.	6		79.	042
Paid interest	3.	6	Paid	3.	6
	60			75.	442
Borrowed	10		Borrowed	10	

-------------------- page 379 --------------------

38 • COMMERCE & CONTROVERSY IN EARLIER TIMES

Dr.	£70			£85.	442
Eighth year interest	4.	2	Eighth year profits	10.	253
	74.	2		95.	695
Paid interest	4.	2	Paid	4.	2
	70			91.	495
Borrowed	10		Borrowed	10	
	80			101.	495
Ninth year interest	4.	8	Ninth year profits	12.	178
	84.	8		113.	673
Paid interest	4.	8	Paid	4.	8
	80			108.	873
Borrowed	10		Borrowed	10	
	90			118.	873
Tenth year interest	5.	4	Tenth year profits	14.	264
	95.	4		113.	137
Paid interest	5.	4	Paid	5.	4
	90			127.	737
Borrowed	10		Borrowed	10	
	100			137.	737
End of tenth year interest	6		End of tenth profits	16.	528
	106			154.	265
Paid interest	6		Paid	6	
	100			148.	265
Yearly interest	6		Yearly profits	17.	791
			Deduct interest	6	
				11.	791

> **GLOSSARY**
>
> **husbandman:** a farmer
>
> **perfidy:** treacherous and dishonest
>
> **poll tax:** a tax paid by every person, not based on their income or the property they own
>
> **remonstrance:** a forceful rebuke or denunciation
>
> **specie:** money that consists of precious metals such as gold or silver, as opposed to paper money.
>
> **uncontrovertible:** archaic form of "incontrovertible," meaning unable to be denied or argued against.

Document Analysis

Morris begins his letter to Alexander by making reference to the "remonstrance and petition" from Blair McClenachan, acknowledging that the issue of "public loans"—that is, governments borrowing money from a variety of sources, including their own citizens in the form of bonds and paper currency—was controversial. Morris expresses sympathy with those who are uncomfortable with public debt, particularly those who are "saddled with the debts of a preceding generation." However, he that while debt resulting from "negligence, folly, or profusion" is a bad thing, revenue raised through taxation can be wasted as well. The problem, then, is not necessary the use of credit but the ways in which governments manage their money, from whatever source it's derived. Morris argues that taxes are the best revenue option for "vicious" (in the sense of being immoral or dishonest) governments because there is a more immediate reaction from the public to unjust and wasteful taxation, thus it can be corrected. Loans, on the other hand, benefit governments who spend money in a manner that is "honest and wise."

There is a delicate balance, Morris explains in the second paragraph, between taxation that encourages "the industry of individuals" and taxation that is "burthensome and oppressive." Loans are a wiser option than oppressive taxes, Morris argues. In order to illustrate this, he spends several paragraphs (with references to the chart at the end of the document) discussing the relative benefits of loans over taxation, in many cases. Taxes, however, are necessary and, Morris argues, beneficial because they "stimulate industry" and "encourage economy." Basically, taxes encourage people to be productive because they need to earn money to pay the taxes and they will also be thrifty because they need to set aside some of the money they earn to pay those taxes.

Morris then compares the use of domestic loans and foreign loans, outlining the benefits and pitfalls of each. Domestic loans, Morris argues, have the benefit of "giv[ing] stability to Government by combining together the interests of monied men for its support." Domestic loans relied upon investment from residents of the nation, thus there is a considerable incentive to see the nation's economy grow and the government to remain solvent. Morris also dismisses one of the common objects to loans from foreign nations—that they created an unfavorable balance and "and drain the Country of the Specie," or hard currency of gold and silver. While both domestic and foreign loans have benefits, Morris asserts that it is necessary to establish public credit—that is the creditworthiness of the nation—on the domestic front before it is possible to obtain foreign credit on favorable terms. A primary way this public credit can be established is through a solid national currency. Morris points to the "confidence" shown by the American people when the Continental currency was first introduced—and the decrease in that confidence when the value of that currency vanished.

Morris continues his arguments about public credit and taxation at some length and closes his letter to Governor Martin with discussion of the problems of collecting import duties that Congress has passed—noting that Rhode Island, in particular, has been lax in collecting them—and paying out the possibility that revenue could, potentially, be raised from the government sale of "the Back Lands"—the western lands belonging to the states in order to retire the public debt. In particular, he observes that "the money of Foreigners be brought in for the purpose" of the land sales.

Essential Themes

When, in his letter to governor Martin, Robert Morris writes "In every Society also there must be some Taxes, because the necessity of supporting Government & defending the State always exist" he is stating in the simplest terms an issue that would be at the heart of many debates in the halls of American government in the eighteenth and nineteenth centuries (and, of course, even to our own time). In wrestling with the very basic question of "how do we pay for all of the things we need to do?" Morris anticipated the issues that would lead not only of the Constitutional Convention of 1787 but also of the fiscal reforms that his successor, Alexander Hamilton, would call for at the dawn of the federalist era in the 1790s. Morris, in this letter, is responding to the demands of those who are losing faith in the government's ability to pay down debts but uses the opportunity to work through larger questions of how to construct systems of revenue that are as equitable as possible. While the Continental Congress does not have the authority to implement all of the revenue-raising plans Morris discusses here, this long letter was a crucial link in the chain that would eventually lead the young nation to greater solvency in the future.

—*Aaron James Gulyas, MA*

Bibliography and Additional Reading

Hogeland, William. *Founding Finance: How Debt, Speculation, Foreclosures, Protests, and Crackdowns Made Us a Nation.* Austin: University of Texas Press, 2012.

Rappleye, Charles. *Robert Morris: Financier of the American Revolution.* New York: Simon & Schuster, 2010.

Smith, Ryan K. *Robert Morris's Folly: The Architectural and Financial Failures of an American Founder.* New Haven, CT: Yale University Press, 2014.

Wright, Robert E., and David J. Cowen. *Financial Founding Fathers: The Men Who Made America Rich.* Chicago: University of Chicago Press, 2006.

Federalist No. 35 (Concerning the General Power of Taxation)

Date: January 5, 1788
Author: Alexander Hamilton (writing as Publius)
Genre: essay

Summary Overview

From September 17, 1787, when participants in the Constitutional Convention in Philadelphia finished their work, through June 21, 1788, when New Hampshire became the ninth state to ratify the Constitution (thus putting it into effect), debate raged in the young United States over the proper role and ideal makeup of the national government. The questions of how the new government should be organized and what powers it should possess had implications for many aspects of society. In *Federalist*, no. 35, published in January 1788, Alexander Hamilton responds to concerns about the proposed federal government's power to tax. In doing so, Hamilton addresses not only the issue of the U.S. government's power to tax but also the overarching question of how the new U.S. Constitution addressed congressional representation. Hamilton shares his insight into the ways that taxation policy had the power and ability to either promote or stifle economic innovation and growth depending on how governments applied that power. In doing so, he presents his perception that various parts of the American economy are far more intertwined than might appear on the surface. A broad or "general" ability of the federal government was, he would argue, an important power for managing and encouraging economic growth throughout the nation.

Defining Moment

In September 1787, the Constitutional Convention in Philadelphia saw delegates complete the work of creating a new framework for the national government of the United States. The new system of government aimed to replace the Articles of Confederation—a relatively basic compact between the states established during the War for Independence. The Articles prioritized the individual sovereignty of each state, with a weak national government providing a minimal amount of coordination. Two of the key faults critics of the Articles of Confederation pointed to were the system of Congressional representation that granted each state equal power—regardless of its population or economic power—and the inability of the Confederation government to levy taxes. Instead, the national government was limited to requesting a contribution from each state—a contribution states rarely paid. In order to raise revenue for their own purposes, individual states on the Atlantic coast relied heavily on import duties from trade. This led to competition between ports for trade and disproportionately affected some sectors of the economy. The Confederation Congress had made attempts to modify the articles to remedy these issues, but these efforts were unsuccessful.

The Constitutional Convention's solution was to grant Congress the power to levy taxes as well as to collect import duties. Article I, section 8 of the Constitution granted Congress the authority to "lay and collect Taxes, Duties, Imposts and Excises" and that these must be "uniform throughout the United States." With regard to taxes on imported goods, the new constitution proclaimed that "No Preference shall be given by any Regulation of Commerce or Revenue to the Ports of one State over those of another." This was far more power than the Confederation Congress possessed.

There were many opposed to this enlargement of the powers of the national government. To counter arguments against the constitution, James Madison, John Jay, and Alexander Hamilton composed eighty-five essays (collectively known as *The Federalist Papers*) to defend the new constitution and promote its ratification. These *Federalist* essays appeared in a number of New York City newspapers from October 1787 to April 1788. They began circulating through the rest of the states when the first collected editions of the essays were published in January 1788. *The Federalist Papers* were instrumental in persuading state ratification assemblies to adopt the new constitution and usher in a new age of American governance.

Author Biography

Alexander Hamilton's early life and family history is shrouded in more mystery than most of the other founders of the American republic. Even the year he was born is uncertain, but be it 1755 or 1757, he was born to an unwed mother on the Caribbean island of Nevis, part of the British West Indies. Abandoned by his father and left an orphan by his mother's death when he was a child, young Alexander found work as a clerk with a trading company that did business with British colonies in North America, including New York. In late 1772, Alexander emigrated to North America, landing at Boston and eventually settling in New York. A year later he became a student at King's College (now Columbia University) and in 1774 became involved in the growing debates over British policy toward its American colonies, giving eloquent speeches and writing persuasive essays for the American cause.

When fighting broke out in 1775, Hamilton joined a militia unit in New York and took part in engagements in New York City, eventually securing the rank of captain and command of an artillery company. Hamilton eventually became commanding General George Washington's aide, handling correspondence and intelligence duties as well as often serving as Washington's representative when consulting with other officers. He commanded several battalions in the war's climactic battle near Yorktown, Virginia.

After the war, Hamilton practiced law and became involved in politics, including serving as part of New York's delegation to Congress. Like many others, Hamilton worried that the national government's lack of authority was a detriment to the United States as a whole. In 1787, when the Constitutional convention began in Philadelphia, Hamilton was appointed as a delegate from New York. He took an active role in the debates and, afterward, joined with John Jay and James Madison in composing *The Federalist Papers* in support of the new Constitution (see "Defining Moment").

Following the ratification of the Constitution, Hamilton served as the nation's first secretary of the treasury under President George Washington. The forward-thinking vision for America's economic future presented in *Federalist*, no. 35 would find expressing in his policies for a national bank and proposals for the encouragement of manufacturing.

HISTORICAL DOCUMENT: *Federalist* No. 35

To the People of the State of New York:

BEFORE we proceed to examine any other objections to an indefinite power of taxation in the Union, I shall make one general remark; which is, that if the jurisdiction of the national government, in the article of revenue, should be restricted to particular objects, it would naturally occasion an undue proportion of the public burdens to fall upon those objects. Two evils would spring from this source: the oppression of particular branches of industry; and an unequal distribution of the taxes, as well among the several States as among the citizens of the same State.

Suppose, as has been contended for, the federal power of taxation were to be confined to duties on imports, it is evident that the government, for want of being able to command other resources, would frequently be tempted to extend these duties to an injurious excess. There are persons who imagine that they can never be carried to too great a length; since the higher they are, the more it is alleged they will tend to discourage an extravagant consumption, to produce a favorable balance of trade, and to promote domestic manufactures. But all extremes are pernicious in various ways. Exorbitant duties on imported articles would beget a general spirit of smuggling; which is always prejudicial to the fair trader, and eventually to the revenue itself: they tend to render other classes of the community tributary, in an improper degree, to the manufacturing classes, to whom they give a premature monopoly of the markets; they sometimes force industry out of its more natural channels into others in which it flows with less advantage; and in the last place, they oppress the merchant, who is often obliged to pay them himself without any retribution from the consumer. When the demand is equal to the quantity of goods at market, the consumer generally pays the duty; but when the markets happen to be overstocked, a great proportion falls upon the merchant, and sometimes not only exhausts his profits, but breaks in upon his capital. I am apt to think that a division of the duty, between the seller and the buyer, more often happens than is commonly imagined. It is not always possible to raise the price of a commodity in exact proportion to every additional imposition laid upon it. The merchant, especially in a country of small commercial capital, is often under a necessity of keeping prices down in order to a more expeditious sale.

> *Exorbitant duties on imported articles would beget a general spirit of smuggling; which is always prejudicial to the fair trader.*

The maxim that the consumer is the payer, is so much oftener true than the reverse of the proposition, that it is far more equitable that the duties on imports should go into a common stock, than that they should redound to the exclusive benefit of the importing States. But it is not so generally true as to render it equitable, that those duties should form the only national fund. When they are paid by the merchant they operate as an additional tax upon the importing State, whose citizens pay their proportion of them in the character of consumers. In this view they are productive of inequality among the States; which inequality would be increased with the increased extent of the duties. The confinement of the national revenues to this species of imposts would be attended with inequality, from a different cause, between the manufacturing and the non-manufacturing States. The States which can go farthest towards the supply of their own wants, by their own manufactures, will not, according to their numbers or wealth, consume so great a proportion of imported articles as those States which are not in the same favorable situation. They would not, therefore, in this mode alone contribute to the public treasury in a ratio to their abilities. To make them do this it is necessary that recourse be had to excises, the proper objects of which are particular kinds of manufactures. New York is more deeply interested in these considerations than such of her citizens as contend for limiting the power of the Union to external taxation may be aware of. New York is an importing State, and is not likely speedily to be, to any great extent, a manufacturing State. She would, of course, suffer in a double light from restraining the jurisdiction of the Union to commercial imposts.

So far as these observations tend to inculcate a danger of the import duties being extended to an injurious extreme it may be observed, conformably to a remark made in another part of these papers, that the interest of the revenue itself would be a sufficient guard against such an extreme. I readily admit that this would be the case, as long as other resources were open; but if the avenues to them were closed, HOPE, stimulated by necessity, would beget experiments, fortified by rigorous precautions and additional penalties, which, for a time, would have the intended effect, till there had been leisure to contrive expedients to elude these new precautions. The first success would be apt to inspire false opinions, which it might require a long course of subsequent experience to correct. Necessity, especially in politics, often occasions false hopes, false reasonings, and a system of measures correspondingly erroneous. But even if this supposed excess should not be a consequence of the limitation of the federal power of taxation, the inequalities spoken of would still ensue, though not in the same degree, from the other causes that have been noticed. Let us now return to the examination of objections.

One which, if we may judge from the frequency of its repetition, seems most to be relied on, is, that the House of Representatives is not sufficiently numerous for the reception of all the different classes of citizens, in order to combine the interests and feelings of every part of the community, and to produce a due sympathy between the representative body and its constituents. This argument presents itself under a very specious and seducing form; and is well calculated to lay hold of the prejudices of those to whom it is addressed. But when we come to dissect it with attention, it will appear to be made up of nothing but fair-sounding words. The object it seems to aim at is, in the first place, impracticable, and in the sense in which it is contended for, is unnecessary. I reserve for another place the discussion of the question which relates to the sufficiency of the representative body in respect to numbers, and shall content myself with examining here the particular use which has been made of a contrary supposition, in reference to the immediate subject of our inquiries.

The idea of an actual representation of all classes of the people, by persons of each class, is altogether visionary. Unless it were expressly provided in the Constitution, that each different occupation should send one or more members, the thing would never take place in practice. Mechanics and manufacturers will always be inclined, with few exceptions, to give their votes to merchants, in preference to persons of their own professions or trades. Those discerning citizens are well aware that the mechanic and manufacturing arts furnish the materials of mercantile enterprise and industry. Many of them, indeed, are immediately connected with the operations of commerce. They know that the merchant is their natural patron and friend; and they are aware, that however great the confidence they may justly feel in their own good sense, their interests can be more effectually promoted by the merchant than by themselves. They are sensible that their habits in life have not been such as to give them those acquired endowments, without which, in a deliberative assembly, the greatest natural abilities are for the most part useless; and that the influence and weight, and superior acquirements of the merchants render them more equal to a contest with any spirit which might happen to infuse itself into the public councils, unfriendly to the manufacturing and trading interests. These considerations, and many others that might be mentioned prove, and experience confirms it, that artisans and manufacturers will commonly be disposed to bestow their votes upon merchants and those whom they recommend. We must therefore consider merchants as the natural representatives of all these classes of the community.

With regard to the learned professions, little need be observed; they truly form no distinct interest in society, and according to their situation and talents, will be indiscriminately the objects of the confidence and choice of each other, and of other parts of the community.

Nothing remains but the landed interest; and this, in a political view, and particularly in relation to taxes, I take to be perfectly united, from the wealthiest landlord down to the poorest tenant. No tax can be laid on land which will not affect the proprietor of millions of acres as well as the proprietor of a single acre. Every landholder will therefore have a common interest to keep the taxes on land as low as possible; and common interest may always be reckoned upon as the surest bond of sympathy. But if we even could suppose a distinction of interest between the opulent landholder and the middling farmer, what reason is there to conclude, that the first would stand a better chance of being deputed to the national legislature than the last? If we take fact as our guide, and look into our own senate and assembly, we shall find that moderate proprietors of land prevail in both; nor is this less the case in the senate, which consists of a smaller number, than in the assembly, which is composed of a greater number. Where the qualifications of the electors are the same, whether they have to choose a small or a large number, their votes will fall upon those in whom they have most confidence; whether these happen to be men of large fortunes, or of moderate property, or of no property at all.

It is said to be necessary, that all classes of citizens should have some of their own number in the representative body, in order that their feelings and interests may be the better understood and attended to. But we have seen that this will never happen under any arrangement that leaves the votes of the people free. Where this is the case, the representative body, with too few exceptions to have any influence on the spirit of the government, will be composed of landholders, merchants, and men of the learned professions. But where is the danger that the interests and feelings of the different classes of citizens will not be understood or attended to by these three descriptions of men? Will not the landholder know and feel whatever will promote or insure the interest of landed property? And will he not, from his own interest in that species of property, be sufficiently prone to resist every attempt to prejudice or encumber it? Will not the merchant understand and be disposed to cultivate, as far as may be proper, the interests of the mechanic and manufacturing arts, to which his commerce is so nearly allied? Will not the man of the learned profession, who will feel a neutrality to the rivalships between the different branches of industry, be likely to prove an impartial arbiter between them, ready to promote either, so far as it shall appear to him conducive to the general interests of the society?

If we take into the account the momentary humors or dispositions which may happen to prevail in particular parts of the society, and to which a wise administration will never be inattentive, is the man whose situation leads to extensive inquiry and information less likely to be a competent judge of their nature, extent, and foundation than one whose observation does not travel beyond the circle of his neighbors and acquaintances? Is it not natural that a man who is a candidate for the favor of the people, and who is dependent on the suffrages of his fellow-citizens for the continuance of his public honors, should take care to inform himself of their dispositions and inclinations, and should be willing to allow them their proper degree of influence upon his conduct? This dependence, and the necessity of being bound himself, and his posterity, by the laws to which he gives his assent, are the true, and they are the strong chords of sympathy between the representative and the constituent.

There is no part of the administration of government that requires extensive information and a thorough knowledge of the principles of political economy, so much as the business of taxation. The man who understands those principles best will be least likely to resort to oppressive expedients, or sacrifice any particular class of citizens to the procurement of revenue. It might be demonstrated that the most productive system of finance will always be the least burdensome. There can be no doubt that in order to a judicious exercise of the power of taxation, it is necessary that the person in whose hands it should be acquainted with the general genius, habits, and modes of thinking of the people at large, and with the resources of the country. And this is all that can be reasonably meant by a knowledge of the interests and feelings of the people. In any other sense the proposition has either no meaning, or an absurd one. And in that sense let every considerate citizen judge for himself where the requisite qualification is most likely to be found.

PUBLIUS.

GLOSSARY

acquirements: achievements or skills that have been obtained

duties: fees imposed on imported goods as a means of raising government revenue

impracticable: unable to be implemented

revenue: money raised to support the activities of the government

Document Analysis

Hamilton opens the essay with a "general remark" that will inform much of what follows. He argues that limiting the power of the government to tax only specific items would cause "undue proportion of the public burdens to fall upon those objects." This would result in some sectors of the economy being unequally (and negatively) affected by tax policy and that this inequality would also, as a consequence, affect some states of the country more than others.

He then moves to address specific arguments against the national government possessing a broadly defined power to tax. The first is the argument that the taxing power should be "confined to duties on imports." Hamilton contends that if this was the only way the government could raise funds, the result would be extremely high import duties because there would be no other option for the government to obtain income. Contrary to what some believe, Hamilton says, import duties need to have limits: if they are too high, merchants will resort to smuggling, which not only deprives the government of its funds but also harms merchants who play by the rules and pay their taxes. Hamilton also addresses the argument that merchants are not harmed by high import duties because those costs are passed on to the consumer. This is not, he responds, always the case. In most instances, Hamilton asserts, high import duties make costs higher for consumers while, at the same time, decreasing overall profits for merchants. Limiting the government's authority to tax to the imposition of duties on imports also places importers and merchants at an economic disadvantage compared to other sectors of the economy such as manufacturers or farmers.

Hamilton then moves onto an objection that is not entirely economic but, rather, is connected to larger questions of how Americans were to be represented in the national government under the new Constitution. This objection is that the House of Representatives (to which states would send delegations in proportion to their

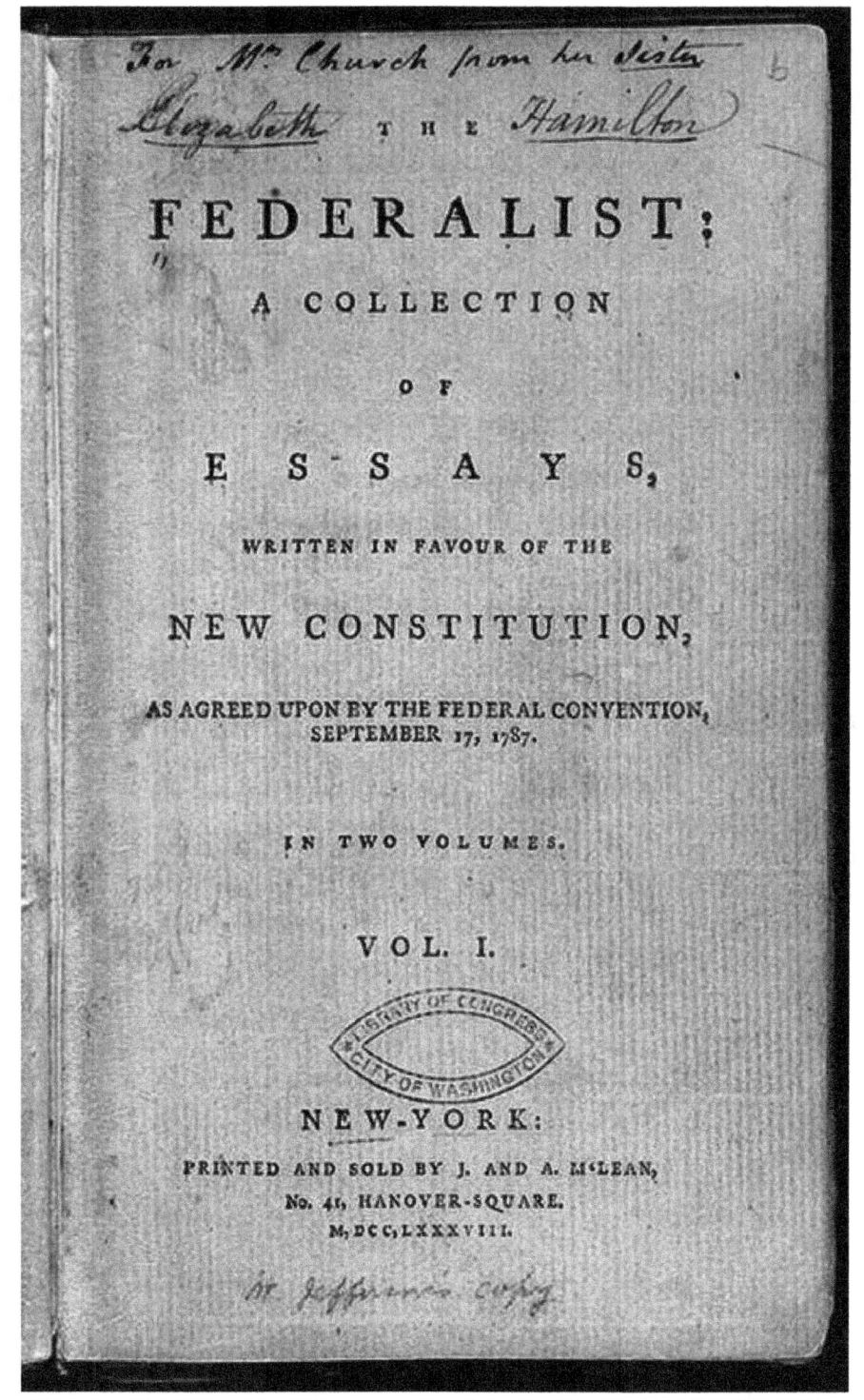

Alexander Hamilton wrote 51 essays in the Federalist Papers, including No. 35 on Taxation. This image was sent from Eliza Hamilton to her sister Angelica Schuyler Church

population—that is, the more people lived in a state, the more representatives it would send) was not large enough to sufficiently represent the views of "all the different classes of citizens." In this instance, Hamilton seems to be using "classes of citizens" to mean citizens working in various sectors of the economy. He argues that, even if the Constitution outlined such a system, it would be "impracticable" to proportionately represent merchants, manufacturers, and all other occupations in the legislature. Rather, he argues, the system put in place by the Constitution is adequate to represent all sectors of the economy because all sectors of the economy are interconnected and interdependent. Merchants and manufacturers have interests in common. Members of "the learned professions," regardless of their field of expertise often have similar political and economic interests. Landowners—regardless of the amount of land they possess—have (at least with regard to taxation), in Hamilton's opinion, views that are "perfectly united." Thus, the makeup of Congress defining by the Constitution will be representative of all sectors of the economy without the need to resort to finding a system to specifically represent individual occupational groups.

This broad array of representatives Congress, and the "strong chords of sympathy between the representative and the constituent" that results from it will, Hamilton argues, help ensure that knowledgeable members of Congress, will create systems of taxation that will be "productive" without being "burdensome" to the American people. By defending the nature of representation proposed by the Constitution, Hamilton is able to address concerns about the new, broad powers to tax granted to those representatives.

Essential Themes

In *Federalist*, no. 35, Hamilton moves beyond simply defending Congress's ability to tax under the proposed Constitution. Rather, he offers a defense for the very concept of a broad taxing and revenue-raising power as well as a defense for the structure of the House of Representatives, as defined in the Constitution. Although he places his focus and tailors his examples for an audience of New York readers, the lessons he presents are applicable to Americans in all regions of the country and who are involved in a variety of economic pursuits. Hamilton also emphasizes the role of the House of Representatives in providing a valuable cross-section of the American economy, with members who are engaged in enough different types of financial pursuits to craft tax policy that will benefit the nation as a whole.

—*Aaron James Gulyas, MA*

Bibliography and Additional Reading

Chernow, Ron. *Alexander Hamilton*. New York: Penguin, 2005.

Federici, Michael P. *The Political Philosophy of Alexander Hamilton*. Baltimore: Johns Hopkins University Press, 2012.

McCraw, Thomas K. *The Founders and Finance: How Hamilton, Gallatin, and other Immigrants Forged a New Economy*. Cambridge, MA: Harvard University Press, 2012.

Wood, Gordon. *Empire of Liberty: A History of the Early Republic, 1789-1815*. New York: Oxford University Press, 2009.

An ACT to promote the Progress of useful Arts.

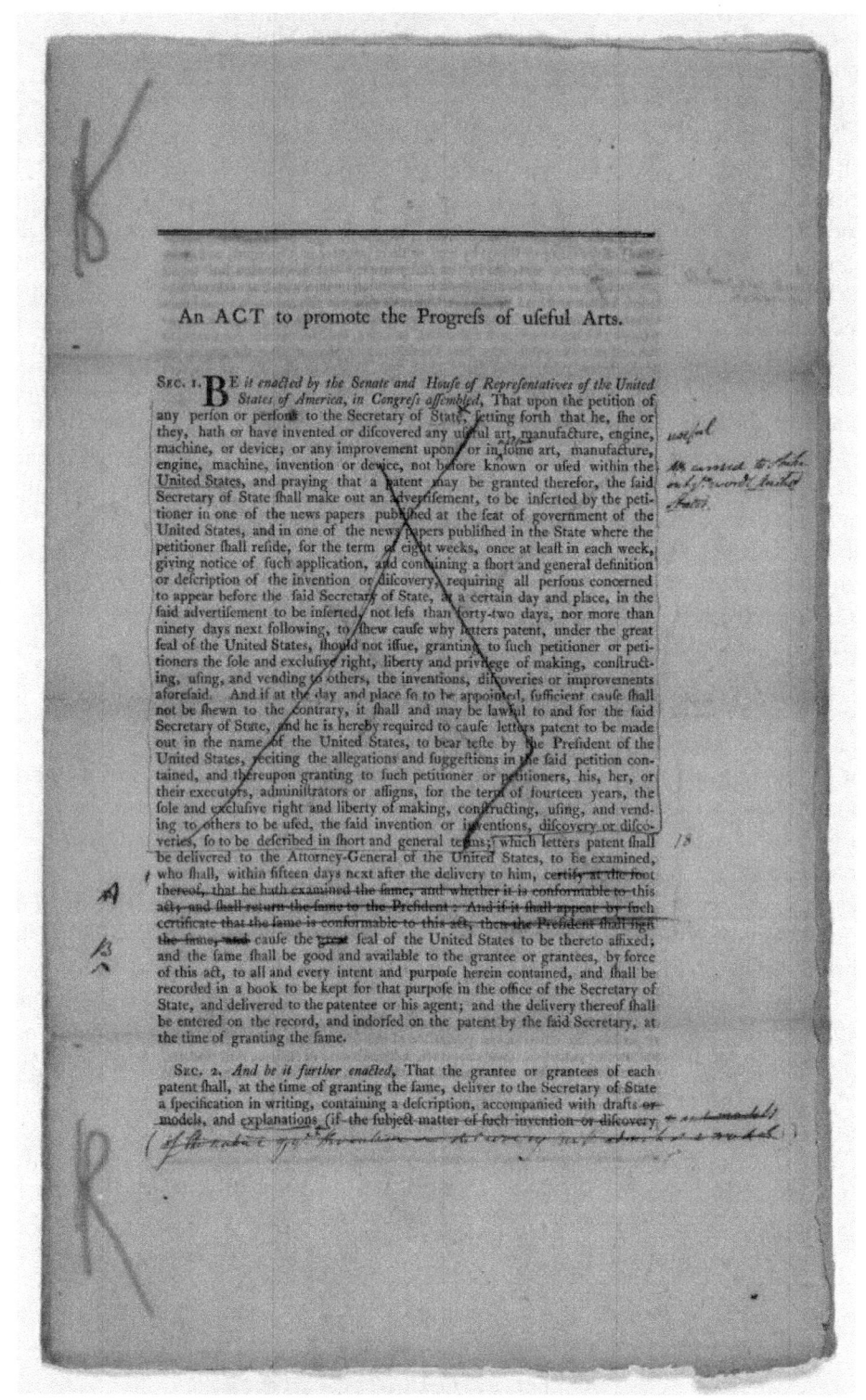

SEC. 1. BE it enacted by the Senate and House of Representatives of the United States of America, in Congress assembled, That upon the petition of any person or persons to the Secretary of State, setting forth that he, she or they, hath or have invented or discovered any useful art, manufacture, engine, machine, or device; or any improvement upon or in some art, manufacture, engine, machine, invention or device, not before known or used within the United States, and praying that a patent may be granted therefor, the said Secretary of State shall make out an advertisement, to be inserted by the petitioner in one of the news papers published at the seat of government of the United States, and in one of the news papers published in the State where the petitioner shall reside, for the term of eight weeks, once at least in each week, giving notice of such application, and containing a short and general definition or description of the invention or discovery, requiring all persons concerned to appear before the said Secretary of State, at a certain day and place, in the said advertisement to be inserted, not less than forty-two days, nor more than ninety days next following, to shew cause why letters patent, under the great seal of the United States, should not issue, granting to such petitioner or petitioners the sole and exclusive right, liberty and privilege of making, constructing, using, and vending to others, the inventions, discoveries or improvements aforesaid. And if at the day and place so to be appointed, sufficient cause shall not be shewn to the contrary, it shall and may be lawful to and for the said Secretary of State, and he is hereby required to cause letters patent to be made out in the name of the United States, to bear teste by the President of the United States, reciting the allegations and suggestions in the said petition contained, and thereupon granting to such petitioner or petitioners, his, her, or their executors, administrators or assigns, for the term of fourteen years, the sole and exclusive right and liberty of making, constructing, using, and vending to others to be used, the said invention or inventions, discovery or discoveries, so to be described in short and general terms; which letters patent shall be delivered to the Attorney-General of the United States, to be examined, who shall, within fifteen days next after the delivery to him, certify at the foot thereof, that he hath examined the same, and whether it is conformable to this act; and shall return the same to the President: And if it shall appear by such certificate that the same is conformable to this act, then the President shall sign the same, and cause the great seal of the United States to be thereto affixed; and the same shall be good and available to the grantee or grantees, by force of this act, to all and every intent and purpose herein contained, and shall be recorded in a book to be kept for that purpose in the office of the Secretary of State, and delivered to the patentee or his agent; and the delivery thereof shall be entered on the record, and indorsed on the patent by the said Secretary, at the time of granting the same.

SEC. 2. And be it further enacted, That the grantee or grantees of each patent shall, at the time of granting the same, deliver to the Secretary of State a specification in writing, containing a description, accompanied with drafts or models, and explanations (if the subject matter of such invention or discovery

The Patent Act of 1790 was designed to encourage innovation, but inventors and designers have argued about its effectiveness ever since.

Patent Act of 1790

Date: April 10, 1790
Authors: The First Congress (originating with a committee consisting of Aedanus Burke, Lambert Cadwalader, and Benjamin Huntington)
Genre: legislation

Summary Overview

The Patent Act of 1790—with its official, and more poetic, title being "An Act to promote the progress of useful Arts"—was the first patent legislation implemented in the United States and provided for a system that would protect the rights of an increasing number of inventors who were at the forefront of American ingenuity. The Patent Act of 1790, though Congress would supplant it with a new law three years later (see "Essential Themes"), was a milestone for technological innovation.

Defining Moment

The new, recently ratified Constitution for the United States of America granted a level of authority to the federal Congress that did not exist in the earlier, less powerful legislature under the Articles of Confederation. An aspect of this, enumerated in Article I, Section 8, was the power "To promote the Progress of Science and useful Arts, by securing for limited Times to Authors and Inventors the exclusive Right to their respective Writings and Discoveries." This is the Constitutional source of the First Congress's ability to pass the Patent Act of 1790. Virginia's James Madison, one of the driving forces of the 1787 Constitutional Convention discussed the appropriateness of this specific power in *The Federalist Papers*, no. 42. Madison wrote that "The utility of this power will scarcely be questioned" because "the public good fully coincides in both cases with the claims of individuals" to their useful creations. Furthermore, Madison argued, this should be within the purview of the federal government since "the States cannot separately make effectual provisions" for securing patents.

There was the potential for competing patent claims between inventors in different states of the country. In the *Journal of the House of Representatives* for January 29, 1790, we see that a number of petitions had been presented to Congress. Aaron Putnam of Massachusetts requested "that an exclusive privilege may be granted him in the use of an improved method of distilling, which he has discovered, whereby the spirit is rendered much more pure." Francis Bailey, of Philadelphia wanted the same privilege for "an invention which he has discovered, of forming types for printing devices to surround or make parts of printed papers for any purpose, which cannot be counterfeited." The Speaker of the House, Frederick Muhlenberg, ordered that the petitions be referred to a committee which was preparing a bill "for securing to Authors and Inventors the exclusive right to their respective writings and discoveries." This committee had been at work for several weeks and throughout the Spring of that year Congress worked to create a law that would recognize the rights of inventors and their interests. The result was House Resolution 41, which would form the basis of the Patent Act of 1790.

Author Biography

The Patent Act of 1790 was enacted by the First U.S. Congress, which was in session from 1789 to 1791, and signed into law by President George Washington. While a committee in the House of Representatives (consisting of Aedanus Burke of South Carolina, Lambert Cadwalader of New Jersey, and Benjamin Huntington of Connecticut) was tasked with creating the initial resolution, the First Congress, in its three sessions, implemented a vast array of legislation. Some of this legislation, like the Patent Act, the Copyright Act of 1790, and the Judiciary Act of 1789, were the result of fulfilling the declaration of the types of laws Congress had the Constitutional authority to make. Other laws involved setting up the Executive Branch—establishing the Departments of State and War, for example—or attempting to solve the young nation's continuing fiscal crisis by imposing tariffs on imported goods and establishing a national bank.

HISTORICAL DOCUMENT: Patent Act of 1790

An Act to promote the progress of useful Arts.

SEC. 1. Be it enacted by the Senate and House of Representatives of the United States of America in Congress assembled, That upon the petition of any person or persons to the Secretary of State, the Secretary for the department of war, and the Attorney General of the United States, setting forth, that he, she, or they, hath or have invented or discovered any useful art, manufacture, engine, machine, or device, or any improvement therein not before known or used, and praying that a patent may be granted therefor, it shall and may be lawful to and for the Secretary of State, the Secretary for the department of war, and the Attorney General, or any two of them, if they shall deem the invention or discovery sufficiently useful and important, to cause letters patent to be made out in the name of the United States, to bear teste by the President of the United States, reciting the allegations and suggestions of the said petition, and describing the said invention or discovery, clearly, truly and fully, and thereupon granting to such petitioner or petitioners, his, her or their heirs, administrators or assigns for any term not exceeding fourteen years, the sole and exclusive right and liberty of making, constructing, using and vending to others to be used, the said invention or discovery; which letters patent shall be delivered to the Attorney General of the United States to be examined, who shall, within fifteen days next after the delivery to him, if he shall find the same conformable to this act, certify it to be so at the foot thereof, and present the letters patent so certified to the President, who shall cause the seal of the United States to be thereto affixed, and the same shall be good and available to the grantee or grantees by force of this act, to all and every intent and purpose herein contained, and shall be recorded in a book to be kept for that purpose in the office of the Secretary of State, and delivered to the patentee or his agent, and the delivery thereof shall be entered on the record and endorsed on the patent by the said Secretary at the time of granting the same.

SEC 2. And be it further enacted, That the grantee or grantees of each patent shall, at the time of granting the same, deliver to the Secretary of State a specification in writing, containing a description, accompanied with drafts or models, and explanations and models (if the nature of the invention or discovery will admit of a model) of the thing or things, by him or them invented or discovered, and described as aforesaid, in the said patents; which specification shall be so particular, and said models so exact, as not only to distinguish the invention or discovery from other things before known and used, but also to enable a workman or other person skilled in the art or manufacture, whereof it is a branch, or wherewith it may be nearest connected, to make, construct, or use the same, to the end that the public may have the full benefit thereof, after the expiration of the patent term; which specification shall be filed in the office of the said Secretary, and certified copies thereof, shall be competent evidence in all courts and before all jurisdictions, where any matter or thing, touching or concerning such patent, right, or privilege, shall come in question.

SEC. 3. And be it further enacted, That upon the application of any person to the Secretary of State, for a copy of any such specification, and for permission to have similar model or models made, it shall be the duty of the Secretary to give such copy, and to permit the person so applying for a similar model or models, to take, or make, or cause the same to be taken or made, at the expense of such applicant.

SEC. 4. And be it further enacted, That if any person or persons shall devise, make, construct, use, employ, or vend within these United States, any art, manufacture, engine, machine or device, or any invention or improvement upon, or in any art, manufacture, engine, machine or device, the sole and exclusive right of which shall be so as aforesaid granted by patent to any person or persons, by virtue and in pursuance of this act, without the consent of the patentee or patentees, their executors, administrators or assigns, first had and obtained in writing, every person so offending, shall forfeit and pay to the said patentee or patentees, his, her or their executors, administrators or assigns such damages as shall be assessed by a jury, and moreover shall forfeit to the person aggrieved, the thing or things so devised, made, constructed, used, employed or vended, contrary to the true intent of this act, which may be recovered in an action on the case founded on this act.

> *An Act to promote the progress of useful Arts.*

SEC. 5. And be it further enacted, That upon oath or affirmation made before the judge of the district court, where the defendant resides, that any patent which shall be issued in pursuance of this act, was obtained surreptitiously by, or upon false suggestion, and motion made to the said court, within one year after issuing the said patent, but not afterwards, it shall and may be lawful to and for the judge of the said district court, if the matter alleged shall appear to him to be sufficient, to grant a rule that the patentee or patentees, his, her, or their executors, administrators or assigns, show cause why process should not issue against him, her, or them, to repeal such patents; and if sufficient cause shall not be shown to the contrary, the rule shall be made absolute, and thereupon the said judge shall order process to be issued as aforesaid, against such patentee or patentees, his, her, or their executors, administrators, or assigns. And in case no sufficient cause shall be shown to the contrary, or if it shall appear that the patentee was not the first and true inventor or discoverer, judgment shall be rendered by such court for the repeal of such patent or patents; and if the party at whose complaint the process issued, shall have judgment given against him, he shall pay all such costs as the defendant shall be put to in defending the suit, to be taxed by the court, and recovered in such manner as costs expended by defendants, shall be recovered in due course of law.

SEC. 6. And be it further enacted, That in all actions to be brought by such patentee or patentees, his, her, or their executors, administrators or assigns, for any penalty incurred by virtue of this act, the said patents or specifications shall be prima facie evidence, that the said patentee or patentees was or were the first and true inventor or inventors, discoverer or discoverers of the thing so specified, and that the same is truly specified; but that nevertheless the defendant or defendants may plead the general issue, and give this act, and any special matter whereof notice in writing shall have been given to the plaintiff, or his attorney, thirty days before the trial, in evidence, tending to prove that the specification filed by the plaintiff does not contain the whole of the truth concerning his invention or discovery; or that it contains more than is necessary to produce the effect described; and if the concealment of part, or the addition of more than is necessary, shall appear to have been intended to mislead, or shall actually mislead the public, so as the effect described cannot be produced by the means specified, then, and in such cases, the verdict and judgment shall be for the defendant.

SEC. 7. And be it further enacted, That such patentee as aforesaid, shall, before he receives his patent, pay the following fees to the several officers employed in making out and perfecting the same, to wit: For receiving and filing the petition, fifty cents; for filing specifications, per copy-sheet containing one hundred words, ten cents; for making out patent, two dollars; for affixing great seal, one dollar; for indorsing the day of delivering the same to the patentee, including all intermediate services, twenty cents.

APPROVED, April 10, 1790.

GLOSSARY

aforesaid: stated previously

assigns: people designated to act on someone's behalf

prima facie evidence: evidence that is accepted as true unless and until proved otherwise.

thereupon: immediately following

vend: to sell

Document Analysis

The Patent Act of 1790 is divided into seven sections. Section One outlines the makeup of the team that would evaluate patent applications. The law establishes that the Secretary of State, the Secretary of War, and the Attorney General were responsible for evaluating the applications of "any person or persons" who "invented or discovered any useful art, manufacture, engine, machine, or device, or any improvement therein not before known or used." This is a fairly broad array of applications and the law does not—in subsequent sections—provide much more in the way of guidance for what was or was not allowed. We should also, at this point, note the relatively inclusive language with regard to gender provided in Section One, for the law specifies that "he, she, or they" might bring a petition. Section One goes on to direct that a petition for a patent must be granted if two of the three members of the board agree that the "invention or discovery" is "sufficiently useful and important." Again, there is a degree of vagueness. An "invention" is easy enough to comprehend, but "discovery" is much less specific. Patents, the law specifies, would be granted for up to fourteen years. A limit on the life of the patent serves as a compromise between an environment where intellectual property is undefended and a situation where inventors or developers might hold an unfair monopoly.

Section Two outlines the requirements for the description of the "invention or discovery." While there are not incredibly detailed instructions, there are important general guidelines and, significantly, a well-founded explanation of the reasoning for the guidelines. They are twofold. First, the description must be detailed enough to enable to the board to determine whether or not the invention or discovery is truly unique. Second, it is to provide enough information that people may replicate the invention or discovery in order that "that the public may have the full benefit" of how to make use of the object after the term of the patent has expired. In this way, the Patent Act was not only for the benefit of the inventor or innovator, but was intended to be of value to the people of the United States as a whole. Section Three provides for copies of patent paperwork to be provided to those willing to pay the costs of doing so.

Section Four outlines the legal remedy for those whose patent rights had been violated. In such cases, the violations and damages are to be determined in a jury trial. In addition to financial damages, the patent holder will also receive "the thing or things" that violated his or her patent. Somewhat similarly, Section Five deals with the possibility of a patent having been issued based "upon false suggestion." Once again, the remedy for such an occurrence lies with the judicial system. Section Six lays out the procedures and standards for presenting evidence to the courts in these cases.

Finally, Section Seven presents the schedule of fees for various aspects of the patent process. These costs were not exorbitant (adjusted for inflation, the total cost was well under $100 in twenty-first century terms). This range of costs placed patent-holding well-within reach of many Americans, broadening access to economic growth and security for many.

Essential Themes

One of the most striking things about the Patent Act of 1790 is that Congress attempted to implement a system to evaluate patent applications and grant patents without creating a bureaucratic infrastructure to accomplish this. Placing responsibility for administering this law in the hands of a variety of cabinet officials highlights the degree to which the federal government was far smaller not only than it is in the twenty-first century, but how much smaller it would be just a few decades later. The system established by the 1790 act had many flaws—enough that a new law would replace it only three years later.

The structure for patent approval was slow—the first patent under the law was granted on July 31, 1790. It was for a method of producing potash (a substance used in glassmaking); only two additional patents were granted in 1790. As it transpired, cabinet-level officials had enough duties to which they had to attend without reviewing patent claims, leading to a logjam of applications to be worked through. In all, fifty-five inventions successfully navigated the process of the 1790 act before it was supplanted by the new 1793 law. The final patent granted under the system was to John Fitch, who developed a steam engine for ships.

Though only in effect for a short time before being improved upon, the Patent Act of 1790 established important precedents for safeguarding the rights of inventors and innovators, just in time for the industrial revolution to sweep through the United States in the years to come. It also demonstrated the manner in which the provisions of the new Constitution contributed to national standards and, in time, a national economy.

—*Aaron James Gulyas, MA*

Bibliography and Additional Reading

First Federal Congress Project: Documenting the History of the First Federal Congress, 1789-1791. George Washington University, https://www2.gwu.edu/~ffcp/.

Hovenkamp, Herbert J. "The Emergence of Classical American Patent Law." Faculty Scholarship at Penn Law, 2016. https://scholarship.law.upenn.edu/faculty_scholarship/1799.

Mossoff, Adam. "Who Cares What Thomas Jefferson Thought about Patents—Reevaluating the Patent Privilege in Historical Context," *Cornell Law Review* 92 (2007): 953.

Walterscheid, Edward C. "Charting a Novel Course: The Creation of the Patent Act of 1790." *AIPLA Quarterly Journal* 25 (1997): 445.

Thomas Jefferson on the Constitutionality of a National Bank

Date: February 15, 1791
Author: Thomas Jefferson
Genre: essay; white paper

Summary Overview

The Bank of the United States, commented on by Thomas Jefferson in his "Opinion on the Constitutionality of a National Bank" in 1791, was one of the keystones of Treasury Secretary Alexander Hamilton's plan for refinancing the Revolutionary War debt of the United States. After weeks of heated congressional debate, which included questions about the proposed bank's constitutionality, President George Washington requested statements from Hamilton and Secretary of State Thomas Jefferson. Hamilton justified the bank by broadly construing the constitutional powers of Congress. Jefferson, on the other hand, rejected that argument and claimed that the Constitution created a federal government that was strictly limited in its political and financial power.

The statements of these two respected political minds encapsulated the growing legal gulf that separated advocates of "loose construction" from those who supported a "strict construction" of the Constitution, a gulf manifested in the emerging political party system between the Federalists and the Republicans (i.e., the Democratic-Republicans). Additionally, the debate over the bank's constitutionality revealed an even more contentious debate over the role of the federal government in the economic life of the nation. In short, the debate over the bank went far beyond finance to question the very meaning of federalism.

Defining Moment

The American Revolution was one of the longest-fought wars in American history, certainly the longest on North American soil, and one of the most costly. Immediately following the battles of Lexington and Concord (Massachusetts), in 1775, delegates to the Second Continental Congress made several fateful decisions regarding the future of the war, such as the choice to fight the British using conventional means, including a large standing army of regular troops. A national army, of course, would necessarily be armed, fed, clothed, and housed at the Continental Congress's expense.

Congress financed the Continental army by issuing a variety of debt instruments to be liquidated after the war by redemption and taxation. Congress also created a fiat currency of "continentals," which were declared legal tender by Congress without the backing of specie. As the war dragged on, Congress simply issued more currency and debt instruments, creating an inflationary spiral as leaders tried printing their way out of the financial crisis. The value of the currency and debt instruments both plummeted, leaving Americans the victors in war but nearing financial catastrophe.

By early 1786, a national solution appeared to be a lost cause, and debt holders increasingly turned to the state governments for assistance.

In that year alone, interest on half of the total debt was paid by the states of Pennsylvania, New York, and Massachusetts. With the states now leading the way toward eliminating the Continental debt, nationalists feared for the worst, as they had planned to use that issue to grant more power and authority to the central government. Fortunately for the nationalists, the states failed to satisfy all creditors, to address British threats on the western frontier, or to squelch Shays's Rebellion in Massachusetts (which was spawned, in part, by the imposition of a liquor tax). Enough people were frightened by the circumstances to warrant the calling of a national convention in Philadelphia in 1787, where delegates boldly proposed a new federal government strong enough to gain economic controls over the states.

Following the ratification of the U.S. Constitution, Congress and President George Washington spent most of the first session, in 1789, creating the federal bureaucracy and tax structure. With those tasks completed, the newly minted secretary of the treasury, Alexander Hamilton, pressed for a major fiscal program for the new government. Commonly called "Hamiltonian finance," his plan was laid out in a series of reports issued between 1790 and 1791. The "Report on the Public Credit" (January 9, 1790) called on Congress to pay off all of the remaining Revolutionary War debt—including that of the states—at face value by issuing new federal debt certificates. Interest on and the principal of this new national debt would be paid by direct taxes (especially on distilled spirits like whiskey), a tariff, and land sales. The "Report on a National Bank" (December 13, 1790) defended the chartering of a federal bank that would issue a paper currency ostensibly based on its specie holdings, be a lender to the national government, and facilitate the collection of taxes. The "Report on the Subject of a Mint" (January 28, 1791) proposed the creation of a mint to coin gold and silver for national circulation. Finally, the "Report on the Subject of Manufacturers" (December 5, 1791) suggested that the government dispense direct subsidies to stimulate domestic industry, but Congress decided against the recommendation.

Opponents of the proposed national bank—Jefferson, among them—drew heavily on classical liberal political economy as well as on the history of the Bank of England to show that a national bank's inflationary policies, though perhaps funding an initial boom for the economy, would surely bring a financial crash. Defenders of the national bank wavered in the face of such attacks but eventually argued that regardless of the long-term consequences, the government would be more effective with a bank than without one. The dynamics of the debate shifted away from economic considerations to political ones, leading both sides to support their positions with constitutional claims.

Opponents believed that the purpose of the U.S. Constitution was to carefully delineate those powers expressly granted to the federal government by the states and by the people. They rejected the arguments of bank supporters as mere semantics that could be used to justify virtually any prerogative. To opponents, "necessary" meant "absolutely indispensable," and efficiency was not as important as "limitation." Those against the bank relied upon the explicit wording of Article I as well as on the Ninth and Tenth Amendments.

Congressional debate on the bank's constitutionality stalled, giving way to a free-for-all, as fledgling party newspapers assaulted and mercilessly slandered their opponents. The coalition built by Hamilton began to fragment, and with it the bank bill's chances of being passed dwindled. It was in the midst of this crisis—the first genuine political deadlock faced by Congress—that President Washington requested written positions from three of his cabinet members: the attorney general Edmund Randolph, Hamilton, and Jefferson. Randolph opposed the national bank on constitutional grounds, but the low caliber of his treatise warranted scant attention, thus placing the focus on Jefferson and Hamilton. The treatises then written by these two men are among the first attempts to interpret the Constitution in light of a policy issue not directly addressed in the text.

Author Biography

Born April 13, 1743, into a planter family in the Tidewater region of Virginia, Thomas Jefferson received the best his world could offer. He studied at the College of William and Mary, married into a prominent family, and would have been content to spend the rest of his life as a tobacco planter. When hostilities broke out in 1775, however, Jefferson rose through the ranks of Virginia politics, serving as a delegate to the Second Continental Congress—where he drafted the Declaration of Independence—and as the state's governor. When conflict subsided, Jefferson traveled to France on behalf of the fledgling United States before returning home at the beginning of the Washington administration. He subsequently served as secretary of state, vice president, and, for two terms, president of the United States. Jefferson believed that an agrarian society would best perpetuate American liberty, which he typically defined as independence and self-government rather than as financial success.

He retired to Monticello, his family estate near Charlottesville, Virginia, where he also founded the University of Virginia. He died July 4, 1826.

HISTORICAL DOCUMENT: Thomas Jefferson on the Constitutionality of a National Bank

The bill for establishing a National Bank undertakes among other things:
1. To form the subscribers into a corporation.
2. To enable them in their corporate capacities to receive grants of land; and so far is against the laws of Mortmain.
3. To make alien subscribers capable of holding lands, and so far is against the laws of Alienage.
4. To transmit these lands, on the death of a proprietor, to a certain line of successors; and so far changes the course of Descents.
5. To put the lands out of the reach of forfeiture or escheat, and so far is against the laws of Forfeiture and Escheat.
6. To transmit personal chattels to successors in a certain line and so far is against the laws of Distribution.
7. To give them the sole and exclusive right of banking under the national authority; and so far is against the laws of Monopoly.
8. To communicate to them a power to make laws paramount to the laws of the States; for so they must be construed, to protect the institution from the control of the State legislatures, and so, probably, they will be construed.

I consider the foundation of the Constitution as laid on this ground: That "all powers not delegated to the United States, by the Constitution, nor prohibited by it to the States, are reserved to the States or to the people." [XIIth amendment.] To take a single step beyond the boundaries thus specially drawn around the powers of Congress, is to take possession of a boundless field of power, no longer susceptible of any definition.

The incorporation of a bank, and the powers assumed by this bill, have not, in my opinion, been delegated to the United States, by the Constitution.

I. They are not among the powers specially enumerated: for these are: 1st A power to lay taxes for the purpose of paying the debts of the United States; but no debt is paid by this bill, nor any tax laid. Were it a bill to raise money, its origination in the Senate would condemn it by the Constitution.

2. "To borrow money." But this bill neither borrows money nor ensures the borrowing it. The proprietors of the bank will be just as free as any other money holders, to lend or not to lend their money to the public. The operation proposed in the bill first, to lend them two millions, and then to borrow them back again, cannot change the nature of the latter act, which will still be a payment, and not a loan, call it by what name you please.

3. To "regulate commerce with foreign nations, and among the States, and with the Indian tribes." To erect a bank, and to regulate commerce, are very different acts. He who erects a bank, creates a subject of commerce in its bills, so does he who makes a bushel of wheat, or digs a dollar out of the mines; yet neither of these persons regulates commerce thereby. To make a thing which may be bought and sold, is not to prescribe regulations for buying and selling. Besides, if this was an exercise of the power of regulating commerce, it would be void, as extending as much to the internal commerce of every State, as to its external. For the power given to Congress by the Constitution does not extend to the internal regulation of the commerce of a State, (that is to say of the commerce between citizen and citizen,) which remain exclusively with its own legislature; but to its external commerce only, that is to say, its commerce with another State, or with foreign nations, or with the Indian tribes. Accordingly the bill does not propose the measure as a regulation of trace, but as "productive of considerable advantages to trade." Still less are these powers covered by any other of the special enumerations.

II. Nor are they within either of the general phrases, which are the two following:

1. To lay taxes to provide for the general welfare of the United States, that is to say, "to lay taxes for *the purpose of* providing for the general welfare." For the laying of taxes is the *power*, and the general welfare the *purpose* for which the power is to be exercised. They are not to lay taxes *ad libitum for any purpose they please*; but only *to pay the debts or provide for the welfare of the Union*. In like manner, they are not *to do anything they please* to provide for the general welfare, but only *to lay taxes* for that purpose. To consider the latter phrase, not as describing the purpose of the first, but as giving a distinct and independent power to do any act they please, which might be

for the good of the Union, would render all the preceding and subsequent enumerations of power completely useless.

It would reduce the whole instrument to a single phrase, that of instituting a Congress with power to do whatever would be for the good of the United States; and, as they would be the sole judges of the good or evil, it would be also a power to do whatever evil they please.

> *The incorporation of a bank, and the powers assumed by this bill, have not, in my opinion, been delegated to the United States, by the Constitution.*

It is an established rule of construction where a phrase will bear either of two meanings, to give it that which will allow some meaning to the other parts of the instrument, and not that which would render all the others useless. Certainly no such universal power was meant to be given them. It was intended to lace them up straitly within the enumerated powers, and those without which, as means, these powers could not be carried into effect. It is known that the very power now proposed *as a means* was rejected as *an end* by the Convention which formed the Constitution. A proposition was made to them to authorize Congress to open canals, and an amendatory one to empower them to incorporate. But the whole was rejected, and one of the reasons for rejection urged in debate was, that then they would have a power to erect a bank, which would render the great cities, where there were prejudices and jealousies on the subject, adverse to the reception of the Constitution.

2. The second general phrase is, "to make all laws *necessary* and proper for carrying into execution the enumerated powers." But they can all be carried into execution without a bank. A bank therefore is not *necessary*, and consequently not authorized by this phrase.

If has been urged that a bank will give great facility or convenience in the collection of taxes, Suppose this were true: yet the Constitution allows only the means which are "*necessary*," not those which are merely "convenient" for effecting the enumerated powers. If such a latitude of construction be allowed to this phrase as to give any non-enumerated power, it will go to everyone, for there is not one which ingenuity may not torture into a *convenience* in some instance *or other*, to *some one* of so long a list of enumerated powers. It would swallow up all the delegated powers, and reduce the whole to one power, as before observed. Therefore it was that the Constitution restrained them to the *necessary* means, that is to say, to those means without which the grant of power would be nugatory.

But let us examine this convenience and see what it is. The report on this subject, page 3, states the only *general* convenience to be, the preventing the transportation and re-transportation of money between the States and the treasury, (for I pass over the increase of circulating medium, ascribed to it as a want, and which, according to my ideas of paper money, is clearly a demerit.) Every State will have to pay a sum of tax money into the treasury; and the treasury will have to pay, in every State, a part of the interest on the public debt, and salaries to the officers of government resident in that State. In most of the States there will still be a surplus of tax money to come up to the seat of government for the officers residing there. The payments of interest and salary in each State may be made by treasury orders on the State collector. This will take up the greater part of the money he has collected in his State, and consequently prevent the great mass of it from being drawn out of the State. If there be a balance of commerce in favor of that State against the one in which the government resides, the surplus of taxes will be remitted by the bills of exchange drawn for that commercial balance. And so it must be if there was a bank. But if there be no balance of commerce, either direct or circuitous, all the banks in the world could not bring up the surplus of taxes, but in the form of money. Treasury orders then, and bills of exchange may prevent the displacement of the main mass of the money collected, without the aid of any bank; and where these fail, it cannot be prevented even with that aid.

Perhaps, indeed, bank bills may be a more *convenient* vehicle than treasury orders. But a little *difference* in the degree of *convenience* cannot constitute the necessity which the Constitution makes the ground for assuming any non-enumerated power.

Besides, the existing banks will, without a doubt, enter into arrangements for lending their agency, and the more favorable, as there will be a competition among them for it; whereas the bill delivers us up bound to the national bank, who are free to refuse all arrangement, but on their own terms, and the public not free, on such refusal, to employ any other bank. That of Philadelphia I believe, now does this business, by their post-notes, which, by an arrangement with the treasury, are paid by any State collector to whom they are presented. This expedient alone suffices to prevent the existence of that *necessity* which may justify the assumption of a non-enumerated power as a means for carrying into effect an enumerated one. The thing may be done, and has been done, and well done, without this assumption, therefore it does not stand on that degree of *necessity* which can honestly justify it.

It may be said that a bank whose bills would have a currency all over the States, would be more convenient than one whose currency is limited to a single State. So it would be still more convenient that there should be a bank, whose bills should have a currency all over the world. But it does not follow from this superior conveniency, that there exists anywhere a power to establish such a bank; or that the world may not go on very well without it.

Can it be thought that the Constitution intended that for a shade or two of *convenience*, more or less, Congress should be authorized to break down the most ancient and fundamental laws of the several States; such as those against Mortmain, the laws of Alienage, the rules of descent, the acts of distribution, the laws of escheat and forfeiture, the laws of monopoly? Nothing but a necessity invincible by any other means, can justify such a prostitution of laws, which constitute the pillars of our whole system of jurisprudence. Will Congress be too strait-laced to carry the Constitution into honest effect, unless they may pass over the foundation-laws of the State government for the slightest convenience of theirs?

The negative of the President is the shield provided by the Constitution to protect against the invasions of the legislature: 1. The right of the Executive. 2. Of the Judiciary. 3. Of the States and State legislatures. The present is the case of a right remaining exclusively with the States, and consequently one of those intended by the Constitution to be placed under its protection,

It must be added, however, that unless the President's mind on a view of everything which is urged for and against this bill, is tolerably clear that it is unauthorized by the Constitution; if the pro and the con hang so even as to balance his judgment, a just respect for the wisdom of the legislature would naturally decide the balance in favor of their opinion. It is chiefly for cases where they are clearly misled by error, ambition, or interest, that the Constitution has placed a check in the negative of the President.

GLOSSARY

acts of distribution: rules allowing for the transfer of a person's property if there is no will; typically, states allowed property to go to surviving blood relatives

bills of exchange: exchange instruments allowing a merchant to receive goods by providing a note promising full payment at a later date in a currency chosen by the seller; occasionally circulated as a money substitute

circulating medium: money or money substitute, such as banknotes, specie, or promissory notes of public debt, being used to facilitate economic exchange

commercial balance: the amount owed to a seller or group of sellers

enumerated powers: those areas of authority specifically listed in a constitution

forfeiture and escheat: the transfer of a person's property to the government if he or she dies intestate (without a will) or without legal heirs

laws of Alienage: restrictions under English common law whereby foreigners could not own or inherit land because they were not under the jurisdiction of the king

laws of Monopoly: rules regulating enterprises that do not have competition; early corporations were often granted monopoly status to encourage economic development

laws of Mortmain: regulations regarding property held by corporate entities, which by definition never die, or figuratively possess a main mort, French for "dead hand"

> **paper (as a currency medium):** a fiat currency whereby a government may print currency notes irrespective of specie or other holdings to back it; the currency becomes legal tender owing to the "fiat" of the state
>
> **plenary and sovereign authority:** complete power over a particular matter
>
> **treasury orders:** promissory notes issued by treasury officials stipulating payment with interest at a future date

Document Analysis

Jefferson's opinion was written prior to Alexander Hamilton's. In fact, Hamilton had the benefit of reading Jefferson's opinion before writing his own. It may seem odd that Jefferson began his opinion by listing eight legal dilemmas posed by the national bank legislation. However, any well-trained lawyer or anyone well versed in land policy in the 1790s understood what was at stake, as these laws related to the ownership of land, its distribution upon the death of the owner, and how states regulated incorporated land companies. In effect, Jefferson argues that the national bank would be a privileged corporation beyond the scope of regulation because of its federal charter. Jefferson appears to be employing a standard states' rights argument, but he is actually attacking Hamilton. James Madison probably told Jefferson that Alexander Hamilton wrote Federalist no. 33 to help secure the ratification of the Constitution in New York. Therein, Hamilton bluntly states that the federal government would not have the power "to vary the law of descent" (one of Jefferson's stated legal dilemmas) and that the ability to do so would constitute a "tyrannical power" (Carey and McClellan, p. 160).

In Jefferson's view, the authority of the states and of the federal government rested on two different types of power. In that the states preceded the national government, they served as the primary basis of political authority in the United States of America. Thus, the states were the proper projections of the people's sovereignty, exercising all aspects of that sovereignty unless the people expressly reserved the exercise of a power for themselves. The federal government possessed no such inherent exercise of sovereignty, being limited to only those powers explicitly given by the people through the state ratifying conventions. Since the Constitution contains no mention of a national bank and, more important, no express delegation of the power to create federally chartered enterprises, the bank bill was unconstitutional. Such a power, Jefferson suggests, is further prohibited by the Tenth Amendment, which he calls the "Twelfth" because it was the twelfth submitted for ratification.

Jefferson offers some economic arguments against the bank, and he also alludes to the framers' voting down an attempt to give chartering power to Congress. He denies that a bank could be created simply to pay the debts of the country, to lend money to the federal government, or help regulate interstate commerce. Indeed, Jefferson argues that a national bank would actually harm business interests by interfering in intrastate commerce, an area most believed to fall outside the jurisdiction of the federal government.

Jefferson's most stinging criticism, however, is aimed against the broad interpretation of powers employed by bank supporters to defend it. He fears that their arguments ultimately opposed the reason for having a constitution in the first place, which in his mind was to limit the power of the national government. Clearly, Jefferson was no ardent nationalist who believed that social order and happiness depended upon the exercise of strong political power by a central government. To his final days, Jefferson insisted that a massive, activist government was a burden for the citizenry. He understood that social order must flow from liberty, not vice versa.

He also believed that the federal government must be a government of limited powers. To Jefferson, this meant that it would be limited in its ends and in its means; the fact that Congress could levy taxes did not mean that it could levy taxes for anything it wanted. (It was still widely considered at the time that "general welfare," as mentioned in the Constitution, meant those things that fell *generally* throughout the nation, not those things confined to specific states or interest groups.) Like other bank detractors, Jefferson defines *necessary* as "essential" rather than as "convenient." A bank was not essential for any of the government's activities, and congressmen would be wrong to sacrifice constitutional prerogatives for the sake of convenience.

Jefferson concludes his opinion by returning to states' rights, which he believed best guarded against encroachments on liberty. He holds that the president must safeguard these rights, especially when confronted with a concerted effort in Congress to jeopardize popular liberties for the sake of pecuniary interests.

Essential Themes

Historians have typically sided with Hamilton in regard to the national bank, either because they agree with his interpretation of the Constitution or owing to the perceived benefits of stabilizing the currency and funding the national debt. Hamilton's proposals were far from radical, as the British had a national bank, and a similar institution had been created under the Articles of Confederation. Nonetheless, many Americans considered these policies to be "un-American," and some politicians insisted that Hamilton was overly fascinated with British forms because he was an Anglophile.

The passage of the bank bill affected American politics in two ways. First, it provided a forum in which manners of constitutional interpretation were widely discussed. Neither Hamilton nor Jefferson conceded his argument, and their political descendants continued to defend their positions for decades to come. More significantly, the debate on the bank bill polarized national politics and proved instrumental to the creation of the first party system. Newspapers were formed, rallies were held, and myriad local movements—some of which were organized against the national bank—slowly coalesced into a formal structure of political activity.

Once under operation, the Bank of the United States further fueled the party system when its inflationary activity quickly brought about depression centered in New York City in 1792. Pamphleteers pilloried the bank as a sign of corruption, whereby "monied" interests used the federal government to enrich themselves at the public's expense. This characterization carried over to Republican rhetoric, which portrayed the Federalists as a commercial elite who had warped the Constitution to suit their purposes. Federalists responded by attacking the Republicans as inept farmers who would wreck the economy.

The elections of 1800 seemed to settle the matter, with the Republicans taking office. In fact, even though they changed the policies of the Bank of the United States to reflect their insistence on founding currency on hard money rather than allowing inflation, the Republicans did not suspend the bank's operation. In effect, the Republicans used Hamiltonian means to secure Jeffersonian ends. They kept a national bank but used it to extinguish the national debt as quickly as possible. The bank's charter expired in 1811.

—*Carey M. Roberts, PhD*

Bibliography and Additional Reading

Carey, George W., and James McClellan, eds. *The Federalist*. Indianapolis, Ind.: Liberty Fund, 2001.

Chernow, Ron. *Alexander Hamilton*. New York: Penguin Press, 2004.

Cowen, David J. *The Origins and Economic Impact of the First Bank of the United States, 1791–1797*. New York: Garland Publishing, 2000.

Cunningham, Noble E., Jr. *Jefferson vs. Hamilton: Confrontations That Shaped a Nation*. New York: Palgrave Macmillan, 2000.

Elkins, Stanley, and Eric McKitrick. *The Age of Federalism*. New York: Oxford University Press, 1993.

Holloway, Carson. *Hamilton versus Jefferson in the Washington Administration*. New York: Cambridge University Press, 2015.

Madison, James. *Notes of the Debates of the Federal Convention of 1787*. New York: W. W. Norton, 1966.

Perkins, Edwin. *American Public Finance and Financial Services, 1700–1815*. Columbus: Ohio State University Press, 1994.

■ Alexander Hamilton on the Constitutionality of a National Bank

Date: February 23, 1791
Author: Alexander Hamilton
Genre: essay; white paper

Summary Overview

The Bank of the United States, commented on by Treasury Secretary Alexander Hamilton in his "Opinion as to the Constitutionality of the Bank of the United States" in 1791, was one of the keystones of his plan for refinancing the Revolutionary War debt of the United States of America. After weeks of heated congressional debate that included questions about the proposed bank's constitutionality, President George Washington requested statements from Hamilton and Secretary of State Thomas Jefferson, who opposed the bank. In his "Opinion on the Constitutionality of a National Bank," Jefferson claimed that the ratified Constitution created a federal government that was strictly limited in its political and financial power. Hamilton justified the bank by broadly construing the constitutional powers of Congress.

The statements of these two respected political minds encapsulated the growing legal gulf that separated advocates of "loose construction" from those who supported a "strict construction" of the Constitution, a gulf manifested in the emerging political party system between the Federalists and Republicans (often referred to as Democratic-Republicans), respectively. Additionally, the debate over the bank's constitutionality revealed an even more contentious debate over the role of the federal government in the economic life of the nation. In short, the debate over the bank went far beyond finance to question the very meaning of federalism.

Defining Moment

The American Revolution was one of the longest-fought wars in American history, certainly the longest on North American soil, and one of the most costly. Immediately following the battles of Lexington and Concord (Massachusetts), in 1775, delegates to the Second Continental Congress made several fateful decisions regarding the future of the war, such as the choice to fight the British using conventional means, including a large standing army of regular troops. A national army, of course, would necessarily be armed, fed, clothed, and housed at the Continental Congress's expense.

Congress financed the Continental army by issuing a variety of debt instruments to be liquidated after the war by redemption and taxation. Congress also created a fiat currency of "continentals," which were declared legal tender by Congress without the backing of specie. As the war dragged on, Congress simply issued more currency and debt instruments, creating an inflationary spiral as leaders tried printing their way out of the financial crisis. The value of the currency and debt instruments both plummeted, leaving Americans the victors in war but nearing financial catastrophe.

By early 1786, a national solution appeared to be a lost cause, and debt holders increasingly turned to the state governments for assistance.

In that year alone, interest on half of the total debt was paid by the states of Pennsylvania, New York, and Massachusetts. With the states now leading the way toward eliminating the Continental debt, nationalists feared for the worst, as they had planned to use that issue to grant more power and authority to the central government. Fortunately for the nationalists, the states failed to satisfy all creditors, to address British threats on the western frontier, or to squelch Shays's Rebellion in Massachusetts (which was spawned, in part, by the imposition of a liquor tax). Enough people were frightened by the circumstances to warrant the calling of a national convention in Philadelphia in 1787, where delegates boldly proposed a new federal government strong enough to gain economic controls over the states.

Following the ratification of the U.S. Constitution, Congress and President George Washington spent most of the first session, in 1789, creating the federal bureaucracy and tax structure. With those tasks completed, the newly minted secretary of the treasury, Alexander Hamilton, pressed for a major fiscal program for the new government. Commonly called "Hamiltonian finance," his plan was laid out in a series of reports issued between 1790 and 1791. The "Report on the Public Credit" (January 9, 1790) called on Congress to pay off all of the remaining Revolutionary War debt—including debt held by the states—at face value by issuing new federal debt certificates. Interest on and the principal of this new national debt would be paid by direct taxes (especially on distilled spirits like whiskey), a tariff, and land sales. The "Report on a National Bank" (December 13, 1790) defended the chartering of a federal bank that would issue a paper currency ostensibly based on its specie holdings, be a lender to the national government, and facilitate the collection of taxes. The "Report on the Subject of a Mint" (January 28, 1791) proposed the creation of a mint to coin gold and silver for national circulation. Finally, the "Report on the Subject of Manufacturers" (December 5, 1791) suggested that the government dispense direct subsidies to stimulate domestic industry, but Congress decided against the recommendation.

Opponents of the proposed national bank drew heavily on classical liberal political economy as well as on the history of the Bank of England to show that a national bank's inflationary policies, though perhaps funding an initial boom for the economy, would surely bring a financial crash. Defenders of the national bank wavered in the face of such attacks but eventually argued that regardless of the long-term consequences, the government would be more effective with a bank than without one. The dynamics of the debate shifted away from economic considerations to political ones, leading both sides to support their positions with constitutional claims.

Defenders—Hamilton, among them—relied on the "necessary and proper" clause of the Constitution (Article I, Section 8). They believed that anything allowing the federal government to more easily meet its delegated powers was constitutional; the preamble of the Constitution gave the government the power to promote the general welfare of the country, which is exactly what they expected the bank to do. A national bank would ease government functions by providing a national currency, making the collection of taxes easier, and providing the federal government with loans when needed. Thus, bank supporters resorted to an "efficiency" defense.

Congressional debate on the bank's constitutionality stalled, giving way to a free-for-all, as fledgling party newspapers assaulted and mercilessly slandered their opponents. The coalition built by Hamilton began to fragment, and with it the bank bill's chances of being passed dwindled. It was in the midst of this crisis—the first genuine political deadlock faced by Congress—that President Washington requested written positions from three of his cabinet members: the attorney general Edmund Randolph, Hamilton, and Jefferson. Randolph opposed the national bank on constitutional grounds, but the low caliber of his treatise warranted scant attention, thus placing the focus on Jefferson and Hamilton. The treatises written by these two men are among the first attempts to interpret the Constitution in light of a policy issue not directly addressed in the Constitution's text.

Author Biography

Alexander Hamilton was born on the island of Nevis, in the West Indies, on January 11, 1757, grew up in a port town, and was forced to work in a countinghouse at an early age. Realizing the lack of opportunity on the island, Hamilton moved to New York City, where he quickly rose through the financial ranks. He served as General Washington's aide-de-camp and private secretary during the American Revolution, as a member of the Continental Congress, and as a delegate to the Philadelphia Convention before becoming secretary of the treasury. To Hamilton, the future of America lay in commerce, progress, and development. While he worried that too much political control could hamper economic progress, he did not fully endorse free markets and unfettered capitalism. He viewed economic exchange as inherently unstable—indeed, chaotic—without the overarching hand of governing institutions, led by something like the Bank of England. Rather than simply trusting rural property holders like planters and yeoman farmers, Hamilton placed his faith in a commercial class of merchants like those who dominated British politics during the eighteenth century. Economic progress meant international trade and local commercial development, not the sprawling agrarian society envisioned by men like Thomas Jefferson. A national bank, he thought, would encourage the creation of commercial banks, which would then lend funds to merchants and urban businessmen. In turn, the economy would prosper as these figures invested in foreign trade, manufacturing, and transportation improvements.

After his retirement from office in 1795, Hamilton practiced law in New York City. He died July 12, 1804, from wounds sustained in a duel with Vice President Aaron Burr.

HISTORICAL DOCUMENT: Alexander Hamilton on the Constitutionality of a National Bank

The Secretary of the Treasury having perused with attention the papers containing the opinions of the Secretary of State and Attorney General, concerning the constitutionality of the bill for establishing a National Bank, proceeds, according to the order of the President, to submit the reasons which have induced him to entertain a different opinion.

...

In entering upon the argument, it ought to be premised that the objections of the Secretary of State and Attorney General are founded on a general denial of the authority of the United States to erect corporations. The latter, indeed, expressly admits, that if there be anything in the bill which is not warranted by the Constitution, it is the clause of incorporation.

Now it appears to the Secretary of the Treasury that this general principle is inherent in the very definition of government, and essential to every step of progress to be made by that of the United States, namely: That every power vested in a government is in its nature sovereign, and includes, by force of the term, a right to employ all the means requisite and fairly applicable to the attainment of the ends of such power, and which are not precluded by restrictions and exceptions specified in the Constitution, or not immoral, or not contrary to the essential ends of political society.

This principle, in its application to government in general, would be admitted as an axiom; and it will be incumbent upon those who may incline to deny it, to prove a distinction, and to show that a rule which, in the general system of things, is essential to the preservation of the social order, is inapplicable to the United States.

The circumstance that the powers of sovereignty are in this country divided between the National and State governments, does not afford the distinction required. It does not follow from this, that each of the portion of powers delegated to the one or to the other, is not sovereign with regard to its proper objects. It will only follow from it, that each has sovereign power as to certain things, and not as to other things. To deny that the government of the United States has sovereign power, as to its declared purposes and trusts, because its power does not extend to all cases would be equally to deny that the State governments have sovereign power in any case, because their power does not extend to every case. The tenth section of the first article of the Constitution exhibits a long list of very important things which they may not do. And thus the United States would furnish the singular spectacle of a political society without sovereignty, or of a people governed, without government.

> "The truth is, that difficulties on this point are inherent in the nature of the Federal Constitution; they result inevitably from a division of the legislative power."

If it would be necessary to bring proof to a proposition so clear, as that which affirms that the powers of the federal government, as to its objects, were sovereign, there is a clause of its Constitution which would be decisive. It is that which declares that the Constitution, and the laws of the United States made in pursuance of it, and all treaties made, or which shall be made, under their authority, shall be the serene law of the land. The power which can create the supreme law of the land in any case, is doubtless sovereign as to such case.

This general and indisputable principle puts at once an end to the abstract question, whether the United States have power to erect a corporation; that is to say, to give a legal or artificial capacity to one or more persons, distinct from the natural. For it is unquestionably incident to sovereign power to erect corporations, and consequently to that of the United States, in relation to the objects intrusted to the management of the government. The difference is this: where the authority of the government is general, it can create corporations in all cases, where it is confined to certain branches of legislation, it can create corporations only in those cases.

...

The first of these arguments is, that the foundation of the Constitution is laid on this ground: "That all powers not delegated to the United States by the Constitution, nor prohibited to it by the States, are reserved for the States, or to the people." Whence it is meant to be inferred, that Congress can in no case exercise any power not included in those not enumerated in the Constitution. And it is affirmed, that the power of erecting a corporation is not included in any of the enumerated powers.

...

It is not denied that there are implied well as express powers, and that the former are as effectually delegated as the tatter. And for the sake of accuracy it shall be mentioned, that there is another class of powers, which may be properly denominated resting powers. ...

It is conceded that implied powers are to be considered as delegated equally with express ones. Then it follows, that as a power of erecting a corporation may as well be implied as any other thing, it may as well be employed as an instrument or mean of carrying into execution any of the specified powers, as any other instrument or mean whatever. The only question must be in this, as in every other case, whether the mean to be employed or in this instance, the corporation to be erected, has a natural relation to any of the acknowledged objects or lawful ends of the government. Thus a corporation may not be erected by Congress for superintending the police of the city of Philadelphia, because they are not authorized to regulate the police of that city. But one may be erected in relation to the collection of taxes, or to the trade with foreign countries, or to the trade between the States, or with the Indian tribes; because it is the province of the federal government to regulate those objects, and because it is incident to a general sovereign or legislative power to regulate a thing, to employ all the means which relate to its regulation to the best and greatest advantage.

A strange fallacy seems to have crept into the manner of thinking and reasoning upon the subject. Imagination appears to have been unusually busy concerning it. An incorporation seems to have been regarded as some great independent substantive thing; as a political end of peculiar magnitude and moment; whereas it is truly to be considered as a quality, capacity, or mean to an end. Thus a mercantile company is formed, with a certain capital, for the purpose of carrying on a particular branch of business. Here the business to be prosecuted is the end. ...

To this mode of reasoning respecting the right of employing all the means requisite to the execution of the specified powers of the government, it is objected, that none but necessary and proper means are to be employed; and the Secretary of State maintains, that no means are to be considered as necessary but those without which the grant of the power would be nugatory. Nay, so far does he go in his restrictive interpretation of the word, as even to make the case of necessity which shall warrant the constitutional exercise of the power to depend on casual and temporary circumstances; an idea which alone refutes the construction. The expediency of exercising a particular power, at a particular time, must, indeed depend on circumstances, but the constitutional right of exercising it must be uniform and invariable, the same to-day as to-morrow.

All the arguments, therefore, against the constitutionality of the bill derived from the accidental existence of certain State banks, institutions which happen to exist to-day, and, for aught that concerns the government of the United States, may disappear tomorrow, must not only be rejected as fallacious, but must be viewed as demonstrative that there is a radical source of error in the reasoning.

...

It is certain that neither the grammatical nor popular sense of the term requires that construction. According to both, necessary often means no more than needful, requisite, incidental, useful, or conducive to. It is a common mode of expression to say, that it is necessary for a government or a person to do this or that thing, when nothing more is intended or understood, than that the interests of the government or person require, or will be promoted by, the doing of this or that thing. The imagination can be at no loss for exemplifications of the use of the word in this sense. And it is the true one in which it is to be understood as used in the Constitution. The whole turn of the clause containing it indicates, that it was the intent of the Convention, by that clause, to give a liberal latitude to the exercise of the specified powers. The expressions have peculiar comprehensiveness. They are, "to make all laws necessary and proper for carrying into execution the foregoing powers, and all other powers vested by the Constitution in the government of the United States, or in any department or officer thereof."

To understand the word as the Secretary of State does, would be to depart from its obvious and popular sense, and to give it a restrictive operation, an idea never before entertained. It would be to give it the same force as if the word absolutely or indispensably had been prefixed to it.

Such a construction would beget endless uncertainty and embarrassment. The cases must be palpable and extreme, in which it could be pronounced, with certainty, that a measure was absolutely necessary, or one, without which, the exercise of a given power would be nugatory. There are few measures of any government which would stand so severe a test. ...

It may be truly said of every government, as well as of that of the United States, that it has only a right to pass such laws as are necessary and proper to accomplish the objects intrusted to it. For no government has a right to do merely what it pleases. ...

The degree in which a measure is necessary, can never be a test of the legal right to adopt it; that must be a matter of opinion, and can only be a test of expediency. The relation between the measure and the end; between the nature of the mean employed toward the execution of a power, and the object of that power must be the criterion of constitutionality, not the more or less of necessity or utility.

The practice of the government is against the rule of construction advocated by the Secretary of State. ...

This restrictive interpretation of the word necessary is also contrary to this sound maxim of construction, namely, that the powers contained in a constitution of government, especially those which concern the general administration of the affairs of a country, its finances, trade, defense, etc., ought to be construed liberally in advancement of the public good. This rule does not depend on the particular form of a government, or on the particular demarcation of the boundaries of its powers, but on the nature and object of government itself. The means by which national exigencies are to be provided for, national inconveniences obviated, national prosperity promoted, are of such infinite variety, extent, and complexity, that there must of necessity be great latitude of discretion in the selection and application of those means. Hence, consequently, the necessity and propriety of exercising the authorities intrusted to a government on principles of liberal construction.

The Attorney General admits the rule, but takes a distinction between a State and the Federal Constitution. The latter, he thinks, ought to be construed with greater strictness, because there is more danger of error in defining partial than General powers. But the reason of the rule forbids such a distinction. This reason is, the variety and extent of public exigencies, a far greater proportion of which, and of a far more critical kind, are objects of National than of State administration. The greater danger of error, as far as it is supposable, may be a prudential reason for caution in practice, but it cannot be a rule of restrictive interpretation.

...

It is no valid objection to the doctrine to say, that it is calculated to extend the power of the government throughout the entire sphere of State legislation. The same thing has been said, and may be said, with regard to every exercise of power by implication or construction.

The moment the literal meaning is departed from, there is a chance of error and abuse. And yet an adherence to the letter of its powers would at once arrest the motions of government. ...

The truth is, that difficulties on this point are inherent in the nature of the Federal Constitution; they result inevitably from a division of the legislative power. The consequence of this division is, that there will be cases clearly within the power of the national government; others, clearly without its powers; and a third class, which will leave room for controversy and difference of opinion, and concerning which a reasonable latitude of judgment must be allowed.

But the doctrine which is contended for is not chargeable with the consequences imputed to it. It does not affirm that the national government is sovereign in all respects, but that it is sovereign to a certain extent; that is, to the extent of the objects of its specified powers.

It leaves, therefore, a criterion of what is constitutional, and of what is not so. This criterion is the end, to which the measure relates as a mean. If the end be clearly comprehended within any of the specified powers, and if the measure have an obvious relation to that end, and is not forbidden by any particular provision of the Constitution, it may safely be deemed to come within the compass of the national authority. There is also this further criterion, which may materially assist the decision: Does the proposed measure abridge a pre-existing right of any State or of any individual? If it does not, there is a strong presumption in favor of its constitutionality, and slighter relations to any declared object of the Constitution may be permitted to turn the scale.

...

Another argument made use of by the Secretary of State is, the rejection of a proposition by the Convention to empower Congress to make corporations, either generally, or for some special purpose.

What was the precise nature or extent of this proposition, or what the reasons for refusing it, is not ascertained by any authentic document, or even by accurate recollection. ...

But whatever may have been the nature of the proposition, or the reasons for rejecting it, nothing is included by it, that is the proposition, in respect to the real merits of the question. The Secretary of State will not deny, that, whatever may have been the intention of the framers of a constitution, or of a law, that intention is to be sought for in the instrument itself, according to the usual and established rules of construction. Nothing is more common than for laws to express and elect more or less than was intended. If, then, a power to erect a corporation in any case be deducible, by fair inference, from the whole or any part of the numerous provisions of the Constitution of the United States arguments drawn from extrinsic circumstances regarding the intension of the Convention must be rejected.

...

Those [arguments] of the Attorney General will now properly come under view.

His first objection is, that the power of incorporation is not expressly given to Congress. This shall be conceded, but in this sense only, that it is not declared in express terms that Congress may erect a corporation. But this cannot mean, that there are not certain express powers which necessarily include it. ...

Surely it can never be believed that Congress, with exclusive powers of legislation in all cases whatsoever, cannot erect a corporation within the district which shall become the seat of government, for the better regulation of its police. And yet there is an unqualified denial of the power to erect corporations in every case on the part both of the Secretary of State and of the Attorney General; the former, indeed, speaks of that power in these emphatical terms: That it is a right remaining exclusively with the States.

...

A general legislative authority implies a power to erect corporations in all cases. A particular legislative power implies authority to erect corporations in relation to cases arising under that power only. Hence the affirming that, as incident to sovereign power, Congress may erect a corporation in relation to the collection of their taxes, is no more to affirm that they may do whatever else they please, than the saying that they have a power to regulate trade, would be to affirm that they have a power to regulate religion; or than the maintaining that they have sovereign power as to taxation, would be to maintain that they have sovereign power as to everything else.

...

The proposed bank is to consist of an association of persons, for the purpose of creating a joint capital, to be employed chiefly and essentially in loans. So far the object is not only lawful, but it is the mere exercise of a right which the law allows to every individual. The Bank of New York, which is not incorporated, is an example of such an association. The bill proposed ill addition that the government shall become a joint proprietor in this undertaking, and that it shall permit the bills of the company, payable on demand, to be receivable in its revenues; and stipulates that it shall not grant privileges, similar to those which are to be allowed to this company, to any others. All this is incontrovertibly within the compass of the discretion of the government. The only question is, whether it has a right to incorporate this company, in order to enable it the more effectually to accomplish ends which are in themselves lawful.

To establish such a right, it remains to show the relation of such an institution to one or more of the specified powers of the government. Accordingly it is affirmed that it has a relation, more or less direct, to the power of collecting taxes, to that of borrowing money, to that of regulating trade between the States, and to those of raising and maintaining fleets and armies. ...

It now remains to show, that the incorporation of a bank is within the operation of the provision which authorizes Congress to make all needful rules and regulations concerning the property of the United States. But it is previously necessary to advert to a distinction which has been taken by the Attorney General.

He admits that the word property may signify personal property, however acquired, and yet asserts that it cannot signify money arising from the sources of revenue pointed out in the Constitution, "because," says he, "the disposal and regulation of money is the final cause for raising it by taxes."

But it would be more accurate to say that the object to which money is intended to be applied is thermal cause for raising it, than that the disposal and regulation of it is such.

The support of government—the support of troops for the common defense—the payment of the public debt, are the true final causes for raising money. The disposition and regulation of it, when raised, are the steps by which it is applied to the ends for which it was raised, not the ends themselves. Hence, therefore, the money to be raised by taxes, as well as any other personal property, must be supposed to come within the meaning, as they certainly do within the letter, of authority to make all needful rules and regulations concerning the property of the United States.

...

There is an observation of the Secretary of State to this effect which may require notice in this place:—Congress, says he, are not to lay taxes ad libitum, for any purpose they please, but only to pay the debts or provide for the welfare of the Union. Certainly no inference can be drawn from this against the power of applying their money for the institution of a bank. It is true that they cannot without breach of trust lay taxes for any other purpose than the general welfare; but so neither can any other government. The welfare of the community is the only legitimate end for which money can be raised on the community. Congress can be considered as under only one restriction which does not apply to other governments, they cannot rightfully apply the money they raise to any purpose merely or purely local.

But, with this exception, they have as large a discretion in relation to the application of money as any legislature whatever. The constitutional test of a right application must always be, whether it be for a purpose of general or local nature. If the former, there can be no want of constitutional power. The quality of the object as how far it will really promote or not the welfare of the Union must be matter of conscientious discretion, and the arguments for or against a measure in this light must be arguments concerning expediency or inexpediency, not constitutional right. Whatever relates to the general order of the finances, to the general interests of trade, etc., being general objects, are constitutional ones for the Application of money.

A bank, then, whose bills are to circulate in all the revenues of the country, is evidently a general object, and, for that very reason, a constitutional one, as far as regards the appropriation of money to it. ...

To suppose, then, that the government is precluded from the employment of so usual and so important an instrument for the administration of its finances as that of a bank, is to suppose what does not coincide with the general tenor and complexion of the constitution, and what is not agreeable to impressions that any new spectator would entertain concerning it.

Little less than a prohibitory clause can destroy the strong presumptions which result from the general aspect of the government. Nothing but demonstration should exclude the idea that the power exists.

In all questions of this nature, the practice of mankind ought to have great weight against the theories of individuals.

The fact, for instance, that all the principal commercial nations have made use of trading corporations or companies, for the purpose of external commerce, is a satisfactory proof that the establishment of them is an incident to the regulation of the commerce.

This other fact, that banks are an usual engine in the administration of national finances, and an ordinary and the most effectual instrument of loan, and one which, in this country, has been found essential, pleads strongly against the supposition that a government, clothed with most of the most important prerogatives of sovereignty in relation to its revenues, its debts, its credits, its defense, its trade, its intercourse with foreign nations, is forbidden to make use of that instrument as an appendage to its own authority.

GLOSSARY

bank circulation: banknotes being exchanged as money, typically as based on the amount of specie (money in coin) in holding

Bank of New York: formed in 1784 by Alexander Hamilton, the first commercial bank in New York City

bills of exchange: exchange instruments allowing a merchant to receive goods by providing a note promising full payment at a later date in a currency chosen by the seller; occasionally circulated as a money substitute

bounties: direct subsidies provided by a government to business operations in the form of payments of goods or services rendered

circulating medium: money or money substitute, such as banknotes, specie, or promissory notes of public debt, being used to facilitate economic exchange

custom-house regulation: a statute or rule related to the collection of taxes imposed on imported goods

doctrine of implied powers: the belief that the U.S. Constitution allows Congress (or the executive) the authority to exercise any power to achieve another power explicitly granted

dollar out of the Nines: a mathematical formula for checking the addition of large numbers in a sequence, by which those digits adding up to nine are made equal to zero, thus "casting" the nine away

douceurs: tips or emoluments provided for a service

duties: taxes on imported goods

escheat and forfeiture: the transfer of a person's property to the government if he or she dies intestate (without a will) or without legal heirs

> **excises:** taxes on imported goods
>
> **exportation of commodities:** the selling of goods from a specific area, such as a state or nation, outside that area's territorial boundaries
>
> **imposts:** taxes on imported goods
>
> **laws of alienage:** restrictions under English common law whereby foreigners could not own or inherit land because they were not under the jurisdiction of the king
>
> **laws of monopoly:** rules regulating enterprises that do not have competition; early corporations were often granted monopoly status to encourage economic development
>
> **mercantile company:** a business involved in the transfer of staple goods, usually overseas
>
> **plenary and sovereign authority:** complete power over a particular matter
>
> **regulation of pilots:** statutes governing ship captains
>
> **rules of construction:** the manner in which a law, statute, or constitution is interpreted
>
> **taxes in kind:** payments made to the state with goods or services rather than with currency

Document Analysis

In his treatise, Alexander Hamilton does little to alleviate Thomas Jefferson's suspicions about the creation of the bank. Jefferson portrays political power as the great corrupter: If congressmen thought a national bank was constitutional, then there could be no limit to what they might propose next. Hamilton is more restrained, offering a measured response to the situation at hand. The country's economy was in trouble, and a national bank would help rescue it.

Lacking the prosaic elegance typical of a refined Virginia planter, Hamilton delivers a point-by-point refutation that drowns his opponents in verbiage and rhetorical might. Essentially, his argument closely follows his belief that the national government must possess complete sovereignty and, as such, must possess all the means and powers requisite to the fulfillment of its purpose of securing "social order." These powers are supreme and cannot be undermined by any other institution, including the state governments. He agrees that the federal government possesses expressly delegated powers, but these are understood to be supplemented by "implied" powers and what Hamilton calls "resting powers." The power to erect or incorporate a national bank falls within the latter two spheres, not that of express delegations. For a policy to be constitutional to Hamilton, it merely needs "a natural relation to any of the acknowledged objects or lawful ends of the government."

Hamilton then attacks Jefferson's contention that the "necessary and proper" clause limits the federal government to engaging in matters deemed essential. Such was not the popular meaning of the term *necessary*, he claims, and would "beget endless uncertainty and embarrassment" in addition to making most policies inoperative. Anything deemed essential to the "advancement of the public good," he holds, should be "construed liberally." Hamilton insists that the national government is the bedrock of American society. While not admitting "that the national government is sovereign in all respects," Hamilton writes that "it is sovereign to a certain extent; that is, to the extent of the objects of its specified powers."

With little patience for Jefferson's "originalist" doctrines, Hamilton insists that one could trust neither the memories of the delegates to the Philadelphia Convention nor the conflicting accounts of what the framers intended the new government to be. Instead, intention must "be sought for in the instrument [the Constitution] itself, according to the usual and established rules of construction." Hamilton honestly thinks that these rules allowed for the creation of a national bank. He asserts that these circumstances did not imply, as Jefferson and Randolph were contending, that federal government officials could simply do as they pleased.

After dismissing Jefferson's and Randolph's opinions, Hamilton spends considerable effort tracing the legality of a national bank outside the realm of constitutional jurisprudence. Equally impressive is his subsequent justification of banks in general and the important role that they could play in improving the economy and in funding future wars. He even goes so far as to claim that "the support of troops" depended on whether Congress could successfully create a national bank—an argument sure to move Washington, if he were to manage to read that far.

Hamilton clearly had the upper hand in the argument, not because of his rhetorical skill but because of the nature of the subject. Jefferson accepted the terms of the debate when he echoed James Madison's reasoning on the floor of the House of Representatives, treating the bank bill as a matter of constitutionalism rather than sound economic policy. Jefferson's opinion, though perhaps more elegant, leaves open the question of whether a national bank would actually help the economy. Hamilton enjoys free reign in touting the economic virtues of the proposed bank, which makes his argument appear sounder than Jefferson's.

It is not clear who gained ground in the argument either in the president's cabinet or in Congress following the delivery of Jefferson's and Hamilton's opinions. The national bank bill did pass, but neither Hamilton nor Jefferson could be said to have claimed total victory or to have conceded defeat.

Essential Themes

Historians have typically sided with Hamilton in regard to the national bank, either because they agree with his interpretation of the Constitution or owing to the perceived benefits of stabilizing the currency and funding the national debt. Hamilton's proposals were far from radical, as the British had a national bank, and a similar institution had been created under the Articles of Confederation. Nonetheless, many Americans considered these policies to be "un-American," and some politicians insisted that Hamilton was overly fascinated with British forms because he was an Anglophile.

The passage of the bank bill affected American politics in two ways. First, it provided a forum in which manners of constitutional interpretation were widely discussed. Neither Hamilton nor Jefferson conceded his argument, and their political descendants continued to defend their positions for decades to come. More significantly, the debate on the bank bill polarized national politics and proved instrumental to the creation of the first party system. Newspapers were formed, rallies were held, and myriad local movements—some of which were organized against the national bank—slowly coalesced into a formal structure of political activity.

Once under operation, the Bank of the United States further fueled the party system when its inflationary activity quickly brought about depression centered in New York City in 1792. Pamphleteers pilloried the bank as a sign of corruption, whereby "monied" interests used the federal government to enrich themselves at the public's expense. This characterization carried over to Republican rhetoric, which portrayed the Federalists as a commercial elite who had warped the Constitution to suit their purposes. Federalists responded by attacking the Republicans as inept farmers who would wreck the economy.

The elections of 1800 seemed to settle the matter, with the Republicans taking office. In fact, even though they changed the policies of the Bank of the United States to reflect their insistence on founding currency on hard money rather than allowing inflation, the Republicans did not suspend the bank's operation. In effect, the Republicans used Hamiltonian means to secure Jeffersonian ends. They kept a national bank but used it to extinguish the national debt as quickly as possible. The bank's charter expired in 1811.

—*Carey M. Roberts, PhD*

Bibliography and Additional Reading

Carey, George W., and James McClellan, eds. *The Federalist*. Indianapolis: Liberty Fund, 2001.

Chernow, Ron. *Alexander Hamilton*. New York: Penguin Press, 2004.

Cowen, David J. *The Origins and Economic Impact of the First Bank of the United States, 1791–1797*. New York: Garland Publishing, 2000.

Cunningham, Noble E., Jr. *Jefferson vs. Hamilton: Confrontations That Shaped a Nation*. New York: Palgrave Macmillan, 2000.

Elkins, Stanley, and Eric McKitrick. *The Age of Federalism*. New York: Oxford University Press, 1993.

Holloway, Carson. *Hamilton versus Jefferson in the Washington Administration*. New York: Cambridge University Press, 2015.

Madison, James. *Notes of the Debates of the Federal Convention of 1787*. New York: W.W. Norton, 1966.

Perkins, Edwin. *American Public Finance and Financial Services, 1700–1815*. Columbus: Ohio State University Press, 1994.

■ The Whiskey Tax of 1791 and George Washington's Proclamation Regarding the Whiskey Rebellion

Dates: March 3, 1791 (tax passed by Congress); September 15, 1792 (Washington's proclamation)
Authors: Alexander Hamilton; President George Washington
Genres: legislative document; presidential proclamation

Summary Overview

One of the early pieces of legislation passed by the recently formed U.S. Congress, the Whiskey Tax of 1791 was passed by the federal legislative branch on March 3 of that year. It placed a federal excise tax on "ardent sprits" produced from agricultural products as well as a tax on each still used for the production of such spirits. While the major impetus for the tax was to provide revenue for the government, which had incurred debts stemming from the War of Independence, some who supported the tax hoped it might also serve to curb Americans' consumption of alcohol. Opposition to the Whiskey Tax led to the so-called Whiskey Rebellion in western Pennsylvania. Although there was little actual combat, the Whiskey Rebellion was the first violent resistance to laws passed by the new constitutional government, and led President George Washington to send a large militia force to see that the rebellion was put down.

Defining Moment

The U.S. Constitution was ratified in 1788. One of the major problems of the previous framework of government, the Articles of Confederation, was that it provided no efficient taxing power for the federal government. Alexander Hamilton, President Washington's secretary of the treasury, pursued a nationalist economic policy. Pursuant to this nationalist goal, Hamilton had persuaded Congress to assume responsibility for paying off the debt of the states from the Revolutionary War. Hamilton believed that if the national government paid off these debts, the interests of those owed money (some of the wealthiest people in America) would be tied to the strength and stability of the federal government. Of course, this also signaled that the government needed more revenue. Hamilton had proposed a tax on whiskey in his *Report on Public Credit*, sent to Congress in 1790.

The Whiskey Tax, passed by Congress in March 1791, was one of the first federal excise taxes. The law was opposed by small-scale distillers on the western frontier (i.e., the Allegheny Mountain region), who often made whiskey because their corn crop was expensive to ship unless they had access to water transportation. Making whiskey produced a value-added product that was much less bulky to ship and could be readily sold locally to raise cash.

Passage of the excise tax produced opposition and eventually led to the Whiskey Rebellion. President Washington's remarks, included in this entry, were in response to that uprising. The region where resistance was strongest was in the Monongahela River Valley in western Pennsylvania, but unrest affected a wide area from western New York state to eastern Kentucky. The resistance was often passive—refusal either to pay the tax or to help enforce the law. In some communities, officials in charge of collecting the tax resigned, and no one would fill the position. Some who were tried for breaking the law were acquitted by sympathetic juries. When the federal government mobilized a large militia force from neighboring states, the resistance of the whiskey rebels faded away. Many people were arrested, but few were convicted. Two leaders of the movement were convicted of treason, which carried the death penalty, but Washington pardoned both of them. A major factor in Washington's strong response to the Whiskey Rebellion was to send the message that in a republic, dissatisfaction with the law was to be handled within the political system and not by taking up arms.

Author Biographies

Secretary of the Treasury Alexander Hamilton was the major author of the Whiskey Tax. Hamilton was born in the British West Indies on June 11, 1755. He migrated to colonial New York in 1773 and quickly became involved in the Patriot cause, writing several pamphlets promoting American independence. During the American Revolution, he served as aide de camp to General George Washington. He was one of the authors of *The Federalist Papers*, which were published in New York and urged the ratification of the Constitution. Hamilton resigned from Washington's cabinet in 1794 and practiced law in New York City, where he continued to be active in politics. Political disputes between Hamilton and the New York politician Aaron Burr led to Burr challenging Hamilton to a duel. In the duel, Burr mortally wounded Hamilton, who died the following day, July 12, 1804, in New York City.

The leader of the Continental Army in the War of Independence and the first president of the United States, George Washington, was born in Westmoreland County, Virginia, on February 27, 1732. As an officer in the Virginia militia, he was involved in the French and Indian War (1754–1763). He presided over the Constitutional Convention, and when the U.S. Constitution was adopted, many thought he was the obvious choice to be the first president. Initially, he was reluctant to seek the office but agreed to run and was elected in 1789, and again in 1792. After leaving the presidency, he retired to his plantation at Mount Vernon, Virginia, where he died on December 14, 1799.

HISTORICAL DOCUMENT: Excise Tax of 1791 and Whiskey Rebellion Proclamation

Chap. XV—*An Act repealing, after the last day of June next, the duties heretofore laid upon Distilled Spirits imported from abroad, and laying others in their stead; and also upon Spirits distilled within the United States, and for appropriating the same.*

Section 1. Be it enacted by the Senate and House of Representatives of the United States of America in Congress assembled, That after the last day of June next, the duties laid upon distilled spirits by the act entitled "An act making further provision for the payment of the debts of the United States," shall cease; and that upon all distilled spirits which shall be imported into the United States after that day, from any foreign port or place, there shall be paid for their use the duties following; that is to say—For every gallon of those spirits more than ten per cent. below proof, according to Dicas's hydrometer, twenty cents. For every gallon of those spirits under five, and not more than ten per cent. below proof, according to the same hydrometer, twenty-one cents. For every gallon of those spirits of proof, and not more than five per cent. below proof, according to the same hydrometer, twenty-two cents. For every gallon of those spirits above proof, but not exceeding twenty per cent. according to the same hydrometer, twenty-five cents. For every gallon of those spirits more than twenty, and not more than forty per cent. above proof, according to the same hydrometer, thirty cents. For every gallon of those spirits more than forty per cent. above proof, according to the same hydrometer, forty cents.

SEC. 2. *And be it further enacted,* That the said duties shall be collected in the same manner, by the same persons, under the same regulations, and subject to the same forfeitures and other penalties, as those heretofore laid; the act concerning which shall be deemed to be in full force for the collection of the duties herein before imposed, except as to the alterations contained in this act.

SEC. 3. *And be it further enacted,* That the said duties, when the amount thereof shall not exceed fifty dollars, shall be immediately paid; but when the said amount shall exceed fifty, and shall not amount to more than five hundred dollars, may, at the option of the proprietor, importer or consignee, be either immediately paid, or secured by bond, with condition for the payment thereof in four months; and if the amount of the said duties shall exceed five hundred dollars, the same may be immediately paid or secured by bond, with condition for the payment thereof in six months; which bond, in either case, at the like option of the proprietor, importer or consignee, shall either include one or more sureties to the satisfaction of the collector, or person acting as such, or shall be accompanied with a deposit in the custody of the said collector, or person acting as such, of so much of the said spirits as shall in his judgment be a sufficient security for the amount of the duties for which the said bond shall have been given, and the charges of the safe keeping and sale of the spirits so deposited; which deposit shall and may be accepted in lieu of the said surety or sureties, and shall be kept by the said collector, or person acting as such, with due and reasonable care at the expense and risk of the party or parties on whose account the same shall have been made; and if at the expiration of the time mentioned in the bond for the payment of the duties thereby intended to be secured, the same shall not be paid, then the said deposited spirits shall be sold at public sale, and the proceeds thereof, after deducting the charges of keeping and sale, shall be applied to the payment of the whole sum of the duties for which such deposit shall have been made, rendering the overplus of the said proceeds, and the residue of the said spirits, if any there be, to the person or persons by whom such deposit shall have been made, or to his, her or their representatives.

SEC. 4. In order to a due collection of the duties imposed by this act, *Be it further enacted,* That the United States shall be divided into fourteen districts, each consisting of one state, but subject to alterations by the President of the United States, from time to time, by adding to the smaller such portions of the greater as shall in his judgment best tend to secure and facilitate the collection of the revenue; which districts it shall be lawful for the President of the United States to subdivide into surveys of inspection, and the same to alter at his discretion. That the President be authorized to appoint, with the advice and consent of the Senate, a supervisor to each district, and as many inspectors to each survey therein as he shall judge necessary, placing the latter under the direction of the former. *Provided always,* That it shall and may be lawful for the President, with the advice and consent of the Senate, in his discretion to appoint, such and so many officers of the customs to be inspectors in any survey of inspection as he shall deem advisable to employ in the execution of this act: *Provided also,* That where, in the judgment of the President, a supervisor can discharge the duties of that office, and also that of inspector, he may direct the same: *And provided further,* That if the appointment of the inspectors of surveys, or any part of them, shall not be made during the present session of Congress, the President may, and he is hereby empowered to make such appointments during the recess of the Senate, by granting commissions which shall expire at the end of their next session.

SEC. 5. *And be it further enacted,* That the supervisors, inspectors and officers to be appointed by virtue of this act, and who shall be charged to take bonds for securing the payment of the duties upon spirits distilled within the United States, and with the receipt of monies in discharge of such duties, shall keep fair and true accounts and records of their transactions in their respective offices, in such manner and form as may be directed by the proper department or officer having the superintendence of the collection of the revenue, and shall at all times submit their books, papers and accounts to the inspection of such persons as are or may be appointed for that purpose, and shall at all times pay to the order of the officer, who is or shall be authorized to direct the payment thereof, the whole of the monies which they may respectively receive by virtue of this act, and shall also once in every three months, or oftener if they shall be required, transmit their accounts for settlement to the officer or officers whose duty it is, or shall be to make such settlement.

SEC. 6. *And be it further enacted,* That all officers and persons to be appointed pursuant to this act, before they enter on the duties of their respective offices, shall take an oath or affirmation diligently and faithfully to execute the duties of their said offices respectively, and to use their best endeavours to prevent and detect frauds, in relation to the duties on spirits imposed by this act, which oath or affirmation may be taken before any magistrate authorized to administer oaths within the district or survey to which he belongs, and being certified under the hand and seal of the magistrate by whom the same shall have been administered, shall within three months thereafter be transmitted to the comptroller of the treasury, in default of taking which oath or affirmation, the party failing shall forfeit and pay two hundred dollars for the use of the United States, to be recovered with costs of suit.

Sec. 7. *And be it further enacted,* That the supervisor of the revenue for each district, shall establish one or more offices within the same, as may be necessary; and in order that the said offices may be publicly known, there shall be painted or written in large legible characters upon some conspicuous part outside and in front of each house, building or place in which any such office shall be kept, these words, "Office of Inspection;" and if any person shall paint or write, or cause to be painted or written, the said words, upon any other than such house or building, he or she shall forfeit and pay for so doing, one hundred dollars.

Sec. 8. *And be it further enacted,* That within forty-eight hours after any ship or vessel, having on board any distilled spirit brought in such ship or vessel from any foreign port or place, shall arrive within any port of the United States, whether the same be the first port of arrival of such ship or vessel, or not, the master or person having the command or charge thereof, shall report to one of the inspectors of the port at which she shall so arrive, the place from which she last sailed, with her name and burthen, and the quantity and kinds of the said spirits on board of her, and the casks, vessels or cases containing them, with their marks and numbers; on pain of forfeiting the sum of five hundred dollars.

Sec. 9. *And be it further enacted,* That the collector or other officer, or person acting as collector, with whom entry shall have been made of any of the said spirits, pursuant to the act entitled "An act to provide more effectually for the collection of the duties imposed by law on goods, wares and merchandises imported into the United States, and on the tonnage of ships or vessels," shall forthwith after such entry certify and transmit the same, as particularly as it shall have been made with him, to the proper officer of inspection, of the port where it shall be intended to commence the delivery of the spirits so entered, or any part thereof: for which purpose, every proprietor, importer or consignee, making such entry, shall deliver two manifests of the contents (upon one of which the said certificate shall be given) and shall at the time thereof declare the port at which the said delivery shall be so intended to be commenced, to the collector or officer with whom the same shall be made. And every permit granted by such collector, for the landing of any of the said spirits, shall previous to such landing, be produced to the said officer of inspection, who shall make a minute in some proper book, of the contents thereof, and shall endorse thereupon the word "Inspected," the time when, and his own name: after which he shall return it to the person by whom it shall have been produced; and then, and not otherwise it shall be lawful to land the spirits therein specified; and if the said spirits shall be landed without such endorsement upon the permit for that purpose granted, the master or person having charge of the ship or vessel from which the same shall have been so landed, shall for every such offence forfeit the sum of five hundred dollars.

SEC. 10. *And be it further enacted,* That whenever it shall be intended that any ship or vessel shall proceed with the whole or any part of the spirits which shall have been brought in such ship or vessel from any foreign port or place, from one port in the United States to another port in the said United States, whether in the same or in different districts, the master or person having the command or charge of such ship or vessel, shall previous to her departure, apply to the officer of inspection, to whom report was made, for the port from which she is about to depart, for a certificate of the quantity and particulars of such of the said spirits as shall have been certified or reported to him to have been entered as imported in such ship or vessel, and of so much thereof as shall appear to him to have been landed out of her at such port; which certificate the said officer shall forthwith grant. And the master or person having the command or charge of such ship or vessel, shall within twenty-four hours after her arrival at the port to which she shall be bound, deliver the said certificate to the proper officer of inspection of such last mentioned port. And if such ship or vessel shall proceed from one port to another within the United States, with the whole or any part of the spirits brought in her as aforesaid, without having first obtained such certificate; or if within twenty-four hours after her arrival at such other port, the said certificate shall not be delivered to the proper officer of inspection there, the master or person having the command or charge of the said ship or vessel, shall in either case forfeit the sum of five hundred dollars; and the spirits on board of her at her said arrival, shall be forfeited, and may be seized by any officer of inspection....

SEC. 14. *And be it further enacted,* That upon all spirits which after the said last day of June next, shall be distilled within the United States, wholly or in part from molasses, sugar, or other foreign materials, there shall be paid for their use the duties following; that is to say—For every gallon of those spirits more than ten per cent. below proof, according to Dicas's hydrometer, eleven cents. For every gallon of those spirits under five and not more than ten per cent. below proof, according to the same hydrometer, twelve cents. For every gallon of those spirits of proof and not more than five per cent. below proof, according to the same hydrometer, thirteen cents. For every gallon of those spirits above proof, and not exceeding twenty per cent., according to the same hydrometer, fifteen cents. For every gallon of those spirits more than twenty and not more than forty per cent. above proof, according to the same hydrometer, twenty cents. For every gallon of those spirits more than forty per cent. above proof, according to the same hydrometer, thirty cents.

SEC. 15. *And be it further enacted,* That upon all spirits which after the said last day of June next, shall be distilled within the United States, from any article of the growth or produce of the United States, in any city, town or village, there shall be paid for their use the duties following; that is to say—For every gallon of those spirits more than ten per cent. below proof, according to Dicas's hydrometer, nine cents. For every gallon of those spirits under five and not more than ten per cent. below proof, according to the same hydrometer, ten cents. For every gallon of those spirits of proof, and not more than five per cent. below proof, according to the same hydrometer, eleven cents. For every gallon of those spirits above proof, but not exceeding twenty per cent., according to the same hydrometer, thirteen cents. For every gallon of those spirits more than twenty and not more than forty per cent. above proof, according to the same hydrometer, seventeen cents. For every gallon of those spirits more than forty per cent. above proof, according to the same hydrometer, twenty-five cents.

SEC. 16. *And be it further enacted,* That the said duties on spirits distilled within the United States, shall be collected under the management of the supervisors of the revenue.

SEC. 17. *And be it further enacted,* That the said duties on spirits distilled within the United States, shall be paid or secured previous to the removal thereof from the distilleries at which they are respectively made. And it shall be at the option of the proprietor or proprietors of each distillery, or of his, her or their agent having the superintendence thereof, either to pay the said duties previous to such removal, with an abatement at the rate of two cents for every ten gallons, or to secure the payment of the same, by giving bond quarter-yearly, with one or more sureties, to the satisfaction of the chief officer of inspection within whose survey such distillery shall be, and in such sum as the said officer shall direct, with condition for the payment of the duties upon all such of the said spirits as shall be removed from such distillery, within three months next ensuing the date of the bond, at the expiration of nine months from the said date.

SEC. 18. *And be it further enacted,* That the supervisor of each district shall appoint proper officers to have the charge and survey of the distilleries within the same, assigning to each, one or more distilleries as he may think proper, who shall attend such distillery at all reasonable times, for the execution of the duties by this act enjoined on him.

SEC. 19. *And be it further enacted,* That previous to the removal of the said spirits from any distillery, the officer within whose charge and survey the same may be, shall brand or otherwise mark each cask containing the same, in durable characters, and with progressive numbers, and with the name of the acting owner or other manager of such distillery, and of the place where the same was situate, and with the quantity therein, to be ascertained by actual gauging, and with the proof thereof. And the duties thereupon having been first paid, or secured, as above provided, the said officer shall grant a certificate for each cask of the said spirits, to accompany the same wheresoever it shall be sent, purporting that the duty thereon hath been paid or secured, as the case may be, and describing each cask by its marks; and shall enter in a book for that purpose to be kept, all the spirits distilled at such distillery, and removed from the same; and the marks of each cask, and the persons for whose use, and the places to which removed and the time of each removal, and the amount of the duties on the spirits so removed. And if any of the said spirits shall be removed from any such distillery without having been branded or marked as aforesaid, or without such certificate as aforesaid, the same, together with the cask or casks containing, and the horses or cattle, with the carriages, their harness and tackling, and the vessel or boat with its tackle and apparel employed in removing them, shall be forfeited, and may be seized by any officer of inspection. And the superintendent or manager of such distillery, shall also forfeit the full value of the spirits so removed, to be computed at the highest price of the like spirits in the market.

SEC. 20. *And be it further enacted,* That no spirits shall be removed from any such distillery at any other times than between sun rising and sun setting, except by consent and in presence of the officer having the charge and survey thereof, on pain of forfeiture of such spirits, or of the value thereof at the highest price in the market, to be recovered with costs of suit from the acting owner or manager of such distillery.

SEC. 21. *And be it further enacted,* That upon stills which after the last day of June next, shall be employed in distilling spirits from materials of the growth or production of the United States, in any other place than a city, town or village, there shall be paid for the use of the United States, the yearly duty of sixty cents for every gallon, English wine-measure, of the capacity or content of each and every such still, including the head thereof.

SEC. 22. *And be it further enacted,* That the evidence of the employment of the said stills shall be, their being erected in stone, brick or some other manner whereby they shall be in a condition to be worked.

SEC. 23. *And be it further enacted,* That the said duties on stills shall be collected under the management of the supervisor in each district, who shall appoint and assign proper officers for the surveys of the said stills and the admeasurement thereof, and the collection of the duties thereupon; and the said duties shall be paid half-yearly, within the first fifteen days of January and July, upon demand of the proprietor or proprietors of each still, at his, her or their dwelling, by the proper officer charged with the survey thereof:

And in case of refusal or neglect to pay, the amount of the duties so refused or neglected to be paid, may either be recovered with costs of suit in an action of debt in the name of the supervisor of the district, within which such refusal shall happen, for the use of the United States, or may be levied by distress and sale of goods of the person or persons refusing or neglecting to pay, rendering the overplus (if any there be after payment of the said amount and the charges of distress and sale) to the said person or persons.

SEC. 24. *And be it further enacted,* That if the proprietor of any such still, finding himself or herself aggrieved by the said rates, shall enter or cause to be entered in a book to be kept for that purpose, from day to day when such still shall be employed, the quantity of spirits distilled therefrom, and the quantity from time to time sold or otherwise disposed of, and to whom and when, and shall produce the said book to the officer of inspection within whose survey such still shall be, and shall make oath or affirmation that the same doth contain to the best of his or her knowledge and belief, true entries made at their respective dates, of all the spirits distilled within the time to which such entries shall relate, from such still, and of the disposition thereof; and shall also declare upon such oath or affirmation, the quantity of such spirits then remaining on hand, it shall be lawful in every such case for the .said officer to whom the said book shall be produced, and he is hereby required to estimate the duties upon such still, according to the quantity so stated to have been actually made therefrom at the rate of nine cents per gallon, which, and no more, shall be paid for the same: *Provided,* That if the said entries shall be made by any person other than the said proprietor, a like oath or affirmation shall be made by such person....

APPROVED, March 3, 1791.

* * * * *

George Washington's Proclamation of
September 15, 1792

Whereas certain violent and warrantable proceedings have lately taken place tending to obstruct the operation of the laws of the United States for raising a revenue upon spirits distilled within the same, enacted pursuant to express authority delegated in the Constitution of the United States, which proceedings are subversive of good order, contrary to the duty that every citizen owes to his country and to the laws, and of a nature dangerous to the very being of a government; and

    Whereas such proceedings are the more unwarrantable by reason of the moderation which has been heretofore shown on the part of the Government and of the disposition which has been manifested by the Legislature (who alone have authority to suspend the operation of laws) to obviate causes of objection and to render the laws as acceptable as possible; and

Whereas it is the particular duty of the Executive "to take care that the laws be faithfully executed," and not only that duty but the permanent interests and happiness of the people require that every legal and necessary step should be pursued as well to prevent such violent and unwarrantable proceedings as to bring to justice the infractors of the laws and secure obedience thereto:

Now, therefore, I, George Washington, President of the United States, do by these presents most earnestly admonish and exhort all persons whom it may concern to refrain and desist from all unlawful combinations and proceedings whatsoever having for object or tending to obstruct the operation of the laws aforesaid, inasmuch as all lawful ways and means will be strictly put in execution for bringing to justice the infractors thereof and securing obedience thereto.

And I do moreover charge and require all courts, magistrates, and officers whom it may concern, according to the duties of their several offices, to exert the powers in them respectively vested by law for the purposes aforesaid, hereby also enjoining and requiring all persons whomsoever, as they tender the welfare of their country, the just and due authority of Government, and the preservation of the public peace, to be aiding and assisting therein according to law.

In testimony whereof I have caused the seal of the United States to be affixed to these presents, and signed the same with my hand. [SEAL.] Done this 15th of September, A.D. 1792, and of the Independence of the United States the seventeenth.

GO WASHINGTON.

Document Analysis

The Whiskey Tax was one of the first excise taxes created by the United States Congress. Excise taxes were taxes on domestically produced items; in early America and in Great Britain, they were sometimes called "interior" or "inland" taxes, to distinguish them from import taxes. The new Congress under the Constitution passed a number of import tariffs. Such import taxes were a familiar part of trade, and generated little opposition in the early republic. Excise taxes would prove to be more controversial.

The Whiskey Tax bill was a long, complicated piece of legislation, with 62 sections. The first thirteen sections of the bill dealt with the repeal of earlier import duties on "distilled spirits," and the replacement of these with new duties. As in later parts of the bill dealing with taxing whiskey, the tax varied according to the "proof" of the beverage. Proof is a measure of the alcoholic content, and the law specifies that the standard to measure this was the "Dicus hydrometer"— a device for proof testing invented by a British instrument maker, John Dicus (1741–1797), in the 1780s.

To most Americans, the most significant parts of the law would have been Sections 14 and 15. Section 14 imposed a tax on alcoholic beverages produced from "foreign materials." Much rum was distilled in the United States from imported sugar or molasses. Section 15 imposed a tax on beverages distilled from "any article of the growth or produce of the United States," thus taxing ardent spirits made from farm commodities grown in the United States. While whiskey can be made from rye and other crops, since corn was grown extensively in early America, this tax would primarily be on whiskey distilled from corn.

Section 21 imposed a tax on the capacity of stills used to produce whiskey. Small-scale producers of alcohol believed that the regulations favored large distillers. Those who produced large quantities of whiskey could post bond to pay the tax later, but small operators had to pay the tax immediately. The bill also taxed whiskey made for home consumption rather than for sale. Congress later amended the bill to remove some of the most objectionable measures. Nevertheless, the law sparked the short-lived Whiskey Rebellion in western Pennsylvania and frontier areas of neighboring states, which led President Washington to send a large force of militia to put down the uprising, and to issue the proclamation included in this document.

Essential Themes

A major theme illustrated in the passage of the Whiskey Tax is 1791 was the new federal government's need for revenue. Import taxes were not raising enough funds, and the Constitution, until amended in 1913, prohibited an income tax. Hamilton considered a land tax, but with the majority of Americans being involved in agriculture, he knew that such a tax would be very unpopular. While he expected some opposition to the Whiskey Tax, it is unlikely that he envisioned the extent of the resistance that arose.

Besides the need for revenue, some also hoped that the tax would lessen the consumption of "ardent spirits." Hamilton had written in *The Federalist Papers* (No. 21) that a national tax on whiskey "should tend to diminish the consumption of it," and that such a result would be "an effect [which] would be equally favorable to the agriculture, to the economy, to the morals, and to the health of society." Hamilton was not always consistent his arguments on this issue. In messages to Congress regarding the tax, he argued that the demand for whiskey was "inelastic," or consistent and unchanging. Consumers, that is, wanted their whiskey, and likely would not be deterred from purchasing it because of a tax. In that context, Hamilton was arguing that a tax would not lessen consumption.

To many American leaders and opinion-makers at the time, the chief danger of the Whiskey Rebellion was that the people involved in it claimed that they were doing what the patriots had done in the American Revolution—taking up arms to resist government oppression. Their opponents, on the other hand, argued that in a republic citizens should work within the political system to change the laws, not revert to armed conflict. In Washington's proclamation regarding the rebellion, therefore, he calls the actions of the rebels "subversive of good order . . . and of a nature dangerous to the very being of a government." Washington argued that some aspects of the original law had been amended to "obviate causes of objection and to render the laws as acceptable as possible." He called upon the rebels to end their resistance, and for all government officials to enforce the law. Ultimately, his view won the day.

—*Mark S. Joy, PhD*

Bibliography and Additional Reading

Berkin, Carol. *A Sovereign People: The Crises of the 1790s and the Birth of American Nationalism.* New York: Basic Books, 2017.

Chernow, Ron. *Alexander Hamilton.* New York: The Penguin Press, 2004.

Railton, Ben. "Considering History: How Whiskey and Taxes Helped Create the United States." *The Saturday Evening Post,* April 15, 2019.

■ *McCulloch v. Maryland*

Date: March 6, 1819
Author: Marshall, John
Genre: court opinion

Summary Overview

McCulloch v. Maryland is a US Supreme Court case that was decided on March 6, 1819, under the leadership of Chief Justice John Marshall. The Second Bank of the United States was operating a branch in Baltimore when the state of Maryland passed legislation effectively taxing its operation. James McCulloch, an officer of the Baltimore branch, refused to pay the tax and appealed to the US Supreme Court after the Maryland state courts decided the issue in favor of Maryland. *McCulloch v. Maryland* specifically addresses whether the United States Congress has the power under the US Constitution to establish a federal bank, and whether the states have the authority to tax a federal bank's operation within their borders. However, this case carries significance beyond these facts, because its rulings affected the balance of power between the federal government and the states, and shaped the future of US expansion during the nineteenth century.

Defining Moment

During the drafting of the US Constitution, the division of power between the federal and state governments was a hotly debated issue, with respected leaders holding strong opinions on both sides. Some, including the first US treasury secretary, Alexander Hamilton, and future US Supreme Court chief justice John Marshall, argued that a strong federal government was necessary to unite the people of the new nation. Others, including future president Thomas Jefferson, hesitated to give a centralized government too much control, still wary after the recent struggles against England's heavyhanded rule from afar.

In the end, perhaps as a matter of compromise, the Constitution addressed this matter in a rather vague way: it grants only a few specific powers to the federal government, and places only a few clear limitations on those powers. This is further complicated by a clause in article 1, section 8 known as the "Necessary and Proper Clause," which states that Congress has the authority to "make all Laws which shall be necessary and proper for carrying into Execution" the powers granted to it by the Constitution. From the early days of the United States, opinion was divided as to whether this clause should be interpreted as affirmatively granting Congress the power to pass any laws it deems necessary to carry out its constitutional duties, or intentionally limiting Congress's power to write only those laws that are deemed absolutely necessary to carry out its duties.

This interpretive difference has great meaning, because the Tenth Amendment reserves to the states any powers not explicitly granted to the federal government, and article 1, section 10 forbids the states from interfering with the exercise of those explicit federal powers. Thus, the broader "granting" interpretation of the Necessary and Proper Clause effectively reduces the states' autonomy in favor of stronger national regulation that states cannot challenge. By contrast, the narrower "limiting" interpretation skews the balance of power more toward the states.

On its face, the Supreme Court in *McCulloch v. Maryland* simply needed to decide whether the Constitution authorized Congress to charter a federal bank, and whether the state of Maryland had the right to tax its operation. However, all parties involved knew that the case would have a far-reaching impact on the ideological split between those who favored a strong, centralized federal government, and those who championed more autonomous states.

Author Biography

John Marshall was born near Germantown, Virginia, on September 24, 1755. His formal education on the Virginia frontier was sparse but classical, consisting of one year at a private academy and some home tutoring. At age twenty, he joined a Virginia militia as a lieutenant to fight in the Revolutionary War. In 1780, he left the military and returned to Virginia, where he briefly studied law at the College of William and Mary. He was admitted to the Virginia bar and moved to Richmond, where he set up a law practice and established a strong reputation for his work in the state's appeals court. Marshall also served in a legislative capacity as a member of the Virginia House of Delegates from 1782 to 1789, and in 1788 he was appointed as a delegate to the Virginia convention charged with ratifying or rejecting the newly proposed US Constitution.

Marshall's first federal appointment in the young United States government was to a diplomatic mission to France in 1797 under President John Adams. Upon his return, at the request of former president George Washington, Marshall successfully ran for the Richmond seat in the US House of Representatives as a member of the Federalist Party. He took this seat in late 1799, and by May of the following year, President Adams had appointed him secretary of state. In 1801, Adams appointed Marshall chief justice of the Supreme Court of the United States.

Marshall served on the Supreme Court for thirty four years, during which time he wrote 519 of the 1,215 opinions issued by the court, including several landmark cases defining the court's powers to interpret the Constitution, such as *Marbury v. Madison* (1803). During the early years of his tenure, Marshall had considerable influence among his fellow justices, reflected in the strong Federalist leaning of many decisions from that time. This started to change around 1804, when President Thomas Jefferson, a distant cousin of Marshall's and a strong anti-Federalist, appointed the first of three new justices to the court. The country's rapid economic growth and western expansion in the 1810s and early 1820s led to many decisions on the balance of power between the federal and state governments, including *McCulloch v. Maryland*. By the late 1820s, Marshall's influence further declined as President Andrew Jackson's appointees arrived on the court, skewing the bench further in favor of states' rights.

Chief Justice John Marshall continued to serve on the US Supreme Court until his death in Philadelphia on July 6, 1835.

HISTORICAL DOCUMENT: *McCullough v. Maryland*

Chief Justice Marshall delivered the opinion of the Court.

In the case now to be determined, the defendant, a sovereign State, denies the obligation of a law enacted by the legislature of the Union, and the plaintiff, on his part, contests the validity of an act which has been passed by the legislature of that State. The constitution of our country, in its most interesting and vital parts, is to be considered; the conflicting powers of the government of the Union and of its members, as marked in that constitution, are to be discussed; and an opinion given, which may essentially influence the great operations of the government. No tribunal can approach such a question without a deep sense of its importance, and of the awful responsibility involved in its decision. But it must be decided peacefully, or remain a source of hostile legislation, perhaps of hostility of a still more serious nature; and if it is to be so decided, by this tribunal alone can the decision be made. On the Supreme Court of the United States has the constitution of our country devolved this important duty.

The first question made in the cause is, has Congress power to incorporate a bank? It has been truly said that this can scarcely be considered as an open question, entirely unprejudiced by the former proceedings of the nation respecting it. The principle now contested was introduced at a very early period of our history, has been recognized by many successive legislatures, and has been acted upon by the judicial department, in cases of peculiar delicacy, as a law of undoubted obligation. . . .

The power now contested was exercised by the first Congress elected under the present constitution. The bill for incorporating the Bank of the United States did not steal upon an unsuspecting legislature, and pass unobserved. Its principle was completely understood, and was opposed with equal zeal and ability. After being resisted, first in the fair and open field of debate, and afterwards in the executive cabinet, with as much persevering talent as any measure has ever experienced, and being supported by arguments which convinced minds as pure and as intelligent as this country can boast, it became a law. The original act was permitted to expire; but a short experience of the embarrassments to which the refusal to revive it exposed the government, convinced those who were most prejudiced against the measure of its necessity, and induced the passage of the present law. It would require no ordinary share of intrepidity to assert that a measure adopted under these circumstances was a bold and plain usurpation, to which the constitution gave no countenance.

These observations belong to the cause; but they are not made under the impression that, were the question entirely new, the law would be found irreconcilable with the constitution.

In discussing this question, the counsel for the State of Maryland have deemed it of some importance, in the construction of the constitution, to consider that instrument not as emanating from the people, but as the act of sovereign and independent States. The powers of the general government, it has been said, are delegated by the

States, who alone are truly sovereign; and must be exercised in subordination to the States, who alone possess supreme dominion.

It would be difficult to sustain this proposition. The Convention which framed the constitution was indeed elected by the State legislatures. But the instrument, when it came from their hands, was a mere proposal, without obligation, or pretensions to it. It was reported to the then existing Congress of the United States, with a request that it might "be submitted to a convention of delegates, chosen in each State by the people thereof, under the recommendation of its legislature, for their assent and ratification." This mode of proceeding was adopted; and by the convention, by Congress, and by the State legislatures, the instrument was submitted to the people. They acted upon it in the only manner in which they can act safely, effectively, and wisely, on such a subject, by assembling in convention. It is true, they assembled in their several States—and where else should they have assembled? No political dreamer was ever wild enough to think of breaking down the lines which separate the States, and of compounding the American people into one common mass. Of consequence, when they act, they act in their States. But the measures they adopt do not, on that account, cease to be the measures of the people themselves, or become the measures of the State governments.

From these conventions the constitution derives its whole authority. The government proceeds directly from the people; is "ordained and established" in the name of the people; and is declared to be ordained, "in order to form a more perfect union, establish justice, ensure domestic tranquility, and secure the blessings of liberty to themselves and to their posterity." The assent of the States, in their sovereign capacity, is implied in calling a convention, and thus submitting that instrument to the people. But the people were at perfect liberty to accept or reject it; and their act was final. It required not the affirmance, and could not be negatived, by the State governments. The constitution, when thus adopted, was of complete obligation, and bound the State sovereignties. . . .

This government is acknowledged by all to be one of enumerated powers. The principle, that it can exercise only the powers granted to it . . . is now universally admitted. But the question respecting the extent of the powers actually granted, is perpetually arising, and will probably continue to arise, as long as our system shall exist. . . .

Among the enumerated powers, we do not find that of establishing a bank or creating a corporation. But there is no phrase in the instrument which, like the articles of confederation, excludes incidental or implied powers; and which requires that everything granted shall be expressly and minutely described. Even the 10th amendment . . . omits the word "expressly," and declares only, that the powers "not delegated to the United States, nor prohibited to the states, are reserved to the states or to the people." . . . A constitution, to contain an accurate detail of all the subdivisions of which its great powers will admit, and of all the means by which they may be carried into execution . . . would, probably, never be understood by the public. Its nature, therefore, requires, that only its great outlines should be marked.

Although, among the enumerated powers of government, we do not find the word "bank" or "incorporation," we find the great powers, to lay and collect taxes; to borrow money; to regulate commerce; to declare and conduct a war; and to raise and support armies and navies. . . . But it may with great reason be contended, that a government, entrusted with such ample powers . . . must also be entrusted with ample means for their execution. The power being given, it is the interest of the nation to facilitate its execution. . . .

But the constitution of the United States has not left the right of Congress to employ the necessary means, for the execution of the powers conferred on the government, to general reasoning. To its enumeration of powers is added that of making "all laws which shall be necessary and proper for carrying into execution the foregoing powers, and all other powers vested by this constitution, in the government of the United States, or in any department thereof."

The counsel for the State of Maryland have urged various arguments, to prove that this clause, though in terms a grant of power, is not so in effect; but is really restrictive of the general right, which might otherwise be implied, of selecting means for executing the enumerated powers. . . .

Let this be done in the case under consideration. The subject is the execution of those great powers on which the welfare of a nation essentially depends. It must have been the intention of those who gave these powers, to insure, as far as human prudence could insure, their beneficial execution. This could not be done by confiding the choice of means to such narrow limits as not to leave it in the power of Congress to adopt any which might be appropriate, and which were conducive to the end. This provision is made in a constitution intended to endure for ages to come, and, consequently, to be adapted to the various crises of human affairs. To have prescribed the means by which government should, in all future time, execute its powers, would have been to change, entirely, the character of the instrument, and give it the properties of a legal code. It would have been an unwise attempt to provide, by immutable rules, for exigencies which, if foreseen at all, must have been seen dimly, and which can be best provided for as they occur. To have declared that the best means shall not be used, but those alone without which the power given would be nugatory, would have been to deprive the legislature of the capacity to avail itself of experience, to exercise its reason, and to accommodate its legislation to circumstances. If we apply this principle of construction to any of the powers of the government, we shall find it so pernicious in its operation that we shall be compelled to discard it. . . .

Let the end be legitimate, let it be within the scope of the constitution, and all means which are appropriate, which are plainly adapted to that end, which are not prohibited, but consist with the letter and spirit of the constitution, are constitutional. . . .

Should Congress, in the execution of its powers, adopt measures which are prohibited by the constitution; or should Congress, under the pretext of executing its powers, pass laws for the accomplishment of objects not entrusted to the government; it would become the painful duty of this tribunal, should a case requiring such a decision come before it, to say that such an act was not the law of the land. But where the law is not prohibited, and is really calculated to effect any of the objects entrusted to the government, to undertake here to inquire into the degree of its necessity, would be to pass the line which circumscribes the judicial department, and to tread on legislative ground. This court disclaims all pretensions to such a power.

After this declaration, it can scarcely be necessary to say that the existence of State banks can have no possible influence on the question. No trace is to be found in the constitution of an intention to create a dependence of the government of the Union on those of the States, for the execution of the great powers assigned to it. Its means are adequate to its ends; and on those means alone was it expected to rely for the accomplishment of its ends. To impose on it the necessity of resorting to means which it cannot control, which another government may furnish or withhold, would render its course precarious, the result of its measures uncertain, and create a dependence on other governments, which might disappoint its most important designs, and is incompatible with the language of the constitution. But were it otherwise, the choice of means implies a right to choose a national bank in preference to State banks, and Congress alone can make the election.

After the most deliberate consideration, it is the unanimous and decided opinion of this Court, that the act to incorporate the Bank of the United States is a law made in pursuance of the constitution, and is a part of the supreme law of the land. . . .

It being the opinion of the Court, that the act incorporating the bank is constitutional; and that the power of establishing a branch in the State of Maryland might be properly exercised by the bank itself, we proceed to inquire—

Whether the State of Maryland may, without violating the constitution, tax that branch? . . .

There is no express provision for the case, but the claim has been sustained on a principle which so entirely pervades the constitution. . . . This great principle is, that the constitution and the laws made in pursuance thereof are supreme; that they control the constitution and laws of the respective states, and cannot be controlled by them. From this . . . other propositions are deduced as corollaries. . . .

That the power to tax involves the power to destroy. . . . If the states may tax one instrument, employed by the government in the execution of its powers, they may tax any and every other instrument. They may tax the mail; they may tax the mint; they may tax patent-rights; they may tax the papers of the custom-house; they may tax judicial process; they may tax all the means employed by the government, to an excess which would defeat all the ends of government. This was not intended by the

American people. They did not design to make their government dependent on the states. . . .

The result is a conviction that the states have no power, by taxation or otherwise, to retard, impede, burden, or in any manner control, the operations of the constitutional laws enacted by congress to carry into execution the powers vested in the general government. This is, we think, the unavoidable consequence of that supremacy which the constitution has declared. We are unanimously of opinion, that the law passed by the legislature of Maryland, imposing a tax on the Bank of the United States, is unconstitutional and void.

GLOSSARY

affirmance: affirmation

charter: legal document establishing a corporation and defining its operations

devolved: passed on to

enumerated powers: powers explicitly granted to Congress in the US Constitution, primarily in article 1, section 8

intrepidity: fearlessness

nugatory: inconsequential; without force

plaintiff: an individual, business, or other entity suing another in a court of law

sovereign: having supreme power

Document Analysis

In the early days of the United States, there was much debate about whether a national bank should be established, and whether doing so would be permissible under the US Constitution. In 1791, the Congress chartered the First Bank of the United States, with the goals of establishing a consistent and stable currency, extending credit to encourage further expansion of US territory, and facilitating the collection of taxes from the states for the benefit of the newly founded nation. The bank was championed by those in the administration of President George Washington with Federalist leanings, including Treasury Secretary Alexander Hamilton, but was opposed by those who supported states' rights, including Secretary of State Thomas Jefferson. Under its charter, the First Bank of the United States was limited to twenty years of operation; in 1811, Congress debated renewing the charter, and the bank's opponents won the day: the charter was not renewed, and the First Bank of the United States ceased operations.

However, the War of 1812 and the Napoleonic Wars led to worldwide financial instability, and it became clear that some intervention was needed to keep the fledgling US economy on track. Some of the national bank's earlier opponents conceded that the bank had served a useful function during its tenure, and in 1817, the Second Bank of the United States began operations under a new twenty-year charter. The Second Bank's headquarters were in Philadelphia, Pennsylvania, but the bank established branch locations in a number of cities across the United States.

The Second Bank had opened and was operating a branch in Baltimore, Maryland, in 1817 when the state passed legislation that amounted to a tax on the operations of any bank not chartered in Maryland, which included the Second Bank. The new law required that out-of-state banks must print their notes on special paper purchased from the state, or pay $15,000 per year to be exempt from the requirement. Noncompliant banks would face stiff fines. This law was controversial, as it was reminiscent of the stamp taxes that England had forced upon legal documents prepared in the United States prior to the American Revolution.

James McCulloch, who was then acting as the head of the Baltimore branch of the Second Bank, refused to pay the tax. He was reported to the state and ordered to pay the fine for noncompliance, but the Second Bank fought back. The fine was first appealed in the Maryland state court, where a judge ruled against Mc- Culloch and the Second Bank on the grounds that the entire notion of a federal bank was unconstitutional, as the Constitution did not explicitly authorize Congress to establish such a bank. The case was then appealed to the US Supreme Court—which, in its decision, reaffirmed the court's authority to determine the constitutionality of state and federal legislative actions with respect to the US Constitution.

The Trial

Oral argument in *McCulloch v. Maryland* began before the US Supreme Court on February 22, 1819, and lasted for nine days. The members of the Supreme Court, as well as the Congress and numerous state leaders, were quite interested in the arguments and the outcome of the case. So, moreover, was the general public: a quote from the letters of Justice Joseph Story noted that the arguments took place before "a crowded audience of ladies and gentlemen; the hall was full almost to suffocation, and many went away for want of room" (325). Indeed, it was widely recognized that this case held more significance than the simple taxation of a single bank branch.

Altogether, six attorneys argued before the Supreme Court. Arguing on behalf of McCulloch and the Second Bank of the United States was Daniel Webster, a well-respected attorney from Massachusetts who frequently appeared before the court; William Wirt, the attorney general of the United States; and William Pinkney, former US attorney general under President James Madison. Arguing on behalf of the state of Maryland was Joseph Hopkinson, a well-known attorney from Philadelphia; Walter Jones, a private attorney from Washington, DC, with a reputation for extensive legal knowledge; and Luther Martin, attorney general for the state of Maryland.

The Supreme Court issued its opinion on March 6, 1819, just three days after the conclusion of oral arguments— impressively fast for an opinion that filled more than 150 written pages. Chief Justice John Marshall wrote the opinion, which, to the surprise of many observers, was unanimous. The ruling established that Congress did indeed have the authority to charter a federal bank, and that Maryland did not have the power to tax that bank's operations. However, the legal justification behind the decision gave the case significant and long-lasting impact.

The Decision
In writing for the court, Chief Justice Marshall lays out four arguments explaining why Congress did in fact have the authority to establish a national bank. First, the court states that, since Congress had created the First Bank of the United States, it likewise had the authority to create the second. This logic seems dubious, but Chief Justice Marshall explains that the decision to create the First Bank was made by "minds as pure and as intelligent as this country can boast." He notes that "its principle was completely understood, and was opposed with equal zeal and ability," and that Congress nonetheless voted to charter the First Bank. He reasoned that, since the decision to charter a federal bank was not made lightly the first time around, the judgment of those who made that decision should be trusted and allowed to stand. Chief Justice Marshall further noted that the chartering of the Second Bank occurred after a "short experience of the embarrassments to which the refusal to revive it exposed the government"; in other words, the Second Bank was chartered in a somewhat rushed manner. Marshall acknowledges that laws passed in this way might be more suspect than those that are extensively debated, but that fact alone does not mean the law is "irreconcilable with the constitution." This is particularly true in this case, since the First Bank was chartered only after lengthy discussion.

Second, the court rejected Maryland's argument that the states retain full sovereignty because they were the entities that ratified the Constitution in the first place. Drafted in 1787 at the Constitutional Convention held in Philadelphia, the Constitution was then ratified over a period of two years by state-level ratification conventions. The fact that the Constitution was ratified at the state level formed the basis of Maryland's argument that it was really the states, not the people, who adopted the Constitution, therefore making the states the locus of sovereignty from which federal power is derived. Chief Justice Marshall writes, however, that "it is true, [the ratification conventions] assembled in their several States," but that "the measures they adopt do not, on that account, cease to be the measures of the people themselves."

The third and fourth arguments are tied closely together, and address the provisions of the Constitution directly. The court agreed that the power to charter a national bank was not explicitly granted to Congress in article 1, section 8 of the Constitution. However, Marshall writes that "there is no phrase in the instrument which . . . requires that everything granted shall be expressly and minutely described." In other words, there was nothing in the Constitution that restricted Congress's powers to that which was specifically enumerated. He further elaborates that the Constitution does provide for "great powers, to lay and collect taxes; to borrow money; to regulate commerce; to declare and conduct a war; and to raise and support armies and navies," and that as a result Congress "must also be entrusted with ample means for their execution." So while Congress may not explicitly have the power to establish a national bank, it implicitly has that power if establishing such a bank will help to execute constitutional duties such as collecting taxes and borrowing money. Marshall particularly emphasized that, because the Constitution was meant to be a living document subject to interpretation, any rulings on the extent of its provisions must be considered in a broader context, and not limited to a strict reading of the text.

This led into Marshall's final argument, which relied upon the Necessary and Proper Clause. This clause, which is found in article 1, section 8, clause 18, states that Congress can pass any law that is "necessary" and "proper" to carry out the powers granted to it by the Constitution. However, the word "necessary" led to disagreement over its interpretation: Maryland argued that it meant Congress could only enact laws that were absolutely necessary in order to carry out its powers, and that establishing a national bank was not absolutely necessary for the government to function. However, Chief Justice Marshall ultimately said that it referred to "all means which are appropriate" and was not intended to limit Congress to actions that were essentially a last resort. He justified this interpretation by noting that the Necessary and Proper Clause was listed among Congress's powers in article 8, rather than among its limitations in article 9, and also by noting again that the US Constitution was intended to be a flexible document subject to contextual interpretation. If this were not the case, he argues, it would "deprive the legislature of the capacity to avail itself of experience, to exercise its reason, and to accommodate its legislation to circumstances."

The decision on this point was significant in the long-running battle between federalism and states' rights. Chief Justice Marshall stated that the Necessary and Proper Clause was meant to be "an additional power" granted to Congress, rather than "a restriction on those already granted." This gave Congress broad authority to pass many specific provisions not explicitly addressed in the Constitution, as long as they could be justifiably related to a power that Congress was specifically granted by the Constitution. Further complicating the issue is that the Tenth Amendment, which was ratified as part of the Bill of Rights in 1791, states that any power "not delegated to the United States by the Constitution, nor prohibited by it to the States, are reserved to the States respectively, or to the people." This meant that any decision that expanded the power of the federal government necessarily limited the power of the states to legislate in that same area.

This tension informed the second part of the court's decision in *McCulloch v. Maryland*: once it was determined that the federal government had the authority to create the Second Bank of the United States, the Supreme Court had to decide whether it was permissible for the state of Maryland to tax the operations of the Baltimore branch.

On this point, the court established that Maryland did not have the power to tax the operation of the federal bank within its borders. Chief Justice Marshall clearly stated that "the power to tax involves the power to destroy," and that a state cannot "retard impede, burden, or in any manner control, the operations of the Constitutional laws enacted by congress to carry into execution" its powers and duties. To support this ruling, Marshall makes what is commonly referred to as a "slippery slope" argument: he suggests that, if the state is allowed to tax the bank, next it will tax the mail, the mint, the judicial process, the patent system, and any other federal government operation that occurs within its borders. He notes that this would effectively allow a state to shut down the operation of the federal government in that state, which would directly contradict the will of the people as expressed in the ratification of the US Constitution.

Reaction
The decision in *McCulloch v. Maryland* was not well received in states known for anti-Federalist views, primarily in the South. The decision was widely criticized in newspapers, including the *Richmond Enquirer*, of Marshall's own hometown. Within a few days of the court's opinion being issued, a writer using the pen name "Amphictyon" wrote an editorial criticizing Marshall on several points, including the issuance of a single court opinion (when, until a few years prior, each justice had generally issued his own opinion), and suggesting that his ruling might have been a result of political influence. The writer likewise noted that the ruling would have broad implications for the future development of the United States, particularly with respect to westward expansion and the creation of railroads, canals, and other matters affecting interstate travel and commerce; the decision in *McCulloch v. Maryland* would ensure that the federal government could always have the final say on these matters if it so desired. In a rare move, Marshall felt it necessary to defend the ruling in the popular media, publishing a piece titled "A Friend to the Union" in the Philadelphia newspapers. This piece reiterated a significant point in the original opinion, namely that it was the people and not the states who had ratified the Constitution, and expressed Marshall's belief that it was within the federal government's authority to take any actions necessary to preserve the nation on behalf of the people that had chosen to form it.

Alas, there was no clear resolution of this ideological split, either at the time of the McCulloch decision, or at present; the issue of the division of power between the federal and state governments continues to be debated.

Essential Themes

McCulloch v. Maryland was a landmark case for the US Supreme Court because of its ruling on the balance of power between federal and state governments, and the constitutional justifications provided for its decision. In the early days of the United States, opinion was starkly divided between those who favored strong federal regulation and those who favored state autonomy. This issue was addressed only vaguely in the Constitution itself. The federal government was granted several specifically enumerated powers, with only a few explicit limitations. Any power not specifically granted to the federal government was reserved for the states by operation of the Tenth Amendment. However, the Necessary and Proper Clause of article 1, section 8 complicated the interpretation of these provisions, and the balance of federal power and state autonomy hinged upon whether that clause was interpreted in a broad "power-granting" sense or a narrow "power-limiting" sense.

McCulloch v. Maryland was significant because, in writing for the court, Chief Justice Marshall stated that the Necessary and Proper Clause should be interpreted broadly. This meant that Congress did indeed have authority to pass laws on matters not explicitly mentioned in the Constitution, as long as those laws were "necessary and proper" to carrying out its constitutional duties. This extended to the establishment of the Second Bank of the United States, because Congress did have explicit authority in several related areas, including levying taxes, lending money, and funding armies and navies. Additionally, by prohibiting the state from taxing the national bank, the court clearly established a limit on states' power: a state cannot take an action that interferes with the federal government's exercise of its constitutionally authorized powers.

The ruling in *McCulloch v. Maryland* had far-reaching consequences for the growth and development of the United States and its government. This theme was present quite often during the early days of the United States, as common infrastructure was being established. For example, it frequently arose in the context of the Interstate Commerce Clause, a clause of the US Constitution that granted Congress the authority to regulate any economic activity that would cross state lines. This effectively gave the federal government ultimate authority over the establishment of railroads, canals, and roadways in new states and territories, which was vitally important as the United States expanded across North America. Additionally during Franklin D. Roosevelt's presidency, much of the legislation that formed the New Deal was upheld as constitutional because of the precedent establishing broad powers for the federal government. This expansiveness has been called into question many times throughout history, and sometimes Congress's acts are struck down as unconstitutional if they are deemed insufficiently closely related to its enumerated powers. But since the established precedent is for broad legislative authority, any reduction in this power must be justified by the court, rather than the other way around. As a result, this ideology and the US Supreme Court's decision in *McCulloch v. Maryland* had a significant impact on the federal-state balance of power throughout the history of the United States.

—Tracey M. DiLascio, JD

Bibliography and Additional Reading

Catterall, Ralph C. H. *The Second Bank of the United States*. Chicago: U of Chicago P, 1968. Print.

Crompton, Samuel Willard. McCulloch v. Maryland: *Implied Powers of the Federal Government*. New York: Infobase, 2007. Print.

Cushman, Clare, Ed. *The Supreme Court Justices: Illustrated Biographies, 1789–1993*. Washington, DC: Congressional Quarterly, 1993. Print.

Gunther, Gerald, Ed. *John Marshall's Defense of* McCulloch v. Maryland. Stanford: Stanford UP, 1969. Print.

Hall, Kermit L., ed. *The Oxford Guide to United States Supreme Court Decisions*. New York: Oxford UP, 1999. Print. Harrison, Maureen, and Steve Gilbert, eds. *Landmark Decisions of the United States Supreme Court IV*. La Jolla: Excellent, 1994. Print.

Killenbeck, Mark R. M'Culloch v. Maryland: *Securing a Nation*. Lawrence: UP of Kansas, 2006. Print.

Story, Joseph. *Life and Letters of Joseph Story*. Boston: Little, 1851. Print.

Henry Clay's Speech on American Industry

Date: 1824
Author: Henry Clay
Genre: speech

Summary Overview

Reproduced here is an excerpt from a speech by Henry Clay, one of the most influential American politicians in the first half of the nineteenth century. Clay espoused an economic model that he called the American System. This model had several basic tenets: protective tariffs, a federal bank, and investment in physical infrastructure, such as roads and bridges. It was firmly rooted in the American School of economics, founded by Alexander Hamilton and later taken up by Abraham Lincoln. In this speech, Clay focuses on one of the American System's main pillars: tariffs. He gave the speech as Speaker of the House in attempt to garner support for the Tariff of 1824, which he eventually helped pass. The speech describes the status quo as in desperate need of change and tariffs as the ideal remedy. Clay acknowledges the common perception of tariffs as negative and unfair before asserting that this is a misperception and claiming an inherent fairness in tariffs.

Defining Moment

Henry Clay gave this speech in support of the Tariff of 1824, which eventually became law. Tariffs were a part of Clay's economic model, the American System, which itself was a part of the influential American School.

Alexander Hamilton founded the American School, shortly after the nation's inception. He believed that the United States would never be truly independent until it was financially independent and self-sufficient. The main tenets of his economic policies were threefold: create a national bank, promote protectionism (through tariffs and the like), and invest in physical infrastructure. Despite resistance from his peers such as Thomas Jefferson, Hamilton was largely successful in pushing his agenda as the first treasurer of the United States. He helped form a national bank that assumed the various debts of the state banks. He and his allies helped push through a system of tariffs. The Tariff Act of 1789, for example, was the first major legislation to pass through Congress and become law following the Constitution itself. Finally, the young U.S. government funded a system of physical infrastructure dubbed Internal Improvements.

Others took up Hamilton's policies and the American School's model after his death. The economist Friedrich List supported this set of policies, dubbing them the National System. Another economist, Henry Carey, likewise championed the same basic ideas in what he called a Harmony of Interests. Beyond economists theorizing on these policies, a number of politicians attempted to continue to turn these policies into law. Chief among them was Henry Clay. He called his version of these policies the American System and advocated for it throughout his long and influential political career. He gave the speech featured in this document as Speaker of the House in support of the Tariff of 1824, which he helped pass into law. Under his influence, first the National Republican Party then the Whig Party made this set of policies central to their platforms.

There were many politicians that opposed Clay's American System and the broader American School. The Democratic Party as a whole proved inimical to Clay and his policies. Andrew Jackson, in particular, consistently railed against tariffs and the American System. He viewed tariffs as benefitting special interest groups while harming the majority of Americans, especially Southern plantation owners. The American School came roaring back with the election of Abraham Lincoln. His administration passed a body of policies during the Civil War that brought the American School policies to fruition. By the twentieth century, most analysts stopped discussing these policies under the names of the American School or the American System. However, their various tenets continued to be debated, enacted, and revoked. Even into the twenty-first century, American politicians consistently debate the efficacy of tariffs and infrastructure spending.

Author Biography

Henry Clay was a prominent American politician of the first half of the nineteenth century. He was born in Virginia in 1777, amidst the Revolutionary War. He became a successful lawyer in Lexington, Kentucky, where, among other accomplishments, he successfully defended Aaron Burr in the so-called Burr Conspiracy. Clay quickly rose through the ranks of the Kentucky state government, becoming a member of and then speaker of the State House of Representatives. He moved from state to national politics, serving as a senator and Speaker of the U.S. House of Representatives. As Speaker of the House, he played an influential role in driving the United States into the War of 1812, and as a diplomat, he helped negotiate its peace terms. He made three serious but ultimately unsuccessful bids for the presidency, in 1824, 1832, and 1844. John Quincy Adams appointed him secretary of state in 1825. He became known for the American System; his economic plan centered on tariffs. He gained a reputation for brokering compromises and together with Daniel Webster and John C. Calhoun made up the influential so-called Great Triumvirate. He and his wife Lucretia Hart had eleven children together.

HISTORICAL DOCUMENT: Henry Clay's Speech on American Industry

It is my intention, with the permission of the committee, to avail myself also of this opportunity, to present to its consideration those general views, as they appear to me, of the true policy of this country, which imperiously demand the passage of this bill. I am deeply sensible, Mr. Chairman, of the high responsibility of my present situation. But that responsibility inspires me with no other apprehension than that I shall be unable to fulfill my duty; with no other solicitude than that I may, at, least, in some small degree, contribute to recall my country from the pursuit of a fatal policy, which appears to me inevitably to lead to its impoverishment and ruin. I do feel most awfully this responsibility ...

In casting our eyes around us, the most prominent circumstance which fixes our attention and challenges our deepest regret is the general distress which pervades the whole country. It is forced upon us by numerous facts of the most incontestable character. It is indicated by the diminished exports of native produce; by the depressed and reduced state of our foreign navigation; by our diminished commerce; by successive unthrashed crops of grain, perishing in our barns and barn-yards for the want of a market; by the alarming diminution of the circulating medium; by the numerous bankruptcies, not limited to the trading classes, but extending to all orders of society; by a universal complaint of the want of employment, and a consequent reduction of the wages of labor . . . This distress pervades every part of the Union, every class of society; all feel it, though it may be felt at different places, in different degrees. It is like the atmosphere which surrounds us,—all must inhale it, and none can escape it ...

What, again I would ask, is the cause of the unhappy condition of our country, which I have faintly depicted? It is to be found in the fact that, during almost the whole existence of this government, we have shaped our industry, our navigation, and our commerce, in reference to an extraordinary war in Europe, and to foreign markets which no longer exist; in the fact that we have depended too much upon foreign sources of supply, and excited too little the native; in the fact that, whilst we have cultivated, with assiduous care, our foreign resources, we have suffered those at home to wither in a state of neglect and abandonment. The consequence of the termination of the war of Europe has been the resumption of European commerce, European navigation, and the extension of European agriculture and European industry in all its branches. Europe, therefore, has no longer occasion, to anything like the same extent as that she had during her wars, for American commerce, American navigation, the produce of American industry ...

The committee will agree with me in thinking that it is the solemn duty of government to apply a remedy to the evils which afflict our country, if it can apply one. Is there no remedy within the reach of the government? Are we doomed to behold our industry languish and decay, yet more and more? But there is a remedy, and that remedy consists in modifying our foreign policy, and in adopting a genuine American system. We must naturalize the arts in our country; and we must naturalize them by the only means which the wisdom of nations has yet discovered to be effectual, by adequate protection against the otherwise overwhelming influence of foreigners. This is only to be accomplished by the establishment of a tariff, to the consideration of which I am now brought.

And what is this tariff? It seems to have been regarded as a sort of monster, huge and deformed,—a wild beast, endowed with tremendous powers of destruction, about to be let loose among our people, if not to devour them, at least to consume their substance. But let us calm our passions, and deliberately survey this alarming, this terrific being. The sole object of the tariff is to tax the produce of foreign industry, with the view of promoting American industry. The tax is exclusively leveled at foreign industry. That is the avowed and the direct purpose of the tariff. If it subjects any part of American industry to burdens, that is an effect not intended, but is altogether incidental, and perfectly voluntary.

It has been treated as an imposition of burdens upon one part of the community by design, for the benefit of another; as if, in fact, money were taken from the pockets of one portion of the people and put into the pockets of another. But is that a fair representation of it? No man pays the duty assessed on the foreign article by compulsion, but voluntarily; and this voluntary duty, if paid, goes into the common exchequer, for the common benefit of all.

> *Are we doomed to behold our industry languish and decay...? The remedy consists in [providing] adequate protection against the otherwise overwhelming influence of foreigners ... by the establishment of a tariff.*

Henry Clay's Speech on American Industry • 109

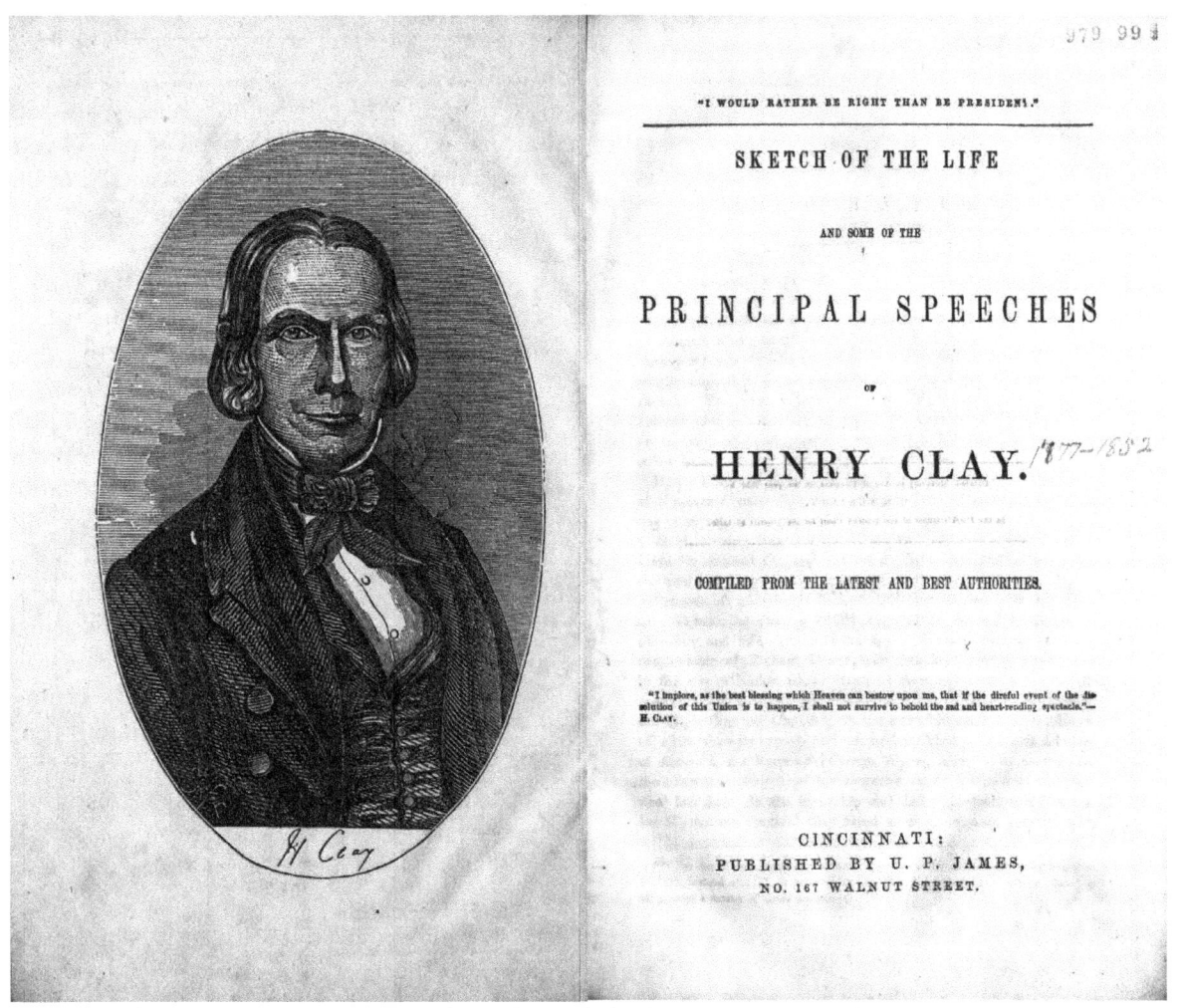

Throughout his time in Congress, Henry Clay spoke regularly about tariffs; his speech in 1832 is considered to have been the best in his life.

Document Analysis

Henry Clay gave this speech to champion the Tariff of 1824. His message is tripartite and straightforward. He starts by describing a status quo in need of changing; he then proposes a remedy; he concludes by explaining and defending his stated remedy.

He begins by stating his intention to describe "those general views, as they appear to me, of the true policy of this country, which imperiously demand the passage of this bill." He does not explain policy so much as the dire circumstance of the nation. He strives to paint a particularly desperate picture to make the nation look in need of change. He depicts many signs of the national "distress," saying it is indicated "by the diminished exports of native produce; by the depressed and reduced state of our foreign navigation; by our diminished commerce; by successive unthrashed crops of grain, perishing in our barns and barn-yards for the want of a market." These first indicators pertain to the United States' unfavorable import/export market. He continues his list, "by the alarming diminution of the circulating medium; by the numerous bankruptcies, not limited to the trading classes, but extending to all orders of society; by a universal complaint of the want of employment, and a consequent reduction of the wages of labor." The scope of the various distress signals thereby expands to incorporate a broader sense of economic trouble.

From the negative state of affairs, Clay constructs a duty for Congress to act: "The committee will agree with me in thinking that it is the solemn duty of government to apply a remedy to the evils which afflict our country, if it can apply one." The remedy is a shift in foreign policy and the passage of his personal economic model: "That remedy consists in modifying our foreign policy, and in adopting a genuine American system." He namechecks his economic model ("American system"), but it is not pertinent for him to detail it in its entirety here. He focuses instead on the relevant aspect of it, tariffs: "We must naturalize the arts in our country; and we must naturalize them by the only means which the wisdom of nations has yet discovered to be effectual,—by adequate protection against the otherwise overwhelming influence of foreigners. This is only to be accomplished by the establishment of a tariff." He utilizes the concept of protection to illustrate tariffs in a positive, assuring light.

The last portion of the document aims to dispel any counterarguments against the tariff that he is proposing. He acknowledges that the tariff is often seen in a very unfavorable light. It is, he says, understood to be "a sort of monster, huge and deformed,—a wild beast, endowed with tremendous powers of destruction, about to be let loose among our people, if not to devour them, at least to consume their substance." Yet he claims that this negative characterization is unfounded. "The sole object of the tariff," he explains, "is to tax the produce of foreign industry, with the view of promoting American industry. The tax is exclusively leveled at foreign industry. That is the avowed and the direct purpose of the tariff." Critics would find fault with his claims. Both American industries that rely on foreign imports and American export industries that would be hurt by retaliatory tariffs, for instance, may be injured by tariffs. Nevertheless, Clay's speech proved successful insofar as the Tariff of 1824 became law.

Essential Themes

Henry Clay develops the theme of tariffs' fairness in attempt to dispel opposition to the Tariff of 1824. He claims that tariffs have been impugned unfairly as "a sort of monster, huge and deformed." He uses the theme of fairness to counter these claims. No one, he argues, is forced to pay a tariff on a foreign import: "If it subjects any part of American industry to burdens, that is an effect not intended, but is altogether incidental, and perfectly voluntary." He further unfurls this point: "No man pays the duty assessed on the foreign article by compulsion, but voluntarily; and this voluntary duty, if paid, goes into the common exchequer, for the common benefit of all." Tariffs are not as simple—nor, necessarily, as fair—as Clay portrays them to be. If one's business and livelihood depend on foreign imports, then paying a tariff may not feel voluntary. Yet Clay's development of the theme of fairness helped him illustrate his point and, eventually, pass this piece of legislation.

—Anthony Vivian, PhD

Bibliography and Additional Reading

Brands, H.W. *Heirs of the Founders: The Epic Rivalry of Henry Clay, John Calhoun and Daniel Webster, the Second Generation of American Giants.* New York: Doubleday, 2018.

Heidler, David S., and Jeanne T. Heidler. Henry Clay: *The Essential American.* New York: Random House, 2011..

Klotter, James C. *Henry Clay: The Man Who Would Be President.* Oxford: Oxford University Press, 2018.

Unger, Harlow Giles. Henry Clay: America's Greatest Statesman. Boston: Da Capo Press, 2015.

■ Gibbons v. Ogden

Date: March 2, 1824
Author: Marshall, John
Genre: court opinion; constitution; law

Summary Overview

The decision by Chief Justice John Marshall in the 1824 Supreme Court case of *Gibbons v. Ogden* was a landmark ruling that ended the steamboat navigation monopoly originally granted to Robert R. Livingston and Robert Fulton by the New York State legislature. The Livingston-Fulton monopoly controlled all steamboat traffic between New York City and Albany along the Hudson River. Their successful manufacture and operation of steamboats on the Hudson River revolutionized the speed and efficiency, not to mention the cost, at which goods and passengers could be transported regionally. A crucial channel for interstate trade and travel, the New York monopoly prevented any outside steam-powered vessel from entering New York waterways. The monopoly held by Livingston and Fulton, therefore, was widely reviled and after years of litigation defending the steamboat monopoly, the *Gibbons v. Ogden* decision declared the state-granted monopoly to be in conflict with Congress's right to regulate commerce. The *Gibbons* decision abolished the right of any state to protect transportation monopolies that affected interstate commerce.

Defining Moment

In 1808, American engineer Robert Fulton succeeded in launching the Clermont, a steamboat able to move upriver faster than five miles per hour. The Clermont made it possible to travel from New York City to Albany on the Hudson River within thirty-two hours. The New York legislature, impressed by the success of this joint venture by Fulton and his business partner Robert Livingston, not only provided them with a monopoly on state steamboat transportation, but included provisions in the monopoly that expanded their entitlement for thirty years and dictated that any steamboat entering New York waters without the consent of Livingston and Fulton be seized by the state. The monopoly kept out other entrepreneurial steamboat ventures that sought navigational routes in New York waterways and forced peripheral routes to pay significant licensing fees to operate. The Livingston-Fulton monopoly was deeply unpopular with regional business and the public alike, and the monopoly endured a significant number of legal challenges while in effect. The strong familial and political connections of Robert Livingston in the New York legislature and court system, however, secured the injunction's legacy until challenged in the Supreme Court in 1824. Though Livingston and Fulton were often the direct targets of cases challenging their exclusive navigation rights, the case that ultimately reached the Supreme Court and dismantled these exclusive rights involved neither of the men so famously associated with the monopoly.

The complainant in the critical constitutional case was Aaron Ogden, a former governor of New Jersey, who held the majority interest in a steamboat line between New York City and Elizabethtown, New Jersey. Although he had at one point been an aggressive challenger of the Livingston-Fulton monopoly, Ogden was unsuccessful in his efforts and instead joined the monopoly as a licensed operator. Thomas Gibbons had moved from Georgia to Elizabethtown, New Jersey, and entered into a business venture with Ogden upon his arrival. The contentious relationship that developed between Ogden and Gibbons, however, had as much to do with personal animosity as with business matters. Gibbons had long been involved in a family conflict over matters of inheritance with his daughter and her husband. Ogden, at one point, inserted himself into the Gibbons' family matter, taking the side of Gibbons's daughter against Gibbons himself. After this event, the two men's relationship devolved quickly. The following year, Gibbons began a steamboat operation that ran the same route Ogden had claimed under the Livingston-Fulton monopoly. Ogden took Gibbons to court for violating the dictates of the monopoly, and the two men pursued their case all the way to the Supreme Court. The decision handed down in Gibbons v. Ogden presented a broad interpretation of what constituted interstate commerce, and ultimately reserved for the Supreme Court the right to determine when state law was in violation of congressional power to regulate interstate commerce. Marshall's majority opinion in the case employed his well-known use of narrow constitutional interpretation, which worked to strengthen the authority of the federal government without dismantling the rights of the states.

Author Biography

John Marshall, the fourth chief justice of the US Supreme Court, was born in 1755 and grew up in the developing counties of Virginia's frontier territories. Marshall's formative years were spent engaged in the political challenges and physical battles of the Revolutionary War. He became an officer in the Continental army in his early twenties and experienced firsthand the challenges and hardships that accompanied fighting a war in a new country that had yet to form a central government authoritative enough to draw military provisions and resources from its states to relieve suffering troops. Despite the organizational challenges, Marshall was profoundly influenced by the nationalistic goals of the Revolutionary War.

Marshall's only formal training in the legal profession came from George Wythe, a prominent Virginia judge. The future Supreme Court justice attended a brief course taught by Wythe in Williamsburg, Virginia, while he was on leave from his duties with the army. Though aspiring for a career in law, the disruption of the Revolutionary War prevented Marshall from starting his own law practice. Instead, Marshall joined the Virginia legislature. Though unsatisfied with the slow process of the legislature, Marshall spent a good portion of his career in and out of office in Virginia. Marshall's experiences with the Revolutionary War, both positive and negative, as well as his familiarity with the important but often inefficient function of state legislatures profoundly influenced Marshall's conviction in the need for a federalist system supported by a strong, centralized government.

Marshall held positions in both legislative and legal institutions for twenty years in the state of Virginia. In 1799, however, Marshall embarked on a national political career. Marshall served in the House of Representatives and as President John Adams's secretary of state. Marshall retained that position for only one year, however, before he was appointed by Adams to the position of chief justice of the Supreme Court in 1801. Over the course of his career, Marshall wrote the deciding opinions for several landmark Supreme Court cases. Marshall's legacy as chief justice has proven to be one of the most enduring and significant in the history of the Supreme Court. The Marshall Court advanced foundational court opinions that continue to shape constitutional law through the present.

HISTORICAL DOCUMENT: *Gibbons v. Ogden*

The appellant contends that this decree is erroneous because the laws which purport to give the exclusive privilege it sustains are repugnant to the Constitution and laws of the United States. They are said to be repugnant: first, to that clause in the Constitution which authorizes Congress to regulate commerce; second, to that which authorizes Congress to promote the progress of science and useful arts.

As preliminary to the very able discussions of the Constitution which we have heard from the bar, and as having some influence on its construction, reference has been made to the political situation of these states, anterior to its formation. It has been said that they were sovereign, were completely independent, and were connected with each other only by a league. This is true. But, when these allied sovereigns converted their league into a government, when they converted their congress of ambassadors, deputed to deliberate on their common concerns, and to recommend measures of general utility, into a legislature, empowered to enact laws on the most interesting subjects, the whole character in which the states appear underwent a change, the extent of which must be determined by a fair consideration of the instrument by which that change was effected.

This instrument contains an enumeration of powers expressly granted by the people to their government. It has been said that these powers ought to be construed strictly. But why ought they to be so construed? Is there one sentence in the Constitution which gives countenance to this rule? In the last of the enumerated powers, that which grants, expressly, the means for carrying all others into execution, Congress is authorized to make all laws which shall be necessary and proper for the purpose. But this limitation on the means which may be used is not extended to the powers which are conferred; nor is there one sentence in the Constitution, which has been pointed out by the gentlemen of the bar, or which we have been able to discern, that prescribes this rule. We do not, therefore, think ourselves justified in adopting it. . . .

We know of no rule for construing the extent of such powers other than is given by the language of the instrument which confers them, taken in connection with the purposes for which they were conferred.

The words are: Congress shall have power to regulate commerce with foreign nations, and among the several states, and with the Indian tribes. The subject to be regulated is commerce; and our Constitution being, as was aptly said at the bar, one of enumeration and not of definition, to ascertain the extent of the power it becomes necessary to settle the meaning of the word. . . .

Commerce, undoubtedly, is traffic, but it is something more—it is intercourse. It describes the commercial intercourse between nations, and parts of nations, in all its branches, and is regulated by prescribing rules for carrying on that intercourse. The mind can scarcely conceive a system for regulating commerce between nations which shall exclude all laws concerning navigation, which shall be silent on the admission of the vessels of the one nation into the ports of the other, and be confined to prescribing rules for the conduct of individuals in the actual employment of buying and selling or of barter. If commerce does not include navigation, the government of the Union has no direct power over that subject, and can make no law prescribing what shall constitute American vessels, or requiring that they shall be navigated by American seamen.

Yet this power has been exercised from the commencement of the government, has been exercised with the consent of all, and. has been understood by all to be a commercial regulation. All America understands, and has uniformly understood, the word commerce to comprehend navigation.

If the opinion that "commerce," as the word is used in the Constitution, comprehends navigation also, requires any additional confirmation, that additional confirmation is, we think, furnished by the words of the instrument itself. . . .

The word used in the Constitution, then, comprehends, and has been always understood to comprehend, navigation within its meaning, and a power to regulate navigation is as expressly granted as if that term had been added to the word "commerce". . . .

This principle is, if possible, still more clear, when applied to commerce "among the several States". . . . What is commerce "among" them, and how is it to be conducted? Can a trading expedition between two adjoining States, commence and terminate outside of each? And if the trading intercourse be between two States remote from each other, must it not commence in one, terminate in the other, and probably pass through a third? . . . The power of Congress, then, whatever it may be, must be exercised within the territorial jurisdiction of the several States. . . .

We are now arrived at the inquiry—What is this power? It is the power to regulate, that is, to prescribe the rule by which commerce is to be governed. This power, like all others vested in Congress, is complete in itself, may be exercised to its utmost extent, and acknowledges no limitations other than are prescribed in the Constitution. . . .

When a State proceeds to regulate commerce with foreign nations, or among the several States, it is exercising the very power that is granted to Congress, and is doing the very thing which Congress is authorized to do. There is no analogy, then, between the power of taxation and the power of regulating commerce. . . .

We must first determine whether the act of laying "duties or imposts on imports or exports" is considered in the Constitution as a branch of the taxing power, or of the power to regulate commerce. We think it very clear that it is considered as a branch of the taxing power. . . . The power of imposing duties on imports is classed with the power to levy taxes, and that seems to be its natural place. But the power to levy taxes could never be considered as abridging the right of the States on that subject, and they might, consequently, have exercised it by levying duties on imports or exports, had the Constitution contained no prohibition on this subject. This prohibition, then, is an exception from the acknowledged power of the States to levy taxes, not from the questionable power to regulate commerce. . . .

So, if a State, in passing laws on subjects acknowledged to be within its control . . . shall adopt a measure of the same character with one which Congress may adopt, it does not derive its authority from the particular power which has been granted, but from some other, which remains with the State and may be executed by the same means. . . .

Since, in exercising the power of regulating their own purely internal affairs the States may sometimes enact laws the validity of which depends on their interfering with, and being contrary to, an act of Congress passed in pursuance of the Constitution, the Court will enter upon the inquiry whether the laws of New York, as expounded by the highest tribunal of that State, have, in their application to this case, come into collision with an act of Congress and deprived a citizen of a right to which that act entitles him. . . . In one case and the other, the acts of New York must yield to the law of Congress, and the decision sustaining the privilege they confer against a right given by a law of the Union must be erroneous. . . .

It will at once occur that, when a Legislature attaches certain privileges and exemptions to the exercise of a right over which its control is absolute, the law must imply a power to exercise the right. The privileges are gone if the right itself be annihilated. It would be contrary to all reason, and to the course of human affairs, to say that a State is unable to strip a vessel of the particular privileges attendant on the exercise of a right, and yet may annul the right itself; that the State of New York cannot prevent an enrolled and licensed vessel, proceeding from Elizabethtown, in New Jersey, to New York, from enjoying, in her course, and on her entrance into port, all the privileges conferred by the act of Congress, but can shut her up in her own port, and prohibit altogether her entering the waters and ports of another State. To the Court, it seems very clear that the whole act on the subject of the coasting trade, according to those principles which govern the construction of statutes, implies unequivocally an authority to licensed vessels to carry on the coasting trade. . . .

If, as our whole course of legislation on this subject shows, the power of Congress has been universally understood in America to comprehend navigation, it is a very persuasive, if not a conclusive, argument to prove that the construction is correct, and if it be correct, no clear distinction is perceived between the power to regulate vessels employed in transporting men for hire and property for hire. . . . A coasting vessel employed in the transportation of passengers is as much a portion of the American marine as one employed in the transportation of a cargo. . . .

Vessels have always been employed to a greater or less extent in the transportation of passengers, and have never been supposed to be, on that account, withdrawn from the control or protection of Congress. . . .

If, then, it were even true that the Bellona and the Stoudinger were employed exclusively in the conveyance of passengers between New York and New Jersey, it would not follow that this occupation did not constitute a part of the coasting trade of the United States, and was not protected by the license annexed to the answer. . . .

The laws of New York, which grant the exclusive privilege set up by the respondent, take no notice of the employment of vessels, and relate only to the principle by which they are propelled. Those laws do not inquire whether vessels are engaged in transporting men or merchandise, but whether they are moved by steam or wind. If by the former, the waters of New York are closed against them, though their cargoes be dutiable goods, which the laws of the United States permit them to enter and deliver in New York. If by the latter, those waters are free to them though they should carry passengers only. . . .

The questions, then, whether the conveyance of passengers be a part of the coasting trade and whether a vessel can be protected in that occupation by a coasting license are not, and cannot be, raised in this case. The real and sole question seems to be whether a steam machine in actual use deprives a vessel of the privileges conferred by a license. . . .

The first idea which presents itself is that the laws of Congress for the regulation of commerce do not look to the principle by which vessels are moved. That subject is left entirely to individual discretion, and, in that vast and complex system of legislative enactment concerning it . . . there is not . . . one word respecting the peculiar principle by which vessels are propelled through the water, except what may be found in a single act granting a particular privilege to steamboats. . . .

But all inquiry into this subject seems to the Court to be put completely at rest by the act already mentioned, entitled, "An act for the enrolling and licensing of steamboats."

This act authorizes a steamboat employed, or intended to be employed, only in a river or bay of the United States, owned wholly or in part by an alien, resident within the United States, to be enrolled and licensed as if the same belonged to a citizen of the United States.

This act demonstrates the opinion of Congress that steamboats may be enrolled and licensed, in common with vessels using sails. They are, of course, entitled to the same privileges, and can no more be restrained from navigating waters and entering ports which are free to such vessels than if they were wafted on their voyage by the winds, instead of being propelled by the agency of fire. . . .

Powerful and ingenious minds, taking as postulates that the powers expressly granted to the government of the Union are to be contracted by construction into the narrowest possible compass and that the original powers of the States are retained if any possible construction will retain them may, by a course of well digested but refined and metaphysical reasoning founded on these premises, explain away the Constitution of our country and leave it a magnificent structure indeed to look at, but totally unfit for use. They may so entangle and perplex the understanding as to obscure principles which were before thought quite plain, and induce doubts where, if the mind were to pursue its own course, none would be perceived. In such a case, it is peculiarly necessary to recur to safe and fundamental principles to sustain those principles, and when sustained, to make them the tests of the arguments to be examined.

> **GLOSSARY**
>
> **alien:** nonresident
>
> **appellant:** party appealing a court decision
>
> **Belladona and Stoudinger:** names of the steamboats owned by Thomas Gibbons
>
> **coasting trade:** commerce operating via waterway between adjacent harbors within the same nation, as opposed to
>
> **international or long-distance commerce.**
>
> **levy:** to impose charges
>
> **postulates:** presumptions without supporting evidence
>
> **sovereignty:** absolute statutory power inside territorial boundaries
>
> **steam machine:** steamboat

Document Analysis

The *Gibbons v. Ogden* opinion, considered to be one of the most important Supreme Court decisions in the nation's history, allowed Chief Justice John Marshall to affirm the government's authority over interstate commerce by asserting a broad definition of commerce while also providing a narrow legal basis for his decision, which endeavored to preserved the equilibrium between state and federal power. The opinion delivered by Marshall in the *Gibbons v. Ogden* case clearly demonstrates Marshall's tendency toward making measured and narrow decisions in controversial cases. Certainly, the chief justice was a proponent of a strong central government and a defender of the Supreme Court's role in judicial review, which allowed the Supreme Court to nullify the actions of the executive and judiciary branches as well as state laws deemed to be unconstitutional. Understanding the delicate balance of power in a federalist system that granted simultaneous sovereignties to both the state and federal governments, Marshall was careful in writing the *Gibbons* opinion to assert the primacy of federal law while also managing to avoid establishing a legal precedent that would make significant restrictions on states' rights. As such, Marshall's opinion in the *Gibbons* case avoided making any sweeping claims about the commerce clause's ability to grant absolute exclusivity to Congress in implementing laws concerning commerce and trade. Instead, Marshall's decision rested on the conflict between the New York steamboat law and the federal Coasting Act of 1793. The Coasting Act was a congressional act that enrolled and licensed seafaring vessels engaged in trade and fishing along the coast. Marshall's opinion rested on the conflict between the New York monopoly and the federal government's authority to regulate the vessels involved in transportation and trade according to the Coasting Act. The supremacy of the federal law lay in Congress's power to regulate commerce. Granted by the Commerce Clause of the Constitution, Congress holds the power "to regulate commerce with foreign nations, and among the several states, and with the Indian Tribes" (Section I, Article 8, Clause 3).

In framing the court decision, Marshall directly addressed the arguments advanced by the attorneys for both Thomas Gibbons and Aaron Ogden. Gibbons was represented by Daniel Webster and William Wirt, who argued for Gibbons's right to run his steamboats freely due to the unconstitutional nature of the New York monopoly. They argued for the exclusive right of Congress to regulate interstate commerce under the Commerce Clause. To support their argument for federal exclusivity, they sought to make a clear distinction between the powers of the state, which regulated the health, safety, and well-being of its residents, and the powers of the federal government, which were put in place to regulate national concerns such as commerce. Webster and Wirt also contended that the New York monopoly violated the federal Coasting Act of 1793, which required all vessels involved in coastal trade to register with the federal government. The attorneys argued that the Coasting Act provided ship captains with right of entry to all American ports. Ogden's lawyers, Thomas J. Oakley and Thomas A. Emmet, provided a counterargument that defended states' rights by claiming that the state and federal governments held concurrent power over regulating commerce. In other words, the states had the right to regulate commerce within their borders as they saw fit, as long as their commerce laws did not conflict with federal regulations. They also sought to portray the legislature's allowance of a steamboat monopoly not as a commercial statute, but instead as a navigation law, permissible under the powers reserved for the states. Additionally, Ogden's lawyers sought to define commerce narrowly, to be applied only to the transport and sale of merchandise.

When examining Marshall's decision, the opinion clearly shows the influence of both arguments submitted before the Court. Chief Justice Marshall appeared to integrate into his opinion both the concept of concurrent state and federal power over commerce presented by Ogden's attorneys, as well as the argument that the state of New York's monopoly was in violation of the federal Coasting Act of 1793, as presented by Gibbons's lawyers. The narrowly defined decision by Marshall allowed him to assert the supremacy of federal over state law by upholding the Coasting Act while avoiding making any constitutional claims to the federal exclusivity over commerce law.

Concurrent Commerce Power

In tackling the issues brought to bear in the *Gibbons v. Ogden* case, Marshall carefully addressed the relationship between the federal government and state governments on the issue of commerce law. Chief Justice Marshall delineated the way in which state and federal law were to operate in relation to one another. Marshall took pains to outline the idea that each states was free to make laws concerning its own operation and well-being, even if the laws the state enacted were "of the same character with one which Congress may adopt." If, however, the state adopted a law that came into conflict with laws passed by Congress under the authority of the Constitution, the state law "must yield to the law of Congress, and the decision sustaining the privilege they confer against a right given by a law of the Union must be erroneous." In the *Gibbons* case, ruled Marshall, the New York steamboat monopoly directly conflicted with the federal Coasting Act of 1793 and was therefore in violation of a federal law regulating commerce. The state law, therefore, had to yield to the supremacy of the federal law.

What Marshall failed to touch on in his opinion, however, was whether or not state laws regulating interstate commerce were automatically in violation of Congress's power to regulate commerce, even if Congress had passed no contradictory law. His affirmation of the states' ability to pass laws "of the same character with one which Congress may adopt" seemed to indicate that as long as Congress adopted no conflicting law, the states were free to regulate commerce as their needs dictated. The Supreme Court, therefore, did not rule in Gibbons v. Ogden that the power to regulate commerce was exclusive to Congress, but instead that the federal government and the states held concurrent powers. Marshall preserved, in his decision, a sense of balance between the authority of states and the federal government over the issue of commerce, and tasked the Court with deciding on a case-by-case basis whether a state law infringed on the congressional authority over regulating commerce. Knowing the limits to the federal government's ability to address the individual needs of the states in regulating transportation, communication, and trade—especially as the nation expanded further west—Marshall's decision made room for the states to control unique problems that might arise related to matters of commerce. Despite this careful balance struck by Marshall in the Gibbons case, in avoiding addressing the nature of the commerce clause, his opinion left open the possibility that, in the future, the Supreme Court could rule that Congress retained a discrete right to regulate commerce and that states were prohibited from enacting any laws of that nature.

Expanding the Meaning of "Commerce"
Marshall's opinion in Gibbons is most widely known for the legal longevity of his broad definition of commerce. Ogden's attorneys appealed to a narrow understanding of commerce, which encompassed only the movement and sale of goods. As steamboats were a system of navigation and not goods themselves, and as they most often transported passengers and not just goods, Ogden's attorneys argued that the regulation of steamboat routes was outside the purview of federal regulation of commerce. Marshall rejected this line of reasoning and instead defined commerce in expansive terms. Marshall noted firmly in his opinion that "the mind can scarcely conceive a system for regulating commerce between nations which shall exclude all laws concerning navigation." This statement by the chief justice worked to establish the authority of the federal government to regulate navigational routes that traversed state boundaries. Nodding to the popular interest in the case, as well as the legitimacy of his assessment, Marshall stated definitively that "all America understands, and has uniformly understood, the word commerce to comprehend navigation." The restricted use of steamboats on waterways was not only an issue of navigation, Marshall acknowledged, but also an issue of the expanding uses of technology.

The basis on which New York restricted boats entering it waters was based solely on the technology used to propel it, as sail boats were not restricted from New York waterways under the steamboat monopoly. If the actions of New York state, in granting Livingston—and, by proxy, Ogden—a monopoly on the use of steamboat technology, became the standard in all states, the possibility of restricting advancing transportation technology across the nation was a genuine possibility. If every state were able to grant exclusive rights over transportation to different parties in every state, the conflict between states would only grow as means of transportation expanded. Marshall's opinion served to diminish these potential conflicts, but also managed to expand the reach of the federal government beyond the limits of technological advancements. Marshall's expansion of the constitutional definition of commerce beyond trade and subsequently even beyond navigation can be seen in the passage which asserts that, "commerce, undoubtedly, is traffic, but it is something more—it is intercourse. It describes the commercial intercourse between nations, and parts of nations, in all its branches, and is regulated by prescribing rules for carrying on that intercourse." The use of the vague and sweeping term "intercourse" provided an incomparably wide category under which myriad forms of interstate dealings could be regulated by the federal government. This far-reaching definition of commerce provided the possibility for the government to expand its regulatory authority over the advancing transportation and communication technology that was rapidly emerging just as the nation was about to begin its westward expansion.

Though careful to preserve the legal balance between state and federal authority, Marshall concluded his majority opinion by leveling an impassioned warning against the excessive advocacy of state authority in matters clearly under the purview of the federal government. Chief Justice Marshall cautioned those within the nation's legal institutions to avoid trying to find ways to diminish the powers that the Constitution bestows to Congress. Always a commanding advocate for a strong central government, Marshall took to task those who would reduce federal powers into "the narrowest possible compass" while finding "any possible construction" through which states may assert their regulatory rights. For Marshall, a continual expansion of regulatory rights retained by the states could "explain away the Constitution of our country and leave it a magnificent structure indeed to look at, but totally unfit for use." Marshall's call for preservation of fundamental constitutional principles and the acknowledgement of the federal government's primary authority in broadly defined matters of commerce resulted in one of the most important and influential Supreme Court decisions on federal power in the nation's history.

Essential Themes

The immediate aftermath of the *Gibbons v. Ogden* decision resulted in widespread popular support for the decision. The cost of using steamboat transportation fell significantly as the number of active steamboats between Baltimore and New York City increased from four to forty-three in just one year. Commerce in Hudson River ports expanded measurably in the wake of opening the waterway to significant growth in the number of steamboat lines. Beyond the immediate benefits, however, Marshall's broad interpretation of interstate commerce in the Gibbons decision had a lasting impact on the government's ability to regulate the rapidly expanding transportation and communication technology facilitating the swift national expansion into western territory. The Gibbons decision also had incredible longevity in providing the constitutional authority to expand the regulatory powers of government. The Great Depression and the subsequent implementation of the New Deal by the Roosevelt administration created new legal importance for the *Gibbons v. Ogden* decision. The broad reading of commerce allowed the federal government to expand its regulatory powers to national labor, industry, agricultural, and banking issues. Considered one of the most important cases in constitutional history, the *Gibbons v. Ogden* decision reinforced the primacy of federal laws that conflicted with those implemented by the states, assisted the rapid expansion of national transportation and communication, and paved the way for an expanding definition of what constituted commerce under the regulatory power of the federal government.

—*Amanda Beyer-Purvis, MA*

Bibliography and Additional Reading

Baxter, Maurice G. *The Steamboat Monopoly*: Gibbons V. Ogden, 1824. New York: Knopf, 1972. Print.

Coenen, Dan T. *Constitutional Law: The Commerce Clause*. New York: Foundation, 2004. Print.

Cooke, Fred'k H. "The Gibbons v. Ogden Fetish." *Michigan Law Review* 9.4 (1911): 324–33. Print.

Cox, Thomas H. Gibbons v. Ogden, *Law, and Society in the Early Republic*. Athens: Ohio UP, 2009. Print.

Fribourg, Marjorie G. *The Supreme Court in American History: Ten Great Decisions; the People, the Times and the Issues*. Philadelphia: Macrae, 1965. Print.

Johnson, Herbert A. Gibbons v. Ogden: *John Marshall, Steamboats, and the Commerce Clause*. Lawrence: UP of Kansas, 2010. Print.

May, Christopher N, and Allan Ides. *Constitutional Law, National Power and Federalism: Examples and Explanations*. New York: Aspen, 2007. Print.

Mendelson, Wallace. "New Light on Fletcher v. Peck and Gibbons v. Ogden." *Yale Law Journal* 58.4 (1949): 567–73. Print.

Paskoff, Paul F. *Troubled Waters: Steamboat Disasters, River Improvements, and American Public Policy*, 1821–1860. Baton Rouge: Louisiana State UP, 2007. Print.

"Steamboats on the Hudson: An American Saga: Two Bobs, Three Johns, Three Jims, a Nick, an Aaron, a Tom and a Boat." New York State Library Database. New York State Library, 2012. Web. 29 Oct. 2012.

Andrew Jackson's Bank Veto Message

Date: July 10, 1832
Author: Andrew Jackson
Genre: presidential proclamation

Summary Overview

The Second Bank of the United States was created by legislation passed in 1816. The Bank had a twenty-year charter and would be up for re-charter in 1836. Henry Clay, who hoped to challenge Jackson for the presidency in the 1832 election, pushed a re-charter bill through Congress four years early, hoping that Jackson's opposition to the bank would become a campaign issue. Congress passed the bill in July 1832, but Jackson quickly vetoed it, and Congress failed to override the veto. Jackson's veto message was an emotional attack on what he believed were the undemocratic and monopolistic characteristics of the bank. He charged that the bank really benefitted only the wealthy who had invested in stock in the bank, many of whom were foreigners. Jackson's veto of the bank bill was part of the "Bank War" Jackson conducted against members of Congress who supported the bank, and against Nicholas Biddle, president of the bank.

Defining Moment

Banking in the early United States was a notoriously unstable and controversial business. Only the federal government could coin money out of precious metal, and this money was called specie. There was never enough gold and silver coin money in circulation, so private banks often issued their own paper money. This money was basically a promise that the holder could bring the money to the issuing bank and redeem it for specie. But banks often went out of business, or suffered setbacks in their financial health and soundness, and sometimes just suspended the redemption of their own paper money.

In 1791, Congress created the Bank of the United States. It was a private bank, operating under a charter from the federal government. Part of its reserves had to be held in government bonds, and some of its board of directors were appointed by the government. This bank issued paper money that was widely accepted and provided a reasonable secure currency for conducting business. Yet there had been widespread opposition to the creation of the bank, and many people feared that ultimately, any kind of paper money might be risky to the holder. The bank had a twenty-year charter, and Congress failed to renew the charter in 1811.

However, a bill to create the Second Bank of the United States was passed in 1816. It was in most ways exactly like the First Bank, and also successful in providing a trusted paper currency.

The Second Bank's charter was also for twenty years, so it would be up for renewal in 1836. Henry Clay was planning to run against President Andrew Jackson in the election of 1832, and he pushed through a re-charter bill for the bank four years ahead of schedule. He knew that Jackson opposed the bank, and he hoped that Jackson's opposition would become a political issue in the 1832 campaign, which it did.

The re-charter bill was passed by Congress in July 1832, but Jackson vetoed it later that month. Congress did not vote to override the veto. The bank continued to operate until its original charter ran out in 1836, but Jackson began taking federal funds out of deposit accounts in the bank, thus depriving the bank of capital that could be used for making loans. Jackson's struggle with the supporters of the bank, including its president, Nicholas Biddle, became known as "The Bank War." The ins and outs of the Bank War caused a financial panic, but it did not hit until 1837, after Jackson had left office and his vice president, Martin Van Buren, had been elected his successor.

Author Biography

Andrew Jackson was born near Waxhaw, South Carolina, on March 15, 1767. In his late teens, Jackson began studying law while working in a law office in Salisbury, North Carolina. He was admitted to the bar in 1787, and settled in Nashville, where he practiced law and was elected as Tennessee's first member of the U.S. House of Representatives in 1796. He became a national hero as a result of his record in the War of 1812, during which he defeated the Creek Indians, allies of the British, at the Battle of Horseshoe Bend; and then in early in January 1815, he won a decisive victory against the British at the Battle of New Orleans. Jackson ran for president in 1824, winning more Electoral College votes than any other candidate. Since he did not have the majority, however, the election was decided by the House of Representatives. The House selected John Quincy Adams, and Jackson and his supporters charged that Henry Clay, the Speaker of the House, had thrown his support behind Adams after the two men made a "corrupt bargain." Jackson easily defeated Adams in the election of 1828, and in 1832 defeated Henry Clay. After leaving the presidency in March 1837, he retired to his estate, The Hermitage, outside of Nashville. He died there on June 8, 1845.

HISTORICAL DOCUMENT: Andrew Jackson's Bank Veto Message

The present corporate body, denominated the president, directors, and company of the Bank of the United States, will have existed at the time this act is intended to take effect twenty years. It enjoys an exclusive privilege of banking under the authority of the General Government, a monopoly of its favor and support, and, as a necessary consequence, almost a monopoly of the foreign and domestic exchange. The powers, privileges, and favors bestowed upon it in the original charter, by increasing the value of the stock far above its par value, operated as a gratuity of many millions to the stockholders....

The act before me proposes another gratuity to the holders of the same stock, and in many cases to the same men, of at least seven millions more....It is not our own citizens only who are to receive the bounty of our Government. More than eight millions of the stock of this bank are held by foreigners. By this act the American Republic proposes virtually to make them a present of some millions of dollars.

Every monopoly and all exclusive privileges are granted at the expense of the public, which ought to receive a fair equivalent. The many millions which this act proposes to bestow on the stockholders of the existing bank must come directly or indirectly out of the earnings of the American people....

It appears that more than a fourth part of the stock is held by foreigners and the residue is held by a few hundred of our own citizens, chiefly of the richest class.

Is there no danger to our liberty and independence in a bank that in its nature has so little to bind it to our country? The president of the bank has told us that most of the State banks exist by its forbearance. Should its influence become concentered, as it may under the operation of such an act as this, in the hands of a self-elected directory whose interests are identified with those of the foreign stockholders, will there not be cause to tremble for the purity of our elections in peace and for the independence of our country in war? Their power would be great whenever they might choose to exert it; but if this monopoly were regularly renewed every fifteen or twenty years on terms proposed by themselves, they might seldom in peace put forth their strength to influence elections or control the affairs of the nation. But if any private citizen or public functionary should interpose to curtail its powers or prevent a renewal of its privileges, it can not be doubted that he would be made to feel its influence.

It is to be regretted that the rich and powerful too often bend the acts of government to their selfish purposes. Distinctions in society will always exist under every just government. Equality of talents, of education, or of wealth can not be produced by human institutions. In the full enjoyment of the gifts of Heaven and the fruits of superior industry, economy, and virtue, every man is equally entitled to protection by law; but when the laws undertake to add to these natural and just advantages artificial distinctions, to grant titles, gratuities, and exclusive privileges, to make the rich richer and the potent more powerful, the humble members of society the farmers, mechanics, and laborers who have neither the time nor the means of securing like favors to themselves, have a right to complain of the injustice of their Government. There are no necessary evils in government. Its evils exist only in its abuses. If it would confine itself to equal protection, and, as Heaven does its rains, shower its favors alike on the high and the low, the rich and the poor, it would be an unqualified blessing. In the act before me there seems to be a wide and unnecessary departure from these just principles.

Nor is our Government to be maintained or our Union preserved by invasions of the rights and powers of the several States. In thus attempting to make our General Government strong we make it weak. Its true strength consists in leaving individuals and States as much as possible to themselves in making itself felt, not in its power, but in its beneficence; not in its control, but in its protection; not in binding the States more closely to the center, but leaving each to move unobstructed in its proper orbit.

Experience should teach us wisdom. Most of the difficulties our Government now encounters and most of the dangers which impend over our Union have sprung from an abandonment of the legitimate objects

> *Every monopoly and all exclusive privileges are granted [to the bank] at the expense of the public, which ought to receive a fair equivalent.*

of Government by our national legislation, and the adoption of such principles as are embodied in this act. Many of our rich men have not been content with equal protection and equal benefits, but have besought us to make them richer by act of Congress. By attempting to gratify their desires we have in the results of our legislation arrayed section against section, interest against interest, and man against man, in a fearful commotion which threatens to shake the foundations of our Union. It is time to pause in our career to review our principles, and if possible revive that devoted patriotism and spirit of compromise which distinguished the sages of the Revolution and the fathers of our Union. If we can not at once, in justice to interests vested under improvident legislation, make our Government what it ought to be, we can at least take a stand against all new grants of monopolies and exclusive privileges, against any prostitution of our Government to the advancement of the few at the expense of the many, and in favor of compromise and gradual reform in our code of laws and system of political economy....

Document Analysis

Andrew Jackson had a lifelong fear and distrust of virtually all banking institutions and the paper money they issued. Modern economic historians have suggested that Jackson had only the most basic understanding of how banking and financial institutions worked, which is probably true; but as one scholar has said, the more Jackson learned about banking, the less he liked any of it. While his message accompanying the veto of the legislation for the re-charter of the Second Bank of the United States reflects his own views, two members of his informal "Kitchen Cabinet" contributed to its creation—Amos Kendall and Francis Blair.

Jackson based his criticism primarily on the idea that the bank served the interests only of a wealthy elite—those who could borrow money from it to invest in profit-making ventures, and those who could buy stock in and profit from the growing value of that stock. It would benefit the wealthy, he charged, but not "the humble members of society, the farmers, mechanics, and laborers." He also believed the bank had virtually monopolistic powers. It was the only financial institution in the nation that operated under a charter from the federal government, and its stability was somewhat guaranteed by the fact that some of its board of directors were appointed by the government, and that some of its reserves had to be held in federal bonds. When Jackson wrote that the bank had "almost a monopoly of the foreign and domestic exchange," he was admitting what many thought was a strength of the bank—that its paper money was widely accepted at or near face value in most domestic transactions, and was the only paper money that many foreign firms would accept.

Jackson also charged that the bank's power threatened the power of the states. Nicholas Biddle, the president of the bank, had said that it could control state-chartered banks by refusing to accept the paper money issued by those institution. Thus, as Jackson saw it, Biddle had threatened that these state banks could exist only by the "forbearance" of the Bank of the United States.

Jackson positioned himself in this matter, as he often did, as a champion of the common man, and he believed that the people would support his veto. There is some evidence that

In expressing his now-famous veto of the bill that would have re-chartered the Second Bank, Andrew Jackson gave several reasons, including calling the bank unconstitutional.

voters letting members of Congress know that they supported Jackson was a factor in the failure of Congress to override the veto.

Essential Themes

Andrew Jackson rose from humble roots to become a wealthy owner of a plantation and slaves, and a man of considerable social and political influence. Yet throughout his career he positioned himself as a champion of the "common man" and pursued policies he believed would protect their economic opportunities and political power. In the past, historians often referred to Jackson's time as the era of "Jacksonian Democracy." That term is not commonly used today, because it is generally clear that when Jackson spoke of the "common man" it was only white men to whom he referred. Native Americans, African Americans, and women of any race were largely outside the "democracy" he envisioned. Despite the contradictions in Jackson's personal life and political actions, many of the working-class white males of his era were fervently loyal to him, and did believe that he pursued policies which were in their best interest.

Since Jackson wanted to appeal to the working-class male voters, he couched his attack on the Second Bank of the United States on the characteristics of the bank that he believed were undemocratic and monopolistic. He believed that the bank benefitted only those who could invest in it, or borrow money from it, and noted that many of the bank's stockholders were foreigners. He pictured men of wealth and influence using the bank to make themselves richer or at least to protect their wealth.

There is also a strong theme of fear in Jackson's veto message—the fear of possible repercussions of perpetuating an institution like the bank. Because the bank could refuse to redeem the paper money from state-chartered banks, Jackson believed that it threatened the rights and independence of those institutions and of the state governments that had chartered them. He argued that creating an institution like the bank had led to arraying "section against section, interest against interest, and man against man." He believed that government must give equal protection to all, but in the bill to re-charter the bank he saw "a wide and unnecessary departure from these just principles."

—Mark S. Joy, PhD

Bibliography and Additional Reading

Feller, Daniel. "King Andrew and the Bank." *Humanities* 29, no. 1 (Jan./Feb. 2008): 28–32.

Kahan, Paul. *The Bank War: Andrew Jackson, Nicholas Biddle, and the Fight for American Finance.* Yardley, PA: Westholme Publishing, 2015.

Pessen, Edward. *Jacksonian America: Society, Personality, and Politics*, rev. ed. Belmont, CA: Dorsey Press, 1978.

Remini, Robert V. *Andrew Jackson and the Bank War: A Study in the Growth of Presidential Power.* New York: W.W. Norton, 1967.

Charles River Bridge v. Warren Bridge

Date: February 14, 1837
Author: Chief Justice Roger B. Taney
Genre: court opinion

Summary Overview

Just as the expansion of the Boston metropolitan area necessitated the need for an easier means to cross the Charles River in the latter half of the 18th century, continued growth in the early 19th century put pressure on the commonwealth to expand cross-river transportation options. Thus, the Charles River Bridge, built to handle the needs of the 1780s, was overwhelmed by the 1820s. As a result of Massachusetts giving permission for the construction of the much needed Warren Bridge, the owners of the Charles River Bridge, a toll bridge with the tolls going to the owners, filed suit claiming economic injury as the result of Massachusetts, allegedly, not meeting its contractual obligations. This, the owners of the Charles River Bridge claimed, violated Article I, Section 10, of the United Stats' Constitution, in which governments were supposed to uphold legally made contracts.

Chief Justice Taney, writing for the majority, found against the Charles River Bridge company, and for the Warren Bridge and the Commonwealth of Massachusetts. His opinion was written, broadly, on the topic of the rights of states versus private entities. A narrow ruling in this case would have focused only on the fact that the contract with the Charles River Bridge company did not contain a clause granting it an exclusive right to operate. Thus Massachusetts could give another company the right to construct a second bridge connecting Boston and Cambridge. However, Taney went beyond this, stating that there was no "implied contract" between Massachusetts and the Charles River Bridge company, only the contract which was written on paper. Taney asserted that as technology advanced, and other transportation possibilities came into existence, it could be claimed that the state had an obligation to allow these new transportation options the chance to prove themselves. Thus the rights of the community take precedence over the rights of private economic entities, when no formal explicit legal contract has been made granting the private concern, or individual, extraordinary rights in that particular venue.

Defining Moment

In 1785, the Massachusetts legislature granted a charter to the Charles River Bridge Company to build a bridge connecting Boston with nearby Cambridge. The company was given the right to collect tolls for forty years (later extended to seventy years, when another company proposed to build a competing bridge), after which time bridge ownership would revert to the state. The endeavor proved hugely successful, and the profits of the company's shareholders rose with the population of Boston and its environs. In 1828, the state granted a second charter, to the Warren Bridge Company, to build another bridge near the Charles River Bridge. This contract permitted the Warren Bridge Company to collect only enough tolls to pay for the bridge's construction, or only for a maximum of six years, after which the public would be permitted to use the new bridge free of charge. As might be expected, Charles River Bridge shareholders cried foul and filed suit, declaring that Massachusetts had violated the terms of its original contract, which they said implicitly conferred a monopoly on their company.

The Supreme Court of Massachusetts found against the Charles River Bridge Company, declining to grant an injunction preventing construction of the Warren Bridge. The Charles River Bridge Company then appealed its case to the U.S. Supreme Court, citing the Massachusetts constitutional guarantee of "life, liberty and property" as well as Article I, Section 10, of the Constitution, which reads in pertinent part: "No State shall ... pass any Bill of Attainder, ex post facto Law, or Law impairing the Obligation of Contracts." Construction of the Warren Bridge, the appellant claimed, would jeopardize both their property rights and public confidence in government undertakings.

The case initially went to the Supreme Court in 1831, when the Court was under the leadership of John Marshall. Three members of the Marshall Court, which originally heard arguments in the case, apparently agreed with the appellant company, but owing largely to illness and vacancies on the Court, it was not possible to have a full Court of seven justices hear the case. Thus, a decision was postponed. When the case was re-argued, nearly six years later, the Court had been transformed. On the 1831 Marshall Court, five justices were pre-Jackson appointees and two had been appointed by President Jackson.

The Taney Court was dominated by Jacksonian Democrats, with five Jackson appointees versus two from before Jackson's tenure as president. Jackson, and his appointees, tended to favor the kind of economic progress represented by the case of the Warren Bridge Company. To them, the government, as a representative of the people, had the right and responsibility to assist in the development and expansion of the United States economy and territory. The broadly construed judicial opinion in *Charles River Bridge v. Warren Bridge* was one step in this process of governmental support to enable new opportunities for American citizens (which in Jackson's mind meant white men, definitely not African-American slaves, Native Americans, or women).

Author Biography

Roger Brooke Taney, the second son of Michael Taney V and Monica Taney, was born in Maryland on March 17, 1777. Raised on a tobacco farm, but not in line to inherit it, Roger studied law at Dickinson College across the border in Pennsylvania. He began his law practice in 1799. Taney married Anne Key in 1806 and they had five daughters who survived to adulthood. (Anne was the sister of Francis Scott Key.) He was active in politics as political process and parties evolved in the early nineteenth century. He served in both houses of the Maryland state legislature, first as a Federalist, then as a Democratic-Republican. He later served as the state's attorney general. Taney then became a Democrat and was a strong supporter of Andrew Jackson. Taney served as U.S. Attorney General and then temporarily as Secretary of the Treasury. (He held the latter position due to a recess appointment, and when his name was submitted to the Senate to become the permanent Secretary of the Treasury, he was rejected by the Senate. This was the first time in U.S. history, that any Cabinet nominee had been rejected by the Senate.) He was unpopular with the senators, because he had been Jackson's chief agent in doing away with the Second National Bank.

In 1835 Jackson nominated Taney to the Supreme Court but, by Whig Party parliamentary action, no vote was taken during that session of Congress. After Congress adjourned for the year, Chief Justice John Marshall died in July, 1835, which meant that for the balance of the year only five of the seven Supreme Court seats were filled. As a new session of Congress opened in December, 1835, Jackson nominated Taney to become Chief Justice, and the Senate finally confirmed Taney in this position in March, 1836. He served until his death on October 12, 1864.

Although Taney, and the Taney Court, are best known for rulings on slavery in the later years of his tenure (*Dred Scott v. Sandford* being the most famous), in the first term of the Taney Court, economic issues made up the major cases. Prior to 1820, Taney seemed not to have supported slavery, freeing those he inherited and defending a man charged with inciting a slave insurrection. However, over the decades, Taney seems to have moved toward greater support of slavery, in addition to his strong position of pro-state power and anti-federal. As part of the 1860 election, Abraham Lincoln strongly criticized many of the rulings of the Taney Court. In Taney's final years on the bench, his power was greatly limited by the opposition of President Lincoln and the limitations placed on the Court by the Civil War.

HISTORICAL DOCUMENT: *Charles River Bridge v. Warren Bridge*

We are not now left to determine, for the first time, the rules by which public grants are to be construed in this country ... the principle recognised, that in grants by the public, nothing passes by implication....

The case now before the court is, in principle, precisely the same. It is a charter from a state; the act of incorporation is silent in relation to the contested power. The argument in favor of the proprietors of the Charles River bridge, is the same, almost in words, with that used by the Providence Bank; that is, that the power claimed by the state, if it exists, may be so used as to destroy the value of the franchise they have granted to the corporation. The argument must receive the same answer; and the fact that the power has been already exercised, so as to destroy the value of the franchise, cannot in any degree affect the principle. The existence of the power does not, and cannot, depend upon the circumstance of its having been exercised or not....

While the rights of private property are sacredly guarded, we must not forget, that the community also have rights, and that the happiness and well-being of every citizen depends on their faithful preservation.

Adopting the rule of construction above stated as the settled one, we proceed to apply it to the charter of 1785, to the proprietors of the Charles River bridge.... There is no exclusive privilege given to them over the waters of Charles river, above or below their bridge; no right to erect another bridge themselves, nor to prevent other persons from erecting one, no engagement from the state, that another shall not be erected; and no undertaking not to sanction competition, nor to make improvements that may diminish the amount of its income. Upon all these subjects, the charter is silent; and nothing is said in it about a line of travel, so much insisted on in the argument, in which they are to have exclusive privileges. No words are used, from which an intention to grant any of these rights can be inferred; if the plaintiff is entitled to them, it must be implied, simply, from the nature of the grant; and cannot be inferred, from the words by which the grant is made....

It results from this statement, that the legislature, in the very law extending the charter, asserts its rights to authorize improvements over Charles river which would take off a portion of the travel from this bridge and diminish its profits; and the bridge company accept the renewal thus given, and thus carefully connected with this assertion of the right on the part of the state. Can they, when holding their corporate existence under this law, and deriving their franchises altogether from it, add to the privileges expressed in their charter, an implied agreement, which is in direct conflict with a portion of the law from which they derive their corporate existence? Can the legislature be presumed to have taken upon themselves an implied obligation, contrary to its own acts and declarations contained in the same law? It would be difficult to find a case justifying such an implication, even between individuals; still less will it be found, where sovereign rights are concerned, and where the interests of a whole community would be deeply affected by such an implication. It would, indeed, be a strong exertion of judicial power, acting upon its own views of what justice required, and the parties ought to have done, to raise, by a sort of judicial coercion, an implied contract, and infer it from the nature of the very instrument in which the legislature appear to have taken pains to use words which disavow and repudiate any intention, on the part of the state, to make such a contract....

Amid the multitude of cases which have occurred, and have been daily occurring, for the last forty or fifty years, this is the first instance in which such an implied contract has been contended for, and this court called upon to infer it, from an ordinary act of incorporation, containing nothing more than the usual stipulations and provisions to be found in every such law. The absence of any such controversy, when there must have been so many occasions to give rise to it, proves, that neither states, nor individuals, nor corporations, ever imagined that such a contract could be implied from such charters. It shows, that the men who voted for these laws, never imagined that they were forming such a contract; and if we maintain that they have made it, we must create it by a legal fiction, in opposition to the truth of the fact, and the obvious intention of the party. We cannot deal thus with the rights reserved to the states; and by legal intendments and mere technical reasoning, take away from them any portion of that power over their own internal police and improvement, which is so necessary to their well-being and prosperity.

And what would be the fruits of this doctrine of implied contracts, on the part of the states, and of property in a line of travel, by a corporation, if it would now be sanctioned by this court? To what results would it lead us? ... The millions of property which have been invested in railroads and canals, upon lines of travel which had been before occupied by turnpike corporations, will be put in jeopardy. We shall be thrown back to the improvements of the last century, and obliged to stand still, until the claims of the old turnpike corporations shall be satisfied; and they shall consent to permit these states to avail themselves of the lights of modern science, and to partake of the benefit of those improvements which are now adding to the wealth and prosperity, and the convenience and comfort, of every other part of the civilized world. Nor is this all. This court will find itself compelled to fix, by some arbitrary rule, the width of this new kind of property in a line of travel; for if such a right of property exists, we have no lights to guide us in marking out its extent, unless, indeed, we resort to the old feudal grants, and to the exclusive rights of ferries, by prescription, between towns; and are prepared to decide that when a turnpike road from one town to another, had been made, no railroad or canal, between these two points, could afterwards be established. This Court are not prepared to sanction principles which must lead to such results.

GLOSSARY

Franchises: a legal term that generally refers to the rights of an organization to sell its products or services with permission from the local government.

Implied contract: a legal term referring to a contractual obligation arising out of the actions of the parties rather than from the wording of a written contract.

Intendments: ways in which the legal system interprets something, in particular the meaning of a law.

Providence Bank: reference to an 1830 Supreme Court case, *Providence Bank v. Billings*, in which the Court ruled that the imposition of a state tax on a state-chartered bank was not inconsistent with the contracts clause of the Constitution and was therefore legal.

Document Analysis

The Historical Document section of this text contains an excerpt from the much longer opinion written by Chief Justice Taney. However, the heart of his opinion is contained within that section. Foremost, in virtually all Taney opinions, was the belief that the states which composed the United States should hold most of the power within the American political system. It would have taken an extraordinary set of circumstances for Taney to see otherwise. In addition, as this case dealt with a contractual issue, Taney was inclined to read the contract literally. Thus, Taney would tend not to see any type of implied obligation or privilege. Together, these formed the basis for the majority opinion written by Taney, giving the Commonwealth of Massachusetts the power to charter a second bridge across the Charles River, without owing any compensation to the Charles River Bridge company, the owners of the initial bridge across the river.

The opinion began with a basic affirmation regarding government grants or charters that "nothing passes by implication." Thus, a literal reading of the grant or charter would be necessary to discover the obligations, rights, or privileges. For Taney, and the others agreeing with him, this was the only way in which to undertake this type of discovery. Doing this, in the case of *Charles River Bridge v. Warren Bridge*, clearly gave Taney the foundation for his ruling. While the Charles River Bridge Company had been given the right to construct a bridge over the Charles River and to charge a toll, the charter the corporation received from the state did not give the Charles River Bridge Company an "exclusive privilege" to construct a bridge over the river (to connect Boston and Cambridge). Nothing was said one way or another about whether or not competition would be allowed in this situation. In Taney's view, only a state (commonwealth) could give away its powers over internal economic issues. Without the a statement from the Commonwealth of Massachusetts limiting the state's (commonwealth's) powers to grant additional charters for other bridges over the Charles River, for Taney there was no limitation upon Massachusetts' powers. Thus, by not specifically granting the Charles River Bridge Company the exclusive right to provide a means of transportation across the Charles River, the Commonwealth had the power to grant charters to any number of companies, or individuals, to construct bridges, or any other means of transportation across the river.

Related to this issue, Taney went on to assert that it would be improper to use "judicial coercion" to expand the rights of the Charles River Bridge Company, or to decrease the rights of the state, acting as an agent for the "whole community." He was adamant that the use of legal arguments should not take away any of the "rights reserved to the states." Thus, for Taney, the Supreme Court, and the lower federal courts, should not limit the powers of a state. Only those powers specifically granted to the federal government by the Constitution, and those powers which a state specifically gives up in a legal agreement with some entity, are not available to the various states. In normal situations, for Taney, the states have virtually all powers necessary for "their well-being and prosperity."

Expanding this argument, Taney went on to discuss the possible result of accepting the Charles River Bridge Company's assertion that there had been an implied contract. Taney wondered whether any economic progress could be made, if the concept of an implied contract was applied to all the various transportation companies which states had chartered. He mused that advances of "modern science" might disappear from the transportation industry, as holders of charters from previous centuries might put forward claims similar to the Charles River Bridge Company. In reviewing this, Taney wrote that the justices were not willing to issue a ruling which might "lead to such results."

Chief Justice Taney wrote the opinion for the four-member majority (the Court only had seven members at that time). The opinion, which Charles River Bridge Company counsel Daniel Webster of called both "smooth and plausible" and "cunning and jesuitical" managed to uphold the sanctity of contract while also advancing the interests of the state legislature, itself representing the sovereign power of the people. While asserting that private property was held to be virtually sacred, Taney also stated that "the object and end of all government is to promote the happiness and prosperity of the community." Massachusetts had chartered the first bridge to promote the public good, but a second bridge was now needed for exactly the same reason. The leaders of Massachusetts believed that both economic progress and equal opportunity required a ruling favoring the Warren Bridge Company, unless—and here is the heart of the matter—the contract included language expressly granting monopoly rights to the Charles River Bridge Company. It did not.

Essential Themes

During the administration of President Jackson there were many economic twists and turns, some caused by his policies and others the result of the ongoing growth of the United States. Thus, when Roger Taney became Chief Justice of the Supreme Court, the most important cases of the first year of his tenure were all related to economic concerns of various states. In all of these (*Mayor of the City of New York v. Miln*, *Charles River Bridge v. Warren Bridge*, and *Briscoe v. Commonwealth Bank of Kentucky*) the Taney Court held in favor of the state, or the agent of the state. Thus, the landmark ruling in Charles Bridge v. Warren Bridge did not occur in isolation; rather it was part of a focus by the Court on upholding states' rights. This was the key philosophical issue in Charles River Bridge v. Warren Bridge, although it was strongly supported by the wording of the charter which Massachusetts had granted to the Charles River Bridge Company.

The right of the Commonwealth of Massachusetts to charter a second bridge over the Charles River was something Taney saw as a given, no matter how many bridges or ferry companies were already in operation. For him, only the commonwealth's legislature could give up that right, by specifically granting an exclusive charter, or contract, to a company. Barring a clear statement granting this right, no company, such as the Charles River Bridge Company, had a claim upon the commonwealth, either to block the construction of another bridge, or for economic damages if one were constructed. This was the clear theme of his opinion in this case and of his judicial philosophy.

Conservative observers feared that American corporate law had been forever damaged, but in fact Taney had accomplished something subtle: by warning against the dangers of vested economic interests and political power, he made way for technological innovation that would advance both corporate and public welfare. Contrary to what the Marshall Court holdover Justice Joseph Story argued in dissent, the majority's opinion actually increased incentives for economic investment. And although Taney insisted that the Court must not engage in nullification of legislation passed to advance the public good, by emphasizing the importance of the state's support for corporate development, his opinion actually increased the Court's influence. For Taney, the advancement of social welfare, although only for American citizens, was a key responsibility of state government, and something best performed at the state, rather than the national level.

—*Donald A. Watt, PhD*

Bibliography and Additional Reading

Graff, Henry F. "The Charles River Bridge Case." *The Quarrels That Have Shaped the Constitution* John A. Garrity, ed., revised and expanded ed. New York: Harper and Row Publishers, Inc., 1987. Print and Web. (Houston Community College) 10 August 2017.

McBride, Alex. "Charles River Bridge v Warren Bridge (1837)." *The Supreme Court: The First Hundred Years.* New York: Thirteen/WNET and Educational Broadcasting Corporation, 2006. Web. 10 August 2017.

Newmyer, R. Kent. "Justice Joseph Story, the Charles River Bridge Case and the Crisis of Republicanism." *Faculty Articles and Papers.* Hartford: University of Connecticut School of Law, 1973. Web. 10 August 2017.

Smith, Charles W. Jr., *Roger B. Taney: Jacksonian Jurist.* Chapel Hill: University of North Carolina Press, 1936. Print and Web. (Hathi Trust Digital Library). 13 August 2017.

Swisher, Carle B. *History of the Supreme Court of the United States.* The Oliver Wendell Homes History of the Supreme Court of the United States, vol. 5. Cambridge: Cambridge University Press, 2010. (earlier edition 1974 Macmillan Library Reference). Print.

The Discovery of Gold in California

Date: November 1857
Author: John A. Sutter
Genre: article; memoir

Summary Overview

In *Hutchings' California Magazine* in 1857, John Augustus Sutter recounted the events surrounding the discovery of gold at his mill near Coloma, California, some nine years earlier. He explained how word of the discovery spread and how the discovery affected him personally. Sutter, a Swiss immigrant who became an early California landowner, could have become extremely wealthy as a result of the discovery of gold on his land, but it ran counter to his goals and eventually became the catalyst for a series of business failures that would characterize much of his later life. Within the context of American history, however, the discovery of gold in California helped to justify the country's belief in Manifest Destiny. It also set into motion large-scale and rapid immigration, and forced the nation to further address whether slavery would be allowed to expand westward.

Defining Moment

In January 1848, the United States was already preparing to expand its holdings in the Southwest. The war with Mexico was ending, and the goals of Manifest Destiny—the belief that the United States was destined by Providence to expand all the way across the North American continent—were becoming realities with the negotiation of the Treaty of Guadalupe Hidalgo, under which Mexico ceded to the United States all the land from Texas to the Pacific. This Mexican Cession, as it was called, included the territory of Alta California, or Upper California, a name the Americans shortened to California.

Prior to Mexican independence in 1821, Alta California was a Spanish colony, and the search to find wealth in the Southwest dates back to the earliest Spanish entradas, or explorations, in the 1530s and 1540s. Stories of riches such as the mythical Seven Cities of Cibola had fuelled the imagination of explorers like Francisco Vásquez de Coronado, but in truth, the Spanish colonies of Texas, New Mexico, and Alta California had been a drain on Spanish resources. The riches the Spanish had found in their other colonies, such as Peru and Mexico, seemed not to be in evidence in Spain's northern holdings. Therefore, relatively few Spaniards colonized Alta California, although a vibrant Hispanic culture, based around the large landholdings of a number of wealthy Californios (Spanish-speaking inhabitants of California) and the numerous Franciscan missions, was well established by the time the Americans arrived. Before US annexation, the future cities of San Diego, Los Angeles, and San Francisco (then called Yerba Buena) were nothing more than small towns in a region far from the corridors of Spanish, Mexican, or American power.

The events that John Sutter describes, however, would change everything. California would almost overnight go from a primitive expanse occupied by Mexican landowners to a bustling and wild frontier region dominated by mostly young, single men from the eastern United States, Europe, and China. Prior to the gold rush, Americans had gradually been moving across the continent. Afterward, as historian J. S. Holliday aptly put it, "the world rushed in." The gold that flowed out of California, which had remained hidden until just after the Americans took over, seemed to justify the American notion of Manifest Destiny and the country's preordained right to inhabit the continent.

Author Biography

Born in Baden, Germany, to Swiss parents in 1803, Johann August Sutter emigrated from Berne, Switzerland, to the United States in 1834 in order to avoid mounting debt, changing his first two names to John Augustus. He left his wife and family behind, though he hoped to bring them to the United States when his fortunes turned. He found his way to California in 1839, after stops in St. Louis, the Oregon Territory, and Hawaii. Along the way, Sutter relied on inflated stories of his past and his considerable "gift of gab" to get him out of financial difficulties and convince merchants to extend him credit and government officials to view him as a valuable new member of the community. Even the nickname "Captain" was the result of exaggerating his time as an under lieutenant in the Bernese reserve corps into service as a commander in the famed Swiss Guard (Hurtado 19–20). He tried his hand at trading along the Santa Fe Trail, raising horses and cattle, and building a hotel before leaving for California in order to avoid being sued for default on his debts in Missouri.

Once in California, Sutter impressed both American traders and Mexican government officials with his stories and apparent wealth, claiming, for instance, that he owned a ship. He applied for and received Mexican citizenship and then received a grant of 50,000 acres near present-day Sacramento, where he hoped to raise horses, cattle, and sheep. Once he made peace with the local Nisenan and Miwok Indians, whom he employed as laborers and as his own personal military force, his compound, which he named Sutter's Fort, became the social, political, and commercial center for the entire inland region. Because the area was so isolated from the centers of Mexican power closer to the coast, Sutter became the de facto authority of the region. But the events that would change the history of California and the United States as a whole occurred on another part of Sutter's land grant, about forty-five miles away from Sutter's Fort at a sawmill he had commissioned in the Coloma Valley, named for a nearby Maidu Indian settlement.

HISTORICAL DOCUMENT: The Discovery of Gold in California

It was in the first part of January, 1848, when the gold was discovered at Coloma, where I was then building a sawmill. The contractor and builder of this mill was James W. Marshall, from New Jersey. In the fall of 1847, after the mill seat had been located, I sent up to this place Mr. P. L. Wimmer with his family, and a number of laborers, from the disbanded Mormon Battalion; and a little later I engaged Mr. Bennet from Oregon to assist Mr. Marshall in the mechanical labors of the mill. Mr. Wimmer had the team in charge, assisted by his young sons, to do the necessary teaming, and Mrs. Wimmer did the cooking for all hands.

I was very much in need of a new saw-mill, to get lumber to finish my large flouring mill, of four run of stones, at Brighton, which was commenced at the same time, and was rapidly progressing; likewise for other buildings, fences, etc., for the small village of Yerba Buena, (now San Francisco.) In the City Hotel, (the only one) at the dinner table this enterprise was unkindly called "another folly of Sutter's," as my first settlement at the old fort near Sacramento City was called by a good many, "a folly of his," and they were about right in that, because I had the best chances to get some of the finest locations near the settlements; and even well stocked rancho's had been offered to me on the most reasonable conditions; but I refused all these good offers, and preferred to explore the wilderness, and select a territory on the banks of the Sacramento. It was a rainy afternoon when Mr. Marshall arrived at my office in the Fort, very wet. I was somewhat surprised to see him, as he was down a few days previous; and then, I sent up to Coloma a number of teams with provisions, mill irons, etc., etc. He told me then that he had some important and interesting news which he wished to communicate secretly to me, and wished me to go with him to a place where we should not be disturbed, and where no listeners could come and hear what we had to say. I went with him to my private rooms; he requested me to lock the door; I complied, but I told him at the same time that nobody was in the house except the clerk, who was in his office in a different part of the house; after requesting of me something which he wanted, which my servants brought and then left the room, I forgot to lock the doors, and it happened that the door was opened by the clerk just at the moment when Marshall took a rag from his pocket, showing me the yellow metal: he had about two ounces of it; but how quick Mr. M. put the yellow metal in his pocket again can hardly be described.

The clerk came to see me on business, and excused himself for interrupting me, and as soon as he had left I was told, "now lock the doors; didn't I tell you that we might have listeners?" I told him that he need fear nothing about that, as it was not the habit of this gentleman; but I could hardly convince him that he need not to be suspicious. Then Mr. M. began to show me this metal, which consisted of small pieces and specimens, some of them worth a few dollars; he told me that he had expressed his opinion to the laborers at the mill, that this might be gold; but some of them were laughing at him and called him a crazy man, and could not believe such a thing.

After having proved the metal with aqua fortis, which I found in my apothecary shop, likewise with other experiments, and read the long article "gold" in the Encyclopedia Americana, I declared this to be gold of the finest quality, of at least 23 carats. After this Mr. M. had no more rest nor patience, and wanted me to start with him immediately for Coloma; but I told him I could not leave as it was late in the evening and nearly supper time, and that it would be better for him to remain with me till the next morning, and I would travel with him, but this would not do: he asked me only "will you come to-morrow morning?" I told him yes, and off he started for Coloma in the heaviest rain, although already very wet, taking nothing to eat. I took this news very easy, like all other occurrences good or bad, but thought a great deal during the night about the consequences which might follow such a discovery. I gave all my necessary orders to my numerous laborers, and left the next morning at 7 o'clock, accompanied by an Indian soldier, and vaquero, in a heavy rain, for Coloma. About half way on the road I saw at a distance a human being crawling out from the brushwood.

I asked the Indian who it was: he told me "the same man who was with you last evening." When I came nearer I found it was Marshall, very wet; I told him that he would have done better to remain with me at the fort than to pass such an ugly night here but he told me that he went up to Coloma, (54 miles) took his other horse and came half way to meet me; then we rode up to the new Eldorado. In the afternoon the weather was clearing up, and we made a prospecting promenade. The next morning we went to the tail-race of the mill, through which the water was running during the night, to clean out the gravel which had been made loose, for the purpose of widening the race; and after the water was out of the race we went in to search for gold. This was done every morning: small pieces of gold could be seen remaining on the bottom of the clean washed bed rock. I went in the race and picked up several pieces of this gold, several of the laborers gave me some which they had picked up, and from Marshall I received a part. I told them that I would get a ring made of this gold as soon as it could be done in California; and I have had a heavy ring made, with my family's cost of arms engraved on the outside, and on the inside of the ring is engraved, "The first gold, discovered in January, 1848." Now if Mrs. Wimmer possesses a piece which has been found earlier than mine Mr. Marshall can tell, as it was probably received from him. I think Mr. Marshall could have hardly known himself which was exactly the first little piece, among the whole.

The next day I went with Mr. M. on a prospecting tour in the vicinity of Coloma, and the following morning I left for Sacramento. Before my departure I had a conversation with all hands: I told them that I would consider it as a great favor if they would keep this discovery secret only for six weeks, so that I could finish my large flour mill at Brighton, (with four run of stones,) which had cost me already about from 24 to 25,000 dollars—the people up there promised to keep it secret so long. On my way home, instead of feeling happy and contented, I was very unhappy, and could not see that it would benefit me much, and I was perfectly right in thinking so; as it came just precisely as I expected. I thought at the same time that it could hardly be kept secret for six weeks, and in this I was not mistaken, for about two weeks later, after my return, I sent up several teams in charge of a white man, as the teamsters were Indian boys. . . .

Mr. Brannan made a kind of claim on Mormon Island, and put a tolerably heavy tax on "The Latter Day Saints." I believe it was 30 per cent, which they paid for some time, until they got tired of it, (some of them told me that it was for the purpose of building a temple for the honor and glory of the Lord.)

So soon as the secret was out my laborers began to leave me, in small parties first, but then all left, from the clerk to the cook, and I was in great distress; only a few mechanics remained to finish some very necessary work which they had commenced, and about eight invalids, who continued slowly to work a few teams, to scrape out the mill race at Brighton. The Mormons did not like to leave my mill unfinished, but they got the gold fever like everybody else. After they had made their piles they left for the Great Salt Lake. So long as these people have been employed by me they have behaved very well, and were industrious and faithful laborers, and when settling their accounts there was not one of them who was not contented and satisfied.

Then the people commenced rushing up from San Francisco and other parts of California, in May, 1848: in the former village only five men were left to take care of the women and children. The single men locked their doors and left for "Sutter's Fort," and from there to the Eldorado. For some time the people in Monterey and farther south would not believe the news of the gold discovery, and said that it was only a 'Ruse de Guerre' of Sutter's, because he wanted to have neighbors in his wilderness. From this time on I got only too many neighbors, and some very bad ones among them.

What a great misfortune was this sudden gold discovery for me! It has just broken up and ruined my hard, restless, and industrious labors, connected with many dangers of life, as I had many narrow escapes before I became properly established....

At the same time I was engaged in a mercantile firm in Coloma, which I left in January, 1849—likewise with many sacrifices. After this I would have nothing more to do with the gold affairs. At this time, the Fort was the great trading place where nearly all the business was transacted. I had no pleasure to remain there, and moved up to Hock Farm, with all my Indians, and who had been with me from the time they were children. The place was then in charge of a Major Domo.

It is very singular that the Indians never found a piece of gold and brought it to me, as they very often did other specimens found in the ravines. I requested them continually to bring me some curiosities from the mountains, for which I always recompensed them. I have received animals, birds, plants, young trees, wild fruits, pipe clay, stones, red ochre, etc., etc., but never a piece of gold. Mr. Dana of the scientific corps of the expedition under Com. Wilkes' Exploring Squadron, told me that he had the strongest proof and signs of gold in the vicinity of Shasta Mountain, and furthers south. A short time afterwards, Doctor Sandels, a very scientific traveler, visited me, and explored a part of the country in a great hurry, as time would not permit him to make a longer stay.

He told me likewise that he found sure signs of gold, and was very sorry that he could not explore the Sierra Nevada. He did not encourage me to attempt to work and open mines, as it was uncertain how it would pay and would probably be only for a government. So I thought it more prudent to stick to the plow, notwithstanding I did know that the country was rich in gold, and other minerals. An old attached Mexican servant who followed me here from the United States, as soon as he knew that I was here, and who understood a great deal about working in placers, told me he found sure signs of gold in the mountains on Bear Creek, and that we would go right to work after returning from our campaign in 1845, but he became a victim to his patriotism and fell into the hands of the enemy near my encampment, with dispatches for me from Gen. Micheltorena, and he was hung as a spy, for which I was very sorry.

By this sudden discovery of the gold, all my great plans were destroyed. Had I succeeded for a few years before the gold was discovered, I would have been the richest citizen on the Pacific shore; but it had to be different. Instead of being rich, I am ruined, and the cause of it is the long delay of the United States Land Commission of the United States Courts, through the great influence of the squatter lawyers. Before my case will be decided in Washington, another year may elapse, but I hope that justice will be done me by the last tribunal—the Supreme Court of the United States. By the Land Commission and the District Court it has been decided in my favor. The Common Council of the city of Sacramento, composed partly of squatters, paid Adelpheus Felch, (one of the late Land Commissioners, who was engaged by the squatters during his office), $5,000, from the fund of the city, against the will of the tax-payers, for which amount he has to try to defeat my just and old claim from the Mexican government, before the Supreme Court of the United States in Washington.

GLOSSARY

aqua fortis: a solution of nitric acid that dissolves most metals other than gold

Eldorado: an area of great wealth, based on the Spanish legend of El Dorado, a city of gold

major domo: an administrator who acts on behalf of an absent landowner or supervises an owner's business

Mormon Battalion: a military unit made up of members of the Church of Jesus Christ of Latter-Day Saints, which were then known as Mormons, that served during the Mexican-American War, many of whom settled in California

Document Analysis

John Sutter had an ambition that was certainly as big as the events that swept through his land grant starting in January 1848, and though he personally did not profit from the gold rush that followed, he was an integral member of the drama that played out in California, transforming the area from a sparsely populated Mexican backwater to one of the economic engines of the United States in a matter of less than five years.

One might think that someone with Sutter's ambitions who also had the good fortune to have gold discovered on his land would be well positioned to profit from the discovery. However, Sutter achieved all he had more by force of personality and slyness than business acumen, and this became readily apparent in the years following the discovery. By the time Sutter told his story to a popular journal—nearly a decade after the discovery— the gold rush was already well known across the nation. But the details Sutter revealed demonstrate much about who he was as a man as well as the importance of the California gold rush in the history of the state, the region, and the nation.

Sutter had chosen the then-remote area near the confluence of the American and Sacramento Rivers as his land grant some seven years earlier, despite having the chance to acquire land closer to the coast. However, being at a distance from the centers of power suited Sutter well, as he wished to have complete control over the development of his land grant as well as the people residing on it. In Sutter's vision, what was wilderness at the time would become a profitable operation, producing cowhides, beef, horses, and lumber for the slowly growing cities of Monterey and Yerba Buena on the coast. Development had been slower than Sutter anticipated, though, and Sutter's Fort was not yet self-sufficient. As a result, he was often seeking credit from suppliers on the coast to keep his operation functioning, something with which he had quite a bit of experience. Sutter had additional reasons for apprehension about what the future might bring in late 1847 and early 1848, as the United States was still at war with Mexico. Although California was still technically Mexican territory, it was by that time under the control of the United States, and a permanent change in government was almost inevitable. Sutter's authority in the region was largely based upon the fact that the Mexican government in Alta California was weak, and his grant was far enough from the Mexican territorial capitol at Monterey that he had unrestrained control over his land (Brands, 17–18).

In late 1847, Sutter had entered a partnership with James W. Marshall to build a sawmill on the South Fork of the American River. Marshall was a mechanic from New Jersey who, like Sutter, had gradually made his way west. Like Sutter, he had briefly settled in the Oregon Territory, but, disliking the weather, moved farther south into California. Men like Marshall who had extensive experience with tools and construction were in high demand in the West, and he had no problem finding work with Sutter. The main portion of Sutter's 50,000-acre land grant was near the present city of Sacramento, California, but he also had an additional grant in the Coloma Valley, which was in the foothills of the Sierra Nevada. Being close to the mountains and on a stream made a perfect location for a sawmill that would provide Sutter's Fort and the surrounding area with the wood needed for construction, and Sutter and Marshall had agreed to share equally in the lumber that the mill produced.

By January, the workers building the mill were digging out the millrace that was to bring the water from the river into the sawmill, turning the wheel that would power the operation. On January 24, 1848, as the water flowed through the millrace, Marshall noticed flakes of a gleaming yellow metal left behind. As the flowing water would have washed away any dirt or lighter minerals, it was clear to Marshall that the metal left behind was gold. Quickly, Marshall collected the flakes and, together with a number of his workers, performed several tests to verify the identity of the metal. Convinced that it was gold he possessed, four days later Marshall embarked on the forty-five mile trip to from Coloma to Sutter's Fort to discuss this development with his business partner.

As Sutter enters into his description of Marshall's arrival at Sutter's Fort, it is interesting that he veers into what others thought of his decision to settle on the Sacramento River rather than nearer to the coast. It appears that he is using the discovery of gold on his property to justify his decision and make his detractors look like fools, which is ironic considering the fact that Sutter profited very little from the discovery. In Sutter's account, when Marshall does arrive, he appears to have a full sense of the significance of the discovery, as he asked to discuss the matter in "a place where we should not be disturbed, and where no listeners could come and hear what we had to say." Marshall asks Sutter to lock the door, and Sutter portrays himself as somewhat incompetent when he forgets to lock the door and his clerk comes into the room just as Marshall is removing the gold from his pocket.

After Marshall shows Sutter the gold, Sutter does exactly what Marshall did at the mill, chemically testing the metal to ensure that it actually was gold and reading up on the material to determine its quality. Satisfied that this was, indeed, high-quality gold, Marshall returned to Coloma, and Sutter left to join him the next morning. Sutter, too, was well aware of the consequences of the discovery, and he became determined to keep the secret for as long as possible. Although Sutter asks the workers at the mill to keep the discovery secret, he states that he knew that it would be nearly impossible to prevent the workers from talking. After the visit, Sutter explained that "On my way home, instead of feeling happy and contented, I was very unhappy, and could not see that it would benefit me much, and I was perfectly right in thinking so; as it came just precisely as I expected." The workers at the mill were well acquainted with the workers at Sutter's Fort, so Sutter concludes that it was inevitable that word would escape. At the same time, Sutter takes great pride in describing the ring that he had made with the first gold taken from the millrace, which he stated he did very soon after, so Sutter himself could have been responsible for spreading news of the discovery. Rather than seeking a way to profit from the discovery personally, Sutter laments the fact that he could see no way to profit, as it did not fit with his plans to build a flour mill and continue his other operations at Sutter's Fort. Rather than seizing the opportunity to profit from gold before the world rushed in, Sutter remains steadfast in his own operations, "as it was uncertain how it would pay and would probably be only for a government. So I thought it more prudent to stick to the plow, notwithstanding I did know that the country was rich in gold, and other minerals." In fact, finding no way to participate in the gold rush itself, Sutter's other operations suffered as his workers left his employ in droves, looking instead to enrich themselves by being among the first in the gold fields.

Interestingly, Sutter mentions in passing Sam Brannan of Mormon Island, who he said placed a tax on his people to mine there. What he does not mention is that Brannan was also a merchant who ran a store at Sutter's Fort. Perhaps if Sutter had possessed the business acumen of his hero John Jacob Astor, he might have followed Brannan's example. As soon as he learned of the discovery, Brannan bought up all of the mining supplies he could, took a trip to San Francisco, and did everything he could to spread the word of the gold strike. As a result, Brannan became the first millionaire in California, not through joining the rush to the gold fields, but by realizing that he was in the right place at the right time to profit from it. However, Sutter continues to complain about the discovery of gold ruining his dream of setting up his private kingdom: "What a great misfortune was this sudden gold discovery for me! It has just broken up and ruined my hard, restless, and industrious labors, connected with many dangers of life, as I had many narrow escapes before I became properly established." Narrow escapes certainly characterized Sutter's life, though his self-pity was meant to disguise the fact that the narrow escapes were too often from circumstances of his own making.

As the gold rush progressed, Sutter focused on keeping what he had. But the vast majority of those who worked for him, with the exception of American Indian workers who were largely chased away from the gold fields, led the throngs that would come to California from all over the United States and the rest of the world to seek their fortunes. Many of the early miners were successful, as there was a significant portion of gold that could be found in much the same way that Marshall had. Placer gold—gold that is on the surface of the earth rather than underground—was still relatively abundant, and miners quickly descended on the region's streams hoping to follow Marshall's example. Governmental jurisdiction of the land was lax because of the gold fields' distance from the coast and because the Treaty of Guadalupe Hidalgo did not go into effect until July 4, 1848. The absence of effective government restrictions meant that there were no rules and no taxes. Small impresarios like Sutter could no longer hold sway over their land grants, as the miners largely made up their own laws to govern themselves in the mining camps.

As much as Sutter had sought to delay the spreading of the news, those like Brannan, who saw opportunity in the influx of immigrants that was sure to follow, ensured that the word would get out. The first outsiders to seek their fortunes began to arrive during the summer of 1848. News had spread to the neighboring Oregon Territory, where many Americans had already migrated. By the end of the year, miners were appearing from Hawaii, Mexico, and South America, and the first settlers from the eastern United States were beginning to arrive. But those numbers would snowball during 1849, when tens of thousands flocked to the California territory. Most came on the overland route via the California Trail, although those with some means could purchase a ticket to come by ship and sail either around the cape at the southern tip of South America or by the Panama shortcut (the Panama Canal would not be built for another sixty-five years).

Mining became more difficult as the "forty-niners" arrived. Competition over claims in the gold fields was intense, and the prices that miners paid to merchants like Brannan for necessary supplies were often exorbitant. It was said that just to survive, a miner in 1849 or 1850 had to mine one ounce of gold every day. Although those who arrived came looking for easy wealth, mining whatever gold was available was extremely difficult work. Success could still be found during those first few years, but after 1853, the amount of placer gold that was mined began to decrease while the number of miners continued to increase.

It is impossible to separate the history of the gold rush from the story of the rapid population growth in California. Although many of the miners returned home disappointed and destitute, many others decided to stay in the region, which became a state on September 9, 1850. Ironically, it was those very miners who saw the potential of the region as agricultural land who realized many of Sutter's dreams, albeit on a much smaller scale.

Like Sutter's own life, the fate of California was determined by a number of events that seemingly overwhelmed the area. The gold rush, clearly, brought huge numbers of people and made the dream of Manifest Destiny a reality. Only nine days after Marshall's discovery of gold, the Treaty of Guadalupe Hidalgo was signed, which, when ratified by the US Senate, would make California a US territory. The timing of the discovery of gold, combined with the transfer of California from Mexico to the United States, made the fate of the region a national issue, since Congress had been debating for decades whether new states and territories would be admitted into the union as slave or free. The rapid increase in the population of California meant that quick statehood would be a necessity. California was ultimately admitted as a free state, but only as a part of the Compromise of 1850, which allowed for a popular vote on slavery in other parts of the territory gained from Mexico, the continuation of slavery in Washington, DC, and, most importantly to Southerners, the passage of a new Fugitive Slave Act, which stated that Southern slave owners could cross into the nonslave states and territories to capture escaped slaves.

Sutter, however, remained focused not on the transformative impact that the discovery of gold on his land had on the region, but rather on his own personal misfortune that was caused by his poor business decisions. His concluding remarks continue his theme of feeling personally ruined by the discovery of gold. "By this sudden discovery of the gold, all my great plans were destroyed. Had I succeeded for a few years before the gold was discovered, I would have been the richest citizen on the Pacific shore; but it had to be different. Instead of being rich, I am ruined."

Essential Themes

The discovery of gold on John Sutter's land in 1848 had dramatic consequences for many different populations within California. For miners, the impact was felt economically, and for a few of them it was a time of incredible profit and good fortune. For others, it was a fool's errand, and they returned home destitute and in disgrace. Furthermore, for many of California's American Indians, Sutter's discovery was the beginning of the end of their culture. As happened in other regions where Euro-American settlers arrived in large numbers, disease spread rapidly, decimating many communities. The dependency some tribes had on Euro-American trade meant that with the increased prices of those trade goods, many Indians slipped into poverty or even died of starvation. The justice of the gold fields did not include justice for the Indians, who were sometimes killed for their land. Those who remained had their land and their cultures invaded by the flood of Euro-Americans.

The gold rush that resulted from the discovery also greatly diversified the California population. Mexicans and American Indians constituted the majority of native inhabitants in the region at the time of the discovery. That would quickly change, however, as immigrants from all over the world flooded in. The Chinese arrived in greater numbers than any other. By 1850, there were five hundred Chinese in California, and by 1855 the number of Chinese who had made the trip across the Pacific to the "Gold Mountain" reached twenty thousand, over twice the entire population of the region seven years earlier. San Francisco quickly became the center of Chinese American culture, and although many other cities in California developed Chinatowns, San Francisco's remained dominant and iconic. Chinese miners, like Indians, were persecuted and many had their claims stolen by Euro-American miners. However, the Chinese soon earned a reputation for making profitable claims that other miners had abandoned. After the gold rush, discrimination increased, and by 1882, the United States passed the Chinese Exclusion Act, which was the first immigration law restricting the entry of one particular group based on ethnicity.

Finally, the discovery had a dramatic impact on the landscape. Once the placer gold began to run out in 1853, more destructive means were employed to extract gold from beneath the surface. Hydraulic mining decimated entire hillsides by using torrents of water to find the gold hiding underneath. Chemicals such as arsenic, cyanide, and mercury—used to extract the gold from the materials in which it was embedded—poisoned the land and water. The burgeoning population cut down huge stands of timber to fuel the growth of their towns. In the end, the discovery of gold resulted in the creation of a new California, but—as Sutter would have pointed out—at the expense of destroying the old California.

—*Steven L. Danver, PhD*

Bibliography and Additional Reading

Brands, H. W. *The Age of Gold: The California Gold Rush and the New American Dream*. Rev. ed. New York: Random, 2002. Print.

Dillon, Richard. *Fool's Gold: The Decline and Fall of Captain John Sutter of California*. Sanger, CA: Write Thought, 2012. Print.

Holliday, J. S. *The World Rushed In: The California Gold Rush Experience*. New York: Simon, 1981. Print.

———. *Rush for Riches: Gold Fever and the Making of California*. Berkeley: U of California P, 1999. Print.

Hurtado, Albert L. *John Sutter: A Life on the North American Frontier*. Norman: U of Oklahoma P, 2006. Print.

Osborne, Thomas J. *Pacific Eldorado: A History of Greater California*. New York: Wiley-Blackwell, 2013. Print.

Owens, Kenneth N., ed. *John Sutter and a Wider West*. Rev. ed. Lincoln: U of Nebraska P, 2002. Print.

———. *Riches for All: The California Gold Rush and the World*. Lincoln: U of Nebraska P, 2002. Print.

Starr, Kevin. *Americans and the California Dream, 1850–1915*. New York: Oxford UP, 1986. Print.

Trafzer, Clifford E. and Joel R. Hyer, eds. *Exterminate Them! Written Accounts of the Murder, Rape, and Slavery of Native Americans during the California Gold Rush, 1848–1868*. East Lansing: Michigan State UP, 1999. Print.

Vaught, David. *After the Gold Rush: Tarnished Dreams in the Sacramento Valley*. Baltimore: Johns Hopkins UP, 2007. Print.

With an export of $220,000,000 under the present tariff, the South organized separately would have $40,000,000 of revenue. With one-fourth the present tariff, she would have a revenue with the present tariff adequate to all her wants, for the South would never go to war; she would never need an army or a navy, beyond a few garrisons on the frontiers and a few revenue cutters. It is commerce that breeds war. It is manufactures that require to be hawked about the world, and that give rise to navies and commerce. But we have nothing to do but to take off restrictions on foreign merchandise and open our ports, and the whole world will come to us to trade. They will be too glad to bring and carry us, and we never shall dream of a war. Why the South has never yet had a just cause of war except with the North. Every time she has drawn her sword it has been on the point of honor, and that point of honor has been mainly loyalty to her sister colonies and sister States, who have ever since plundered and calumniated her.

But if there were no other reason why we should never have war, would any sane nation make war on cotton? / Without firing a gun, without drawing a sword, should they make war on us we could bring the whole world to our feet. The South is perfectly competent to go on, one, two, or three years without planting a seed of cotton. / I believe that if she was to plant but half her cotton, for three years to come, it would be an immense advantage to her. I am not so sure but that after three years' entire abstinence she would come out stronger than ever she was before, and better prepared to enter afresh upon her great career of enterprise. What would happen if no cotton was furnished for three years? I will not stop to depict what every one can imagine, but this is certain: England would topple headlong and carry the whole civilized world with her, save the South. / No, you dare not make war on cotton. No power on earth dares to make war upon it. Cotton *is* king. / Until lately the Bank of England was king; but she tried to put her screws as usual, the fall before the last, upon the cotton crop, and was utterly vanquished. The last power has been conquered. Who can doubt, that has looked at recent events, that cotton is supreme? When the abuse of credit had destroyed credit and annihilated confidence; when thousands of the strongest commercial houses in the world were coming down, and hundreds of millions of dollars of supposed property evaporating in thin air; when you came to a dead lock, and revolutions were threatened, what brought you up? Fortunately for you it was the commencement of the cotton season, and we have poured in upon you one million six hundred thousand bales of cotton just at the crisis to save you from destruction. That cotton, but for the bursting of your speculative bubbles in the North, which produced the whole of this convulsion, would have brought us $100,000,000. We have sold it for $65,000,000, and saved you. Thirty-five million dollars we, the slaveholders of the South, have put into the charity box for your magnificent financiers, your "cotton lords," your "merchant princes."

But, sir, the greatest strength of the South arises from the harmony of her political and social institutions. This harmony gives her a frame of society, the best in the world, and an extent of political freedom, combined with entire security, such as no other people

In his 1858 speech, Congressman James Henry Hammond argued that while the Southern states could survive without the North, the North could never survive without the South.

■ "Cotton Is King"

Date: March 4, 1858
Author: Sen. James Henry Hammond
Genre: speech

Summary Overview

James Hammond, a slave-owner and a strong supporter of slavery, made this speech as the tension between pro- and antislavery forces was once again building within the United States. The Compromise of 1850 had eased some of these tensions regarding slavery (and the related issue of states' rights), and many hoped the Kansas-Nebraska Act (1854) would continue do the same. However, as open warfare developed in Kansas ("Bleeding Kansas"), and competing political entities claimed to speak for the territory, it was unclear which side would prevail. As the Senate debated statehood for Kansas, based on the proslavery Lecompton Constitution, senators on both sides of the slavery issue gave forceful speeches.

Hammond's speech was in response to two individuals. The first was Stephen Douglas, a fellow Democrat, although from the North, who was one of the swing votes and a key individual pushing the Senate to allow Kansas to enter but only as a free-state. The second was William Seward, an abolitionist from New York, whose remarks were interpreted by Hammond as sanctioning the Northern oppression of the South. In this context, Hammond gave one of his most eloquent speeches, although for morally suspect ends and in a losing political cause.

Defining Moment

Although regional differences between the North and the South had existed in the United States since its inception, the 1820s and early 1830s brought an increase in the tension between the two. Tariff acts passed by the federal government made the importation of manufactured goods more expensive, which was of benefit primarily to the Northern states. The Southern states, whose economies were more agricultural than those of the North, objected to what their leaders saw as increased costs with no major benefits. The movement that began in response to the tariffs was the Nullification movement, which had the basic tenet that states should be able to nullify, essentially veto, any federal law to which the state objected. This was essentially the beginning of the version of the states' rights argument used prior to (and in some respects since) the Civil War. Hammond's political activism began when he espoused the Nullification position. The ongoing argument over slavery fit into this philosophy.

As the United States expanded westward, the central issue for many was whether or not slavery should be allowed in the new states. With the law stating that the decision in Kansas was to be made by its citizens in its application for statehood, two competing groups wrote proposed constitutions for consideration by Congress. The first, rejected by Congress, was antislavery, but was written by a group with questionable authority. With bloodshed already occurring in Kansas, how well this issue was handled was seen by many as an indication as to what might lie ahead for the United States. A second constitution for Kansas, the proslavery Lecompton Constitution, was sent to Congress.

The acrimonious debate on this document demonstrated that secession by the Southern states was a real possibility. This implicit threat created the need for leaders on both sides to understand the viability of each region's future as a united or divided nation. Hammond made it clear that the South would be viable as an independent nation. He made it clear that, in his opinion, the South was the stronger region, not only economically but in political heritage. For Hammond, the North created the conditions leading to wars, not the South. He made it clear in his argument for slavery, that he regarded the laborers in the North to be the equivalent of the slaves in the South. While he admitted that Northern laborers did have political rights, for Hammond the possibility of starvation for Northern laborers put them in a worse position than the slaves. For Hammond, it seemed that a split was coming; it seemed he hoped it would be peaceful, but he believed that a strong South would be able to continue on its own and repel any attempts to force it to change its politics or slave-based economic system. Cotton, the nation's most lucrative crop and export, would insure the future of the South.

Author Biography

James Henry Hammond (1807–64) was from South Carolina and a graduate of South Carolina College. He was admitted to the bar in 1828, practicing law in Columbia, and starting a newspaper that strongly supported states' rights and opposed federal tariffs and economic policy. In 1831, he married Catherine Fitzsimmons (seven years his junior), with whom he had eight children, and through her acquired a fortune which gave him entry to the state's political elite groups. A staunch proslavery, antistrong government politician, he served in the U.S. House of Representatives (1835–36, resigned), governor (1842–44), and U.S. Senate (1857–60, resigned). He often wrote and spoke in support of slavery, seeing the American form of it as stemming from a divine mandate.

Hammond seemed to have a voracious sexual appetite. Although unknown to the general public at the time, he had a homosexual relationship while in college. Later, the public did know about his rape (he called them "familiarities and dalliances") of four of his teenage nieces, which caused him to sit out politics for several years. Of lesser concern to many of his contemporaries were the multiple rapes of his slaves, with clear documentation regarding two of them with whom he had children.

HISTORICAL DOCUMENT: "Cotton is King"

[…]

But, sir, the true object of the discussion on the other side of the Chamber, is to agitate the questions of slavery. I have very great doubts whether the leaders on the other side of the house really wish to defeat this bill. I think they would consider it a vastly greater victory to crush out the Democratic party in the North, and destroy the authors of the Kansas-Nebraska bill; and I am not sure that they have not brought about this m for the very purpose. They tell us that year after year the majority in Kansas was beaten at the polls! They have always had a majority, but they always get beaten! How could that be? It does seem, from the most reliable sources of information, that they have a majority, and have had a majority for some time. Why has not this majority come forward and taken possession of the government, and made a free-State constitution and brought it here? We should all have voted for its admission cheerfully. There can be but one reason; if they had brought, as was generally supposed at the time the Kansas-Nebraska act was passed would be the case, a free-State constitution here, there would have been no difficulty among the northern Democrats; they would have been sustained by their people. The statement made by some of them, as I understood, that that act was a good free-State act, would have been verified, and the northern Democratic party would have been sustained. But its coming here a slave State, it is hoped, will kill that party, and that is the reason they have refrained from going to the polls; that is the reason they have refrained from making it a free-State when they had the power. They intend to make it a free-State as soon as they have effected their purpose of destroying the Democratic Party at the North, and now their chief object here is, to agitate slavery. For one, I am not disposed to discuss that question here in any abstract from. I think the time has gone by for that. Our minds are all made up. I may be willing to discuss it—and that is the way it should be and must be discussed—as a *practical thing*, as a thing that *is*, and *is to be*; and to discuss its effect upon our political institutions, and ascertain how long those institutions will hold together with slavery *ineradicable*.

The Senator from New York entered very fairly into this field yesterday. I was surprised, the other day, when he so openly said "the battle had been fought and won." Although I knew, and had long known it to be true, I was surprised to hear him say so. I thought that he had been entrapped into a hasty expression by the sharp rebukes of the Senator from New Hampshire; and I was glad to learn yesterday they had been well considered—that they meant all that I thought they meant; that they meant that the South is a conquered province, and that the North intends to rule it. He said that was their intention "to take this Government from unjust and unfaithful hands, and place it in just and faithful hands;" that it was their intention to consecrate all the Territories of the Union to free labor; and that, to effect their purposes, they intended to reconstruct the Supreme Court.

Yesterday, the Senator said, suppose we admit Kansas with the Lecompton constitution—what guarantees are there that Congress will not again interfere with the affairs of Kansas? meaning, I suppose, that if she abolished slavery, what guarantee there was that Congress would not force it upon her again. So far as we of the South are concerned, you have, at least, the guarantee of good faith that never has been violated. But what guarantee have we, when you have this Government in your possession, in all its departments, even if we submit quietly to what the Senator exhorts us to submit to—the limitation of slavery to its present territory, and even to the reconstruction of the Supreme Court—that you will not plunder us with tariffs; that you will not bankrupt us with internal improvements and bounties on *your* exports; that you will not cramp us with navigation laws, and other laws impeding the facilities of transportation to southern produce? What guarantee have we that you will not create a new bank, and concentrate all the finances of this country at the North, where already, for the want of direct trade and a proper system of banking in the South, they are ruinously concentrated? Nay, what guarantee have we that you will not emancipate our slaves, or, at least, make the attempt? We cannot rely on your faith when you have the power. It has been always broken whenever pledged.

As I am disposed to see this question settled as soon as possible, and am perfectly willing to have a final and conclusive settlement *now*, after what the Senator from New York has said, I think it not improper that I should attempt to bring the North and South fact to face, and see what resources each of us might have in the contingency of separate organization.

If we never acquire another foot of territory for the South, look at her. Eight hundred and fifty thousand square miles. As large as Great Britain, France, Austria, Prussia, and Spain. Is not that territory enough to make an empire that shall rule the world? With the finest soil, the most delightful climate, whose staple productions none of those great countries can grow, we have three thousand miles of continental shore line, so indented with bays and crowded with islands, that, when their shore lines are added, we have twelve thousand miles. Through the heart of our country runs the great Mississippi, the father of waters, into whose bosom are poured thirty-six thousand miles of tributary streams; and beyond we have the desert prairie wastes, to protect us in our rear. Can you hem in such a territory as that? You talk of putting up a wall of fire around eight hundred and fifty thousand square miles so situated! How absurd.

But, in this territory lies the great valley of the Mississippi, now the real, and soon to be the acknowledged seat of the empire of the world. They sway of that valley will be as great as ever the Nile knew in the earlier ages of mankind. We own the most of it. The most valuable part of it belongs to us now; and although those who have settled above us are now opposed to us, another generation will tell a different tale. They are ours by all the laws of nature; slave-labor will go over every foot of this great valley where it will be found profitable to use it, and some of those who may not use it are soon to be united with us by such ties as will make us one and inseparable. The iron horse will soon be clattering over the sunny plains of the South to bear the products of its upper tributaries to our Atlantic ports, as it now does through the ice-bound North. There is the great Mississippi, a bond of union made by Nature herself. She will maintain it forever.

On this fine territory we have a population four times as large as that with which these colonies separated from the mother country, and a hundred, I might say a thousand fold as strong. Our population is now sixty per cent. greater than that of the whole United States when we entered into the second war of independence. It is as large as the whole population of the United States was ten years after the conclusion of that war, and our exports are three times as great as those of the whole United States then. Upon our muster-rolls we have a million of men. In a defensive war, upon an emergency, every one of them would be available. At any time, the South can raise, equip, and maintain in the field, a larger army than any Power of the earth can send against her, and an army of soldiers—men brought up on horseback, with guns in their hands.

If we take the North, even when the two large States of Kansas and Minnesota shall be admitted, her territory will be one hundred thousand square miles less than ours. I do not speak of California and Oregon; there is no antagonism between the South and those countries, and never will be. The population of the North is fifty per cent. greater than ours. I have nothing to say in disparagement either of the soil of the North, or the people of the North, who are a brave, and energetic race, full of intellect. But they produce no great staple that the South does not produce; while we produce two or three, and those the very greatest, that she can never produce. As to her men, I may be allowed to say, they have never proved themselves to be superior to those of the South, either in the field or in the Senate.

But the strength of a nation depends in a great measure upon its wealth, and the wealth of a nation, like that of a man, is to be estimated by its surplus production. You may go to your trashy census books, full of falsehood and nonsense—they tell you, for example, that in the State of Tennessee, the whole number of house-servants is not equal to one-half those in my own house, and such things as that. You may estimate what is made throughout the country from these census books, but it is no matter how much is made if it is all consumed. If a man is worth millions of dollars and consumes his income, is he rich? Is he competent to embark in any new enterprise? Can he build ships or railroads? And could a people in that condition build ships and roads or go to war? All the enterprises of peace and war depend upon the surplus productions of a people. They may be happy, they may comfortable, they may enjoy themselves in consuming what they make; but they are not rich, they are not strong. It appears, by going to the reports of the Secretary of the Treasury, which are authentic, that last year the United States exported in round numbers $279,000,000 worth of domestic produce, excluding gold and foreign merchandise re-exported. Of this amount

$158,000,000 worth is the clear produce of the South; articles that are not and cannot be made at the North. There are then $80,000,000 worth of exports of products of the forest, provisions, and breadstuffs. If we assume that the South made out one-third of these, and I think that is a low calculation, our exports were $185,000,000, leaving to the North less than $95,000,000.

In addition to this, we sent to the North $30,000,000 worth of cotton, which is not counted in the exports. We sent to her $7, or $8,000,000 worth of tobacco, which is not counted in the exports. We sent naval stores, lumber, rice, and many other minor articles. There is no doubt that we sent to the North $40,000,000 in addition; but suppose the amount to be $35,000,000, it will give us a surplus production of $222,000,000. But the *recorded* exports of the South now are greater than the whole exports of the United States in any year before 1856. They are greater than the whole average exports of the United States for the last twelve years including the two extraordinary years of 1856 and 1857. They are nearly double the amount of the average exports of the twelve preceding years. If I am right in my calculations as to $220,000,000 of surplus produce, there is not a nation on the face of the earth, with any numerous population, that can compete with us in produce *per capita*. It amounts to $16 66 per head, supposing that we have twelve million people. England with all her accumulated wealth, with her concentrated and educated energy, makes but sixteen-and-a-half dollars of surplus production per head. I have not made a calculation as to the North, with her $95,000,000 surplus; admitting that she exports as much as we do, with her eighteen millions of population it would be but little over twelve dollars a head. But she cannot export to us and abroad exceeding ten dollars a head against our sixteen dollars. I know well enough that the North sends to the South a vast amount of the productions of her industry. I take it for granted that she, at least, pays us in that way for the thirty or forty million dollars worth of cotton and other articles we send her. I am willing to admit that she sends us considerable more; but to bring her up to our amount of surplus production, to bring her up to $220,000,000 a year, the South must take from her $125,000,000; and this, in addition to our share of the consumption of the $333,000,000 worth introduced into the country from abroad, and paid for chiefly by our own exports. The thing is absurd; it is impossible; it can never appear anywhere but in a book of statistics.

With an export of $220,000,000 under the present tariff, the South organized separately would have $40,000,000 of revenue. With one-fourth the present tariff she would have a revenue adequate to all her wants, for the South would never go to war; she would never need an army or a navy, beyond a few garrisons on the frontiers and a few revenue cutters. It is commerce that breeds war. It is manufactures that require to be hawked about the world, that give rise to navies and commerce. But we have nothing to do but to take off restrictions on foreign merchandise and open our ports, and the whole world will come to us to trade. They will be too glad to bring and carry for us, and we never shall dreams of a war. Why the South has never yet had a just cause of war. Every time she has drawn her sword it has been on the point of honor, and that point of honor has been mainly loyalty to her sister colonies and sister Sates, who have ever since plundered and calumniated her.

But if there were not other reason why we should never have war, would any sane nation make war on cotton? Without firing a gun, without drawing a sword, should they make war on us we could bring the whole world to our feet. The South is perfectly competent to go on, one, two, or three years without planting a seed of cotton. I believe that if she was to plant but half her cotton, for three years to come, it would be an immense advantage to her. I am not so sure but that after three total years' abstinence she would come out stronger than ever she was before, and better prepared to enter afresh upon her great career of enterprise. What would happen if no cotton was furnished for three years? I will not stop to depict what every one can imagine, but this is certain: England would topple headlong and carry the whole civilized world with her, save the South. No, you dare not make war on cotton. No power on earth dares to make war upon it. Cotton *is* king. Until lately the Bank of England was king, but she tried to put her screws as usual, the fall before last, upon the cotton crop, and was utterly vanquished. The last power has been conquered. Who can doubt tat has looked at recent events, that cotton is supreme? When the abuse of credit had destroyed credit and annihilated confidence, when thousands of the strongest commercial houses in the world were coming down, and hundreds of millions of dollars of supposed property evaporating in thin air, when you came to a dead lock, and revolutions were threatened, what brought you up? Fortunately for you it was the commencement of the cotton season, and we have poured in upon you one million six hundred thousand bales of cotton just at the crisis to save you from destruction. That cotton, but for the bursting of your speculative bubbles in the North, which produced the whole of this convulsion, would have brought us $1,000,000,000. We have sold it for $65,000,000, and saved you. Thirty-five million dollars we, the slaveholders of the South, have put into the charity box for your magnificent financiers, your "cotton lords," your "merchant princes."

But sir, the greatest strength of the South arises from the harmony of her political and social institutions. This harmony gives her a frame of society, the best in the world, and an extent of political freedom, combined with entire security, such as no other people ever enjoyed upon the face of the earth. Society precedes government; creates it, and ought to control it; but as far as we can look back in historical times we find the case different; for government is not sooner created than it becomes too strong for society, and shapes and moulds, as well as controls it. In later centuries the progress of civilization and of intelligence has made the divergence so great as to produce civil wars and revolutions; and it is nothing now but the want of harmony between governments and societies which occasions all the uneasiness and trouble and terror that we see abroad. It was this that brought on the American Revolution. We threw off a Government not adapted to our social system, and made one for ourselves. The question is how far have we succeeded: The South so far as that is concerned, is satisfied, harmonious, and prosperous.

In all social systems there must be a class to do the menial duties, to perform the drudgery of life. That is, a class requiring but a low order of intellect and but little skill. Its requisites are vigor, docility, fidelity. Such a class you must have, or you would not have that other class which leads progress, civilization, and refinement. It constitutes the very mud-sill of society and of political government; and you might as well attempt to build a house in the air, as to build either the one or the other, except on this mud-sill. Fortunately for the South, she found a race adapted to that purpose to her hand. A race inferior to her own, but eminently qualified in temper, in vigor, in docility, in capacity to stand the climate, to answer all her purposes. We use them for our purpose, and call them slaves. We found them slaves by the "common consent of mankind," which, according to Cicero, lex naturae est. The highest proof of what is Nature›s law. We are old-fashioned at the South yet; it is a word discarded now by «ears polite;» I will not characterize that class at the North with that term; but you have it; it is there; it is everywhere; it is eternal.

The Senator from New York said yesterday that the whole world had abolished slavery. Aye, the name, but not the thing; all the powers of the earth cannot abolish that. God only can do it when he repeals the fiat, "the poor ye always have with you;" for the man who lives by daily labor, and scarcely lives at that, and who has to put out his labor in the market, and take the best he can get for it; in short, your whole class of manual laborers and "operatives," as you call them, are essentially slaves. The difference between us is, that our slaves are hired for life and well compensated; there is no starvation, no begging, no want to employment among our people, and not too much employment either. Yours are hired by the day, not cared for, and scantily compensated, which may be proved in the most painful manner, at any hour in any street in any of your large towns. Why, you meet more beggars in one day, in any single street of the city of New York, when you would meet in a lifetime in the whole South. We do not think that whites should be slaves either by law or necessity. Our slaves are black, of another and inferior race. The status in which we have placed them is an elevation. They are elevated from the condition in which God first created them, by being made our slaves. None of that race on the whole face of the globe can be compared with the slaves of the South. They are happy, content, unaspiring, and utterly incapable, from the intellectual weakness, ever to give us any trouble by their aspirations. Yours are white, of your own race; you are brothers of one blood. They are your equals in natural endowment of intellect, and they feel galled by their degradation. Our slaves do not vote. We give them not political power. Yours do vote, and being the majority, they are the depositaries of all your political power. If they knew the tremendous secret, that the ballot-box is stronger than «an army with banners,» and could combine, where would you be? Your society would be reconstructed, your government overthrown, your property divided, not as they have mistakenly attempted to initiate such proceedings by meeting in parks, with arms in their hands, but by the quiet process of the ballot-box. You have been making war upon us to our very hearthstones. How would you like for us to send lecturers and agitators North, to teach these people this, to aid in combining, and to lead them?

Mr. WILSON and others. Send them along.

Mr. HAMMOND. You say send them along. There is no need of that. Your people are awaking. They are coming here. They are thundering at our doors for homesteads, one hundred and sixty acres of land for nothing, and Southern Senators are supporting them. Nay, they are assembling, as I have said, with arms in their hands, and demanding work at $1,000 a year for six hours a day. Have you heard that the ghosts of Mendoza and Torquemada are stalking in the streets of your great cities? That the inquisition is at hand? There is afloat a fearful rumor that there have been consultations for Vigilance Committees. You know what that means.

Transient and temporary causes have thus far been your preservation. The great West has been open to your surplus population, and your hordes of semi-barbarian immigrants, who are crowding in year by year. They make a great movement, and you call it progress. Whither? It is progress; but it is progress towards Vigilance Committees. The South have sustained you in a great measure. You are our factors. You bring and carry for us. One hundred and fifty million dollars of our money passes annually through your hands. Much of its sticks; all of it assists to keep your machinery together and in motion. Suppose we were to discharge you; suppose we were to take our business out of your hands; we should consign you to anarchy and poverty. You complain of the rule of the South; that has been another cause that has preserved you. We have kept the Government conservative to the great purposes of Government. We have placed her, and kept her, upon the Constitution; and that has been the cause of your peace and prosperity. The Senator from New York says that that is about to be at an end; that you intend to take the Government from us; that it will pass from our hands. Perhaps what he says is true; it may be; but do not forget—it can never be forgotten—it is written on the brightest page of human history—that we, the slaveholders of the South, took our country in her infancy, and, after ruling her for sixty out of the seventy years of her existence, we shall surrender her to you without a stain upon her honor, boundless in prosperity, incalculable in her strength, the wonder and the admiration of the world. Time will show what you will make of her; but no time can ever diminish our glory or your responsibility.

> **GLOSSARY**
>
> **calumniated:** to have made false statements
>
> **Free-State:** a state in which slavery was not permitted
>
> **imbroglio:** a messy misunderstanding
>
> **ineradicable:** permanent, not able to be removed
>
> **Lecompton Constitution:** in territorial Kansas, a proposed proslavery constitution adopted in Lecompton, Kansas
>
> **mud-sill:** the bottom horizontal support for a structure, set on or in the ground

Document Analysis

As Hammond addressed the Senate, he had a clear understanding of the strengthening division in the United States between the North and the South. The proposal for Kansas statehood as a proslavery state, forwarded to Congress by President Buchanan, was a proxy before Congress as regarded the strongest reason for the division. In this section of his speech, Hammond did little to address the issue of Kansas statehood, rather he spoke forcefully upholding his position that slavery was a just institution. In his mind, slaves were the "mud-sill," the people with "little skill" who undergirded the broader Southern society. He was certain that the international demand for cotton ("Cotton Is King") made the South secure and able to protect its economic, social, and political interests.

Although he addressed many of his comments toward Senator Seward (a Whig who had become a Republican), he was in many ways more concerned with the northern Democratic party, specifically Stephen Douglas. Hammond hoped that the Democrats might once again become unified, at least on the issue of Kansas. If that were not to be the case, then he would celebrate the strengths of the South that would enable it to go it alone. Among his arguments were those concerning territorial and population sizes and the ease of transportation relating to exports. However, the key to Southern success would be its economic strength, basically being the strength of cotton. He was correct that, during the 1850s, cotton was the primary export of the United States and a significant part of the U.S. economy. In normal circumstances, if cotton had been removed from the economy, it would have meant that more than half the American exports would disappear and New York City would become much poorer, since it was estimated that about 40 percent of the cotton revenues ended up with companies based there. Hammond understood Britain's demand for cotton, since about 20 percent of its population worked directly in cotton textile manufacturing or trade. Three quarters of the cotton for British companies came from the South. Thus, Hammond was accurate in his statistics, and even in his catch phrase, "Cotton Is King."

To a certain extent, Hammond was also accurate in his projections regarding the ability of the antislavery North and proslavery South to coexist in the future. Trying to overcome this divide created the need to justify slavery to those who were not Southern slaveholders or their dependents. Although he did not develop the theory of the disparity between races, Hammond spoke forcefully on this issue. He claimed that those who had been brought from Africa were a "race inferior," and that these individuals were able to "answer all her purposes"—that is, perform all the labor and tasks that the white population did not want to undertake. He continued, "We use them for our purpose, and call them slaves." For Hammond, and many others, this made them the South's "mud-sill," the foundation for what Hammond saw as the greater achievements of the white population. Hammond's economic theory was that every society had a mud-sill, including the North's manual laborers. For him, slaves and manual laborers were essentially interchangeable, the difference being that the slaves were guaranteed food and housing while the laborers had exchanged this guarantee for the vote. Hammond believed slavery to be a more stable system, because the slaves were "docile" while laborers might use their votes to take control in the North and wreak havoc. Thus, Hammond believed the Northern leaders would be fools for confronting the South because of its inherent strengths, political and social.

Essential Themes

The central aspect of this section of Hammond's speech was the role cotton played in the American economic system. "Cotton Is King," was more than just a political phrase, it was an economic reality. His assertion that "you dare not make war on cotton" was a warning to the North, and the rest of the world, of the economic turmoil that would arise from interfering in the South's way of life. Slavery was a basic part of a cotton plantation, and for Hammond this was as it should be. Those forcefully brought from Africa were "elevated from the condition in which God first created them," according to Hammond. This is why Hammond believed the slaves were "happy, content" individuals. While he did believe whites should not be slaves, he believed that the Northern system created great poverty as exemplified by begging on the streets of New York. Thus, for Hammond, the South had the superior system that undergirded America. If a split occurred (if the government would "pass from our hands"), he hoped it would be peaceful but if not, in Hammond's mind, the South had the strength to prevail.

Hammond did not seem to sway anyone regarding slavery. However, Stephen Douglas, as a leader of the northern Democrats, did respond to Hammond's call for unity. President Buchanan's proposal that the Lecompton Constitution be the document upon which Kansas would be admitted into the Union was facing defeat. Douglas pushed, and succeeded in passing, an alternative, the English bill, which would allow Kansas to enter the Union under the Lecompton Constitution if a majority of the voters in Kansas voted in favor of it. (When presented to the voters of Kansas, less than 14 percent voted in favor of the Lecompton Constitution.) Kansas eventually became a state under the antislavery Wyandotte Constitution after Southern senators began to resign in 1861, as their states seceded from the Union.

The economic strength of the South, its massive cotton trade with Great Britain and the North, was ultimately its downfall when the Civil War was fought. Obviously, the North would not buy cotton from its adversary. Then the British decided not to try to break the North's blockade of the Southern ports, resulting in the South not being able to obtain many of the military supplies needed for the war effort. Although there were other factors that resulted in the South losing the war, its dependence upon the cotton trade was the major economic factor. Cotton might have been king, but a nation could not exist without a broader foundation.

—Donald A. Watt, PhD

Bibliography and Additional Reading

American Battlefield Trust. "Cotton is King." *American Battlefield Trust*. Washington, DC: American Battlefield Trust, 2020. Web. 22 Nov. 2020.

Bleser, Carol K. *Secret and Sacred: The Diaries of James Henry Hammond, A Southern Slaveholder*. Oxford: Oxford University Press, 1988.

Elliott, E. N., ed. *Cotton Is King and Pro-Slavery Arguments: Comprising the Writings of Hammond, Harper, Christy, Stringfellow, Hodge, Bledsoe, and Cartwright*. Augusta, GA: Pritchard, Abbott & Loomis, 1860. Web. (Gilderlehrman.org). 21 Nov. 2020.

Hammond, James Henry. "James Henry Hammond of South Carolina, speech." *Kansas Memory: Kansas Historical Society*. (The text in the Historical Document section of this article begins on page 7.) Topeka: The Kansas Historical Society, 2020. Web. 22 Nov. 2020.

McPherson, James M. *Battle Cry of Freedom: The Civil War Era*. (Illustrated edition.) Oxford: Oxford University Press, 2003.

Sinha, Manisha. "Hammond, James Henry." *South Carolina Encyclopedia*. Columbia: University of South Carolina, Institute for Southern Studies, 2016. Web. 22 Nov. 2020.

Treaty between the United States and Great Britain for the Suppression of the Slave Trade

Date: April 7, 1862
Author: Seward, William Henry
Genre: treaty

Summary Overview

By the mid-nineteenth century, efforts to end the transportation of slaves from Africa to various locations in the Western Hemisphere had been underway for decades. In 1807, Great Britain outlawed the slave trade within its empire, with a few exceptions in Asia, and the United States outlawed the importation of slaves in the same year, effective in 1808. In 1862, the United States was involved in the Civil War, a central cause of which was slavery. Great Britain and the United States had just come to an agreement regarding the *Trent* Affair, which dealt with stopping ships in international waters. Sensing that the time was right for further agreements, the British ambassador, Lord Richard Lyons, proposed to Secretary of State William Henry Seward an agreement that would expand efforts to totally eliminate the slave trade. This included allowing each country the freedom to board and inspect any ships suspected of being involved in the slave trade, not just their own. Within weeks, the two countries agreed, and without any senators from the Southern states, the treaty was quickly ratified.

Defining Moment

The relationship between the United States and Great Britain had fluctuated widely during the almost eighty years since the end of the Revolutionary War, but through the decades, ties had gradually become stronger. Agreements regarding the northern border of the United States and increased trade had brought the two countries into a more harmonious relationship. However, with the secession of the Southern states and the beginning of the American Civil War, the relationship between the two countries again became strained. The supply of American cotton to British mills was greatly diminished, and United States ships were intercepting British freighters as the Union blockade of the South tried to put economic pressure on the Confederates. To strengthen this effort, the American ships that had been patrolling near Africa to block the slave trade were withdrawn to American waters. The November 1861 *Trent* Affair, in which two Confederate emissaries were taken off the British ship RMS *Trent* in international waters, also put the British firmly at odds with the American government.

In addition to these elements, the British view of the American secretary of state, William Seward, was highly negative. Seward had been the favorite to become the Republican nominee for president in 1860, but his strongly belligerent views on slavery and other issues diminished support for him, and the more moderate Abraham Lincoln was nominated. When Seward and others were convinced to take steps to relieve the tension with the British over the *Trent* Affair, the British ambassador to the United States, Lord Richard Lyons, came to change his opinion of Seward. After they had jointly solved one crisis, Lord Lyons pushed forward to address another issue related to the *Trent* Affair.

Although the international slave trade had been outlawed by most nations, it was still occurring. Based on understandings reached at the end of the War of 1812 and the *Trent* Affair, British naval officers would be taking a major risk by stopping any American ships in international waters. With the American navy focusing on the blockade in American coastal waters, many slave ships near Africa were flying the American flag to avoid being stopped by the British. Based on the common interest of the United States and Great Britain in ending the illegal slave trade, Lyons proposed a treaty to cooperate in apprehending ships and crews involved in the trade. Seward saw the treaty's advantage to the United States as well as to his own antislavery views. He and Lyons quickly negotiated the specifics of the treaty, and it was ratified by both countries.

Author Biography

Born May 16, 1801, to Samuel Sweezy Seward and Mary Jennings, William Henry Seward was one of five children in a strong and prosperous household in Florida, New York. He graduated from Union College with a law degree and began practicing law in 1821. He moved to Auburn, New York, to practice law with his fiancée's father. In 1824, he married Frances Adeline Miller, with whom he had five children. Having grown up in a household with slaves, he understood the inequality of the system. His wife was a strong abolitionist, pushing him further in that direction and opening their home to fugitive slaves.

During the 1830s, Seward entered politics, serving in the state Senate as a member of the Anti-Masonic Party. After losing a race to become governor of New York, Seward traveled throughout the state giving speeches, including one on the need for universal education. He was elected governor in 1838 and 1840 as a Whig. In 1849, he was chosen to be a US senator and led the antislavery wing of the Whig Party. Seward was reelected in 1855 and moved to the Republican Party, as most Whigs did when the Whig Party disintegrated. In 1858, he made a divisive and prophetic speech stating that the American system could not endure the split between slave and free states; he said it would become all one or the other. Seward was favored for the 1860 Republican nomination, and while he had the plurality on the first nominating ballet, his support rapidly dropped. He campaigned for the eventual nominee, Abraham Lincoln, and when Lincoln won the general election, Seward agreed to join his cabinet.

As secretary of state, Seward had an expansionist vision for America. Even during the Civil War, he spoke of expanding not just in North America but into the Pacific Ocean and the Caribbean. This, in addition to his aggressive nature, set him at odds with European leaders, who saw him as intruding into their areas. The most dangerous task that confronted him during the Civil War was the *Trent* Affair, when he had to work with the British to diffuse a situation that might have led to war with Britain. As this was handled very professionally, Seward's standing with British leaders increased, and they were willing to negotiate with him on a number of other matters, including ending the slave trade.

After the war, Seward's only acquisition was the purchase of Alaska. However, he strengthened relations with China and Japan, as well as helping establish a stronger American influence in Hawaii. He retired at the end of President Andrew Johnson's term of office and traveled widely until shortly before his death on October 10, 1872.

HISTORICAL DOCUMENT: Lyons-Seward Treaty

Treaty between the United States and Great Britain for the Suppression of the Slave Trade. Concluded at Washington, April 7, 1862. Ratifications exchanged at London, May 25, 1862. Proclaimed by the President of the United States, June 7, 1862.

BY THE PRESIDENT OF THE UNITED STATES OF AMERICA: A PROCLAMATION.

Whereas a treaty between the United States of America and her Majesty the Queen of the United Kingdom of Great Britain and Ireland was concluded and signed by their respective Plenipotentiaries, at the city of Washington, on the seventh day of April last, which treaty is, word for word, as follows:

Treaty between the United States of America and her Majesty the Queen of the United Kingdom of Great Britain and Ireland, for the suppression of the African slave trade.

The United States of America and her Majesty the Queen of the United Kingdom of Great Britain and Ireland, being desirous to render more effectual the means hitherto adopted for the suppression of the slave trade carried on upon the coast of Africa, have deemed it expedient to conclude a treaty for that purpose, and have named as their Plenipotentiaries, that is to say:

The President of the United States of America, William H. Seward, Secretary of State;

And her Majesty the Queen of the United Kingdom of Great Britain and Ireland, the right honorable Richard Bickerton Pemell, Lord Lyons, a peer of her United Kingdom, a knight grand cross of her most honorable Order of the Bath, and her Envoy Extraordinary and Minister Plenipotentiary to the United States of America;

Who, after having communicated to each other their respective full powers, found in good and due form, have agreed upon and concluded the following articles:

ARTICLE I. The two high contracting parties mutually consent that those ships of their respective navies which shall be provided with special instructions for that purpose, as hereinafter mentioned, may visit such merchant vessels of the two nations as may, upon reasonable grounds, be suspected of being engaged in the African slave trade, or of having been fitted out for that purpose; or of having, during the voyage on which they are met by the said cruisers, been engaged in the African slave trade, contrary to the provisions of this treaty; and that such cruisers may detain, and send or carry away, such vessels, in order that they may be brought to trial in the manner hereinafter agreed upon.

In order to fix the reciprocal right of search in such a manner as shall be adapted to the attainment of the object of this treaty, and at the same time avoid doubts, disputes, and complaints, the said right of search shall be understood in the manner and according to the rules following:

First. It shall never be exercised except by vessels of war, authorized expressly for that object, according to the stipulations of this treaty.

Secondly. The right of search shall in no case be exercised with respect to a vessel of the navy of either of the two Powers, but shall be exercised only as regards merchant-vessels; and it shall not be exercised by a vessel of war of either contracting party within the limits of a settlement or port, nor within the territorial waters of the other party.

Thirdly. Whenever a merchant-vessel is searched by a ship of war, the commander of the said ship shall, in the act of so doing, exhibit to the commander of the merchant-vessel the special instructions by which he is duly authorized to search; and shall deliver to such commander a certificate, signed by himself, stating his rank in the naval service of his country, and the name of the vessel he commands, and also declaring that the only object of the search is to ascertain whether the vessel is employed in the African slave trade, or is fitted up for the said trade. When the search is made by an officer of the cruiser who is not the commander, such officer shall exhibit to the captain of the merchant-vessel a copy of the before-mentioned special instructions, signed by the commander of the cruiser; and he shall in like manner deliver a certificate signed by himself, stating his rank in the navy, the name of the commander by whose orders he proceeds to make the search, that of the cruiser in which he sails, and the object of the search, as above described. If it appears from the search that the papers of the vessel are in regular order, and that it is employed on lawful objects, the officer shall enter in the log-book of the vessel that the search has been made in pursuance of the aforesaid special instructions; and the vessel shall be left at liberty to pursue its voyage. The rank of the officer who makes the search must not be less than that of lieutenant in the navy, unless the command, either by reason of death or other cause, is at the time held by an officer of inferior rank.

Fourthly. The reciprocal right of search and detention shall be exercised only within the distance of two hundred miles from the coast of Africa, and to the southward of the thirty-second parallel of north latitude, and within thirty leagues from the coast of the Island of Cuba.

ARTICLE II. In order to regulate the mode of carrying the provisions of the preceding article into execution, it is agreed—

First. That all the ships of the navies of the two nations which shall be hereafter employed to prevent the African slave trade shall be furnished by their respective Governments with a copy of the present treaty, of the instructions for cruisers annexed thereto, (marked A,) and of the regulations for the mixed courts of justice annexed thereto, (marked B,) which annexes respectively shall be considered as integral parts of the present treaty.

Secondly. That each of the high contracting parties shall, from time to time, communicate to the other the names of the several ships furnished with such instructions, the force of each, and the names of their several commanders. The said commanders shall hold the rank of captain in the navy, or at least that of lieutenant; it being nevertheless understood that the instructions originally issued to an officer holding the rank of lieutenant of the navy, or other superior rank, shall, in case of his death or temporary absence, be sufficient to authorize the officer on whom the command of the vessel has devolved to make the search, although such officer may not hold the aforesaid rank in the service.

Thirdly. That if at any time the commander of a cruiser of either of the two nations shall suspect that any merchant-vessel under the escort or convoy of any ship or ships-of-war of the other nation carries negroes on board, or has been engaged in the African slave trade, or is fitted out for the purpose thereof, the commander of the cruiser shall communicate his suspicions to the commander of the convoy, who, accompanied by the commander of the cruiser, shall proceed to the search of the suspected vessel; and in case the suspicions appear well founded, according to the tenor of this treaty, then the said vessel shall be conducted or sent to one of the places where the mixed courts of justice are stationed, in order that it may there be adjudicated upon.

Fourthly. It is further mutually agreed that the commanders of the ships of the two navies, respectively, who shall be employed on this service, shall adhere strictly to the exact tenor of the aforesaid instructions.

ARTICLE III. As the two preceding articles are entirely reciprocal, the two high contracting parties engage mutually to make good any losses which their respective subjects or citizens may incur by an arbitrary and illegal detention of their vessels; it being understood that this indemnity shall be borne by the Government whose cruiser shall have been guilty of such arbitrary and illegal detention; and that the search and detention of vessels specified in the first article of this treaty shall be effected only by ships which may form part of the two navies, respectively, and by such of those ships only as are provided with the special instructions annexed to the present treaty, in pursuance of the provisions thereof. The indemnification for the damages of which this article treats shall be paid within the term of one year, reckoning from the day in which the mixed court of justice pronounces its sentence.

ARTICLE IV. In order to bring to adjudication with as little delay and inconvenience as possible, the vessels which may be detained according to the tenor of the first article of this treaty, there shall be established, as soon as may be practicable, three mixed courts of justice, formed by an equal number of individuals of the two nations, named for this purpose by their respective Governments. These courts shall reside, one at Sierra Leone, one at the Cape of Good Hope, and one at New York.

But each of the two high contracting parties reserves to itself the right of changing, at its pleasure, the place of residence of the court or courts held within its own territories.

These courts shall judge the causes submitted to them according to the provisions of the present treaty, and according to the regulations and instructions which are annexed to the present treaty, and which are considered an integral part thereof; and there shall be no appeal from their decision.

ARTICLE V. In case the commanding officer of any of the ships of the navies of either country, duly commissioned according to the provisions of the first article of this treaty, shall deviate in any respect from the stipulations of the said treaty, or from the instructions annexed to it, the Government which shall conceive itself to be wronged thereby shall be entitled to demand reparation; and in such case the Government to which such commanding officer may belong binds itself to cause inquiry to be made into the subject of the complaint, and to inflict upon the said officer a punishment proportioned to any wilful transgression which may be proved to have committed.

ARTICLE VI. It is hereby further mutually agreed, that every American or British merchant-vessel which shall be searched by virtue of the present treaty may lawfully be detained, and sent or brought before the mixed courts of justice established in pursuance of the provisions thereof, if, in her equipment, there shall be found any of the things hereinafter mentioned, namely:

First. Hatches with open gratings, instead of the close hatches, which are usual in merchant vessels.

Second. Divisions or bulk-heads in the hold or on deck, in greater number than are necessary for vessels engaged in lawful trade.

Third. Spare plank fitted for laying down as a second or slave deck.

Fourth. Shackles, bolts, or handcuffs.

Fifth. A larger quantity of water in casks or in tanks than is requisite for the consumption of the crew of the vessel as a merchant-vessel.

Sixth. An extraordinary number of water casks, or of other vessels for holding liquid; unless the master shall produce a certificate from the custom-house at the place from which he cleared outwards, stating that a sufficient security had been given by the owners of such vessel that such extra quantity of casks, or of other vessels should be used only to hold palm oil, or for other purposes of lawful commerce.

Seventh. A greater number of mess-tubs or kids than requisite for the use of the crew of the vessel as a merchant-vessel.

Eighth. A boiler, or other cooking apparatus, of an unusual size, and larger, or capable of being made larger, than requisite for the use of the crew of the vessel as a merchant-vessel; or more than one boiler, or other cooking apparatus, of the ordinary size.

Ninth. An extraordinary quantity of rice, of the flour of Brazil, of manioc or cassada, commonly called farinha, of maize, or of Indian corn, or of any other article of food whatever, beyond the probable wants of the crew; unless such rice, flour, farinha, maize, Indian corn, or other article of food, be entered on the manifest as part of the cargo for trade.

Tenth. A quantity of mats or matting greater than is necessary for the use of the crew of the vessel as a merchant-vessel, unless such mats or matting be entered on the manifest as part of the cargo for trade.

If it be proved that any one or more of the articles above specified is or are on board, or have been on board during the voyage in which the vessel was captured, that fact shall be considered as *primâ facie* evidence that the vessel was employed in the African slave trade, and she shall in consequence be condemned and declared lawful prize; unless the master or owners shall furnish clear and incontrovertible evidence, proving to the satisfaction of the mixed court of justice, that at the time of her detention or capture the vessel was employed in a lawful undertaking, and that such of the different articles above specified as were found on board at the time of detention, or as may have been embarked during the voyage on which she was engaged when captured, were indispensable for the lawful object of her voyage.

ARTICLE VII. If any one of the articles specified in the preceding article as grounds for condemnation should be found on board a merchant-vessel, or should be proved to have been on board of her during the voyage on which she was captured, no compensation for losses, damages, or expenses consequent upon the detention of such vessel, shall in any case be granted either to the master, the owner, or any other person interested in the equipment or in the lading, even though she should not be condemned by the mixed court of justice.

ARTICLE VIII. It is agreed between the two high contracting parties, that in all cases in which a vessel shall be detained under this treaty, by their respective cruisers, as having been engaged in the African slave trade, or as having been fitted out for the purposes thereof, and shall consequently be adjudged and condemned by one of the mixed courts of justice to be established as aforesaid, the said vessel shall, immediately after its condemnation, be broken up entirely, and shall be sold in separate parts, after having been so broken up; unless either of the two Governments should wish to purchase her for the use of its navy, at a price to be fixed by a competent person chosen for that purpose by the mixed court of justice, in which case the Government whose cruiser shall have detained the condemned vessel shall have the first option of purchase.

ARTICLE IX. The captain, master, pilot, and crew of any vessel condemned by the mixed courts of justice shall be punished according to the laws of the country to which such vessel belongs, as shall also the owner or owners and the persons interested in her equipment or cargo, unless they prove that they had no participation in the enterprise.

For this purpose, the two high contracting parties agree that, in so far as it may not be attended with grievous expense and inconvenience, the master and crew of any vessel which may be condemned by a sentence of one of the mixed courts of justice, as well as any other persons found on board the vessel, shall be sent and delivered up to the jurisdiction of the nation under whose flag the condemned vessel was sailing at the time of capture; and that the witnesses and proofs necessary to establish the guilt of such master, crew, or other persons, shall also be sent with them.

The same course shall be pursued with regard to subjects or citizens of either contracting party who may be found by a cruiser of the other on board a vessel of any third Power, or on board a vessel sailing without flag or papers, which may be condemned by any competent court for having engaged in the African slave trade.

ARTICLE X. The negroes who are found on board of a vessel condemned by the mixed courts of justice, in conformity with the stipulations of this treaty, shall be placed at the disposal of the Government whose cruiser has made the capture; they shall be immediately set at liberty, and shall remain free, the Government to whom they have been delivered guarantying their liberty.

ARTICLE XI. The acts or instruments annexed to this treaty, and which it is mutually agreed shall form an integral part thereof, are as follows:

(A.) Instructions for the ships of the navies of both nations, destined to prevent the African slave trade.

(B.) Regulations for the mixed courts of justice.

ARTICLE XII. The present treaty shall be ratified, and the ratifications thereof shall be exchanged at London in six months from this date, or sooner if possible. It shall continue and remain in full force for the term of ten years from the day of exchange of the ratifications, and further, until the end of one year after either of the contracting parties shall have given notice to the other of its intention to terminate the same, each of the contracting parties reserving to itself the right of giving such notice to the other at the end of said term of ten years: And it is hereby agreed between them, that, on the expiration of one year after such notice shall have been received by either from the other party, this treaty shall altogether cease and determine.

In witness whereof the respective plenipotentiaries have signed the present treaty, and have thereunto affixed the seal of their-arms.

Done at Washington the seventh day of April, in the year of our Lord one thousand eight hundred and sixty-two.

[L. S.] WILLIAM H. SEWARD.

[L. S.] LYONS.

GLOSSARY

Cape of Good Hope: the site of the British Cape Colony in what is now South Africa, the principal settlement of which was Cape Town

mess-tubs or kids: large bowls or small tubs with rope handles, used for holding food

mixed courts of justice: the courts established by the treaty with judges appointed by both governments jointly overseeing the trial

plenipotentiaries: diplomatic officials with the power to represent a government on all issues

***primâ facie* evidence:** evidence "at first sight," sufficient to establish guilt without further examination unless disproved

Document Analysis

By 1862, the transportation of Africans to the Americas for the purpose of enslavement had existed for around 360 years. However, since 1836, no country had recognized participation in the international slave trade as a legitimate activity. Although slave trading had declined greatly since the end of the eighteenth century, the continued existence of slavery in several countries and colonies made it a profitable criminal endeavor for those who were willing to risk capture. With one of the major slaveholding countries in the midst of a civil war between the slaveholding and non-slaveholding sections, the opportunity existed to push for further steps to end the exploitation of Africans. Lord Lyons, envoy to the United States from Great Britain, and William Seward, US secretary of state, discussed this issue and drew up an agreement that, within a few years, effectively put an end to the transportation of slaves from Africa to the Americas.

Ever since the Portuguese began the practice in the fifteenth century, European and, later, American powers had sought economic gain via slave labor. However, beginning in the 1800s, slavery and the slave trade began to be examined from a human-rights perspective. As a result, both were slowly outlawed by the major Western powers. However, the legal changes outlawing both practices were not uniform, nor were they implemented at the same time in all places. Thus, as long as slavery was legal, the possibility for slave trade existed. Cuba, which allowed slavery until 1884, was the focal point for the Caribbean slave trade, including shipments to the United States, which were illegal after 1808. With the United States outlawing the participation of its citizens in slave trading between foreign countries in 1800, Great Britain's similar law in 1807, and the US ban on the importation of slaves going into effect in 1808, the international slave trade did decline. By the end of the 1830s, virtually all other European powers had similar laws, with enforcement varying from country to country. Under various treaties, the British fleet was the principal enforcement mechanism, and it posted numerous ships near the African coast.

In 1842, the United States signed the Webster-Ashburton Treaty, in which the United States promised to establish a fleet off the west coast of Africa to intercept slave ships flying the American flag. When the United States withdrew the ships to assist in the blockade of Southern ports in 1861, many slave ships began flying the American flag in order to avoid being stopped by the British. The British and most Union leaders wanted to end slavery, and they saw a treaty on the slave trade as one step toward that goal. Although the Lyons-Seward Treaty was signed and ratified, none of the Union leaders actually believed that ships were going to run the naval blockade of the South to bring in additional slaves. The last documented group of slaves illegally brought into the United States was in 1859. However, the treaty was a forceful statement of the American government's vision for the future.

The treaty itself is fairly straightforward, with provisions allowing for the conviction of slave traders even if no slaves were present. This means that anyone sailing a ship equipped to transport slaves was always at risk. Lyons and Seward tried to be as comprehensive as possible in drawing up the provisions under which a ship could be seized for participating in the slave trade. The opening of the treaty follows the traditional formulation of treaties by describing the nations involved and giving the credentials of those making the agreement. In line with the tradition established by President George Washington, references to the United States and its leaders are very simple compared to the British embellishments.

Having established the credentials of the negotiators, the twelve articles of the treaty outline three basic areas of agreement: who is authorized to undertake searches, the legal procedure for searches for evidence (including what constitutes evidence), and the adjudication of the treaty through "mixed courts of justice." Article 1 of the treaty begins with a statement reflecting these three themes of the treaty, as well as introducing the reason for the treaty's existence. The treaty "for the Suppression of the Slave Trade," as the formal title states, applies to the use of "their respective navies" to undertake the task. If a commercial vessel were suspected of having "been engaged in the African slave trade," then, as would be expected from democracies, the accused would "be brought to trial" and a verdict issued by a court. This summation of the treaty is then clarified throughout the remainder of the document, as well as through two annexes to the treaty, negotiated simultaneously with the formal treaty.

As to the first general principle of the treaty—who was authorized to undertake the mission to stop the slave trade—the ships authorized to undertake this mission are described in articles 1 and 2, as well as in annex A. In order for the goal to be reached, ships from either navy could stop commercial vessels from either country to inspect for signs of slave trading. (Prior to the treaty, only British naval vessels could stop British ships and American naval vessels, American ships.) However, in order to reduce any problems that might arise from possible interference with legitimate commercial enterprises, the treaty limits the scope of the search for slave traders in several ways. The first is by giving this task not to the whole navy but only to certain ships. Thus, as stated in article 1, only ships "authorized expressly for that object" were to undertake operations against suspected slave ships. The ship to be stopped had to be a private vessel; official (i.e., naval) ships of either country could not be stopped. In addition, the fourth section of article 1 delimits the geographical areas in which ships were subject to being searched. The northern border of the African search area was the thirty-second parallel north, which cuts approximately through the middle of the current nation of Morocco. Thus, the search area included essentially all the ocean adjacent to the entire west coast of Africa, as well as the area within thirty leagues of Cuba. Due to the success of the patrols, in 1863, the area within thirty leagues of Madagascar, Puerto Rico, and Santo Domingo (Hispaniola) was added to the search area.

In article 2, further clarification is given regarding those who were authorized to enforce the treaty. Naval vessels that were authorized to carry out the mission of stopping the slave trade were to be specifically named by their respective governments and given copies of the treaty, as well as the two annexes. While this would not be important when stopping a ship from their own country, having the document that authorized stopping a foreign ship would make discussions with the captain of the merchant ship easier. Naming specific ships made it easier to coordinate efforts. Section 2 of article 2 provides that ships assigned to this mission have as commander a person with at least the rank of lieutenant.

In annex A, not printed in this text, specific directions are given for the boarding of a ship suspected of participating in the slave trade. Anyone up to the commander of the naval vessel stopping the merchant ship could be part of the boarding crew. However, annex A tries to give assurance that a senior officer will participate in boarding the suspected ship and overseeing the search for evidence, stating that at least a lieutenant should be in charge of the boarding crew, or if the officer corps on board were depleted, then at least the "second in command of the ship" should participate in the search.

Most of the treaty deals with the procedure by which the search, and any evidence found, would be documented. This second aspect of the treaty, the procedure, was the first step to ensure that due process would be carried out in the investigation and in preparations for any possible trial. The third section of article 1 gives specific guidelines on the paperwork necessary when stopping and boarding a merchant ship. The captain of the naval vessel was to give a copy of his orders showing he was "authorized to search" to the captain of the merchant vessel. When someone other than the captain of the naval vessel did the actual boarding and search, this other officer also had to complete paperwork documenting his role in the action. This was to provide documentation regarding evidence to be used in any trial and to ensure that any innocent ship that was stopped had the necessary documents to explain its delay in transit and to make certain it was not stopped and searched by any other naval vessel. As previously mentioned, the treaty expresses a preference for an officer with at least the rank of lieutenant, with provisions for an exception in the unusual circumstance that no one with that rank or above was available. In order for the system to work correctly, the treaty states that the naval commanders should "adhere strictly to the exact tenor of the aforesaid instructions."

Annex A also states that the search was to "be conducted with the courtesy and consideration which ought to be observed between allied and friendly nations." Under provisions in article 2, if any ship in a convoy were suspected of being a slave ship, then the entire convoy would be stopped and the commander of the convoy would be allowed to participate in the search, along with the naval officials and the commander of the suspected ship. If nothing was found, then the ship would, as article 1 states, "be left at liberty to pursue its voyage." However, if sufficient evidence was found to cause the boarding party to take the merchant ship to be tried in court, three potential locations were given for this to happen. The naval commander was charged to take the merchant ship to the nearest or most easily reached court. Annex A gives stipulations as to how the merchant ship should be crewed during the trip to court. The merchant ship, and everyone and everything on it, was to be taken to the port, where a court could make a final ruling on the guilt or innocence of the captain and crew. It also directs the individual in charge of the search to draw up a document listing all the papers, people, and cargo found on the merchant ship.

As for the evidence necessary for the naval vessel to take the merchant ship to a court of justice, the most obvious piece of evidence would be Africans found on board en route to the Americas. However, as that was only possible on the westbound voyage, article 6 of the treaty lists ten items that were commonly identified as being integral to the slave trade. Thus, items such as "hatches with open gratings" or "a greater number of mess-tubs or kids than requisite for the use of the crew" could constitute enough evidence to take a ship into custody. As with many legal cases, there could be gray areas, such as how many mess-tubs a crew might need. This was the type of question for the court to rule on; a naval officer finding any of these items, or large enough quantities to raise questions, would be authorized to take possession of the merchant ship.

The "mixed courts of justice" were considered "mixed" because judges from both countries jointly presided at the trials. Annex B gives directions for the trials in line with its title, "Regulations for the Mixed Courts of Justice." Assuming that all the procedures had been correctly followed and one or more of the suspicious items listed in article 6 were found, even if a merchant captain and crew were found innocent, then there would be no compensation for the merchant or those shipping cargo on the vessel. However, if none of the suspicious items were found, then the naval officer and the nation that he served would be liable to pay compensation for delay and damages.

If the merchant captain and crew were found guilty of participating in the slave trade, then they were to be punished by the country whose flag they flew. Since both the United States and Great Britain had been signatories to an agreement to charge slave traders as pirates, the punishment would be similar. The ship itself would be destroyed, although provision was made for it to be purchased by one of the governments if it "should wish to purchase her for the use of its navy." Any cargo, except for persons from Africa being taken into slavery, became the property of the government whose flag the merchant vessel was flying. If it could be clearly proved that those shipping cargo on such a ship did not know of it being used for the slave trade, then they could get their cargo returned. The Africans on board a captured ship would "be immediately set at liberty, and shall remain free, the Government to whom they have been delivered guarantying their liberty." If Africans were found on board a slave ship, it might not be possible for them to be returned to their homes; however, the two countries did give the strongest assurances possible that those who might have become slaves would at least regain their freedom. The strength of the treaty lay in the fact that what might have been called circumstantial evidence in other cases was defined in the treaty as *"primâ facie* evidence" that the vessel was employed in the African slave trade.

Essential Themes

The Treaty for the Suppression of the Slave Trade was written in such a way as to follow as closely as possible the normal procedures of international law at the time. It includes provisions for compensation for those unjustly detained. However, the two countries' intent to end the slave trade could be seen in the list of prima facie evidence for conviction, which goes far beyond just finding chained Africans on board. The fact that shackles or extra sleeping mats could convict a slave trader made engaging in the slave trade a much more greater risk. While that could be avoided by stripping the ship when the slaves were sold and then reinstalling everything in the African port when new slaves were purchased, doing so negated the profits. As a result of this treaty, the transatlantic African slave trade finally came to an end. Although slavery lasted until the 1880s in Cuba and Brazil, there is no record of any people brought from Africa after the 1860s. The new era of closer US-British relations, which had started with the peaceful conclusion of the *Trent* Affair, was strengthened by the cooperation established by this treaty, often called the Lyons-Seward Treaty. These two individuals, who at the beginning of Abraham Lincoln's presidency seemed to be as far apart as their homelands, became effective partners in developing a close alliance. Even though there was still a long way to go toward full equality of all peoples, the successful suppression of the slave trade was a landmark on that path.

—*Donald A. Watt, PhD*

Bibliography and Additional Reading

"British-American Diplomacy: Treaty between United States and Great Britain for the Suppression of the Slave Trade; April 7, 1862." *Avalon Project*. Lillian Goldman Law Lib., 2008. Web. 18 Apr. 2013.

Ferris, Norman B. *Desperate Diplomacy: William H. Seward's Foreign Policy, 1861*. Knoxville: U of Tennessee P, 1976. Print.

Foreman, Amanda. *A World on Fire: Britain's Crucial Role in the American Civil War*. New York: Random, 2010. Print.

Goodwin, Doris Kearns. *Team of Rivals: The Political Genius of Abraham Lincoln*. New York: Simon, 2005. Print.

Hill, Walter B., Jr. "Living with the Hydra: The Documentation of Slavery and the Slave Trade in Federal Records." *Prologue* 32.4 (2000): n. pag. *National Archives and Records Administration*. Web. 18 Apr. 2013.

Jenkins, Brian. "The 'Wise Macaw' and the Lion: William Seward and Britain, 1861–1863." *University of Rochester Library Bulletin* 31.1 (1978): n. pag. *River Campus Libraries: University of Rochester*. Web. 18 Apr. 2013.

Jones, Howard. *Abraham Lincoln and a New Birth of Freedom: The Union and Slavery in the Diplomacy of the Civil War*. Lincoln: U of Nebraska P, 1999. Print.

Stahr, Walter. *Seward: Lincoln's Indispensable Man*. New York: Simon, 2012. Print.

Taylor, John M. *William Henry Seward: Lincoln's Right Hand*. New York: Harper, 1991. Print.

"Timeline of Atlantic Slave Trade." *ABCNews.com*. ABC News, 2 July 2000. Web. 18 Apr. 2013.

Van Deusen, Glyndon G. *William Henry Seward*. New York: Oxford UP, 1967. Print.

Lincoln in February 1865, two months before his death. (Alexander Gardner - Library of Congress)

■ "The Money Power"

Date: November 21, 1864
Author: Abraham Lincoln (attributed to)
Genre: letter

Summary Overview

In this excerpt from a letter to Colonel William F. Elkins, attributed to President Abraham Lincoln, the author expresses fears about the growth of the "money power" in the United States. The notion of a shadowy "money power" exercising undue influence over government policies at the state and federal level had surfaced in American political rhetoric at various times over the previous decades, often in response to specific controversies. With the rapid growth of industry in the second half of the nineteenth century and the accompanying rise in the wealth and power of those who controlled these industries, the specter of the "money power" once again flourished.

The language in the letter is dramatic, verging on apocalyptic, framing the emerging dominance of the "money power" as the greatest challenge the nation could face—and as a calamity even more destructive to the United States than the Civil War, which in 1864 was nearing its conclusion.

Historians have long debated the authenticity of this letter; the question of Lincoln's authorship provides an additional layer of significance to the document. At the most basic level, this is a denunciation of corporate dominance. Subsequent debates over authorship illustrate the ways in which people seek to "claim" historical figures as representatives for their views.

Regardless of the ultimate authorship of these words, they provide insight into concerns about the changing American business landscape in the nineteenth century and beyond.

Defining Moment

The letter is dated November 21, 1864. At that time, the American Civil War would continue on for nearly six months until it finally ended. At this point, however, the eventual Union victory was all but assured. President Abraham Lincoln, and others, began to look to developing policies that would shape the postwar United States. While the status of former slaves and reincorporating the seceded Confederate states back into the Union were of primary concern, this excerpt illustrates emerging fears about the growing economic and political dominance of business, industrial, and financial entities in the United States.

While the explosive growth of the financial and industrial sectors in the United States is usually seen as a phenomenon of the later nineteenth and early twentieth centuries, this growth and development had been incubating for several decades. Lincoln's own history working with and for some of these entities is discussed in the Author Biography below; but, broadly, the political party with which Lincoln was affiliated for most of his career—the Whig party—was a powerful force for a growing, national economy. The policies supported by the Whigs recognized the importance of both the agricultural and developing industrial sectors and called for the federal government to support the development of business through protective tariffs, infrastructure improvements, and a central banking system to manage the money supply. Thus, the question of business and corporate influence on the political system was an established concern in the United States.

The Democratic party—particularly under President Andrew Jackson—opposed the use of the federal government's resources to support economic growth, largely because they perceived this support as primarily benefiting a narrow sector of the economy: the burgeoning industrial manufacturing sector. The Democratic opposition to the central banking system, controlled by the Second Bank of the United States, is one of the first historical episodes where the concept of the "money power" emerged (although the phrase "money power" was not prevalent until later in the century).

This letter, with its concern about the growth of the money power and the dominance of industry over the United States, began to be cited in the early twentieth century (one of the reasons for its disputed authorship) during the progressive era's push for increased regulation and public oversight of corporations. These concerns, however, had persisted in American politics for decades.

Author Biography

Abraham Lincoln was born in Kentucky on February 12, 1809. His father, Thomas, engaged in a number of jobs, including farming and land speculation. The confusing and easily contestable nature of land titles in Kentucky was a key factor in encouraging the family's move across the Ohio River to Indiana (where land was surveyed and property described using the more accurate "township and range" system) in 1816. Lincoln's time in formal schools was limited, as their family was far enough out on the western frontier that there were few teachers who were in the area consistently. As a result, he was self-taught in a number of areas, particularly enjoying reading a wide variety of literature. The family moved west to Illinois in 1831, but Abraham, now in his early 20s, moved out on his own, settling in New Salem, Illinois. There, he co-owned a store and attempted to begin a political career running, but losing, a race for the Illinois state legislature.

During the 1830s, he also served in the Illinois militia during the Black Hawk War. His eclectic career continued with stints as a land surveyor and postmaster. Eventually, he began teaching himself from legal textbooks, hoping to become a lawyer. His attempts to enter politics succeeded in 1834 when he was elected to the Illinois legislature, where he served four terms and he passed the bar exam in 1836 and moved to Springfield and began his legal career.

Lincoln married Mary Todd in 1840. His political career expanded in 1847, when he served a single term in the U.S. House of Representatives. Returning to Illinois fulltime in 1849, Lincoln continued his legal practice, often representing railroad companies.

He returned to politics in the 1850s, joining the new Republican Party that had emerged following the collapse of the Whigs in 1856. Losing a contest for the U.S. Senate, Lincoln emerged as the moderate Republican nominee for President in 1860. His election triggered the first wave of southern secession and the establishment of the Confederate States of America.

Aside from the Civil War, Lincoln's policies as president reflected the long-standing goals of the defunct Whig party that had been adopted by the Republicans. Lincoln signed into law the Pacific Railways Acts in 1862 and 1864, which provided support from the federal government for a transcontinental railroad. He supported tariffs to promote domestic industrial growth. Under Lincoln's leadership, the federal government issued paper currency for the first time—a move back toward the central banking of earlier decades. Lincoln's track record of business activity and corporate-friendly policies and positions is one reason why his authorship of these document has been challenged.

HISTORICAL DOCUMENT: "The Money Power"

We may congratulate ourselves that this cruel war is nearing its end. It has cost a vast amount of treasure and blood. . . . It has indeed been a trying hour for the Republic; but I see in the near future a crisis approaching that unnerves me and causes me to tremble for the safety of my country. As a result of the war, corporations have been enthroned and an era of corruption in high places will follow, and the money power of the country will endeavor to prolong its reign by working upon the prejudices of the people until all wealth is aggregated in a few hands and the Republic is destroyed.

I feel at this moment more anxiety for the safety of my country than ever before, even in the midst of war. God grant that my suspicions may prove groundless.

GLOSSARY

enthroned: placed in a position of power and authority

"the money power": a pejorative term that characterizes the financial elite as a corrupt and destructive influence in American politics

"the Republic": a reference to the United States

Document Analysis

In this brief passage in his letter to Colonel Elkins, the author begins by observing (or, perhaps, hopefully predicting) that the "cruel" Civil War is approaching its conclusion. Despite the massive manhunts of money spent and lives lost in the War, the author claims to be "unnerve[d]" by a future "crisis": the fact that "corporations have been enthroned" is the cause for his concern and he predicts that corruption in "high places" will follow. The "high places" referred to here is left undefined but can reasonably be assumed to refer to corruption in the federal government. The author also outlines his suspicions of a campaign in which the "money power" will exploit divisions and "prejudices" among the American people in an effort to concentrate wealth "in a few hands."

Like the reference to "high places," the discussion of the means and method by which the "money power" will "work" upon the peoples' prejudices is left vague; likewise, the concern that the American republic will be "destroyed" is left up to the imagination. Rhetorically, we see the "money power" referred to in monarchical terms, with terms such as "enthroned" and "reign." This is contrasted with the nation, which is explicitly referred to as "the Republic"—a way of contrasting the sides of the struggle between the wealthy elite and the American people in a manner that causes readers to recall the American War of Independence. The author explains that he is more concerned about these potential developments than about the ongoing Civil War and concludes with a prayer that his "suspicions may prove groundless."

Essential Themes

The vague and almost prophetic nature of this excerpt is akin to what we often see in writing from a viewpoint of conspiracy theory or political paranoia. At the same time, it is also possible to interpret the vagueness as being due to this being a brief personal letter rather than an organized, well thought-out treatise. From the standpoint of late 1864, we can see the roots of the author's concern being clear in the growth of northern industry during the Civil War, supported by the many hundreds of contracts with the federal government for weapons, ammunition, food, uniforms, and other supplies needed for the war effort, in addition to the increasing amount of consumer goods being produced. The war itself provided fuel for the growth of the corporations that the author predicts will be the next enemy of the American people.

—*Aaron James Gulyas, MA*

Bibliography and Additional Reading

Appleby, Joyce. *The Relentless Revolution: A History of Capitalism*. New York: W.W. Norton, 2011.

Boritt, Gabor S. *Lincoln and the Economics of the American Dream*. Champaign-Urbana: University of Illinois Press, 1994.

Licht, Walter. *Industrializing America: The Nineteenth Century*. Baltimore: The Johns Hopkins University Press, 1995.

McPherson, James M. *Abraham Lincoln*. London and New York: Oxford University Press, 2009.

Booms & Busts In A Growing Economy

Unlike Europe, the United States from the outset had no strong guild tradition to tie its workers together in a common purpose. It had no officially established state church to intervene in (and benefit from) commercial activity. It had no hereditary aristocracy to control wealth and stifle competition from upstarts. It had no powerful standing army to threaten rivals regarding trade or other matters. As a result, business competition thrived, even coming to be understood as something of a moral imperative (or so said the sociologists Max Weber in *The Protestant Ethic and the Spirit of Capitalism* [English trans., 1930]). In fact, the most important US government intervention in business affairs was not the control of activity but the enforcement of an established set of laws, including patent rights and property laws. Meanwhile, state governments made it relatively easy to secure corporate charters for banks, port facilities, transport operations, factories, and other enterprises. In general, the United States has regulated its economy less than other countries have done. At the same time, it has been subject to cycles of boom and bust perhaps more than other industrialized countries.

The post–Civil War growth of the railroad industry—including the completion of the first transcontinental line—allowed business owners in this and related fields (e.g., steel) to establish national corporations having influence in most states and territories. With the rise of such firms in the 1870s and 1880s, state governments responded in some cases with antitrust legislation aimed at preventing "big business" from muscling out smaller competition. In 1890, the US Congress passed the Sherman Anti-Trust Act, outlawing cartels and monopolies. It would not, however, be until the administration of Theodore Roosevelt in the early twentieth century that federal prosecutors would start to break up some of the larger corporations (or threaten to do so unless they changed their ways).

The period between the 1890s and the 1920s came to be known as the Progressive Era for these and other such socioeconomic reform measures. However, there were also those who, amid the progressive surge, cultivated the idea of "survival of the fittest" based on a flimsy understanding of Darwinian evolution and its application to human social life. These same people were often at a loss, though, to explain the operation of business cycles—booms and busts. That responsibility instead came to rest with a new breed of academic economists, even as politicians continued to have their say in the public arena. By the nineteen-teens, after a few such cycles, it was time to enact economic strengthening measures in the form of a Federal Reserve—i.e., a strong central banking system—along with a federal income tax. These measures displeased many at the time and even today remain sticking points in some corners.

The economists gained further credence during World War I, when, working at the War Industries Board, they helped gauge America's war readiness and prepare the nation for military action abroad and financial stability at home (as much as that was possible). After the war, the National Bureau of Economic Research continued to collect and analyze data in the hope of anticipating harmful fluctuations in the economy. No one, however, foresaw the coming of the Great Depression of the 1930s (much to the dismay of the economists themselves). Once the depression was underway, the ideas of the British economist John Maynard Keynes came to dominate economic theory and practice. Keynes endorsed the notion of a more active government role in the economy, including implementing changes to taxes and expenditures. He also endorsed the actions taken by US president Franklin D. Roosevelt in addressing the many problems created by the depression. In some sense, in fact, FDR's policies represented Keynesianism in action.

■ Documents Relating to Black Friday, 1869

Date: 1869 and September 24, 1869
Authors: Currier & Ives; New York Gold Exchange
Genre: editorial, report

Summary Overview

The Currier & Ives editorial cartoon reproduced here, along with the picture of the chalkboard tracking gold prices at the New York Gold Exchange, were two images representing one of several scandals occurring during the administration of President Ulysses S. Grant—although this particular one, the financial crash known as Black Friday (1869), was not of Grant's making. Attempts to rig markets that traded in various commodities have happened for centuries. In 1869, two wealthy financiers, Jay Gould and James Fisk, decided to rig the gold market; they also sought at least tacit consent from the president. The scheme seemed to be working well for the two investors until September 24, when Grant determined that the dramatic increase in gold prices was not welcome. The results of the president's actions came to be reflected in the price board, which showed the price of gold peaking at $162.50 at 11:36 a.m., holding most of its value for the next few hours, and then plummeting to $133.375 at 2:52 p.m., when trading closed for a short time. The illustrators Currier & Ives captured the situation by depicting Fisk prodding bulls and bears—symbols of Wall Street growth and decline, respectively—just as Grant comes charging out from the Treasury. Both of these graphic portrayals of events proved effective in conveying the dramatic developments of that day to the public.

Defining Moment

The economic pressures wrought by the Civil War forced great changes on the operation of the government of the United States. In 1861, Congress authorized the printing of paper money, "Demand Notes," to help finance the war. Prior to that, June 1776 had been the last time that paper money (a $2 Continental note) had been authorized by the central government (such as it was at the time). In the interim, currency meant coins, which contained precious metals such as gold or silver; this gave them an intrinsic value in addition to the face value ascribed to them by the federal government. The "Demand Notes" of 1861 were followed in 1862 by "Legal Tender Notes," which were not received enthusiastically by the public. At times during the Civil War, one hundred paper dollars were valued at only thirty-seven gold or silver dollars. In the years after the war, when both forms of currency were still widely circulated, the "exchange" rate settled at about one hundred thirty-seven paper to one hundred gold/silver.

Early in 1869, the price of gold rose to $131, and Jay Gould was able to buy it and make a handsome profit by selling it at $145 before the price settled back to its normal range. This started him thinking about the profits that could be made if gold rose to $200. With James Fisk, Jr., as his major partner, Gould began strategically buying gold to force up the price. On September 24, Grant realized that he had been led by Gould into indirectly supporting this scheme, by agreeing to not sell government gold during September. Now Grant, however, authorized the immediate sale of $5-million worth of gold (some sources say $4 million) by the Treasury, an amount that was actually more than the government had on hand (or at least readily available). The authorization served its purpose. The price of gold, which had been at $132 in August, was at $150 on September 10, according to the data on the chalkboard. After fluctuations, the price closed at $145 on September 23. Thus, on the 24 of September gold had a swing from up twelve points to down nine points, before trading was temporarily halted. The price board documented this change, while the cartoon ridiculed Fisk and Gould for the attempt. Yet, Gould had discovered on the 23rd that Grant was considering making a change, which caused him to begin selling more than he was buying. In the end the financier netted about $12 million from his scheme.

Author Biography

Nathan Currier (1813-1888) and James Merritt Ives (1824-1895) were artists and lithographers, running the most successful lithography studio in nineteenth century America. While today, the partnership is best known for its sentimental Victorian-style illustrations of life in the United States, Currier's initial success was in depicting through lithography current and historically significant events. His depictions of disasters, such as the fire at the New York Merchant's Exchange, gained him a contract with the *New York Sun* for weekly prints. This was the venue for the publication of items such as "The Boy of the Period Stirring up the Animals." Ives had joined the firm by the mid-1850s, and became a partner in 1857. His understanding of trends and demands for lithographs was his contribution to the firm. While the two published their own work (which ranged over the breadth of life in the United States), they also brought the work of other artists to the general population, making and coloring lithographs of artists' works. It was estimated that during the pair's partnership, their company produced over 7,000 distinct lithographs, printing hundreds of thousands of copies overall.

The chalkboard was the ongoing record of the prices of transactions and the time of those transactions, kept by the New York Gold Exchange. This was established in 1862, when the government began printing paper money. The New York Gold Exchange became part of the New York Stock Exchange in 1865, and closed its operations in 1897. This board was used as evidence before the Committee of Banking and Currency in 1870, which may explain why the caption, which was written then, mistakenly gives the year of Black Friday as 1870 rather than 1869.

Documents Relating to Black Friday, 1869 • 183

HISTORICAL DOCUMENT

A cartoon showing Jim Fisk stirring up the gold market in New York. Grant is shown running holding a bag of gold. By Currier & Ives, 1869 - Library of Congress.

Photograph of the blackboard in the New York Gold Room, September 24, 1869, showing the collapse of the price of gold. Handwritten caption by James A. Garfield indicates it was used as evidence before the Committee of Banking & Currency during hearings in 1870.

Documents Relating to Black Friday, 1869 • 185

> **GLOSSARY**
>
> **Black Friday:** refers to a day when financial markets collapse, such as Black Friday, September 24, 1869, and Black Monday, October 19, 1987

Document Theme and Analysis

The chalkboard (called a bulletin board in the photo's caption) showing the price of gold during the day of September 24, 1869, was captured in a photograph that was used as evidence in a Congressional hearing occurring in 1870. When Rep. James A. Garfield, as chairperson of the House Committee on Banking and Currency, was given the task of coordinating a full investigation of what had occurred, he made certain that the task was completed in such a manner that Grant, a fellow Republican, might once again have the public's confidence. While there have been times when a dramatic price increase for a stock or commodity has been justified, the significant increase during that month, and even the past twenty-four hours, indicate that the market was not operating efficiently. Prior to September 1869, the U.S. government held weekly gold auctions to keep the supply relatively equal to the demand. However, Gould, making use of Grant's brother-in-law (Abel Corbin) and a political ally (Daniel Butterfield) who was sub-treasurer in New York, convinced Grant that it would be beneficial to farmers if the government did not hold gold sales in September. (Many famers' profits depended on the crop prices which were pegged to the international price of their crops, with international sales being conducted in gold currency, not paper money; thus with high gold prices, they would be better off when they converted their revenue into paper currency.) When Grant finally realized that he had been tricked and issued an order to release gold from the Treasury, the collapse in prices was reflected on the board. Among other things, the price collapse caused many farmers to lose money on that year's crops. While the judgment of history has been that Grant did not knowingly participate in the plan to corner the gold market, it was one of a number of scandals that seemed to indicate he was an incompetent chief executive.

When Currier and Ives produced their editorial cartoon about the events surrounding Black Friday, they depicted the "zoo" that the New York Gold Exchange (often referred to as the Gold Room) had become. Jim Fisk, a key driver of the turmoil, is shown using a prod to stir up the bears and bulls in the cage. Although it was unclear when, or why, these animals first became associated with an upward market (bull) or a downward market (bear), by the time of this cartoon these images were coming to be widely understood in America. Fisk (the "boy of the period") was attempting to stir up a bull market to get the price of gold to climb another $40. He partially succeeded, by having his agents announce on the morning of September 24 that they would pay $160 for the commodity, up to $1-million worth, hence the inscription on the prod. Fisk is clearly identified by the toy Erie Railroad engine in his hip pocket, a rail line he owned with Gould, and by other possessions of his. Attempting to calm the disturbance, President Grant runs out from the U.S. Treasury building toward the Gold Room, carrying a bag marked "5 million gold." Even without a sale of that much gold, a statement that such a sale could take place is enough to cause a collapse in gold prices.

In this case, when the bursting of the bubble occurred and brought gold prices back to their

Panic in Gold room on Black Friday.

normal range, it spilled over into the stock market, which similarly lost about 25 percent of its value. The millions that were lost led to great financial hardship, widespread bankruptcies, and some suicides. Because Gould and Fisk were allies of William Marcy Tweed, who controlled New York politics, when they were brought to trial a combination of good lawyers and Tweed-appointed judges meant that they were found innocent on all charges. An 1870 Congressional hearing, in which the picture of the blackboard was used, found President Grant innocent of any involvement in the scheme and identified the true culprits as Gould and Fisk.

—*Donald A. Watt, PhD*

Bibliography and Additional Reading

American Experience. "Black Friday, September 24, 1869." *PBS: American Experience*. Boston: WGBH Educational Foundation, 2018. Web. 13 July 2018.

Armstrong Economics. "Panic of 1869" *Armstrong Economics*. Princeton: Armstrong Economics, 2018. Web. 13 July 2018.

Garfield, James A. and the House Committee on Banking and Currency. Investigation into the causes of the gold panic. Report of the majority of the Committee on banking and currency. March 1, 1870. Washington: United States Printing Office, 1870 at Internet Archive. San Francisco: Internet Archive, 2009. Web. 13 July 2018.

Renehan, Edward J., Jr. *Dark Genius of Wall Street: The Misunderstood Life of Jay Gould, King of the Robber Barons*. New York: Basic Books, 2005. Print.

Observations Regarding the Transcontinental Railroad

Date: July 2, 1867; May 10, 1869 (published 1923)
Author: Editors of *Harper's Weekly*; Alexander Toponce
Genre: editorial; memoir

Summary Overview

Congress authorized the building of the first railroad across the western parts of the United States in the summer of 1862 with the passage of the Pacific Railroad Act. The two excerpts included here deal with the building of this railroad, the combined Union Pacific and Central Pacific. The editorial from *Harper's Weekly* was written almost two years before the railroad was completed, and speculates grandly about the impact that the railroad could be expected to have. It is typical of the kind of enthusiasm many Americans had for the project and the benefits they expected to flow from it. The second excerpt is from the reminiscences of Alexander Toponce, a Western businessman who supplied beef to the railroad's construction crews and was at Promontory Summit when the railroad was completed on May 10, 1869. He describes the celebratory spirit of that occasion, when a special ceremony was held to commemorate the driving of the "last spike."

Defining Moment

In the 1840s, the United States settled the controversy with Great Britain over the Pacific Northwest and also acquired most of the American Southwest as a result of the war with Mexico from 1846 to 1848. Almost immediately, speculation arose about the possibility of building a railroad across the western region. Before the Civil War, however, Congressional debates over the railroad invariably became entangled in the sectional controversy, as Northern and Southern interests each wanted the first line in their region. During the Civil War, when Southern congressmen were not present, the Republican-controlled Congress passed the Pacific Railroad Act, which was signed by President Abraham Lincoln on July 1, 1862. The bill gave a federal business charter to a new railroad corporation, the Union Pacific, to build westward from the Missouri River. It also gave a charter to the Central Pacific Railroad, an existing short line in California, to build eastward from Sacramento, CA. In order to finance this massive construction venture, the government gave generous aid, including massive land grants and cash loans, to the two corporations. The land grants included ten square miles of government land for each mile of track built; this was later increased to twenty square miles per mile of track. The government also agreed to negotiate with the Indians to obtain title to the lands the railroads would cross. The railroads could sell their land to settlers to raise money for construction. However, since the settlers were not likely to come until the railroad was built, in practice the railroads had to borrow money through bond sales, hoping that later shipping revenues and land sales would generate the funds to repay these obligations. Together, the Union Pacific and Central Pacific received about 45,000,000 acres of federal land.

While the gold rush of the late 1840s had brought much settlement and development to California, the first transcontinental railroad was largely built through unsettled land, with few customers needing the transportation services the railroad would provide. In a sense, then, the railroads were built for future needs—creating the railroad would bring the farms, ranches, mines, lumbering companies, and other businesses that would need to ship their products and buy manufactured goods from the East. Economists describe this concept as "building ahead of demand." Because they had vast lands they needed to sell, all of the western railroads that received land grants were heavily involved in promotion of settlement and townsite development, often sending agents to Europe to attract immigrants to come and buy land from the railroads. Even if settlers bought land from the government, or got land free through homesteading, the railroads stood to benefit from the traffic that their economic activity would stimulate. These two excerpts ably illustrate the sense of expectancy and the hopes for the future that surrounded the building of the first transcontinental railroad.

Author Biography

The 1867 editorial from *Harper's Weekly* was an unsigned piece by the editorial staff. *Harper's Weekly* was one of the most prominent American journals of its day. It was founded in 1850 by the book publishers Harper and Brothers. Alexander Toponce (1839–1923), the author of the reminiscence about the "Golden Spike" ceremony, was an emigrant from France who had his hand in several different business ventures on the western frontier. Most of his later life was spent in Idaho, the southern parts of Montana, and northern Utah. He prospected for gold, ran freighting businesses with wagon trains, and when the transcontinental railroad was being built, he contracted with both the Central Pacific and Union Pacific to provide beef for their work camps. His *Reminiscences of Alexander Toponce*, from which this excerpt is taken, was published by his wife shortly after his death.

HISTORICAL DOCUMENT: Observations Regarding the Transcontinental RR

[*Harper's Weekly* editorial on the transcontinental railroad, 1867]

We have ... expressed the belief that the constantly changing wants and exigencies of a growing country like ours demand, and will compel, a radical change in our present railway system; that with the completion of the grand arterial road across the continent to the Pacific, all other roads must become tributary and subservient to it—the direction of railway traffic (freights) being traverse to the water communication that cuts the country from north to south. A consolidation of railroad interests will naturally result, as well as a change in the mode of operating and running. The future requirements are already foreseen and felt; the first movement toward the new order of things is the proposed combination of leading railroads to form a great Western route under one management. The parties to the combination are the New York Central, Lake Shore, Cleveland and Toledo, Michigan Southern, and those other roads that constitute the northernmost tier of transverse communication. Another rival organization is promised, to include a more southern route, and will embrace the Pennsylvania Central, Pittsburg, Fort Wayne and Chicago, etc. Their interests will not conflict; on the contrary, the commercial necessities of the country will on the course of time require one or two more routes still further south to convey the produce of the sea-board States to their western destination.

When the Pacific Railroad is completed in 1870, all these gigantic tributaries will converge toward the main stem, like the fingers of a hand. All the immense and richly productive districts of the Atlantic and the East will contribute to supply the vital fluid that courses through them. Even the vast domain of the "New Dominion" [i.e., Canada] ... will be induced to furnish its quota of subsistence. But the seat of the vital principle will be in the city of New York. There will the mighty beat of its palpitation be heard. Already the commercial centre of America, it will then, by its geographical position, become the commercial centre of the world. We do not assume that the Pacific Railway will supersede vessels in the carrying trade, for that would be impossible; a dozen lines of railroad could not furnish the required transportation, even if it could carry as cheaply. But from its closer relations and proximity to other countries, New York could command the commerce. It would be as nearly united to Asia as it has been to Europe. The distance to China, now accomplished in forty-three to forty-five days, will be shortened to thirty days. A letter will reach Hong Kong by way of San Francisco much quicker than when it went by way of Liverpool, just as our enterprise had shortened the time of our communication with Brazil. The London banker would no longer pocket the commissions and the exchange on the immense trade carried on between New York and China, as well as South American and the West Indies; but New York would become, to America at least, what London is not to the rest of the world, namely, the place on which exchange is universally drawn. Millions of dollars would thereby be saved to our merchants annually, to say nothing of the difference of time, which is as precious as money.

We have heretofore spoken of the advantages to be obtained by the operation of the Pacific Railroad in developing the treasures of California and the Rocky Mountain region, and the easy access it afford to Asiatic trade. The gains, to be sure, are for the present purely speculative, but it is easy to conjecture the results from past experience. And we are to obtain all this by an estimated outlay of $45,000,000 currency for a road 1565 miles long ... It will take time to overcome the commercial and financial derangement which the late war inflicted upon the court, and to stimulate the productive interests of the several sections to their full capacity; but by the time the Pacific Railroad is completed we hope to lie upon the top wave of prosperity, and to tax our new lines of intercommunication to their utmost limit.

* * *

[Alexander Topance on the Golden Spike ceremonies, Promontory Summit, Utah, May 10, 1869]

I saw the Golden Spike driven at Promontory, Utah, on May 10th, 1869. I had a beef contract to furnish meat to the construction camps of Benson and West. This West was my good friend. Bishop Chauncey W. West of Ogden. They had a grading contract with the Central Pacific and their camp was near Blue Creek. I also furnished beef for some of the Union Pacific contractors.

The Golden Spike could have been driven a couple of weeks earlier than it was. But the two companies had settled on Promontory as the meeting place some days prior to the actual meeting.

The Central Pacific had been planning to make the junction at Ogden as to be in touch with Salt Lake City and the settlements in Utah. But the Union Pacific planned to lay their iron as far west as Humboldt Wells, in Nevada, and had most of their grade completed that far west.

If the Union Pacific had crowded their work as hard as the Central Pacific did in the last two weeks the Golden Spike would have been driven a good many miles to the west. The Union Pacific employed white labor, largely Irish, and the Central Pacific had Chinese labor. The Irish and Chinese met on Promontory Hill.

The Union Pacific sold to the Central Pacific fifty-six miles of road, which brought the real junction back to a point five miles north of the Ogden depot, and then leased that five miles to the Central Pacific, making Ogden the junction.

On the last day only about 100 feet were laid and everybody tried to have a hand in the work. I took a shovel from an Irishman and threw a shovel full of dirt on the ties just to tell about it afterward.

A special train from the west brought Governor Leland Stanford of California and C. P. Huntington, Crocker, Hopkins and lots of California wine.

Another special train from the east brought Sidney Dillon, General Dodge, T. C. Durant, John R. Duff, S. A. Seymour, a lot of newspaper men, and plenty of the best brands of champagne.

Another train made up at Ogden carried the band from Fort Douglas, the leading men of Utah Territory, and a small, but efficient supply, of Valley Tan.

It was a very hilarious occasion, everybody had all they wanted to drink all the time. Some of the participants got "sloppy" and these were not all Irish and Chinese, by any means.

California furnished the Golden Spike. Governor Tuttle of Nevada furnished one of silver. General [i.e., Governor] Stanford presented one of gold, silver and iron from Arizona. The last tie was of California laurel.

When they came to drive the last spike. Governor Stanford, president of the Central Pacific, took the sledge and the first time he struck he missed the spike and hit the rail.

What a howl went up! Irish, Chinese, Mexicans, and everybody yelled with delight. Everybody slapped everybody else on the back and yelled "He missed it. Yee." The engineers blew the whistles and rang their bells. Then Stanford tried it again and tapped the spike and the telegraph operators had fixed their instruments so that the tap was reported in all the offices, east and west, and set bells to tapping in hundreds of towns and cities. W. N. Shilling was one of the telegraph operators.

Then Vice President T. C. Durant of the Union Pacific took up the sledge and he missed the spike the first time. Then everybody slapped everybody else again and yelled, "He missed it, [too], yow!"

It was a great occasion, everyone carried off souvenirs and there are enough splinters of the last tie in museums to make a good bonfire. When the connection was finally made the U. P. and the C. P. engineers ran their engines up until their pilots touched. Then the engineers shook hands and had their pictures taken and each broke a bottle of champagne on the pilot of the other's engine and had their pictures taken again.

The [C. P.] engine, the "Jupiter," was driven by my good friend, George Lashus, who still lives in Ogden.

Both before and after the spike driving ceremony there were speeches, which were cheered heartily. I do not remember what any of the speakers said now, but I do remember that there was a great abundance of champagne.

Document Analysis

These two excerpts clearly illustrate the excitement that surrounded the subject of the first railroad across the American West. Great things were expected to result from the completion of the first line, the combined Union Pacific and Central Pacific route from Omaha, Nebraska to Sacramento, California. The editorial in *Harper's Weekly*, written nearly two years before the line was completed, envisioned that all eastern railroads would become "tributary and subservient to it." The editors also predicted a merger or "combination" of all the leading roads in the East to form one "Western route under one management." While there have been many mergers in the history of American railroading, this prediction did not become true. Instead, the different railroads continued to operate independently, but interchanged traffic to create a national transportation network. The prediction that when the Pacific Railroad was completed, these tributary railroads "will converge toward the main stem, like the fingers of a hand," did come to pass in a sense. Eventually, five major railroad lines were built across the American West, and each of these companies built branches that reached north and south off of their trunk lines, and smaller regional railroads also interconnected with the transcontinental lines. Likewise, the prediction that New York would become a major world trade center was also fulfilled.

The second excerpt is from Alexander Toponce's memoirs of his days on the western frontier. Toponce had contracted with the railroads to provide beef for the camps of the construction crews. The Central Pacific Railroad had built 881 miles eastward from Sacramento, CA, and the Union Pacific had built 1,032 miles westward from Omaha, NE. Since the two companies received generous land grants and loans from the government for each mile of track built, they competed to build the most track and refused to coordinate a meeting place until Congress dictated that the two lines would meet at Promontory, near Ogden in the Utah Territory. As Toponce notes, much of the Central Pacific's work force was immigrant Chinese labor, while the Union Pacific employed many Irish laborers. African Americans workers, many of them former slaves, also worked on the Union Pacific construction crews.

With his frequent references to the quantities and varieties of alcoholic beverages consumed, Toponce captures the celebratory mood of the day when the railroad was completed. Commemorative spikes of precious metals were temporarily installed, but the final spike was an iron one attached to telegraph lines. When Leland Stanford, former governor of California and president of the Central Pacific, hammered in the last spike, the message was to be instantly telegraphed across the nation. Stanford missed when he swung at the spike, but the telegraphers sent the message anyway. Nearly six years after Congress had authorized its construction, the Pacific Railroad was completed on May 10, 1869.

Essential Themes

These excerpts illustrate the sense of expectancy and promise that accompanied the building of the first transcontinental railroad. Although the railroad was built through regions that had very few non-Indian inhabitants, many political leaders, businessmen, editors and journalists believed the railroad would lead to widespread settlement and development throughout the region. Many of these predictions came true; farming and ranching in the Great Plains region, for example, boomed in the last decades of the nineteenth century. Little of this development would have been possible without the railroad to bring people and supplies to the frontier and to ship the commodities produced there to market. The railroad companies were heavily involved in "boosterism," extolling the virtues of the land they owned in the West in order to attract settlers. People who settled these lands sometimes charged that they were misled about the quality of the land and the climate. Eventually, four transcontinental lines were completed across the West, which all received government land grants. Besides the Union Pacific and Central Pacific, these included the Atchison, Topeka, and Santa Fe; the Southern Pacific; and the Northern Pacific—the latter three all being finished in 1883. A fifth transcontinental, the Great Northern, was completed in 1895, but did not receive a land grant from the federal government.

In time, the enthusiasm for the western railroads cooled. Farmers and businessmen who settled in the West realized the railroad made their commerce possible, but they also realized that, with few viable alternative forms of transportation, they were captive to the railroads' interests. The building of the transcontinental railroads also involved considerable mismanagement, waste, and outright fraud. When scandals such as the Crédit Mobilier affair became widely known, public opinion began to turn against the railroad companies. In the late nineteenth century, agrarian protest movements, such as the Grangers and the Populists, attacked the railroads and called for government ownership, or failing that, strict government regulation of railroad business practices. Many laws regulating the railroads were enacted during the Progressive Era in the early twentieth century.

—Mark S. Joy, PhD

Bibliography and Additional Reading

Ambrose, Stephen E. *Nothing Like It in the World: The Men Who Built the Transcontinental Railroad, 1863–1869.* New York: Simon and Schuster, 2000. Print.

Bain, David Hayward. *Empire Express: Building the First Transcontinental Railroad.* New York: Penguin Books, 1999. Print.

White, Richard. *Railroaded: The Transcontinentals and the Making of Modern America*. New York: W. W. Norton, 2011. Print.

Williams, John Hoyt. *A Great and Shining Road: The Epic Story of the Transcontinental Railway*. Lincoln: University of Nebraska Press, 1996. Print.

■ Cornelius Vanderbilt Cartoon, Map, and Illustration

Dates: 1870; c. 1890; 1876
Authors: Currier and Ives; unknown; unknown
Genres: cartoon; map; and drawing

Summary Overview

Each of the illustrations reproduced here invokes aspects of Cornelius Vanderbilt's struggle to gain control of the Erie Railroad during the late-1860s. Vanderbilt already controlled the two railroad lines he stands over in the Currier and Ives cartoon: The Hudson Rover Railroad and the New York Central. Those two lines, running north from New York City and west to the Great Lakes, were a popular path between New York City and Chicago, not to mention all the rest of the American West during this era. The Erie Railroad also crossed New York State from east to west. Vanderbilt wanted to control the Erie so that he would have a monopoly over this important route.

Upstart stock traders Jay Gould and Jim Fisk controlled the Erie when Vanderbilt began to accumulate stock in the line in 1867. In response to that effort, they and Erie Director Daniel Drew issued an increasing amount of worthless stock in order to make Vanderbilt's objective more expensive or ultimately impossible. When a New York State judge got involved, Gould and Fisk fled to New Jersey in order to maintain control of the railroad. Eventually, Vanderbilt brokered a deal with Gould and Fisk, allowing them to keep control of the railroad and getting the money he had paid for the worthless stock returned to him.

Defining Moment

The so-called Erie War was a historic struggle in late-nineteenth century America because it showed off many of industrial capitalism's worst traits. First, while he denied that he wanted a monopoly, Vanderbilt himself was primarily interested in the railroad in order to restrict competition with his own lines. While there were other ways to travel between the east and west besides these railroads, at least controlling the Erie would have allowed him to end the price war that threatened his extensive investments. There was the corruption involved: Jay Gould bribed New York State legislators to keep control of the railroad, yet nobody was punished for this malfeasance. Finally, the Erie itself was a badly run railroad that was not particularly good at transporting people or cargo. This is evidence that most large American businesses simply did not care about consumers.

Railroads were the first gigantic industrial concerns in the United States. They took a lot of capital to build and maintain. Therefore, the men who ran them wanted a good return for their investment. Railroad profits, in turn, fueled the growth of other American industries as these corporations grew larger. For example, railroads consumed huge amounts of pig iron and coal. Their demand helped fuel the industrialization and consolidation of those industries for the remainder of the nineteenth century.

Had Vanderbilt won the struggle over the Erie Railroad, the growth of railroad lines between New York and Chicago might have proceeded very differently. When Vanderbilt consolidated his two lines into the New York Central & Hudson River Railroad, he created the first great bureaucratic corporation in American history. While a complete monopoly over railroad travel was impossible, Vanderbilt's aspirations to prevent ruinous competition set the stage for leaders in other industries like Andrew Carnegie and James "Buck" Duke who grew their businesses to extraordinary size in order to prevent the same thing.

Subject Biography

Born in 1794, Cornelius Vanderbilt got his start commanding a steamship that transported oysters from his native Staten Island to market in Manhattan. This explains his nickname "Commodore." Early in his career, he worked for Thomas Gibbons, who successfully challenged a steamship monopoly granted to Aaron Ogden in a celebrated 1824 Supreme Court case. In this work, he developed considerable skill coordinating business activity over a wide geographic area.

Vanderbilt began his business career investing in other steamships and running ferry lines around the New York/Jersey area. He started investing in oceangoing steamships when the California Gold Rush began in 1849. Vanderbilt ran steamships from New York to Nicaragua, stagecoaches across Nicaragua, and more ships between the West Coast of Nicaragua and California during this time. During the 1850s, he was involved in a failed effort to build a canal across Nicaragua that was surrounded by intrigue.

Vanderbilt became a director in several railroads during the 1850s. In 1863, he took control of the New York and Harlem and became its president. He gained control of the Hudson Railroad in 1864 and the New York Central in 1867. The Grand Central Depot, finished in 1871, was the terminus of his railroad routes between the Great Lakes and New York City. The better known Grand Central Station replaced that building in 1913. Vanderbilt died in 1877, leaving enough money to his many children to keep the Vanderbilt name as synonymous with wealth down to today.

HISTORICAL DOCUMENTS: Cornelius Vanderbilt Cartoon, Map and Illus.

Vanderbilt jockeying for control of railroads against Jim Fisk (by Currier and Ives, 1870).

Map of the New York Central and Hudson Railroad, circa 1890.

Grand Central Depot in Manhattan, early 1870s.

Document Analysis

Cornelius Vanderbilt was a legendarily quiet man. He didn't speak much, and when he did he kept his sentences short and sweet. "He talked very little," one acquaintance recalled. "Vanderbilt, as is well known, is remarkable for terseness of expression, a compacted force of argument, and Spartan simplicity, rarely to be equalled" (Stiles, p. 223). He also avoided public speaking because of his lack of education, so it is little wonder that he wrote very little. That is largely why we look here at illustrations concerning Vanderbilt and his business rather than text documents.

The cartoon labeled "The Great Race for the Western Stakes" is surprisingly literal for the cartoons of this era. Vanderbilt and Jim Fisk, standing on top of railroad engines representing their holdings compete over whom could get the biggest head of steam going to win the race for the prize of Western markets. Vanderbilt is depicted as bigger, not because he has two railroads, but because he was well known to be the wealthier competitor in the race for the control of the Erie. Fisk's retort, "Don't stop for water or you'll be beat," implies that Fisk was getting the best of him by issuing watered stock.

The map of the New York Central and Hudson River Railroad simultaneously implies that the railroad has no competition and implies that it is better than its competition. The giant hand covers the Pennsylvania Railroad, the main competition to Vanderbilt's line and omits the Erie Railroad altogether. That's because it's only a map of lines owned or affiliated with the Vanderbilt interests. Of course, passengers and freight didn't care how they got from place to place as long as the voyage was completed. All the competition between lines was an inconvenience to people who had to constantly change trains, and the intrigue symbolized by the Erie War only served to drive up prices.

The Grand Central Depot, built by Vanderbilt's Harlem Railroad at 42nd Street and 4th Avenue in 1871, was the largest railway station in North America at that time. Vanderbilt actually paid for it out of his own pocket, which meant that the building was on some level a monument to himself. Indeed, it was an ornate arches and elaborate finish, designed to impress the passengers who came and went through it every day. As the end of the line in New York City and the only terminus for a railroad inside the borough at that time, it became an important symbol of Vanderbilt's influence. Unfortunately, the building was poorly designed. People had to exit the building and go back in again in order to change lines. It was also too small for a growing city, which explains its short lifespan.

In the end, Vanderbilt was most interested in his own wealth rather than any kind of service to the public. With a weak government and few real competitors, this proved a winning strategy for long-term economic success.

Essential Themes

The cartoon invokes many aspects of the culture of industrial capitalism. Businessmen being drawn as large enough to straddle railroad engines suggests both their wealth and their importance to the American economy. Many later cartoons would depict trusts as giant people, but these men are seen as synonymous with their railroads even though neither of them had controlled either for a particularly long time. The idea of a race for the west suggests both the American spirit of Manifest Destiny and the extraordinarily competitive attitude of American capitalists during this era.

Railroad lines, like buildings, were temporary landmarks of the industrial age. Vanderbilt's New York Central and Hudson was in some ways his most lasting legacy, but even this huge mostly private endeavor could no longer thrive a few decades later when cars and trucks became the most common way for people to get around the country. Even on a map that doesn't show every railroad line, the general orientation of lines running between east and west speaks volumes about the relationship between the regions during industrialization. So does the relative lack of railway lines in the South.

The Grand Central Depot was an urban landmark built by private interests, as so many of the best-known buildings of the time were. Its ornate nature hearkened back to earlier eras even though railroads were the most important modern industry of the age. The flaws of the building demonstrated the limits of private enterprise and the limited role of government in regulating anything at that time. It is also interesting that the view of the building doesn't show any of the trains that explain the reason that the building existed. Trains were too dirty and too dangerous to operate in crowded cities, which is why New York City banned steam engines south of 42nd Street. Vanderbilt's ability to locate his depot on the very border of this steam-free zone was therefore an achievement in its own right.

—Jonathan Rees, PhD

Bibliography and Additional Reading

Gordon, John Steele. *The Scarlet Woman of Wall Street: Jay Gould, Jim Fisk, Cornelius Vanderbilt, the Erie Railway Wars, and the Birth of Wall Street*. New York: Weidenfeld & Nicolson, 1988.

Renehan, Edward J., Jr. *Commodore: The Life of Cornelius Vanderbilt*. New York: Basic Books, 2007.

Stiles, T.J. *The First Tycoon: The Epic Life of Cornelius Vanderbilt*. New York: Random House, 2009.

■ Bell Telephone Patent

Date: March 7, 1876
Author: Alexander Graham Bell
Genre: legal document

Summary Overview

In the latter half of the nineteenth century, many individuals were working to improve communication over long distances via electronic devices. Alexander Graham Bell was one of these, and in 1876 filed a patent application. On March 10, based on the specifications of this patent, Graham used the first working model, based on this patent, of what came to be called the telephone. Although telephones have changed dramatically since 1876, the basic concept and some of the technology described in this patent application are still at the heart of the instrument used almost one hundred and fifty years later.

The significance of this patent went beyond Bell being given credit, and monetary income, as the "inventor" of the telephone. Having had most of his research funded by his future father-in-law, Gardiner Hubbard, it was Hubbard who commercialized the invention by forming the Bell Telephone Company in 1877. (Bell held shares in the company and was hired as its technical adviser.) Although other individuals developed similar devices, and some non-Bell devices were even used for a time in a few localities, these were not compatible with Bell's telephone. As a result, the Bell Telephone Company developed a natural monopoly on the provision of telephone service throughout much of the United States, and in supplying and repairing equipment while its patents were in force.

Defining Moment

Although the first telegraph system was developed and constructed in England, in the United States during the 1830s Samuel Morse and his associates developed a simpler telegraph mechanism. From that time forward, people sought ways to improve this system. By the early 1860s, Western Union had become the dominate telegraph company, with lines running from coast to coast. To limit competition, it hired people, such as Thomas Edison, to develop improved transmission mechanisms for it to patent, thereby limiting competition. One improvement Edison made was an instrument that allowed the transmission of four messages at one time. Bell, among others, sought to create a device that would transmit more than four messages, thereby demonstrating that it did not infringe on any of Western Union's patents. While undertaking that "corporate style" research, with funding from Gardiner Hubbard (founder and financial backer of the Clarke School for the Deaf, where Bell taught), Bell's personal interest was in the development of a machine that could transmit speech.

By late 1874, Bell notified Gardiner that he had developed a harmonic telegraph that could operate on up to ten "channels," each being sent/received by a different pitch. In 1875, Bell developed plans for a more complex device that would transmit not just a few pitches but the whole range of human speech. Two competitors, Elisha Gray and Antonia Meucci, both disputed Graham's 1876 patent for his mechanism to transmit the human voice. Meucci had filed a caveat with the Patent Office in 1871 for such a device, but never followed through and it did not mention the use of electromagnetic transmission of a voice. Gray filed a caveat with the Patent Office the same day Bell's attorney filed his patent application. Bell's was stamped as the fifth entry of the day, while Gray's was stamped as the thirty-ninth. Thus, Bell's patent was granted, and Gray's caveat was rejected. Although Bell won the hundreds of legal cases filed regarding his work, which gave him legal title to the invention of the telephone, many historians debate who did what and when—that is, who actually was the first to create a device that could transmit human speech.

Shortly after his successful test of his new device with his assistant, Thomas Watson, Bell wrote a letter to his father indicating (using different words) that he believed in the not too distant future that every home would be connected to a telephone system, just like they were to water and gas. Although in 1876 he offered to sell his patent to Western Union, his offer was rejected, as Western Union executives did not believe it was a serious competitor to their business. Bell Telephone Company soon proved them wrong.

Author Biography

Alexander Graham Bell (1847–1922) was born in Edinburgh, Scotland. Growing up he attended school there, then in London, prior to his family moving to Canada in 1870. In 1871, he moved to Boston and began teaching deaf children, later teaching in other schools for the deaf in New England. He married Mabel Hubbard, a former student, and they had two daughters who survived to become adults.

Building on the work of others, Bell began researching how to send more than four telegraph messages simultaneously through the same wire. One result was the patent granted in 1876. Going beyond the telephone, he continued research in the field of electronics. The results included a sound recording/playback machine and a device, important in World War I, which used electronic waves to locate bullets in wounded soldiers. Other work, such as using light to transmit sound, did not have practical applications until technology caught up with it almost a century later. He supported others, such as his work assisting Glenn Curtiss's aviation advances. In 1880, France gave Bell the Volta Prize, and he used these funds to establish a laboratory to study deafness and ways to improve the lives of the deaf. He also helped found the National Geographic Society and the American Association for the Advancement of Science's journal, *Science*.

> **HISTORICAL DOCUMENT: Bell Telephone Patent**
>
> ### UNITED STATES PATENT OFFICE.
>
> ### ALEXANDER GRAHAM BELL, OF SALEM, MASSACHUSETTS.
>
> ### IMPROVEMENT IN TELEGRAPHY.
>
> Specification forming part of Letters Patent No. 174,465, dated March 7, 1876; application filed February 14, 1876.
>
> To all whom it may concern:
>
> (1) Be it known that I, ALEXANDER GRAHAM BELL, of Salem, Massachusetts, have invented certain new and useful Improvements in Telegraphy, of which the following is a specification:—
>
> In Letters Patent granted to me April 6, 1875, No. 161,739, I have described a method of, and apparatus for, transmitting two or more telegraphic signals simultaneously along a single wire by the employment of transmitting instruments, each of which occasions a succession of electrical impulses differing in rate from the others; and of receiving instruments, each tuned to a pitch at which it will be put in vibration to produce its fundamental note by one only of the transmitting instruments; and of vibratory circuit-breakers operating to convert the vibratory movement of the receiving instrument into a permanent make or break (as the case may be) of a local circuit, in which is placed a Morse sounder, register, or other telegraphic apparatus. I have also therein described a form of autograph-telegraph based upon the action of the above-mentioned instruments.
>
> In illustration of my method of multiple telegraphy I have shown in the patent aforesaid, as one form of transmitting instrument, an electro-magnet having a steel-spring armature, which is kept in vibration by the action of a local battery. This armature in vibrating makes and breaks the main circuit, producing an intermittent current upon the line wire. I have found, however, that upon this plan the limit to the number of signals that can be sent simultaneously over the same wire is very speedily reached; for, when a number of transmitting instruments, having different rates of vibration, (2) are simultaneously making and breaking the same circuit, the effect upon the main line is practically equivalent to one continuous current.
>
> In a pending application for Letters Patent, filed in the United States Patent Office February 25, 1875, I have described two ways of producing the intermittent current—the one by actual make and break of contact, the other by alternately increasing and diminishing the intensity of the current without actually breaking the circuit. The current produced by the latter method I shall term, for distinction sake, a pulsatory current.

My present invention consists in the employment of a vibratory or undulatory current of electricity in contradistinction to a merely intermittent or pulsatory current, and of a method of, and apparatus for, producing electrical undulations upon the line-wire.

The distinction between an undulatory and a pulsatory current will be understood by considering that electrical pulsations are caused by sudden or instantaneous changes of intensity, and that electrical undulations result from gradual changes of intensity exactly analogous to the changes in the density of air occasioned by simple pendulous vibrations. The electrical movement, like the aerial motion, can be represented by a sinusoidal curve or by the resultant of several sinusoidal curves.

Intermittent or pulsatory and undulatory currents may be of two kinds, accordingly as the successive impulses have all the same polarity or are alternately positive and negative.

The advantages I claim to derive from the use of an undulatory current in place of merely intermittent one are, first, that a very much larger number of signals can he transmitted simultaneously on the same circuit; second, that a closed circuit and single main battery may be used; third, that communication in both directions is established without the necessity of special induction-coils; fourth, that cable dispatches may be transmitted more rapidly than by means of intermittent current or by the methods at present in use; for, as it is unnecessary to discharge the cable before a new signal can he made, the lagging of cable signals is prevented; fifth, and that as the circuit is never broken a spark-arrester becomes unnecessary.

(3) It has long been known that when a permanent magnet is caused to approach the pole of an electro-magnet a current of electricity is induced in the coils of the latter, and that when it is made to recede a current of opposite polarity to the first appears upon the wire. When, therefore, a permanent magnet is caused to vibrate in front of the pole of an electro-magnet an undulatory current of electricity is induced in the coils of the electro-magnet, the undulations of which correspond, in rapidity of succession, to the vibrations of the magnet, in polarity to the direction of its motion, and in intensity to the amplitude of its vibration.

That the difference between an undulatory and an intermittent current may be more clearly understood I shall describe the condition of the electrical current when the attempt is made to transmit two musical notes simultaneously—first upon the one plan and then upon the other. Let the interval between the two sounds be a major third; then their rates of vibration are in the ratio of 4 to 5. Now, when the intermittent current is used the circuit is made and broken four times by one transmitting-instrument in the same time that five makes and breaks are caused by the other. A and B, Figs. 1, 2, and 3, represent the intermittent currents produced, four impulses of B being made in the same time as five impulses of A. c c c, &c., show where and for how long time the circuit is made, and d d d, &c., indicate the duration of the breaks of the circuit. The line A and B shows the total effect upon the current when the transmitting-instruments for A and B are caused simultaneously to make and break the same circuit. The resultant effect depends very much upon the duration of the make relatively to the break. Fig. 1 the ratio is as 1 to 4; in Fig. 2, as 1 to 2; and in Fig. 3 the makes and breaks are of equal duration. The combined effect A and B, Fig. 3, is very nearly equivalent to a continuous current.

I have described a method of, and apparatus for, transmitting two or more telegraphic signals simultaneously along a single wire.

When many transmitting instruments of different rates of vibration are simultaneously making and breaking the same circuit the current upon the main line becomes for all practical purposes continuous.

Next, consider the effect when an undulatory current is employed. Electrical undulations, induced by the vibration of a body capable of inductive action, can be represented graphically, without error, (4) by the same sinusoidal curve which expresses the vibration of the inducing body itself, and the effect of its vibration upon the air; for, as above stated, the rate of oscillation in the electrical body—that is, to the pitch of the sound produced. The intensity of the current varies with the amplitude of the vibration—that is, with the loudness of the sound; and the polarity of the current corresponds to the direction of the vibrating body—that is, to the condensations and rarefactions of air produced by the vibration. Hence, the sinusoidal curve A or B, Fig. 4, represents, graphically, the electrical undulations induced in a circuit by the vibration of a body capable of inductive action.

The horizontal line *a d e f*, &c., represents the zero of current. The elevation *b b b*, &c., indicate impulses of positive electricity. The depressions *c c c*, &c., show impulses of negative electricity. The vertical distance *b d* or *c f* of any portion of the curve from the zero line expresses the intensity of the positive or negative impulse at the part observed, and the horizontal distance *a a* indicates the duration of the electrical oscillation. The vibrations represented by the sinusoidal curves B and A, Fig. 4, are in the ratio aforesaid, of 4 to 5—that is, four oscillations of B are made in the same time as five oscillations of A.

The combined effect of A and B, when induced simultaneously on the same circuit, is expressed by the curve A+B, Fig. 4, which is the algebraic sum of the sinusoidal curves A and B. This curve A+B also indicates the actual motion of the air when the two musical notes considered are sounded simultaneously. Thus, when electrical undulations of different rates are simultaneously induced in the same circuit, an effect is produced exactly analogous to that occasioned in the air by the vibration of the inducing bodies. Hence, the co-existence upon a telegraphic circuit of electrical vibrations to different pitch is manifested, not by the peculiarities in the shapes of the electrical undulations, or, in other words, by the peculiarities in the shapes of the curves which represent those undulations.

There are many ways of producing undulatory currents of electricity, dependent for effect upon the vibrations or motions of bodies (5) capable of inductive action. A few of the methods that may be employed I shall here specify. When a wire, through which a continuous current of electricity is passing, is caused to vibrate in the neighborhood of another wire, an undulatory current of electricity is induced in the latter. When a cylinder, upon which are arranged bar-magnets, is made to rotate in front of the pole of an electro-magnet, an undulatory current is induced in the coils of the electro-magnet.

Undulations are caused in a continuous voltaic current by the vibration of motion of bodies capable of inductive action; or by the vibration of the conducing-wire itself in the neighborhood of such bodies. Electrical undulations may also be caused by alternately increasing and diminishing the resistance of the circuit, or by alternately increasing and diminishing the power of the battery. The internal resistance of a battery is diminished by bringing the voltaic elements nearer together, and increased by placing them further apart. The reciprocal vibration of the elements of a battery, therefore, occasions an undulatory action in the voltaic current. The external resistance may also be varied. For instance, let mercury or some other liquid form part of a voltaic current, then the more deeply the conducting-wire is immersed in the mercury or other liquid, the less resistance does the liquid offer to the passage of the current. The vertical vibration of the elements of a battery in the liquid in which they are immersed produces an undulatory action in the current by alternately increasing and diminishing the power of the battery.

In illustration of the method of creating electrical undulations, I shall show and describe one form of apparatus for producing the effect. I prefer to employ for this purpose an electro-magnet A, Fig. 5, having a coil upon only one of its legs b. A steel-spring armature, c, is firmly clamped by one extremity to the uncovered leg d of the magnet, and its free end is allowed to project above the pole of the uncovered leg. The armature c can be set in vibration in a variety of ways, one of which is by wind, and, in vibrating, it produces a musical note of a certain definite pitch.

(6) When the instrument A is placed in a voltaic circuit, $g\ b\ e\ f\ g$, the armature c becomes magnetic, and the polarity of its free end is opposed to that of the magnet underneath. So long as the armature c remains at rest, no effect is produced upon the voltaic current, but the moment it is set in vibration to produce its musical note a powerful induction action takes place, and electrical undulations transverse the circuit $g\ b\ e\ f\ g$. The vibratory current passing through the coil of the electro-magnet f causes vibration in its armature h when the armature $c\ h$ of the two instruments A I are normally in unison with one another; but the armature h is unaffected by the passage of the undulatory current when the pitches of the two instruments are different.

A number of instruments may be placed upon a telegraphic circuit, instruments is set in vibration all the other instruments upon the circuit which are in unison wiht it respond, but those which have normally a different rate of vibration remain silent. Thus, if A, Fig. 6, is set in vibration, the armatures of A1 and A2 will vibrate also, but all the others will remain still. So, if B1 is caused to emit its musical note the instruments B B2 respond. They continue sounding so long as the mechanical vibration of B1 is continued, but become silent with the cessation of its motion. The duration of the sounds may be used to indicate the dot or dash of the Morse alphabet, and thus a telegraphic dispatch may be indicated by alternately interrupting and renewing the sound. When two or more instruments of different pitch are simultaneously caused to vibrate, all the instruments of corresponding pitches upon the circuit are set in vibration, each responding to that one only of the transmitting instruments with which it is in unison. Thus the signals of A, Fig. 6, are repeated by A1 and A2, but by no other instrument upon the circuit; the signals of B2 by B and B1; and the signals of C1 by C and C2—whether A, B2, and C1 are successively or simultaneously caused to vibrate. Hence by these instruments two or more telegraphic signals or messages may be sent simultaneously over the same circuit without interfering with one another.

I desire here to remark that there are many other uses to which these instruments may be put, such as the simultaneous transmission (7) of musical notes, differing in loudness as well as in pitch, and the telegraphic transmission of noises or sounds of any kind.

When the armature c, Fig. 5, is set in motion the armature h responds not only in pitch, but in loudness. Thus, when c vibrates with little amplitude, a very soft musical note proceeds from h; and when c vibrates forcibly the amplitude of the vibration of h is considerably increased, and the resulting sound becomes louder. So, if A and B, Fig. 6, are sounded simultaneously (A loudly and B softly), the instruments A1 and A2 repeat loudly the signals of A, and B1 B2 repeat softly those of B.

One of the ways in which the armature c, Fig. 5, may be set in motion has been stated above to by by wind. Another mode is shown in Fig. 7, whereby motions can be imparted to the armature by the human voice or by means of a musical instrument.

The armature c, Fig. 7, is fastened loosely by one extremity to the uncovered leg d of the electro-magnet b, and its other extremity is attached to the centre of a stretched membrane, a. A cone, A, is used to converge sound-vibrations upon the membrane. When a sound is uttered in the cone the membrane a is set in vibration, the armature c is forced to partake of the motion, and thus electrical undulations are created upon the circuit E $b\ e\ f\ g$. These undulations are similar in sound to the air vibrations caused by the sound—that is, they are represented graphically by similar curves. The undulatory current passing through the electro-magnet f influences its armature h to copy the motions of the armature c. A similar sound to that uttered into A is the heard to proceed from L.

In this specification the three words "oscillation," "vibration," and "undulation," are used synonymously, and in contradistinction to the terms "intermittent" and "pulsatory." By the term "body capable of inductive action," I mean a body which, when in motion, produces dynamical electricity. I include in the category of bodies capable of inductive action—brass, copper, and other metals, as well as iron and steel.

Having described my invention, what I claim, and desire to secure by Letters Patent, is as follows:

1. A system of telegraphy in which the receiver is set in vibration (8) by the employment of undulatory currents of electricity, substantially as set forth.

2. The combination, substantially as set forth, of a permanent magnet or other body capable of inductive action, with a closed circuit, so that the vibration of the one shall occasion electrical undulations in the other, or in itself, and this I claim, whether the permanent magnet be set in vibration in the neighborhood of the conducting-wire forming the circuit, or whether the conducting-wire be set in vibration in the neighborhood of the permanent magnet, or whether the conducting wire and the permanent magnet both simultaneously be set in vibration in each other's neighborhood.

3. The method of producing undulations in a continuous voltaic current by the vibration of motion of bodies capable of inductive action, or by the vibration or motion of the conducting-wire itself, in the neighborhood of such bodies, as set forth.

4. The method of producing undulations in a continuous voltaic circuit by gradually increasing and diminishing the resistance of the circuit, or by gradually increasing and diminishing the power of the battery, as set forth.

5. The method of, and apparatus for, transmitting vocal or other sounds telegraphically, as herein described, by causing electrical undulations, similar in form to the vibrations of the air accompanying the said vocal or other sounds, substantially as set forth.

In testimony whereof I have hereunto signed my name this 20th day of January, A.D. 1876.

ALEX. GRAHAM BELL.

Witnesses :
   Thomas E. Barry.
   P. D. Richards.

> **GLOSSARY**
>
> **autograph-telegraph:** an early attempt (1861) to transmit drawings by telegraph, doable, but too expensive to operate
>
> **contradistinction:** contrast
>
> **pendulous vibrations:** repeated fluctuations
>
> **sinusoidal:** a wave based on the mathematical sine function
>
> **telegraphy:** having to do with a telegraph system
>
> **undulatory:** moving in the form of a wave

Document Analysis

Although Bell's patent application for an "Improvement in Telegraphy" made no mention of its economic value, as is the case for most patents, what he described and ultimately built had a monumental effect on commerce and people's lives. The technical specifications of this device, and how it differed from previous devices, contained in the patent application were slow and difficult reading for anyone not conversant with mid-nineteenth century electronics. And for some, such as the executives at Western Union who rejected Bell's offer to sell them the patent, the economic value of such a device was also difficult to understand. However, what Bell had created was the basis for a system which would transform the world via simple "electrical undulations" being transmitted from one mechanism to another.

Technologically, Bell introduced the use of variations and vibrations in the electromagnetic waves/circuits as the means to carry the message, rather than using the much simpler circuit on/off function of Morse's telegraph system. As he described in his patent application, while it was possible to send more than one message using the simpler system, any attempt to increase it dramatically resulted in the mechanism's line having "practically equivalent to one continuous current." Thus, Bell's change to the "undulatory currents of electricity" would result in the receiving apparatus replicating the vibrations that had been applied to the sending apparatus. Most of the patent application is a description of the applied physics that made this possible. However, the result of Bell's work was not a system for producing coded messages, such as Morse had developed, although that type of message could be sent using Bell's equipment. What Bell sought, and achieved, was a much more encompassing means of transmission that could go far beyond the on/off of the original telegraph. Bell's "undulatory currents" could be initiated by many things, including the complex waves of human speech. While this was the crowning achievement for Bell, it is interesting to note that it was not mentioned until the next-to-last page of the patent application.

The mechanism described in Bell's patent application was not overly expensive to build or to operate. Thus, while Bell's first telephone looks unwieldy from a twenty-first century vantage point, with a few tweaks it was a practical means of communication once enough sets were put into operation. From the point of view of skeptics, such as the executives of Western Union, the economic value of the new system was minimal, because messages could already be sent efficiently from one Western Union office to another. However, Bell saw his new device as something that would allow direct communication between homes or businesses, not needing to use an intermediary such as Western Union. Once the Bell Telephone Company was established, it quickly became the dominant company for electronic communications, with regional and international companies created to provide equipment and service in various localities and with American Telephone & Telegraph (AT&T) as its long-distance division. At the end of 1899, the company was reorganized under the AT&T name, with the regional systems, laboratories, and manufacturing (Western Electric) as subsidiaries.

Essential Theme

Although Alexander Graham Bell and his associates had to fend off close to six hundred lawsuits relating to Bell's patent, it was money well spent for those who became owners of the new corporation. Bell was fortunate to have had the support, financial and professional, of Gardiner Greene Hubbard and Thomas Sanders. They and Bell were the major shareholders, with two other members of the Hubbard family and Thomas Watson as minor shareholders, when the Bell Telephone Company was incorporated. Bell was not that interested in corporate operations or finance, even transferring 99 percent of his shares to his wife when they married.

Bell's successful patent did not break new ground in terms of electromagnetic theories in physics. However, it did expand the understanding of how to apply those laws to achieve the desired physical results. "Electrical undulations" were demonstrated to be a reliable means of reproducing sounds that had originated near the sending device. This principle was not just applicable to telephones; in fact, it became the foundation to the modern entertainment industry. It can be seen that radios and televisions use almost the exact same system, just updated as technology advanced. While the original "record players" used physical means to amplify the sound, modern audio devices use amplification derived from Bell's work, as did the devices to play movie soundtracks. Thus, while the economic consequences of people having telephones is almost beyond our ability to compute, adding in other electronics that use the same or similar applications of the laws of physics indicates the astronomical impact of Bell's work and patent. Many refer to Bell's patent as the most valuable one ever issued.

Early corporate decisions made Bell's patent worth substantially more than might have been the case. A decision made by his father-in-law resulted in Bell Telephone merely leasing equipment to consumers, not selling it. This insured a continuous income stream, which because of the lack of competition was guaranteed to endure. Eventually, the virtual monopoly on almost all aspects of the telephone industry brought about lawsuits, with AT&T being broken up by regulators in 1984. While this changed the dynamics of the telecommunications industry, it did not diminish the value and impact of Bell's work.

—*Donald A. Watt, PhD*

Bibliography and Additional Reading

Beauchamp, Christopher. *Invented by Law: Alexander Graham Bell and the Patent That Changed America.* Cambridge, MA: Harvard University Press, 2015.

Bruce, Robert V. "Bell, Alexander Graham." *American National Biography.* Oxford: Oxford University Press, 2020. Web. 22 Oct. 2020.

Franklin Institute, The. "Case Files' Alexander Graham Bell." *The Franklin Institute Awards.* Philadelphia: The Franklin Institute, 2020. Web. 22 Oct. 2020.

Grosvenor, Edwin S., and Morgan Wesson. *Alexander Graham Bell: The Life and Times of the Man Who Invented the Telephone.* New York: Harry N Abrams, 1997.

History.Com Editors. "Alexander Graham Bell." *History.* New York: A&E Television Networks LLC, 2020. Web. 20 Oct. 2020.

Shulman, Seth. *The Telephone Gambit: Chasing Alexander Graham Bell's Secret.* (Illustrated edition.) New York: W.W. Norton & Company, 2009.

From *Progress and Poverty*

Date: 1879
Author: Henry George
Genre: book excerpt; political tract

Summary Overview

The subtitle of *Progress and Poverty* gives the reader a good understanding of the overall content and purpose of the book. While generally known by the brief title, the subtitle is more revealing: *An Inquiry Into the Causes of Industrial Depressions, and of Increase of Want with Increase of Wealth: The Remedy*. Author Henry George sought to explain why, in an industrializing nation such as the United States, there could be an immense increase in wealth creation while poverty and want increase simultaneously. Many economists and politicians had tried to address this, but George believed that none had succeeded. This excerpt does not include George's ultimate answer—a proposal for a "single tax" on the unearned increase in the value of land, but this portion of the book does hint at the author's conclusion by discussing the key concept that no one should have the right to wealth based on increased land values when, ultimately, the land originally belonged to all people in common.

Defining Moment

In the late 1800s, the United States underwent a rapid transformation from a nation that was largely rural and agrarian to a nation that was predominantly urban and industrial. At the time of the Civil War, the nation was perhaps third in the world as an industrial power, behind Great Britain and Germany. By the beginning of the twentieth century, however, the United States was the largest and most up-to-date industrial economy in the world.

Industrialization created vast fortunes for those who founded new businesses and those that invested in these ventures. Yet the prosperity was not shared throughout society. The distribution of wealth was vastly unequal. A small number of people at the very top of the economic ladder controlled a huge percentage of the nation's wealth. The discontent of urban workers and rural farmers intensified as this growing cleavage between the "haves" and the "have-nots" became more and more evident. Skilled workers, and the small percentage of workers who belonged to labor unions, managed to make substantial gains. A new managerial class arose to run the huge corporations that dominated the business world, and the mid-level workers in these businesses were generally well-paid. But unskilled workers saw little improvement in their standard of living. Many who had made decent livings as craftsmen saw their trades become obsolete as machines were developed that could replace human workers. The working class came to include many women and children; in 1900, one-fifth of the children under sixteen were working outside of their homes.

In general, unskilled workers endured low wages, unhealthy working conditions, and frequent periods of unemployment. Perhaps the only mitigating factor that worked in favor of low-income employees was that the prices for the goods they needed were generally low and the cost of living was not rising. Ironically, the same mechanization and efficiencies of manufacturing that threw many people out of work also functioned to keep consumer prices generally low. In the late 1800s, various popular schemes emerged for addressing these problems of inequality, often offering what seemed to be simple solutions to complex problems. Many journalists and academics tried to identify the reasons for the trend of increasing prosperity for some, coexisting with persistent poverty for others. None of these writers captured the mind of the reading public like Henry George did with his book *Progress and Poverty*, published in 1879. The book sold three million copies in a brief time, and made George a household name in many parts of the world. The work is often cited as perhaps the best-selling book on economic issues ever published.

Author Biography

Henry George was born in Philadelphia on September 2, 1839. His father was a devout member of the Episcopal church, and ran a bookstore and publishing business that published religious materials. Although never completing high school, George educated himself through voracious reading. When he was fifteen, he sailed as a crewman on a ship to Australia and India. He came to San Francisco in 1858, where he became a printer with various newspapers; he also wrote articles for these papers. He became an established journalist and for a time edited his own newspaper. In December 1861, he married Annie Corsina Fox, a young woman from Australia.

His major work, *Progress and Poverty*, was published in 1879. The success of this book, which quickly sold three million copies, led George to travel widely, giving lectures to promote his ideas. In 1880, he moved to New York City, where he ran unsuccessfully for mayor in 1886. George's fame and influence soon spread overseas, and in many parts of the world groups were formed to promote the single-tax message, or what was sometimes called Georgism. In 1897, George suffered a fatal stroke while campaigning for mayor of New York City and died on October 29, 1897.

HISTORICAL DOCUMENT: From *Progress and Poverty*

This association of poverty with progress is the great enigma of our times. It is the central fact from which spring industrial, social, and political difficulties that perplex the world, and with which statesmanship and philanthropy and education grapple in vain. From it come the clouds that overhang the future of the most progressive and self-reliant nations. It is the riddle which the Sphinx of Fate puts to our civilization, and which not to answer is to be destroyed. So long as all the increased wealth which modern progress brings goes but to build up great fortunes, to increase luxury and make sharper the contrast between the House of Have and the House of Want, progress is not real and cannot be permanent. The reaction must come. The tower leans from its foundations, and every new story but hastens the final catastrophe. To educate men who must be condemned to poverty, is but to make them restive; to base on a state of most glaring social inequality political institutions under which men are theoretically equal, is to stand a pyramid on its apex.

All-important as this question is, pressing itself from every quarter painfully upon attention, it has not yet received a solution which accounts for all the facts and points to any clear and simple remedy. This is shown by the widely varying attempts to account for the prevailing depression. They exhibit not merely a divergence between vulgar notions and scientific theories, but also show that the concurrence which should exist between those who avow the same general theories breaks up upon practical questions into an anarchy of opinion. Upon high economic authority we have been told that the prevailing depression is due to over-consumption; upon equally high authority, that it is due to over-production; while the wastes of war, the extension of railroads, the attempts of workmen to keep up wages, the demonetization of silver, the issues of paper money, the increase of labor-saving machinery, the opening of shorter avenues to trade, etc., are separately pointed out as the cause, by writers of reputation.

> This association of poverty and progress is the great enigma of our time.

And while professors thus disagree, the ideas that there is a necessary conflict between capital and labor, that machinery is an evil, that competition must be restrained and interest abolished, that wealth may be created by the issue of money, that it is the duty of government to furnish capital or to furnish work, are rapidly making way among the great body of the people, who keenly feel a hurt and are sharply conscious of a wrong. Such ideas, which bring great masses of men, the repositories of ultimate political power, under the leadership of charlatans and demagogues, are fraught with danger; but they cannot be successfully combated until political economy shall give some answer to the great question which shall be consistent with all her teachings, and which shall commend itself to the perceptions of the great masses of men. . .

I propose in the following pages to attempt to solve by the methods of political economy the great problem I have outlined. I propose to seek the law which associates poverty with progress, and increases want with advancing wealth; and I believe that in the explanation of this paradox we shall find the explanation of those recurring seasons of industrial and commercial paralysis which, viewed independently of their relations to more general phenomena, seem so inexplicable. . .

What constitutes the rightful basis of property? What is it that enables a man justly to say of a thing, "It is mine"? From what springs the sentiment which acknowledges his exclusive right as against all the world? Is it not, primarily, the right of a man to himself, to the use of his own powers, to the enjoyment of the fruits of his own exertions? Is it not this individual right, which springs from and is testified to by the natural facts of individual organization-the fact that each articular pair of hands obey a particular brain and are related to a particular stomach; the fact that each man is a definite, coherent, independent whole, which alone justifies individual owner ship? As a man belongs to himself, so his labor when put in concrete form belongs to him. . .

Now, this is not only the original source from which all ideas of exclusive ownership arise—as is evident from the natural tendency of the mind to revert to it when the idea of exclusive ownership is questioned, and the manner in which social relations develop but it is necessarily the only source. There can be to the ownership of anything no rightful title which is not derived from the title of the producer and does not rest upon the natural right of the man to himself. There can be no other rightful title, because (1st) there is no other natural right from which any other title can be derived, and (2d) because the recognition of any other title is inconsistent with and destructive of this.

For (1st) what other right exists from which the right to the exclusive possession of anything can be derived, save the right of a man to himself? With what other power is man by nature clothed, save the power of exerting his own faculties? How can he in any other way act upon or affect material things or other men? Paralyze the motor nerves, and your man has no more external influence or power than a log or stone. From what else, then, can the right of possessing and controlling things be derived? If it spring not from man himself, from what can it spring? Nature acknowledges no ownership or control in man save as the result of exertion. In no other way can her treasures be drawn forth, her powers directed, or her forces utilized or controlled. She makes no discriminations among men, but is to all absolutely impartial. She knows no distinction between master and slave, king and subject, saint and sinner. All men to her stand upon an equal footing and have equal rights. She recognizes no claim but that of labor, and recognizes that without respect to the claimant. If a pirate spread his sails, the wind will fill them as well as it will fill those of a peaceful merchantman or missionary bark; if a king and a common man be thrown overboard, neither can keep his head above water except by swimming; birds will not come to be shot by the proprietor of the soil any quicker than they will come to be shot by the poacher; fish will bite or will not bite at a hook in utter disregard as to whether it is offered them by a good little boy who goes to Sunday-school, or a bad little boy who plays truant; grain will grow only as the ground is prepared and the seed is sown; it is only at the call of labor that ore can be raised from the mine; the sun shines and the rain falls, alike upon just and unjust. The laws of nature are the decrees of the Creator. There is written in them no recognition of any right save that of labor; and in them is written broadly and clearly the equal right of all men to the use and enjoyment of nature; to apply to her by their exertions, and to receive and possess her reward. Hence, as nature gives only to labor, the exertion of labor in production is the only title to exclusive possession.

2d. This right of ownership that springs from labor excludes the possibility of any other right of ownership. If a man be rightfully entitled to the produce of his labor, then no one can be rightfully entitled to the ownership of anything which is not the produce of his labor, or the labor of some one else from whom the right has passed to him. If production give to the producer the right to exclusive possession and enjoyment, there can rightfully be no exclusive possession and enjoyment of anything not the production of labor, and the recognition of private property in land is a wrong. For the right to the produce of labor cannot be enjoyed without the right to the free use of the opportunities offered by nature, and to admit the right of property in these is to deny the right of property in the produce of labor. When non-producers can claim as rent a portion of the wealth created by producers, the right of the producers to the fruits of their labor is to that extent denied.

There is no escape from this position. To affirm that a man can rightfully claim exclusive ownership in his own labor when embodied in material things, is to deny that any one can rightfully claim exclusive ownership in land. To affirm the rightfulness of property in land, is to affirm a claim which has no warrant in nature, as against a claim founded in the organization of man and the laws of the material universe.

What most prevents the realization of the injustice of private property in land is the habit of including all the things that are made the subject of ownership in one category, as property, or, if any distinction is made, drawing the line, according to the unphilosophical distinction of the lawyers, between personal property and real estate, or things movable and things immovable. The real and natural distinction is between things which are the produce of labor and things which are the gratuitous offerings of nature; or, to adopt the terms of political economy, between wealth and land.

These two classes of things are in essence and relations widely different, and to class them together as property is to confuse all thought when we come to consider the justice or the injustice, the right or the wrong of property.

A house and the lot on which it stands are alike property, as being the subject of ownership, and are alike classed by the lawyers as real estate. Yet in nature and relations they differ widely. The one is produced by human labor, and belongs to the class in political economy styled wealth. The other is a part of nature, and belongs to the class in political economy styled land.

The essential character of the one class of things is that they embody labor, are brought into being by human exertion, their existence or non-existence, their increase or diminution, depending on man. The essential character of the other class of things is that they do not embody labor, and exist irrespective of human exertion and irrespective of man; they are the field or environment in which man finds himself; the storehouse from which his needs must be supplied, the raw material upon which and the forces with which alone his labor can act.

The moment this distinction is realized, that moment is it seen that the sanction which natural justice gives to one species of property is denied to the other; that the rightfulness which attaches to individual property in the produce of labor implies the wrongfulness of individual property in land; that, whereas the recognition of the one places all men upon equal terms, securing to each the due reward of his labor, the recognition of the other is the denial of the equal rights of men, permitting those who do not labor to take the natural reward of those who do.

Whatever may be said for the institution of private property in land, it is therefore plain that it cannot be defended on the score of justice.

The equal right of all men to the use of land is as clear as their right to breathe the air—it is a right preclaimed by the fact of their existence. For we cannot suppose that some men have a right to be in this world and others no right. . .

The wide-spreading social evils which everywhere oppress men amid an advancing civilization spring from a great primary wrong—the appropriation, as the exclusive property of some men, of the land on which and from which all must live. From this fundamental injustice flow all the injustices which distort and endanger modern development, which condemn the producer of wealth to poverty and pamper the non-producer in luxury, which rear the tenement house with the palace, plant the brothel behind the church, and compel us to build prisons as we open new schools.

There is nothing strange or inexplicable in to phenomena that are now perplexing the world. It is not that material progress is not in itself a good; it is not that nature has called into being children for whom she has failed to provide; it is not that the Creator has left us natural laws a taint of injustice at which even the human mind revolts, that material progress brings such bitter fruits. That amid our highest civilization men faint and die with want is not due to the niggardliness of nature, but to the injustice of man. Vice and misery, poverty and pauperism, are not the legitimate results of increase of population and industrial development; they only follow increase of population and industrial development because land is treated as private property—they are the dire—and necessary results of the violation of the supreme law of justice, involved in giving to some men the exclusive possession of that which nature provides for all men.

Whether in the present drifts of opinion and tasks there are as yet any indications of retrogression, it is not necessary to inquire; but there are many things about which there can be no dispute, which go to show that our civilization has reached a critical period, and that unless a new start is made in the direction of social equality, the nineteenth century may to the future march its climax. These industrial depressions, which cause much waste and suffering as famines or wars, are leading the twinges and shocks which precede paralysis. Every where is it evident that the tendency to inequality, which is the necessary result of material progress where land is monopolized, cannot go much further without carrying our civilization into that downward path which is so easy to enter and so hard to abandon. Everywhere the increasing intensity of the struggle to live, the increasing necessity for straining every nerve to prevent being thrown down and trodden under foot in the scramble for wealth, is draining the forces which gain and maintain improvements. In every civilized country pauperism, crime, insanity, and suicides are increasing. In every civilized country the diseases are increasing which come from overstrained nerves, from insufficient nourishment, from squalid lodgings, from unwholesome and monotonous occupations, from premature labor of children, from the tasks and crimes which poverty imposes upon women. In every highly civilized country the expectation of life, which gradually rose for several centuries, and which seems to have culminated about the first quarter of this century, appears to be now diminishing.

It is not an advancing civilization that such figures show. It is a civilization which in its undercurrents has already begun to recede. When the tide turns in bay or river from flood to ebb, it is not all at once; but here it still runs on, though there it has begun to recede. When the sun passes the meridian, it can be told only by the way the short shadows fall; for the heat of the day yet increases. But as sure as the turning tide must soon run full ebb; as sure as the declining sun must bring darkness, so sure is it, that though knowledge yet increases and invention marches on, and new states are being settled, and cities still expand, yet civilization has begun to wane when, in proportion to population, we must build more and more prisons, more and more almshouses, more and more insane asylums. It is not from top to bottom that societies die; it is from bottom to top.

But there are evidences far more palpable than any that can be given by statistics, of tendencies to the ebb of civilization. There is a vague but general feeling of disappointment; an increased bitterness among the working classes; a widespread feeling of unrest and brooding revolution. If this were accompanied by a definite idea of how relief is to be obtained, it would be a hopeful sign; but it is not. Though the schoolmaster has been abroad some time, the general power of tracing effect to cause does not seem a whit improved. The reaction toward protectionism, as the reaction toward other exploded fallacies of government, shows this. And even the philosophic freethinker cannot look upon that vast change in religious ideas that is now sweeping over the civilized world without feeling that this tremendous fact may have most momentous relations, which only the future can develop. For what is going on is not a change in the form of religion, but the negation and destruction of the ideas from which religion springs. Christianity is not simply clearing itself of superstitions, but in the popular mind it is dying at the root, as the old paganisms were dying when Christianity entered the world. And nothing arises to take its place. The fundamental ideas of an intelligent Creator and of a future life are in the general mind rapidly weakening. Now, whether this may or may not be in itself an advance, the importance of the part which religion has played in the world's history shows the importance of the change that is now going on. Unless human nature has suddenly altered in what the universal history of the race shows to be its deepest characteristics, the mightiest actions and reactions are thus preparing. Such stages of thought have heretofore always marked periods of transition. On a smaller scale and to a less depth (for I think any one who will notice the drift of our literature, and talk upon such subjects with the men he meets, will see that it is sub-soil and not surface plowing that materialistic ideas are now doing), such a state of thought preceded the French Revolution. But the closest parallel to the wreck of religious ideas now going on is to be found in that period in which ancient civilization began to pass from splendor to decline. What

> change may come, no mortal man can tell, but that some great change must come, thoughtful men begin to feel.
>
> The civilized world is trembling on the verge of a great movement. Either it must be a leap upward, which will open the way to advances yet undreamed of, or it must be a plunge downward which will carry us back toward barbarism.

Document Analysis

Many scholars have noted that Henry George's thinking in *Progress and Poverty* was influenced by some of the classical economists of the preceding generation, including David Ricardo, Thomas Malthus, and Adam Smith. The influence of Smith is suggested in the subtitle of George's book. The full title Adam Smith's classic work was *An Inquiry into the Nature and Causes of the Wealth of Nations*. In a similar vein, the subtitle of *Progress and Poverty* is *An Inquiry into the Causes of Industrial Depressions, and of Increase of Want with Increase of Wealth: The Remedy*.

George asserted that "This association of poverty and progress is the great enigma of our time." He notes that there had been varied explanations for the ongoing depression at the time, which was the aftermath of the Panic of 1877. Most economic experts had blamed the economic depression on overconsumption, while others, "upon equally high authority," saw the cause as overproduction. That these conclusions are contradictory illustrates the fact no one had definitive answers to the problem George was investigating.

Although the conclusion that George eventually develops in his book is not part of this excerpt, it is foreshadowed here. George proposes that there should be a tax upon the value of land—the value raw or undeveloped land, without any buildings or improvements. Over time, as settlement and development occurred around a piece of land, the value of the land tended to increase, even though the owner had done nothing to earn that increased value. George believed that land should never have been considered private property, but, ultimately, is part of the common good. Yet rather than propose the drastic step of confiscation of land, George proposed a tax on the unearned increase in the land's value. If, that is, landowners were to be taxed on the increased value of their holdings, they would be encouraged to develop their land, instead of just holding it for speculation and future development. If owners were to build something on their land, workers would be employed in the construction effort and in whatever subsequent economic activities were carried on there; and this will help the overall economy. In this excerpt, George gives the reader a hint of where he ultimately is going, arguing that no one should profit from anything but their own labor. Landowners who have profited from the rising value of their land had done nothing to earn that profit, and thus they should give back a part of it in the tax that George envisioned.

PROGRESS AND POVERTY:

AN INQUIRY INTO THE

CAUSE OF INDUSTRIAL DEPRESSIONS,

AND OF

INCREASE OF WANT WITH INCREASE OF WEALTH.

THE REMEDY.

BY

HENRY GEORGE.

NEW YORK:
D. APPLETON AND COMPANY,
1, 3, AND 5 BOND STREET.
1881.

In 1881, Henry George wrote Progress and Poverty, *exploring the social theory and economics behind why progress so often increases poverty.*

Essential Themes

A sense of astonishment is found throughout this document. In this, George was reflecting a widespread appraisal of many in the industrialized world. The author was asking what many were thinking: How could there be such great increases in wealth in the modern industrial economy, while poverty and want were also persistent realities? The tremendous popular response to George's book suggests that many people were asking the same question, and were anxious to learn about his remedy.

Even for those not in the investor class, the industrial economy had improved life in many ways. The railroads had made overland transportation easier and more rapid than ever. The telegraph had made swift, long-distance communication possible for the first time. Many urban homes had gas lighting, and were heated with coal- or oil-fired furnaces. Yet, George argued that because of the continued existence of widespread poverty, even among those who had relatively steady employment, all of this apparent progress was illusory, and likely was not permanent.

Throughout this excerpt there is also a sense of crisis and a warning that the socioeconomic problem described must be addressed. George calls it the "riddle which the Sphinx of fate puts to our civilization, and which not to answer is to be destroyed." He pictures industrial society, with its imbalance in the share of wealth, as a tower leaning on its foundation; adding to the tower at the top will only hasten its fall.

In seeking to introduce his solution to the problem, George appeals to the theme of justice. He argues that no one has the right to earnings or profits that were not produced by their own labor. Raw land, even with no improvements, will increase in value as settlement and development naturally arise. The owner of that land thus will enjoy a profit that they did nothing to earn, aside from speculating on its prospects. Such a situation is unjust, George argued. The solution that he proposed later in the book was a tax on the rising value of undeveloped land, the so-called single tax.

In the end, George's solution proved more a popular sop than a sustainable economic argument or workable answer. Economists and investors ultimately won the day by claiming that land ownership, even if "speculative" (i.e., based on future development), represented a financial risk on the part of owners and therefore was a valid form of private interest—one, moreover, that generally served the economy at large.

—Mark S. Joy, PhD

Bibliography and Additional Reading

Hudson, Michael. "Henry George's Political Critics." *American Journal of Economics and Sociology* 61, no. 1 (January 2008):1–45.

O'Donnell, Edward. *Henry George and the Crisis of Inequality: Progress and Poverty in the Gilded Age.* New York: Columbia University Press, 2017.

Thomas, John L. *Alternative America: Henry George, Edward Bellamy, Henry Demarest Lloyd and the Adversary Tradition.* Cambridge, MA: Belknap Press, 1983.

■ Sharecropping Contract

Date: January 18, 1879
Author: Solid South
Genre: contract

Summary Overview

The period after the Civil War was a time of uncertainty and chaos for both Southern landowners and former slaves. Agricultural land was devastated by the effects of neglect and war damage, and the new terms of labor in a racially-charged environment were uncertain. Former slaves believed initially that they would be granted land as part of their emancipation, but by the end of the 1860s, it was clear that this would not happen. For poor blacks and landless whites with only farming experience, the options were few. Landowners devised systems of land rental that returned many former slaves to a position of complete dependence. Sharecropping contracts, such as the one between the company Solid South and John Dawson, set terms on things, like equipment use and seed prices, which ensured that the tenant would always be in debt to the landowner and could be removed from the land at any time. It was a very precarious existence.

Defining Moment

By 1880, over half of black farmers in the deep South worked on farms that operated on a sharecropping system. When the Civil War ended with no widespread land grants to freed slaves, landowners who once owned slaves were left with land that was difficult to work with free-market labor. At the same time, many former slaves were left with very limited skills, except for agricultural work, but were unable to secure farmland. The system of sharecropping was a way for poor people, who owned very little, to be able to have access to equipment, seed, and a piece of farmland. During Reconstruction, the Freedman's Bureau saw the need for former slaves to be able to rent parcels of land on plantations, actively encouraged the sharecropping system, and became nominally responsible for the enforcement of freedmen's contracts. One Freedman's Bureau official, M. R. Delany, devised a model sharecropping contract that was equitable and spelled out the duties and obligations of the landowner as well as the tenant. Unfortunately, the Freedman's Bureau did not see the need to institute standardized contracts and, thus, dismissed Delany's concept in favor of allowing landowners and sharecroppers to write their own.

When this contract was written in 1879, sharecropping contracts gave the tenant no rights and exclusively protected the interest of the landowner. Sharecroppers were obligated by the terms of their contract to rent nearly everything, including housing, seed, equipment, and draft animals. They did not control the crops that were grown, how they were sold, or the price paid for those crops. They were often bound to plots of land insufficient to raise the quantity of crops that would be necessary just to pay the rent on the land and equipment, so they were kept desperately poor and in mounting debt.

Many sharecroppers rented land that they or their families had once worked as slaves, and they were extremely vulnerable to exploitation by landowners, who resented their new status as freedmen. Many sharecroppers were illiterate, meaning that they were easily cheated, as the landowner was the keeper of accounts and records, and the farmer simply had to pay what he was told was due. There was no recourse if theft or fraud occurred, or if the terms of the contract were violated, since the contract stipulated that a sharecropper could be removed from the land for any reason. The sharecropper was also obligated to pay for the upkeep and improvement of land that could be taken away at any time.

Most sharecroppers lived from harvest to harvest, going into debt each year and then hoping that the crop would be sufficient to settle the debt when it was sold. If the crop failed for any reason, the farmer still owed the full amount of the debt, which could be carried over from year to year at exorbitant interest rates set by the landowner and merchant, who were often the same entity. Even in successful years, these farmers often ended up with little to nothing after their debts were paid. Were the sharecropper to fall sick or become injured even temporarily, additional fees could be levied for missed work. If sharecroppers left the land while in debt, they could be jailed, but a landowner could remove tenants at any time and for any reason, including age, injury, or illness.

Author Biography

Little is known about John Dawson other than his lease of fifteen acres of Waterford Plantation in Madison Parish, Louisiana. As was the case with many sharecroppers, he could neither read nor write, as evidenced by his mark on the contract rather than a signature. The author of the contract is a company called Solid South, which is an intriguing choice of name. Solid South is the nickname for the results of the Compromise of 1877, which effectively ended Reconstruction by removing federal troops from the former Confederacy. Without the monitoring of the federal government, discriminatory practices were put in place to ensure that Democratic candidates would win elections, establishing the Democratic "Solid South" and ensuring that laws could be passed that effectively disenfranchised black people and stripped them of their rights. It was in such an environment that contracts, such as this one, which was clearly exploitative and discriminatory, were allowed to stand.

HISTORICAL DOCUMENT: Sharecropping Contract

Agreement between Landlord and Sharecropper

This agreement, made and entered into this 18th day of January, 1879, between Solid South, of the first part, and John Dawson, of the second part.

Witnesseth: that said party of the first part for and in consideration of eighty-eight pounds of lint cotton to be paid to the said Solid South, as hereinafter expressed, hereby leases to said Dawson, for the year A. D. 1879, a certain tract of land, the boundaries of which are well understood by the parties hereto, and the area of which the said parties hereby agree to be fifteen acres, being a portion of the Waterford Plantation, in Madison Parish, Louisiana.

The said Dawson is to cultivate said land in a proper manner, under the general superintendence of the said Solid South, or his agent or manager, and is to surrender to said lessor peaceable possession of said leased premises at the expiration of this lease without notice to quit. All ditches, turn-rows, bridges, fences, etc. on said land shall be kept in proper condition by said Dawson, or at his expense. All cotton-seed raised on said land shall be held for the exclusive use of said plantation, and no goods of any kind shall be kept for sale on any said land unless by consent of said lessor.

If said Solid South shall furnish to said lessee money or necessary supplies, or stock, or material, or either or all of them during this lease, to enable him to make a crop, the amount of said advances, not to exceed $475 (of which $315 has been furnished in two mules, plows, etc.), the said Dawson agrees to pay for the supplies and advances so furnished, out of the first cotton picked and saved on said land from the crop of said year, and to deliver said cotton of the first picking to the said Solid South, in the gin on said plantation, to be by him bought or shipped at his option, the proceeds to be applied to payment of said supply bill, which is to be fully paid on or before the 1st day of January, 1880.

After payment of said supply bill, the said lessee is to pay to said lessor, in the gin of said plantation, the rent cotton herein before stipulated, said rent to be fully paid on or before the 1st day of January, 1880. All cotton raised on said land is to be ginned on the gin of said lessor, on said plantation, and said lessee is to pay $4 per bale for ginning same.

To secure payment of said rent and supply bill, the said Dawson grants unto said Solid South a special privilege and right of pledge on all the products raised on said land, and on all his stock, farming implements, and personal property, and hereby waives in favor of said Solid South the benefit of any and all homestead laws and exemption laws now in force, or which may be in force, in Louisiana, and agrees that all his property shall be seized and sold to pay said rent and supply bill in default of payment thereof as herein agreed. Any violation of this contract shall render the lease void

[signed]

Solid South

John Dawson

X *(his mark)*

GLOSSARY

first part, second part: legal parties; persons or entities party to a contract

gin: cotton gin

said party: the party named previously

Document Analysis

This document lays out the terms under which an illiterate man may rent a parcel of land on a former slave plantation in Louisiana. Its primary goal was to control every aspect of John Dawson's business, from the rent he paid to the seed he bought, and to ensure that he remained in the debt of the landowner, Solid South. Dawson had no control over the land he was contracted to farm, and his rent of eighty-eight pounds of lint cotton (deseeded and cleaned) was just the beginning of his obligations to Solid South. Dawson's relationship to the landowner is spelled out clearly in the second paragraph: "All cotton-seed raised on said land shall be held for the exclusive use of said plantation, and no goods of any kind shall be kept for sale on any said land unless by consent of said lessor." In other words, no matter how much cotton John Dawson managed to raise, it could only be sold to the landowner, at his prices, and seed could also only be bought from him. The cotton could only be processed at the cotton gin owned by the landlord at the sharecropper's expense. It was a closed system.

In addition to owning the land and any cotton grown on it, Solid South also sold or rented tools, equipment, draft animals (in this case, a pair of mules), and housing. John Dawson was under obligation to pay first for the cleaning and processing of his cotton (he needed to pay his rent with cleaned cotton, so this was not optional); but since the payment of any debts and his rent were to come out of his crop before he was allowed to sell any (to the plantation, on their terms), there was no way to avoid significant debt. The eighty-eight pounds of cotton that Dawson was to pay in rent would cost him an additional four dollars per bale to clean before he made a penny from any of his other cotton.

Everything that John Dawson owned was surety on his rent: "Dawson grants unto said Solid South a special privilege and right of pledge on all the products raised on said land, and on all his stock, farming implements, and personal property." Under Louisiana law, he was also liable to imprisonment if he failed to pay the debt, but only after "all his property shall be seized and sold to pay said rent and supply bill." John Dawson signed away any rights to laws protecting him from such exploitation in this contract as well. Since he was in perpetual debt, Dawson's land, tools, equipment, and all of his other property were liable to be taken from him at any time and without notice.

Essential Themes

This contract highlights the exploitative and discriminatory environment that existed for landless freedmen after the Civil War and the end of Reconstruction. John Dawson agreed to a relationship with a landowner that was, in many ways, a form of continued slavery. Sharecroppers were tied to the land and its owner by debt and obligation, while the landowner did not have to worry about paying wages or providing living quarters. In the end, the owner of the land had no obligation to the sharecroppers and could remove them from the property they and their families had worked.

There was no real ability to go outside this system. The legal system did not offer effective recourse for sharecroppers, as they had signed contracts that were binding, and the courts were often biased in favor of white landowners. Moreover, in some states, a black claimant could be penalized with fines or jail time if found to have brought "false suit" against a white landowner. From seed to finished product, nearly every aspect of sharecropping was controlled by the landowner-merchant, who could ensure that the families who worked their land could never leave it and could not own it either.

—*Bethany Groff, MA*

Bibliography and Additional Reading

Alexander, Danielle. "Forty Acres and a Mule: The Ruined Hope of Reconstruction." *Humanities* 25.1 (2004): 26–29. Print.

Du Bois, W. E. B. *Black Reconstruction in America, 1860–1880*. New York: Simon, 1935. Print.

Feldman, Glenn. *The Irony of the Solid South: Democrats, Republicans, and Race, 1865–1944*. Tuscaloosa: U of Alabama P, 2013. Print.

Foner, Eric. *Reconstruction: America's Unfinished Revolution, 1863–1877*. New York: HarperCollins, 2002. Print.

Ransom, Roger L. and Richard Sutch. *One Kind of Freedom: The Economic Consequences of Emancipation*. 2nd ed. Cambridge: Cambridge UP, 2001. Print.

Sterling, Dorothy, ed. *The Trouble They Seen: The Story of Reconstruction in the Words of African Americans*. New York: Da Capo, 1994. Print.

■ Dawes Severalty Act

Date: February 8, 1887
Authors: Henry Dawes; U.S. Congress
Genre: legislation

Summary Overview

Named after the Massachusetts senator Henry L. Dawes, who headed the U.S. Senate's Committee on Indian Affairs, the Dawes Severalty Act of 1887 was the culmination of decades of policy work designed to free up western land for white settlers and acculturate American Indians to American values and practices. The Dawes Severalty Act broke the land of most remaining reservations into parcels to be farmed by individual American Indians or nuclear American Indian families. Partitioning Indian land in this manner, Congress hoped, would force native peoples to give up communal living and to adopt American farming practices. Eventually, policy makers reasoned, American Indians would embrace all American cultural norms and become integrated into U.S. society.

When the Dawes Act passed in 1887, Americans' views of native peoples varied considerably. Some groups, particularly evangelicals, dedicated themselves to both the religious and the cultural conversion of American Indians. Viewing themselves as benevolent teachers, they believed that they had a duty to acculturate American Indians. Others thought that American Indians were inassimilable, racially inferior savages who were destined for extinction. Few felt that Indian tribes deserved to be treated as sovereign nations as they had been in the past.

While the crafters of the Dawes Act believed themselves to have the best interests of American Indians at heart, the act ultimately hurt native peoples, dispossessing them of their lands and further marginalizing them. People unsympathetic to American Indians manipulated the Dawes Act for their own financial gain, resulting in the massive displacement of native peoples. As a consequence, by 1900 the American Indian population had fallen to its lowest point in U.S. history.

Defining Moment

Following the Civil War, Americans had a reinvigorated interest in western migration. Transnational railroads made western migration safer and faster than it had been in the past. At the same time, rapid population growth resulting largely from immigration contributed to overcrowding of urban areas and competition for jobs. Many saw the Jeffersonian hope for a nation of independent homesteaders as less and less realistic. Nevertheless, many Americans resisted "wage slavery," determined to pursue the dream of homesteading. The federal government aided potential homesteaders by passing the Homestead Act in 1862, providing land grants to hundreds of thousands of Americans.

White American migration into the West did not occur without opposition, however. The trans-Mississippi West was home to both American Indians native to that region and tribes that had been forcibly migrated from the eastern United States in the eighteenth and early nineteenth centuries. These groups did not passively accept homesteaders' claims to their land. Those who posed the greatest obstacle to

American homesteaders were the Plains Indians. Primarily semisedentary people, the Plains Indians, including the Cheyenne, the Comanche, the Crow, the Kiowa, and the Sioux, subsisted mainly by hunting buffalo. Homesteaders impeded their ability to survive by breaking land into parcels protected as private property, preventing both the buffalo and the Plains Indians from roaming freely. In many cases Native Americans responded violently in an effort to deter settlers. Homesteaders in turn complained that the government should protect them from Indian attacks. The situation in the West was exacerbated because businessmen, homesteaders, and railroad companies also wanted to remove the American Indians living on reservations in the West. Although the federal government had initially set up reservations in areas considered undesirable for white settlement, as land grew scarcer, the appeal of reservation land increased. In addition, in some cases, such as in the Dakota Territory, valuable natural resources like gold were discovered on Indian lands.

Throughout the second half of the nineteenth century, Native Americans responded to white settlers in a number of ways. Many tribal leaders appealed to U.S. politicians to recognize their equality as men and to appreciate tribal sovereignty. Those who made treaties with the federal government or received promises of land rights lacked recourse when the agreements were ignored or forgotten. Consequently, many Native Americans escalated attacks on American settlers and troops in an effort to protect their way of life. However, even protracted Indian wars, such as that waged by the Apache in the Southwest, eventually resulted in Indian surrender. Indian victories, such as the Sioux and Cheyenne defeat of General George Armstrong Custer and his troops at Little Bighorn, resulted in harsher retribution by American settlers and troops. By the 1880s many Native Americans saw acquiescence to U.S. policies as their best chance for survival.

Author Biography

Crafted by the U.S. Congress, the Dawes Act was based on the contribution of many individuals, although it is primarily credited to Senator Henry L. Dawes of Massachusetts, who chaired the Senate's Indian Affairs Committee. Dawes was initially skeptical about attempts to acculturate American Indians through land allotment but was persuaded by advocates to promote the act. Dawes made an exceptional candidate because he both chaired the Indian Affairs Committee and represented the state with the largest contingent of participants in the Indian reform movement.

Henry Laurens Dawes was born in Cummington, Massachusetts, on October 30, 1816. Trained as a lawyer, Dawes entered politics at a young age. As the Republican candidate, he was elected to the Massachusetts House of Representatives at age thirty-two and continued his political career in the Massachusetts State Senate followed by the U.S. House of Representatives and the U.S. Senate. During the 1850s, 1860s, and 1870s Dawes adamantly supported antislavery and Reconstruction policies. During the 1880s he became an advocate for Indian reform groups in the Senate. The meetings held by groups sympathetic to the plight of American Indians at Lake Mohonk, New York, particularly influenced Dawes. Dawes increasingly advocated allotment of reservation lands to acculturate American Indians and to integrate them into American society. He remained an active advocate for Indian rights until his death on February 5, 1903.

HISTORICAL DOCUMENT: Dawes Severalty Act

Be it enacted by the Senate and House of Representatives of the United States of America in Congress assembled, That in all cases where any tribe or band of Indians has been, or shall hereafter be, located upon any reservation created for their use, either by treaty stipulation or by virtue of an act of Congress or executive order setting apart the same for their use, the President of the United States be, and he hereby is, authorized, whenever in his opinion any reservation or any part thereof of such Indians is advantageous for agricultural and grazing purposes, to cause said reservation, or any part thereof, to be surveyed, or resurveyed if necessary, and to allot the lands in said reservation in severalty to any Indian located thereon in quantities as follows:

To each head of a family, one-quarter of a section;

To each single person over eighteen years of age, one-eighth of a section;

To each orphan child under eighteen years of age, one-eighth of a section; and

To each other single person under eighteen years now living, or who may be born prior to the date of the order of the President directing an allotment of the lands embraced in any reservation, one-sixteenth of a section:

Provided, That in case there is not sufficient land in any of said reservations to allot lands to each individual of the classes above named in quantities as above provided, the lands embraced in such reservation or reservations shall be allotted to each individual of each of said classes pro rata in accordance with the provisions of this act: And provided further, That where the treaty or act of Congress setting apart such reservation provides the allotment of lands in severalty in quantities in excess of those herein provided, the President, in making allotments upon such reservation, shall allot the lands to each individual Indian belonging thereon in quantity as specified in such treaty or act: And provided further, That when the lands allotted are only valuable for grazing purposes, an additional allotment of such grazing lands, in quantities as above provided, shall be made to each individual.

Sec. 2. That all allotments set apart under the provisions of this act shall be selected by the Indians, heads of families selecting for their minor children, and the agents shall select for each orphan child, and in such manner as to embrace the improvements of the Indians making the selection. where the improvements of two or more Indians have been made on the same legal subdivision of land, unless they shall otherwise agree, a provisional line may be run dividing said lands between them, and the amount to which each is entitled shall be equalized in the assignment of the remainder of the land to which they are entitled under his act: Provided, That if any one entitled to an allotment shall fail to make a selection within four years after the President shall direct that allotments may be made on a particular reservation, the Secretary of the Interior may direct the agent of such tribe or band, if such there be, and if there be no agent, then a special agent appointed for that purpose,to make a selection for such Indian, which selection shall be allotted as in cases where selections are made by the Indians, and patents shall issue in like manner.

Sec. 3. That the allotments provided for in this act shall be made by special agents appointed by the President for such purpose, and the agents in charge of the respective reservations on which the allotments are directed to be made, under such rules and regulations as the Secretary of the Interior may from time to time prescribe, and shall be certified by such agents to the Commissioner of Indian Affairs, in duplicate, one copy to be retained in the Indian Office and the other to be transmitted to the Secretary of the Interior for his action, and to be deposited in the General Land Office.

Sec. 4. That where any Indian not residing upon a reservation, or for whose tribe no reservation has been provided by treaty, act of Congress, or executive order, shall make settlement upon any surveyed or unsurveyed lands of the United States not otherwise appropriated, he or she shall be entitled, upon application to the local land-office for the district in which the lands are located, to have the same allotted to him or her, and to his or her children, in quantities and manner as provided in this act for Indians residing upon reservations; and when such settlement is made upon unsurveyed lands, the grant to such Indians shall be adjusted upon the survey of the lands so as to conform thereto; and patents shall be issued to them for such lands in the manner and with the restrictions as herein provided. And the fees to which the officers of such local land-office would have been entitled had such lands been entered under the general laws for the disposition of the public lands shall be paid to them, from any moneys in the Treasury of the United States not otherwise appropriated, upon a statement of an account in their behalf for such fees by the Commissioner of the General Land Office, and a certification of such account to the Secretary of the Treasury by the Secretary of the Interior.

Sec. 5. That upon the approval of the allotments provided for in this act by the Secretary of the Interior, he shall cause patents to issue therefor in the name of the allottees, which patents shall be of the legal effect, and declare that the United States does and will hold the land thus allotted, for the period of twenty-five years, in trust for the sole use and benefit of the Indian to whom such allotment shall have been made, or, in case of his decease, of his heirs according to the laws of the State or Territory where such land is located, and that at the expiration of said period the United States will convey the same by patent to said Indian, or his heirs as aforesaid, in fee, discharged of said trust and free of all charge or incumbrance whatsoever: Provided, That the President of the United States may in any case in his discretion extend the period. And if any conveyance shall be made of the lands set apart and allotted as herein provided, or any contract made touching the same, before the expiration of the time above mentioned, such conveyance or contract shall be absolutely null and void: Provided, That the law of descent and partition in force in the State or Territory where such lands are situate shall apply thereto after patents therefor have been executed and delivered, except as herein otherwise provided; and the laws of the State of Kansas regulating the descent and partition of real estate shall, so far as practicable, apply to all lands in the Indian Territory which may be allotted in severalty under the provisions of this act: And provided further, That at any time after lands have been allotted to all the Indians of any tribe as herein provided, or sooner if in the opinion of the President it shall be for the best interests of said tribe, it shall be lawful for the Secretary of the Interior to negotiate with such Indian tribe for the purchase and release by said tribe, in conformity with the treaty or statute under which such reservation is held, of such portions of its reservation not allotted as such tribe shall, from time to time, consent to sell, on such terms and conditions as shall be considered just and equitable between the United States and said tribe of Indians, which purchase shall not be complete until ratified by Congress, and the form and manner of executing such release prescribed by Congress: Provided however, That all lands adapted to agriculture, with or without irrigation so sold or released to the United States by any Indian tribe shall be held by the United States for the sale purpose of securing homes to actual settlers and shall be disposed of by the United States to actual and bona fide settlers only tracts not exceeding one hundred and sixty acres to any one person, on such terms as Congress shall prescribe, subject to grants which Congress may make in aid of education: And provided further, That no patents shall issue therefor except to the person so taking the same as and homestead, or his heirs, and after the expiration of five years occupancy therof as such homestead; and any conveyance of said lands taken as a homestead, or any contract touching the same, or lieu thereon, created prior to the date of such patent, shall be null and void. And the sums agreed to be paid by the United States as purchase money for any portion of any such reservation shall be held in the Treasury of the United States for the sole use of the tribe or tribes Indians; to whom such reservations belonged; and the same, with interest thereon at three per cent per annum, shall be at all times subject to appropriation by Congress for the

> *In all cases where any tribe or band of Indians has been ... located upon any reservation created for their use, ... the President of the United States ... is authorized to allot the lands ... in severalty to any Indian located thereon.*

education and civilization of such tribe or tribes of Indians or the members thereof. The patents aforesaid shall be recorded in the General Land Office, and afterward delivered, free of charge, to the allottee entitled thereto. And if any religious society or other organization is now occupying any of the public lands to which this act is applicable, for religious or educational work among the Indians, the Secretary of the Interior is hereby authorized to confirm such occupation to such society or organization, in quantity not exceeding one hundred and sixty acres in any one tract, so long as the same shall be so occupied, on such terms as he shall deem just; but nothing herein contained shall change or alter any claim of such society for religious or educational purposes heretofore granted by law. And hereafter in the employment of Indian police, or any other employees in the public service among any of the Indian tribes or bands affected by this act, and where Indians can perform the duties required, those Indians who have availed themselves of the provisions of this act and become citizens of the United States shall be preferred.

Sec. 6. That upon the completion of said allotments and the patenting of the lands to said allottees, each and every member of the respective bands or tribes of Indians to whom allotments have been made shall have the benefit of and be subject to the laws, both civil and criminal, of the State or Territory in which they may reside; and no Territory shall pass or enforce any law denying any such Indian within its jurisdiction the equal protection of the law. And every Indian born within the territorial limits of the United States to whom allotments shall have been made under the provisions of this act, or under any law or treaty, and every Indian born within the territorial limits of the United States who has voluntarily taken up, within said limits, his residence separate and apart from any tribe of Indians therein, and has adopted the habits of civilized life, is hereby declared to be a citizen of the United States, and is entitled to all the rights, privileges, and immunities of such citizens, whether said Indian has been or not, by birth or otherwise, a member of any tribe of Indians within the territorial limits of the United States without in any manner affecting the right of any such Indian to tribal or other property.

Sec. 7. That in cases where the use of water for irrigation is necessary to render the lands within any Indian reservation available for agricultural purposes, the Secretary of the Interior be, and he is hereby, authorized to prescribe such rules and regulations as he may deem necessary to secure a just and equal distribution thereof among the Indians residing upon any such reservation; and no other appropriation or grant of water by any riparian proprietor shall permitted to the damage of any other riparian proprietor.

Sec. 8. That the provisions of this act shall not extend to the territory occupied by the Cherokees, Creeks, Choctaws, Chickasaws, Seminoles, and Osage, Miamies and

Peorias, and Sacs and Foxes, in the Indian Territory, nor to any of the reservations of the Seneca Nation of New York Indians in the State of New York, nor to that strip of territory in the State of Nebraska adjoining the Sioux Nation on the south added by executive order.

Sec. 9. That for the purpose of making the surveys and resurveys mentioned in section two of this act, there be, and hereby is, appropriated, out of any moneys in the Treasury not otherwise appropriated, the sum of one hundred thousand dollars, to be repaid proportionately out of the proceeds of the sales of such land as may be acquired from the Indians under the provisions of this act.

Sec. 10. That nothing in this act contained shall be so construed to affect the right and power of Congress to grant the right of way through any lands granted to an Indian, or a tribe of Indians, for railroads or other highways, or telegraph lines, for the public use, or condemn such lands to public uses, upon making just compensation.

Sec. 11. That nothing in this act shall be so construed as to prevent the removal of the Southern Ute Indians from their present reservation in Southwestern Colorado to a new reservation by and with consent of a majority of the adult male members of said tribe.

Approved, February, 8, 1887.

GLOSSARY

aforesaid: previously mentioned; already referred to

allot: to allocate a portion

allottee: the receiver of an allotment

appropriation: something set aside for a specific purpose

deem: to regard as

disposition: bestowal

embrace: to contain

patent: a document granting an exclusive right

pro rata: in proportion

riparian: relating to a body of water

> **severalty:** the quality of being distinct or autonomous
>
> **stipulation:** an agreed-to condition in a contract

Document Analysis

Section 1 of the Dawes Act states the main purpose of the act. The act provides the president of the United States with the right to survey and divide reservation lands among individual American Indians and American Indian families. It also stipulates the manner in which the land will be divided, providing every head of household with one-quarter section of land, every single person over age eighteen or orphan under age eighteen with one-eighth section of land, and all other unmarried people under the age of eighteen with one-sixteenth section of land. Section 1 does not specify the actual size of a section but suggests that sections will be determined based on government survey of reservations and the size of the Indian population living on each. If an American Indian receives an allotment suitable only for ranching and not for agriculture, the act guarantees that he will get an additional allotment.

Section 2 guarantees the right of each American Indian to choose the area of land that will become his allotment. Heads of household are charged with choosing plots in the name of their minor children, and Bureau of Land Management agents are responsible for choosing land on behalf of orphaned children. If two people entitled to allotments want the same tract of land, the parcel will be divided between them, and they will receive from another area the remainder of land due to them. After Indians make their selections, agents are responsible for drawing preliminary boundaries, which they are to revise after resurveying the land and adding or subtracting from the various plots to standardize their size.

Section 2 also anticipates potential problems arising from the act. It insists that the agents responsible for choosing land on behalf of orphaned children choose land based on the best interests of those children. Suspecting some resistance to land division and allotment, Section 2 states that if an American Indian entitled to a portion of the newly divided reservations does not stake his claim to a partition of land within four years, the secretary of the interior should have a land agent choose a parcel on behalf of that Indian and issue a patent to the Indian in question for the plot of land in his name.

The purpose of Section 3 is to establish the manner in which allotments will be made, who will make them, who will appoint the officers who grant allotments, and how allotments will be documented. It states that the president will assign agents responsible for overseeing the allotment process. Records of allotment will be stored in both the Indian Office and the General Land Office.

Section 4 explains how the system of allotment will apply to American Indians who do not live on reservations. It states that an Indian residing off a reservation has the right to an allotment parcel equal to that of a native living on a reservation and that he can choose a parcel from any area of unsettled land. Although American Indians can choose their allotment from areas of unsurveyed land, the allotments will be adjusted once the land is surveyed. Section 4 also explains that the U.S. Treasury will compensate local land offices for the land settled by Indians.

Section 5 specifies the requirements for American Indians to gain ownership of their allotments. It states that once American Indians choose their plots of lands, those plots will be patented to them but held in trust by the U.S. government for twenty-five years. During those twenty-five years American Indians cannot sell the land. Furthermore, Section 5 nullifies any sale of allotted land prior to the end of the twenty-five-year period. If an allottee dies during the period in which the government holds his land in trust, his heirs will inherit the right to the land.

Additionally, Section 5 discusses options for reservation land not allotted to individuals under the provision of the act. It states that the federal government can negotiate with tribes to purchase unallotted reservation land but that land purchased from tribes can be used only to encourage actual settlers. Settlers will be restricted to land grants no larger than 160 acres per person. Religious organizations engaged in converting or educating native people are also entitled to tracts of land of no more than 160 acres. Like American Indians living on allotments, nonnative settlers will have their land held in trust by the federal government, but only for five years.

The fees paid by homesteaders for tracts of former Indian land are relegated to the American Indians who had previously held the rights to the land in question. The money can be used by Congress for educating or otherwise "civilizing" the American Indians from the reservation in question. Section 5 concludes by stating that American Indians who have taken advantage of the allotment policy as well as those who have become U.S. citizens will have preference in the hiring of public employees working in American Indian communities.

Section 6 deals with the legal and citizenship status of American Indians who participate in the allotment program. All American Indians who receive allotments, it states, will become American citizens and have all of the rights of American citizens. It stipulates that no local or state government can pass laws denying equal protection by law to American Indians who have taken part in the allotment program. In addition, Section 6 specifies that all American Indians who take part in the allotment process will become subject to the laws of the state or territory in which they reside.

Section 7 endows the secretary of the interior with the authority to regulate water resources, if they are needed to make reservation land fertile for agricultural use. The secretary is charged with equitably distributing water among the American Indians living on a reservation. Section 7 also forbids giving water rights to one individual if doing so would hurt another.

Section 8 excludes certain tribes (Cherokee, Creek, Choctaw, Chickasaw, Fox, Osage, Miami, Peoria, Sac, and Seminole) and certain regions (Seneca Nation of New York reservations and Sioux Nation territory in Nebraska) from the provisions of the act. Section 9 states that the cost of surveying lands authorized by the act will be paid out of a $100,000 account in the Treasury. (The $100,000 will be repaid to the Treasury from the sale of land acquired from American Indians based on the standards set forth by the act.) Section 10 protects the federal government's right to exercise eminent domain over land allotted to American Indians. And, finally, Section 11 certifies that the act cannot be used to halt the relocation of the Southern Ute Indians from their current reservation in southwestern Colorado to a new reservation.

Essential Themes

Few American Indians converted to American styles of farming or adopted American cultural norms as a result of the Dawes Act. The act assigned plots of land to individual Indians but did not include a provision to train them in farming practices. Few American Indians had experience farming. They did not have the required equipment and goods to begin farming, and most encountered difficulty if they tried to buy things on credit. Although in the 1880s and 1890s Congress approved small grants for American Indians to purchase seeds and farming equipment, the grants were far too small and inconsistent to aid American Indians significantly in converting to sedentary living and farming. Those American Indians who tried to mimic American homesteaders therefore usually reaped small, unprofitable harvests and quickly abandoned their efforts.

American Indians did not immediately feel the effects of the Dawes Act. Although speculators began making agreements for the trade or sale of Indian lands almost as soon as the act passed, they rarely began settling or developing the land for fear of expropriation. Ironically, although the Dawes Act intended to Americanize Indians, because the federal government held the allotments in trust for twenty-five years, American Indians were able to maintain their traditional ways of life in the years immediately following the passage of the Dawes Act. While many made agreements regarding their allotments that would ultimately lead to their displacement, during the years in which the land remained in trust, American Indians were able to continue to hunt game and to use resources throughout their reservations. Few American Indians accepted the notion of private property, and on most reservations they continued to live as though they held their lands communally.

Within the first decade of the Dawes Act's inception, state and local governments found loopholes allowing outsiders to purchase American Indian allotments. Once speculators and businesses gained ownership of Indian lands, American Indians felt the effects of the Dawes Act swiftly. Fences went up, restricting the movement of Indians as well as the game they hunted. Key resources, such as rivers and forests, were relegated to private, non-Indian owners, often eliminating the subsistence ability of American Indians.

In addition, the funds made from the sale of reservation land that the Dawes Act had earmarked for programs to improve American Indians' lives were grossly mismanaged. Compensation for land sales often did not make its way to Indian accounts for decades. Even when payments for reservation land made it to the federally held Indian accounts, they were used for ends that few Native Americans viewed as beneficial. In her study of the effects of the Dawes Act on the American Indians of Minnesota, the historian Melissa L. Meyer writes, "Facile generalizations about Anishinaabe dependence on welfare gratuities mask the fact that they essentially financed their own 'assimilation.'" (p. 388). Money from the sale of Indian lands usually funded schools and social welfare programs aimed at Americanizing Indians. In 1934, when the Dawes Act was reversed through the Indian Reorganization Act, American Indians owned less than half the land that they had owned in 1887.

—G. Mehera Gerardo, PhD

Bibliography and Additional Reading

Carlson, Leonard A. *Indians, Bureaucrats, and Land: The Dawes Act and the Decline of Indian Farming*. Westport, CT: Greenwood Press, 1981.

Ellinghous, Katherine. *Blood Will Tell: Native Americans and Assimilation Policy.* Lincoln: University of Nebraska Press, 2017.

Greenwald, Emily. *Reconfiguring the Reservation: The Nez Perces, Jicarilla Apaches, and the Dawes Act*. Albuquerque: University of New Mexico Press, 2002.

Hauptman, Laurence M., and L. Gordon McLester, III. *The Oneida Indians in the Age of Allotment, 1860–1920*. Norman: University of Oklahoma Press, 2006.

Johnston, Robert D., and Catherine McNicol Stock, eds. *The Countryside in the Age of the Modern State: Political Histories of Rural America. Ithaca, NY: Cornell University Press, 2001.

McDonnell, Janet A. *The Dispossession of the American Indian, 1887–1934*. Bloomington: Indiana University Press, 1991.

Meyer, Melissa L. "'We Can Not Get a Living as We Used To': Dispossession and the White Earth Anishinaabeg, 1889–1920." *American Historical Review* 96, no. 2 (Apr. 1991): 368–394.

Otis, D.S. *The Dawes Act and the Allotment of Indian Lands*, ed. Francis Paul Prucha. Norman: University of Oklahoma Press, 1973.

Stubben, Jerry D. *Native Americans and Political Participation: A Reference Handbook*. Santa Barbara, CA: ABC-CLIO, 2006.

■ Andrew Carnegie: "The Gospel of Wealth"

Date: June 1889
Author: Andrew Carnegie
Genre: article; editorial; essay

Summary Overview

For the extremely wealthy, the Gilded Age of the late nineteenth century was a time of excess. Many of the so-called robber barons amassed huge fortunes while spending extravagantly on themselves and giving little thought to the morality of what they did with their wealth. However, one of the wealthiest men in the world, who also happened to grow up in poverty, would speak to and define the responsibility of the wealthy toward society at large and the poor in particular. Andrew Carnegie, owner of the largest steel company in the world, was certainly a product of his time, and the way he treated his employees was not much different than the way many of his contemporaries treated theirs. But after selling his company, Carnegie put his words into action by using his vast fortune to improve society and offer the poor an opportunity to change their futures themselves.

Defining Moment

The term "Gilded Age" may imply a sense of glamour, but when Mark Twain wrote his 1873 novel *The Gilded Age: A Tale of Today*, he had something else in mind, satirizing the wealthy and powerful, who gave the illusion of glitter and shine but instead were hollow and corrupt. "Robber barons" is a derogatory term popularized in the nineteenth century. It was used to refer to wealthy businessmen who amassed even more wealth through dishonest or unscrupulous means, particularly when dealing with one another, smaller business owners, or with the workers they employed.

In some ways, Carnegie agreed with Twain's assessment of Gilded Age business practices and social relations, and in some ways he embodied them; more significantly, however, he viewed the accumulation of wealth by the robber barons as beneficial. Indeed, these businessmen were instrumental in transforming the United States from a predominantly agricultural, rural nation to an urbanized, industrialized world power. Carnegie believed that the actions of the robber barons were the engine of the American economy, which, in turn, led to an increase in industrial jobs, the start of the American Industrial Revolution, and ultimately the creation of the middle class.

Carnegie was as ruthless as other businessmen of the era in stifling dissent and minimizing the strength of unions among his workers. Though his partner, Henry Clay Frick, did the dirty work, Carnegie gave Frick a free hand, making him chairman of Carnegie Steel. In 1892, Frick shut down Carnegie's massive Homestead mill rather than accede to union demands that he not cut wages. He hired Pinkerton detectives to act as the company's army, waging a gun battle with strikers that resulted in ten deaths. After the National Guard arrived to establish order, Homestead reopened as a nonunion mill.

Carnegie saw no benefit in giving workers wages higher than the market would force him to pay, and he viewed giving money to the poor as morally bankrupting the recipients. His goal was to give common people the chance to succeed in the same way he had: by pulling themselves up from poverty through determination, hard work, and force of will. His "Gospel of Wealth" embodied this ethos. Carnegie was willing to use the bulk of his massive fortune to provide the tools for those people who had the kind of determination to achieve through their own efforts.

Author Biography

Andrew Carnegie was born the son of a linen weaver in the town of Dunfermline, Scotland, in 1835. When the burgeoning Industrial Revolution in Britain put his father out of work, the Carnegies moved to the United States when Andrew was thirteen. He then began work as a bobbin boy in a cotton factory, but his drive for knowledge and self-improvement enabled him to move up. After making a good living at the Pennsylvania Railroad, he left to take over the Keystone Bridge Company, and there, he saw that the future of the nation's prosperity lay in steel. Investing in the new Bessemer steelmaking process, he quickly outstripped his competitors' profits by producing steel at a lower cost. Wanting to use his fortune to pursue his vision of social uplift, he sold Carnegie Steel to financier J. P. Morgan in 1903, becoming the wealthiest man in the world. He devoted the rest of his life to philanthropy, building libraries and supporting cultural and higher educational institutions.

HISTORICAL DOCUMENT: "The Gospel of Wealth"

The problem of our age is the proper administration of wealth, so that the ties of brotherhood may still bind together the rich and poor in harmonious relationship. The conditions of human life have not only been changed, but revolutionized, within the past few hundred years. In former days there was little difference between the dwelling, dress, food, and environment of the chief and those of his retainers. The Indians are to-day where civilized man then was. When visiting the Sioux, I was led to the wigwam of the chief. It was just like the others in external appearance, and even within the difference was trifling between it and those of the poorest of his braves. The contrast between the palace of the millionaire and the cottage of the laborer with us to-day measures the change which has come with civilization.

This change, however, is not to be deplored, but welcomed as highly beneficial. It is well, nay, essential for the progress of the race, that the houses of some should be homes for all that is highest and best in literature and the arts, and for all the refinements of civilization, rather than that none should be so. Much better this great irregularity than universal squalor. Without wealth there can be no Maecenas. The "good old times" were not good old times. Neither master nor servant was as well situated then as to-day. A relapse to old conditions would be disastrous to both—not the least so to him who serves—and would sweep away civilization with it. But whether the change be for good or ill, it is upon us, beyond our power to alter, and therefore to be accepted and made the best of. It is a waste of time to criticise the inevitable.

Objections to the foundations upon which society is based are not in order, because the condition of the race is better with these than it has been with any others which have been tried. Of the effect of any new substitutes proposed we cannot be sure.

The Socialist or Anarchist who seeks to overturn present conditions is to be regarded as attacking the foundation upon which civilization itself rests, for civilization took its start from the day that the capable, industrious workman said to his incompetent and lazy fellow, "If thou dost net sow, thou shalt net reap," and thus ended primitive Communism by separating the drones from the bees. One who studies this subject will soon be brought face to face with the conclusion that upon the sacredness of property civilization itself depends—the right of the laborer to his hundred dollars in the savings bank, and equally the legal right of the millionaire to his millions. To these who propose to substitute Communism for this intense Individualism the answer, therefore, is: The race has tried that. All progress from that barbarous day to the present time has resulted from its displacement. Not evil, but good, has come to the race from the accumulation of wealth by those who have the ability and energy that produce it. But even if we admit for a moment that it might be better for the race to discard its present foundation, Individualism—that it is a nobler ideal that man should labor, not for himself alone, but in and for a brotherhood of his fellows, and share with them all in common, realizing Swedenborg's idea of Heaven, where, as he says, the angels derive their happiness, not from laboring for self, but for each other—even admit all this, and a sufficient answer is, This is not evolution, but revolution. It necessitates the changing of human nature itself a work of eons, even if it were good to change it, which we cannot know. It is not practicable in our day or in our age. Even if desirable theoretically, it belongs to another and long-succeeding sociological stratum. Our duty is with what is practicable now; with the next step possible in our day and generation. It is criminal to waste our energies in endeavoring to uproot, when all we can profitably or possibly accomplish is to bend the universal tree of humanity a little in the direction most favorable to the production of good fruit under existing circumstances. We might as well urge the destruction of the highest existing type of man because he failed to reach our ideal as favor the destruction of Individualism, Private Property, the Law of Accumulation of Wealth, and the Law of Competition; for these are the highest results of human experience, the soil in which society so far has produced the best fruit. Unequally or unjustly, perhaps, as these laws sometimes operate, and imperfect as they appear to the Idealist, they are, nevertheless, like the highest type of man, the best and most valuable of all that humanity has yet accomplished.

We start, then, with a condition of affairs under which the best interests of the race are promoted, but which inevitably gives wealth to the few. Thus far, accepting conditions as they exist, the situation can be surveyed and pronounced good. The question then arises—and, if the foregoing be correct, it is the only question with which we have to deal—What is the proper mode of administering wealth after the laws upon which civilization is founded have thrown it into the hands of the few? And it is of this great question that I believe I offer the true solution. It will be understood that *fortunes* are here spoken of, not moderate sums saved by many years of effort, the returns on which are required for the comfortable maintenance and education of families. This is not *wealth*, but only *competence* which it should be the aim of all to acquire.

There are but three modes in which surplus wealth can be disposed of. It call be left to the families of the descendants; or it can be bequeathed for public purposes; or, finally, it can be administered during their lives by its possessors. Under the first and second modes most of the wealth of the world that has reached the few has hitherto been applied. Let us in turn consider each of these modes. The first is the most injudicious. In monarchical countries, the estates and the greatest portion of the wealth are left to the first son, that the vanity of the parent may be gratified by the thought that his name and title are to descend to succeeding generations unimpaired. The condition of this class in Europe to-day teaches the futility of such hopes or ambitions. The successors have become impoverished through their follies or from the fall in the value of land. Even in Great Britain the strict law of entail has been found inadequate to maintain the status of an hereditary class. Its soil is rapidly passing into the hands of the stranger. Under republican institutions the division of property among the children is much fairer, but the question which forces itself upon thoughtful men in all lands is: Why should men leave great fortunes to their children? If this is done from affection, is it not misguided affection? Observation teaches that, generally speaking, it is not well for the children that they should be so burdened. Neither is it well for the state. Beyond providing for the wife and daughters moderate sources of income, and very moderate allowances indeed, if any, for the sons, men may well hesitate, for it is no longer questionable that great suns bequeathed oftener work more for the injury than for the good of the recipients. Wise men will soon conclude that, for the best interests of the members of their families and of the state, such bequests are an improper use of their means.

Poor and restricted are our opportunities in this life; narrow our horizon; our best work most imperfect; but rich men should be thankful for one inestimable boon. They have it in their power during their lives to busy themselves in organizing benefactions from which the masses of their fellows will derive lasting advantage, and thus dignify their own lives. The highest life is probably to be reached, not by such imitation of the life of Christ as Count Tolstoi gives us, but, while animated by Christ's spirit, by recognizing the changed conditions of this age, and adopting modes of expressing this spirit suitable to the changed conditions under which we live; still laboring for the good of our fellows, which was the essence of his life and teaching, but laboring in a different manner.

This, then, is held to be the duty of the man of Wealth: First, to set an example of modest, unostentatious living, shunning display or extravagance; to provide moderately for the legitimate wants of those dependent upon him; and after doing so to consider all surplus revenues which come to him simply as trust funds, which he is called upon to administer, and strictly bound as a matter of duty to administer in the manner which, in his judgment, is best calculated to produce the most beneficial results for the community—the man of wealth thus becoming the mere agent and trustee for his poorer brethren, bringing to their service his superior wisdom, experience and ability to administer, doing for them better than they would or could do for themselves.

We are met here with the difficulty of determining what are moderate sums to leave to members of the family; what is modest, unostentatious living; what is the test of extravagance. There must be different standards for different conditions. The answer is that it is as impossible to name exact amounts or actions as it is to define good manners, good taste, or the rules of propriety; but, nevertheless, these are verities, well known although indefinable. Public sentiment is quick to know and to feel what offends these. So in the case of wealth. The rule in regard to good taste in the dress of men or women applies here. Whatever makes one conspicuous offends the canon. If any family be chiefly known for display, for extravagance in home, table, equipage, for enormous sums ostentatiously spent in any form upon itself, if these be its chief distinctions, we have no difficulty in estimating its nature or culture. So likewise in regard to the use or abuse of its surplus wealth, or to generous, freehanded cooperation in good public uses, or to unabated efforts to accumulate and hoard to the last, whether they administer or bequeath. The verdict rests with the best and most enlightened public sentiment. The community will surely judge and its judgments will not often be wrong.

The best uses to which surplus wealth can be put have already been indicated. These who, would administer wisely must, indeed, be wise, for one of the serious obstacles to the improvement of our race is indiscriminate charity. It were better for mankind that the millions of the rich were thrown in to the sea than so spent as to encourage the slothful, the drunken, the unworthy. Of every thousand dollars spent in so called charity to-day, it is probable that $950 is unwisely spent; so spent, indeed as to produce the very evils which it proposes to mitigate or cure. A well-known writer of philosophic books admitted the other day that he had given a quarter of a dollar to a man who approached him as he was coming to visit the house of his friend. He knew nothing of the habits of this beggar; knew not the use that would be made of this money, although he had every reason to suspect that it would be spent improperly. This man professed to be a disciple of Herbert Spencer; yet the quarter-dollar given that night will probably work more injury than all the money which its thoughtless donor will ever be able to give in true charity will do good. He only gratified his own feelings, saved himself from annoyance—and this was probably one of the most selfish and very worst actions of his life, for in all respects he is most worthy.

In bestowing charity, the main consideration should be to help those who will help themselves; to provide part of the means by which those who desire to improve may do so; to give those who desire to use the aids by which they may rise; to assist, but rarely or never to do all. Neither the individual nor the race is improved by almsgiving. Those worthy of assistance, except in rare cases, seldom require assistance. The really valuable men of the race never do, except in cases of accident or sudden change. Every one has, of course, cases of individuals brought to his own knowledge where temporary assistance can do genuine good, and these he will not overlook. But the amount which can be wisely given by the individual for individuals is necessarily limited by his lack of knowledge of the circumstances connected with each. He is the only true reformer who is as careful and as anxious not to aid the unworthy as he is to aid the worthy, and, perhaps, even more so, for in alms-giving more injury is probably done by rewarding vice than by relieving virtue.

The rich man is thus almost restricted to following the examples of Peter Cooper, Enoch Pratt of Baltimore, Mr. Pratt of Brooklyn, Senator Stanford, and others, who know that the best means of benefiting the community is to place within its reach the ladders upon which the aspiring can rise—parks, and means of recreation, by which men are helped in body and mind; works of art, certain to give pleasure and improve the public taste, and public institutions of various kinds, which will improve the general condition of the people;—in this manner returning their surplus wealth to the mass of their fellows in the forms best calculated to do them lasting good.

Thus is the problem of Rich and Poor to be solved. The laws of accumulation will be left free; the laws of distribution free. Individualism will continue, but the millionaire will be but a trustee for the poor; entrusted for a season with a great part of the increased wealth of the community, but administering it for the community far better than it could or would have done for itself. The best minds will thus have reached a stage in the development of the race in which it is clearly seen that there is no mode of disposing of surplus wealth creditable to thoughtful and earnest men into whose hands it flows save by using it year by year for the general good. This day already dawns. But a little while, and although, without incurring the pity of their fellows, men may die sharers in great business enterprises from which their capital cannot be or has not been withdrawn, and is left chiefly at death for public uses, yet the man who dies leaving behind many millions of available wealth, which was his to administer during life, will pass away "unwept, unhonored, and unsung," no matter to what uses he leaves the dross which he cannot take with him. Of such as these the public verdict will then be: "The man who dies thus rich dies disgraced."

Such, in my opinion, is the true Gospel concerning Wealth, obedience to which is destined some day to solve the problem of the Rich and the Poor, and to bring "Peace on earth, among men Good-Will."

> **GLOSSARY**
>
> **Maecenas:** Gaius Maecenas, the first Emperor of Rome (as Caesar Augustus)
>
> **Herbert Spencer:** (1820–1903): British philosopher and sociologist who was a proponent of Social Darwinism (survival of the fittest)
>
> **Swedenborg:** Emanuel Swedenborg (1688–1772), Swedish philosopher, theologian, and mystic

Document Analysis

When Andrew Carnegie wrote "The Gospel of Wealth" in 1889, he transferred the notion of *noblesse oblige* (the social responsibility of the European nobility) to the context of industrialized America. He believed that the business leaders of the time had a responsibility to use their wealth not just for self-aggrandizement but also for the common good of humanity. The idea of the common good was shaped by one of the most popular ideologies among the wealthy of the time, Social Darwinism.

It is ironic that a man who would become the wealthiest man in the world would state, "the man who dies thus rich dies disgraced," but the saying, which Carnegie often repeated, encapsulated his viewpoint. Carnegie also believed that an increased gap between the wealthy and the poor defined civilization in a positive way. Earlier, less "civilized" societies, Carnegie argues, had equality, but only an equality of poverty, meaning civilization could not progress because there were no wealthy individuals to fund it.

Following the ideas of Herbert Spencer, who coined the term "survival of the fittest" as it relates to societal organization, Carnegie believes that individualism and the drive to become wealthy were "the soil in which society so far has produced the best fruit." He states that collectivism and forced equality were to be abhorred, and the wealthy were obligated by their position in society to lead and to provide opportunities for others who had the ability to achieve more, thus uplifting civilization as a whole. Charity, as it was commonly practiced—giving money or other necessities to the poor—is an unwise use of money according to Carnegie because it only serves to perpetuate the social ills they were trying to cure.

Though a product of the ideas of his time, Carnegie's application of those ideas was far ahead of his contemporaries. He criticizes those who bequeathed their wealth to their children as both depriving society and doing a disservice to their children by not forcing them to earn their success. Instead, the wealthy are obligated by their position to use their wealth "in the manner which, in his judgment, is best calculated to produce the most beneficial results for the community." The wealthy are trustees for the poor, "doing for them better than they would or could do for themselves."

Essential Themes

Carnegie proposed a new and different solution to the crisis of poverty in the United States in his "Gospel of Wealth" essay. Indeed, the fact that he was so willing to tell his fellow millionaires what to do with their money was controversial, as were his ideas about Social Darwinism and the futility of the most common type of charity. Regardless of the debate his ideas generated, he would not back down and continued to write on the topic of philanthropy. He devoted his life and fortune to realizing his vision after he sold Carnegie Steel. At the time of his death in 1919, he had given away more than ninety-five percent of his personal fortune.

Though very few of the wealthy have followed Carnegie's advice to the extent that he did, many have followed the Carnegie pattern of donating and dispersing their money. Today, the Carnegie Corporation, the Carnegie Foundation for the Advancement of Teaching, and the Carnegie Endowment for the Humanities still carry on the philanthropic work started by Carnegie's fortune.

Even if the terminology has changed, the Social Darwinistic bent of Carnegie's philanthropy has lived far beyond his years. Many among the wealthy see themselves as possessing a unique responsibility to society. Additionally, some political philosophies common to the wealthy hold to this view of the proper use of wealth: not giving direct charity to the poor, but instead enabling them to rise out of poverty if they possess the drive to do so.

—Steven L. Danver, PhD

Bibliography and Additional Reading

Burgoyne, Arthur G. *The Homestead Strike of 1892*. Pittsburgh: U of Pittsburgh P, 1979. Print.

Josephson, Matthew. *The Robber Barons: The Great American Capitalists, 1861–1901*. New Brunswick: Transaction, 2011. Print.

Kahan, Paul. *The Homestead Strike: Labor, Violence, and American Industry*. New York: Routledge, 2014. Print.

Lagemann, Ellen Condliff. *The Politics of Knowledge: The Carnegie Corporation, Philanthropy, and Public Policy*. Chicago: U of Chicago P, 1989. Print.

Nasaw, David. *Andrew Carnegie*. New York: Penguin, 2007. Print.

Eugene Debs: "What Can We Do for Working People?"

Date: April 1890
Author: Eugene V. Debs
Genre: article; editorial; essay

Summary Overview

During the so-called Gilded Age of the late nineteenth century, two competing visions of America were propagated. One, put forth by people such as industrialist Andrew Carnegie, emphasized the beneficial role of the wealthy in society. The other, which was held by union and Socialist Party leader Eugene Victor Debs, was more focused on working-class Americans whose well-being was often at the mercy of factory owners' desire for more wealth. In his essay "What Can We Do for Working People?," Debs presents the case that organizing into unions will allow working people to control their destiny and throw off the ideals of the wealthy, whose goal is to ensure that workers are employed for as little money as possible. By utilizing the power of the ballot box during elections and incorporating collective action in the workplace, working people will be better able to determine the course of their lives.

Defining Moment

Debs wrote his essay at a very difficult time for America's nascent labor movement. The prosperity of Gilded Age America was concentrated in the hands of those who owned the means of production. Men such as John D. Rockefeller, Andrew Carnegie, and John Pierpont Morgan controlled entire industries and spent as little as possible on their workers' wages and safety. The working class saw little, if any, benefit from the booming economy of the Industrial Revolution, and they exercised little power over the terms of their employment.

Though trade unions had worked to organize skilled workers for over a century, common laborers had no such protection until the rise of the Knights of Labor, which sought to bring together common workers and collectively negotiate to improve their lot. However, because of the violence that occurred during a labor rally at Chicago's Haymarket Square in 1886, many US citizens associated unions with foreign radicalism and the ideologies of anarchism and socialism.

Debs would not be deterred, however, and he continued to argue in favor of unions as the only way for working people to achieve higher wages, safe working conditions, and an eight-hour day. But the labor movement did not come together to create a united front: as trade unions such as the American Federation of Labor (AFL) organized to improve the conditions of specially skilled workers, the Knights of Labor, which represented the interests of common workers, declined in influence as they became associated with radicalism. The AFL sought to distance itself from partisan politics, whereas Debs encouraged workers to take action both in the workplace and at the polling place in order to elect pro-labor candidates who would institute the long-term goals of the labor movement. Whereas AFL leader Samuel Gompers preferred an issues-based alliance with politicians from the major parties, Debs encouraged workers to become active participants in the political organizations dedicated to the working peoples' agenda, such as the Socialist Labor Party (SLP) and the People's Party (also known as the Populist Party).

Debs's perspective was much more in line with the view espoused two years earlier by utopian novelist Edward Bellamy in *Looking Backward* (1888). A thorough critique of Gilded Age capitalism, Bellamy's view appealed to working people, with whom his ideal society, free of social divisions and conflict, resonated. But the only way to achieve a utopia such as Bellamy espoused was through voting and through organizing industrial workers to take control of their own fate.

Author Biography

Eugene V. Debs was born in Terre Haute, Indiana, on November 5, 1855. Like many young men at that time, he left school and entered the workplace at the age of fourteen. Around 1870, he became active in the railways employees union, the Brotherhood of Locomotive Firemen and Enginemen, and started a career as an advocate for working people. During the 1880s, Debs, still a member of the Democratic Party, won a seat in the Indiana state legislature. However, his true calling was with the railroad workers, and he became national secretary of the Brotherhood in 1880. It was during this period that his essay, "What Can We Do for Working People?" appeared in the union's periodical, the *Locomotive Firemen's Magazine*.

During the 1890s, Debs would expand his role nationally and found and lead the American Railway Union (ARU) in 1893. The ARU, which would soon become the largest organized union in the nation, accepted any white railway worker below the position of foreman, and Debs became instrumental in some of the union's most important labor actions before becoming a national political figure and running for president of the United States as a Socialist in 1900, 1904, 1908, and 1912.

HISTORICAL DOCUMENT: "What Can We Do for Working People?"

In one form or another certain persons are continually asking, "What can we do, or, What can be done for working people?" Why should such a question be asked at all in the United States? What gives rise to it? Are there circumstances and conditions warranting such an interrogatory? Who propounds it?....

Philanthropists of a certain type ask, "What can be done for working people?" and recommend soup houses, free baths, and more stringent laws against idleness and tramping, together with improved machinery in penitentiaries.

Another class devote time and investigation to diet, to show if wages decline that a man can live on ten cents a day and keep his revolting soul within his wretched body.

Another class, in answering the question, "What can we do for the working people?" reply by saying, "We will organize an Insurance Bureau which shall insure workingmen against accident, sickness, and death. We will supply them with medicine, doctors, and hospitals, taking so much from their wages to maintain the Bureau, and then, by compelling them to sign a contract which virtually reduces them to chattels, and makes them a part of our machinery, we will permit them to work for such pay as we choose to determine."

Another class answer the question, "What can we do for working people?" by telling them that unless they consent to abandon their labor organizations, absolve themselves from all obligations to such organizations, so far as they are concerned they shall have no work at all.

There are others, still, who discuss schemes for doing great and good things for working people, excepting, so far as it has come under the notice of the writer, to pay fair, honest wages.

This whole business of doing something for working people is disgusting and degrading to the last degree. It is not desirable to deny that in some quarters the question is asked honestly, but in such cases it is always in order to manifest pity for the questioner.

He is not inconvenienced by a surplus of brains. The question, "What can we do for working people?" as a general proposition, finds its resemblance in a question that might be asked by the owner of a sheep ranch, "What can I do for the sheep?" The reply would be, doubtless, "shear them." The ranch man takes care of the sheep that he may shear them, and it will be found that the men who ask with so much pharisaical solicitude, "What can we do for working men?" are the very ones who shear them the closest when the opportunity offers—strip them of everything of value that they may the more easily subjugate them by necessities of cold and hunger and nakedness, degrade and brutalize them to a degree that they become as fixed in their servitude as the wheels, cogs, cranks, and pins in the machinery they purchase and operate.

The real question to be propounded is, "What can workingmen do for themselves?" The answer is ready. They can do all things required, if they are independent, self-respecting, self-reliant men.

Workingmen can organize. Workingmen can combine, federate, unify, cooperate, harmonize, act in concert. This done, workingmen could control governmental affairs. They could elect honest men to office. They could make wise constitutions, enact just laws, and repeal vicious laws. By acting together they could overthrow monopolies and trusts. They could squeeze the water out of stocks, and decree that dividends shall be declared only upon cash investments. They could make the cornering of food products of the country a crime, and send the scoundrels guilty of the crime to the penitentiary. Such things are not vagaries. They are not Utopian dreams. They are practical. They are honest, they are things of good report.

Workingmen are in the majority. They have the most votes. In this God-favored land, where the ballot is all powerful, peaceful revolutions can be achieved. Wrongs can be crushed — sent to their native hell, and the right can be enthroned by workingmen acting together, pulling together.

What can workingmen do for themselves? They can teach capitalists that they do not want and will not accept their guardianship; that they are capable of self-management, and that they simply want fair pay for an honest day's work, and this done, "honors are easy." Fidelity to obligation is not a one-sided affair. Mutual respect is not the offspring of arrogance. There may have been a time when it was proper for the Southern slave owner to ask himself, "What can I do to better the condition of my slaves?" He owned them, they were his property; he controlled their destiny. He made them work as he did his cattle, mules, and horses, and appropriated all their earnings. Their children were his property as were the calves and colts of his cows and mares. But there never was a time beyond the dark boundary line of slavery when an employer of American workingmen could ask himself such a question without offering a degrading insult to every self-respecting workingman, and when a workingman hears it or anything like it and his cheek does not burn with righteous indignation he may know that he is on the road to subjugation, and if there exists a more humiliating spectacle within the boundaries of all the zones that belt the earth, what is it?

At every turn the question recurs, "What can workingmen do for themselves?" The question demands an answer, and unbidden a thousand are ready. We have not space for them. Let each workingman answer for himself. For one, we say the workingman can educate himself. He can read, study, and vote. He can improve his time and perfect his skill. He can see as clearly as others coming events, and prepare for their advent.

GLOSSARY

chattel: property; a slave

pharisaical: hypocritically self-righteous; condemnatory

tramping: wandering, vagabondage

Document Analysis

Having been involved in the trade union movement for over a decade, Debs was adjusting his beliefs as the labor movement began to transform. Rather than concern himself with the betterment of working conditions of a particular industry, Debs's essay reflects a growing awareness of the commonality of all industrial workers, skilled and unskilled. Debs was one of a growing number of reformers, often from the upper classes of American society, who were considering ways to appease American workers who were voicing and demonstrating their dissatisfaction with their pay, working conditions, or terms of employment.

Debs begins the essay by noting that reformers in his time sought to ensure that industrial workers were pacified enough to continue to provide the cheapest possible labor for the benefit of America's factory owners and industrialists (much as slaveholders had before them). Each group of reformers is addressed by Debs, who analyzes their proposals and notes that each refuses to consider paying "fair, honest wages," which, Debs claims, is "disgusting and degrading to the last degree." Debs asks, "What can workingmen do for themselves?," and then answers that they can organize into unions to collectively bargain for what is in their best interests and can utilize their voting power to choose candidates who will best represent them in state and federal government.

Essential Themes

After "What Can We Do for Working People?" was published, Debs became increasingly outspoken. His speeches became dominated by the ideals of socialism and argued that the model of industrial capitalism was fundamentally flawed. Many in the middle and upper classes condemned the labor movement for promoting what they considered to be radical ideologies, but Debs and the ideas he expressed persisted.

Debs led the American Railway Union through tumultuous times, including the April 1894 strike against robber baron Jay Gould's Great Northern Railroad and the massive Pullman Strike the following month. Debs was imprisoned for six months for his role in the Pullman Strike, and when he was released he announced he was a socialist and helped to form the Social Democratic Party, which then became the Socialist Party. Debs ran as the Socialist Party candidate for US president for four consecutive elections between 1900 and 1912.

In 1905, Debs helped to found the Industrial Workers of the World (IWW), which best represented his ideas about American industrial workers and socialism. The IWW's goal was to create "one big union" of industrial workers across the nation. Debs's ideas, however, were again considered too radical, and the IWW lacked the support of the American middle and upper classes.

Though Debs and AFL leader Samuel Gompers disagreed on some aspects of unionism, they saw each other as allies, and the AFL eventually became more inclusive of workers from across the broad spectrum of American industry, though it still organized on a per-industry basis. After losing the 1912 presidential election, Debs won an Indiana congressional seat in the 1916 election, running on a pacifist platform and in opposition to America's involvement in World War I. He continued to voice his opposition when the United States entered the war in 1918, which resulted in his arrest and incarceration for sedition and violation of the Espionage Act. Nominated for the presidency by the Socialist Party in 1920, Debs ran his campaign from prison and received six percent of the popular vote. He was released upon the order of President Warren Harding on Christmas Day 1921. Debs died in 1926.

—*Steven L. Danver, PhD*

Bibliography and Additional Reading

Ginger, Ray. *The Bending Cross: A Biography of Eugene Victor Debs*. Chicago: Haymarket, 2007 Print.

Kloppenberg, James T. *Uncertain Victory: Social Democracy and Progressivism in European and American Thought, 1870–1920*. New York: Oxford UP, 1988. Print.

Lipset, Seymour Martin, and Gary Marks. *It Didn't Happen Here: Why Socialism Failed in the United States*. New York: Norton, 2000. Print.

Salvatore, Nick. *Eugene V. Debs: Citizen and Socialist*. 2nd ed. Urbana: U of Illinois P, 2007. Print.

Standard Oil (Refinery No. 1 in Cleveland, Ohio, pictured) was a major company broken up under United States antitrust laws.

Sherman Antitrust Act

Date: 1890
Author: Senator John Sherman of Ohio
Genre: legislation

Summary Overview

A trust is a way of organizing a company that allows a firm to operate on a very large scale. The Sherman Antitrust Act was one of the two most important pieces of legislation passed by Congress in the late nineteenth century. It enshrined in American law and to a certain degree American culture that a company that controls too much of the market for a particular good or service is not good for the nation as a whole and should be broken up into separate pieces. It is the basis of all subsequent antitrust legislation in American history.

Defining Moment

Industrialization during the late nineteenth century favored companies that were first movers and companies that could achieve economies of scale. Businessmen like James "Buck" Duke and Andrew Carnegie employed technology to manufacture products cheaper than their competitors. These firms could then use their efficiencies to harm competition. By underselling those competitors or buying them out, it became possible for one (or sometimes a few) large companies to dominate whole industries. Once this situation came about, these dominant firms could raise prices on consumers and make their stockholders even richer.

The Sherman Antitrust Act was a response to this tendency in industries of all kinds. By giving the federal government the power to sue to break up trusts, it held the potential to restore competition and benefit consumers. Unfortunately, the federal government seldom used the law during its first decade of existence. More importantly, the U.S. Supreme Court, which invariably reviewed major antitrust cases, was loathe to let the Justice Department's interpretation of the act stand, even though they agreed that the law itself was constitutional because of Congress' power under the Commerce Clause. In the law's first major test, the Supreme Court let the E.C. Knight Company (better known as the Sugar Trust) remain intact even though it controlled 98 percent of the market for that product.

Despite the existence of this act, the United States went through a great merger movement that began in the 1860s, but greatly accelerated during the 1890s. By the end of that movement, one or two giant companies controlled over half the market in seventy-eight different industries. What gradually changed was the public attitude towards this situation as the nineteenth century transitioned into the Progressive era.

The real difference in the antitrust situation came with the ascension of Theodore Roosevelt to the Presidency in 1901. Roosevelt was willing to distinguish between what he considered "good" and "bad" trusts, employing the Sherman Antitrust Act against the ones he thought hurt consumers and not employing it against the others. The Supreme Court showed more willingness to allow those decisions to stand, most notably in cases against the Northern Securities Company (a railroad holding company) and the infamous Standard Oil trust. While the existence of this act did not change the general trajectory of capitalism in the United States towards large corporations, it did set an outer limit on the anticompetitive behavior in which those large companies could engage.

Author Biography

John Sherman (1823–1900), Republican of Ohio, was a congressman, U.S. senator, secretary of the treasury, and secretary of state. He played a pivotal role in Congress on the slavery issue before the Civil War and on many pressing issues during the late nineteenth century such as Chinese immigration and Civil Service reform. His greatest impact, however, was on American economic policy through legislation such as the Sherman Silver Purchase Act and the Sherman Antitrust Act.

Sherman's brother was William Tecumseh Sherman, the Civil War general who marched through Georgia. Unlike his brother, John Sherman twice unsuccessfully sought the presidential nomination of his party, in 1880 and 1884. Unfortunately for him, his campaigns never caught on because he was an uninspiring leader and poor public speaker. Sherman's primary historical importance derives from the wide range of legislation he championed through Congress.

HISTORICAL DOCUMENT: Sherman Antitrust Act

An act to protect trade and commerce against unlawful restraints and monopolies.
Be it enacted by the Senate and House of Representatives of the United States of America in Congress assembled,

Sec. 1. Every contract, combination in the form of trust or other- wise, or conspiracy, in restraint of trade or commerce among the several States, or with foreign nations, is hereby declared to be illegal. Every person who shall make any such contract or engage in any such combination or conspiracy, shall be deemed guilty of a misdemeanor, and, on conviction thereof, shall be punished by fine not exceeding five thousand dollars, or by imprisonment not exceeding one year, or by both said punishments, at the discretion of the court.

Sec. 2. Every person who shall monopolize, or attempt to monopolize, or combine or conspire with any other person or persons, to monopolize any part of the trade or commerce among the several States, or with foreign nations, shall be deemed guilty of a misdemeanor, and, on conviction thereof; shall be punished by fine not exceeding five thousand dollars, or by imprisonment not exceeding one year, or by both said punishments, in the discretion of the court.

Sec. 3. Every contract, combination in form of trust or otherwise, or conspiracy, in restraint of trade or commerce in any Territory of the United States or of the District of Columbia, or in restraint of trade or commerce between any such Territory and another, or between any such Territory or Territories and any State or States or the District of Columbia, or with foreign nations, or between the District of Columbia and any State or States or foreign nations, is hereby declared illegal. Every person who shall make any such contract or engage in any such combination or conspiracy, shall be deemed guilty of a misdemeanor, and, on conviction thereof, shall be punished by fine not exceeding five thousand dollars, or by imprisonment not exceeding one year, or by both said punishments, in the discretion of the court.

Sec. 4. The several circuit courts of the United States are hereby invested with jurisdiction to prevent and restrain violations of this act; and it shall be the duty of the several district attorneys of the United States, in their respective districts, under the direction of the Attorney-General, to institute proceedings in equity to prevent and restrain such violations. Such proceedings may be by way of petition setting forth the case and praying that such violation shall be enjoined or otherwise prohibited. When the parties complained of shall have been duly notified of such petition the court shall proceed, as soon as may be, to the hearing and determination of the case; and pending such petition and before final decree, the court may at any time make such temporary restraining order or prohibition as shall be deemed just in the premises.

Sec. 5. Whenever it shall appear to the court before which any proceeding under section four of this act may be pending, that the ends of justice require that other parties should be brought before the court, the court may cause them to be summoned, whether they reside in the district in which the court is held or not; and subpoenas to that end may be served in any district by the marshal thereof.

Sec. 6. Any property owned under any contract or by any combination, or pursuant to any conspiracy (and being the subject thereof) mentioned in section one of this act, and being in the course of transportation from one State to another, or to a foreign country, shall be forfeited to the United States, and may be seized and condemned by like proceedings as those provided by law for the forfeiture, seizure, and condemnation of property imported into the United States contrary to law.

Sec. 7. Any person who shall be injured in his business or property by any other person or corporation by reason of anything forbidden or declared to be unlawful by this act, may sue therefor in any circuit court of the United States in the district in which the defendant resides or is found, without respect to the amount in controversy, and shall recover three fold the damages by him sustained, and the costs of suit, including a reasonable attorney's fee.

Sec. 8. That the word "person," or " persons," wherever used in this act shall be deemed to include corporations and associations existing under or authorized by the laws of either the United States, the laws of any of the Territories, the laws of any State, or the laws of any foreign country.

> **GLOSSARY**
>
> **antitrust:** opposed to a trust, which was a form of legal organization that first appeared during the late nineteenth century and which helped large companies become very large companies; antitrust legislation was designed to allow the federal government to break those companies into pieces or dissolve them entirely
>
> **monopoly:** any company that has total or near-total domination of a market in a particular good; while all monopolies in this era were trusts, not all trusts were monopolies

Document Analysis

The Sherman Antitrust Act passed unanimously in the House of Representatives and with only one dissenting vote in the Senate. On the surface, this seems odd for such a seemingly significant piece of legislation. However, the reason it passed so easily was that it actually did very little to change fundamental business law. Companies that were in restraint of trade were already technically illegal under common law before its passage and remained so afterwards.

The most important section of the law is the part that reads: "Every contract, combination in the form of trust or otherwise, or conspiracy, in restraint of trade or commerce…is hereby declared illegal." The wording comes from common law, but is extraordinarily vague. The essential question became how exactly would the Executive Branch and the courts that reviewed antitrust cases define "in restraint of trade?" Moreover, who exactly would the government enforce the act against because, after all, more than just companies signed contracts. Many Americans believed that very large companies were the inevitable result of free-market capitalism, and did not think it would be right to enforce the law against those combinations.

The hole that courts most often used to gut the intention of the framers of the act was its failure to distinguish between manufacturing and commerce. Sherman had spoken of passing a bill that outlawed "trusts and combinations in restraint of trade and production." The final text of the law only covered "restraint of trade or commerce," not production or manufacturing. That explains how the Supreme Court, in its tortured decision in the E.C. Knight case (1895), could let such an obvious monopolist to remain intact. Sugar refining was manufacturing, not commerce. This monopoly obviously affected commerce, but the Court was unwilling to extend Congress' powers from the Commerce Clause to enact legislation that had indirect effects upon commerce until the New Deal cases of the late 1930s.

Essential Themes

Despite its problems, the Sherman Antitrust Act is still important because it essentially federalized the enforcement of limitations on capitalism that already existed. While states retained the power to give and withdraw charters, this was one of the first laws that allowed the federal government to regulate their conduct for the sake of the public good. It is nonetheless conservative in the sense that it reaffirmed the traditional notion that competition was the best way to check economic power, not the action of a central government, even if it required action by the federal government to keep competition alive.

The primary weakness of the law was its failure to define basic terms like "trust," "restraint of trade," and "monopoly." John Sherman defended that decision since the common law defined them for anyone who looked there for guidance, but this nonetheless allowed judges enormous discretion in how it was enforced. Indeed, the law would prove a greater bane to trade unions than to large corporations in the years immediately following its passage. Nonetheless, all future antitrust laws would build upon the assumptions behind this legislation, filling in more than a few of the gaps that this law left open.

—*Jonathan Rees, PhD*

Bibliography and Additional Reading

Garraty, John A. *The New Commonwealth: 1877–1890*. New York: Harper & Row, 1968.

Merry, Robert W. *President McKinley: Architect of the American Century*. New York: Simon & Schuster, 2017.

Painter, Nell Irvin. *Standing at Armageddon: A Grassroots History of the Progressive Era*. New York: W.W. Norton, 2008.

Rees, Jonathan. *Industrialization and the Transformation of American Life: A Brief Introduction*. Armonk, NY: M.E. Sharpe, 2013.

■ "Wall Street Owns the Country"

Date: ca. 1890
Author: Mary Elizabeth Lease
Genre: speech

Summary Overview

The late nineteenth century marked a significant point in US history. Following the Civil War, the United States expanded its reach, reincorporating the Southern states into the Union, as well as adding many new ones, especially in the West. The economies of these regions depended heavily on agriculture, but food prices and various policies that significantly affected farmers were not set by the farmers themselves. Instead, they were set by corporate and political interests that largely resided in the East. As farmers felt the burden of these policies, they banded together to form organizations such as the Farmers' Alliance and the Populist Party—officially known as the People's Party—in hopes of bringing their interests to the national stage and motivating significant change. Mary Elizabeth Lease was heavily involved in this movement in the early 1890s, and her speech "Wall Street Owns the Country" succinctly captures many of the issues and frustrations faced by farmers during this time.

Defining Moment

In the wake of the Civil War, many regions of the United States faced serious economic depression, especially in the West and South, where the economy relied heavily on agriculture. As droughts damaged crops and cotton prices plummeted, many farmers—especially tenant farmers, who rented the land on which they grew their crops—were severely in debt. Even once crop yield improved, farmers found their livelihoods dependent upon prices, taxes, availability of transportation and storage, and myriad other regulations established by corporate and political powers mainly located in the East.

These hardships paved the way for the rise of a new political party, focused primarily in the Western and Southern states. The People's Party focused on strengthening farmers' rights, as well as asserting economic and political independence from the manufacturing- and industry-dominated East Coast. Populists fought for fair crop pricing, improved and expanded options for transportation and storage, and freedom from regulations on implements, such as grain elevators, that had a serious negative impact on the economic viability of farming.

In 1890, the Populists won control of the Kansas state legislature and successfully elected their first US senator. With these successes, the party set its sights on increasing its presence on the national stage, a role that speakers such as Lease undertook. They traveled the country sharing their ideals and ideas with voters in areas similar to their own, in hopes of gaining enough support to win national elections.

Unfortunately, there was disagreement within the party over how to best accomplish this goal. Some believed teaming up with a mainstream political party such as the Democrats, who already had a strong following in the South, would help build national credibility and provide the channels necessary to reach a larger audience. Others believed this would dilute the Populist message by trying to appeal to moderates and that it was not worth the risk. By the time the

Populist Convention took place in St. Louis, Missouri, in July of 1896, tension within the party ran high. Loyalties split between "fusion" Populists who favored a merger with the Democratic Party, and "mid-roaders" who believed such a merger would only help the Democrats suppress the third-party influence they had already gained. The rift proved to be too great, and the People's Party soon fell out of favor in both national and state politics.

Author Biography

Mary Elizabeth Lease was born Mary Clyens in Ridgway, Pennsylvania, in either 1850 or 1853. Her parents immigrated to the United States from Ireland during the Irish Famine; her father and brother died fighting for the Union Army in the Civil War. In the early 1870s, she moved to Kansas to teach at a Catholic missionary school, and shortly thereafter married pharmacist Charles L. Lease. The couple lost everything in the financial panic of 1873 and relocated to Texas, where Lease became active in several causes, including prohibition and women's suffrage. She and her husband had several children during this time.

When the family moved back to Kansas, Lease became involved with the labor movement, joining the Farmers' Alliance and People's Party. Between 1890 and 1896, she toured the United States, speaking at campaign rallies and political conventions. Lease eventually divorced her husband and moved to New York City with her children, where she continued her career as a lecturer and activist until her death in 1933.

HISTORICAL DOCUMENT: "Wall Street Owns the Country"

This is a nation of inconsistencies. The Puritans fleeing from oppression became oppressors. We fought England for our liberty and put chains on four million of blacks. We wiped out slavery and our tariff laws, and national banks began a system of white wage slavery worse than the first. Wall Street owns the country. It is no longer a government of the people, by the people, and for the people, but a government of Wall Street, by Wall Street, and for Wall Street. The great common people of this country are slaves, and monopoly is the master. The West and South are bound and prostrate before the manufacturing East. Money rules, and our Vice-President is a London banker. Our laws are the output of a system which clothes rascals in robes and honesty in rags. The [political] parties lie to us and the political speakers mislead us. We were told two years ago to go to work and raise a big crop, that was all we needed. We went to work and plowed and planted; the rains fell, the sun shone, nature smiled, and we raised the big crop that they told us to; and what came of it? Eight-cent corn, ten-cent oats, two-cent beef and no price at all for butter and eggs—that's what came of it. The politicians said we suffered from overproduction. Overproduction, when 10,000 little children, so statistics tell us, starve to death every year in the United States, and over 100,000 shopgirls in New York are forced to sell their virtue for the bread their niggardly wages deny them... We want money, land and transportation. We want the abolition of the National Banks, and we want the power to make loans direct from the government. We want the foreclosure system wiped out... We will stand by our homes and stay by our fireside by force if necessary, and we will not pay

> our debts to the loan-shark companies until the government pays its debts to us. The people are at bay; let the bloodhounds of money who dogged us thus far beware.

GLOSSARY

niggardly: scanty or meager

sell ... virtue: a euphemism for engaging in sex work, or prostitution

shopgirl: a woman employed in a retail store or shop

Document Analysis

Lease begins her speech by noting that the United States is a "nation of inconsistencies." She observes that the United States was founded by individuals who sought freedom from the control of England during the seventeenth and eighteenth centuries, but then used that freedom to enslave Africans and black Americans. Once slavery was technically abolished, she says, Congress passed tax laws and established national banks that enabled rich people to remain wealthy, while trapping the "common people" into a life that Lease describes as "wage slavery."

Lease then calls attention to the sharp regional divide in economic prosperity within the United States: She notes that the West and South—regions heavily dependent on agriculture—are subject to the financial whims of eastern business and political interests. She clearly expresses her personal feelings about the individuals in charge, saying that "the [political] parties lie to us and the political speakers mislead us."

To illustrate her point, Lease describes a scenario where, two years prior to her speech, politicians and corporate leaders encouraged farmers in the South and West to raise a large yield to ensure their future prosperity. With some help from good weather, the farmers' work proved quite effective, and food was plentiful that year. However, when the time came to sell the crops, the farmers found that the purchase price offered for the crops had dropped dramatically—to the point, she claims, where no one would even pay at all for butter or eggs. The same politicians claimed that prices had fallen because the farmers had "overproduced," but Lease observes that in that same year, an estimated ten thousand children starved to death in the United States, and a hundred thousand young girls in cities engaged in prostitution just to afford food.

Finally, Lease lays out the demands she and her supporters have for future policy reform. Specifically, they want money, land, and transportation, as well as the power to obtain loans directly from the government rather than through private loan sharks. She also wants to end the foreclosure system. She concludes her speech with a warning to the "bloodhounds of money": The people who have been harmed by these corporations are ready to take action, and reform is on its way.

Essential Themes

At the time of her speech, Lease and her family were living in Kansas, surrounded by farmers and others whose livelihoods relied upon agriculture. As the United States admitted new western states following the Civil War, many felt disconnected from the money-controlling corporate powers in the East and struggled to make ends meet despite the importance of their role in producing food for the country.

Lease's speech expressed the frustration felt by many farmers in the West and South at the control these economic powers had over their livelihood, particularly with respect to setting crop prices. Many felt duped by politicians who had assured farmers that they would be able to provide for themselves and their families by producing a large amount of high-quality crops. Yet when the time came for harvest, those same powers used their influence to suppress prices to satisfy their own self-interest; the set prices were often too low for the farmers to recoup their expenses and keep up with payments on their land. Many were forced to borrow money at exorbitant rates to keep their land, repay debts incurred during the farming and harvest seasons, or move their product to market.

Some farmers who could not keep up with mortgage or debt payments lost their land to foreclosure. They wound up as tenant farmers, renting land from wealthier owners to continue making a living. Lease and others argued to end the foreclosure system hoping to protect farmers and other working poor from being forced from their homes.

Lease's anecdote about plummeting crop prices illustrates yet another "inconsistency" in the U.S. approach. Politicians claimed that overproduction caused the low prices, since the amount of supply exceeded the demand. But Lease points out that many people in the United States literally starved to death that year, so she cannot accept the argument that there is simply too much food available in the country to demand a fair price. Overall, her speech captures the frustrations and hardships faced by farmers in the United States during a time when manufacturing, corporate interests, and other hallmarks of industrialization dominated policy and political concerns. Lease's speech is sometimes quoted today to draw parallels between the Gilded Age and now.

—*Tracey M. DiLascio, JD*

Bibliography and Additional Reading

Edwards, Rebecca. "Mary E. Lease." 1896: *The Presidential Campaign*. Vassar College, 2000. Web. 24 Apr. 2014.

Edwards, Rebecca. "The Populist Party." 1896: *The Presidential Campaign*. Vassar College, 2000. Web. 24 Apr. 2014.

Goodwyn, Lawrence. The Populist Moment: *A Short History of the Agrarian Revolt in America*. New York: Oxford UP, 1978. Print.

Nugent, Walter. *The Tolerant Populists: Kansas Populism and Nativism*. 2d ed. Chicago: The U of Chicago P, 2013. Print.

Woestman, Kelly A. "Mary Elizabeth Lease: Populist Reformer." *Gilder Lehrman Institute of American History*: History by Era. Gilder Lehrman Institute of American History, 2014. Web. 12 Apr. 2014.

Zinn, Howard. *A People's History of the United States: 1492 to Present*. New York: Harper, 2005. Print.

■ Populist Party Platform

Date: July 4, 1892
Authors: Ignatius Donnelly; People's Party
Genre: political tract

Summary Overview

The People's Party—widely known as the Populist Party—grew out of the agrarian crisis of the late nineteenth century. Many American farmers faced serious problems resulting from declining commodity prices, rising debt, and transportation issues. The People's Party stemmed from the Granger movement and the regional Farmers' Alliance. In February 1892, leaders from various reform organizations met in St. Louis, Missouri, to discuss forming a new party. They issued a call for a national convention, held in July 1892, in Omaha, Nebraska, to create the party. While the party's platform addressed some of the concerns of the urban poor and the labor movement, most of its planks dealt with agrarian issues, including monetary and banking issues; government land policies; and transportation and farm-commodities storage issues.

Defining Moment

The People's Party had only a brief moment on the national political scene, but the movement encapsulated the problems facing rural Americans (and some urban workers) in the late nineteenth century. Farmers struggling with mortgage debt, falling commodity prices, and transportation issues came to believe both that they were at the mercy of social and economic forces beyond their control and that the American economy was controlled by a conspiracy of the wealthy and the powerful, who had little incentive to change the status quo. These issues, as well as the perception that neither the Democratic nor the Republican parties cared about the concerns of farmers, led to a sense of crisis. The Populists sought to address these issues by creating a new political party. Farmers had first tried to address some of their concerns through the Granger movement. The Grange began primarily as a social organization, but turned to politics when economic conditions for farmers deteriorated in the 1870s. Rather than form a third party, they backed Democratic or Republican candidates who promised to address farmers' concerns, and in many farm states, Grange backing was integral to candidates' election to local or state offices. The People's Party also had roots in the Farmers' Alliance. Like the Grange, the alliances initially had little to do with politics; they simply aimed at creating cooperative purchasing and marketing associations for farmers. But like the Grange, the Alliances eventually began to back candidates who seemed sympathetic to farmers' needs. When the People's Party announced its platform at the Omaha Convention in July 1892, outsiders considered many of the group's proposals radical. In 1896, when the Populists "fused" with the Democratic Party by endorsing William Jennings Bryan, whom the Democrats had already nominated for president, many of the Populist's other goals were eclipsed by the issue of "free silver," the focus of Bryan's campaign against the Republican candidate William McKinley. Bryan's defeat in that election marked the beginning of the Populists' decline on the national scene. While the Populists never succeeded as a national party and never elected anyone to national office, many of the reforms for which they advocated were enacted during the Progressive Era.

Author Biography

At the preliminary meeting in St. Louis in February 1892, the group appointed a committee on resolutions to draft planks for a potential party platform. The preamble to the platform, the most-often quoted portion of the document, was largely the work of Ignatius Donnelly, a journalist and political activist with a long career in third-party politics promoting reform causes. He was born on November 3, 1831, in Philadelphia, Pennsylvania, and in 1857 moved to Minnesota, where he held several elected offices, including lieutenant governor and a seat in the US House of Representatives from 1863 to 1869. He was a candidate for the Populist presidential nomination in 1892, but his many idiosyncrasies made him too great a risk. He died on January 1, 1901.

HISTORICAL DOCUMENT: Populist Party Platform

Assembled upon the 116th anniversary of the Declaration of Independence, the People's Party of America, in their first national convention, invoking upon their action the blessing of Almighty God, put forth in the name and on behalf of the people of this country, the following preamble and declaration of principles:

Preamble

The conditions which surround us best justify our cooperation; we meet in the midst of a nation brought to the verge of moral, political, and material ruin. Corruption dominates the ballot-box, the Legislatures, the Congress, and touches even the ermine of the bench.

The people are demoralized; most of the States have been compelled to isolate the voters at the polling places to prevent universal intimidation and bribery. The newspapers are largely subsidized or muzzled, public opinion silenced, business prostrated, homes covered with mortgages, labor impoverished, and the land concentrating in the hands of capitalists. The urban workmen are denied the right to organize for self-protection, imported pauperized labor beats down their wages, a hireling standing army, unrecognized by our laws, is established to shoot them down, and they are rapidly degenerating into European conditions. The fruits of the toil of millions are badly stolen to build up colossal fortunes for a few, unprecedented in the history of mankind; and the possessors of these, in turn, despise the Republic and endanger liberty. From the same prolific womb of governmental injustice we breed the two great classes—tramps and millionaires. The national power to create money is appropriated to enrich bond-holders; a vast public debt payable in legal-tender currency has been funded into gold-bearing bonds, thereby adding millions to the burdens of the people.

Silver, which has been accepted as coin since the dawn of history, has been demonetized to add to the purchasing power of gold by decreasing the value of all forms of property as well as human labor, and the supply of currency is purposely abridged to fatten usurers, bankrupt enterprise, and enslave industry. A vast conspiracy against mankind has been organized on two continents, and it is rapidly taking possession of the world. If not met and overthrown at once it forebodes terrible social convulsions, the destruction of civilization, or the establishment of an absolute despotism.

We have witnessed for more than a quarter of a century the struggles of the two great political parties for power and plunder, while grievous wrongs have been inflicted upon the suffering people. We charge that the controlling influences dominating both these parties have permitted the existing dreadful conditions to develop without serious effort to prevent or restrain them. Neither do they now promise us any substantial reform. They have agreed together to ignore, in the coming campaign, ever issue but one. They propose to drown the outcries of a plundered people with the uproar of a sham battle over the tariff, so that capitalists, corporations, national banks, rings, trusts, watered stock, the demonetization of silver and the oppressions of the usurers may all be lost sight of. They propose to sacrifice our homes, lives, and children on the altar of mammon; to destroy the multitude in order to secure corruption funds from the millionaires.

Assembled on the anniversary of the birthday of the nation, and filled with the spirit of the grand general and chief who established our independence, we seek to restore the government of the Republic to the hands of the "'plain people," with which class it originated. We assert our purposes to be identical with the purposes of the National Constitution; to form a more perfect union and establish justice, insure domestic tranquility, provide for the common defense, promote the general welfare, and secure the blessings of liberty for ourselves and our posterity. . . .

Our country finds itself confronted by conditions for which there is not precedent in the history of the world; our annual agricultural productions amount to billions of dollars in value, which must, within a few weeks or months, be exchanged for billions of dollars' worth of commodities consumed in their production; the existing currency supply is wholly inadequate to make this exchange; the results are falling prices, the formation of combines and rings, the impoverishment of the producing class. We pledge ourselves that if given power we will labor to correct these evils by wise and reasonable legislation, in accordance with the terms of our platform. We believe that the power of government—in other words, of the people—should be expanded (as in the case of the postal service) as rapidly and as far as the good sense of an intelligent people and the teaching of experience shall justify, to the end that oppression, injustice, and poverty shall eventually cease in the land. . . .

Platform

We declare, therefore—

First.—That the union of the labor forces of the United States this day consummated shall be permanent and perpetual; may its spirit enter into all hearts for the salvation of the republic and the uplifting of mankind.

Second.—Wealth belongs to him who creates it, and every dollar taken from industry without an equivalent is robbery. "If any will not work, neither shall he eat." The interests of rural and civil labor are the same; their enemies are identical.

Third.—We believe that the time has come when the railroad corporations will either own the people or the people must own the railroads; and should the government enter upon the work of owning and managing all railroads, we should favor an amendment to the constitution by which all persons engaged in the government service shall be placed under a civil-service regulation of the most rigid character, so as to prevent the increase of the power of the national administration by the use of such additional government employees.

FINANCE.—We demand a national currency, safe, sound, and flexible issued by the general government only, a full legal tender for all debts, public and private, and that without the use of banking corporations; a just, equitable, and efficient means of distribution direct to the people, at a tax not to exceed 2 per cent, per annum, to be provided as set forth in the sub-treasury plan of the Farmers' Alliance, or a better system; also by payments in discharge of its obligations for public improvements.

1. We demand free and unlimited coinage of silver and gold at the present legal ratio of 16 to 1.
2. We demand that the amount of circulating medium be speedily increased to not less than $50 per capita.
3. We demand a graduated income tax.
4. We believe that the money of the country should be kept as much as possible in the hands of the people, and hence we demand that all State and national revenues shall be limited to the necessary expenses of the government, economically and honestly administered. We demand that postal savings banks be established by the government for the safe deposit of the earnings of the people and to facilitate exchange.

TRANSPORTATION—Transportation being a means of exchange and a public necessity, the government should own and operate the railroads in the interest of the people. The telegraph and telephone, like the post-office system, being a necessity for the transmission of news, should be owned and operated by the government in the interest of the people.

LAND—The land, including all the natural sources of wealth, is the heritage of the people, and should not be monopolized for speculative purposes, and alien ownership of land should be prohibited. All land now held by railroads and other corporations in excess of their actual needs, and all lands now owned by aliens should be reclaimed by the government and held for actual settlers only.

Expressions of Sentiments

Your Committee on Platform and Resolutions beg leave unanimously to report the following: Whereas, Other questions have been presented for our consideration, we hereby submit the following, not as a part of the Platform of the People's Party, but as resolutions expressive of the sentiment of this Convention.

1. RESOLVED, That we demand a free ballot and a fair count in all elections and pledge ourselves to secure it to every legal voter without Federal Intervention, through the adoption by the States of the unperverted Australian or secret ballot system.
2. RESOLVED, That the revenue derived from a graduated income tax should be applied to the reduction of the burden of taxation now levied upon the domestic industries of this country.
3. RESOLVED, That we pledge our support to fair and liberal pensions to ex-Union soldiers and sailors.
4. RESOLVED, That we condemn the fallacy of protecting American labor under the present system, which opens our ports to the pauper and criminal classes of the world and crowds out our wage-earners; and we denounce the present ineffective laws against contract labor, and demand the further restriction of undesirable emigration.
5. RESOLVED, That we cordially sympathize with the efforts of organized workingmen to shorten the hours of labor, and demand a rigid enforcement of the existing eight-hour law on Government work, and ask that a penalty clause be added to the said law.
6. RESOLVED, That we regard the maintenance of a large standing army of mercenaries, known as the Pinkerton system, as a menace to our liberties, and we demand its abolition. . . .
7. RESOLVED, That we commend to the favorable consideration of the people and the reform press the legislative system known as the initiative and referendum.
8. RESOLVED, That we favor a constitutional provision limiting the office of President and Vice-President to one term, and providing for the election of Senators of the United States by a direct vote of the people.

9. RESOLVED, That we oppose any subsidy or national aid to any private corporation for any purpose.

10. RESOLVED, That this convention sympathizes with the Knights of Labor and their righteous contest with the tyrannical combine of clothing manufacturers of Rochester, and declare it to be a duty of all who hate tyranny and oppression to refuse to purchase the goods made by the said manufacturers, or to patronize any merchants who sell such goods.

GLOSSARY

circulating medium: currency or coin

ermine of the bench: a reference to the white fur trim adorning some judge's robes

Pinkerton: a private detective agency that was used by business owners to put down workers' strikes

usurer: an exploitative moneylender

Document Analysis

The Populists had three major concerns: currency and monetary policy, transportation issues, and federal land policies. In this political tract, they call for the "free and unlimited coinage of silver and gold at the present legal ratio of 16 to 1, a policy often dubbed "free silver." Congress had ended the production of silver dollars in 1873, but the Populists wanted the government to resume coining silver dollars and to return to an 1830s policy that had pegged the value of silver at one-sixteenth that of gold. They believed that resuming silver coinage would increase the money supply, benefitting debtors. In the 1890s, the market price of silver was far lower than one-sixteenth the price of gold, so this policy would have increased the price of silver, appealing to people in mining states where silver production was important, as well as to debtors; however, its inflationary underpinning frightened middle-class and wealthy people with assets.

The Populists also call for a graduated (progressive) income tax, meaning that tax rates should increase with the level of income. No federal income tax existed at this time, and on the state and local level, real estate taxes were often a major component of government revenues; thus, the tax burden fell heavily on farmers.

Transportation costs and service issues also presented problems for farmers. The Populists advocate government ownership of the railroads, arguing that "the railroad corporations will either own the people or the people must own the railroads." Since communication services also had great impact on all the people, the Populists argue that the government should also operate telephone and telegraph services.

Land issues were also of major importance to the Populists. The federal government had given huge land grants to western railroads; the Populists want the remnants of these grants returned to the government. They also call for an end to absentee "alien ownership" of land—foreigners should not be allowed to own land in the United States unless they actually became residents.

In the section of the document entitled "Expressions of Sentiments," the Populists list items not formally part of the party platform but "expressive of the sentiment of this Convention." Some deal with direct democracy issues such as initiative and recall and electing US senators by a direct vote of the people (rather than by the legislatures of the states, as provided for in the Constitution prior to ratification of the Seventeenth Amendment in 1913). Populists express support for the concerns of urban workers and demand "further restriction of undesirable emigration." The secondary status of these issues in the platform underlines one of the problems the Populists faced: while they exhibited some concern for the needs of urban workers, they were not able to attract large numbers of the laboring class to support their party. The Populists advocated primarily rural, agrarian issues in an urbanizing nation in which the cities were increasingly the center of power and influence.

Essential Themes

Scholars consider the 1892 *Populist* platform one of the most comprehensive reform agendas in American history. The central theme evident in the preamble is the sense of crisis, connected to which is the notion of a suspected conspiracy among the wealthy, big business, and corrupt politicians that greatly endangered the American economic system, according to the Populists. "The fruits of the toil of millions are badly stolen to build up colossal fortunes for a few," the preamble asserts. A key element of this "vast conspiracy against mankind," according to the preamble, was the federal government's refusal to coin silver dollars.

In this document, the Populists also stress that the will of the people had been ignored. Republicans and Democrats had not addressed many of the issues that concerned the average worker, focusing instead on a fight over the protective tariff. To give real political power to the people, the Populists called for several "direct democracy" reforms.

In many ways, the Populists were ahead of their time, although scholars have often framed their movement as seeking to restore a lost agrarian ideal. On the national scene, the Populists failed and faded into obscurity. But as historian Richard Hofstadter has pointed out, third parties are not necessarily failures, even if they lose at the ballot box. If sound, their policies will be adopted by one of the major parties, and eventually reforms may result. Indeed, many of the reforms the Populists called for in 1892 came to fruition within the following two or three decades in the Progressive Era.

—*Mark S. Joy, PhD*

Bibliography and Additional Reading

Goodwyn, Lawrence. *Democratic Promise: The Populist Moment in America*. New York: Oxford UP, 1976. Print.

Hofstadter, Richard. *The Age of Reform: From Bryan to F.D.R.* New York: Vintage, 1955. Print.

Kazin, Michael. *The Populist Persuasion: An American History*. Rev. ed. Ithaca: Cornell UP, 1998. Print.

Stock, Catherine McNicol. *Rural Radicals: Righteous Rage in the American Grain*. Ithaca: Cornell UP, 1996. Print.

■ President Grover Cleveland on Repeal of the Sherman Silver Purchase Act

Date: August 8, 1893
Authors: Grover Cleveland
Genre: speech

Summary Overview

During the Panic of 1893, President Grover Cleveland attempted to protect dwindling US gold reserves by making the unpopular decision to repeal the Sherman Silver Purchase Act of 1890. Cleveland called for a special session of Congress and on August 8, 1893, delivered a message arguing that the law was contributing heavily to the depletion of the US gold supply. Cleveland called upon Congress to enact gold and silver standards that were reflective of the policies of other countries, thereby stabilizing gold and silver sales on the international stage.

Defining Moment

During the late 1880s, concerns arose about the sustainability of the explosive economic growth the United States had experienced following the Civil War. Farmers sought debt relief, calling for cheaper paper currency to pay their bills, especially when droughts wiped out much of their crops. By this period, the nation had gained more states, many of which were in mineral-rich areas of the Midwest and mountain regions. The increased number of silver mines from those states was flooding the market with their product, thus lowering the price of silver both in the United States and worldwide.

In 1890, the so-called Free Silver movement spurred a push in Congress for a solution to the country's rampant deflation. Ohio senator John Sherman, along with fellow Ohio senator and future president William McKinley, produced a bill known as the Sherman Silver Purchase Act, which was signed into law in June of that year. The bill required the government to purchase millions of ounces of silver using paper money that would be redeemable for either silver or gold coins. The government's purchases would, in theory, drive up the price of silver and spur inflation, thereby serving the interests of both mine owners and farmers. The government had already been required to purchase millions of ounces of silver by the 1878 Bland-Allison Act, which had been passed in a similar attempt to reinvigorate the American economy, and advocates of the act saw the need to expand greatly upon this premise.

By 1893, however, it had become clear to many that the Sherman Silver Purchase Act was not as effective as its proponents had hoped. Most notably, Americans preferred to redeem their paper money for gold rather than silver, thus drawing heavily on American gold reserves. Meanwhile, a crisis was brewing in the American economy. Railroads, which had been built throughout the country, were by that point overextended. Some fell to bankruptcy and receivership, and many banks, whose gold supplies had dwindled, also closed their doors. The Panic of 1893, as it was known, spurred a depression that would last until 1897.

President Cleveland and others believed that the Sherman Silver Purchase Act was one of the major causes of the panic. During the summer of 1893, he called a special session of Congress to debate the law's repeal. The move would be widely unpopular, as the law had the support of some of the most powerful industries in the United States, so Cleveland needed to tread lightly but deliberately. With the aid of his advisers, particularly Attorney General Richard Olney, Cleveland issued a carefully worded message to the members of Congress, calling for repeal but attempting to avoid offending the law's many supporters.

Author Biography

Stephen Grover Cleveland was born in Caldwell, New Jersey, on March 18, 1837. His father died when Cleveland was sixteen, so he opted not to attend college and instead worked to support his large family. After working as a law clerk in Buffalo, New York, Cleveland was admitted to the bar at twenty-two, despite having no college education. During the Civil War, he served as assistant district attorney in Erie County, New York. In 1870, he was elected sheriff of that county, and he was later elected mayor of Buffalo. In light of his success as a reformer, the Democratic Party nominated him for governor of New York, a position he assumed in 1883. The following year, Democrats and reform Republicans (known as Mugwumps) collectively helped Cleveland win the presidency. He was defeated by Republican challenger Benjamin Harrison in the presidential election of 1888 but returned to office in 1893, becoming the only US president to serve two nonconsecutive terms. Despite winning a second term, his hard stance with organized labor and the ongoing economic depression cost him favor in his own party. He left the White House in 1897 and retired in Princeton, New Jersey, where he died on June 24, 1908.

HISTORICAL DOCUMENT: On Repeal of the Sherman Silver Purchase Act

The existence of an alarming and extraordinary business situation, involving the welfare and prosperity of all our people, has constrained me to call together in extra session the people's representatives in Congress, to the end that through a wise and patriotic exercise of the legislative duty, with which they solely are charged, present evils may be mitigated and dangers threatening the future may be averted.

Our unfortunate financial plight is not the result of untoward events nor of conditions related to our natural resources, nor is it traceable to any of the afflictions which frequently check national growth and prosperity. With plenteous crops, with abundant promise of remunerative production and manufacture, with unusual invitation to safe investment, and with satisfactory assurance to business enterprise, suddenly financial distrust and fear have sprung up on every side. . . . Values supposed to be fixed are fast becoming conjectural, and loss and failure have invaded every branch of business.

I believe these things are principally chargeable to Congressional legislation touching the purchase and coinage of silver by the General Government.

This legislation is embodied in a statute passed on the 14th day of July, 1890, which was the culmination of much agitation on the subject involved, and which may be considered a truce, after a long struggle, between the advocates of free silver coinage and those intending to be more conservative. . . .

This law provides that in payment for the 4,500,000 ounces of silver bullion which the Secretary of the Treasury is commanded to purchase monthly there shall be issued Treasury notes redeemable on demand in gold or silver coin, at the discretion of the Secretary of the Treasury, and that said notes may be reissued. It is, however, declared in the act to be "the established policy of the United States to maintain the two metals on a parity with each other upon the present legal ratio or such ratio as may be provided by law."

This declaration so controls the action of the Secretary of the Treasury as to prevent his exercising the discretion nominally vested in him if by such action the parity between gold and silver may be disturbed. Manifestly a refusal by the Secretary to pay these Treasury notes in gold if demanded would necessarily result in their discredit and depreciation as obligations payable only in silver, and would destroy the parity between the two metals by establishing a discrimination in favor of gold.

The policy necessarily adopted of paying these notes in gold has not spared the gold reserve of $100,000,000 long ago set aside by the Government for the redemption of other notes, for this fund has already been subjected to the payment of new obligations amounting to about $150,000,000 on account of silver purchases, and has as a consequence for the first time since its creation been encroached upon.

We have thus made the depletion of our gold easy and have tempted other and more appreciative nations to add it to their stock. . . .

Unless Government bonds are to be constantly issued and sold to replenish our exhausted gold, only to be again exhausted, it is apparent that the operation of the silver-purchase law now in force leads in the direction of the entire substitution of silver for the gold in the Government Treasury, and that this must be followed by the payment of all Government obligations in depreciated silver.

At this stage gold and silver must part company and the Government must fail in its established policy to maintain the two metals on a parity with each other. Given over to the exclusive use of a currency greatly depreciated according to the standard of the commercial world, we could no longer claim a place among nations of the first class, nor could our Government claim a performance of its obligation, so far as such an obligation has been imposed upon it, to provide for the use of the people the best and safest money.

If, as many of its friends claim, silver ought to occupy a larger place in our currency and the currency of the world through general international cooperation and agreement, it is obvious that the United States will not be in a position to gain a hearing in favor of such an arrangement so long as we are willing to continue our attempt to accomplish the result single-handed. . . .

The people of the United States are entitled to a sound and stable currency and to money recognized as such on every exchange and in every market of the world. Their Government has no right to injure them by financial experiments opposed to the policy and practice of other civilized states, nor is it justified in permitting an exaggerated and unreasonable reliance on our national strength and ability to jeopardize the soundness of the people's money.

This matter rises above the plane of party politics. It vitally concerns every business and calling and enters every household in the land. There is one important aspect of the subject which especially should never be overlooked. At times like the present, when the evils of unsound finance threaten us, the speculator may anticipate a harvest gathered from the misfortune of others, the capitalist may protect himself by hoarding or may even find profit in the fluctuations of values; but the wage earner-the first to be injured by a depreciated currency and the last to receive the benefit of its correction-is practically defenseless. He relies for work upon the ventures of confident and contented capital. This failing him, his condition is without alleviation, for he can neither prey on the misfortunes of others nor hoard his labor....

It is of the utmost importance that such relief as Congress can afford in the existing situation be afforded at once. The maxim "He gives twice who gives quickly" is directly applicable. It may be true that the embarrassments from which the business of the country is suffering arise as much from evils apprehended as from those actually existing. We may hope, too, that calm counsels will prevail, and that neither the capitalists nor the wage earners will give way to unreasoning panic and sacrifice their property or their interests under the influence of exaggerated fears. Nevertheless, every day's delay in removing one of the plain and principal causes of the present state of things enlarges the mischief already done and increases the responsibility of the Government for its existence. Whatever else the people have a right to expect from Congress, they may certainly demand that legislation condemned by the ordeal of three years' disastrous experience shall be removed from the statute books as soon as their representatives can legitimately deal with it.

It was my purpose to summon Congress in special session early in the coming September, that we might enter promptly upon the work of tariff reform, which the true interests of the country clearly demand, which so large a majority of the people, as shown by their suffrages, desire and expect, and to the accomplishment of which every effort of the present Administration is pledged. But while tariff reform has lost nothing of its immediate and permanent importance and must in the near future engage the attention of Congress, it has seemed to me that the financial condition of the country should at once and before all other subjects be considered by your honorable body.

I earnestly recommend the prompt repeal of the provisions of the act passed July 14, 1890, authorizing the purchase of silver bullion, and that other legislative action may put beyond all doubt or mistake the intention and the ability of the Government to fulfill its pecuniary obligations in money universally recognized by all civilized countries.

GLOSSARY

depreciation: a decrease in value because of age or market conditions

parity: equality; equivalence

pecuniary: pertaining to money

remunerative: providing a profit or compensation

tariff: a tax on imports

Document Analysis

Cleveland's message to Congress, delivered in August 1893, was designed to identify the economic crisis and its causes as well as prompt Congress to react appropriately. He begins his message by explaining that the special session was called to enact true reform and not what he dubs "unsound" fiscal policies, such as the Sherman Silver Purchase Act. The act, in Cleveland's opinion, had done more damage than good. Cleveland therefore urges Congress to take bipartisan action to repeal the 1890 law.

Through his message, Cleveland reminds senators and representatives of the ongoing fiscal crisis. Banking institutions and business enterprises once considered juggernauts on the open markets were closing their doors. Unemployment was spiking, and gold reserves were depleted. However, this crisis was, according to Cleveland, not the product of some catastrophic event, nor was it some natural retraction that would be expected after a long period of explosive growth. Rather, Cleveland argues, the panic was the result of the Sherman Silver Purchase Act of 1890. This law was creating unnecessary parity between gold and silver, rapidly draining gold reserves and fostering a general sense of fear among investors and business enterprises. The law, he explains, was introduced to settle the "long struggle" between Free Silver advocates and conservatives. However, the act's provisions had major implications for the Treasury Department, on whose discretion (which the law hampered, according to Cleveland) the country relied to guard against fiscal instability.

The main problem with the act, according to the president, was the shortage of gold it caused. Because people were redeeming the newly issued paper money for gold, the country's gold reserves were being depleted at an alarming rate. Even if substantial investment in gold returned the reserves to their previous levels, the act would only continue to drain these reserves. The only course of action, he states, was to repeal the Sherman Silver Purchase Act.

Cleveland also uses the message to criticize lawmakers for putting the United States at a disadvantage in comparison to the rest of the world. The US government, he urges, should eschew "financial experiments" such as the Sherman Silver Purchase Act and instead enact "sound and stable" currency reform. Repealing the law would likely prove unpopular, he notes, as some business owners and speculators profited during the years it was in force. Despite this, Cleveland argues that Congress must act quickly to prevent the act from causing any further harm to the American economy.

Essential Themes

In his message to Congress, Cleveland focuses on identifying the crisis at hand and establishing the Sherman Silver Purchase Act of 1890 as its cause. He understood that its repeal would not be a popular move, but in his estimation, the depletion of the nation's gold reserves and the continuation of the developing fiscal depression required immediate action, regardless of the political consequences.

Cleveland's original message allegedly contained much more pointed and critical language, but he reportedly toned down that verbiage in order to appeal to both sides of the political aisle. Still, his address to Congress nevertheless refers to the law as an "experiment" and notes that no other nation in the world shared the view that such an experimental move should be taken. Indeed, he suggests, this experiment was ill-conceived, removing the Treasury's typical discretion over gold and silver prices. The perceived benefits were never realized, he argues, but the risks were clear.

In admitting to Congress that there would be many influential parties who would oppose the repeal of the law, Cleveland revealed that he had a clear understanding of the multifaceted nature of the issue. At the same time, he was solidly in favor of repealing the Silver Purchase Act, having weighed the benefits of the law against their harmful effects on the nation and found them lacking. He was ultimately successful in convincing Congress of the law's dangerous financial consequences, and the Sherman Silver Purchase Act was repealed in October of 1893.

—*Michael P. Auerbach, MA*

Bibliography and Additional Reading

Pafford, John M. *The Forgotten Conservative: Rediscovering Grover Cleveland.* Washington: Regenery History, 2013. Print.

Reed, Lawrence W. *A Lesson from the Past: The Silver Panic of 1893.* Irvington: Foundation for Economic Education, 1993. Print.

Steeples, Douglas W., and David O. Whitten. *Democracy in Desperation: The Depression of 1893.* Westport: Praeger, 1998. Print.

Wells, Merle W. *Gold Camps and Silver Cities.* Moscow: U of Idaho P, 2002. Print.

■ "Political Causes of the Business Depression"

Date: December 1893
Authors: William E. Russell
Genre: article

Summary Overview

Massachusetts governor William E. Russell, in a December 1893 article published in *North American Review*, attempts to identify the political underpinnings of the Panic of 1893 and the subsequent depression. The Democratic governor places blame for the crisis on the Republican Party, which he says forced through Congress the Sherman Silver Purchase Act and enacted other laws that entrenched poor economic policies before the Democrats could undo them.

Defining Moment

Although the national elections of the latter 1880s were considered by many to be less substantive and contested than other campaign seasons, there were some concerns about the sustainability of the explosive economic growth the United States experienced following the Civil War. Farmers sought debt relief, calling for cheaper paper currency to pay their bills, especially when droughts wiped out much of their crops. Silver mines in new Midwestern and mountain states were flooding the market with their product—the value of silver (not just in the United States, but around the world) dropped as a result.

In 1890, the so-called free silver movement spurred a push in Congress for a solution. In a bipartisan compromise that guaranteed the passing of tariff legislation, Republicans put their support behind a bill known as the Sherman Silver Purchase Act (the Sherman Act), which would require that the government purchase millions of ounces of silver using paper money. The paper notes would be redeemable for either silver or gold coins. In theory, the government's purchases would drive up the price of silver and inflation and, therefore, satisfy the interests of the mines and farmers, respectively. The government had already been required to purchase millions of ounces of silver in the 1878 Bland-Allison Act—advocates such as Sherman saw the need to expand greatly upon this premise, and the bill was pushed through Congress.

In 1893, however, it became clear to many that the Sherman Silver Purchase Act was not as effective as its proponents had hoped. It did increase the price of silver somewhat, for example, but the fact that silver was so prevalent in the world markets meant that the price increase would not be significant. Additionally, Americans preferred to redeem their silver with gold, in essence making the two metals interchangeable in investors' eyes and drawing heavily on American gold reserves.

Meanwhile, a crisis was brewing in the American economy. Railroads, which had been built throughout the country, were overextended. The Philadelphia and Reading Railroad, for example, filed for bankruptcy shortly before Grover Cleveland began his second term as president. Other railroads fell to bankruptcy and receivership, and many banks (whose gold supplies had dwindled during this period) also closed their doors. A series of tariffs on imports also contributed to the crisis, experts argued—the protections put in place on American goods were in fact having an ill effect on revenues as well as manufacturing. The Panic of 1893, as it was known, would spur a depression that lasted until 1897.

Whether to repeal the Sherman Act and laws that increased tariffs on imports became a major issue during what was supposed to be a low-key congressional session. However, many experts and leaders pointed at the Sherman Silver Purchase Act as the main culprit. One such leader was Massachusetts governor William E. Russell, who offered his thoughts in an article published in the December 1893 edition of *North American Review*.

Author Biography

William Eustis Russell was born on January 6, 1857, in Cambridge, Massachusetts. He graduated from Harvard University in 1877 and, in 1879, graduated from Boston University Law School. He worked at his father's law firm before deciding to enter politics, gaining a seat on the Cambridge Board of Aldermen in 1883. In 1884, he was elected mayor of Cambridge, Massachusetts, a post he held until 1887. After two unsuccessful campaigns for governor, he won his third attempt in 1890, winning as a Democrat in the heavily Republican state. He remained in office until 1894, when he decided not to run for a fourth one-year term. He remained active in Massachusetts politics until his death on July 14, 1896.

HISTORICAL DOCUMENT: "Political Causes of the Business Depression"

That business depression exists and has existed since mid-summer no one doubts. Much as we deplore this fact, the painful proof of it is manifest; confident as we are that the worst is over and the country is now on the road to recovery, it is certainly true that a general depression, starting with stringency of money and a financial panic, has extended through all branches of business and has brought suffering and misery. It is equally true that this condition has not been limited to our country, but has been world-wide in extent, and is in part due to world-wide causes which it is quite beyond the power of legislation here, past or future, to control.

The fact remains, however, that legislation cannot escape its share of responsibility. Unwise laws can impair confidence, shake credit and disturb industrial stability, until the people, under the stress of suffering, demand and get remedial legislation by repeal or otherwise. Political action in this country can and does to a large extent affect our industrial interests. How far this connection of business with politics is wise or proper, it is not my purpose now to discuss.

Because it exists, economic and financial questions have, especially in late years, received prominent attention in political campaigns. Carefully, thoughtfully, the people have considered these matters in the firm belief that political action would affect their own material welfare. Since 1888 the political issues have been largely on these lines, and while other and sometimes local questions have also been considered, the attention of the country has been directed most to important matters of national and economic policy.

It is not strange then that again this year the old questions should have arisen. While it is an "off year," with only a few State elections, and those involving largely local issues, yet business depression and popular belief that its cause and remedy are to be found in legislation have brought both parties sharply to face the issue of responsibility for present conditions.

Unfortunately the issue is complicated by the political situation. The Democratic Party is in power, but Republican laws and policy are still in force. There has not been time yet to change or repeal these with the exception of a single measure, and that one only by a special session of a Democratic Congress convened by a Democratic President.

All other laws remain. The Republican policy upon tariff and finance, with this exception, is still the law of the land. Our revenue is still raised under Republican taxation, and our money spent under Republican appropriations. If mills are closed and men idle, it is well to remember that the McKinley Bill and high protection are still in full force; if the cause of sound money is threatened, that the Sherman law has only just been repealed; if there is an increasing deficit in the Treasury approaching fifty million dollars a year, that the Democratic Party left in March, 1889, a surplus of over one hundred millions, and that our income and expenses since have been determined by Republican laws.

There has been a change only of the Party in power with no fair chance yet to make the people's will and Democratic policy the law of the land. As measures are more important than men, so the acts and laws of a Party have the larger share of responsibility for results dependent upon political control. A Democratic administration with Republican laws to enforce is not responsible for those laws, nor for their evil results, until at least it has had opportunity to change them.

No doubt a suffering people are apt to lay their ills to the Party in power. It is easy to say to an idle workingman: "Your Party has won a national victory, and now you are out of a job," and to ask him to believe that the one fact has caused the other. However untrue this conclusion, it is hard to reach him, and to show him the real facts and the true causes of his idleness, especially in the haste and excitement of a short campaign. No doubt this Republican appeal to idle men, and this tendency to attribute hard times to the governing Party, were important factors in the recent elections, and the Democratic Party had to suffer for causes it did not create and over which it had little control. Now that the election is over the people will more carefully and fairly consider the situation and measure Party responsibility for it.

Realizing its responsibility for present laws, the Republican Party seeks to escape from it by claiming that not these laws but the fear of laws which are to be enacted has shaken confidence and brought adversity. This then is the issue? Is our admitted distress due to existing Republican legislation which the country has condemned and ordered to be repealed, or to impending Democratic legislation which is to carry out the people's will?

Let us see what the situation is: We find the country suffering from a diminished revenue, increased expenditures, a reduced gold reserve and a flood of useless silver. The Republican Party through its McKinley Bill declared its purpose to shut off imports and so reduce revenue. Then it set the precedent of a billion-dollar Congress, and by its laws fastened this expenditure on the future. Then for partisan purposes, and with the aid of Territories which it created States, protection and silver through the Republican Party made their coalition for a double burden on the people and passed the Silver Bill against the unanimous protest of the Democratic Party. Pour years of reckless, extravagant legislation had to be paid for by impaired confidence, with the inevitable result of panic and distress. Although the evil of the Sherman Bill was continually becoming more clear and burdensome, its authors in their State and National conventions either openly indorsed it or uttered no word of protest against it, until at last a financial crisis, due principally to it, broke their silence and forced them to lend their aid in undoing their own mischief. Then they claimed that the bill was passed to prevent the free coinage of silver. But at the time of its passage the House had already defeated free coinage, and it was known that the President would veto it. Their excuse means that over a Presidential veto a Republican Senate and a Republican House by a two-thirds vote would have supported free coinage though a majority of the House had just voted the other way. The country does not credit this excuse. It believes that the Sherman Bill was passed less from a patriotic purpose to avert danger than from a political purpose to risk a danger in order to save the silver-mining States to the Republican Party and to facilitate the passage of the McKinley Bill. So Republicans themselves have declared. Senator Teller, in the recent debate upon the repeal of the Sherman Bill, said:

> I want to refer to the statement made by the Senator from Ohio (Mr. Sherman) that the Sherman law was passed to save the country from a free coinage act. The Senator from Ohio was the Chairman of the Conference Committee which framed that act; and on the floor of the Senate, when he made the report, he stated in the most emphatic manner that the House of Representatives had determined in a very positive way that no free coinage bill could pass that body. Mr. President, I say here now with all due deference to the honorable Senator, and trying to keep as closely within the rules of senatorial decency and courtesy as the circumstances will admit, that his present statement was an afterthought. The records will not support it. The matter was brought here in that shape for the reason that it was supposed it would quiet the agitation and would maintain intact in the Northwest the Republican column of States. We were told in plain, unmistakable language that this might be a sop to our people which would save us and save our political organization in that great section of the country and that we could get nothing better. I repeat, Mr. President, there was not a man in this body nor anywhere else, who gave

attention to this subject,—who did not know we had reached a point where it was absolutely impossible to pass a free coinage bill.

Another Republican, Senator Jones, of Nevada, is quoted in the *Boston Daily Advertiser* of September 6, 1893, as having said to his associates in the Conference Committee, which framed the Sherman Bill, these words:

> Now I want to tell you, gentlemen, that the McKinley Bill will be over in the Senate in a very short time. If you reject our ultimatum on the silver proposition the silver men in the Senate will move the free coinage bill as an amendment to the McKinley Bill, and there are enough Democrats who will vote with us to carry it. Now after that amendment is adopted in the Senate, all the Democrats will vote against the McKinley Bill because it is a protective measure, and the Eastern protectionists will vote against it because it contains free silver. The free silver Republicans in the Senate will be the only men who will vote for it; and being protectionists they will be the only consistent men in the Senate, being for protection and for the free coinage of silver. When I got through they were listening to me, and before the conference broke up the silver purchase law known as the Sherman Act was agreed to. If there are many more misrepresentations on the floor of the Senate as to the reasons why the act of 1890 was agreed to and came about, I will take the floor and explain what occurred and how it came to be adopted.

And again, but a few days ago, in the closing debate on the repeal of the Sherman Bill, at least one other Republican Senator in effect repeated the charge and served notice that the coalition of silver and protection was ended because the Republican Party had not kept faith with silver.

It is true that neither Party is united upon this question, but the difference between them is that at the critical moment the Republican Party yields to financial heresy in its ranks and the Democratic Party conquers it. This was strikingly shown by the Democratic administration from 1884 to 1888. Its unflinching stand for sound money was met by the criticism and opposition of the Republican Party, expressed in the Republican national convention of 1888, later by Republican leaders, notably by Mr. McKinley, who said in his speech at Toledo, February, 1891:

During all of his (Cleveland's) years as the head of the Government he was dishonoring one of our precious metals, one of our great products, discrediting silver and enhancing the price of gold. He endeavored even before his inauguration to stop the coinage of silver dollars, and afterwards and to the end of his administration persistently used his power to that end. He was determined to contract the circulating medium and demonetize one of the coins of commerce, limit the volume of money among the people, make money scarce and therefore dear. He would have increased the value of money and diminished the value of everything else; money the master, everything else the servant.

This was followed by Republican acts in admitting the silver Territories and in the passage of the Sherman Bill. Always the spirit of compromise was dominating that Party and giving new life and vigor to its financial unsoundness. Contrast with this the action of the Democratic Party not only from 1884 to 1888, but later in meeting division within its ranks upon this question. With an overwhelming majority in the House of Representatives in 1892 it fought and conquered the demand for the passage of silver legislation, believed by the country to be unsound and unsafe. It faced the issue again in its national convention, and settled it not by compromise, but by argument and the triumphant assertion of a sound principle and policy; and then, as its pledge for the future, it nominated as its candidate the one man most conspicuous before the country for consistent, steadfast devotion to such policy. Again, within a few weeks, when a general demand arose for the repeal of so much of the Sherman Bill as business men believed had been the great cause of depression, and the Democratic Party properly was called upon to face this responsibility, it found united action impossible and the only course open concession or a fight. It chose the latter, although the fatal spirit of compromise was in the air. Such compromise was suggested by Republican precedents, but Democratic precedents and pledges prevailed, and unconditional repeal, through a fight, obtained a great and deserved victory. Ex-Speaker Reed has recently said that this was a victory of the Democratic President over his Party. A Democratic President was indeed at the helm, but a Democratic crew was aboard the ship, and, while he "kept the rudder true," together they sailed the ship out of financial shoals into safe waters. The President stood for right and led his Party, instead of following the precedent set by his predecessor, who yielded to wrong because led by his Party. Democratic State conventions have, almost without exception, declared this leadership to be the expression and enforcement of true Democratic principles. I believe that Republican action on the silver question, marked as it has been by bargains, concessions and compromises culminating in the Sherman Bill, has been the chief cause of business depression. That bill cannot escape responsibility, as Republicans contend, on the ground that the panic did not come until three years after its passage. It took time for it to make its evil fully felt, and it will take time to recover from that evil now that the cause has ceased.

Through these three years the Sherman Bill has steadily been doing its mischievous work, heaping up silver, driving out gold and impairing the public confidence that our increasing currency could be kept at par with gold. During the [administration of President Harrison, from March, 1889, to March, 1893, the treasury gold, outside of the reserve of $100,000,000, fell from $96,000,000 to $3,000,000, while our paper currency, outside of the $346,000,000 of legal tenders, rose from $246,000,000 to $448,000,000. The proportion of free gold to this currency fell from thirty-nine to less than one per cent. Time was constantly making matters worse. The crisis had got to come. The man who fell from the third story window to the sidewalk declared that it was not the fall that hurt him, but bringing up so suddenly on the ground. Under the Sherman Bill the country had been steadily falling and was certain to bring up with a round turn at the end. The best proof that this was the cause of the business depression comes from business itself. In the midst of its distress it knew and stated the cause of it and the remedy. From boards of trade and business centres all over the country there came a unanimous demand. For what? To let the tariff alone? No, but to repeal the Sherman Bill. Impatient of delay, as if its very life depended upon this action, business watched the movement for repeal. Every step in that movement it felt and indicated as keenly as the barometer does a change of weather. It said emphatically through its representative boards that the one predominant cause of its trouble was the financial legislation of a Republican Congress and the one remedy was its repeal. As this remedy was delayed by weeks and months of discussion and obstruction, the business depression became more serious and so deep rooted that now the repeal itself cannot produce an immediate cure.

But the Republican Party, anxious to escape its responsibility, insists that the crisis was due, not to its laws, but to impending Democratic laws; that we have not been reaping the whirlwind Republicans have sown, but are suffering because the country, by a large majority, has thrust them from power and condemned their financial and tariff policy. Let us examine their claim. What is or was the impending Democratic legislation at the time of the crisis? First, the repeal of the mischievous provisions of the Republican Sherman Bill. To that the Democratic Party was pledged; for that a Democratic President had called together a Democratic Congress in special session, which now has redeemed the pledge and met the responsibility that rested upon it. Undoubtedly this impending legislation was not feared as a cause of trouble, but hoped for as a necessary remedy. Next is the repeal of the McKinley Bill. It is true the Democratic Party has, by the deliberate, repeated judgment of the people, been charged with this duty, which it means faithfully to meet, and so obey the people's mandate to reduce the tariff. But we emphatically assert that the promise of such reduction has not caused present depression; but on the contrary that the reduction, when accomplished, will be only a blessing to the people and their industries. We know that the Republicans tell the laborer out of work that a Democratic victory which condemned unjust taxation, and promised that the power of the people's government would be used not for selfish interests but for the equal benefit of all, that this has brought him idleness and poverty.

They neglect to tell him that he is still living under high protection and the McKinley Bill, or that after three years of trial it has failed to give him its promised benefits of work, high wages and prosperity. If called upon to meet this fact, they excuse the failure of that law by asserting in the words of Mr. Reed that "The McKinley Bill is in prison under sentence of death," and they ask with him, "How can it help you or me?" No doubt that is its condition. It was charged with the crime of robbery, tried before the people fairly and fully, with proof of the influences by which it was produced, its purposes and effect, it was found guilty, sentenced and is in prison awaiting execution.

But this was last November. And even before that it had been tried and condemned. It is an old offender. It was first tried in 1890, when the facts in the case were fresh in the public mind, and was then found guilty. True, a Republican Senate and President could for a while stay proceedings. A little time might be given it for repentance and to prepare for death. But it was in prison then and has been for three years with the condemnation of the country upon it and with the certainty that it must go. Timid manufacturers who really believed that their prosperity was dependent upon it ought to have been shortening sail since 1890.

Let us look a little into the past and see how far the promise or fear of tariff reduction has injured business or caused depression. There has scarcely been a year from the close of the war until 1888 when there has not been promised and impending tariff reduction. The war tariff itself was passed with the pledge that it should be reduced when the necessity for a war revenue was over. Presidents Grant and Arthur and their Secretaries of the Treasury repeatedly recommended such reduction. Some measures in that direction, like the removal of the duty on hides in 1872, were passed. Then the tariff commission of 1882 took up the subject, and after a thorough examination recommended a reduction of duties of from twenty to twenty-five per cent; and later, in 1884, the Republican Party became very largely in favor of some reduction. Then followed the earnest recommendation of President Cleveland in 1887, and the introduction of the Mills Bill. In all these years there were promise and hope of tariff reduction through both the Republican and Democratic parties, and though these efforts failed, some of them unexpectedly, nowhere did the anticipation of tariff reduction cause panic or business distress. Then came the tariff reform victories of 1890 and 1892, and not for many months after the last was there a panic or business depression. Not until our revenue fell off, and gold was exported, and the gold reserve impaired, and silver purchase enormously increased, all acts directly chargeable to Republican Legislation, not until then was confidence destroyed. After that business became stagnant and mills idle. That these were the true causes of the trouble Republicans and Protectionists have admitted. In a recent interview Mr. Thomas Dolan, the well-known protectionist of Philadelphia and of its Manufacturers' Club, said:

> I believe that the depression is almost wholly due to the silver policy. If the alarm was due to the victory of the Democrats, why was it not manifested last November? The people knew then as well as they know now that it was within the power of the new administration to repeal the tariff laws, yet no uneasiness was felt. In fact, in the woollen business everything went along swimmingly until the first of July.

The American Wool Reporter, a standard authority, corroborates this statement. It says:

> For those who believe the tariff has been and is the paramount factor in the present depression in the industrial and business world, it may be of interest to note that certain descriptions of wools actually advanced in prices in the spring months clothing wools were fully one cent per pound higher in March than in January, and some wools two cents per pound higher. If the tariff was a factor it had not made itself manifest in prices during these months. As we have shown in previous issues, the goods market was in good shape, the manufacturers with large orders in hand right through the spring months. The depression is due to a lack of confidence in the stability of our currency.

And no less an authority than Senator Sherman, in the debate in the Senate on October 17, 1893, said:

> If we would try it (repeal of the Sherman act) to-morrow, after all the long debate that has been had, and dispose of this question as we think best for the people of the United States, while you are assuming your responsibility, we would gladden the hearts of millions of laboring men who are now being turned out of employment; we would relieve the business cares of thousands of men whose whole fortunes are embarked in trade; we would relieve the farmer and his product for free transportation to foreign countries now clogged for the want of money. In the present condition of affairs there is no money to bay cotton or corn and wheat for foreign consumption. Break down the barrier now maintained by the Senate of the United States, check this viper called obstruction to the will of the majority, give the Senate free power and play, and in ten days from this time the skies will brighten, business will resume its ordinary course, and "the clouds that lower upon our house will be in the deep bosom of the ocean buried."

Let us go a step further and see what the Democratic tariff policy is, and whether it can be an injury or cause of alarm to our industries. Its policy, as often stated, is a revenue tariff with reduction of duties to cheapen the necessaries of life, and give free raw materials to our industries. This it has declared in National and State platforms, formulated into bills and voted for in Congress. This it is pledged to give in its new bill. It means free wool, coal, iron ore and other raw materials, with fair and proper reduction on finished products.

It is something in favor of such a policy that since 1890 it has, after thorough consideration, been twice indorsed by a large majority of our people; that great manufacturing States like New York, New Jersey and Connecticut have constantly supported it, and even Massachusetts voted for it in 1890; that it has been the policy of our nation through most of its life; that, after thorough trial of the low tariff of 1846, manufacturing New England joined with the rest of the country in demanding the lower tariff of 1857, and under these low tariffs many of our great manufacturing cities were founded, and their industries established and prospered. Can such a policy now, after a generation more of active industrial life, with our industries older, with our labor more efficient, with our progress in inventions and greater aptitude for manufacturing, can it, with its assured benefit of free raw material, be a just cause for alarm?

Let us consider some pertinent facts upon this point gathered from the industries themselves, and, first, a bit of evidence from New England. In February, 1889, its iron and steel industries prepared a statement and petition, setting forth their condition and asking Congress for free coal, iron ore and reduced duties on pig and scrap iron. That statement declared that the tendency of these duties had been "to wipe out the iron and steel industries, large and small, of New England." It gives the facts to support this claim. Again, it says: "It is then clearly the duty on coal and crude iron that is strangling in New England one of the largest of all the wonderful industries of our modern days." It adds: "There is no necessity for letting it die; that it is only the existing duties on coal, ore and crude iron that are strangling it; and that the abolition of those duties will not only keep it alive, but will insure it a tremendous vitality and large increase."

This statement and petition were signed by 598 iron and steel industries of New England, including almost without exception every one of importance, and by men of both political parties, including the then Republican Governor of Massachusetts. Certainly to that industry there is hope of new life and growth when a Democratic tariff bill takes the place of the McKinley law.

Turn next to the woollen industry. The burden today of a duty upon wool is clearly shown by the fact that this industry asks and gets an additional duty on its finished products called compensatory, because given to offset this burden. The industry itself asked Congress in 1866 for free wool, and said that with it a duty of twenty-five per cent, on its finished products was sufficient, and recently over 700 woollen manufacturers and dealers, including some of the largest in the country, have again asked for this benefit. They have no fear that free wool, which in all other civilized countries has been a help to this industry, will here work it harm; and they remember that since 1888 the Democratic Party has twice formulated its policy into bills which gave free wool, still leaving a duty on its product larger than the labor cost of the product and much larger than the twenty-five percent, asked by the woollen industry in 1866.

Turn next to the boot and shoe and leather industries. What better proof could be given of the benefit of the Democratic policy of free raw materials than the growth and prosperity of those industries after the duty on hides was removed in 1872, and their unanimous protest against the proposition to reimpose that duty by the McKinley Bill? With their principal raw material free, they export annually over thirteen million dollars worth of goods, competing in the markets of the world with the labor of the world. Mr. McKinley said there was no reason for a duty on wool which did not equally apply to hides. He was right, but he did not put back the duty against this protest. The Democratic Party says that every reason which made hides free demands that wool be free, and it proposes to act upon this belief. The great advantage of free silk to the silk industry, of free rags to the paper industry, of free hides to the boot and shoe and leather industries, can and ought to be extended to other industries as a benefit not only to all the people as consumers, but to the industries themselves, giving them a larger market here and a better chance to send their products into foreign markets.

This is the policy of the Democratic Party as declared in its platforms, formulated in its measures and supported by its votes. It advocates a revenue tariff, remembering that revenue has been the basis of every tariff, even our war tariff, until 1888, when another principle, controlling the Republican Party, supplanted it and found expression in the McKinley Bill. It believes that a tariff, which gives free raw materials and cheaper necessaries of life and which is required to raise a revenue of nearly two hundred million dollars, is a conservative measure, and a benefit to industries as well as to the people. It does not believe in tariff taxation which has for its purpose and result taking from one to give to another, or burdening all to enrich the few. It opposes the principle of the McKinley Bill that taxation can be laid not for revenue, a public purpose, but solely for private interests, to kill competition, encourage trusts and cut off revenue.

The country deliberately, emphatically said in 1890 and 1892 that the Democratic policy was right in principle and would be beneficial in its results. It is hardly conceivable that its mature judgment, twice expressed, was wholly wrong. It certainly is no proof of this that a great business depression has come under another tariff policy, which by the same judgment the country condemned and ordered to be repealed.

Document Analysis

Governor Russell's comments recognize that the United States and the rest of the world, as a result of the Panic of 1893, were entering a severe economic depression, one that would impact every industrial sector. Some of the causes of this depression went beyond the scope of any legislative action, he wrote. However, some of the causes could have been avoided altogether if "unwise" legislation had not been passed into law, he adds.

Russell acknowledged that it was difficult to legislate on matters of business. Striking a balance between passing laws that protect the American economy and interfering in business matters was a vexing endeavor, he writes. Nevertheless, legislators frequently made attempts on this front. The Democratic governor says that the Republican Congress was culpable for the ongoing fiscal crisis, as these leaders—before the elections of 1892—were responsible for passing legislation that negatively affected the business and economic interests of the country. Among these missteps, he claims, were protectionist and monetary policies enacted by the Republican-controlled legislature. Even though Congress returned to Democratic control, it would take time, he writes, to undo the Republican-passed laws that were to blame for the crisis.

Russell cites two major Republican-passed laws that he said contributed to the crisis. The first was a series of bills that increased tariffs and applied taxes on other items. Democrats had criticized such measures (including one filed by Senator William McKinley) on the grounds that, by raising tariff rates, the laws were dramatically impacting revenues, generating fewer imports.

The second law—the Sherman Act—was even more impactful, Russell says. There was a great deal of political posturing when the Senate took up the act's passage, Russell states. "Silver men" strong-armed both Democrats and Republicans alike into ensuring its passage as well as the admission into the Union of silver-rich states. The debate over the act's merits and risks, Russell says, was certainly not evenly split along party lines. However, Russell points at the Republicans for their uncompromising approach to passage.

When the aforementioned taxation and silver laws began to have ill effects on the American economy, Russell says, Republicans were quick to place blame not on the Sherman Act but on the laws passed later by Democrats. Russell argues that, while the Republicans sought to escape their culpability, the Democrats were unified in undoing these two measures (the Sherman Act and the McKinley tariff law). Russell cites the testimony of a number of key industry leaders, organizations, and officials (including Sherman himself) who, when these laws were being passed, argued in favor, only to reverse their positions when the economy went sour.

Russell then turns to several industries in his home state as evidence of the need to follow the Democratic course. The wool industry, he said, would benefit greatly from a reduction in tariffs, as would the shoe and leather industries. The oil, coal, and iron industries, he adds, all stood in favor of repealing McKinley's tariffs. The Democrats, Russell concludes, offered sound policies that included the repeal of both Sherman and McKinley's respective laws.

Essential Themes

Russell was elected governor in a state that was predominantly Republican, and although he had a reputation for attaining bipartisan support on a number of issues in Massachusetts, his experience working in the political minority brought out a sense of defiance. His defiance is evident in this article, wherein he offered his opinions on the causes of the Panic of 1893 and the subsequent depression. He assigned blame for the crisis to the Republicans, whom he said had forced onerous tariff increases and the Sherman Act through Congress and into law.

After the Civil War, Russell argued, the Republicans had introduced a series of tariffs that many (Russell included) believed became too prohibitive for US industries to maintain international business. Meanwhile, the so-called silver men (leaders who strongly advocated for the Sherman Act's passage on behalf of the silver mines and farmers) refused to compromise on the silver issue, and Republicans simply acquiesced, Russell said. Some Democrats were willing to work with Republicans to establish sound policy, Russell insisted, but the Democrats were in the minority. Even now, he added, with the Democrats finally back in power in Congress, it would take a long time to undo those laws, especially when the Republicans shied away from taking responsibility for them.

Russell's article is not just replete with political rhetoric. It includes a careful analysis of the depreciation of gold as a result of the Sherman Act. It also includes commentary from a number of leaders of key industries (such as the wool, steel, and coal sectors), all of whom argue that the McKinley tariffs and other tax laws were adversely impacting their businesses. Perhaps most integral to his argument is the inclusion of testimony from industry and political leaders who had originally advocated for Sherman and McKinley's initiatives and who, when the crisis began, immediately recognized that the Sherman Act and the tariff increases were the main culprits. Russell's politically charged comments aside, statements such as these were highly influential in bringing about both measures' repeal as the depression took hold.

—Michael P. Auerbach, MA

Bibliography and Additional Reading

Hogarty, Richard A. *Massachusetts Political and Public Policy: Studies in Power and Leadership*. Amherst: U of Massachusetts P, 2002. Print.

"Massachusetts Governor William Eustis Russell." *Former Governors' Bios*. National Governors Assoc., 2014. Web. 25 Apr. 2014.

Morgan, Howard Wayne. *William McKinley and His America*. Rev. ed. Kent: Kent State UP, 2003. Print.

"Panic of 1893." *The Life and Times of Florence Kelley in Chicago 1891–1899*. Northwestern Univ. School of Law, 2008. Web. 25 Apr. 2014.

Reed, Lawrence W. *A Lesson from the Past: The Silver Panic of 1893*. Irvington: Foundation for Economic Educ., 1993. Print.

Steeples, Douglas, and David O. Whitten. *Democracy in Desperation: The Depression of 1893*. Westport: Greenwood, 1998. Print.

"William Eustis Russell." *Mass.gov*. Commonwealth of Massachusetts, 2014. Web. 25 Apr. 2014.

■ "The Absurd Effort to Make the World Over"

Date: March 1894
Author: William Graham Sumner
Genre: editorial

Summary Overview

Writing in the *Forum*, a leading American general-interest intellectual magazine, Yale sociologist William Graham Sumner published an essay critiquing the push for "social reform" in the late nineteenth century. Sumner attacks Progressive-Era efforts to bring about social and economic reform, claiming that these efforts were both wrong-headed and doomed to failure because of the Progressive inability to come to grips with the intractable nature of social reality. According to Sumner, Progressives are also frequently in error in their assertions about change for the conditions of the working class, which had actually improved since the colonial era despite the Progressive claims that industrialization harmed workers. Sumner sketches a picture of economic progress celebrating the rise of the industrial organization that dominates society and provides a level of prosperity unequaled in history.

Defining Moment

The late nineteenth century in the United States was a time of capitalist economic transformation. The wealth and power of business magnates or "robber barons" was being challenged by Progressive reformers hoping to regulate it and by nascent labor unions organizing workers seeking better working conditions and higher wages. The extremely wealthy, whose wealth was not based as in the colonial era on land but rather on money, were an increasingly prominent presence in American life. Businesses, particularly large businesses, were more frequently organized into corporations. In reaction, socialism, an import from Europe, was also attracting much interest among Americans. The so-called Gilded Age saw a dramatic increase in the influence of business on government.

The growing power of capitalists was connected to an even more fundamental economic transformation: the rise of industry with the growth of the railroad system and the expansion of manufacturing. America, which had since colonial times had been a predominantly agricultural economy, was becoming a more industrialized one. The Northeast, where Sumner spent his life, was a leading region in this transformation. Along with this transformation, the relatively high wages paid by American industry attracted increasing immigration from Europe and elsewhere. By fostering immigration, industrialization made the United States a more diverse and multicultural country, and by concentrating populations in industrial and commercial cities, it made the nation more urbanized. As enterprises grew larger, managers and business owners grew more removed from workers than they had been in small workshop enterprises.

Sumner was also writing at a time when the study of society was becoming professionalized and secularized, as exemplified by his own decision to leave the ministry and enter the world of the university. Influences from Europe were leading to the creation of the discipline of sociology, the study of society, of which Sumner was a leading early practitioner. Along with secularism went a growing tendency toward materialism, analyzing society not in terms of abstract principles but material benefits. Classical economics, with its exaltation of free trade and suspicion of government intervention in the economy, had arrived in the United States from Britain in the mid-nineteenth century, but its influence was continuing to grow in Sumner's time. This was frequently combined with the influence of Darwinian ideas about advances through struggle and the positivist prioritizing of facts over theory. The new ideas were arriving at a time when the academic curriculum was in turmoil, as the old curriculum based on religion and the Greek and Roman classics was increasingly seen as irrelevant to modern life, and academics like Sumner contended over what students should be required and expected to learn.

Author Biography

William Graham Sumner (1840–1910) was born to an English immigrant couple in Paterson, New Jersey. He briefly served as an Episcopal clergyman, but in 1872, he left the ministry to become professor of political economy at Yale University. Although his interests later shifted to the study of society, Sumner remained deeply influenced by the orthodox free-trade economics of the nineteenth century. Like other American economic conservatives, he supported a gold-backed currency, opposing the free silver movement and protectionism. He was also highly suspicious of labor unions, although he believed that they served morale-building and information-disseminating purposes. Later deemed a Social Darwinist (a term not widely used at the time), he became embroiled in a controversy with the Yale administration for employing the English Social Darwinist Herbert Spencer's *The Study of Sociology* (1873) as a textbook. Sumner pioneered the establishment of sociology as an academic discipline in America, teaching the first sociology course at an American university in 1875 and being elected the second president of the American Sociological Society in 1908.

HISTORICAL DOCUMENT: "The Absurd Effort to Make the World Over"

The burden of proof is on those who affirm that our social condition is utterly diseased and in need of radical regeneration! My task at present, therefore, is entirely negative and critical: to examine the allegations of fact and the doctrines which are put forward to prove the correctness of the diagnosis and to warrant the use of the remedies proposed.

The propositions put forward by social reformers nowadays are chiefly of two kinds. There are assertions in historical form, chiefly in regard to the comparison of existing with earlier social states, which are plainly based on defective historical knowledge, or at most on current stock historical dicta which are uncritical and incorrect….

The other class of propositions consists of dogmatic statements which, whether true or not, are unverifiable. This class of propositions is the pest and bane of current economic and social discussion. [Upon a more or less superficial view of some phenomenon a suggestion arises which is embodied in a philosophical proposition and promulgated as a truth. From the form and nature of such propositions they can always be brought under the head of "ethics." This word at least gives them an air of elevated sentiment and purpose, which is the only warrant they possess….

When anyone asserts that the class of skilled and unskilled manual laborers of the United States is worse off now in respect to diet, clothing, lodgings, furniture, fuel, and lights; in respect to the age at which they can marry; the number of children they can provide for; the start in life which they can give to their children, and their chances accumulating capital, than they ever have been at any former time, he makes a reckless assertion for which no facts have been offered in proof. Upon an appeal to facts, the contrary of this assertion would be clearly established. It suffices, therefore, to challenge those who are responsible for the assertion to make it good.

If it is said that the employed class are under much more stringent discipline than they were thirty years ago or earlier, it is true. It is not true that there has been any qualitative change in this respect within thirty years, but it is true that a movement which began at the first settlement of the country has been advancing with constant acceleration and has become a noticeable feature within our time.

This movement is the advance in the industrial organization. The first settlement was made by agriculturists, and for a long time there was scarcely any organization. There were scattered farmers, each working for himself, and some small towns with only rudimentary commerce and handicrafts. As the country has filled up, the arts and professions have been differentiated and the industrial organization has been advancing.

This fact and its significance has hardly been noticed at all; but the stage of the industrial organization existing at any time, and the rate of advance in its development, are the absolutely controlling social facts. Nine-tenths of the socialistic and semi-socialistic, and sentimental or ethical, suggestions by which we are overwhelmed come from failure to understand the phenomena of the industrial organization and its expansion. It controls us all because we are all in it. It creates the conditions of our existence, sets the limits of our social activity, regulates the bonds of our social relations, determines our conceptions of good and evil, suggests our life-philosophy, molds our inherited political institutions, and reforms the oldest and toughest customs, like marriage and property.

I repeat that the turmoil of heterogeneous and antagonistic social whims and speculations in which we live is due to the failure to understand what the industrial organization is and its all-pervading control over human life, while the traditions of our school of philosophy lead us always to approach the industrial organization, not from the side of objective study, but from that of philosophical doctrine. Hence it is that we find that the method of measuring what we see happening by what are called ethical standards, and of proposing to attack the phenomena by methods thence deduced, is so popular.

* * *

All organization implies restriction of liberty. The gain of power is won by narrowing individual range. The methods of business in colonial days were loose and slack to an inconceivable degree. The movement of industry has been all the time toward promptitude, punctuality, and reliability. It has been attended all the way by lamentations about the good old times; about the decline of small industries; about the lost spirit of comradeship between employer and employee; about the narrowing of the interests of the workman; about his conversion into a machine or into a "ware," and about industrial war.

These lamentations have all had reference to unquestionable phenomena attendant on advancing organization. In all occupations the same movement is discernible—in the learned professions, in schools, in trade, commerce, and transportation. It is to go on faster than ever, now that the continent is filled up by the first superficial layer of population over its whole extent and the intensification of industry has begun. The great inventions both make the intention of the organization possible and make it inevitable, with all its consequences, whatever they may be....

Now the intensification of the social organization is what gives us greater social power. It is to it that we owe our increased comfort and abundance. We are none of us ready to sacrifice this. On the contrary, we want more of it. We would not return to the colonial simplicity and the colonial exiguity if we could. If not, then we must pay the price. Our life is bounded on every side by conditions. We can have this if we will agree to submit to that. In the case of industrial power and product the great condition is combination of force under discipline and strict coordination. Hence the wild language about wage-slavery and capitalistic tyranny.

In any state of society no great achievements can be produced without great force. Formerly great force was attainable only by slavery aggregating the power of great numbers of men. Roman civilization was built on this. Ours has been built on steam. It is to be built on electricity. Then we are all forced into an organization around these natural forces and adapted to the methods or their application; and although we indulge in rhetoric about political liberty, nevertheless we find ourselves bound tight in a new set of conditions, which control the modes of our existence and determine the directions in which alone economic and social liberty can go.

If it is said that there are some persons in our time who have become rapidly and in a great degree rich, it is true; it if is said that large aggregations of wealth in the control of individuals is a social danger, it is not true....

If this poor old world is as bad as they say, one more reflection may check the zeal of the headlong reformer. It is at any rate a tough old world. It has taken its trend and curvature and all its twists and tangles from a long course of formation. All its wry and crooked gnarls and knobs are therefore stiff and stubborn. If we puny men by our arts can do anything at all to straighten them, it will only be by modifying the tendencies of some of the forces at work, so that, after a sufficient time, their action may be changed a little and slowly the lines of movement may be modified. This effort, however, can at most be only slight, and it will take a long time. In the meantime spontaneous forces will be at work, compared with which our efforts are like those of a man trying to deflect a river, and these forces will have changed the whole problem before our interferences have time to make themselves felt.

The great stream of time and earthly things will sweep on just the same in spite of us. It bears with it now all the errors and follies of the past, the wreckage of all the philosophies, the fragments of all the civilizations, the wisdom of all the abandoned ethical systems, the debris of all the institutions, and the penalties of all the mistakes. It is only in imagination that we stand by and look at and criticize it and plan to change it. Everyone of us is a child of his age and cannot get out of it. He is in the stream and is swept along with it. All his sciences and philosophy come to him out of it.

Therefore the tide will not be changed by us. It will swallow up both us and our experiments. It will absorb the efforts at change and take them into itself as new but trivial components, and the great movement of tradition and work will go on unchanged by our fads and schemes. The things which will change it are the great discoveries and inventions, the new reactions inside the social organism, and then changes in the earth itself on account of changes in the cosmic forces.

These causes will make of it just what, in fidelity to them, it ought to be. The men will be carried along with it and be made by it. The utmost they can do by their cleverness will be to note and record their course as they are carried along, which is what we do now, and is that which leads us to the vain fancy that we can make or guide the movement. That is why it is the greatest folly of which a man can be capable, to sit down with a slate and pencil to plan out a new social world.

GLOSSARY

dicta: (pl. of dictum): authoritative pronouncements; maxims

exiguity: meagerness or scantiness

warrant: justification

Document Analysis

Sumner's focus in this essay is less on the ends of progressive reform than on the "absurd" reforming instinct itself, which he finds incompatible with the enormous difficulty of changing social habits and customs. Sumner believes that the reformers are intellectually sloppy, using words without a rigorous understanding of their meaning and making assertions, particularly about past societies, without awareness of their truth or falsity. This leads them to paint contemporary society as declining when it is in many ways improving.

All claims about the deteriorating condition of American workers are, in Sumner's belief, false and based on an inadequate knowledge of the past. Sentimentality and a tendency for making broad, abstract statements without a basis in social reality are also problems for Progressive activists and thinkers. Calling for more rigorous fact-checking of claims about society would also benefit his position as an academic by promoting professionalization of social thought. All social analysis that is not based on rigorous factual analysis Sumner attacks as "sentimental" or "ethical"; his use of the word "ethical" in a derogatory sense broke with its use in mainstream American culture.

Sumner's picture of history is one where the great forces underlying social and historical change are largely immune to conscious action. (In his emphasis on changes in economic relations driving history, his awareness of the significance of the rise of industry, and his materialism, Sumner resembles his older contemporary, Karl Marx, whose politics he held in low regard.) The great economic change of Sumner's own period as he saw it was the rise of large, disciplined organizations associated with the growth of industry. Sumner does not use the term "Industrial Revolution," generally accepted as having been popularized by the British economic historian Arnold Toynbee (1852–83), but it is clear he sees the rise of industry as connected to major social transformation. These organizations regulate the life of the worker to a degree unprecedented in the less organized enterprises of the colonial and early national periods, giving rise to (in his view) baseless charges of "wage slavery," but they have also, and far more importantly, delivered an unparalleled prosperity. Trying to pass laws to moderate the impact of these changing social forces is a waste of time, in Sumner's view.

Economic prosperity is close to a supreme good for Sumner, although he seems to prefer that all classes benefit. He argues that the material condition of American workers has improved greatly since the colonial era and that the increasing regimentation of work is a small price to pay.

Essential Themes

Sumner became one of America's leading and most respected intellectuals. His brand of laissez-faire conservatism, built on the defense of capitalism and economic inequality, has had a great influence on the politics of American business and has always had its champions among university professors (more economists than practitioners of Sumner's own discipline of sociology) and other scholars. There has also been a revival of interest in Sumner's economic thought among libertarians. However, if he thought his essay would stop the Progressive movement in its tracks, he was destined for disappointment. The anti-trust campaign under the administrations of Republicans Theodore Roosevelt and William Howard Taft attempted to rein in the power of the wealthy with some success, and the New Deal of the 1930s saw the further expansion of the regulatory state as a response to the Great Depression. Labor unions, which attempted to ameliorate the conditions of work and increase wages through collective action, also survived and grew in the subsequent decades. Although Sumner believed that government should interfere with business as little as possible, he also feared the influence of business on government, and there is some evidence that by the early twentieth century, he was more skeptical of the extremely wealthy.

Debates about the effectiveness of social reform and the value of economic controls versus economic freedom have continued to the present day. Although Sumner and his intellectual allies are often referred to as "classical liberals," the skeptical position against reform movements and the belief that large enterprises and wealthy people should be allowed to go their own ways with minimal interference he put forth is now identified with conservative forces in American political and intellectual life. Furthermore, great concentrations of wealth and their effect on American society are now usually discussed under the heading of inequality.

—*William E. Burns, PhD*

Bibliography and Additional Readings

Curtis, Bruce. *William Graham Sumner*. Boston: Twayne, 1981. Print.

Hofstadter, Richard. *Social Darwinism in American Thought*. Boston: Beacon, 1992. Print.

McCloskey, Robert Green. *American Conservatism in the Age of Enterprise 1865–1910: A Study of William Graham Sumner, Stephen J. Field, and Andrew Carnegie*. New York: Harper, 1964. Print.

Sumner, William Graham. *On Liberty, Society and Politics: The Essential Essays of William Graham Sumner*. Ed. Robert C. Bannister. Indianapolis: Liberty Fund, 1992. Print.

■ "Cross of Gold" Speech

Date: July 9, 1896
Author: William Jennings Bryan
Genre: speech

Summary Overview

The Cross of Gold speech was given by the young but ambitious politician William Jennings Bryan at the Democratic Party's 1896 national convention during a period in which the United States was divided on the issue of its monetary system. The nation effectively followed a gold standard for currency, but supporters of adding a silver standard—a policy known as "bimetallism"—were increasingly vocal in their belief that increasing the money supply would more widely distribute prosperity. Bryan's advocacy of silver helped him become the Democrats' presidential candidate for the 1896 election and a longstanding party leader.

Defining Moment

The Cross of Gold speech occurred in an election year that saw intense debate over monetary policy both within the Democratic Party and throughout the nation as a whole. In 1873 the Coinage Act had essentially made gold the only legal tender of the United States following the Civil War. The late nineteenth century was marked by tumultuous economic conditions, including a fall in agricultural prices and the Panic of 1893, and a growing populist movement blamed the gold standard. By the 1890s the so-called Free Silver movement had become a significant political force and had some success reintroducing silver currency, but the issue remained divisive.

Monetary policy particularly split the ranks of the Democratic Party. The "Bourbon" or "Gold Bug" Democrats, such as President Grover Cleveland and other politicians from urban Eastern states, represented the gold standard status quo. The Free Silver movement was associated with rural Western states and argued that the adoption of silver as a monetary standard at a ratio of sixteen-to-one with gold would raise prices, thus benefiting farmers and others of the working class. Gold Bugs argued that the adoption of silver would lead to inflation and make it more difficult for the United States to trade with countries such as Great Britain (then the leading economic power) that followed a gold standard. The debate over bimetallism was the central element of the party's national convention in 1896 as Democrats sought to establish a platform and select a presidential candidate.

Author Biography

William Jennings Bryan was born on March 19, 1860, in Illinois. After getting a law degree and practicing for a few years he moved to Lincoln, Nebraska, in 1887. There he was elected to the U.S. Congress in 1890 as a Democrat and re-elected in 1892, but a Senate run in 1894 ended in failure. He worked as a public lecturer, honing his skills as a gifted and persuasive speaker.

Bryan became active in the Free Silver movement and saw bimetallism as a way to unite the fractured Democratic Party. His Cross of Gold speech at the party's 1896 convention was so stirring that he was nominated as the Democratic presidential candidate despite his youth and inexperience. Yet despite support from the populist movement he lost the general election. He was again nominated and defeated in both 1900 and 1908 as well. Still, he remained an important Democratic leader and was named President Woodrow Wilson's secretary of state in 1912.

Bryan's later career continued to be marked by his strong convictions on controversial subjects. As a pacifist he opposed U.S. involvement in World War I. He was also deeply religious, and in 1925, he joined the prosecution in the highly publicized Scopes trial, in which a teacher in Tennessee was charged for teaching evolution. Bryan died shortly after the trial on July 26, 1925.

HISTORICAL DOCUMENT: "Cross of Gold" Speech

I would be presumptuous, indeed, to present myself against the distinguished gentlemen to whom you have listened if this were a mere measuring of abilities; but this is not a contest between persons. The humblest citizen in all the land, when clad in the armor of a righteous cause, is stronger than all the hosts of error. I come to speak to you in defense of a cause as holy as the cause of liberty-the cause of humanity.

When this debate is concluded, a motion will be made to lay upon the table the resolution offered in commendation of the Administration, and also, the resolution offered in condemnation of the Administration. We object to bringing this question down to the level of persons. The individual is but an atom; he is born, he acts, he dies; but principles are eternal; and this has been a contest over a principle.

Never before in the history of this country has there been witnessed such a contest as that through which we have just passed. Never before in the history of American politics has a great issue been fought out as this issue has been, by the voters of a great party. On the fourth of March 1895, a few Democrats, most of them members of Congress, issued an address to the Democrats of the nation, asserting that the money question was the paramount issue of the hour; declaring that a majority of the Democratic party had the right to control the action of the party on this paramount issue; and concluding with the request that the believers in the free coinage of silver in the Democratic party should organize, take charge of, and control the policy of the Democratic party. Three months later, at Memphis, an organization was perfected, and the silver Democrats went forth openly and courageously proclaiming their belief, and declaring that, if successful, they would crystallize into a platform the declaration which they had made. Then began the struggle. With a zeal approaching the zeal which inspired the Crusaders who followed Peter the Hermit, our silver Democrats went forth from victory unto victory until they are now assembled, not to discuss, not to debate, but to enter up the judgment already rendered by the plain people of this country. In this contest brother has been arrayed against brother, father against son. The warmest ties of love, acquaintance, and association have been disregarded; old leaders have been cast aside when they have refused to give expression to the sentiments of those whom they would lead, and new leaders have sprung up to give direction to this cause of truth. Thus has the contest been waged, and we have assembled here under as binding and solemn instructions as were ever imposed upon representatives of the people.

We do not come as individuals. As individuals we might have been glad to compliment the gentleman from New York [Senator Hill], but we know that the people for whom we speak would never be willing to put him in a position where he could thwart the will of the Democratic Party. I say it was not a question of persons; it was a question of principle, and it is not with gladness, my friends, that we find ourselves brought into conflict with those who are now arrayed on the other side.

When you [turning to the gold delegates] come before us and tell us that we are about to disturb your business interests, we reply that you have disturbed our business interests by your course.

We say to you that you have made the definition of a business man too limited in its application. The man who is employed for wages is as much a business man as his employer; the attorney in a country town is as much a business man as the corporation counsel in a great metropolis; the merchant at the cross-roads store is as much a business man as the merchant of New York; the farmer who goes forth in the morning and toils all day, who begins in the spring and toils all summer, and who by the application of brain and muscle to the natural resources of the country creates wealth, is as much a business man as the man who goes upon the Board of Trade and bets upon the price of grain; the miners who go down a thousand feet into the earth, or climb two thousand feet upon the cliffs, and bring forth from their hiding places the precious metals to be poured into the channels of trade are as much business men as the few financial magnates who, in a back room, corner the money of the world. We come to speak of this broader class of business men.

Ah, my friends, we say not one word against those who live upon the Atlantic Coast, but the hardy pioneers who have braved all the dangers of the wilderness, who have made the desert to blossom as the rose, the pioneers away out there [pointing to the West] who rear their children near to Nature's heart, where they can mingle their voices with the voices of the birds-out there where they have erected schoolhouses for the education of their young, churches where they praise their Creator, and cemeteries where rest the ashes of their dead-these people, we say, are as deserving of the consideration of our party as any people in this country. It is for these that we speak. We do not come as aggressors. Our war is not a war of conquest; we are fighting in the defense of our homes, our families, and posterity. We have petitioned, and our petitions have been scorned; we have entreated, and our entreaties have been disregarded; we have begged, and they have mocked when our calamity came. We beg no longer; we entreat no more; we petition no more. We defy them!

The gentleman from Wisconsin [Vilas] has said that he fears a Robespierre. My friends, in this land of the free you need not fear that a tyrant will spring up from among the people. What we need is an Andrew Jackson to stand, as Jackson stood, against the encroachments of organized wealth.

Judge *magazine criticized Bryan for sacrilege in his speech. He is shown with crown and cross, but trampling the Bible. (Cartoon by Grant Hamilton, printed in* Judge *magazine, 1896.)*

They tell us that this platform was made to catch votes. We reply to them that changing conditions make new issues; that the principles upon which Democracy rests are as everlasting as the hills, but that they must be applied to new conditions as they arise. Conditions have arisen, and we are here to meet those conditions. They tell us that the income tax ought not to be brought in here; that it is a new idea. They criticize us for our criticism of the Supreme Court of the United States. My friends, we have not criticized; we have simply called attention to what you already know. If you want criticisms read the dissenting opinions of the court. There you will find criticisms. They say that we passed an unconstitutional law; we deny it. The income tax was not unconstitutional when it was passed; it was not unconstitutional when it went before the Supreme Court for the first time; it did not become unconstitutional until one of the judges changed his mind, and we cannot be expected to know when a judge will change his mind. The income tax is just. It simply intends to put the burdens of government justly upon the backs of the people. I am in favor of an income tax. When I find a man who is not willing to bear his share of the burdens of the government which protects him, I find a man who is unworthy to enjoy the blessings of a government like ours.

They say that we are opposing national bank currency; it is true. If you will read what Thomas Benton said, you will find he said that, in searching history, he could find but one parallel to Andrew Jackson; that was Cicero, who destroyed the conspiracy of Cataline and saved Rome. Benton said that Cicero only did for Rome what Jackson did for us when he destroyed the bank conspiracy and saved America. We say in our platform we believe that the right to coin and issue money is a function of government. We believe it. We believe that it is a part of sovereignty, and can no more with safety be delegated to private individuals than we could afford to delegate to private individuals the power to make penal statutes or levy taxes. Mr. Jefferson, who was once regarded as good Democratic authority, seems to have differed in opinion from the gentleman who has addressed us on the part of the minority. Those who are opposed to this proposition tell us that the issue of paper money is a function of the bank, and that the government ought to go out of the banking business. I stand with Jefferson rather than with them, and tell them, as he did, that the issue of money is a function of government, and that the banks ought to go out of the governing business.

They complain about the plank which declares against life tenure in office. They have tried to strain it to mean that which it does not mean. What we oppose by that plank is the life tenure which is being built up in Washington, and which excludes from participation in official benefits the humbler members of society.

And now, my friends, let me come to the paramount issue. If they ask us why it is that we say more on the money question than we say upon the tariff question, I reply that, if protection has slain its thousands, the gold standard has slain its tens of thousands. If they ask us why we do not embody in our platform all the things that we believe in, we reply that when we have restored the money of the Constitution, all other necessary reform will be possible; but that until this is done, there is no other reform that can be accomplished.

Why is it that within three months such a change has come over the country? Three months ago when it was confidently asserted that those who believed in the gold standard would frame our platform and nominate our candidates, even the advocates of the gold standard did not think that we could elect a President. And they had good reason for their doubt, because there is scarcely a State here today asking for the gold standard which is not in the absolute control of the Republican Party. But note the change. Mr. McKinley was nominated at St. Louis upon a platform which declared for the maintenance of the gold standard until it can be changed into bimetallism by international agreement. Mr. McKinley was the most popular man among the Republicans, and three months ago everybody in the Republican Party prophesied his election. How is it today? Why, the man who was once pleased to think that he looked like Napoleon-that man shudders today when he remembers that he was nominated on the anniversary of the battle of Waterloo.

Not only that, but as he listens, he can hear with ever-increasing distinctness the sound of the waves as they beat upon the lonely shores at St Helena.

Why this change? Ah, my friends, is not the reason for the change evident to any one who will look at the matter? No private character, however pure, no personal popularity, however great, can protect from the avenging wrath of an indignant people a man who will declare that he is in favor of fastening the gold standard upon this country, or who is willing to surrender the right of self-government and place the legislative control of our affairs in the hands of foreign potentates and powers.

We go forth confident that we shall win. Why? Because upon the paramount issue of this campaign there is not a spot of ground upon which the enemy will dare to challenge battle. If they tell us that the gold standard is a good thing, we shall point to their platform and tell them that their platform pledges the party to get rid of the gold standard and substitute bimetallism. If the gold standard is a good thing why try to get rid of it? I call your attention to the fact that some of the very people who are in this Convention today and who tell us that we ought to declare in favor of international bimetallism—thereby declaring that the gold standard is wrong and that the principle of bimetallism is better-these very people four months ago were open and avowed advocates of the gold-standard, and were then telling us that we could not legislate two metals together, even with the aid of all the world. If the gold standard is a good thing, we ought to declare in favor of its retention and not in favor of abandoning it; and if the gold standard is a bad thing why should we wait until other nations are willing to help us to let go? Here is the line of battle, and we care not upon which issue they force the fight; we are prepared to meet them on either issue or on both. If they tell us that the gold standard is the standard of civilization, we reply to them that this, the most enlightened of all the nations of the earth, has never declared for a gold standard and that both the great parties this year are declaring against it. If the gold standard is the standard of civilization, why, my friends, should we not have it? If they come to meet us on that issue we can present the history of our nation. More than that; we can tell them that they will search the pages of history in vain to find a single instance where the common people of any land have ever declared themselves in favor of the gold standard. They can find where the holders of fixed investments have declared for a gold standard, but not where the masses have. Mr. Carlisle said in 1878 that this was a struggle between the "idle holders of idle capital" and "the struggling masses, who produce the wealth and pay the taxes of the country," and, my friends, the question we are to decide is: Upon which side will the Democratic party fight; upon the side of "the idle holders of idle capital" or upon the side of "the struggling masses"? That is the question which the party must answer first, and then it must be answered by each individual hereafter. The sympathies of the Democratic Party, as shown by the platform, are on the side of the struggling masses who have ever been the foundation of the Democratic Party. There are two ideas of government. There are those who believe that if you will only legislate to make the well-to-do prosperous, their prosperity will leak through on those below. The Democratic idea, however, has been that if you legislate to make the masses prosperous, their prosperity will find its way up through every class which rests upon them.

You come to us and tell us that the great cities are in favor of the gold standard; we reply that the great cities rest upon our broad and fertile prairies. Burn down your cities and leave our farms, and your cities will spring up again as if by magic; but destroy our farms and the grass will grow in the streets of every city in the country.

My friends, we declare that this nation is able to legislate for its own people on every question, without waiting for the aid or consent of any other nation on earth; and upon that issue we expect to carry every state in the Union. I shall not slander the inhabitants of the fair state of Massachusetts nor the inhabitants of the state of New York by saying that, when they are confronted with the proposition, they will declare that this nation is not able to attend to its own business. It is the issue of 1776 over again. Our ancestors, when but three millions in number, had the courage to declare their political independence of every other nation; shall we, their descendants, when we have grown to seventy millions, declare that we are less independent than our forefathers?

No, my friends, that will never be the verdict of our people. Therefore, we care not upon what lines the battle is fought. If they say bimetallism is good, but that we cannot have it until other nations help us, we reply, that instead of having a gold standard because England has, we will restore bimetallism, and then let England have bimetallism because the United States has it. If they dare to come out in the open field and defend the gold standard as a good thing, we will fight them to the uttermost. Having behind us the producing masses of this nation and the world, supported by the commercial interests, the laboring interests and the toilers everywhere, we will answer their demand for a gold standard by saying to them: You shall not press down upon the brow of labor this crown of thorns, you shall not crucify mankind upon a cross of gold.

English: Artist's conception of William Jennings Bryan after the Cross of Gold speech at the 1896 Democratic National Convention (By William Robinson Leigh—McClure's Magazine, April 1900, p. 536.)

Document Analysis

Though the central theme of Bryan's speech—that the U.S. should not support the gold standard—is simple, the way he frames and delivers the message is important. He positions himself as a populist champion of the West and the frontier (making no mention of the South, another region that largely supported bimetallism, due to the lingering shadow of the Civil War) in contrast to the established power of the Eastern states and of cities. He describes the movement he leads not only as an insurgency within the Democratic Party but "in defense of a cause as holy as the cause of liberty—the cause of humanity." In this way he builds up the issue as a question of universal morals rather than individual opinions or even simply economic policy.

Bryan uses Christian imagery that is vivid and easily recognizable to his audience. His references to a crown of thorns and a cross of gold put the people—"the producing masses of the nation and the world"—in the position of Jesus Christ at the crucifixion as they allegedly suffer under the gold standard. This powerful symbolism frames gold supporters as harming humankind on a fundamental level. He also evokes the enthusiasm of the crusading warriors of the Middle Ages by comparing the pro-silver Democrats to those who followed the preacher Peter the Hermit on the First Crusade.

In addition to religious imagery Bryan employs the rhetoric of class conflict, railing against the prevailing system that he claims seeks to establish "an office-holding class and excludes . . . the humbler members of our society." Bryan places himself in the tradition of iconic American leaders who represented the interests of the people on monetary issues. He refers to Andrew Jackson and his struggle against the Second Bank of the United States, which ended with a victory "against the encroachments of aggregated wealth" and thereby "saved America." He links himself with Thomas Jefferson, paraphrasing the earlier leader in declaring that the government should control money rather than be controlled by it. He further evokes the spirit of the American Revolution by suggesting that the United States should be able to act independently of England, an upholder of the gold standard. Bryan's rhetoric implies that the United States can and should set its own economic terms and lead by example.

Essential Themes

The Cross of Gold speech had a great immediate impact as audience members at the Democratic National Convention, including many initially hostile to Bryan, expressed their enthusiasm by carrying the speaker around the room as pandemonium broke out. The next day Bryan was nominated as the Democrats' presidential candidate on the fifth ballot, becoming the youngest-ever nominee to that point at thirty-six years old. He also received crossover support as the nominee of both the Populist Party and the Silver Republican Party, a short-lived faction of the Republicans, forming a coalition that would take on the pro–gold standard Republicans in the general election.

In the long run the speech was a failure in that Bryan lost the election to William McKinley and bimetallism was never adopted. Pro-gold Democrats refused to back Bryan and even formed a competing party, the National Democrats. Labor interests also did not provide as much support as expected. The McKinley campaign was able to mobilize America's business community against Bryan, in the process essentially inventing modern campaign financing. The split within the Democratic Party helped lead to a significant shift in U.S. party politics.

Changing economic conditions led to decreasing support for bimetallism in the next few years, and in 1900 the Gold Standard Act officially fixed U.S. monetary policy on gold. Bryan ran for the presidency again that year on a pro-silver platform but was unable to generate the same level of excitement and lost again, as he did once more in 1908. The Democrats would not regain the presidency until Woodrow Wilson's election in 1912. The United States remained on the gold standard until 1933, when the policy was abandoned in the face of the Great Depression.

Perhaps the most lasting effect of Bryan's 1896 speech and candidacy was on the general style and tone of presidential campaigning. He traveled the country giving fiery speeches in contrast to the usual strategy of candidates projecting an aura of being above the fray, and his method soon became standard practice. His highly charged populist rhetoric pitting the working class against the rich continues to be used by politicians from the local to national level and at all points on the political spectrum. The Cross of Gold address is considered one of the strongest political speeches in U.S. history and a key example of the power of rhetoric.

—*William E. Burns, PhD*

Bibliography and Additional Reading

Bensel, Richard Franklin. *Passion and Preferences: William Jennings Bryan and the 1896 Democratic National Convention*. New York: Cambridge UP, 2008. Print.

Bryan, Steven. *The Gold Standard at the Turn of the Twentieth Century: Rising Powers, Global Money and the Age of Empire*. New York: Columbia UP, 2010. Print.

Cherny, Robert W. *A Righteous Cause: The Life of William Jennings Bryan*. Norman: U of Oklahoma P, 1994. Print.

Williams, R. Hal. *Realigning America: McKinley, Bryan and the Remarkable Election of 1896*. Lawrence: UP of Kansas, 2010. Print.

From *The Theory of the Leisure Class*

Date: 1899
Author: Thorstein Veblen
Genre: nonfiction book (excerpt)

Summary Overview

In 1899, Thorstein Veblen's *The Theory of the Leisure Class* was one of the first extensive critiques of modern American conspicuous consumption, or acquiring things not for their usefulness but, rather, as a means of expressing wealth and power. The book was also an attempt to integrate into the study of economics a knowledge of how people actually behave—rather than relying on the traditional economic view that people will act reasonably and in their own self- interest.

Veblen argued that modern industrial societies were socially stratified—that is, organized based on inherited or perceived status rather than on measurable usefulness. In modern societies, he argued, the higher levels of the stratified society are a "leisure class" with time and resources to engage in activities and purchase goods that people of lower status positions are unable to. In this excerpt, from chapter 10, "Modern Survivals of Prowess," Veblen explains that since the leisure class does not engage in labor but, rather, only consumes what is produced by those who do the labor in an industrial society, any success that people in the leisure class enjoy is the result of the type of personality traits that have developed in a consumption-oriented society.

Defining Moment

American writer Mark Twain called it the Gilded Age. Although this phrase was from the title of an 1873 novel about corrupt politicians, since the early twentieth century the term "Gilded Age" has been broadly applied to the United States in the late nineteenth century. It was a time of rapid industrial expansion, the birth of new technologies, and the development of new ways of doing business. These expanding industries provided work for the millions of people who came to the United States from around the world. These growing businesses also led to an increase in wages across the board in the United States. Yet despite the general rise in pay, there was also an increasingly unequal distribution of wealth in the nation. During the second half of the nineteenth century, financial resources were increasingly concentrated in the hands a smaller and smaller portion of Americans.

However, it was not just the ultrawealthy railroad barons and industrial magnates who saw an increase in their wealth. There was an expanding middle class in the United States too, made up of the executives and experts that managed the growing operations of business and industry. These middle-class Americans were the target of an advertising industry that marketed products that not only had utility, but would broadcast status. Whether it was furniture, clothing, household goods, or sports equipment, the brand and style of products that someone bought and used sent messages about the wealth and status of the user. New department stores and mail-order houses provided a greater variety of goods than ever before, with different levels of style, quality, and price that reflected the increasingly stratified society that Veblen described in *The Theory of the Leisure Class*.

Author Biography

Thorstein Veblen was born in 1857 in Cato, Wisconsin, ten years after his parents, Thomas and Kari Veblen, had emigrated from Norway. The family later moved to Minnesota and farmed. Veblen attended local schools and enrolled at Carleton College in Northfield, Minnesota. At college, Veblen studied economics and philosophy at a time when social science as a field of study was beginning to take shape in American higher education. Veblen undertook graduate study at Johns Hopkins University in Baltimore, Maryland, but, unable to receive financial support from the university, moved on to Yale, from which in 1884 he received a PhD in philosophy. Among his instructors at Yale was Charles Graham Sumner, the first American to hold a professorship in sociology. This grounding in the emerging social sciences would inform Veblen's work throughout his career.

Veblen's scholarly career faltered after Yale and, unable to find an academic position, he returned for a time to the family farm in Minnesota. Later, in the 1890s, Veblen shifted his studies to economics, studying first at Cornell University, then obtaining a position at the University of Chicago. There, he published articles in economics and sociology journals and, in 1899, his first and most influential monograph, *The Theory of the Leisure Class*, which is excerpted here.

Veblen's career took him to Stanford University, where he left under a cloud following his involvement in a widely discussed extramarital affair. He briefly taught at the University of Missouri, writing another book. With the outbreak of the First World War in 1914, Veblen began to investigate the connections between war, peace, and economics. He also worked for the federal government during the war and, following, settled in New York City, where he edited *The Dial* magazine for a year. In 1926, Veblen and a group of like-minded academics—who emerged during the Progressive era—established the New School for Social Research in Manhattan.

HISTORICAL DOCUMENT: From *The Theory of the Leisure Class*

The physical vigor acquired in the training for athletic games—so far as the training may be said to have this effect—is of advantage both to the individual and to the collectivity, in that, other things being equal, it conduces to economic serviceability. The spiritual traits which go with athletic sports are likewise economically advantageous to the individual, as contradistinguished from the interests of the collectivity. This holds true in any community where these traits are present in some degree in the population. Modern competition is in large part a process of self-assertion on the basis of these traits of predatory human nature. In the sophisticated form in which they enter into the modern, peaceable emulation, the possession of these traits in some measure is almost a necessary of life to the civilized man. But while they are indispensable to the competitive individual, they are not directly serviceable to the community. So far as regards the serviceability of the individual for the purposes of the collective life, emulative efficiency is of use only indirectly if at all. Ferocity and cunning are of no use to the community except in its hostile dealings with other communities; and they are useful to the individual only because there is so large a proportion of the same traits actively present in the human environment to which he is exposed. Any individual who enters the competitive struggle without the due endowment of these traits is at a disadvantage, somewhat as a hornless steer would find himself at a disadvantage in a drove of horned cattle.

The possession and the cultivation of the predatory traits of character may, of course, be desirable on other than economic grounds. There is a prevalent aesthetic or ethical predilection for the barbarian aptitudes, and the traits in question minister so effectively to this predilection that their serviceability in the aesthetic or ethical respect probably offsets any economic unserviceability which they may give. But for the present purpose that is beside the point. Therefore nothing is said here as to the desirability or advisability of sports on the whole, or as to their value on other than economic grounds.

In popular apprehension there is much that is admirable in the type of manhood which the life of sport fosters. There is self-reliance and good-fellowship, so termed in the somewhat loose colloquial use of the words. From a different point of view the qualities currently so characterized might be described as truculence and clannishness. The reason for the current approval and admiration of these manly qualities, as well as for their being called manly, is the same as the reason for their usefulness to the individual. The members of the community, and especially that class of the community which sets the pace in canons of taste, are endowed with this range of propensities in sufficient measure to make their absence in others felt as a shortcoming, and to make their possession in an exceptional degree appreciated as an attribute of superior merit. The traits of predatory man are by no means obsolete in the common run of modern populations. They are present and can be called out in bold relief at any time by any appeal to the sentiments in which they express themselves—unless this appeal should clash with the specific activities that make up our habitual occupations and comprise the general range of our everyday interests. The common run of the population of any industrial community is emancipated from these, economically considered, untoward propensities only in the sense that, through partial and temporary disuse, they have lapsed into the background of sub-conscious motives. With varying degrees of potency in different individuals, they remain available for the aggressive shaping of men's actions and sentiments whenever a stimulus of more than everyday intensity comes in to call them forth. And they assert themselves forcibly in any case where no occupation alien to the predatory culture has usurped the individual's everyday range of interest and sentiment. This is the case among the leisure class and among certain portions of the population which are ancillary to that class. Hence the facility with which any new accessions to the leisure class take to sports; and hence the rapid growth of sports and of the sporting sentient in any industrial community where wealth has accumulated sufficiently to exempt a considerable part of the population from work.

A homely and familiar fact may serve to show that the predaceous impulse does not prevail in the same degree in all classes. Taken simply as a feature of modern life, the habit of carrying a walking-stick may seem at best a trivial detail; but the usage has a significance for the point in question. The classes among whom the habit most prevails—the classes with whom the walking-stick is associated in popular apprehension—are the men of the leisure class proper, sporting men, and the lower-class delinquents. To these might perhaps be added the men engaged in the pecuniary employments. The same is not true of the common run of men engaged in industry and it may be noted by the way that women do not carry a stick except in case of infirmity, where it has a use of a different kind. The practice is of course in great measure a matter of polite usage; but the basis of polite usage is, in turn, the proclivities of the class which sets the pace in polite usage. The walking-stick serves the purpose of an advertisement that the bearer's hands are employed otherwise than in useful effort, and it therefore has utility as an evidence of leisure. But it is also a weapon, and it meets a felt need of barbarian man on that ground. The handling of so tangible and primitive a means of offense is very comforting to anyone who is gifted with even a moderate share of ferocity. The exigencies of the language make it impossible to avoid an apparent implication of disapproval of the aptitudes, propensities, and expressions of life here under discussion. It is, however, not intended to imply anything in the way of deprecation or commendation of any one of these phases of human character or of the life process. The various elements of the prevalent human nature are taken up from the point of view of economic theory, and the traits discussed are gauged and graded with regard to their immediate economic bearing on the facility of the collective life process. That is to say, these phenomena are here apprehended from the economic point of view and are valued with respect to their direct action in furtherance or hindrance of a more perfect adjustment of the human collectivity to the environment and to the institutional structure required by the economic situation of the collectivity for the present and for the immediate future. For these purposes the traits handed down from the predatory culture are less serviceable than might be. Although even in this connection it is not to be overlooked that the energetic aggressiveness and pertinacity of predatory man is a heritage of no mean value. The economic value—with some regard also to the social value in the narrower sense—of these aptitudes and propensities is attempted to be passed upon without reflecting on their value as seen from another point of view. When contrasted with the prosy mediocrity of the latter-day industrial scheme of life, and judged by the accredited standards of morality, and more especially by the standards of aesthetics and of poetry, these survivals from a more primitive type of manhood may have a very different value from that here assigned them. But all this being foreign to the purpose in hand, no expression of opinion on this latter head would be in place here. All that is admissible is to enter the caution that these standards of excellence, which are alien to the present purpose, must not be allowed to influence our economic appreciation of these traits of human character or of the activities which foster their growth. This applies both as regards those persons who actively participate in sports and those whose sporting experience consists in contemplation only. What is here said of the sporting propensity is likewise pertinent to sundry reflections presently to be made in this connection on what would colloquially be known as the religious life.

The last paragraph incidentally touches upon the fact that everyday speech can scarcely be employed in discussing this class of aptitudes and activities without implying deprecation or apology. The fact is significant as showing the habitual attitude of the dispassionate common man toward the propensities which express themselves in sports and in exploit generally. And this is perhaps as convenient a place as any to discuss that undertone of deprecation which runs through all the voluminous discourse in defense or in laudation of athletic sports, as well as of other activities of a predominantly predatory character. The same apologetic frame of mind is at least beginning to be observable in the spokesmen of most other institutions handed down from the barbarian phase of life. Among these archaic institutions which are felt to need apology are comprised, with others, the entire existing system of the distribution of wealth, together with the resulting class distinction of status; all or nearly all forms of consumption that come under the head of conspicuous waste; the status of women under the patriarchal system; and many features of the traditional creeds and devout observances, especially the exoteric expressions of the creed and the naive apprehension of received observances. What is to be said in this connection of the apologetic attitude taken in commending sports and the sporting character will therefore apply, with a suitable change in phraseology, to the apologies offered in behalf of these other, related elements of our social heritage.

There is a feeling—usually vague and not commonly avowed in so many words by the apologist himself, but ordinarily perceptible in the manner of his discourse—that these sports, as well as the general range of predaceous impulses and habits of thought which underlie the sporting character, do not altogether commend themselves to common sense. "As to the majority of murderers, they are very incorrect characters." This aphorism offers a valuation of the predaceous temperament, and of the disciplinary effects of its overt expression and exercise, as seen from the moralist's point of view. As such it affords an indication of what is the deliverance of the sober sense of mature men as to the degree of availability of the predatory habit of mind for the purposes of the collective life. It is felt that the presumption is against any activity which involves habituation to the predatory attitude, and that the burden of proof lies with those who speak for the rehabilitation of the predaceous temper and for the practices which strengthen it. There is a strong body of popular sentiment in favor of diversions and enterprises of the kind in question; but there is at the same time present in the community a pervading sense that this ground of sentiment wants legitimation. The required legitimation is ordinarily sought by showing that although sports are substantially of a predatory, socially disintegrating effect; although their proximate effect runs in the direction of reversion to propensities that are industrially disserviceable; yet indirectly and remotely—by some not readily comprehensible process of polar induction, or counter-irritation perhaps—sports are conceived to foster a habit of mind that is serviceable for the social or industrial purpose. That is to say, although sports are essentially of the nature of invidious exploit, it is presumed that by some remote and obscure effect they result in the growth of a temperament conducive to non-invidious work. It is commonly attempted to show all this empirically or it is rather assumed that this is the empirical generalization which must be obvious to any one who cares to see it. In conducting the proof of this thesis the treacherous ground of inference from cause to effect is somewhat shrewdly avoided, except so far as to show that the "manly virtues" spoken of above are fostered by sports. But since it is these manly virtues that are (economically) in need of legitimation, the chain of proof breaks off where it should begin. In the most general economic terms, these apologies are an effort to show that, in spite of the logic of the thing, sports do in fact further what may broadly be called workmanship. So long as he has not succeeded in persuading himself or others that this is their effect the thoughtful apologist for sports will not rest content, and commonly, it is to be admitted, he does not rest content. His discontent with his own vindication of the practice in question is ordinarily shown by his truculent tone and by the eagerness with which he heaps up asseverations in support of his position. But why are apologies needed? If there prevails a body of popular sentient in favor of sports, why is not that fact a sufficient legitimation? The protracted discipline of prowess to which the race has been subjected under the predatory and quasi-peaceable culture has transmitted to the men of today a temperament that finds gratification in these expressions of ferocity and cunning. So, why not accept these sports as legitimate expressions of a normal and wholesome human nature? What other norm is there that is to be lived up to than that given in the aggregate range of propensities that express themselves in the sentiments of this generation, including the hereditary strain of prowess? The ulterior norm to which appeal is taken is the instinct of workmanship, which is an instinct more fundamental, of more ancient prescription, than the propensity to predatory emulation. The latter is but a special development of the instinct of workmanship, a variant, relatively late and ephemeral in spite of its great absolute antiquity. The emulative predatory impulse—or the instinct of sportsmanship, as it might well be called—is essentially unstable in comparison with the primordial instinct of workmanship out of which it has been developed and differentiated. Tested by this ulterior norm of life, predatory emulation, and therefore the life of sports, falls short.

The manner and the measure in which the institution of a leisure class conduces to the conservation of sports and invidious exploit can of course not be succinctly stated. From the evidence already recited it appears that, in sentient and inclinations, the leisure class is more favorable to a warlike attitude and animus than the industrial classes. Something similar seems to be true as regards sports. But it is chiefly in its indirect effects, though the canons of decorous living, that the institution has its influence on the prevalent sentiment with respect to the sporting life. This indirect effect goes almost unequivocally in the direction of furthering a survival of the predatory temperament and habits; and this is true even with respect to those variants of the sporting life which the higher leisure-class code of proprieties proscribes; as, e.g., prize-fighting, cock-fighting, and other like vulgar expressions of the sporting temper. Whatever the latest authenticated schedule of detail proprieties may say, the accredited canons of decency sanctioned by the institution say without equivocation that emulation and waste are good and their opposites are disreputable. In the crepuscular light of the social nether spaces the details of the code are not apprehended with all the facility that might be desired, and these broad underlying canons of decency are therefore applied somewhat unreflectingly, with little question as to the scope of their competence or the exceptions that have been sanctioned in detail.

Addiction to athletic sports, not only in the way of direct participation, but also in the way of sentiment and moral support, is, in a more or less pronounced degree, a characteristic of the leisure class; and it is a trait which that class shares with the lower-class delinquents, and with such atavistic elements throughout the body of the community as are endowed with a dominant predaceous trend. Few individuals among the populations of Western civilized countries are so far devoid of the predaceous instinct as to find no diversion in contemplating athletic sports and games, but with the common run of individuals among the industrial classes the inclination to sports does not assert itself to the extent of constituting what may fairly be called a sporting habit. With these classes sports are an occasional diversion rather than a serious feature of life. This common body of the people can therefore not be said to cultivate the sporting propensity. Although it is not obsolete in the average of them, or even in any appreciable number of individuals, yet the predilection for sports in the commonplace industrial classes is of the nature of a reminiscence, more or less diverting as an occasional interest, rather than a vital and permanent interest that counts as a dominant factor in shaping the organic complex of habits of thought into which it enters. As it manifests itself in the sporting life of today, this propensity may not appear to be an economic factor of grave consequence. Taken simply by itself it does not count for a great deal in its direct effects on the industrial efficiency or the consumption of any given individual; but the prevalence and the growth of the type of human nature of which this propensity is a characteristic feature is a matter of some consequence. It affects the economic life of the collectivity both as regards the rate of economic development and as regards the character of the results attained by the development. For better or worse, the fact that the popular habits of thought are in any degree dominated by this type of character can not but greatly affect the scope, direction, standards, and ideals of the collective economic life, as well as the degree of adjustment of the collective life to the environment.

Something to a like effect is to be said of other traits that go to make up the barbarian character. For the purposes of economic theory, these further barbarian traits may be taken as concomitant variations of that predaceous temper of which prowess is an expression. In great measure they are not primarily of an economic character, nor do they have much direct economic bearing. They serve to indicate the stage of economic evolution to which the individual possessed of them is adapted. They are of importance, therefore, as extraneous tests of the degree of adaptation of the character in which they are comprised to the economic exigencies of today, but they are also to some extent important as being aptitudes which themselves go to increase or diminish the economic serviceability of the individual.

As it finds expression in the life of the barbarian, prowess manifests itself in two main directions—force and fraud. In varying degrees these two forms of expression are similarly present in modern warfare, in the pecuniary occupations, and in sports and games. Both lines of aptitudes are cultivated and strengthened by the life of sport as well as by the more serious forms of emulative life. Strategy or cunning is an element invariably present in games, as also in warlike pursuits and in the chase. In all of these employments strategy tends to develop into finesse and chicanery. Chicanery, falsehood, browbeating, hold a well-secured place in the method of procedure of any athletic contest and in games generally. The habitual employment of an umpire, and the minute technical regulations governing the limits and details of permissible fraud and strategic advantage, sufficiently attest the fact that fraudulent practices and attempts to overreach one's opponents are not adventitious features of the game. In the nature of the case habituation to sports should conduce to a fuller development of the aptitude for fraud; and the prevalence in the community of that predatory temperament which inclines men to sports connotes a prevalence of sharp practice and callous disregard of the interests of others, individually and collectively. Resort to fraud, in any guise and under any legitimation of law or custom, is an expression of a narrowly self-regarding habit of mind. It is needless to dwell at any length on the economic value of this feature of the sporting character.

In this connection it is to be noted that the most obvious characteristic of the physiognomy affected by athletic and other sporting men is that of an extreme astuteness. The gifts and exploits of Ulysses are scarcely second to those of Achilles, either in their substantial furtherance of the game or in the éclat which they give the astute sporting man among his associates. The pantomime of astuteness is commonly the first step in that assimilation to the professional sporting man which a youth undergoes after matriculation in any reputable school, of the secondary or the higher education, as the case may be. And the physiognomy of astuteness, as a decorative feature, never ceases to receive the thoughtful attention of men whose serious interest lies in athletic games, races, or other contests of a similar emulative nature. As a further indication of their spiritual kinship, it may be pointed out that the members of the lower delinquent class usually show this physiognomy of astuteness in a marked degree, and that they very commonly show the same histrionic exaggeration of it that is often seen in the young candidate for athletic honors. This, by the way, is the most legible mark of what is vulgarly called "toughness" in youthful aspirants for a bad name.

The astute man, it may be remarked, is of no economic value to the community—unless it be for the purpose of sharp practice in dealings with other communities. His functioning is not a furtherance of the generic life process. At its best, in its direct economic bearing, it is a conversion of the economic substance of the collectivity to a growth alien to the collective life process—very much after the analogy of what in medicine would be called a benign tumor, with some tendency to transgress the uncertain line that divides the benign from the malign growths. The two barbarian traits, ferocity and astuteness, go to make up the predaceous temper or spiritual attitude. They are the expressions of a narrowly self-regarding habit of mind. Both are highly serviceable for individual expediency in a life looking to invidious success. Both also have a high aesthetic value. Both are fostered by the pecuniary culture. But both alike are of no use for the purposes of the collective life.

GLOSSARY

contradistinguish: to draw distinctions between two things by comparing them

deprecation: to demean or dismiss

matriculation: formal entry into a school or course of study

pecuniary occupations; pecuniary employment: Veblen's term for work that is primarily managerial or financial as opposed to physical or industrial

propensity: a habit or common practice

THE THEORY OF THE LEISURE CLASS

CHAPTER I

INTRODUCTORY

The institution of a leisure class is found in its best development at the higher stages of the barbarian culture; as, for instance, in feudal Europe or feudal Japan. In such communities the distinction between classes is very rigorously observed; and the feature of most striking economic significance in these class differences is the distinction maintained between the employments proper to the several classes. The upper classes are by custom exempt or excluded from industrial occupations, and are reserved for certain employments to which a degree of honour attaches. Chief among the honourable employments in any feudal community is warfare; and priestly service is commonly second to warfare. If the barbarian community is not notably warlike, the priestly office may take the precedence, with that of the warrior second. But the rule holds with but slight exceptions that, whether warriors or priests, the upper classes are exempt from industrial employments, and this exemption is the economic expression of their superior rank. Brahmin India affords

The Theory of the Leisure Class, *1924*

Document Analysis

Veblen begins this chapter of *The Theory of the Leisure Class* by establishing the frame of reference he will use throughout—that of sports, or athletic competition. In the opening paragraph, he argues that the physical skills and "spiritual traits" that are associated with sports and athletics are "economically advantageous to the individual." Veblen then asserts that "modern competition" consists of a process of people asserting themselves on the basis of what he calls "traits of predatory human nature." In the modern world, he explains, these traits are "peaceable" but—as is the case with the predation practiced by animals in the wild—they are chiefly of benefit to the individual rather than the community as a whole. Veblen closes out the paragraph by describing some of these predatory traits, such as efficiency, ferocity, and cunning—anyone not possessing these traits, he argues, is at a "disadvantage" in the "competitive struggle." Sports, he argues, help cultivate these traits.

The next paragraph is almost an aside, as Veblen muses on the noneconomic value of the predatory traits encouraged by sports, claiming that "there is a prevalent aesthetic or ethical predilection for the barbarian aptitudes. Here, he is basically observing that athletes and athletic competitions are popular. All of this, he admits, is "beside the point" and he is not going to argue about whether or not sports are valuable on anything other than an economic basis.

In the third paragraph, Veblen's language becomes more complex and—to casual readers—confusing as he expands on his argument about the utility of sports for nurturing the predatory traits necessary for thriving in a competitive economy. He observes that sport features "self-reliance and good-fellowship" (or, expressed in a less charitable manner "truculence and clannishness"). He also discusses the prevalence of the word "manly" to describe the qualities necessary for competition and explains that these aggressive traits continued to be valued by modern society. Veblen points to the popularity of sports and athletics to members of the leisure class, arguing that the popularity will grow "in any industrial community where wealth has accumulated sufficiently to exempt a considerable part of the population from work." Sports require time and practice to master—the upper classes, not having to work 12 hours a day in a factory or other job—have the luxury of the spare time in which to indulge these activities. Thus, they are able to hone their predatory traits in a more efficient way than members of the working classes.

For his next example, Veblen uses the illustration of a walking stick. He explains that the walking stick is—in the popular imagination—associated with the leisure class, sporting men, "lower-class delinquents," and those "engaged in the pecuniary employments"—work which involves, Veblen explained in an earlier chapter, "ownership or acquisition." Similarly, there are groups that are generally not seen to carry walking sticks: women and men "engaged in industry" that is, men who are working. The walking stick, Veblen explains, is a signal or "advertisement" that the person carrying it doesn't have to engage in physical work, either because they are sufficiently wealthy, are engaged in "pecuniary" work, or because they are a criminal. He then connects the walking stick to his theme of predatory traits by reminding the reader that the walking stick is a weapon as well as an accessory and is also associated with sport. Here, Veblen brings together several of his themes such as the importance of sport, and sporting symbolism to modern industrial societies and the ways in which status objects (like walking sticks) may carry multiple layers of meaning.

Veblen, in a very long paragraph, also addresses the seeming contradiction that although the predatory traits nurtured by athletic competition are, in general, perceived as negative "sports are conceived to foster a habit of mind that is serviceable for the social or industrial purpose." In the subsequent paragraph, Veblen reiterates a point from a previous chapter (that the leisure class tends to be "more favorable to a warlike attitude and animus than the industrial classes") and draws a parallel between combat and athletics. The upper classes, however, have developed a refined taste and have rejected sporting events ("prize-fighting, cock-fighting, and other like vulgar expressions of the sporting temper"). Thus, while there are lower-class expressions of sport (the "vulgar" ones), there are also upper-class expressions. The type of sport one enjoys are another signifier of social status.

Essential Themes

Veblen concludes the chapter by continuing the discussion of the leisure class's attraction to sports—both as participants and spectators—and comparing it to the manifestations of sporting life enjoyed by the working classes. He also discusses the concept of "prowess," which (for the "barbarian") is made up of two factors: force and fraud. Force and fraud, he argues, are important not only to sport but modern warfare as well as the pecuniary occupations, or business and finance. Veblen further breaks these ideas down into traits such as strategy, finesse, and chicanery. In all, he sees evidence of the workings of class-informed attitudes and behaviors that are not entirely "rational" in the economic sense and that also bolster his ideas about leisure and consumption in the modern world.

—*Aaron James Gulyas, PhD*

Bibliography and Additional Reading

Diggins, John Patrick. *Thorstein Veblen: Theorist of the Leisure Class*. Princeton, NJ: Princeton University Press, 1999.

Hudson, Michael, and Ahmet Öncü, eds. *Absentee Ownership and its Discontents: Critical Essays on the Legacy of Thorstein Veblen*. Dresden: ISLET, 2016.

Jorgensen, Elizabeth, and Henry Jorgensen. *Thorstein Veblen: Victorian Firebrand*. London: Routledge, 1998.

Plotkin, Sidney, ed. *The Anthem Companion to Thorstein Veblen*. London: Anthem, 2017.

■ Theodore Roosevelt on Corporate Trusts

Date: September 20, 1902
Author: President Theodore Roosevelt
Genre: political speech

Summary Overview

In the late summer of 1902, President Theodore Roosevelt set out on a speaking tour aimed at generating support for Republican congressional candidates in the off-year elections coming in November that year. Roosevelt gave this speech in the Music Hall in Cincinnati, Ohio, on September 20, 1902. This speech focused on the problem of the business trusts, and the need to regulate them. Roosevelt argued that while some action was needed to address the problems associated with the growth of the trusts, it must be done carefully and advisedly. He believed some solutions that had been proposed would hurt all corporations, not just those using trusts as a means of achieving monopoly. Roosevelt argued that a reckless approach to controlling the power of the trusts could destroy the general prosperity that the nation was experiencing at the time.

Defining Moment

The growth of big business in the late nineteenth and early twentieth centuries dramatically altered the American economy. Many of the founders and major stockholders in these new industrial firms grew very wealthy, and many Americans shared in some portion of the newly created prosperity. The growth of big business at this time was somewhat natural. The national railroad system provided relatively fast and reliable transportation, and the telegraph and later the telephone made instant communication possible. The corporate structure of business allowed companies to sell shares of stock to raise huge amounts of capital. In many ways, big business was growing simply because, for the first time, it was possible to do business on a truly large scale.

However, many believed that some of this growth was due to illegitimate business practices. Some consumers, journalists, and political reformers believed that some business firms tried to limit competition and to monopolize their particular industry. The trust was a common means of attempting this. As Roosevelt points out in this speech, many people used the word "trust" in a loose and often incorrect way, referring to any corporate business activity. The first trust that became known to the American public was the Standard Oil Trust, formed in 1882 but unknown to those outside the company for several years. In a business trust, the assets of several companies were put under the control of a group of trustees. Many of the early trusts were informal, with no legal structure, and were secret. But the managers of the trust could run the several businesses whose assets they controlled in such a way that competition was limited and the trust could move toward monopolistic control of the product or services they provided. Standard Oil soon became one of the favorite targets of muckraking journalists and crusading reformers. While Standard Oil apparently pioneered the trust, and became the most infamous example, there were trusts that attempted to control various businesses, such as the tobacco industry, meatpacking, and railroading. Congress had tried to address this issue with the Sherman Antitrust Act of 1890 but the legislation had little effect, in part because it was loosely worded and the types of illegal business combinations were not distinctly defined.

Theodore Roosevelt believed that the public's interest in reining in the power of the trusts needed to be addressed. As the off-year elections of November 1902 drew near, he undertook a speaking tour to stimulate support for Republican candidates in Congress. He believed the Democratic Party would make the trusts a campaign issue, and if the Republicans did not address it they could lose seats in Congress. This was a speech made during that tour.

Author Biography

Theodore Roosevelt, the 26th president of the United States, was born in New York City on October 27, 1857. Roosevelt graduated from Harvard College in 1880, and studied law at Columbia University. He served one term in the New York State Assembly, and then served six years on the United States Civil Service Commission. He was assistant secretary of the Navy in President William McKinley's first administration, but resigned to serve in the army in the Spanish-American War. The notoriety he gained in that war led to his election as governor of New York in 1898. New York City political bosses who were unhappy with Roosevelt as governor and maneuvered to have him nominated for U.S. vice president when McKinley ran for a second term in 1900. McKinley was reelected with Roosevelt on the ticket, but the president was shot by an assassin on September 6, 1901; when he died (on September 14), Roosevelt became president and was easily elected in his own right in 1904.

HISTORICAL DOCUMENT: Theodore Roosevelt on Corporate Trusts

AT MUSIC HALL, CINCINNATI, OHIO, ON THE EVENING OF SEPTEMBER 20, 1902

Mr. Mayor, and you, my fellow-Americans:

I shall ask your attention to what I say to-night, because I intend to make a perfectly serious argument to you, and I shall be obliged if you will remain as still as possible; and I ask that those at the very back will remember that if they talk or make a noise it interferes with the hearing of the rest. I intend to speak to you on a serious subject and to make an argument as the Chief Executive of a nation, who is the President of all the people, without regard to party, without regard to section. I intend to make to you an argument from the standpoint simply of one American talking to his fellow-Americans upon one of the great subjects of interest to all alike; and that subject is what are commonly known as the trusts. The word is used very loosely and almost always with technical inaccuracy. The average man, however, when he speaks of the trusts means rather vaguely all of the very big corporations, the growth of which has been so signal a feature of our modern civilization, and especially those big corporations which, though organized in one State, do business in several States, and often have a tendency to monopoly.

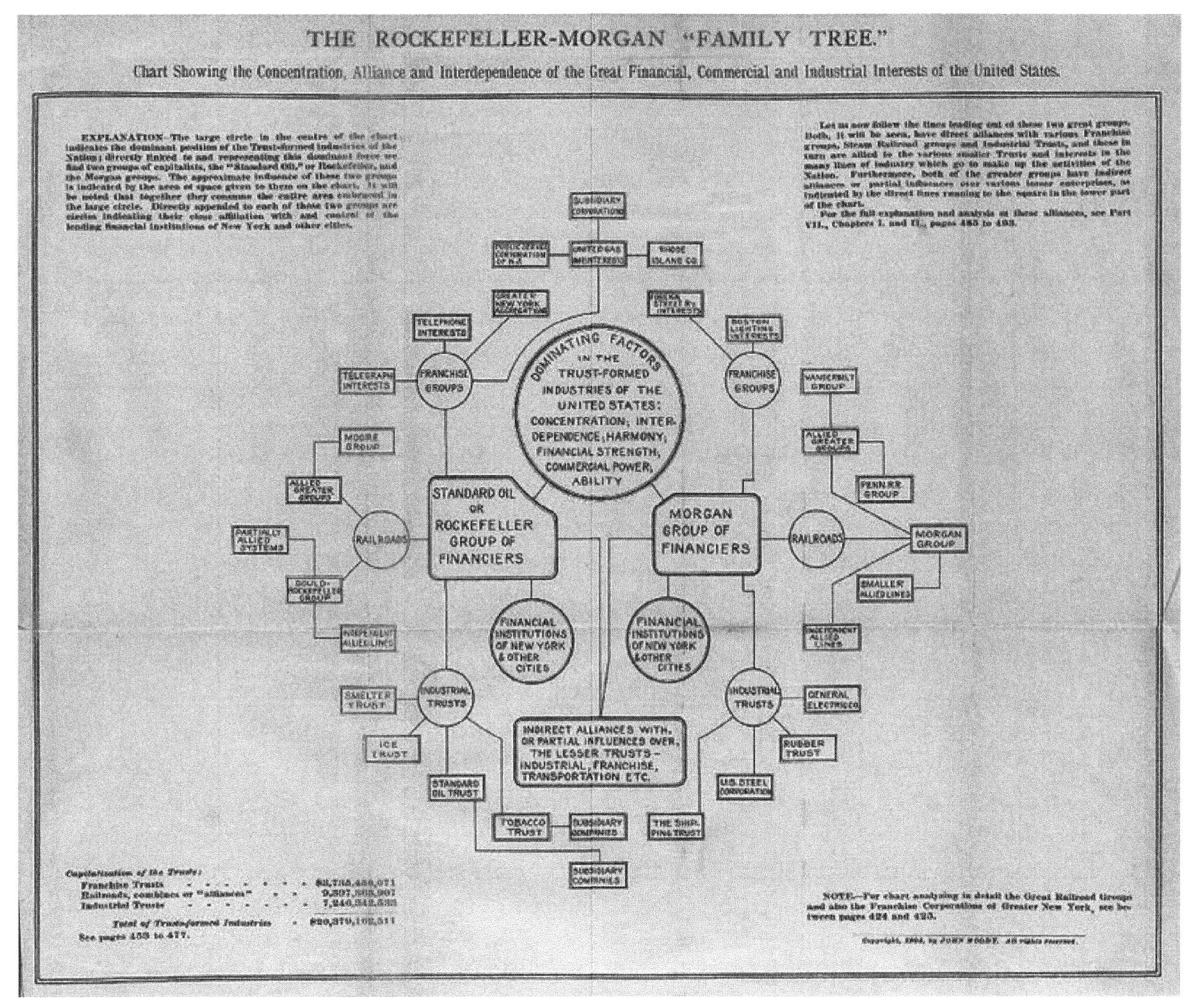

The Rockefeller-Morgan Family Tree (1904), which depicts how the largest trusts at the turn of the 20th century were in turn connected to each other. (John Moody - The Truth about The Trusts: A Description and Analysis of the American Trust Movement. New York: Moody Publishing Company, 1904.)

The whole subject of the trusts is of vital concern to us, because it presents one, and perhaps the most conspicuous, of the many problems forced upon our attention by the tremendous industrial development which has taken place during the last century, a development which is occurring in all civilized countries, notably in our own. There have been many factors responsible for bringing about these changed conditions. Of these, steam and electricity are the chief. The extraordinary changes in the methods of transportation of merchandise and of transmission of news have rendered not only possible, but inevitable, the immense increase in the rate of growth of our great industrial centres that is, of our great cities. I want you to bring home to yourselves that fact. When Cincinnati was founded, news could be transmitted and merchandise carried exactly as had been the case in the days of the Roman Empire. You had here on your river the flatboat, you had on the ocean the sailing-ship, you had the pack-train, you had the wagon, and every one of the four was known when Babylon fell. The change in the last hundred years has been greater by far than the changes in all the preceding three thousand. Those are the facts. Because of them have resulted the specialization of industries, and the unexampled opportunities offered for the employment of huge amounts of capital, and therefore for the rise in the business world of those master minds through whom alone it is possible for such vast amounts of capital to be employed with profit. It matters very little whether we like these new conditions or whether we dislike them; whether we like the creation of these new opportunities or not. Many admirable qualities which were developed in the older, simpler, less progressive life, have tended to atrophy under our rather feverish, high-pressure, complex life of to-day. But our likes and dislikes have nothing to do with the matter. The new conditions are here. You can't bring back the old days of the canal-boat and stage-coach if you wish. The steamboat and the railroad are here. The new forces have produced both good and evil. We cannot get rid of them even if it were not undesirable to get rid of them; and our instant duty is to try to accommodate our social, economic, and legislative life to them, and to frame a system of law and conduct under which we shall get out of them the utmost possible benefit and the least possible amount of harm. It is foolish to pride ourselves upon our progress and prosperity, upon our commanding position in the international industrial world, and at the same time have nothing but denunciation for the men to whose commanding position we in part owe this very progress and prosperity, this commanding position.

Whenever great social or industrial changes take place, no matter how much good there may be to them, there is sure to be some evil, and it usually takes mankind a number of years and a good deal of experimenting before they find the right ways in which, so far as possible, to control the new evil, without at the same time nullifying the new good. I am stating facts so obvious that if each one of you will think them over, you will think them trite, but if you read or listen to some of the arguments advanced, you will come to the conclusion that there is need of learning these trite truths. In these the effort to bring the new tendencies to a standstill is always futile and generally mischievous; but it is possible somewhat to develop them aright. Law can to a degree guide, protect, and control industrial development, but it can never cause it, or play more than a sub ordinate part in its healthy development unfortunately it is easy enough by bad laws to bring it to an almost complete stop.

In dealing with the big corporations which we call trusts, we must resolutely purpose to proceed by evolution and not revolution. We wish to face the facts, declining to have our vision blinded either by the folly of those who say there are no evils, or by the more dangerous folly of those who either see, or make believe that they see, nothing but evil in all the existing system, and who if given their way would destroy the evil by the simple process of bringing ruin and disaster to the entire country. The evils attendant upon over-capitalization alone are, in my judgment, sufficient to warrant a far closer supervision and control than now exist over the great corporations. Wherever a substantial monopoly can be shown to exist, we should certainly try our utmost to devise an expedient by which it can be controlled. Doubtless some of the evils existing in or because of the great corporations, cannot be cured by any legislation which has yet been proposed, and doubtless others, which have really been incident to the sudden development in the formation of corporations of all kinds, will in the end cure themselves. But there will remain a certain number which can be cured if we decide that by the power of the Government they are to be cured. The surest way to prevent the possibility of curing any of them is to approach the subject in a spirit of violent rancor, complicated with total ignorance of business interests, and fundamental incapacity or unwillingness to understand the limitations upon all law-making bodies. No problem, and least of all so difficult a problem as this, can be solved if the qualities brought to its solution are panic, fear, envy, hatred, and ignorance. There can exist in a free republic no man more wicked, no man more dangerous to the people, than he who would arouse these feelings in the hope that they would redound to his own political advantage. Corporations that are handled honestly and fairly, so far from being an evil, are a natural business evolution and make for the general prosperity of our land. We do not wish to destroy corporations, but we do wish to make them subserve the public good. All individuals, rich or poor, private or corporate, must be subject to the law of the land; and the Government will hold them to a rigid obedience thereof. The biggest corporation, like the humblest private citizen, must be held to strict compliance with the will of the people as expressed in the fundamental law. The rich man who does not see that this is in his interest is, indeed, short-sighted. When we make him obey the law we insure for him the absolute protection of the law.

The savings banks show what can be done in the way of genuinely beneficent work by large corporations when intelligently administered and supervised. They now hold over twenty-six hundred millions of the people's money and pay annually about one hundred millions of interest or profit to their depositors. There is no talk of danger from these corporations; yet they possess great power, holding over three times the amount of our present national debt; more than all the currency, gold, silver, greenbacks, etc., in circulation in the United States. The chief reason for there being no talk of danger from them is that they are, on the whole, faithfully administered for the benefit of all, under wise laws which require frequent and full publication of their condition, and which prescribe certain needful regulations with which they have to comply, while at the same time giving full scope for the business enterprise of their managers within these limits.

Now, of course, savings banks are as highly specialized a class of corporations as railroads, and we cannot force too far the analogy with other corporations; but there are certain conditions which I think we can lay down as indispensable to the proper treatment of all corporations which from their size have become important factors in the social development of the community.

Before speaking, however, of what can be done by way of remedy, let me say a word or two as to certain proposed remedies which, in my judgment, would be ineffective or mischievous. The first thing to remember is that if we are to accomplish any good at all it must be by resolutely keeping in mind the intention to do away with any evils in the conduct of big corporations, while steadfastly refusing to assent to indiscriminate assault upon all forms of corporate capital as such. The line of demarcation we draw must always be on conduct, not upon wealth; our objection to any given corporation must be, not that it is big, but that it behaves badly. Perfectly simple again, my friends, but not always heeded by some of those who would strive to teach us how to act toward big corporations. Treat the head of the corporation as you would treat all other men. If he does well stand by him. You will occasionally find the head of a big corporation who objects to that treatment; very good, apply it all the more carefully. Remember, after all, that he who objects because he is the head of a big corporation to being treated like anyone else is only guilty of the same sin as the man who wishes him treated worse than anyone else because he is the head of a big corporation. Demagogic denunciation of wealth is never wholesome and generally dangerous; and not a few of the proposed methods of curbing the trusts are dangerous chiefly because all insincere advocacy of the impossible is dangerous. It is an unhealthy thing for a community when the appeal is made to follow a course which those who make the appeal either do know or ought to know cannot be followed; and which if followed would result in disaster to everybody. Loose talk about destroying monopoly out of hand, without a hint as to how the monopoly should even be defined, offers a case in point.

Nor can we afford to tolerate any proposal which will strike at the so-called trusts only by striking at the general well-being. We are now enjoying a period of great prosperity. The prosperity is generally diffused through all sections and through all classes. Doubtless there are some individuals who do not get enough of it, and there are others who get too much. That is simply another way of saying that the wisdom of mankind is finite; and that even the best human system does not work perfectly. You don t have to take my word for that. Look back just nine years. In 1893 nobody was concerned in downing the trusts. Everybody was concerned in trying to get up himself. The men who propose to get rid of the evils of the trusts by measures which would do away with the general well- being, advocate a policy which would not only be a dam age to the community as a whole, but which would defeat its own professed object. If we are forced to the alternative of choosing either a system under which most of us prosper somewhat, though a few of us prosper too much, or else a system under which no one prospers enough, of course we will choose the former. If the policy advocated is so revolutionary and destructive as to involve the whole community in the crash of common disaster, it is as certain as anything can be that when the disaster has occurred all efforts to regulate the trusts will cease, and that the one aim will be to restore prosperity. A remedy much advocated at the moment is to take off the tariff from all articles which are made by trusts. To do this it will be necessary first to define trusts. The language commonly used by the advocates of the method implies that they mean all articles made by large corporations, and that the changes in tariff are to be made with punitive intent towards these large corporations. Of course, if the tariff is to be changed in order to punish them, it should be changed so as to punish those that do ill, not merely those that are prosperous. It would be neither just nor expedient to punish the big corporations as big corporations; what we wish to do is to protect the people from any evil that may grow out of their existence or mal-administration. Some of those corporations do well and others do ill. If in any case the tariff is found to foster a monopoly which does ill, of course no protectionist would object to a modification of the tariff sufficient to remedy the evil. But in very few cases does the so-called trust really monopolize the market. Take any very big corporation I could mention them by the score which controls say something in the neighborhood of half of the products of a given industry. It is the kind of corporation that is always spoken of as a trust. Surely, in rearranging the schedules affecting such a corporation it would be necessary to consider the interests of its smaller competitors which control the remaining part, and which, being weaker, would suffer most from any tariff designed to punish all the producers; for, of course, the tariff must be made light or heavy for big and little producers alike. Moreover, such a corporation necessarily employs very many thousands, often very many tens of thousands of workmen, and the minute we proceeded from denunciation to action it would be necessary to consider the interests of these workmen. Furthermore, the products of many trusts are unprotected, and would be entirely unaffected by any change in the tariff, or at most very slightly so. The Standard Oil Company offers a case in point; and the corporations which control the anthracite coal output offer another for there is no duty whatever on anthracite coal.

I am not now discussing the question of the tariff as such; whether from the standpoint of the fundamental difference between those who believe in a protective tariff and those who believe in free trade; or from the standpoint of those who, while they believe in a protective tariff, feel that there could be a rearrangement of our schedules, either by direct legislation or by reciprocity treaties, which would result in enlarging our markets; nor yet from the standpoint of those who feel that stability of economic policy is at the moment our prime economic need, and that the benefits to be derived from any change in schedules would not compensate for the damage to business caused by the wide-spread agitation which would follow any attempted general revision of the tariff at this moment. Without regard to the wisdom of any one of those three positions, it remains true that the real evils connected with the trusts cannot be remedied by any change in the tariff laws. The trusts can be damaged by depriving them of the benefits of a protective tariff, only on condition of damaging all their smaller competitors, and all the wage workers employed in the industry. This point is very important, and it is desirable to avoid any misunderstanding concerning it. I am not now considering whether or not, on grounds totally unconnected with the trusts, it would be well to lower the duties on various schedules, either by direct legislation, or by legislation or treaties designed to secure as an offset reciprocal advantages from the nations with which we trade. My point is that changes in the tariff would have little appreciable effect on the trusts save as they shared in the general harm or good proceeding from such changes. No tariff change would help one of our smaller corporations, or one of our private individuals in business, still less one of our wage workers, as against a large corporation in the same business; on the contrary, if it bore heavily on the large corporation, it would inevitably be felt still more by that corporation's weaker rivals, while any injurious result would of necessity be shared by both the employer and the employed in the business concerned. The immediate introduction of substantial free trade in all articles manufactured by trusts, that is, by the largest and most successful corporations, would not affect some of the most powerful of our business combinations in the least, save by the damage done to the general business welfare of the country; others would undoubtedly be seriously affected, but much less so than their weaker rivals, while the loss would be divided between the capitalists and the laborers; and after the years of panic and distress had been lived through, and some return to prosperity had occurred, even though all were on a lower plane of prosperity than before, the relative difference between the trusts and their rivals would remain as marked as ever. In other words, the trust, or big corporation, would have suffered relatively to, and in the interest of, its foreign competitor; but its relative position towards its American competitors would probably be improved; little would have been done towards cutting out or minimizing the evils in the trusts; nothing towards securing adequate control and regulation of the large modern corporations. In other words, the question of regulating the trusts with a view to minimizing or abolishing the evils existent in them, is separate and apart from the question of tariff revision.

You must face the fact that only harm will come from a proposition to attack the so-called trusts in a vindictive spirit by measures conceived solely with a desire of hurting them, without regard as to whether or not discrimination should be made between the good and evil in them, and without even any regard as to whether a necessary sequence of the action would be the hurting of other interests. The adoption of such a policy would mean temporary damage to the trusts, because it would mean temporary damage to all of our business interests; but the effect would be only temporary, for exactly as the damage affected all alike, good and bad, so the reaction would affect all alike, good and bad. The necessary supervision and control in which I firmly believe as the only method of eliminating the real evils of the trusts must come through wisely and cautiously framed legislation which shall aim, in the first place, to give definite control to some sovereign over the great corporations, and which shall be followed, when once this power has been conferred, by a system giving to the Government the full knowledge which is the essential for satisfactory action. Then when this knowledge one of the essential features of which is proper publicity has been gained, what further steps of any kind are necessary can be taken with the confidence born of the possession of power to deal with the subject, and of a thorough knowledge of what should and can be done in the matter.

We need additional power; and we need knowledge. Our Constitution was framed when the economic conditions were so different that each State could wisely be left to handle the corporations within its limits as it saw fit. Nowadays all the corporations which I am considering do what is really an interstate business, and as the States have proceeded on very different lines in regulating them, at present a corporation will be organized in one State, not because it intends to do business in that State, but because it does not, and therefore that State can give it better privileges, and then it will do business in some other States, and will claim not to be under the control of the States in which it does business; and of course it is not the object of the State creating it to exercise any control over it, as it does not do any business in that State. Such a system cannot obtain. There must be some sovereign. It might be better if all the States could agree along the same lines in dealing with these corporations, but I see not the slightest prospect of such an agreement. Therefore I personally feel that ultimately the nation will have to assume the responsibility of regulating these very large corporations which do an interstate business. The States must combine to meet the way in which capital has combined; and the way in which the States can combine is through the National Government. But I firmly believe that all these obstacles can be met if only we face them, both with the determination to overcome them, and with the further determination to overcome them in ways which shall not do damage to the country as a whole; which, on the contrary, shall further our industrial development, and shall help instead of hindering all corporations which work out their success by means that are just and fair towards all men.

Without the adoption of a constitutional amendment my belief is that a good deal can be done by law. It is difficult to say exactly how much, because experience has taught us that in dealing with these subjects where the lines dividing the rights and duties of the States and of the nation are in doubt it has sometimes been difficult for Congress to forecast the action of the courts upon its legislation. Such legislation (whether obtainable now, or obtainable only after a constitutional amendment) should provide for a reasonable supervision, the most prominent feature of which at first should be publicity; that is, the making public both to the governmental authorities and to the people at large the essential facts in which the public is concerned. This would give us exact knowledge of many points which are now not only in doubt but the subject of fierce controversy. Moreover, the mere fact of the publication would cure some very grave evils, for the light of day is a deterrent to wrong-doing. It would doubtless disclose other evils with which for the time being we could devise no way to grapple. Finally, it would disclose others which could be grappled with and cured by further legislative action.

Remember, I advocate the action which the President can only advise, and which he has no power himself to take. Under our present legislative and constitutional limitations, the national executive can work only between narrow lines in the field of action concerning great corporations. Between those lines, I assure you that exact and even-handed justice will be dealt, and is being dealt, to all men, without regard to persons.

I wish to repeat with all emphasis that, desirable though it is that the nation should have the power I suggest, it is equally desirable that it should be used with wisdom and self-restraint. The mechanism of modern business is tremendous in its size and complexity, and ignorant intermeddling with it would be disastrous. We should not be made timid or daunted by the size of the problem; we should not fear to undertake it; but we should undertake it with ever present in our minds dread of the sinister spirits of rancor, ignorance, and vanity. We need to keep steadily in mind the fact that besides the tangible property in each corporation there lies behind the spirit which brings it success, and in the case of each very successful corporation this is usually the spirit of some one man or set of men. Under exactly similar conditions one corporation will make a stupendous success where another makes a stupendous failure, simply because one is well managed and the other is not. While making it clear that we do not intend to allow wrong-doing by one of the captains of industry any more than by the humblest private in the industrial ranks, we must also in the interests of all of us avoid cramping a strength which, if beneficently used, will be for the good of all of us. The marvellous prosperity we have been enjoying for the past few years has been due primarily to the high average of honesty, thrift, and business capacity among our people as a whole; but some of it has also been due to the ability of the men who are the industrial leaders of the nation. In securing just and fair dealing by these men let us to do them justice in return, and this not only because it is our duty, but because it is our interest; not only for their sakes, but for ours. We are neither the friend of the rich man as such nor the friend of the poor man as such; we are the friend of the honest man, rich or poor; and we intend that all men, rich and poor alike, shall obey the law alike and receive its protection alike.

Theodore Roosevelt on Corporate Trusts • 327

THE WASHINGTON SCHOOLMASTER
From the *Chronicle* (Chicago)

"The Washington Schoolmaster," an editorial cartoon about the coal strike of 1902, by Charles Lederer.

Document Analysis

As Theodore Roosevelt moved into the second year of his presidency, he was aware of the public's concerns about the unregulated growth and power of business trusts. Roosevelt noted that many people used the word trust "very loosely and almost always with technical inaccuracy." What the average person called a "trust," Roosevelt contended, was simply a large corporation. He further noted that this common conception of the trusts included large corporations that operated in several states "and often have a tendency to monopoly."

Roosevelt argues that large corporations had developed because of the new technologies in the transportation and communication fields. These changes have happened, and cannot be undone. The challenge, as Roosevelt sees it, is to adopt laws which shall allow society to develop from these changes "the utmost possible benefit and the least possible amount of harm." While Roosevelt believed there had to be regulation of the trusts, he contended that the behavior of a company, not simply its size, is the real issue. Attacking all big businesses could endanger the general prosperity the nation was experiencing at that time.

Roosevelt also addresses one reform that had been suggested—removing the tariff from products that were made by the trusts. Since the Civil War, the Republican Party had supported a high protective tariff—an import tax that made imported goods more expensive, and was therefore thought to protect American manufacturers from competition from cheaper foreign imports. Roosevelt notes that the trusts rarely achieved true monopoly, and removing tariff protections would harm the small businesses that were not part of any illegitimate trust; indeed, it might even harm the small companies more than the trusts.

Throughout his speech, Roosevelt called for sensible reforms, and rejected proposals that sprang from "rancor" or a "vindictive spirit." The government needed the power to regulate big businesses that behaved badly, but that power had to be exercised "with wisdom and self-restraint." While he gave few details of the kinds of reforms he envisioned, he did note that some might be accomplished by simple legislation, while others might require a constitutional amendment. He also suggested that some means was needed to force businesses to make accurate reports to the government about their activities and earnings, and that this information should be made public also, so that the people could know what wrongs were being committed and what needed to be done to correct them.

Essential Themes

President Roosevelt stressed a few key themes throughout this speech. One is the persistence of change. Changes in technology and in the structuring of business had led to the development of large corporations in America, and these changes could not be undone. The nation needed to address the problem of trusts being used in attempts to create monopolies, but the fact that big business exists, and that the technology that allowed such growth has been developed, must be accepted. The clock could not be turned back, even if the nation wished to do so.

While Roosevelt believed some means of regulating big business was needed, he stressed the themes of care and restraint in creating these regulations. He believed that some reforms that had been suggested were simply impossible; others would require amending the Constitution before the government could exercise the powers envisioned. Roosevelt argued these changes should be evolutionary, not revolutionary. This is in keeping with the general approach of the Progressive movement of the early 1900s—Progressivism was pragmatic, liberal reform, not radical utopianism. It aimed at practical reforms that would benefit consumers and workers.

Roosevelt feared that attacking all big businesses, and not just those involved in monopolistic practices, might endanger the overall health of the economy, which benefitted all Americans to some extent.

A third theme Roosevelt emphasizes in this speech was a regular part of his speeches and writings on the trust issue. He argued that the mere size of a corporation was not the issue. The behavior of the company is the issue that must be addressed. Doing business on a large scale brought certain benefits to businesses, which were not necessarily illegitimate. But business combinations like the trusts, or cartels, or pools, which sought to limit competition and tended toward monopoly, had to be prohibited.

—Mark S. Joy, PhD

Bibliography and Additional Reading

Blum, John Morton. *The Republican Roosevelt*. New York: Atheneum, 1974.

Chessman, G. Wallace. *Theodore Roosevelt and the Politics of Power*. Boston: Little, Brown and Company, 1969.

Goodwin, Doris Kearns. *The Bully Pulpit: Theodore Roosevelt, William Howard Taft, and the Golden Ae of Journalism.* New York: Simon and Schuster, 2013.

McGerr, Michael. *A Fierce Discontent: The Rise and Fall of the Progressive Movement in America.* New York: Oxford University Press, 2003.

■ Eugene V. Debs: "How I Became a Socialist"

Date: 1902
Author: Eugene V. Debs
Genre: article

Summary Overview

The American trade union leader, orator, and Socialist Party activist Eugene Debs was a master at making what might look today like radical political ideas seem as American as apple pie. A student of history as well as politics, Debs regularly invoked the memory of the Founding Fathers to make his policy suggestions seem more acceptable. Motivated by an unyielding sense of justice, he often tried to shame authorities to do what he thought was right. Whether addressing audiences at a labor rally or on the campaign trail, Debs invariably came back to a sharp critique of the American political system, touting the virtues of his brand of Socialism. His goal as a politician was not necessarily to win elections but instead to inspire listeners by his own example and to win converts to the Socialist cause. In a country with no Socialist legacy—unlike many European countries where Socialism was established—it is really quite remarkable that Debs had any success at all as a politician. That success was due in no small part to the power of Debs's oratory and prose. In his 1902 article "How I Became a Socialist," Debs traces his path toward growing class consciousness and final embrace of Socialism.

Defining Moment

Debs' greatest struggle throughout his life was trying to realign perceptions of Socialism in American society. In this article and others throughout his life, Debs tried to move people toward a political viewpoint that he believed was more in sync with their best interests. It was only through an embrace of Socialism, Debs believed, could American workers achieve the sort of equality and justice that they deserved. His target for these speeches were chiefly American industrial workers, the men and women toiling in factories, in mines, and, perhaps above all else, laboring on the railroads. Working under hazardous conditions, long hours, and for little pay, American workers were ripe for recruitment into Debs' movement. By documenting his journey to Socialism, Debs hoped to inspire others in similar conditions, and in so doing call them to action.

Author Biography

Eugene Victor Debs was a trade union leader, orator, and frequent Socialist Party candidate for the presidency of the United States. He was born in Terre Haute, Indiana, in 1855. While working his way up through the hierarchy of the Brotherhood of Locomotive Firemen, an important railroad union, he was elected city clerk in Terre Haute in 1879. He also served one term in the Indiana state legislature in 1885. In 1893 Debs cofounded the American Railway Union (ARU), an industrial union that, unlike most exclusive railroad brotherhoods of the era, admitted railroad workers of all skill levels. As the leader of that organization, Debs led the infamous Pullman strike of 1894.

The Pullman strike was an effort to organize workers at the Pullman Palace Car Company of Pullman, Illinois. As part of the strike, ARU members nationwide decided to boycott all trains that carried the company's famous sleeping cars in an effort to force them to recognize the union. As a result, rail traffic stopped nationwide. In response, railroad companies deliberately placed mail cars on trains with Pullman Palace Cars in order to encourage government intervention in the dispute. The legal injunction issued by a federal judge in response to the boycott essentially shut down the strike and destroyed the union. In 1895 Debs was convicted of interfering with the mail as a result of his refusal to abide by that injunction. Debs's political views were greatly affected by the Socialist literature he read during his short stay in jail. Indeed, this incarceration would prove to be the pivotal point of his entire life.

Upon his release Debs announced his conversion to Socialism. He also changed career paths from being a trade union leader to being a political leader. Debs would serve as a Socialist Party presidential candidate five times: 1900, 1904, 1908, 1912, and 1920. His best showing occurred in 1912 when he came close to garnering a million votes. That was 6 percent of the total votes cast in that election. In 1918 Debs was convicted of sedition for a speech he had given in Canton, Ohio, earlier that year. Debs had to run his final campaign for president as a protest candidate from his jail cell. A famous campaign button from 1920 read "For President—Convict No. 9653." Between elections Debs toured the country giving speeches and writing articles that critiqued the American capitalist system and championed the cause of Socialism. Debs died in 1926 at the age of seventy.

Debs represented a vision of Socialism in America that got lost in the anti-Communist hysteria of the cold war era. His political beliefs, though Socialist, were grounded in American ideals like justice, equal rights, and Christianity. Debs's willingness to go to prison for the causes he championed greatly increased his appeal and the popularity of his ideas. While many other figures in American Socialism were immigrants from European countries like Germany, where Socialism was more in the mainstream, Debs attracted native-born Americans to the Socialist cause. His success as a politician came as the result of hundreds of thousands of Americans entertaining the possibility of radical change in American life in an era when the adverse effects of industrialization had made them unhappy with the existing political system.

HISTORICAL DOCUMENT: "How I Became a Socialist"

On the evening of February 27, 1875, the local lodge of the Brotherhood of Locomotive Firemen was organized at Terre Haute, Ind., by Joshua A. Leach, then grand master, and I was admitted as a charter member and at once chosen secretary. "Old Josh Leach" as he was affectionately called, a typical locomotive fireman of his day, was the founder of the brotherhood, and I was instantly attracted by his rugged honesty, simple manner and homely speech. How well I remember feeling his large, rough hand on my shoulder, the kindly eye of an elder brother searching my own as he gently said, "My boy, you're a little young, but I believe you're in earnest and will make your mark in the brotherhood." Of course, I assured him that I would do my best....

My first step was thus taken in organized labor and a new influence fired my ambition and changed the whole current of my career. I was filled with enthusiasm and my blood fairly leaped in my veins. Day and night I worked for the brotherhood. To see its watchfires glow and observe the increase of its sturdy members were the sunshine and shower of my life. To attend the "meeting" was my supreme joy, and for ten years I was not once absent when the faithful assembled....

Through all these years I was nourished at Fountain Proletaire. I drank deeply of its waters and every particle of my tissue became saturated with the spirit of the working class. I had fired an engine and been stung by the exposure and hardship of the rail. I was with the boys in their weary watches, at the broken engine's side and often helped to bear their bruised and bleeding bodies back to wife and child again. How could I but feel the burden of their wrongs? How the seed of agitation fail to take deep root in my heart?

And so I was spurred on in the work of organizing, not the firemen merely, but the brakemen, switchmen, telegraphers, shopmen, track-hands, all of them in fact, and as I had now become known as an organizer, the call came from all sides and there are but few trades I have not helped to organize and less still in whose strikes I have not at some time had a hand.

In 1894 the American Railway Union was organized and a braver body of men never fought the battle of the working class.

Up to this time I had heard but little of Socialism, knew practically nothing about the movement, and what little I did know was not calculated to impress me in its favor. I was bent on thorough and complete organization of the railroad men and ultimately the whole working class, and all my time and energy were given to that end. My supreme conviction was that if they were only organized in every branch of the service and all acted together in concert they could redress their wrongs and regulate the conditions of their employment. The stockholders of the corporation acted as one, why not the men? It was such a plain proposition—simply to follow the example set before their eyes by their masters—surely they could not fail to see it, act as one, and solve the problem....

The skirmish lines of the A. R. U. were well advanced. A series of small battles were fought and won without the loss of a man. A number of concessions were made by the corporations rather than risk an encounter. Then came the fight on the Great Northern, short, sharp, and decisive. The victory was complete—the only railroad strike of magnitude ever won by an organization in America.

Next followed the final shock—the Pullman strike—and the American Railway Union again won, clear and complete. The combined corporations were paralyzed and helpless. At this juncture there were delivered, from wholly unexpected quarters, a swift succession of blows that blinded me for an instant and then opened wide my eyes—and in the gleam of every bayonet and the flash of every rifle *the class struggle was revealed*. This was my first practical lesson in Socialism, though wholly unaware that it was called by that name.

An army of detectives, thugs and murderers were equipped with badge and beer and bludgeon and turned loose; old hulks of cars were fired; the alarm bells tolled; the people were terrified; the most startling rumors were set afloat; the press volleyed and thundered, and over all the wires sped the news that Chicago's white throat was in the clutch of a red mob; injunctions flew thick and fast, arrests followed, and our office and headquarters, the heart of the strike, was sacked, torn out and nailed up by the "lawful" authorities of the federal government; and when in company with my loyal comrades I found myself in Cook County jail at Chicago with the...press screaming conspiracy, treason and murder, and by some fateful coincidence I was given the cell occupied just previous to his execution by the assassin of Mayor Carter Harrison, Sr., overlooking the spot, a few feet distant, where the anarchists were hanged a few years before, I had another exceedingly practical and impressive lesson in Socialism....

The Chicago jail sentences were followed by six months at Woodstock and it was here that Socialism gradually laid hold of me in its own irresistible fashion. Books and pamphlets and letters from socialists came by every mail and I began to read and think and dissect the anatomy of the system in which workingmen, however organized, could be shattered and battered and splintered at a single stroke....

The American Railway Union was defeated but not conquered—overwhelmed but not destroyed. It lives and pulsates in the Socialist movement, and its defeat but blazed the way to economic freedom and hastened the dawn of human brotherhood.

GLOSSARY

Chicago's white throat was in the clutch of a red mob: sarcastic comparison of the city to a woman (white, at that) in danger from "reds," or Socialists

class struggle: fundamental conflict between the workers (proletariat) and business owners (capitalists)

Fountain Proletaire: an expression, apparently of Debs's own coinage, that used the French adjectival format (noun followed by adjective) and presented the struggle of industrial workers as an opportunity to gain wisdom and grow

grand master: a master craftsman, a leading figure in many local union bodies

Great Northern: the Great Northern Railway

homely: down home

watches: shifts at work

> **where the anarchists were hanged a few years before:** a reference to the place of execution of four men out of eight charged for their alleged roles in the Haymarket riot in Chicago on May 4, 1886

Document Analysis

In his article "How I Became a Socialist" Debs does his best to convey that he had always been a kind of Socialist, even though he had explicitly rejected that label for his political ideas before his imprisonment in 1895. His goal in this piece is to suggest that people like him who saw aspects of class conflict all around them but did not understand Socialism would come to embrace the movement once Socialists like Debs taught them to understand the world. Here he describes his own education in the hope that others might follow along his same path.

In the early sections of the essay, Debs conveys his enthusiasm for organizing his fellow members of the working class as a sign of his growing class consciousness. At that point in his life, he thought organization alone was enough to redress the many wrongs that management inflicted upon labor. Debs explains that unlike other labor leaders of that era, he helped organize the ARU because he thought that all railroad men would do best standing together rather than separated into unions organized by skill. This is an implied contrast to the American Federation of Labor, an umbrella organization for unions that was just getting started around the time that Debs first gained prominence in the labor movement. Despite his comparatively broad view of organized labor's potential base, Debs's vision remained limited to what he could do in support of the trade union movement.

Then came the Pullman strike. "In the gleam of every bayonet and the flash of every rifle" Debs writes, *"the class struggle was revealed."* This justifiably famous line not only supports the idea that the Pullman strike converted Debs to Socialism but also helps explain his reasons for supporting Socialism. Since the federal army kept the exploitation of Pullman workers going, ordinary people had to be able to control the state so that it could support their cause rather than the goals of giant corporations. To Debs, then, labor and politics were inseparable. He could not help the working class without entering politics.

This philosophy is in sharp contrast to the predominant labor union philosophy of that era. The American Federation of Labor, led by Samuel Gompers, believed in what Gompers called "pure and simple unionism." This meant that trade unions should worry about raising the wages and improving the working conditions of their members, and absolutely nothing else. Unions that followed this philosophy ignored politics because politics took time and resources away from their core purpose—helping their members. This debate was sometimes referred to as the "political question" within union circles. However, by the time of his death in 1924, Gompers came around to Debs's point of view on this issue even if he never adopted Debs's radical positions.

Essential Themes

The industrial revolution completely transformed not just how products were made but also the relationship between labor and capital. Whereas before products were handcrafter, requiring specialized skill, the industrial revolution allowed, and in fact demanded, large numbers of unskilled workers. To the men who owned the factories, labor became just another resource, on the same order as coal or oil. As need for labor increased, workers began to make demands on owners, including higher pay, shorter hours, and higher safety standards. When owners refused, the clashes often became violent. One industry especially fraught with conflict were the railroads, run with an iron fist by industrialists such as Jay Gould and Cornelius Vanderbilt. These robber barons continuously fought against the rise of unions and bettering conditions for their workers, even going so far as to employ private police to put down work stoppage and protest, violently, if need be. By the 1880s several unions had formed as a counter measure to the power of the industrialists, among them Eugene V. Deb' American Railway Union. Tensions erupted in 1893. When after a panic in the market, George Pullman began to lay off employees and cut wages. Pullman, owner of the Pullman Palace Car Company, required workers to live in a planned community he designed on the south side of Chicago, but despite firing workers and cutting wages, he did not cut the already steep rents he forced his employees to pay. The following year, the ARU organized a mass boycott, in which 125,000 Pullman employees walked off the job at over two dozen railroads. The boycott, along with sympathy strikes launched by other unions, halted railroad transportation across the country. When the railroads responded by hiring strikebreakers, the strikes became violent. In response President Grover Cleveland sent in the army, leading to clashes between armed troops and strikers, resulting in 30 deaths. Ultimately the boycott was a failure with much of the nation against the unions, the press blaming the action on immigrants. Although the government tried to extend an olive branch by making Labor Day a federal holiday, the Pullman strikes had the effect of radicalizing much of the union movement and its leadership, much of whom, Debs among them, were jailed after the boycott. As tensions continued to grow, labor, heavily influenced by the ideas of German philosopher Karl Marx, began to organize around the idea of socialism. In fact, by 1901, following Debs' release from prison, the disparate far left groups came together as a unified Socialist Party of America, setting the stage for a multi-pronged conflict between capital and labor that would dominate industrial relations for the next century. The challenge for union leaders such as Debs was to drive up recruitment for what they saw as a full scale war between capital and labor, especially as an increasingly vocal segment of the population viewed socialism as a threat to the natural order, with the federal government even considering groups such as the Socialist Party as potentially treasonous.

The efforts of Eugene Debs to recruit people into socialism yielded mixed results. Despite his impassioned writing, speaking, and organizing, despite several failed presidential bids, one of them from prison, socialism generally, and the Socialist Party of America specifically, never gained much of a following. Some of this had to do with the rigidity of the far left, as the Socialist Party and its affiliate groups would not form coalitions with other parties or even allow members to vote for other candidates. Another factor was the fact that the United States at the turn of the century had already embarrassed left-leaning policy, with both major parties representing progressive ideas in their platforms, most prominently on display during the 1912 election between Howard Taft, Woodrow Wilson, and Theodore Roosevelt. Finally, the rise of Russian Communism in 1917, had the effect of turning much of public opinion against socialism, as average Americans equated the political ideas of Karl Marx with the authoritarianism of the Soviet Union. Red Scares became a common tactic of the political right to galvanize support against the socialist agenda. However, Debs and his Socialist Party did have a profound effect on organized labor and the form of the liberal agenda in the mainstream parties. Debs won converts across organized labor who then helped shape and influence the political discourse across the nation. Debs' tireless advocacy for the workers and the poor helped normalize concepts such as socialized medical and retirement benefits, in fact, many of the ideas first espoused by Debs later became the basis for Franklin Roosevelt's New Deal, which in turn became the structure on which the Democratic party is built upon today. Debs continues to be a major influence on liberals and progressives, with many prominent members of the left, including Senator Bernie Sanders of Vermont, claiming Debs as a personal hero. Although in life Eugene V. Debs never achieved the kind of social changed he dreamed of, his ideas continue to resonate to this day, influencing public debate and the ongoing relationship between capital and labor.

—*Jonathan Rees, PhD and K.P. Dawes, MA*

Bibliography and Additional Reading

Chace, James. *Wilson, Roosevelt, Taft and Debs -The Election that Changed the Country*. Simon and Schuster, 2009.

Debs, Eugene V. *Writings of Eugene V Debs: A Collection of Essays by America's Most Famous Socialist*. Red and Black Publishers, 2009.

Debs, Eugene V. *Gentle Rebel: Letters of Eugene V. Debs*. University of Illinois Press, 1995.

Freeberg, Ernest. *Democracy's Prisoner*. Harvard University Press, 2009.

Ginger, Ray. *The Bending Cross: A Biography of Eugene Victor Debs*. Haymarket Books, 2007.

Salvatore, Nick. *Eugene V. Debs: Citizen and Socialist*. University of Illinois Press, 1984.

Robert La Follette on Amending the National Banking Laws

Date: March 17, 1908
Author: Robert La Follette
Genre: speech; address

Summary Overview

Throughout much of his adult life, Robert M. La Follette, popularly known as "Fighting Bob," was admittedly combative and suspicious. At the same time, he was an indefatigable investigator and speaker who could often intimidate opponents with mounds of supporting data and his effective speechmaking. He always characterized himself as a spokesperson for a public trampled by predatory capitalists and Wall Street speculators. In 1908, in his speech on the amendment of National Banking Laws, La Follette indicted the entire financial system, which he believed was grinding down the true producers of the nation—common people. He saw the marriage of investment banks with corporations as creating what he termed a "money trust" of groups lining their pockets and putting at peril smaller institutions and businesses.

Defining Moment

In the Senate, La Follette was one of the more vocal members, focusing in particular on giant business, which he saw as an evil in itself. In 1906, breaking the unwritten rule that freshman senators should not speak, he delivered an address on strengthening the pending Hepburn Act, a railroad regulation bill that was so detailed that it filled 148 pages of the Congressional Record. He produced similar documentation in advocating the direct election of senators, more powerful antitrust legislation, income redistribution, lower tariffs, and protection for American workers. He led the attack against the Aldrich-Vreeland bill in 1908, a measure to allow banks to issue emergency currency against securities and bonds. In his presentation, he claimed that fewer than a hundred men dominated and controlled business and industry in America.

On March 17, 1908, La Follette began a series of speeches attacking the money trust. This first speech was triggered by the Aldrich currency bill, proposed in the aftermath of the Panic of 1907. Nelson Aldrich, the powerful chairman of the Senate Finance Committee, proposed the issue of $500 million in emergency currency that would be backed by state, municipal, and private railroad bonds. Edward B. Vreeland of New York offered a similar bill in the House. Aldrich soon renounced the clause involving railroad bonds, acting out of the fear that the proposal would injure the Finance Committee members William B. Allison of Iowa and Chester I. Long of Kansas in their forthcoming races for reelection. La Follette had intended to blast Aldrich's original proposal, but he hastily rewrote his speech, with the result containing some of the most sensationalist charges ever made on the floor of Congress.

Author Biography

Robert Marion La Follette, a son of farmers, was born on June 14, 1855, in Primrose, Wisconsin. At age twenty he entered the University of Wisconsin, graduating in 1879. In 1880, after briefly attending law school, he was elected district attorney of Dane County, where Madison, the capital of Wisconsin, is located. In 1884 he was elected as the youngest member of U.S. House of Representatives, where he was so orthodox in his Republicanism that he ardently supported the high rates of the McKinley Tariff. The victim of a Democratic landslide in 1890, he resumed his law practice in Madison. An attempted bribe by the Wisconsin senator Philetus Sawyer, who asked La Follette to intervene in a case in which his brother-in-law was judge, radicalized the young attorney, who henceforth became a strong foe of entrenched interests.

After two abortive bids for Wisconsin's governorship, La Follette won the race in 1900 and was reelected in both 1902 and 1904. He pushed through a battery of reform measures, including conservation acts, antilobbying laws, regulation of telephone and telegraph companies, educational expansion, public utility controls, consumer protection, tax and civil service legislation, a direct primary, and railroad and industrial commissions. He also pioneered what was called the "Wisconsin idea" by which university experts aided in drafting significant legislation. While still governor, he was chosen in January 1905 by the state legislature to represent Wisconsin in the U.S. Senate, where he would serve until his death in 1925.

Although he was nominally a Republican, he broke with the presidency of William Howard Taft over the high Payne-Aldrich Tariff and over alleged corruption in the Department of the Interior. He sought to gain the Republican presidential nomination of 1912, his platform including collective bargaining, public ownership of water power and railroads, aid to farmers, a ban on child labor, and the recall of federal judges. Nevertheless, his major supporters abandoned him once former President Theodore Roosevelt entered the race.

HISTORICAL DOCUMENT: On Amending the National Banking Laws

Eighteen hundred and ninety-eight was the beginning of great industrial reorganization. Men directly engaged in production brought about in the first instance an association of the independent concerns which they had built up. These reorganizations were at the outset limited to those turning out finished products similar in kind. Within a period of three years following, 149 such reorganizations were effected with a total stock and bond capitalization of $3,784,000,000. In making these reorganizations, the opportunity for a large paper capitalization offered too great a temptation to be resisted. This was but the first stage in the creation of fictitious wealth. The success of these organizations led quickly on to a consolidation of combined industries, until a mere handful of men controlled the industrial production of the country.

The opportunity to associate the reorganization of the industrial institutions of the country with banking capital presented itself. Such connections were a powerful aid to reorganization, and reorganization offered an unlimited field for speculation....

I have compiled a list of about one hundred men with their directorships in the great corporate business enterprises of the United States. It furnishes indisputable proof of the community of interest that controls the industrial life of the country....

It discloses their connections with the transportation, the industrial, and the commercial life of the American people. This exhibit will make it clear to anyone that a small group of men hold in their hands the business of this country.

No student of the economic changes in recent years can escape the conclusion that the railroads, telegraph, shipping, cable, telephone, traction, express, mining, iron, steel, coal, oil, gas, electric light, cotton, copper, sugar, tobacco, agricultural implements, and the food products are completely controlled and mainly owned by these hundred men; that they have through reorganization multiplied their wealth almost beyond their own ability to know its amount with accuracy....

But the country seems not to understand how completely great banking institutions in the principal money centers have become bound up with the control of industrial institutions, nor the logical connection of this relationship to the financial depression which we have so recently suffered, nor the dangers which threaten us from this source in the future....

The closeness of business association between Wall Street and the centralized banking power of New York can, unfortunately, be but imperfectly traced through the official reports. It would seem that the radical changes taking place in the banking business of the country, suggesting to the conservative, economic, and financial authorities the gravest possible dangers to our industrial and commercial integrity, might well have caused the Treasury Department to recognize the necessity of so directing its investigations of the national banks in the greater cities which are centers of speculation and to so classify their returns as to inform itself and the country definitely respecting such changes. This has not been done....

It is, however, possible to find evidence which establishes the diversion of a large volume of the bank resources to securities which are the subject of speculative operation in the stock exchange....

Official figures do not show the real condition. The reports from banks upon which statistics are based fail to make clear the actual investment in speculative securities.... These banks have either established connections with trust companies or have organized inside trust companies as a protection and convenience.... These companies afford a convenient cover for the banks.... Their securities can be borrowed and shuffled back and forth to make a good showing. The trust companies can handle securities which the banks can not touch. They can underwrite bonds and float loans for which the banks could not openly stand sponsor. They can deal with themselves in innumerable ways to their own benefit and the detriment of the public....

The effect of the proposed legislation becomes more apparent as we investigate the grouping together of the great financial institutions holding these railroad bonds and other special securities and then trace their connection with the companies issuing these bonds....

The twenty-three directors of the National City Bank, the head of the Standard Oil group, and the directors of the National Bank of Commerce, thirty-nine in number, hold 1,007 directorships on the great transportation, industrial, and commercial institutions of this country....

Fourteen of the directors of the National City Bank are at the head of fourteen great combinations representing 38 per cent of the capitalization of all the industrial trusts of the country.

The railroad lines represented on the board of this one bank cover the country like a network.... These same twenty-three directors, through their various connections, represent more than 350 other banks, trust companies, railroads, and industrial corporations, with an aggregate capitalization of more than twelve thousand million dollars....

It was inevitable that this massing of banking power should attract to itself the resources of other banks throughout the country. Capital attracts capital. It inspires confidence. It appeals to the imagination....

The law providing that 15 per cent of the deposits of a country bank should be held for the protection of its depositors conveniently permits three-fifths of the amount to be deposited in reserve city banks, and of the 25 per cent of reserve for the protection of depositors in reserve city banks one-half may be deposited with central reserve city banks. As there are but three central reserve cities, one of which, of course, is New York City, the alluring interest rates which these all-powerful groups could offer inevitably tended to draw the great proportion of lawful reserves subject to transfer from the country and reserve banks....

The power which the New York banks derive through these vast accumulations of the resources of other national banks strengthen their position so that they could draw in the surplus money of all the other financial institutions of the country, State, private, and savings banks and trust companies....

The ability of these group banks of New York through their connected interests to engage in underwriting, to finance promotion schemes, where the profits resulting from overcapitalization represent hundreds of millions of dollars, places them beyond let or hindrance from competitors elsewhere in the country. Their ability to take advantage of conditions in Wall Street ... would enable them to command, almost at will, the capital of the country for these speculative purposes.

But one result could follow. Floating the stocks and bonds in overcapitalized transportation, traction, mining, and industrial organizations does not create wealth, but it does absorb capital. Through the agency of these great groups hundreds of millions of dollars of the wealth of the country have been tied up....

The plain truth is that legitimate commercial banking is being eaten up by financial banking. The greatest banks of the financial center of the country have ceased to be agents of commerce and have become primarily agencies of promotion and speculation.... Trained men, who a dozen years ago stood first among the bankers of the world as heads of the greatest banks of New York City, are, in the main, either displaced or do the bidding of men who are not bankers, but masters of organization....

Sir, can any sane man doubt the power of a little group of men in whose hands are lodged the control of the railroads and the industries, outside of agriculture, as well as the great banks, insurance, and trust companies of the principal money center of the country, to give commercial banking and general business a shock at will?...

Taking the general conditions of the country, it is difficult to find any sufficient reason outside of manipulation for the extraordinary panic of October, 1907....

The panic came. It had been scheduled to arrive. The way had been prepared. Those who were directing it were not the men to miss anything in their way as it advanced....

The panic was working well. The stock market had gone to smash. Harriman was buying back Union Pacific shorts, but still smashing the market. Morgan was buying in short steel stocks and bonds, but still smashing the market.... The country banks were begging for their balances. Business was being held up.... On the street and in the brokers' offices the strain of apprehension was intense. In the midst of a Wall Street fight, when fear supersedes reason, it is difficult for those who are in it, but not directing it, to determine how much is real, how much is sham. Some of the guns are loaded only with blank cartridges to alarm; some are loaded with powder and ball to kill....

The floor of the stock exchange was chosen as the scene for the closing act, October 24 the time.

> *This [list] will make it clear to anyone that a small group of men hold in their hands the business of this country.*

The men who had created the money stringency, who had absorbed the surplus capital of the country with promotions and reorganization schemes, who had deliberately forced a panic and frightened many innocent depositors to aid them by hoarding, who had held up the country banks by lawlessly refusing to return their deposits, never lost sight of one of the chief objects to be attained. The cause of currency revision was not neglected for one moment. It was printed day by day in their press; it passed from mouth to mouth.... High interest rates should be made to plead for emergency money through the telegraph dispatches of October 24 in every countinghouse, factory, and shop in America. The banks refused credit to old customers—all business to new customers. Call loans for money were at last denied at any price.... It spelled ruin....

How perfect the stage setting! How real it all seemed! But back of the scenes Morgan and Stillman were in conference. They had made their representations at Washington. They knew when the next installment of aid would reach New York.... They awaited its arrival and deposit. Thereupon they pooled an equal amount. But they held it.... Interest rates soared. Wall street was driven to a frenzy.... The smashing of the market became terrific. Still they waited.... Men looked into each other's ghastly faces. Then, at precisely 2.15, the curtain went up with Morgan and Standard Oil in the center of the stage with money—real money, twenty-five millions of money—giving it away at 10 per cent....

And so ended the panic.

How beautifully it all worked out. They had the whole country terrorized. They had the money of the deposits of the banks of every State in the Union to the amount of five hundred million, nearly all of which was in the vaults of the big group banks. This served two purposes—it made the country banks join in the cry for currency revision and it supplied the big operators with money to squeeze out investors and speculators at the very bottom of the decline, taking in the stock at an enormous profit.... The operations of Morgan and the Standard Oil furnish additional evidence of the character of this panic. We have record proof of their utter contempt for commercial interests.... Did they give aid and support to the distressed merchant and manufacturer?... Alas, no. They pursued the course of the speculating banker.... They let great commercial houses, great manufacturing concerns,... down to ruin and dishonor, while they protected their speculative patrons. No better evidence could be asked to establish the character of this panic or the character of the men who were in command. By their fruits ye shall know them!

GLOSSARY

capitalization: the total value of a company, based usually on the total value of the company's shares of stock

Harriman: E.H. Harriman, father of W. Averell Harriman and director of the Union Pacific Railroad

Morgan: James Pierpont Morgan, American financier in the steel industry

shorts: also called "short sales," an investment technique that involves first selling a stock one does not own with the expectation of later buying the stock back at a lower price when its value falls, thus realizing a profit in a falling market

speculative securities: investments that are highly risky but hold the potential for large profits

Stillman: James Stillman, American financier and banker

trust companies: combinations of companies, usually formed with the purpose of driving out competition

underwrite: to guarantee financial support; to finance stocks or bonds and sell them to the public

Wall Street: the street in Lower Manhattan where the New York Stock Exchange is located; as a figure of speech, the financial sector of the economy

Document Analysis

By the beginning of the twentieth century, the corporation became the linchpin of the American economy. Moreover, thanks to such devices as the trust and the holding company, many of these enterprises became increasingly concentrated in fewer hands. By 1904 two-fifths of all manufacturing was controlled by 305 industrial combinations possessing an aggregate capital of $7 billion. The epitome of such consolidation of power was John D. Rockefeller's Standard Oil Company, a firm that by 1900 dominated the petroleum industry. The imbalanced situation was fostered by Wall Street investment banks, particularly J.P. Morgan & Company. These banks would raise needed capital for new corporations by selling their stocks and bonds and would, at the same time, police these new ventures by placing their own representatives on the boards of directors and by controlling sources of credit. Critics of this new centralization, such as La Follette, referred to the phenomenon as the "money trust."

In his Senate speech of March 17, 1908, La Follette begins with the accusation that about a hundred men "hold in their hands the business of the country." He lists the enterprises they controlled, ranging from railroads to mining, from cotton to food. He then points to the domination of American banking by Wall Street, which he found to be involved in destructive speculation. The Wisconsin senator refers to a special committee, established in 1905 by the New York State Legislature and headed by the state senator William M. Armstrong, which investigated the corrupt use of life insurance funds. Wall Street banks either established connections with trust companies or organized such firms themselves so as to sell securities, underwrite bonds, and float loans that ordinary banks could not openly sponsor. La Follette then produces a massive "List of Men Who Control Industrial, Franchise, Transportation, and Financial Business of the United States, with Their Directorships and Offices in Various Corporations." This document covered ten pages of fine print in the Congressional Record. Here, La Follette argues, was firm evidence showing the control exercised by Morgan and Standard Oil at the expense of ordinary Americans.

In the last part of his speech, La Follette accuses the Morgan and Standard Oil banks of creating the Panic of 1907 so as to line their own pockets. During the October panic, the great New York financial institutions were unable to supply funds to needy banks in the interior of the country. Therefore, bankruptcies took place among several large industrial corporations and many small western and southern banks as well. Only intervention by J.P. Morgan himself, who switched funds from one bank to another as well as to securities markets, could save the day. La Follette, however, does not see Morgan as a redeemer but as one who profited unjustly from the crisis. He quotes predictions of impending disaster made that summer by James J. Hill, chairman of the Great Northern Railway Company, and Edward Payson Ripley, president of the Atchison, Topeka and Santa Fe Railway. He also notes warnings of banking concentration made by Thomas F. Woodlock, former editor of the Wall Street Journal; Charles J. Bullock, an economist at Williams College; and the commercial expert Edward E. Pratt.

Essential Themes

It was Morgan's effort to squeeze out a conglomeration centering on the Heinze United Copper Company that created the panic. Only after it became obvious that "every countinghouse, factory, and shop in America" might be affected did J.P. Morgan and James Stillman, board chairman of the Rockefeller-controlled National City Bank of New York, meet on October 24 to end the crisis. La Follette concludes by denouncing the Morgan and Rockefeller interests for sacrificing "the distressed merchant and manufacturer" to the interests of "the speculating banker." His final remark, "By their fruits ye shall know them!" was taken from Jesus' Sermon on the Mount (Matthew 7:20).

La Follette's claims were widely publicized. Not surprisingly, he was immediately challenged. The president of the First National Bank of Chicago, one of the men on the senator's list, called the speech "worse than rot" and said that it was "a deliberate stirring up of passion and rage among people who have no facility for acquiring knowledge at first hand and are dependent upon men whom they trust" (*New York Times*, March 19, 1908). Such attacks did not faze La Follette, who concluded his series of addresses on March 24. On this occasion he denied that he was attacking such figures as Rockefeller, Morgan, and E.H. Harriman, of the Union Pacific Railroad, as individuals, remarking that they were merely types, the embodiment of an evil. It was what drove them that had to be destroyed in order to safeguard America's free institutions.

Some business interests backed La Follette, among them the New York Board of Trade, which distributed copies of the speech among its most active members. Indeed, in contrast to earlier requests, this time it was companies in the Northeast, not the Midwest, that sought many reprints. Aldrich accepted a La Follette amendment prohibiting banks from investing in the securities of other firms in which they had interlocking directorates. However, defeated by a vote of thirty-seven to thirteen was a La Follette proposal to forbid banks from making loans to people who were officers of the same banks. On May 29, La Follette proved furious enough to start a filibuster of the Aldrich-Vreeland bill. Battling a cold and addressing his Senate colleagues in ninety-degree heat, La Follette spoke for a record nineteen hours, but parliamentary blundering by allies led to the bill's adoption, by a vote of forty-three to twenty-two. Only with the adoption of the Federal Reserve System in 1913 were genuine reforms made to the nation's banking and credit system.

—*Justus D. Doenecke, PhD*

Bibliography and Additional Reading

La Follette, R.M., and Matthew Rothschild. *La Follette's Autobiography: A Personal Narrative of Political Experience*. Madison: University of Wisconsin Press, 2013.

Unger, Nancy C. *Fighting Bob La Follette: The Righteous Reformer*. Chapel Hill: University of North Carolina Press, 2000.

Wicker, Elmus. *The Great Debate on Banking Reform: Nelson Aldrich and the Origins of the Fed*. Columbus: Ohio University Press, 2005.

John D. Rockefeller on Standard Oil

Date: 1909
Author: John D. Rockefeller Sr. (with ghostwriters Frank N. Doubleday and Starr Murphy)
Genre: memoir; book excerpt

Summary Overview

This chapter of John D. Rockefeller's autobiographical musings, *Random Reminiscences*, is a defense of Standard Oil, the company that grew to control the American oil industry and which made Rockefeller one of the richest men in the world. Often attacked as a monopolist, Rockefeller defends his actions, and his firm, as an efficient supplier of petroleum that lowered costs for consumers who bought the company's products. Rockefeller explains that Standard Oil's large size was a product of this success and that the stockholders it enriched were partners in the business. He goes to great lengths to downplay his individual role in the success of the company, praising the people he hired at the beginning and the steady stream of new blood that continually rose in service to the firm. He goes on to defend the firm's wages, arguing that workers deserve only the equivalent of what they put into the company—nothing more. He defends the idea that his company helped men help themselves.

The great significance of this section of Rockefeller's memoir is as a counterattack to efforts to expose the corruption of the company and to break it up under the terms of the Sherman Antitrust Act of 1890. The book cannot be fully appreciated without recognizing the impact on it of Ida B. Tarbell's muckraking *History of the Standard Oil Company*, released in 1904, and the U.S. Justice Department's antitrust suit against the company, filed by the Theodore Roosevelt Administration in 1906.

Defining Moment

Before it was a book, *McClure's* magazine ran Ida Tarbell's "History of the Standard Oil Company" as a series of articles in 1902. This work quickly became a defining example of muckraking journalism, writing designed to promote political change by discovering how the rich abused power in the United States. The abuses she described all centered around Standard Oil abusing the power it held because of its enormous share of the oil refining industry. The victims of this abuse included its competitors, railroads, and ultimately consumers.

Indignation over Tarbell's revelations influenced the decision of President Theodore Roosevelt and Attorney General William Moody to file an antitrust suit against Rockefeller's Standard Oil in 1906. Trusts were very large businesses that threatened competition because of their size. Roosevelt believed that there were good trusts and bad trusts. Tarbell's revelations explaining exactly how Standard Oil got so large helped convince both Roosevelt and most of the American public that Standard Oil was a bad trust. Rockefeller, who seldom made public statements and who had retired from active management of the business long before this point, recorded his reminiscences in order to sway public opinion in the other direction. After all, not only his company but his reputation was at stake.

Like Tarbell, Rockefeller initially published his book in monthly installments. In his case, the magazine that first ran them was *The World's Work,* beginning in October 1908. Publisher Frank N. Doubleday was the ghostwriter for these essays. His aide Starr Murphy assisted in these efforts. The goal of the series was to remake Rockefeller's image as a stern capitalist and turn him into an easygoing, folksy man, relatable to people. Reviews of the book were mixed.

While this effort to improve Rockefeller's reputation succeeded to some degree, that improvement did not help Standard Oil survive the government's antitrust suit. In *Standard Oil v. United States* (1911), the United States Supreme Court ordered the company to divide itself into thirty-four different companies. Eight different firms retained the phrase "Standard Oil" in their names. The Rockefeller family remained a major shareholder in each of them, which meant that John D. Rockefeller's pride was affected much more by this decision than his fortune ever was.

Author Biography

Born in 1839, John D. Rockefeller Sr. was raised in Cleveland, Ohio. He started his career in bookkeeping, but quickly became involved in oil refining because the crude that had brought so much wealth to Western Pennsylvania at that time was worthless in its natural state. He formed Standard Oil of Ohio in 1870. The company grew quickly because it demanded kickbacks from railroads that shipped its product and because it aggressively handled competition by either merging with them or taking over those companies outright. At its height, the firm controlled approximately 90 percent of the American oil market.

Rockefeller retired from active involvement in his business in 1897. Even before that, Rockefeller had become a pioneering philanthropist. Among his most notable legacies in this regard were the University of Chicago and what would eventually be known as Rockefeller University in New York City, which remains devoted to medical research. Ida Tarbell's book and the subsequent successful antitrust suit against Standard Oil hurt Rockefeller's historical reputation, but the size of his wealth grew as the rise of the automobile increased demand for the product of the many oil firms his family partially owned. His son, John D. Rockefeller Jr., who expanded the family's many philanthropies, and his grandson, New York Governor Nelson Rockefeller, continued to keep the Rockefeller name in the public eye many years after John Sr.'s death in 1937.

HISTORICAL DOCUMENT: Standard Oil

CHAPTER III

The Standard Oil Company

It would be surprising if in an organization which included a great number of men there should not be an occasional employee here and there who acted, in connection with the business or perhaps in conducting his own affairs, in a way which might be criticized. Even in a comparatively small organization it is well-nigh impossible to restrain this occasional man who is over-zealous for his own or his company's advancement. To judge the character of all the members of a great organization or the organization itself by the actions of a few individuals would be manifestly unfair.

It has been said that I forced the men who became my partners in the oil business to join with me. I would not have been so short-sighted. If it were true that I followed such tactics, I ask, would it have been possible to make of such men life-long companions? Would they accept, and remain for many years in positions of the greatest trust, and finally, could any one have formed of such men, if they had been so browbeaten, a group which has for all these years worked in loyal harmony, with fair dealing among themselves as well as with others, building up efficiency and acting in entire unity? This powerful organization has not only lasted but its efficiency has increased. For fourteen years I have been out of business, and in eight or ten years went only once to the company's office.

In the summer of 1907 I visited again the room at the top of the Standard Oil Company's building, where the officers of the company and the heads of departments have had their luncheon served for many years. I was surprised to find so many men who had come to the front since my last visit years ago. Afterward I had an opportunity to talk with old associates and many new ones, and it was a source of great gratification to me to find that the same spirit of coöperation and harmony existed unchanged. This practice of lunching together, a hundred or more at long tables in most intimate and friendly association, is another indication of what I contend, slight as it may seem to be at first thought. Would these people seek each other's companionship day after day if they had been forced into this relation? People in such a position do not go on for long in a pleasant and congenial intimacy.

For years the Standard Oil Company has developed step by step, and I am convinced that it has done well its work of supplying to the people the products from petroleum at prices which have decreased as the efficiency of the business has been built up. It gradually extended its services first to the large centers, and then to towns, and now to the smallest places, going to the homes of its customers, delivering the oil to suit the convenience of the actual users. This same system is being followed out in various parts of the world. The company has, for example, three thousand tank wagons supplying American oil to towns and even small hamlets in Europe. Its own depots and employees deliver it in a somewhat similar way in Japan, China, India, and the chief countries of the world. Do you think this trade has been developed by anything but hard work?

This plan of selling our products direct to the consumer and the exceptionally rapid growth of the business bred a certain antagonism which I suppose could not have been avoided, but this same idea of dealing with the consumer directly has been followed by others and in many lines of trade, without creating, so far as I recall, any serious opposition.

This is a very interesting and important point, and I have often wondered if the criticism which centered upon us did not come from the fact that we were among the first, if not the first, to work out the problems of direct selling to the user on a broad scale. This was done in a fair spirit and with due consideration for every one's rights. We did not ruthlessly go after the trade of our competitors and attempt to ruin it by cutting prices or instituting a spy system. We had set ourselves the task of building up as rapidly and as broadly as possible the volume of consumption. Let me try to explain just what happened.

To get the advantage of the facilities we had in manufacture, we sought the utmost market in all lands—we needed volume. To do this we had to create selling methods far in advance of what then existed; we had to dispose of two, or three, or four gallons of oil where one had been sold before, and we could not rely upon the usual trade channels then existing to accomplish this. It was never our purpose to interfere with a dealer who adequately cultivated his field of operations, but when we saw a new opportunity or a new place for extending the sale by further and effective facilities, we made it our business to provide them. In this way we opened many new lines in which others have shared. In this development we had to employ many comparatively new men. The ideal way to supply material for higher positions is, of course, to recruit the men from among the youngest in the company's service, but our expansion was too rapid to permit this in all cases. That some of these employees were over-zealous in going after sales it would not be surprising to learn, but they were acting in violation of the expressed and known wishes of the company. But even these instances, I am convinced, occurred so seldom, by comparison with the number of transactions we carried on, that they were really the exceptions that proved the rule.

Every week in the year for many, many years, this concern has brought into this country more than a million dollars gold, all from the products produced by American labor. I am proud of the record, and believe most Americans will be when they understand some things better. These achievements, the development of this great foreign trade, the owning of ships to carry the oil in bulk by the most economical methods, the sending out of men to fight for the world's markets, have cost huge sums of money, and the vast capital employed could not be raised nor controlled except by such an organization as the Standard is to-day.

To give a true picture of the early conditions, one must realize that the oil industry was considered a most hazardous undertaking, not altogether unlike the speculative mining undertakings we hear so much of to-day. I well remember my old and distinguished friend, Rev. Thomas W. Armitage, for some forty years pastor of a great New York church, warning me that it was worse than folly to extend our plants and our operations. He was sure we were running unwarranted risks, that our oil supply would probably fail, the demand would decline, and he, with many others, sometimes I thought almost everybody, prophesied ruin. None of us ever dreamed of the magnitude of what proved to be the later expansion. We did our day's work as we met it, looking forward to what we could see in the distance and keeping well up to our opportunities, but laying our foundations firmly. As I have said, capital was most difficult to secure, and it was not easy to interest conservative men in this adventurous business. Men of property were afraid of it, though in rare cases capitalists were induced to unite with us to a limited extent. If they bought our stock at all, they took a little of it now and then as an experiment, and we were painfully conscious that they often declined to buy new stock with many beautiful expressions of appreciation.

The enterprise being so new and novel, on account of the fearfulness of certain holders in reference to its success, we frequently had to take stock to keep it from going begging, but we had such confidence in the fundamental value of the concern that we were willing to assume this risk. There are always a few men in an undertaking of this kind who would risk all on their judgment of the final result, and if the enterprise had failed, these would have been classed as visionary adventurers, and perhaps with good reason.

The 60,000 men who are at work constantly in the service of the company are kept busy year in and year out. The past year has been a time of great contraction, but the Standard has gone on with its plans unchecked, and the new works and buildings have not been delayed on account of lack of capital or fear of bad times. It pays its workmen well, it cares for them when sick, and pensions them when old. It has never had any important strikes, and if there is any better function of business management than giving profitable work to employees year after year, in good times and bad, I don't know what it is.

Another thing to be remembered about this so-called "octopus" is that there has been no "water" introduced into its capital (perhaps we felt that oil and water would not have mixed); nor in all these years has any one had to wait for money which the Standard owed. It has suffered from great fires and losses, but it has taken care of its affairs in such a way that it has not found it necessary to appeal to the general public to place blocks of bonds or stock; it has used no underwriting syndicates or stock-selling schemes in any form, and it has always managed to finance new oil field operations when called upon.

It is a commonthing to hear people say that this company has crushed out its competitors. Only the uninformed could make such an assertion. It has and always has had, and always will have, hundreds of active competitors; it has lived only because it has managed its affairs well and economically and with great vigor. To speak of competition for a minute: Consider not only the able people who compete in refining oil, but all the competition in the various trades which make and sell by-products—a great variety of different businesses. And perhaps of even more importance is the competition in foreign lands. The Standard is always fighting to sell the American product against the oil produced from the great fields of Russia, which struggles for the trade of Europe, and the Burma oil, which largely affects the market in India. In all these various countries we are met with tariffs which are raised against us, local prejudices, and strange customs. In many countries we had to teach the people—the Chinese, for example—to burn oil by making lamps for them; we packed the oil to be carried by camels or on the backs of runners in the most remote portions of the world; we adapted the trade to the needs of strange folk. Every time we succeeded in a foreign land, it meant dollars brought to this country, and every time we failed, it was a loss to our nation and its workmen.

One of our greatest helpers has been the State Department in Washington. Our ambassadors and ministers and consuls have aided to push our way into new markets to the utmost corners of the world.

I think I can speak thus frankly and enthusiastically because the working out of many of these great plans has developed largely since I retired from the business fourteen years ago.

The Standard has not now, and never did have a royal road to supremacy, nor is its success due to any one man, but to the multitude of able men who are working together. If the present managers of the company were to relax efforts, allow the quality of their product to degenerate, or treat their customers badly, how long would their business last? About as long as any other neglected business. To read some of the accounts of the affairs of the company, one would think that it had such a hold on the oil trade that the directors did little but come together and declare dividends. It is a pleasure for me to take this opportunity to pay tribute to the work these men are doing, not only for the company they serve, but for the foreign trade of our country; for more than half of all the product that the company makes is sold outside of the United States. If, in place of these directors, the business were taken over and run by anyone but experts, I would sell my interest for any price I could get. To succeed in a business requires the best and most earnest men to manage it, and the best men rise to the top. Of its origin and early plans I will speak later.

The Modern Corporation

Beyond question there is a suspicion of corporations. There may be reason for such suspicion very often; for a corporation may be moral or immoral, just as a man may be moral or the reverse; but it is folly to condemn all corporations because some are bad, or even to be unduly suspicious of all, because some are bad. But the corporation in form and character has come to stay—that is a thing that may be depended upon. Even small firms are becoming corporations, because it is a convenient form of partnership.

It is equally true that combinations of capital are bound to continue and to grow, and this need not alarm even the most timid if the corporation, or the series of corporations, is properly conducted with due regard for the rights of others. The day of individual competition in large affairs is past and gone—you might just as well argue that we should go back to hand labor and throw away our efficient machines—and the sober good sense of the people will accept this fact when they have studied and tried it out. Just see how the list of stockholders in the great corporations is increasing by leaps and bounds. This means that all these people are becoming partners in great businesses. It is a good thing—it will bring a feeling of increased responsibility to the managers of the corporations and will make the people who have their interests involved study the facts impartially before condemning or attacking them.

On this subject of industrial combinations I have often expressed my opinions; and, as I have not changed my mind, I am not averse to repeating them now, especially as the subject seems again to be so much in the public eye.

The chief advantages from industrial combinations are those which can be derived from a coöperation of persons and aggregation of capital. Much that one man cannot do alone two can do together, and once admit the fact that coöperation, or, what is the same thing, combination, is necessary on a small scale, the limit depends solely upon the necessities of business. Two persons in partnership may be a sufficiently large combination for a small business, but if the business grows or can be made to grow, more persons and more capital must be taken in. The business may grow so large that a partnership ceases to be a proper instrumentality for its purposes, and then a corporation becomes a necessity. In most countries, as in England, this form of industrial combination is sufficient for a business co-extensive with the parent country, but it is not so in America. Our Federal form of government making every corporation created by a state foreign to every other state, renders it necessary for persons doing business through corporate agency to organize corporations in some or many of the different states in which their business is located. Instead of doing business through the agency of one corporation they must do business through the agencies of several corporations. If the business is extended to foreign countries, and Americans are not to-day satisfied with home markets alone, it will be found helpful and possibly necessary to organize corporations in such countries, for Europeans are prejudiced against foreign corporations, as are the people of many of our states. These different corporations thus become coöperating agencies in the same business and are held together by common ownership of their stocks.

> *The chief advantages from industrial combinations are those which can be derived from a coöperation of persons and aggregation of capital.*

It is too late to argue about advantages of industrial combinations. They are a necessity. And if Americans are to have the privilege of extending their business in all the states of the Union, and into foreign countries as well, they are a necessity on a large scale, and require the agency of more than one corporation.

The dangers are that the power conferred by combination may be abused, that combinations may be formed for speculation in stocks rather than for conducting business, and that for this purpose prices may be temporarily raised instead of being lowered. These abuses are possible to a greater or less extent in all combinations, large or small, but this fact is no more of an argument against combinations than the fact that steam may explode is an argument against steam. Steam is necessary and can be made comparatively safe. Combination is necessary and its abuses can be minimized; otherwise our legislators must acknowledge their incapacity to deal with the most important instrument of industry.

In the hearing of the Industrial Commission in 1899, I then said that if I were to suggest any legislation regarding industrial combinations it would be: First, Federal legislation under which corporations may be created and regulated, if that be possible. Second, in lieu thereof, state legislation as nearly uniform as possible, encouraging combinations of persons and capital for the purpose of carrying on industries, but permitting state supervision, not of a character to hamper industries, but sufficient to prevent frauds upon the public. I still feel as I did in 1899.

The New Opportunities

I am far from believing that this will adversely affect the individual. The great economic era we are entering will give splendid opportunity to the young man of the future. One often hears the men of this new generation say that they do not have the chances that their fathers and grandfathers had. How little they know of the disadvantages from which we suffered! In my young manhood we had everything to do and nothing to do it with; we had to hew our own paths along new lines; we had little experience to go on. Capital was most difficult to get, credits were mysterious things. Whereas now we have a system of commercial ratings, everything was then haphazard and we suffered from a stupendous war and all the disasters which followed.

Compare this day with that. Our comforts and opportunities are multiplied a thousand fold. The resources of our great land are now actually opening up and are scarcely touched; our home markets are vast, and we have just begun to think of the foreign peoples we can serve—the people who are years behind us in civilization. In the East a quarter of the human race is just awakening. The men of this generation are entering into a heritage which makes their fathers' lives look poverty-stricken by comparison. I am naturally an optimist, and when it comes to a statement of what our people will accomplish in the future, I am unable to express myself with sufficient enthusiasm.

There are many things we must do to attain the highest benefit from all these great blessings; and not the least of these is to build up our reputation throughout the whole world. The great business interests will, I hope, so comport themselves that foreign capital will consider it a desirable thing to hold shares in American companies. It is for Americans to see that foreign investors are well and honestly treated, so that they will never regret purchases of our securities.

I may speak thus frankly, because I am an investor in many American enterprises, but a controller of none (with one exception, and that a company which has not been much of a dividend payer), and I, like all the rest, am dependent upon the honest and capable administration of the industries. I firmly and sincerely believe that they will be so managed.

The American Business Man

You hear a good many people of pessimistic disposition say much about greed in American life. One would think to hear them talk that we were a race of misers in this country. To lay too much stress upon the reports of greed in the newspapers would be folly, since their function is to report the unusual and even the abnormal. When a man goes properly about his daily affairs, the public prints say nothing; it is only when something extraordinary happens to him that he is discussed. But because he is thus brought into prominence occasionally, you surely would not say that these occasions represented his normal life. It is by no means for money alone that these active-minded men labor—they are engaged in a fascinating occupation. The zest of the work is maintained by something better than the mere accumulation of money, and, as I think I have said elsewhere, the standards of business are high and are getting better all the time.

I confess I have no sympathy with the idea so often advanced that our basis of all judgments in this country is founded on money. If this were true, we should be a nation of money hoarders instead of spenders. Nor do I admit that we are so small-minded a people as to be jealous of the success of others. It is the other way about: we are the most extraordinarily ambitious, and the success of one man in any walk of life spurs the others on. It does not sour them, and it is a libel even to suggest so great a meanness of spirit.

In reading the newspapers, where so much is taken for granted in considering things on a money standard, I think we need some of the sense of humor possessed by an Irish neighbor of mine, who built what we regarded as an extremely ugly house, which stood out in bright colors as we looked from our windows. My taste in architecture differed so widely from that affected by my Irish friend, that we planted out the view of his house by moving some large trees to the end of our property. Another neighbor who watched this work going on asked Mr. Foley why Mr. Rockefeller moved all these big trees and cut off the view between the houses. Foley, with the quick wit of his country, responded instantly: "It's invy, they can't stand looking at the ividence of me prosperity."

In my early days men acted just as they do now, no doubt. When there was anything to be done for general trade betterment, almost every man had some good reason for believing that his case was a special one different from all the rest. For every foolish thing he did, or wanted to do, for every unbusiness-like plan he had, he always pleaded that it was necessary in his case. He was the one man who had to sell at less than cost, to disrupt all the business plans of others in his trade, because his individual position was so absolutely different from all the rest. It was often a heart-breaking undertaking to convince those men that the perfect occasion which would lead to the perfect opportunity would never come, even if they waited until the crack o' doom.

Then, again, we had the type of man who really never knew all the facts about his own affairs. Many of the brightest kept their books in such a way that they did not actually know when they were making money on a certain operation and when they were losing. This unintelligent competition was a hard matter to contend with. Good old-fashioned common sense has always been a mighty rare commodity. When a man's affairs are not going well, he hates to study the books and face the truth. From the first, the men who managed the Standard Oil Company kept their books intelligently as well as correctly. We knew how much we made and where we gained or lost. At least, we tried not to deceive ourselves.

My ideas of business are no doubt old-fashioned, but the fundamental principles do not change from generation to generation, and sometimes I think that our quick-witted American business men, whose spirit and energy are so splendid, do not always sufficiently study the real underlying foundations of business management. I have spoken of the necessity of being frank and honest with oneself about one's own affairs: many people assume that they can get away from the truth by avoiding thinking about it, but the natural law is inevitable, and the sooner it is recognized, the better.

One hears a great deal about wages and why they must be maintained at a high level, by the railroads, for example. A laborer is worthy of his hire, no less, but no more, and in the long run he must contribute an equivalent for what he is paid. If he does not do this, he is probably pauperized, and you at once throw out the balance of things. You can't hold up conditions artificially, and you can't change the underlying laws of trade. If you try, you must inevitably fail. All this may be trite and obvious, but it is remarkable how many men overlook what should be the obvious. These are facts we can't get away from—a business man must adapt himself to the natural conditions as they exist from month to month and year to year. Sometimes I feel that we Americans think we can find a short road to success, and it may appear that often this feat is accomplished; but real efficiency in work comes from knowing your facts and building upon that sure foundation.

Many men of wealth do not retire from business even when they can. They are not willing to be idle, or they have a just pride in their work and want to perfect the plans in which they have faith, or, what is of still more consequence, they may feel the call to expand and build up for the benefit of their employees and associates, and these men are the great builders up in our country. Consider for a moment how much would have been left undone if our prosperous American business men had sat down with folded hands when they had acquired a competency. I have respect for all these reasons, but if a man has succeeded, he has brought upon himself corresponding responsibilities, and our institutions devoted to helping men to help themselves need the brain of the American business man as well as part of his money.

Some of these men, however, are so absorbed in their business affairs that they hardly have time to think of anything else. If they do interest themselves in a work outside of their own office and undertake to raise money, they begin with an apology, as if they are ashamed of themselves.

"I am no beggar," I have heard many of them say, to which I could only reply: "I am sorry you feel that way about it."

I have been this sort of beggar all my life and the experiences I have had were so interesting and important to me that I will venture to speak of them in a later chapter.

GLOSSARY

Standard, The: Rockefeller uses this phrase to refer to Standard Oil because the trust that he controlled actually consisted of many different firms acting in concert; each began with "Standard Oil" followed by the name of the state in which it operated (e.g., Ohio; New Jersey)

Document Analysis

John D. Rockefeller was a public figure but not a public intellectual. However, by 1908, others like Andrew Carnegie and William Graham Sumner had begun to spin justifications for industrial capitalism upon which Rockefeller and his ghostwriters could rely. These tropes appear throughout Rockefeller's reminiscences about Standard Oil, albeit in an even more watered-down form than the way earlier business advocates had expressed them because the whole point of these essays was to improve his public image.

When Rockefeller recounts his only visit to Standard Oil since his retirement, he notes how there were many people there whom he did not recognize. His explanation is that the company was a meritocracy, but this is actually a variation of the idea of Social Darwinism—the notion that capitalism operates under the same laws as Darwinian evolution: the strong prosper because they are strongest, not because of any advantages they had such as their race or the resources they had when they were born. Yet, Rockefeller's internal competition is a friendly competition when office backstabbing is forgotten at lunchtime.

Rockefeller also goes to great lengths to highlight the advantages that Standard Oil created for the consumer. Its efficiency led to low prices, he argues, which in turn saved Americans

From 1870 to 1911, Standard Oil controlled all oil production in the US. Ultimately, the company was broken up under monopoly laws.

money. It is worth noting here that when Standard Oil began there were no cars on America's roads. It sold kerosene for lighting, something that all Americans needed. Keeping prices low, however, was one of the ways in which Standard Oil could bankrupt its competitors. Once those competitors were vanquished, monopolies like Standard Oil could then raise prices, or at least artificially prop them up by limiting supply. This was a theme of Congressional hearings held before the publication of Tarbell's book and an argument that Tarbell herself adopted.

Rockefeller's defense of industrial combination as a necessity for American international expansion reflects both earlier opposition to the Sherman Antitrust Act and the state of America's overseas aspirations after the turn of the twentieth century. Our competitors—particularly Germany—had large industrial combinations. Restriction on such combinations were a uniquely American idea, and, in the eyes of the men who ran those combinations, a threat to American national security.

Rockefeller's defense of Standard Oil's wages is similar to that of capitalists in every other American industry: pay people what they are worth, not for the effort that they put into their work. Rockefeller takes the laws of capitalism as a given at a time when some Americans (e.g., the presidential candidate Eugene V. Debs) were beginning to question the assumptions that undergirded the entire American economy. His contributions to what was known at that time as "The Labor Question" were not new, and were probably the least popular section of this entire essay. However, by taking the position that he was unable to change the situation, Rockefeller reinforced the idea that Standard Oil was not nearly as powerful as its critics believed.

Neither was Rockefeller himself powerful any longer. As rich as he was, Rockefeller really was a retired businessman. Other people who aspired to his life of leisure would likely have sympathized with these efforts to humanize him. On the other hand, people who were victims of the decreased opportunities that concentrated wealth created would not have sympathized with him at all.

Essential Themes

Rockefeller's ghostwritten writings were nowhere near as influential as those of other businessmen. Besides his indirect invocation of Social Darwinism, he taps into the idea of laissez-faire capitalism in the effort to keep the federal government from destroying the business that he built earlier in his career. But Rockefeller was writing at the height of the Progressive Era, and the whole notion that the government should leave business alone faced its most severe attack, perhaps in all of American history, at precisely this time. Just two years later, the Progressives would win the battle over Standard Oil—although by retaining and growing his wealth afterwards, Rockefeller probably won the war.

What's good for Standard Oil is good for America, he essentially tells his readers when he notes that his company is prospering and building even while the economy itself was in a severe recession. Judging businessmen by their works had been a popular tactic of their defenders since the beginnings of industrial capitalism and would continue to be so long afterwards. Arguing that your business is a meritocracy was a way to align your firm with the whole notion that rags-to-riches stories were common in American capitalism, even though they were increasingly less common as capital began to concentrate in increasingly few hands.

After the Ludlow Massacre of 1914, when soldiers working on behalf of the Rockefeller-owned Colorado Fuel and Iron Company killed many striking miners and their family members, Rockefeller's son John D. Rockefeller Jr. would try to join the ranks of reformers by experimenting with company unions there and at other Rockefeller facilities. The elder Rockefeller must have signed off on this attempt to improve the family's reputation because the attacks on his son were so vicious. Ultimately, those reforms failed. The best way to clear the Rockefeller name was not through public relations, but through philanthropy. Even private ventures, like the building of Rockefeller Center in New York City during the height of the Depression, was more effective than John D. Rockefeller's tepid defense of capitalism.

—*Jonathan Rees, PhD*

Bibliography and Additional Reading

Chernow, Ron. *Titan: The Life of John D. Rockefeller, Sr.* New York: Random House, 1998.

Nevins, Allan. *John D. Rockefeller: The Heroic Age of American Enterprise*. 2 vols. New York: Charles Scribner's Sons, 1940.

Nevins, Allan. *Study in Power: John D. Rockefeller, Industrialist and Philanthropist*. 2 vols. New York: Charles Scribner's Sons, 1953.

Tarbell, Ida B. *The History of the Standard Oil Company*. 2 vols. New York: McClure, Phillips & Co., 1904.

Remarks on Politics and Business

Date: November 16, 1911
Author: Nicholas Murray Butler
Genre: speech

Summary Overview

In his November 1911 speech to the New York Chamber of Commerce—published the following year as a chapter in his book, *Why Should We Change Our Form of Government?: Studies in Practical Politics*, Columbia University president Nicholas Murray Butler argues that the Progressive impulses to subdue monopolies and emphasize direct popular representation and initiative are wrongheaded and overreach the intent of the framers of the U.S. Constitution. Influential in the non-Progressive wing of the Republican Party, Butler argued that the movement toward Progressive policies promoted by those such as his good friend, Theodore Roosevelt, was emblematic of a movement away from the origins of the American republic and toward socialism, which he was committed to stopping.

Defining Moment

Speaking during the Progressive Era, Columbia University president Nicholas Murray Butler discusses the impact of Progressive reforms on the capitalist economic system and society in the United States. A Republican, Butler was at ideological odds with his good friend and fellow New York resident Theodore Roosevelt on most of the tenets of Progressivism. Reforms such as trust-busting and popular ballot initiatives were anathema to Butler, a Constitutional originalist who thought that such ideas overstepped what America's founders had intended.

Author Biography

Nicholas Murray Butler was president of Columbia University in New York from 1902 until 1945. During that time, he transformed Columbia into what many would call the model for the modern university, adding the first university hospital, the first university extension program, and what would become the Teachers College. He was a staunch advocate for world peace through higher education and was a corecipient of the 1931 Nobel Peace Prize with social reformer Jane Addams. Murray was also active in Republican politics, though he disagreed with the Progressive wing of the party that was ascendent throughout most of the early twentieth century on matters ranging from antitrust litigation, to the referendum and initiative reform efforts, and the prohibition of alcohol.

HISTORICAL DOCUMENT: Remarks on Politics and Business

What is the situation? Government is at war with the economic forces of the body politic… Government armed with the strong weapon of the law is one combatant; economic forces urged on by self-interest and the necessities of the world's business are the other… What has happened in these United States to bring about in fifteen or twenty years an almost complete reversal of business conditions? We are told, on the one hand, that nothing has happened; but that's men's passions have been stirred, that jealousy has been aroused, and that people have been attacking that which they do not like—a most inadequate and helpless explanation. On the other hand, we are told that what has happened has been a new vision of liberty, a new insight into ethical and social conditions, and that this new vision, and this new insight, are finding expression, and will find expression, in these amazing public policies. That is another helpless and inadequate explanation, and it indicates that some of our good friends are dilating with the wrong emotion…

It is necessary to look a little deeper to get at the actual facts. My impression is that what is going on in this country is nothing less than a test of the adaptability of our institutions and a test of our national common sense, a test being imposed by utterly new, strange, unexpected and unpredicted economic conditions and forces working upon a gigantic scale. In other words, we are living in one of those periods of development and movement and change and evolution when institutions established and embodied in law and in political procedure, are put to it to keep pace with natural and orderly and inevitable development in social and economic conditions…

The fact of the matter is, and it may just as well be recognized in this country and in every other country, that the era of unrestricted individual competition has gone forever. And the reason why it has gone is partly because it has done its work, partly because it has been taken up into a new and larger principle of co-operation. What happens in every form of organic evolution is that an old part no longer useful to the structure drops away, and its functions pass over into and are absorbed by a new development. That new development is co-operation, and co-operation as a substitute for unlimited, unrestricted, individual competition has come to stay as an economic fact, and legal institutions will have to be adjusted to it. It cannot be stopped. It ought not to be stopped. It is not in the public interest that it should be stopped.

Now, how has this co-operation manifested itself? This new movement of cooperation has manifested itself in the last sixty or seventy years chiefly in the limited liability corporation. I weigh my words, when I say that in my judgment the limited liability corporation is the greatest single discovery of modern times, whether you judge it by its social, by its ethical, by its industrial or, in the long run,—after we understand it and know how to use it,—by its political, effects. Even steam and electricity are far less important than the limited liability corporation, and they would be reduced to comparative impotence without it. Now, what is this limited liability corporation? It is simply a device by which a large number of individuals may share in an undertaking without risking in that undertaking more than they voluntarily and individually assume. It substitutes co-operation on a large scale for individual, cut-throat, parochial, competition. It makes possible huge economy in production and in trading. It means the steadier employment of labor at an increased wage. It means the modern provision of industrial insurance, of care for disability, old age and widowhood. It means—and this is vital to a body like this—it means the only possible engine for carrying on international trade on a scale commensurate with modern needs and opportunities. ...

I know how unsafe it is for any layman even to mention the Sherman law. I know that there is a prejudice in some political and journalistic circles against a layman saying anything about that law except the single word "Guilty." But let me suggest that you do not agitate for an amendment of the Sherman law. Supplement it, if you like, but do not amend it. The Sherman law has now been subjected to twenty years of the most careful, the most extensive and the most elaborate legal and judicial examination and determination. Under it you are working out a solution slowly, patiently, and with much doubt; but you are working out a solution of the relations of business to that law by the very processes which have always been those governing in our Anglo-Saxon life, the process of the application of the common law, building up from precedent to precedent; and the man who undertakes to amend that law will make it worse. The first thing that will be done in that case will be to except some privileged people from it, and the only people who will be excepted will be those with a large number of votes. ...

There is nothing new about all this conflict over large and new business undertakings. ... As a matter of fact there has not a single thing been said about corporations, about large industrial combinations, which was not said in England about co-partnerships, when co-partnerships were first invented. You may go all the way back five hundred years, and you will find exactly these same expressions. I ran upon this the other day. Let me read it, and perhaps you may guess from what American daily newspaper it comes:

"The merchants form great companies and become wealthy; but many of them are dishonest and cheat one another. Hence the directors of the companies, who have charge of the accounts, are nearly always richer than their associates. Those who thus grow rich are clever, since they do not have the reputation of being thieves."

That was not published in New York, or Chicago or San Francisco. That is found in the Chronicle of Augsburg, Germany, in 1512. In one year more that quotation will be four hundred years old. They were very much disturbed about this problem in those days, and the Diet of Nuremberg appointed a committee in 1522 to investigate monopolies. They sent an inquiry to several cities, to Boards of Trade and Chambers of Commerce, to know what better be done. This is the answer they got from Augsburg:

"It is impossible to limit the size of the companies for that would limit business and hurt the common welfare; the bigger and more numerous they are the better for everybody. If a merchant is not perfectly free to do business in Germany he will go elsewhere to Germany's loss. Any one can see what harm and evil such an action would mean to us. If a merchant cannot do business, above a certain amount, what is he to do with his surplus money? It is impossible to set a limit to business, and it would be well to let the merchant alone and put no restrictions on his ability or capital. Some people talk of limiting the earning capacity of investments. This would be unbearable and would work great injustice and harm by taking away the livelihood of widows, orphans and other sufferers, noble and non-noble, who derive their income from investments in these companies. Many merchants out of love and friendship invest the money of their friends—men, women and children—- who know nothing of business, in order to provide them with an assured income. Hence any one can see that the idea that the merchant companies undermine the public welfare ought not to be seriously considered. ..."

I read that to illustrate that the business and political mind of Europe has been on this question for at least four hundred years. .... . We must learn that economic laws, economic principles, based on everlasting human nature are fundamental and vital, and your care and mine, as citizens of this Republic, is not to interfere with these laws, not to check them; but to see to it that no moral wrong is done in their name.

That is a very different proposition from the one of overturning a great economic and industrial system by statute. You cannot control these fundamental economic processes by human statutes, and it is not in the public interest that you should...

> **GLOSSARY**
>
> **Chronicle of Augsburg:** the Augsburg Chronicle is a historical text detailing life in Germany during the Middle Ages
>
> **limited liability company (LLC):** a type of corporate structure where the owners of the company are legally protected from personal liability for the company's debts; LLC's typically are partnerships where larger numbers of people engage in business together and own a share of the company commensurate with their investment
>
> **Sherman law:** the Sherman Antitrust Act, a federal law enacted in 1890 to regulate competition between companies in order to avoid monopolies that could drive up the prices of goods; it prohibited cooperation between companies to gain an unfair advantage and any attempts to drive competitors out of business

Document Analysis

In his 1911 speech, "Politics and Business," presented before the New York Chamber of Commerce, Butler argues that the role of government is not to be the arm of the people, but rather that it is often "at war with the economic forces of the body politic." But neither is Butler an advocate for a return to the laissez-faire capitalism that had characterized the Gilded Age of the recent past, arguing that "that the era of unrestricted individual competition has gone forever." American capitalism is not the product of natural competition as so many, including Roosevelt, argued it should be. But neither is it ruined by the large monopolies and trusts that Roosevelt had crusaded against.

What Butler sees as taking the place of these two extremes is the recent invention of the limited liability corporation (LLC)—a corporate format characterized less by forceful individualism of the sort that had made titans of Andrew Carnegie and John D. Rockefeller than by nameless, faceless cooperatives of many owners and managers who are neither the face of their corporate identities nor the ones to be held alone legally, and Butler might add morally, responsible for the fate of their companies. As Butler argued, the LLC "substitutes co-operation on a large scale for individual, cut-throat, parochial, competition."

The LLC overcomes the individual owner's force of will by employing large numbers of people who are more capable of increasing the scale of production and profit, resulting not only in increased wages for the employees but also increased benefits for the care of those disabled in the workplace, those who are too old to work, and widows that those workers might leave behind. Butler's vision of the LLC is not the small businesses who compete with one another to make a better "widget" for a lower price, it is the large corporation that is able to compete on a global scale, dominating industries but at the same time improving quality of life. To Butler, any limitations on the size of LLCs are bereft of any common sense, are not based upon the human nature, are economically destructive, and are antithetical to the idea of freedom enshrined in the thoughts of America's founders.

Essential Themes

The economic ideas espoused by Nicholas Murray Butler were characteristic of a time when the Progressive ideas that had been supreme during Theodore Roosevelt's presidency (1901–9) were beginning to be moderated during the presidency of Roosevelt's hand-picked successor, William Howard Taft (1909–13). Though Taft still espoused Progressive ideals, such as economic reform, social welfare, and direct democracy, his actions were much more conservative than those of his predecessor. The way that Butler viewed the Sherman Antitrust Act was very much in line with this more conservative interpretation of Progressivism. Rather than using the law to quickly bring overreaching corporations into submission, Butler thought it would be better used to gradually ensure that those corporations were serving the interests of the people, and that their size or monopolistic status were not the overriding concerns that Roosevelt and others considered them to be.

In the years following his 1911 speech, Butler would remain an active figure in education and politics. In 1916, he worked to promote his friend, Senator Elihu Root, for the presidency, though Root eventually bowed out and supported incumbent Woodrow Wilson since the United States was nearing involvement in the First World War. Butler himself sought the Republican nomination for president in 1920, but only won a small handful of delegates as compared to the party nominee and eventual president, Warren Harding. Butler would go on to be a staunch advocate for world peace, which he thought achievable through education. He received the Nobel Peace Prize in 1931, was president of the American Academy of Arts and Letters, and remained president of Columbia University until 1945.

—*Steven L. Danver, PhD*

Bibliography and Additional Reading

Butler, Nicholas Murray. *Why Should We Change Our Form of Government?: Studies in Practical Politics*. New York: Scribner's, 1912.

Magruder, F.A. Review of Nicholas Murray Butler, *Why Should We Change Our Form of Government?: Studies in Practical Politics*. *The American Political Science Review* 6, no. 4 (November 1912): 657–58.

O'Neill, Johnathan. "Constitutional Maintenance and Religious Sensibility in the 1920s: Rethinking the Constitutionalist Response to Progressivism." *Journal of Church and State* 51, no. 1 (Winter 2009): 24–51.

Review of Nicholas Murray Butler, *Why Should We Change Our Form of Government?: Studies in Practical Politics*. *Journal of Political Economy* 20, no. 6 (June 1912): 651.

■ Federal Reserve Act

Date: 1913
Author: Congress, U.S.
Genre: law; legislation

Summary Overview

The Federal Reserve Act was signed into law by President Woodrow Wilson on December 23, 1913. The purpose of the Federal Reserve Act was to create a central banking system, enabling the US government to manage the nation's money and credit in a more efficient manner. After the expiration of the Second Bank of the United States in 1836, the United States functioned for the remainder of the century without a central bank. But throughout the 1800s the nation experienced several financial panics, notably in 1857, 1873, and 1893. A financial panic in 1907, which led to the failure of several banks, convinced many Americans of the need for a central banking system that could regulate credit and the supply of money.

The Federal Reserve Act was the end product of a highly contentious political debate. On one side of the debate were progressives, populists, and agrarian reformers led by such figures as William Jennings Bryan. Progressives, representing small towns, small-business owners, and farmers, believed that too much economic power was concentrated in the hands of the nation's banks and other "big city" financial institutions—what at the time was dubbed the "money trust." On the other side of the debate were conservative bankers, Wall Street executives, and others who wanted to retain a free hand in the financial markets, without the interference of the federal government, and who believed that the US Constitution did not grant Congress authority to create a central bank.

In this context, the newly elected Wilson relied on two men to for advice: Representative Carter Glass of Virginia, who would become chairman of the House Committee on Banking and Currency and, later, US secretary of the Treasury; and H. Parker Willis, a professor of economics at George Washington University. The two presented Wilson with a draft of a financial reform bill in late 1912. After Wilson took office in 1913, debate continued as the president tried to reconcile the money trust to the bill while simultaneously trying to convince progressives that the bill would provide needed reforms. On September 18, 1913, the House of Representatives overwhelmingly approved the bill; the Senate followed on December 19. Since December 23, 1913, the "Fed" has been the central banking system of the United States.

Defining Moment

In 1907, as he had in 1895, J.P. Morgan, a leading New York banker, organized the effort to keep the American financial system solid in the midst of a widespread panic. As a partial response to this financial panic, in 1908 the National Monetary Commission was created to research what government powers were needed to enable the federal government to take the leadership role in times of financial crisis. After three years of research, and with strong input from banking leaders, a proposal was put forward by Senator Nelson Aldrich for a weak National Reserve Association controlled by the banking industry. In 1912, Woodrow Wilson ran on a platform opposing this proposal, but he was not opposed to the idea of creating a central bank for the United States.

Working with Rep. Glass, Wilson supported Glass's use of many of Aldrich's ideas, but for a stronger system totally under the control of the federal government. However, this was administered through a system of regional banks rather than just one central authority. While Glass was able to get this passed in the house, the politics and concerns of the Senate were different. Taking Glass' bill, Senator Robert Owen made several minor modifications which allowed it to gain the necessary support in the Senate. For the first time in eighty years, the federal government had the ability to create and implement monetary policy.

Author Biography

Rep. Carter Glass (1858-1946) and Sen. Robert L. Owen (1856-1947) are the two individuals who, in 1913, shepherded the bill through the Sixty-Third United States Congress with the support of President Woodrow Wilson (1856-1924). All were Democrats.

Although from a newspaper background, throughout his career Glass was best known for his work with the banking system. In addition to this bill, he was a principle sponsor of three Depression Era banking laws which regulated the industry throughout the remainder of the twentieth century.

Owen, one of the first two Native American senators, was a lawyer and the founder of a small bank. The impact of the 1907 crisis on his bank was a major reason for his interest in this bill.

Woodrow Wilson, the twenty-eighth president of the United States, had served two years as governor of New Jersey. Prior to that, he had worked in higher education, including as president of Princeton University. Wilson ran on a progressive platform, which included opposition to many established corporate interests.

The Sixty-Third Congress was controlled by the Democratic Party with fifty-three of the ninety-six Senators from that party and 291 Democrats in the House versus 134 Republicans. Overall, it was a liberal/progressive Congress which, among the many laws enacted and in addition to the Federal Reserve Act, passed the federal income tax system, established regulations regarding agricultural products, created the Federal Trade Commission, enlarged antitrust powers, and the regulation of narcotic drugs.

HISTORICAL DOCUMENT: Federal Reserve Act

An Act to provide for the establishment of Federal reserve banks, to furnish an elastic currency, to afford means of rediscounting commercial paper, to establish a more effective supervision of banking in the United States, and for other purposes.

SEC. 2. As soon as practicable, the Secretary of the Treasury, the Secretary of Agriculture and the Comptroller of the Currency, acting as "The Reserve Bank Organization Committee," shall designate not less than eight nor more than twelve cities to be known as Federal reserve cities, and shall divide the continental United States, excluding Alaska, into districts, each district to contain only one of such Federal reserve cities. . . . Provided, That the districts shall be apportioned with due regard to the convenience and customary course of business and shall not necessarily be coterminous with any State or States. . . . Such districts shall be known as Federal reserve districts and may be designated by number. . . .

Said organization committee . . . shall supervise the organization in each of the cities designated of a Federal reserve bank, which shall include in its title the name of the city in which it is situated, as "Federal Reserve Bank of Chicago."

Under regulations to be prescribed by the organization committee, every national banking association in the United States is hereby required, and every eligible bank in the United States and every trust company within the District of Columbia, is hereby authorized to signify in writing, within sixty days after the passage of this Act, its acceptance of the terms and provisions hereof. When the organization committee shall have designated the cities in which Federal reserve banks are to be organized, and fixed the geographical limits of the Federal reserve districts, every national banking association within that district shall be required within thirty days after notice from the organization committee, to subscribe to the capital stock of such Federal reserve bank in a sum equal to six per centum of the paid-up capital stock and surplus of such bank. . . .

Any national bank failing to signify its acceptance of the terms of this Act within the sixty days aforesaid, shall cease to act as a reserve agent, upon thirty days' notice, to be given within the discretion of the said organization committee or of the Federal Reserve Board.

Should any national banking association in the United States now organized fail within one year after the passage of this Act to become a member bank or fail to comply with any of the provisions of this Act applicable thereto, all of the rights, privileges, and franchises of such association granted to it under the national-bank Act, or under the provision of this Act, shall be thereby forfeited. . . .

No individual, copartnership, or corporation other than a member bank of its district shall be permitted to subscribe for or to hold at any time more than $20,000 par value of stock in any Federal reserve bank. Such stock shall be known as public stock and may be transferred on the books of the Federal reserve bank by the chairman of the board of directors of such bank. . . .

SEC. 3. Each Federal reserve bank shall establish branch banks within the Federal reserve district in which it is located and may do so in the district of any Federal reserve bank which may have been suspended. . . .

SEC. 5. The capital stock of each Federal reserve bank shall be divided into shares of $100 each. . . .

SEC. 7. After all necessary expenses of a Federal reserve bank have been paid or provided for, the stockholders shall be entitled to receive an annual dividend of six per centum on the paid-in capital stock, which dividend shall be cumulative. After the aforesaid dividend claims have been fully met, all the net earnings shall be paid to the United States as a franchise tax, except that one-half of such net earnings shall be paid into a surplus fund until it shall amount to forty per centum of the paid-in capital stock of such bank.

The net earnings derived by the United States from Federal reserve banks shall, in the discretion of the Secretary, be used to supplement the gold reserve held against outstanding United States notes, or shall be applied to the reduction of the outstanding bonded indebtedness of the United States under regulations to be prescribed by the Secretary of the Treasury. . . .

SEC. 9. Any bank incorporated by special law of any State, or organized under the general laws of any State or of the United States, may make application to the reserve bank organization committee, pending organization, and thereafter to the Federal Reserve Board for the right to subscribe to the stock of the Federal reserve bank organized or to be organized within the Federal reserve district where the applicant is located. . . .

SEC. 10. A Federal Reserve Board is hereby created which shall consist of seven members, including the Secretary of the Treasury and the Comptroller of the Currency, who shall be members ex officio, and five members appointed by the President of the United States, by and with the advice and consent of the Senate. In selecting the five appointive members of the Federal Reserve Board, not more than one of whom shall be selected from any one Federal reserve district, the President shall have due regard to a fair representation of the different commercial, industrial and geographical divisions of the country. The five members of the Federal Reserve Board appointed by the President and confirmed as aforesaid shall devote their entire time to the business of the Federal Reserve Board. . . .

The members of said board, the Secretary of the Treasury, the Assistant Secretaries of the Treasury, and the Comptroller of the Currency shall be ineligible during the time they are in office and for two years thereafter to hold any office, position, or employment in any member bank. Of the five members thus appointed by the President at least two shall be persons experienced in banking or finance. One shall be designated by the President to serve for two, one for four, one for six, one for eight, and one for ten years, and thereafter each member so appointed shall serve for a term of ten years unless sooner removed for cause by the President. Of the five persons thus appointed, one shall be designated by the President as governor and one as vice governor of the Federal Reserve Board. The governor of the Federal Reserve Board, subject to its supervision, shall be the active executive officer. . . .

SEC. 11. The Federal Reserve Board shall be authorized and empowered:

(a) To examine at its discretion the accounts, books and affairs of each Federal reserve bank and of each member bank and to require such statements and reports as it may deem necessary. The said board shall publish once each week a statement showing the condition of each Federal reserve bank and a consolidated statement for all Federal reserve banks. . . .

(b) To permit, or, on the affirmative vote of at least five members of the Reserve Board to require Federal reserve banks to rediscount the discounted paper of other Federal reserve banks at rates of interest to be fixed by the Federal Reserve Board.

(c) To suspend for a period not exceeding thirty days, and from time to time to renew such suspension for periods not exceeding fifteen days, any reserve requirement specified in this Act. . . .

(e) To add to the number of cities classified as reserve and central reserve cities under existing law in which national banking associations are subject to the reserve requirements set forth in section twenty of this Act; or to reclassify existing reserve and central reserve cities or to terminate their designation as such. . . .

(j) To exercise general supervision over said Federal reserve banks.

(k) To grant by special permit to national banks applying therefor, when not in contravention of State or local law, the right to act as trustee, executor, administrator, or registrar of stocks and bonds under such rules and regulations as the said board may prescribe. . . .

SEC. 12. There is hereby created a Federal Advisory Council, which shall consist of as many members as there are Federal reserve districts. Each Federal reserve bank by its board of directors shall annually select from its own Federal reserve district one member of said council. . . . The meetings of said advisory council shall be held at Washington . . . at least four times each year, and oftener if called by the Federal Reserve Board. . . .

The Federal Advisory Council shall have power, by itself or through its officers, (1) to confer directly with the Federal Reserve Board on general business conditions; (2) to make oral or written representations concerning matters within the jurisdiction of said board; (3) to call for information and to make recommendations in regard to discount rates, rediscount business, note issues, reserve conditions in the various districts, the purchase and sale of gold or securities by reserve banks, open-market operations by said banks, and the general affairs of the reserve banking system.

SEC. 13. Any Federal reserve bank may receive from any of its member banks, and from the United States, deposits of current funds in lawful money, national-bank notes, Federal reserve notes, or checks and drafts upon solvent member banks, payable upon presentation; or, solely for exchange purposes, may receive from other

Federal reserve banks deposits of current funds in lawful money, national-bank notes, or checks and drafts upon solvent member or other Federal reserve banks, payable upon presentation.

Upon the indorsement of any of its member banks, with a waiver of demand, notice and protest by such bank, any Federal reserve bank may discount notes, drafts, and bills of exchange arising out of actual commercial transactions; that is, notes, drafts, and bills of exchange issued or drawn for agricultural, industrial, or commercial purposes, or the proceeds of which have been used, or are to be used, for such purposes, the Federal Reserve Board to have the right to determine or define the character of the paper thus eligible for discount, within the meaning of this Act....

Any Federal reserve bank may discount acceptances which are based on the importation or exportation of goods and which have a maturity at time of discount of not more than three months, and indorsed by at least one member bank. The amount of acceptances so discounted shall at no time exceed one-half the paid-up capital stock and surplus of the bank for which the rediscounts are made.

The aggregate of such notes and bills bearing the signature or indorsement of any one person, company, firm, or corporation rediscounted for any one bank shall at no time exceed ten per centum of the unimpaired capital and surplus of said bank; but this restriction shall not apply to the discount of bills of exchange drawn in good faith against actually existing values....

SEC. 14. Any Federal reserve bank may, under rules and regulations prescribed by the Federal Reserve Board, purchase and sell in the open market, at home or abroad, either from or to domestic or foreign banks, firms, corporations, or individuals, cable transfers and bankers' acceptances and bills of exchange of the kinds and maturities by this Act made eligible for rediscount, with or without the indorsement of a member bank.

Every Federal reserve bank shall have power:

(a) To deal in gold coin and bullion at home or abroad, to make loans thereon, exchange Federal reserve notes for gold, gold coin, or gold certificates, and to contract for loans of gold coin or bullion, giving therefor, when necessary, acceptable security, including the hypothecation of United States bonds or other securities which Federal reserve banks are authorized to hold;

(b) To buy and sell, at home or abroad, bonds and notes of the United States, and bills, notes, revenue bonds, and warrants with a maturity from date of purchase of not exceeding six months, issued in anticipation of the collection of taxes or in anticipation of the receipt of assured revenues by any State, county, district, political subdivision, or municipality in the continental United States, including irrigation, drainage and reclamation districts....

(c) To purchase from member banks and to sell, with or without its indorsement, bills of exchange arising out of commercial transactions, as hereinbefore defined;

(d) To establish from time to time, subject to review and determination of the Federal Reserve Board, rates of discount to be charged by the Federal reserve bank for each class of paper, which shall be fixed with a view of accommodating commerce and business;

(e) To establish accounts with other Federal reserve banks for exchange purposes and, with the consent of the Federal Reserve Board, to open and maintain banking accounts in foreign countries, appoint correspondents, and establish agencies in such countries wheresoever it may deem best for the purpose of purchasing, selling, and collecting bills of exchange, and to buy and sell with or without its indorsement, through such correspondents or agencies, bills of exchange arising out of actual commercial transactions which have not more than ninety days to run and which bear the signature of two or more responsible parties.

SEC. 15. The moneys held in the general fund of the Treasury, except the five per centum fund for the redemption of outstanding national-bank notes and the funds provided in this Act for the redemption of Federal reserve notes may, upon the direction of the Secretary of the Treasury, be deposited in Federal reserve banks, which banks, when required by the Secretary of the Treasury, shall act as fiscal agents of the United States; and the revenues of the Government or any part thereof may be deposited in such banks, and disbursements may be made by checks drawn against such deposits.

No public funds of the Philippine Islands, or of the postal savings, or any Government funds, shall be deposited in the continental United States in any bank not belonging to the system established by this Act. . . .

SEC. 16. Federal reserve notes, to be issued at the discretion of the Federal Reserve Board for the purpose of making advances to Federal reserve banks through the Federal reserve agents as hereinafter set forth and for no other purpose, are hereby authorized. The said notes shall be obligations of the United States and shall be receivable by all national and member banks and Federal reserve banks and for all taxes, customs, and other public dues They shall be redeemed in gold on demand at the Treasury Department of the United States, in the city of Washington . . . . or in gold or lawful money at any Federal reserve bank.

Any Federal reserve bank may make application to the local Federal reserve agent for such amount of the Federal reserve notes hereinbefore provided for as it may require. Such application shall be accompanied with a tender to the local Federal reserve agent of collateral in amount equal to the sum of the Federal reserve notes thus applied for and issued pursuant to such application. The collateral security thus offered shall be notes and bills, accepted for rediscount under the provisions of section thirteen of this Act. . . .

Every Federal reserve bank shall maintain reserves in gold or lawful money of not less than thirty-five per centum against its deposits and reserves in gold of not less than forty per centum against its Federal reserve notes in actual circulation, and not offset by gold or lawful money deposited with the Federal reserve agent. . . .

SEC. 24. Any national banking association not situated in a central reserve city may make loans secured by improved and unencumbered farm land, situated within its Federal reserve district, but no such loan shall be made for a longer time than five years, nor for an amount exceeding fifty per centum of the actual value of the property offered as security. . . .

The Federal Reserve Board shall have power from time to time to add to the list of cities in which national banks shall not be permitted to make loans secured upon real estate in the manner described in this section.

SEC. 25. Any national banking association possessing a capital and surplus of $1,000,000 or more may file application with the Federal Reserve Board . . . for the purpose of securing authority to establish branches in foreign countries or dependencies of the United States for the furtherance of the foreign commerce of the United States, and to act, if required to do so, as fiscal agents of the United States. . . . The Federal Reserve Board shall have power to approve or to reject such application if, in its judgment, the amount of capital proposed to be set aside for the conduct of foreign business is inadequate, or if for other reasons the granting of such application is deemed inexpedient. . . .

Approved, December 23, 1913

GLOSSARY

discounting/rediscounting: selling loans (commercial paper, acceptances, etc) at a price based on the interest payable and length of time until mandatory payment

elastic currency: a system in which the amount of currency in circulation can be increased, or decreased, by acts of a governmental entity, i.e. in the US the Federal Reserve

reserve agent: bank eligible to hold federal funds

Document Analysis

The purpose of the Federal Reserve Act, portions of which are reproduced here, is "to provide for the establishment of Federal Reserve banks, to furnish an elastic currency, to afford means of rediscounting commercial paper [that is, allowing banks to convert assets in the form of short-term loans to businesses into money], to establish a more effective supervision of banking in the United States, and for other purposes." To that end, the act created a Reserve Bank Organization Committee consisting of the Secretary of the Treasury, the Secretary of Agriculture, and the Comptroller of the Currency. The committee's job was to establish what would become the nation's twelve Federal Reserve banks, each representing a Federal Reserve district. Each of these banks, in turn, would have its own branches, boundaries, and board of directors.

Essentially, all nationally chartered banks are required to become members of the Federal Reserve System, to purchase stock in their regional Federal Reserve bank, and to set aside reserve currency in that regional bank. (In 1913, because many mistrusted federal power, it was technically possible not to agree to be a part of the Federal Reserve System. However, this was not a realistic option due to several clauses which would prevent non-member banks from participating in normal banking practices.) In turn, every member bank is entitled to certain services, in particular, access to discounted loans. State-chartered banks are allowed, but not required, to purchase stock in the Federal Reserve Bank in its region.

Supervising the system is the Federal Reserve Board, later renamed the Board of Governors of the Federal Reserve System. One of the changes demanded by the Senate, and put into the law, was to lengthen the term of the five appointed members of the Board of Governors to ten years, while the two ex-officio members (Secretary of the Treasury and the Comptroller) would normally serve much shorter terms. (The Board has since changed to a membership of seven appointed members, each serving a fourteen year term, with no ex-officio members. Thus all Board members are now appointed by the president, with Senate confirmation.) The longer terms were demanded, so that normally no president can appoint all the members of the Board. A different bill, which had been introduced in 1912, had proposed that one large board, dominated by banking representatives, be in charge of a new nationwide federal banking agency. However, Glass proposed that the day-to-day operations of the Federal Reserve Bank be given to numerous regional banks, as a way to limit its power and the influence of New York banking interests. During the debate, as many as twenty regional banks were proposed, but a range of eight to twelve appears in the legislation. There are twelve regional banks, as has been the case since the law was implemented in 1914. While the national Board of Governors plays an important role in creating policy, the twelve regional banks handle the operations which allows the modern banking system to exist.

Most of the Federal Reserve Board's powers are enumerated in Section 11. However, tucked into the list of operations which the regional banks undertake, in Section 14 (d), is a short clause, which is the basis for much of the power the Fed has for the implementation of monetary policy. Each regional bank can set "rates of discount" for various classes of loans which it makes to the member banks. As a way to keep some order within the banking industry, these rates are "subject to review and determination" by the national Board. Thus although it sounds like each of the twelve banks sets its own rates, actually, the Fed Rate, determined by the Board of Governors, is the rate used by all twelve banks. Raising and lowering the interest rates on the various types of loans that the regional banks administer, is a key monetary policy tool used to moderate inflationary or deflationary pressures on the economy.

A key provision of the Federal Reserve Act is contained in Section 13:

Any Federal reserve bank may receive from any of its member banks, and from the United States, deposits of current funds in lawful money, national-bank notes, Federal reserve notes, or checks and drafts upon solvent member banks, payable upon presentation; or, solely for exchange purposes, any federal reserve bank may receive from other Federal reserve banks deposits, payable upon presentation, of current funds in lawful money, national-bank notes, or checks and drafts upon solvent member or other Federal reserve banks.

This provision ensures that the system is in fact a *system*, one that permits the free flow of money and credit; promotes stable employment, prices, and interest rates; and moderates the effects of boom-and-bust cycles and seasonal fluctuations in the nation's economy. Keeping liquidity in the financial system is an important aspect of the Fed's responsibilities, although not one which it can totally control. This was exemplified by major liquidity problems within the financial system during 2007–2008, which created the largest recession since the 1930s. In addition to the interest rate power noted above, this section and Section 14 (b) give the Fed additional powers to combat adverse financial cycles through buying, or selling, government or corporate securities. Thus in the period after 2007, the Fed lowered interest rates and purchased private and governmental securities (loans) in two coordinated efforts to revive the economy. The powers granted in this act, and in later legislation, play an important role as the Fed attempts to moderate financial problems when they arise.

Perhaps the one provision of the Federal Reserve Act that is most noticeable to members of the public is the Federal Reserve's authority to issued Federal Reserve notes—the paper currency people carry in their wallets—as legal tender. Section 16 states that "the said notes shall be obligations of the United States and shall be receivable by all national and member banks and Federal Reserve Banks and for all taxes, customs, and other public dues." At the time, each Federal Reserve Bank was required to maintain "reserves in gold of not less than forty per centum against its Federal reserve notes in actual circulation." Indeed, the world's largest stash of gold is located not in Fort Knox, but in a vault beneath the Federal Reserve Bank of New York. This practice continues, even though currency is no longer officially backed by gold or silver, and thus no longer redeemable for precious metals from the government. The requirement in Section 16 that each regional bank hold gold deposits valued at forty percent of the money in circulation in that region has been repealed.

As initially established, the Federal Reserve System had very close ties to the Department of the Treasury. The Secretary of the Treasury was an ex officio voting member of the Board. That is no longer the case. When the United States government received taxes and other income, it was normally deposited in one of the regional banks. The question as to whether the Federal Reserve was, or should be, under partial, or full, control of the Department of the Treasury was debated until 1951 when an agreement was reached that made it clear that the Federal Reserve was a fully independent entity.

Section 12 was included in the bill to make it more acceptable to the banking industry. As conceived by the bill's authors, the Federal Advisory Council is to represent banking interests to the Federal Reserve Boards and Federal Reserve Banks. Although it has no specific powers, it does have the right to communicate directly with the leaders of the Fed as regards issues which are affecting the banking and financial industries. The truth of the phrase "knowledge is power," is assumed in this situation. Those legislators supporting the inclusion of Section

12 in the bill believed that by being able to raise issues and their interpretations of the facts in such a way, the Federal Reserve would make decisions more favorable to the Federal Advisory Council, i.e., bankers and financiers.

Essential Themes

The Federal Reserve Act was a major step toward ending the financial panics that had plagued the United States during the previous five decades. Although the new law could not end all financial panics, it did give the government more tools and authority to deal with the situation. With a national banking system and an agency which could implement monetary policy, semi-independent of political concerns, the Federal Reserve Board (Board of Governors) could have a major effect upon American lives and financial institutions.

Since the end of the Second National Bank in 1836, there had been no true national banking system. The National Banking Act of 1863 had been a major step toward unifying the American financial system, through the push toward a nationally backed currency issued by federally chartered banks. However, as noted above, after the Civil War the economy became very cyclical, with devastating recessions and depressions. With the implementation of the Federal Reserve Act, a system was developed for the smooth movement of funds from one bank to another, as well as a secure place for banks to deposit part of their funds.

More importantly, the Federal Reserve Act gave the Fed the ability to undertake monetary policy in times of crisis, or in times leading up to a crisis. It was challenged quickly by World War I, when trade and financial transactions with Europe were greatly affected. In 1923, when a financial recession threatened, Fed leaders implemented a policy which enabled the country to get back on track. (The person leading this effort had died in 1928, and the Fed did little when signs of a financial collapse began to appear in 1929.) Over the decades since then, the Fed has been given additional powers, but the basic powers of setting discount rates for various loans and the ability to buy and sell government securities are the foundation for monetary policy.

The manner in which the Federal Reserve System was established, with an independent Board of Governors appointed for very long terms, has taken it out of political struggles in the nation's capital. While the appointment of a new Board member every two years does happen within the context of presidential and Congressional politics, with fourteen-year terms, these appointments do not happen often enough to greatly affect the daily operations of the Fed. As happened several times in the period following the 2007 financial meltdown, political leaders harshly criticized Fed leaders and policies, but this did not seem to affect the steps the Fed was taking to, in their opinion, help strengthen the American economy. In retrospect, this seems to be the type of system which was desired when the Federal Reserve Act was passed in 1913.

—*Michael J. O'Neal, PhD and Donald A. Watt, PhD*

Bibliography and Additional Reading

Lowenstein, Roger. *America's Bank: The Epic Struggle to Create the Federal Reserve.* New York: Penguin Press, 2015.

Meltzer, Allan H. *A History of the Federal Reserve: Volume 1: 1913-1951.* Chicago: University of Chicago Press, 2004.

Owen, Robert L. *The Federal Reserve Act: Its Origin and Principles.* (Self-Published 1919) Richmond: Federal Reserve Bank of Richmond, 2013. Web 12 August 2016.

Staff of the Federal Reserve Bank of Kansas City. "Federal Reserve Act Signed by President Wilson." *Federal Reserve History.* Richmond: Federal Reserve Bank of Richmond, 2013. Web. 12 August 2016.

Todd, Tim. *Confidence Restored: The History of the Tenth District's Federal Reserve Bank*. Kansas City: Public Affairs Department of the Federal Reserve Bank of Kansas City, 2008.

Wicker, Elmus. *Great Debate on Banking Reform: Nelson Aldrich and the Origins of the Fed*. Columbus: Ohio State University Press, 2005.

Sixteenth Amendment to the U.S. Constitution

Date: 1913
Authors: Norris Brown, Cordell Hull
Genre: law

Summary Overview

Written by Senator Norris Brown of Nebraska and Representative Cordell Hull of Tennessee, the Sixteenth Amendment to the U.S. Constitution, empowering the federal government to levy an income tax, was adopted in February 1913. After the Supreme Court declared the Wilson-Gorman Tariff Act unconstitutional in 1895, many felt that some sort of tax on income was necessary in order for government revenue to keep pace with the high cost of living. Nearly fifteen years passed before another income tax was proposed and accepted in Congress. Senator Brown, especially, wanted the income tax to be adopted as a constitutional amendment. Written in July 1909, the income tax amendment was not fully ratified by the required three-fourths majority of the states until February 1913. The amendment was signed into effect by Secretary of State Philander C. Knox on February 25, 1913. After the amendment was ratified, an income tax bill officially became law on October 3, 1913.

Defining Moment

The 1913 federal income tax amendment came about as a result of the 1895 court case *Pollock v. Farmers' Loan and Trust Co.* When the Civil War started in 1861, Congress initiated an income tax as a way to help pay for wartime expenses. Going into effect in 1862, this first income tax applied only to incomes over $800 and began at a flat rate of 3 percent; incomes greater than $10,000 were later taxed at 5 percent. Although it was proposed simply as a temporary emergency measure to raise money during the war, this tax remained in effect until 1872. In 1894 Congress instituted another income tax, the first established during peacetime, with the Wilson-Gorman Tariff Act. President Grover Cleveland refused to sign the document, but it was passed by both the House and Senate.

A year later, Charles Pollock, a Farmers' Loan and Trust shareholder from Massachusetts, sued to prevent the Farmers' Loan and Trust Company from having to pay the tax. According to the Constitution, Congress was allowed to institute a direct tax only if it was levied proportionally to the populations of each state. The Supreme Court determined that the Wilson-Gorman tax on income derived from property was a direct tax levied disproportionally and so declared the act unconstitutional.

Author Biography

Senator Norris Brown, a Republican from Nebraska, was born in Maquoketa, Iowa, on May 2, 1863. After finishing law school at the University of Iowa in 1883, he was admitted to the bar the following year. Brown practiced law in Iowa before moving to Nebraska in 1888. From 1892 to 1896 he was the attorney for Buffalo County, Nebraska. He practiced law in Nebraska for a number of years before serving as the state attorney general from 1904 to 1906. In 1906 Brown was elected to the U.S. Senate, where he would serve until 1913. In 1909, in response to several income tax proposals, Senator Brown introduced a bill that would add an amendment to the Constitution allowing for a federal income tax. After his first term, Brown failed to gain reelection for a second. Leaving Congress in 1913, he returned home to Nebraska, where he practiced law until 1942, when he retired and moved to Seattle, Washington. He remained there until his death on January 5, 1960.

Representative Cordell Hull was born in Pickett County, Tennessee, to William and Elizabeth Hull on October 2, 1871. Hull graduated from the Cumberland University School of Law in 1891. When he became old enough, he ran for the state legislature and was elected to the Tennessee House of Representatives from 1893 to 1897; he then left that office to serve in the Spanish-American War. When he returned, Hull was appointed a judge before being elected to the U.S. House of Representatives. He served on the Ways and Means Committee for eighteen of his twenty-two years in the House. In addition to helping draft the Sixteenth Amendment, Hull wrote the Revenue Act of 1916. Elected a U.S. senator in 1931, Hull resigned his position when President Franklin D. Roosevelt appointed him secretary of state in March 1933. In that office, Hull was a leading proponent of international trade agreements and low tariffs. He served as secretary of state until his retirement in December 1944 due to health problems. In 1945 Hull received the Nobel Peace Prize for his role in creating the United Nations. He continued to live in Washington, D.C., until his death on July 23, 1955.

HISTORICAL DOCUMENT: Sixteenth Amendment to the U.S. Constitution

Sixty-first Congress of the United States of America, At the First Session,

Begun and held at the City of Washington on Monday, the fifteenth day of March, one thousand nine hundred and nine.

Joint Resolution

Proposing an amendment to the Constitution of the United States.

Resolved by the Senate and House of Representatives of the United States of America in Congress assembled (two-thirds of each House concurring therein), That the following article is proposed as an amendment to the Constitution of the United States, which, when ratified by the legislature of three-fourths of the several States, shall be valid to all intents and purposes as a part of the Constitution:

"ARTICLE XVI. The Congress shall have power to lay and collect taxes on incomes, from whatever source derived, without apportionment among the several States, and without regard to any census or enumeration."

> **GLOSSARY**
>
> **apportionment:** the proportional distribution of the number of members of the U.S. House of Representatives on the basis of the population of each state
>
> **census:** an official count of the population, with details as to age, sex, occupation, and so forth
>
> **enumeration:** the act of determining the number of; counting or listing one by one
>
> **lay:** to impose as a burden, duty, penalty, or the like

Document Analysis

One of the shortest constitutional amendments, the Sixteenth Amendment consists of just one sentence. The amendment may seem to have instituted the federal income tax; on the contrary, the text therein simply gives Congress the power to impose an income tax. The Sixteenth Amendment specifies that the tax does not have to be allotted according to a state's population, which the Constitution would otherwise require of such a direct tax. The amendment also specifies that income from any source, no matter where, would be subject to the tax.

Following the Supreme Court's ruling, many presidential candidates began to include the income tax on their platforms, and President Theodore Roosevelt advocated for a graduated income tax in 1906. President William Howard Taft, on the other hand, did not see the need for a constitutional amendment for federal income tax, although he did ultimately call a special session of Congress in March 1909 to discuss the issue of a new tariff bill. Democrats and progressive Republicans in the Senate proved resolute in their goal to add an income tax rider to the tariff reform bill. Senators Joseph Bailey and Albert Cummins joined forces in introducing a bill to tax income over $5,000.

Nonetheless, Senator Norris Brown of Nebraska was especially determined to draft a constitutional amendment for the income tax in the hope that such an amendment would result in a Constitution that could not be interpreted two ways. Brown teamed up with Representative Cordell Hull of Tennessee, a member of the House Ways and Means Committee, to draft the amendment. Hull modeled the new tax bill on the defunct 1894 law. After finally being passed in both the Senate and the House in July 1909, the amendment then needed to be approved by a three-fourths majority of the states.

Some people, including Governor Charles Evans Hughes of New York, opposed the amendment because of the inclusion of the phrase "from whatever source derived." To address this concern, Senator Norris Brown remarked, "I am sure I cannot see why, if we are making the taxing of incomes constitutional, we should not tax all incomes regardless of source. It is just as much income if it is derived from National, State, or Municipal securities as it is if derived from railway dividends, interest on corporation boards of any sort, industrial stock dividends, or the profits of ordinary mercantile business" (Ekirch, p. 178). Others in opposition did not want to cede money to the federal government when their own states might need the revenue. Industrialists, like John D. Rockefeller, opposed the tax out of the fear that "wealth must more and more pay the bills" (Ekirch, p. 178). On the other hand, many landowners from the more agricultural regions of the country were in favor of an income tax, fearing that Congress might instead enact a tax on property.

With the election of a new governor, New York ratified the amendment in 1910. The final state needed to ratify the amendment approved it in February 1913, almost four years after the amendment was introduced. With the three-fourths vote from the states to ratify the income tax amendment, Secretary of State Philander C. Knox signed the amendment into effect on February 25, 1913.

Essential Themes

One of the major impacts of the Sixteenth Amendment was that, with an income tax, America would no longer have to rely on tariffs to raise revenue. This fact would prove especially important since the country would enter World War I just a few years later. Indeed, upon America's entry into the war, the need for the income tax was immediately realized, for without it, the financing of the war would have been difficult. In fact, as the historians Baack and Ray contend, "No single element involved with the rapid assumption of economic power by the federal government was more important than the passage of the income tax, the means by which the increasing role of government was financed" (p. 607).

The 1913 tax marked the first time in American history that a tax had been applied so broadly to individuals and corporations alike. By 1916 two cases seeking the abolishment of the tax had made their way to the Supreme Court. In both *Brushaber v. Union Pacific Railroad Co.* and *Stanton v. Baltic Mining Co.*, wealthy stockholders attempted to convince the courts that their companies should not have to pay the tax.

The amendment allowing the federal government to impose an income tax also created more bureaucracy for the institution. Congress apportioned almost one million dollars for the collection of the taxes, and the newly formed Bureau of Internal Revenue—which would eventually be renamed the Internal Revenue Service—had thirty employees responsible for "handl[ing] the letters and telegrams asking about the tax" (Weisman, p. 282). By 1915, the Bureau of Internal Revenue employed more than 350 tax collectors.

—*Nicole Mitchell, PhD*

Bibliography and Additional Reading

Adams, Charles. *Those Dirty Rotten Taxes: The Tax Revolts That Built America*. New York: Free Press, 1998.

Baack, Bennett D., and Edward John Ray. "Special Interests and the Adoption of the Income Tax in the United States." *Journal of Economic History* 45, no. 3 (September 1985): 607–25.

Blakey, Roy G. "The New Income Tax." *American Economic Review* 4, no. 1 (March 1914): 25–46.

Blakey, Roy G., and Gladys C. Blakey. *The Federal Income Tax*. London: Longmans, Green, 1940.

Bowen, Howard R. "The Personal Income Tax and the Economy." *Annals of the American Academy of Political and Social Science* 266 (November 1949): 117–20.

Brownlee, W. Elliot. *Federal Taxation in America: A Short History*. Washington, DC: Woodrow Wilson Center Press, 1996.

Buenker, John D. "The Ratification of the Federal Income Tax Amendment." *Cato Journal* 1, no. 1 (Spring 1981): 183–223.

Carson, Gerald. *The Golden Egg: The Personal Income Tax—Where It Came From, How It Grew*. Boston: Houghton Mifflin, 1977.

Conable, Jr., Barber B. *Congress and the Income Tax*. Norman: University of Oklahoma Press, 1989.

Ekirch, Arthur A., Jr. "The Sixteenth Amendment: The Historical Background." *Cato Journal* 1, no. 1 (Spring 1981): 161–82.

Garrison, John C. *The New Income Tax Scandal: How Congress Hijacked the Sixteenth Amendment.* Philadelphia: Xlibris, 2005.

Herber, Bernard P. "Federal Income Tax Reform in the United States: How Did It Happen? What Did It Do? Where Do We Go from Here?" *American Journal of Economics and Sociology* 47, no. 4 (October 1988): 391–408.

Higgens-Evenson, R. Rudy. *The Price of Progress: Public Services, Taxation, and the American Corporate State, 1877 to 1929.* Baltimore: Johns Hopkins University Press, 2003.

Hill, Joseph A. "The Income Tax of 1913." *Quarterly Journal of Economics* 28, no. 1 (November 1913): 46–68.

Internal Revenue Service. *Income Taxes, 1862–1962: A History of the Internal Revenue Service.* Washington, DC: Government Printing Office, 1963.

Joseph, Richard J. *The Origins of the American Income Tax: The Revenue Act of 1894 and Its Aftermath.* Syracuse, NY: Syracuse University Press, 2004.

Klein, Joseph J. *Federal Income Taxation.* New York: John Wiley & Sons, 1929.

Langenderfer, Harold Q. *The Federal Income Tax, 1861–1872.* New York: Arno Press, 1980.

Mehrotra, Ajay K. "'More Mighty Than the Waves of the Sea': Toilers, Tariffs, and the Income Tax Movement, 1880–1913." *Labor History* 45, no. 2 (May 2004): 165–98.

Seligman, Edwin R. A. "The Income Tax." *Political Science Quarterly* 9, no. 4 (December 1894): 610–48.

Seligman, Edwin R. A. *The Income Tax: A Study of the History, Theory and Practice of Income Taxation at Home and Abroad.* New York: Macmillan, 1911.

Smiley, Gene, and Richard H. Keehn. "Federal Personal Income Tax Policy in the 1920s." *Journal of Economic History* 55, no. 2 (June 1995): 285–303.

Stanley, Robert. *Dimensions of Law in the Service of Order: Origins of the Federal Income Tax, 1861–1913.* New York: Oxford University Press, 1993.

Swisher, Carl Brent. *American Constitutional Development.* Boston: Houghton Mifflin, 1943.

Waltman, Jerold L. *Political Origins of the U.S. Income Tax.* Jackson: University Press of Mississippi, 1985.

Weisman, Steven R. *The Great Tax Wars: Lincoln to Wilson, the Fierce Battles over Money and Power That Transformed the Nation.* New York: Simon & Schuster, 2002.

Witte, John F. *The Politics and Development of the Federal Income Tax.* Madison: University of Wisconsin Press, 1985.

"The Bosses of the Senate" (1889). *Reformers like the cartoonist Joseph Keppler depicted the Senate as controlled by the giant moneybags, who represented the nation's financial trusts and monopolies.*

Clayton Act

Date: 1914
Author: Representative Henry De Lamar Clayton
Genre: legislation

Summary Overview

The Clayton Antitrust Act both clarified and strengthened the Sherman Antitrust Act of 1890. While the wording of that previous legislation was purposefully vague, the Clayton Act listed practices that were definitely antitrust violations such as interlocking directorates and price discrimination for purchasers. While the legislation was originally intended to protect labor unions from legal injunctions, the final compromise provision that appeared in the final legislation proved essentially unenforceable.

Defining Moment

Woodrow Wilson had run on an antitrust platform during his 1912 election campaign. While some important trusts had been and continued to be broken up using the Sherman Antitrust Act of 1890, a new Congress easily passed new legislation designed to limit the discretion of courts in enforcing antitrust law so that more trusts could be busted. The Clayton Act was passed in late 1914, part of a spate of progressive legislation that Woodrow Wilson inspired at the beginning of his first term. This included the creation of the Federal Trade Commission, which is charged with enforcing the Clayton Act and other antitrust laws.

The prime motivation for the act was disappointment in the way that antitrust laws had been enforced over the previous twenty-five years. In particular, small businesses and farmers had expressed disappointment, frustration, and anger because so many trusts benefited from the government's laissez-faire attitude toward anticompetitive practices at their expense. The primary reason that the previous antitrust law was seldom enforced was that the Supreme Court had created a "rule of reason" to guide its decisions. This, in effect, gave the justices total discretion over how the law would be enforced and their interpretation depended more upon their political philosophy than the public good. By explicitly spelling out what practices were illegal, judicial discretion was supposed to disappear.

Another prime mover behind the passage of the Clayton Act was the labor movement, which wanted relief from having antitrust laws enforced against them. What they got in the bill was an unsatisfying compromise that did little to stop this kind of persecution. In the next fifteen years, courts would hand down more labor injunctions than in the twenty-four years before the bill's passage. Other demands by labor unions and other progressive groups were watered down in the first draft of the bill and later watered down further in the Senate. The initial bill passed the House 275–54, with every Democrat but one voting in favor. The final bill passed the House 244–54 and the Senate by a margin of 35–24.

Author Biography

Henry De Lamar Clayton (1857–1929) was a Democratic Representative from Alabama from 1897 to 1914 when he accepted a federal judgeship in his home state. His father, also named Henry Clayton, was a general in the Confederate army during the Civil War. He is primarily remembered for being the primary sponsor of the Clayton Antitrust Act.

> **HISTORICAL DOCUMENT: Clayton Act**
>
> *An Act to supplement existing laws against unlawful restraints and monopolies, and for other purposes.*
>
> Be it enacted by the Senate and House of Representatives of the United States of America in Congress assembled, That "antitrust laws," as used herein, includes the Act entitled "An Act to protect trade and commerce against unlawful restraints and monopolies," approved July second, eighteen hundred and ninety; sections seventy-three to seventy-seven, inclusive, of an Act entitled "An Act to reduce taxation, to provide revenue for the Government, and for other purposes," of August twenty-seventh, eighteen hundred and ninety-four; an Act entitled "An Act to amend sections seventy-three and seventy-six of the Act of August twenty-seventh, eighteen hundred and ninety-four, entitled 'An Act to reduce taxation, to provide revenue for the Government, and for other purposes,'" approved February twelfth, nineteen hundred and thirteen; and also this Act.
>
> "Commerce," as used herein, means trade or commerce among the several States and with foreign nations, or between the District of Columbia or any Territory of the United States and any State, Territory, or foreign nation, or between any insular possessions or other places under the jurisdiction of the United States, or between any such possession or place and any State or Territory of the United States or the District of Columbia or any foreign nation, or within the District of Columbia or any Territory or any insular possession or other place under the jurisdiction of the United States: Provided, That nothing in this Act contained shall apply to the Philippine Islands.
>
> The word "person" or "persons" wherever used in this Act shall be deemed to include corporations and associations existing under or authorized by the laws of either the United States, the laws of any of the Territories, the laws of any State, or the laws of any foreign country.
>
> Section 2. That it shall be unlawful for any person engaged in commerce, in the course of such commerce, either directly or indirectly to discriminate in price between different purchasers of commodities, which commodities are sold for use, consumption, or resale within the United States or any Territory thereof or the District of Columbia or any insular possession or other place under the jurisdiction of the United States, where the effect of such discrimination may be to substantially lessen competition or tend to create a monopoly in any line of commerce: Provided, That nothing herein contained shall prevent discrimination in price between purchasers of commodities

on account of differences in the grade, quality, or quantity of the commodity sold, or that makes only due allowance for difference in the cost of selling or transportation, or discrimination in price in the same or different communities made in good faith to meet competition: And provided further, That nothing herein contained shall prevent persons engaged in selling goods, wares, or merchandise in commerce from selecting their own customers in bona fide transactions and not in restraint of trade.

Section 3. That it shall be unlawful for any person engaged in commerce, in the course of such commerce, to lease or make a sale or contract for sale of goods, wares, merchandise, machinery, supplies or other commodities, whether patented or unpatented, for use, consumption or resale within the United States or any Territory thereof or the District of Columbia or any insular possession or other place under the jurisdiction of the United States, or fix a price charged therefor, or discount from, or rebate upon, such price, on the condition, agreement or understanding that the lessee or purchaser thereof shall not use or deal in the goods, wares, merchandise, machinery, supplies or other commodities of a competitor or competitors of the lessor or seller, where the effect of such lease, sale, or contract for sale or such condition, agreement or understanding may be to substantially lessen competition or tend to create a monopoly in any line of commerce.

Section 4. That any person who shall be injured in his business or property by reason of anything forbidden in the antitrust laws may sue therefor in any district court of the United States in the district in which the defendant resides or is found or has an agent, without respect to the amount in controversy, and shall recover threefold the damages by him sustained, and the cost of suit, including a reasonable attorney's fee.

Section 5. That a final judgment or decree hereafter rendered in any criminal prosecution or in any suit or proceeding in equity brought by or on behalf of the United States under the antitrust laws to the effect that a defendant has violated said laws shall be prima facie evidence against such defendant in any suit or proceeding brought by any other party against such defendant under said laws as to all matters respecting which said judgment or decree would be an estoppel as between the parties thereto: Provided, This section shall not apply to consent judgments or decrees entered before any testimony has been taken: Provided further, This section shall not apply to consent judgments or decrees rendered in criminal proceedings or suits in equity, now pending, in which the taking of testimony has been commenced but has not been concluded, provided such judgments or decrees are rendered before any further testimony is taken.

Whenever any suit or proceeding in equity or criminal prosecution is instituted by the United States to prevent, restrain or punish violations of any of the antitrust laws, the running of the statute of limitations in respect of each and every private right of action arising under said laws and based in whole or in part on any matter complained of in said suit or proceeding shall be suspended during the pendency thereof.

Section 6. That the labor of a human being is not a commodity or article of commerce. Nothing contained in the antitrust laws shall be construed to forbid the existence and operation of labor, agricultural, or horticultural organizations, instituted for the purposes of mutual help, and not having capital stock or conducted for profit, or to forbid or restrain individual members of such organizations from lawfully carrying out the legitimate objects thereof; nor shall such organizations, or the members thereof, be held or construed to be illegal combinations or conspiracies in restraint of trade, under the antitrust laws.

Section 7. That no corporation engaged in commerce shall acquire, directly or indirectly, the whole or any part of the stock or other share capital of another corporation engaged also in commerce, where the effect of such acquisition may be to substantially lessen competition between the corporation whose stock is so acquired and the corporation making the acquisition, or to restrain such commerce in any section or community, or tend to create a monopoly of any line of commerce.

No corporation shall acquire, directly or indirectly, the whole or any part of the stock or other share capital of two or more corporations engaged in commerce where the effect of such acquisition; or the use of such stock by the voting or granting of proxies or otherwise, may be to substantially lessen competition between such corporations, or any of them, whose stock or other share capital is so acquired, or to restrain such commerce in any section or community, or tend to create a monopoly of any line of commerce.

This section shall not apply to corporations purchasing such stock solely for investment and not using the same by voting or otherwise to bring about, or in attempting to bring about, the substantial lessening of competition. Nor shall anything contained in this section prevent a corporation engaged in commerce from causing the formation of subsidiary corporations for the actual carrying on of their immediate lawful business, or the natural and legitimate branches or extensions thereof, or from owning and holding all or a part of the stock of such subsidiary corporations, when the effect of such formation is not to substantially lessen competition.

Nor shall anything herein contained be construed to prohibit any common carrier subject to the laws to regulate commerce from aiding in the construction of branches or short lines so located as to become feeders to the main line of the company so aiding in such construction or from acquiring or owning all or any part of the stock of such branch lines, nor to prevent any such common carrier from acquiring and owning all or any part of the stock of a branch or short line constructed by an independent company where there is no substantial competition between the company owning the branch line so constructed and the company owning the main line acquiring the property or an interest therein, nor to prevent such common carrier from extending any of its lines through the medium of the acquisition of stock or otherwise of any other such common carrier where there is no substantial competition between the company extending its lines and the company whose stock, property, or an interest therein is so acquired.

Nothing contained in this section shall be held to affect or impair any right heretofore legally acquired: Provided, That nothing in this section shall be held or construed to authorize or make lawful anything heretofore prohibited or made illegal by the antitrust laws, nor to exempt any person from the penal provisions thereof or the civil remedies therein provided.

Section 8. That from and after two years from the date of the approval of this Act no person shall at the same time be a director or other officer or employee of more than one bank, banking association or trust company, organized or operating under the laws of the United States, either of which has deposits, capital, surplus, and undivided profits aggregating more than $5,000,000; and no private banker or person who is a director in any bank or trust company, organized and operating under the laws of a State, having deposits, capital, surplus, and undivided profits aggregating more than $5,000,000 shall be eligible to be a director in any bank or banking association organized or operating under the laws of the United States. The eligibility of a director, officer, or employee under the foregoing provisions shall be determined by the average amount of deposits, capital, surplus, and undivided profits as shown in the official statements of such bank, banking association, or trust company filed as provided by law during the fiscal year next preceding the date set for the annual election of directors, and when a director, officer, or employee has been elected or selected in accordance with the provisions of this Act it shall be lawful for him to continue as such for one year thereafter under said election or employment.

No bank, banking association or trust company, organized or operating under the laws of the United States, in any city or incorporated town or village of more than two hundred thousand inhabitants, as shown by the last preceding decennial census of the United States, shall have as a director or other officer or employee any private banker or any director or other officer or employee of any other bank, banking association, or trust company located in the same place: Provided, That nothing in this section shall apply to mutual savings banks not having a capital stock represented by shares: Provided further, That a director or other officer or employee of such bank, banking association, or trust company may be a director or other officer or employee of not more than one other bank or trust company organized under the laws of the United States or any State where the entire capital stock of one is owned by stockholders in the other: And provided further, That nothing contained in this section shall forbid a director of class A of a Federal reserve bank, as defined in the Federal Reserve Act, from being an officer or director or both an officer and director in one member bank.

That from and after two years from the date of the approval of this Act no person at the same time shall be a director in any two or more corporations, any one of which has capital, surplus, and undivided profits aggregating more than $1,000,000, engaged in whole or in part in commerce, other than banks, banking associations, trust companies and common carriers subject to the Act to regulate commerce, approved February fourth, eighteen hundred and eighty seven, if such corporations are or shall have been theretofore, by virtue of their business and location of operation, competitors, so that the elimination of competition by agreement between them would constitute a violation of any of the provisions of any of the antitrust laws. The eligibility of a director under the foregoing provision shall be determined by the aggregate amount of the capital, surplus, and undivided profits, exclusive of dividends declared but not paid to stockholders, at the end of the fiscal year of said corporation next preceding the election of directors, and when a director has been elected in accordance with the provisions of this Act it shall be lawful for him to continue as such for one year thereafter.

When any person elected or chosen as a director or officer or selected as an employee of any bank or other corporation subject to the provisions of this Act is eligible at the time of his election or selection to act for such bank or other corporation in such capacity his eligibility to act in such capacity shall not be affected and he shall not become or be deemed amenable to any of the provisions hereof by reason of any change in the affairs of such bank or other corporation from whatsoever cause, whether specifically excepted by any of the provisions hereof or not, until the expiration of one year from the date of his election or employment.

Section 9. Every president, director, officer or manager of any firm, association or corporation engaged in commerce as a common carrier, who embezzles, steals, abstracts or willfully misapplies, or willfully permits to be misapplied, any of the moneys, funds, credits, securities, property or assets of such firm, association or corporation, arising or accruing from, or used in, such commerce, in whole or in part, or willfully or knowingly converts the same to his own use or to the use of another, shall be deemed guilty of a felony and upon conviction shall be fined not less than $500 or confined in the penitentiary not less than one year nor more than ten years, or both, in the discretion of the court.

Prosecutions hereunder may be in the district court of the United States for the district wherein the offense may have been committed.

That nothing in this section shall be held to take away or impair the jurisdiction of the courts of the several States under the laws thereof; and a judgment of conviction or acquittal on the merits under the laws of any State shall be a bar to any prosecution hereunder for the same act or acts.

Section 10. That after two years from the approval of this Act no common carrier engaged in commerce shall have any dealings in securities, supplies or other articles of commerce, or shall make or have any contracts for construction or maintenance of any kind, to the amount of more than $50,000, in the aggregate, in any one year, with another corporation, firm, partnership or association when the said common carrier shall have upon its board of directors or as its president, manager or as its purchasing or selling officer, or agent in the particular transaction, any person who is at the same time a director, manager, or purchasing or selling officer of, or who has any substantial interest in, such other corporation, firm, partnership or association, unless and except such purchases shall be made from, or such dealings shall be with, the bidder whose bid is the most favorable to such common carrier, to be ascertained by competitive bidding under regulations to be proscribed by rule or otherwise by the Interstate Commerce Commission. No bid shall be received unless the name and address of the bidder or the names and addresses of the officers, directors and general managers thereof, if the bidder be a corporation, or of the members, if it be a partnership or firm, be given with the bid.

Any person who shall, directly or indirectly, do or attempt to do anything to prevent anyone from bidding or shall do any act to prevent free and fair competition among the bidders or those desiring to bid shall be punished as prescribed in this section in the case of an officer or director.

Every such common carrier having any such transactions or making any such purchases shall within thirty days after making the same file with the Interstate Commerce Commission a full and detailed statement of the transaction showing the manner of the competitive bidding, who were the bidders, and the names and addresses of the directors and officers of the corporations and the members of the firm or partnership bidding; and whenever the said commission shall, after investigation or hearing, have reason to believe that the law has been violated in and about the said purchases or transactions it shall transmit all papers and documents and its own views or findings regarding the transaction to the Attorney General.

If any common carrier shall violate this section it shall be fined not exceeding $25,000; and every such director, agent, manager or officer thereof who shall have knowingly voted for or directed the act constituting such violation or who shall have aided or abetted in such violation shall be deemed guilty of a misdemeanor and shall be fined not exceeding $5,000, or confined in jail not exceeding one year, or both, in the discretion of the court.

Section 11. That authority to enforce compliance with sections two, three, seven and eight of this Act by the persons respectively subject thereto is hereby vested: in the Interstate Commerce Commission where applicable to common carriers, in the Federal Reserve Board where applicable to banks, banking associations and trust companies, and in the Federal Trade Commission where applicable to all other character of commerce, to be exercised as follows:

Whenever the commission or board vested with jurisdiction thereof shall have reason to believe that any person is violating or has violated any of the provisions of sections two, three, seven and eight of this Act, it shall issue and serve upon such person a complaint stating its charges in that respect, and containing a notice of a hearing upon a day and at a place therein fixed at least thirty days after the service of said complaint. The person so complained of shall have the right to appear at the place and time so fixed and show cause why an order should not be entered by the commission or board requiring such person to cease and desist from the violation of the law so charged in said complaint. Any person may make application, and upon good cause shown may be allowed by the commission or board, to intervene and appear in said proceeding by counsel or in person. The testimony in any such proceeding shall be reduced to writing and filed in the office of the commission or board. If upon such hearing the commission or board, as the case may be, shall be of the opinion that any of the provisions of said sections have been or are being violated, it shall make a report in writing in which it shall state its findings as to the facts, and shall issue and cause to be served on such person an order requiring such person to cease and desist from such violations, and divest itself of the stock held or rid itself of the directors chosen contrary to the provisions of sections seven and eight of this Act, if any there be, in the manner and within the time fixed by said order. Until a transcript of the record in such hearing shall have been filed in a circuit court of appeals of the United States, as hereinafter provided, the commission or board may at any time, upon such notice and in such manner as it shall deem proper, modify or set aside, in whole or in part, any report or any order made or issued by it under this section.

If such person fails or neglects to obey such order of the commission or board while the same is in effect, the commission or board may apply to the circuit court of appeals of the United States, within any circuit where the violation complained of was or is being committed or where such person resides or carries on business, for the enforcement of its order, and shall certify and file with its application a transcript of the entire record in the proceeding, including all the testimony taken and the report and order of the commission or board. Upon such filing of the application and transcript the court shall cause notice thereof to be served upon such person and thereupon shall have jurisdiction of the proceeding and of the question determined therein, and shall have power to make and enter upon the pleadings, testimony, and proceedings set forth in such transcript a decree affirming, modifying, or setting aside the order of the commission or board. The findings of the commission or board as to the facts, if supported by testimony, shall be conclusive. If either party shall apply to the court for leave to adduce additional evidence, and shall show to the satisfaction of the court that such additional evidence is material and that there were reasonable grounds for the failure to adduce such evidence in the proceeding before the commission or board, the court may order such additional evidence to be taken before the commission or board and to be adduced upon the hearing in such manner and upon such terms and conditions as to the court may seem proper. The commission or board may modify its findings as to the facts, or make new findings, by reason of the additional evidence so taken, and it shall file such modified or new findings, which, if supported by testimony, shall be conclusive, and its recommendation, if any, for the modification or setting aside of its original order, with the return of such additional evidence. The judgment and decree of the court shall be final, except that the same shall be subject to review by the Supreme Court upon certiorari as provided in section two hundred and forty of the Judicial Code.

Any party required by such order of the commission or board to cease and desist from a violation charged may obtain a review of such order in said circuit court of appeals by filing in the court a written petition praying that the order of the commission or board be set aside. A copy of such petition shall be forthwith served upon the commission or board, and thereupon the commission or board forthwith shall certify and file in the court a transcript of the record as hereinbefore provided. Upon the filing of the transcript the court shall have the same jurisdiction to affirm, set aside, or modify the order of the commission or board as in the case of an application by the commission or board for the enforcement of its order, and the findings of the commission or board as to the facts, if supported by testimony, shall in like manner be conclusive.

The jurisdiction of the circuit court of appeals of the United States to enforce, set aside, or modify orders of the commission or board shall be exclusive.

Such proceedings in the circuit court of appeals shall be given precedence over other cases pending therein, and shall be in every way expedited. No order of the commission or board or the judgment of the court to enforce the same shall in any wise relieve or absolve any person from any liability under the antitrust Acts.

Complaints, orders, and other processes of the commission or board under this section may be served by anyone duly authorized by the commission or board, either (a) by delivering a copy thereof to the person to be served, or to a member of the partnership to be served, or to the president, secretary, or other executive officer or a director of the corporation to be served; or (b) by leaving a copy thereof at the principal office or place of business of such person; or (c) by registering and mailing a Copy thereof addressed to such person at his principal office or place of business. The verified return by the person so serving said complaint, order, or other process setting forth the manner of said service shall be proof of the same, and the return post-office receipt for said complaint, order, or other process registered and mailed as aforesaid shall be proof of the service of the same.

Section 12. That any suit, action, or proceeding under the antitrust laws against a corporation may be brought not only in the judicial district whereof it is an inhabitant, but also in any district wherein it may be found or transacts business; and all process in such cases may be served in the district of which it is an inhabitant, or wherever it may be found.

Section 13. That in any suit, action, or proceeding brought by or on behalf of the United States subpoenas for witnesses who are required to attend a court of the United States in any judicial district in any case, civil or criminal, arising under the antitrust laws may run into any other district: Provided, That in civil cases no writ of subpoena shall issue for witnesses living out of the district in which the court is held at a greater distance than one hundred miles from the place of holding the same without the permission of the trial court being first had upon proper application and cause shown.

Section 14. That whenever a corporation shall violate any of the penal provisions of the antitrust laws, such violation shall be deemed to be also that of the individual directors, officers, or agents of such corporation who shall have authorized, ordered, or done any of the acts constituting in whole or in part such violation, and such violation shall be deemed a misdemeanor and upon conviction therefor of any such director, officer, or agent he shall be punished by a fine of not exceeding $5,000 or by imprisonment for not exceeding one year, or by both, in the discretion of the court.

Section 15. That the several district courts of the United States are hereby invested with jurisdiction to prevent and restrain violations of this Act, and it shall be the duty of the several district attorneys of the United States, in their respective districts, under the direction of the Attorney General, to institute proceedings in equity to prevent. and restrain such violations. Such proceedings may be by way of petition setting forth the case and praying that such violation shall be enjoined or otherwise prohibited. When the parties complained of shall have been duly notified of such petition, the court shall proceed, as soon as may be, to the hearing and determination of the case; and pending such petition, and before final decree, the court may at any time make such temporary restraining order or prohibition as shall be deemed just in the premises. Whenever it shall appear to the court before which any such proceeding may be pending that the ends of justice require that other parties should be brought before the court, the court may cause them to be summoned, whether they reside in the district in which the court is held or not, and subpoenas to that end may be served in any district by the marshal thereof.

Section 16. That any person, firm, corporation, or association shall be entitled to sue for and have injunctive relief, in any court of the United States having jurisdiction over the parties, against threatened loss or damage by a violation of the antitrust laws, including sections two, three, seven and eight of this Act, when and under the same conditions and principles as injunctive relief against threatened conduct that will cause loss or damage is granted by courts of equity, under the rules governing such proceeding's, and upon the execution of proper bond against damages for an injunction improvidently granted and a showing that the danger of irreparable loss or damage is immediate, a preliminary injunction may issue: Provided, That nothing herein contained shall be construed to entitle any person, firm, corporation, or association, except the United States, to bring suit in equity for injunctive relief against any common carrier subject to the provisions of the Act to regulate commerce, approved February fourth, eighteen hundred and eighty-seven, in respect of any matter subject to the regulation, supervision. or other jurisdiction of the Interstate Commerce Commission.

Section 17. That no preliminary injunction shall be issued without notice to the opposite party.

No temporary restraining order shall be granted without notice to the opposite party unless it shall clearly appear from specific facts shown by affidavit or by the verified bill that immediate and irreparable injury, loss, or damage will result to the applicant before notice can be served and a hearing had thereon. Every such temporary restraining order shall be indorsed with the date and hour of issuance, shall be forthwith filed in the clerk's office and entered of record, shall define the injury and state why it is irreparable and why the order was granted without notice, and shall by its terms expire within such time after entry, not to exceed ten days, as the court or judge may fix, unless within the time so fixed the order is extended for a like period for good cause shown, and the reasons for such extension shall be entered of record. In case a temporary restraining order shall be granted without notice in the contingency specified, the matter of the issuance of a preliminary injunction shall be set down for a hearing at the earliest possible time and shall take precedence of all matters except older matters of the same character; and when the same comes up for hearing the party obtaining the temporary restraining order shall proceed with the application for a preliminary injunction, and if he does not do so the court shall dissolve the temporary restraining order. Upon two days' notice to the party obtaining such temporary restraining order the opposite party may appear and move the dissolution or modification of the order, and in that event the court or judge shall proceed to hear and determine the motion as expeditiously as the ends of justice may require.

Section two hundred and sixty-three of an Act entitled "An Act to codify, revise, and amend the laws relating to the judiciary," approved March third, nineteen hundred and eleven, is hereby repealed.

Nothing in this section contained shall be deemed to alter, repeal, or amend section two hundred and sixty-six of an Act entitled "An Act to codify, revise, and amend the laws relating to the judiciary," approved March third, nineteen hundred and eleven.

Section 18. That, except as otherwise provided in section 16 of this Act, no restraining order or interlocutory order of injunction shall issue, except upon the giving of security by the applicant in such sum as the court or judge may deem proper, conditioned upon the payment of such costs and damages as may be incurred or suffered by any party who may be found to have been wrongfully enjoined or restrained thereby.

Section 19. That every order of injunction or restraining order shall set forth the reasons for the issuance of the same, shall be specific in terms, and shall describe in reasonable detail, and not by reference to the bill of complaint or other document, the act or acts sought to be restrained, and shall be binding only upon the parties to the suit, their officers, agents, servants, employees, and attorneys, or those in active concert or participating with them, and who shall, by personal service or otherwise, have received actual notice of the same.

Section 20. That no restraining order or injunction shall be granted by any court of the United States, or a judge or the judges thereof, in any case between an employer and employees, or between employers and employees, or between employees, or between persons employed and persons seeking employment, involving, or growing out of, a dispute concerning terms or conditions of employment, unless necessary to prevent irreparable injury to property, or to a property right, of the party making the application, for which injury there is no adequate remedy at law, and such property or property right must be described with particularity in the application, which must be in writing and sworn to by the applicant or by his agent or attorney.

And no such restraining order or injunction shall prohibit any person or persons, whether singly or in concert, from terminating any relation of employment, or from ceasing to perform any work or labor, or from recommending, advising, or persuading others by peaceful means so to do; or from attending at any place where any such person or persons may lawfully be, for the purpose of peacefully obtaining or communicating information, or from peacefully persuading any person to work or to abstain from working; or from ceasing to patronize or to employ any party to such dispute, or from recommending, advising, or persuading others by peaceful and lawful means so to do; or from paying or giving to, or withholding from, any person engaged in such dispute, any strike benefits or other moneys or things of value; or from peaceably assembling in a lawful manner, and for lawful purposes; or from doing any act or thing which might lawfully be done in the absence of such dispute by any party thereto; nor shall any of the acts specified in this paragraph be considered or held to be violations of any law of the United States.

Section 21. That any person who shall willfully disobey any lawful writ, process, order, rule, decree, or command of any district court of the United States or any court of the District of Columbia by doing any act or thing therein, or thereby forbidden to be done by him, if the act or thing so done by him be of such character as to constitute also a criminal offense under any statute of the United States, or under the laws of any State in which the act was committed, shall be proceeded against for his said contempt as hereinafter provided.

Section 22. That whenever it shall be made to appear to any district court or judge thereof, or to any judge therein sitting, by the return of a proper officer on lawful process, or upon the affidavit of some credible person, or by information filed by any district attorney, that there is reasonable ground to believe that any person has been guilty of such contempt, the court or judge thereof, or any judge therein sitting, may issue a rule requiring the said person so charged to show cause upon a day certain why he should not be punished therefor, which rule, together with a copy of the affidavit or information, shall be served upon the person charged, with sufficient promptness to enable him to prepare for and make return to the order at the time fixed therein. If upon or by such return, in the judgment of the court, the alleged contempt be not sufficiently purged, a trial shall be directed at a time and place fixed by the court: Provided, however, That if the accused, being a natural person, fail or refuse to make return to the rule to show cause, an attachment may issue against his person to compel an answer, and in case of his continued failure or refusal, or if for any reason it be impracticable to dispose of the matter on the return day, he may be required to give reasonable bail for his attendance at the trial and his submission to the final judgment of the court. Where the accused is a body corporate, an attachment for the sequestration of its property may be issued upon like refusal or failure to answer.

In all cases within the purview of this Act such trial may be by the court, or, upon demand of the accused, by a jury; in which latter event the court may impanel a jury from the jurors then in attendance, or the court or the judge thereof in chambers may cause a sufficient number of jurors to be selected and summoned, as provided by law, to attend at the time and place of trial, at which time a jury shall be selected and impaneled as upon a trial for misdemeanor; and such trial shall conform, as near as may be, to the practice in criminal cases prosecuted by indictment or upon information.

If the accused be found guilty, judgment shall be entered accordingly, prescribing the punishment, either by fine or imprisonment, or both, in the discretion of the court. Such fine shall be paid to the United States or to the complainant or other party injured by the act constituting the contempt, or may, where more than one is so damaged, be divided or apportioned among them as the court may direct, but in no case shall the fine to be paid to the United States exceed, in case the accused is a natural person, the sum of $1,000, nor shall such imprisonment exceed the term of six months: Provided, That in any case the court or a judge thereof may, for good cause shown, by affidavit or proof taken in open court or before such judge and filed with the papers in the case, dispense with the rule to show cause, and may issue an attachment for the arrest of the person charged with contempt; in which event such person, when arrested, shall be brought before such court or a judge thereof without unnecessary delay and shall be admitted to bail in a reasonable penalty for his appearance to answer to the charge or for trial for the contempt; and thereafter the proceedings shall be the same as provided herein in case the rule had issued in the first instance.

Section 23. That the evidence taken upon the trial of any persons so accused may be preserved by bill of exceptions, and any judgment of conviction may be reviewed upon writ of error in all respects as now provided by law in criminal cases, and may be affirmed, reversed, or modified as justice may require. Upon the granting of such writ of error, execution of judgment shall be stayed, and the accused, if thereby sentenced to imprisonment, shall be admitted to bail in such reasonable sum as may be required by the court, or by any justice, or any judge of any district court of the United States or any court of the District of Columbia.

Section 24. That nothing herein contained shall be construed to relate to contempts committed in the presence of the court, or so near thereto as to obstruct the administration of justice, nor to contempts committed in disobedience of any lawful writ, process, order, rule, decree or command entered in any suit or action brought or prosecuted in the name of, or on behalf of, the United States, but the same, and all other cases of contempt not specifically embraced within section twenty-one of this Act, may be punished in conformity to the usages at law and in equity now prevailing.

Section 25. That no proceeding for contempt shall be instituted against any person unless begun within one year from the date of the act complained of; nor shall any such proceeding be a bar to any criminal prosecution for the same act or acts; but nothing herein contained shall affect any proceedings in contempt pending at the time of the passage of this Act.

Section 26. If any clause, sentence, paragraph, or part of this Act shall, for any reason, be adjudged by any court of competent jurisdiction to be invalid, such judgment shall not affect, impair, or invalidate the remainder thereof, but shall be confined in its operation to the clause, sentence, paragraph, or part thereof directly involved in the controversy in which such judgment shall have been rendered.

> **GLOSSARY**
>
> **common carrier:** a term for any company that transports goods across state lines; in the context of this law at this time, the term applied primarily to railroads
>
> **estoppel:** a way for court to prevent a party to a case from going back on assertions made during the case
>
> **injunction:** an order from a judge designed to get parties to obey a court ruling or final decision; injunctions were a major concern to trade unions that had experienced judicial harassment during strikes and labor actions of all kinds for decades by the time this law was passed

Document Analysis

Sections 2 and 3 of the Clayton Act deal with price discrimination and anticompetitive no-purchase agreements. These are among the most important sections of the Clayton Act because they deal with two very common practices that had helped make large monopolies possible. Most notably, Section 3 prevents companies from have two different pricing strategies in different communities depending on the amount of competition they face in each. If they undersold a competitor in one community, they have to keep the same price in a different community where the competition is less. While difficult to enforce, this provision suggests the important role that government can play in limiting the potential excesses of capitalism.

Another important section of this law is Section 7, which bans corporations from acquiring "the whole or any part of the stock or other share capital of another corporation engaged also in commerce," if that acquisition leads to "substantially lessen competition." This provision applies specifically to mergers, which actually increased after the passage of the Sherman Act. It also applies to holding companies, which aligned the interests of apparently competing companies through mutual stock ownership. These had been a significant cause of monopolistic behavior and were made substantially worse by the fact, as was the case with Standard Oil, that these incestuous relationships were unknown to the public. Here is an important provision of the law that was enforced at the time and strengthened by subsequent legislation in later years.

Another key change in the Clayton Act from previous antitrust law is in Section 4, which states, "That any person who shall be injured in his business or property by reason of anything forbidden in the antitrust laws may sue" and can "recover threefold the damages by him sustained, and the cost of suit, including a reasonable attorney's fee." Only the government could enforce the Sherman Act, but now anyone who could afford an attorney could make an argument that might bankrupt the aggrieved party. Unfortunately for labor unions, their employers were often keen to use the Clayton Act in this way.

For all the controversy over its labor provisions, the Clayton Act is surprisingly weak on trade union concerns. While the language about human labor not being a commodity was supposed to indemnify labor unions from antitrust prosecution, it was really just a restatement of common law principles. Nevertheless, Samuel Gompers of the American Federation of Labor (AFL) proclaimed that the passage of this law was "Labor's Magna Carta," referring to the famous English document that gave English lords rights in opposition to King John in 1215.

What it did do was declare strikes, boycotts, and the existence of labor unions legal, even if they were still subject to judicial harassment under this legislation. This was a theoretical improvement even though these organizations and practices had a long history by this point in time. The key phrase here is "lawfully carrying out the legitimate objects." The existence of unions became institutionalized, but their actions remained subject to review from a largely hostile judiciary.

Essential Themes

While the Clayton Act persists as a crucial part of American antitrust law, its initial impact proved limited. For example, it contained a provision against interlocking directorates. An interlocking directorate was the practice of businessmen serving on the boards of directors of each other's companies, which made coordinating activities and prices much easier since seemingly competitive companies then contained the same leadership. Congress postponed the enforcement of this provision in the text of the law and eventually dropped it entirely. Since the passage of the Clayton Act, its provisions have been amended many times, making its impact much stronger.

Despite its limitations, the Clayton Act still marked a number of other important symbolic changes in American history. Most notably, the use of the Constitution's Commerce Clause to justify the power to enact this legislation marked an important precedent for the legislation of the late New Deal years. Similarly, it is also marked a major milestone in the courtship of labor unions by the Democratic Party. While other antitrust legislation followed this law, its provisions continue to regulate American commerce today.

—Jonathan Rees, PhD

Bibliography and Additional Reading

Cooper, Jr., John Milton. *Woodrow Wilson: A Biography*. New York: Alfred A. Knopf, 2009.

Dawley, Alan. *Struggles for Justice: Social Responsibility and the Liberal State*. Cambridge, MA: Harvard University Press, 1991.

Link, Arthur S. *Woodrow Wilson and the Progressive Era, 1910–1917*. New York: Harper and Row, 1954.

Painter, Nell Irvin. *Standing at Armageddon: A Grassroots History of the Progressive Era*. New York: W.W. Norton, 2008.

■ A Survey of American War Readiness

Date: December 1917
Author: D. F. Houston
Genre: report

Summary Overview

Agriculture Secretary D. F. Houston wrote his account of the US preparations for war in December 1917. He described, in detail, the systems in place to encourage both civil and military production and came to the conclusion that the United States was better prepared to wage war than the primary belligerents in Europe had been, and they were certainly more efficient. Houston addressed not only industrial production, but agriculture and medical preparations. He also described the governing bodies of these efforts, and how impressed Europeans were at the speed and efficiency of the US mobilization, during which there was a rapid expansion of bureaucracy in the United States as thousands of new agencies were established.

Defining Moment

On April 2, 1917, President Woodrow Wilson requested that Congress approve a declaration of war against Germany. Relations had soured in the first months of 1917, with Germany openly violating its pledge to halt unrestricted submarine warfare and secretly attempting to bring Mexico into the war on the German side. Within the week, war was declared by both houses of Congress.

The United States was publicly committed to the principle of neutrality from 1914 to 1917, but had come very close to war with Germany several times. In his report, Houston pointed to several changes made before the war that allowed for greater stability and readiness when it was finally declared. First, the Federal Reserve Act of 1913 established a central bank to promote economic stability. In addition, committees were set up to manage advances in shipping, aviation, manufacturing, transportation, munitions, and labor before the declaration of war.

Despite contemplating war for years, the actual mobilization project was a daunting one. The war came during the Progressive Era, at a time when social progress and the efficiency of political systems were idealized. One of the first acts of Congress after the declaration of war was the establishment of over five thousand new bureaucratic agencies, which were estimated to bring jobs to over half a million people.

The government also decided to enact a draft, or conscription law, rather than rely on an all-volunteer army. The Selective Service Act of 1917 was carefully crafted to deal with many of the negative aspects of the Civil War draft, still in the memory of many Americans. The Selective Service Act allowed exemptions for dependency, essential occupations, and religious reasons, and established a "liability for military service of all male citizens"; from twenty-one to thirty years of age (later, it was expanded to include ages eighteen to forty-five). The act also prohibited substitutions, one of the most contentious elements of the Civil War draft, as well as bounties or the purchase of exemptions. Numbers were drawn in a national lottery, and local boards administered how exemptions were handled. During the two years of American involvement in the war, twenty-four million men were registered for military service, and nearly 2.8 million served.

On August 10, 1917, President Woodrow Wilson created the US Food Administration. This administration, headed by Herbert Hoover, would be responsible for the supply, distribution, and conservation of food during the war and would oversee food transportation systems and enforce government control of food supplies. Hoover's plan was to encourage food production and fair distribution through primarily voluntary methods—to this end, he did not accept pay while in the post, as he felt it gave him the moral authority to ask the American people to sacrifice as well. The administration declared that "food would win the war." Homeowners pledged to conserve food, and Americans embraced national conservation efforts, experimenting with novel foods not considered crucial to the war effort. They grew "victory gardens" and pledged not to eat between meals. Even President Wilson grazed sheep on the White House lawn. In addition to voluntary conservation, Hoover also set wheat prices and organized wheat distribution. As production grew, exports rose, and by 1918, the United States exported grain products, meat, and sugar at around three times the prewar rate.

Despite a willing public and deep investment by the government, there were serious delays in some aspects of mobilization. The coal crisis of 1917 was a failure of transportation and distribution, as coal was being mined in sufficient quantities, but could not get to its destination. There were national coal shortages. The government finally took steps to nationalize the railway system and enforce priority coal access.

Author Biography

David Franklin Houston was born in North Carolina in 1866. He received a master's degree in political science from Harvard University in 1892 and began a career as a university professor and administrator. After a decade of successive university teaching and administrative posts, Houston was appointed by President Woodrow Wilson to the position of US secretary of agriculture from 1913 to 1920. Houston also served as the US treasury secretary from 1920 to 1921. He died in 1940.

HISTORICAL DOCUMENT: A Survey of American War Readiness

The first great step toward winning this war was taken when the President of the United States, on April 2nd, in advising Congress to declare the existence of a state of war with Germany, pointed out what war would involve and demand.

The striking thing about that historic address was not so much the advice it contained, momentous as that was, but rather the clear perception it revealed of the magnitude of the task before the nation.

The response of Congress was prompt and adequate. It authorized and directed the President to employ the entire military and naval forces of the Union and pledged to the government all the resources of the nation to bring the conflict to a successful termination.

The task of making good this pledge was entered upon and discharged in such manner as to startle many at home and to amaze even foreigners who had become habituated to prodigious operations.

I well remember some characteristic remarks of Lord Northcliffe during his visit to Washington. Suddenly stopping and turning to me, he said, "Am I dreaming?"

I asserted that he did not look like a dreamer.

He continued: "I am told that Congress declared war on the sixth of April, authorized the Secretary of the Treasury to borrow approximately eleven and a half billion dollars, enacted a new tax law designed to raise two and a half billions in addition to ordinary revenues, appropriated or authorized nine billions for the army and navy, over a billion for ships, with a maximum authorization of nearly two billions, six hundred and forty millions for aeroplanes, credits to the Allies of seven billions, a total of actual appropriations and authorizations of twenty-one billions, gave power to commandeer plants, ships and materials, provided for conscription, which England had not fully resorted to and Canada had not then adopted, that there had been registered or enlisted nearly ten and a half million men, that Pershing was in France and naval vessels were in Europe, that the food-production and food-control measures had been passed, and that authority had been given for the control of exports and imports and of priorities."

He repeated: "Am I dreaming or is it true?"

I replied that unless I was dreaming it was true.

He said: "I can't believe it."

I told him I could believe it but that I could not comprehend it. It is difficult now to do so. The figures even for particular items are beyond comprehension.

Think of them. For ships an authorization of a billion nine hundred millions, nearly double our former federal budget; for aviation, six hundred and forty millions; for torpedo-boat destroyers, three hundred and fifty millions; for army subsistence and regular quartermaster supplies, eight hundred and sixty millions; for clothing and camp and garrison equipment, five hundred and eighty-one millions; for transportation, five hundred and ninety-seven millions; for medicine, one hundred millions; for mobile artillery, one hundred and fifty-eight millions; for ordnance stores and supplies, seven hundred and seventeen millions; for heavy guns, eight hundred and fifty millions; and for ammunition for the same, one billion eight hundred and seven millions.

Clearly Congress for the time being had taken the necessary steps to make good its pledge of placing the resources of the country at the disposal of the government. At the same time, it created or authorized the creation of essential administrative agencies.

In respect to administrative agencies important developments had already taken place. Most striking and significant of all was the enactment of the federal reserve law and the creation of the reserve board and banks.

This action obviously was taken without suspicion that the world was on the verge of war and that we should soon be involved. It was taken to insure better banking conditions in time of peace, and especially to enable us to weather financial storms.

Before the reserve act was passed the nation, as you well know, had no adequate banking system. Its financial arrangements had never been able to withstand strain either in peace or in war. In each of our considerable struggles we had promptly suspended specie payments, with all the attendant disabilities and burdens.

But now, after four years of world financial strain such as no financier dreamed it possible for the world to bear—I might say six years, because there was a worldwide financial chill for at least two years before 1914, due to apprehension of war and to the undoubted financial preparations made by the Central Powers—after this long strain and the shock of the last six months, our finances are sound and we are proceeding in orderly fashion.

For this reason and because of our obligation to extend liberal credits, it is not extravagant to say that no greater contribution to the winning of this war has been or will be made than through the passage of the Federal Reserve Act in 1913 and the successful establishment of the system well in advance of trouble.

Steps toward preparedness in respect to other highly essential interests were taken much before war was declared. Their significance was not grasped by the public at the time. For the most part they have been overlooked.

Pursuant to an Act of Congress of March 3, 1915, two years before the war, the President appointed the National Advisory Committee for Aeronautics, composed of the most eminent students of the subject. In connection with the work of this committee and in part through its labours has been developed our enormous aviation program and expansion.

Likewise, during the summer of 1915, the secretary of the navy organized the admirable Naval Consulting Board with Edison as chairman and two representatives elected by each of eleven great engineering and scientific societies.

Furthermore, on September 7, 1916, after a long and unfortunate delay caused by unintelligent opposition, the Shipping Act was passed, creating a board with large powers, and appropriating fifty million dollars for the construction, purchase, charter, and operation of merchant vessels suitable for naval auxiliaries in time of war. This was the beginning of the present huge shipbuilding program whose speedy execution is of paramount importance.

But that is not all in the way of early preparedness. On August 29, 1916, the Council of National Defense, consisting of six heads of departments and an advisory commission of seven, nominated by the council and appointed by the President, was created.

The council was charged with the duty of mobilizing military and naval resources, studying the location, utilization and coordination of railroads, waterways and highways, increase of domestic production for civil arid military purposes, the furnishing of requisite information to manufacturers, and the creation of relations which would render possible the immediate concentration of national resources.

The creation of the Council of National Defense was not the result of sudden inspiration. It was directly suggested by the activities of two very important groups of individuals.

In March, 1916, a committee from the five great medical and surgical associations, having an aggregate membership of from 70,000 to 100,000, was formed. It met in Chicago on April 14, 1916, and tendered to the President the services of the medical men of the nation.

In March, also, representatives of five engineering organizations with a membership of 35,000 met in New York and formulated a plan to make an inventory of the country's production and manufacturing resources.

The thought and purposes of these two bodies were brought to the attention of the President, and their consideration resulted in recommendations for the creation of the Council of National Defense.

Thus, a number of months before war was declared, agencies had been created covering at least in outline many of the essential new activities. Seven of these of peculiar importance had begun to find themselves and to chart their course. I refer to the shipping board, the aviation, the medical, the manufacturing, the transportation, the munitions, and the labour committees.

When war came these bodies greatly speeded up their work. Others were created—among them, the Food Administration, the Fuel Administration, the War Trade Council, the War Trade Board, and the War Industries Board.

The last is of unique importance, and yet its work is little understood.

Its members are the direct representatives of the government and of the public interest. The tasks of the board are stupendous. It acts as a clearing-house for the needs of the government, determines the most effective ways of meeting them, the best means of increasing production (including the creation of new facilities), the priority of public needs and also of transportation.

It considers price factors, the labour aspects of industrial operations, and large purchases of commodities where market values are greatly affected, and makes appropriate recommendations to the secretaries of war and the navy.

Judge Lovett is in immediate charge of priorities, Mr. Baruch of raw materials, and Mr. Brookings of finished products. These three constitute a commission for the approval of purchases by the Allies in this country from credits made through the secretary of the treasury.

I need only remind you of the items of the appropriations for supplies, ordnance and other things, to impress you with the magnitude of the board's task. Its machinery is not yet perfect but it is working, and I am sure that no step will be omitted to make it as nearly adequate as possible.

If a better scheme can be devised, it should be promptly adopted. It is obviously of the highest importance that the resources of the nation, made available by Congress, should be administered with the utmost skill and effectiveness.

No machinery is of great value unless it is properly manned. The right sort of men is the first requisite of any kind of successful enterprise. I believe this requisite has been satisfied and that the nation is mobilizing for this emergency additional men of as high character and fine talent as it possesses.

Where so many are involved special mention is invidious, and I cite the names of the following merely as samples: Willard, Gompers, Baruch, Rosenwald, Coffin, Martin, and Godfrey; Hoover, Garfield, Vanderlip, Davison, Vauclain; McCormick, Thos. D. Jones, Lovett, Brookings, and Frayne; Dr. Anna Shaw, Mrs. Phillip Moore, Mrs. Cowles, Mrs. Catt, Miss Wetmore, Mrs. Lamar, Mrs. Funk, Mrs. McCormick, and Miss Nestor; and Drs. Simpson, Crile, Janeway, Flexner, Vaughn, Mayo, and Welch—all fine types of American citizenship, only a few of the hundreds working in their respective spheres in the nation and in the states, having no selfish end to serve, working with an eye single to the public interest and to the winning of this war, giving freely their services in as fine spirit as the nation ever witnessed, revealing the real strength of democracy.

So much, and perhaps more than enough, as to the congressional pledge of resources and the creation of machinery. Let us turn to other matters which I am sure you have in mind. I know you are asking what is being accomplished.

What are the results? Obviously, some of them it would be inadvisable to indicate. Others I can only hint at. For the most part they have been detailed to the public through one agency or another from time to time. I shall try to summarize.

The nation has today in all branches of its military services under arms and in training over 1,800,000 men, some in France, some on the ocean, and others in camps or at their posts of duty at home.

Approximately ten and a half millions of men have been enlisted in the regular army, incorporated in the national guard, or registered under the draft act. Those registered but not yet called out are being classified on the basis of national need.

Rapid headway has been made in training subordinate officers, and the gigantic undertaking of providing suitable quarters or camps for the men in training has practically been finished. The nation now has thirty-five army cantonments, sixteen for the National Army, sixteen for the National Guard, two at points of embarkation and one for the quartermaster's training school, all complete in respect to buildings or tents, lighting, sanitary arrangements, and temporary roads.

The National Army cantonments were completed within the time set by the General Staff. What this involved can not easily be set forth. It entailed the selection of sites, the planning of buildings, the securing of responsible contractors, the mobilization of labour, the assembling of materials, and the construction of modern hospitals and roads.

These camps alone cover 150,000 acres and called for the use of 75,000 carloads of materials, including 500,000,000 feet of lumber. Their cost was approximately one hundred and twenty-eight millions of dollars. The work was begun June 15th and the finishing touches were put on by December 1st.

In addition sixteen canvas camps for the National Guard were completed at a cost of approximately forty-eight millions of dollars. Thus local habitations were quickly provided for the new army, superior in respect to ventilation and conveniences to the best practice of Europe.

Five instrumentalities or factors highly necessary for victory, it may be asserted without hesitation, are destroyers, the enemies of the submarine, airplanes, ships, medical service, and food. What of these?

Of the first, the torpedo-boat destroyers, all I may say is that the construction program of the navy contemplates 787 ships of all types at an estimated cost of $1,150,000,000, including additional destroyers costing $350,000,000.

The latter are to be of uniform standard model, large and fast. Some are to be built within nine months, and all within eighteen months. This vast and urgent undertaking required a great extension of building facilities, and, as private capital was unable or unwilling to make the extensions, the government had to do so.

When completed these plants belong to the nation. I may add that these destroyers will require thousands of men to man them. The men are being trained and when the vessels are completed the crews will be ready.

The work for the control of the air grows apace. Of the great aviation training fields, seventeen in number, two are old, one is rebuilding, seven were practically completed by September 1st, and seven others will be finished within two weeks.

In addition, there are in operation today at leading universities ten ground schools giving preparatory instruction in flying. Finishing courses are being given to our students in most of the Allied countries and more than thirty experienced foreign air veterans have been loaned to us for duty in Washington and elsewhere.

The building program calls for twenty thousand machines. It will be expedited by reason of a great and interesting achievement, that of a standardized engine, something which no European nation has developed even after three and a half years of war.

This accomplishment is in line with the best American traditions, and was made with unique speed. What standardization of the engine and of its parts means in respect to speed and quantitative production, in repairs and economy of materials, need not be dwelt upon.

It has been estimated that the service when in full strength will require a full force of 110,000 officers and enlisted men, an army greater than our regular military force of a few months ago.

All agree that the enemy submarine must be destroyed. In the meantime shipping sunk by them must be replaced. England must not be starved. Supplies to all the Allies must go forward without interruption.

Our own troops must be transported and provided with everything essential for effectiveness and comfort, and domestic transportation of men and commodities must be maintained and greatly increased.

Furthermore, commodities must be brought here from many distant places. Therefore we must have ships, more ships, at once. Nothing more urgent!

How is this matter proceeding? In the first place, the Shipping Board on August 3rd commandeered 426 vessels either in course of construction for domestic or foreign account or contracted for, with a tonnage of over 3,000,000.

Thirty-three of these ships, with a tonnage of 257,000, have been completed and released. German and Austrian ships with a capacity of 750,000 tons have been taken over for government use.

The Fleet Corporation has contracted for 948 vessels with a total tonnage of 5,056,000, of which 375, with a tonnage of one and a third million, are wooden; 58, with a tonnage of 270,000, are composite; and 515, with a capacity of 3,500,000, are steel.

All these ships have an aggregate tonnage of 8,835,000, or nearly a million and a half tons more than the regular merchant marine of the nation in 1916. Contracts for 610,000 tons additional are pending.

The total building program calls for over 10,000,000 tons, and it is proposed that a considerable part of it shall be executed by the end of 1918. The nature of this task may be more easily appreciated when it is remembered that the construction in the United States for 1916 did not exceed 400,000 tons and that the average for the five years preceding was 350,000 tons.

At present there are one hundred yards building ships, exclusive of twenty building the commandeered vessels, and of these one hundred, seventy are new. The policy of standardization has been pursued and five classes of ships have been adopted.

I have already referred to the preliminary steps toward medical organization. Further action was promptly taken. An inventory was made of the medical resources of the nation, of doctors, nurses, and others who could be called by the surgeon general, and of hospitals and supplies.

Courses in modern military medicine and surgery for third and fourth-year students were formulated and adopted by seventy-five of the ninety-five medical schools in January, 1917.

It was known that eighty per cent of the instruments used in this country were made in Germany. It was necessary to develop their production here, and to facilitate this the first essential step was to introduce standardization, to resort to staple articles.

More liberal standards were authorized and the variety of types was greatly reduced. Instead of scores of kinds of scissors a dozen were agreed upon. Instead of many sorts of needles, forceps and retractors, two, three, or four types were adopted.

Manufacturers were given priority of materials and consequently full military orders will be delivered in less than eight months. It is illuminating that one concern, taking its chances, had manufactured according to specifications, by the time it was awarded a contract, enough material to require ten carloads of lumber for packing. This was the result of the efforts of seventy-five of the most eminent medical specialists of the nation, working with the military staff in contact with two hundred and fifty leading manufacturers.

The peace strength of the medical forces of the army was 531 and of the navy 480. Now the surgeon general of the army has in his regular force and in the new enrolment of physicians actually accepting commissions 16,432, a number sufficient for an army of two and one-third millions, and a dental force of 3,441, adequate for an army of 3,400,000.

The navy now has 1,795 medical officers, a number in excess of present needs. The Red Cross has enrolled 15,000 trained nurses, organized forty-eight base hospitals with 9,600 doctors, nurses and enlisted men, sixteen hospital units with smaller staffs to supplement the work of the base hospitals, is furnishing supplies to thirty-five hospitals of all sorts in France, and since May has raised over $100,000,000.

What shall I say about the organization of agriculture for the production of food, clothing and other materials? It is unnecessary to dwell upon the need of an adequate supply of food for the civilians and soldiers of this nation and also for those of the nations with whom we are associated.

When we entered the war, this country was and had been facing an unsatisfactory situation in respect to its supply of foods and feedstuffs. The production in 1916 of the leading cereals was comparatively low, aggregating 4.8 billions of bushels as against 6 for 1915, 5 for 1914, and 4.9 for the five-year average.

The wheat crop had been strikingly small, and it was certain that on account of adverse weather conditions the output for 1917 would be greatly curtailed. The situation was no better in respect to other conspicuously important commodities such as potatoes and meats.

The need of action was urgent and the appeal for direction insistent. The nation looked for guidance primarily to the federal department and to the state agencies which it had so liberally supported for many years.

It was a matter of great good fortune that the nation had had the foresight, generations before, in another time of national stress, in 1862, to lay soundly the foundations of agriculture. In respect to agencies working for the improvement of rural life the nation was prepared.

In point of efficiency, personnel and support, it had establishments excelling those of any other three nations combined, and a great body of alert farmers who were capable of producing two or three times as much per unit of labour and capital as the farmers of Europe.

Steps were quickly taken to speed up production. In a two-day session at St. Louis, the trained agricultural officers of the country conceived and devised a program of legislation and organization, the essential features of which have not been successfully questioned, and the substantial part of which has been enacted into law and set in operation.

Initiative was not wanting in any section of the Union. Effective organizations quickly sprang up in all the states, and the services of experts everywhere immediately were made available. The response of the farmers was prompt and energetic.

Weather conditions for the spring season were favourable and the results are that crop yields have been large and that the nation is able not only to feed itself but in considerable measure to supply the needs of those with whom we are cooperating.

It is no time for any class to hug to its bosom the delusion that it possesses a monopoly of patriotism. Human nature is pretty evenly distributed, and no little selfishness manifests itself in every direction.

Unfortunately there are self-seekers in every group. I have heard manufacturers solemnly assert that, if the government wished them to speed up their operations, to extend their plants, or to take additional trouble in any direction, it must guarantee to them an abnormally large profit in addition to the requisite allowance for amortization.

One of them recently suggested to me that he was getting weary of the burdens he had assumed and that, if the government wished him to continue or to undertake new tasks, it would have to induce him to do so by permitting him greatly to increase his profits.

What would he or others say of a soldier, of a man drafted into the army, who protested that for so much he would go to the seaboard, but, if the government wished him to go abroad, it must stimulate him with a twenty-five-per cent increase in his pay, or, if he went to the front trenches, with fifty per cent?

In the words of the President: Patriotism has nothing to do with profits in a case like this.

Patriotism and profits ought never in the present circumstances to be mentioned together. It is perfectly proper to discuss profits as a matter of business, but it would be absurd to discuss them as a motive for helping to serve and save our country.

In these days of our supreme trial, when we are sending hundreds of thousands of our young men across the seas to serve a great cause, no true man who stays behind to work for them and sustain them by his labour will ask himself what he is personally going to make out of that labour.

No true patriot will permit himself to take toll of their heroism in money or seek to grow rich by the shedding of their blood.

Document Analysis

Houston's report was a glowing review of the changes made both before and after the US entry into the war and painted a very flattering, but fairly accurate, picture of war preparations and readiness. Houston used the opinion of an outsider, in this case Britain's Alfred Harmsworth, Lord Northcliffe, to highlight the speed and scale of US war preparations. The British had, of course, already been at war for years, so the flabbergasted Lord Northcliffe's reaction, "Am I dreaming?" proved the supremacy of the American war effort. Houston himself found the statistics associated with war preparations "beyond comprehension" and laid out the money that had been allocated for weapons, men, and supplies. He concluded that Congress had made "good its pledge of placing the resources of the country at the disposal of the government" and had also created "essential administrative agencies."

Houston was eager to report on the changes that had been made previous to American involvement in the war. This highlighted how stable and forward-thinking the US government, of which he was a part, had been since even before war broke out. Most important, in his opinion, was the Federal Reserve Act and the creation of a central banking system prior to the start of the war. This, he argued, had allowed the nation's finances to remain sound. Houston described various committees and planning groups that had been at work before the war, including the Council of National Defense, set up on August 29, 1916, which was charged with studying the best ways to mobilize military and industrial resources. In addition, the creation of a shipping board, an aviation board, and medical, manufacturing, transportation, and labor committees in the months before the war led to a smooth transition when war was declared.

Houston was particularly impressed with the work of the War Industries Board, which he described as being of "unique importance," although he also acknowledged that "its machinery is not yet perfect." Houston's report then turned to a catalog of the results of all of this planning, with particular attention paid to the type and tonnage of shipping being manufactured or refitted for war, and the number of military personnel and the provisions made for them. Houston also pointed out that manufacturing standardization had resulted in cost savings and efficiency. He was uniquely positioned to comment on the state of agriculture, and he credited "a great body of alert farmers" with the ability to produce food much more efficiently than their counterparts in Europe.

In closing, Houston made a plea for self-sacrifice and volunteerism, a common theme in speeches of that time. This was not a time to look for profit, he argued. It was a time to work for the good of the country, and it was clear that he felt the country was well positioned to successfully wage war.

Essential Themes

The primary theme of this report is the enormous undertaking that was involved in the preparations for America's entry into World War I. Houston's description of the mobilization effort highlighted the vast scale of the endeavor, and he was particularly impressed with the number of agencies and planning bodies set up to administer the effort.

Houston also emphasized that those who were in a position to benefit financially from the war should act selflessly and with a spirit of volunteerism and patriotism. At a time when the considerable force of American industry was being turned to war production, the possibility for hoarding and profiteering was real. These were anti-patriotic impulses, and Houston stressed that they should be resisted.

—*Bethany Groff, MA*

Bibliography and Additional Reading

Breen, William J. *Uncle Sam at Home: Civilian Mobilization, Wartime Federalism, and the Council of National Defense, 1917–1919.* Westport: Greenwood, 1984. Print.

Coffman, Edward M. *The War to End All Wars: The American Military Experience in World War I.* 1968. Lexington: UP of Kentucky, 1998. Print.

"Teaching With Documents: Sow the Seeds of Victory! Posters from the Food Administration During World War I" *National Archives.* US National Archives and Records Administration, n.d. Web. 15 Jan. 2014.

Tuchman, Barbara. *The Guns of August.* New York: Ballantine, New York, 1962. Print.

From *My Life and Work*, by Henry Ford

Date: 1922
Author: Henry Ford, with collaboration by Samuel Crowther
Genre: autobiography; memoir

Summary Overview

Twenty years after the founding of the Ford Motor Company, Henry Ford had recently acquired total ownership and control. Although rumors had circulated that he was going bankrupt and was out of touch, Ford had demonstrated that he had the financial and personal resources to meet the challenges of the early 1920s. As the most respected business leader of that time, Ford wanted to influence others who sought to become entrepreneurs. In this book, he set forth his philosophy of business and of life. The economy of the United States had been in a short, but significant, recession in 1920–21, and many looked to the future with uncertainty. Ford believed that the principles that had guided him in prior years would serve him well in the years to come. Thus, he and Crowther wrote a book that outlined a foundation to assist in strengthening the American economy and improving all levels of American society.

Defining Moment

Although Ford had been a peace activist prior to 1917, when the United States finally entered the First World War he shifted the company's production lines to help support the war effort. Up to that time, the company had been very successful, with its focus on the production of the Model T. In the first months after the end of the war, Ford and the company prospered, owing to the pent-up demand for automobiles. However, in 1920, when the first general economic recession since the development of the auto industry started, Ford was not well positioned to face it. There were pressures from his creditors, who were uneasy due to rumors that the company was insolvent. Adding to the credit problem was the fact that Ford had borrowed twenty million dollars in 1919 to buy out all the other company owners. With decreasing sales of its Model T, the Ford Motor Company and its owner were thought, by some, to be facing their end.

However, Ford, aided by key executives, transformed the company. They refocused their efforts, doing away with many of the products they had added to help the war effort. The number of administrative positions was greatly decreased. In line with Ford's personal philosophy of caring for his workers, most laid-off office employees were offered jobs in the factory. Resources not necessary for the newly focused company were sold. But the most important change was the development of the first just-in-time production system. Ford could pressure his suppliers to insure on-time delivery. This allowed him to reduce his inventory by more than enough to allow him to pay off all the loans. He also pressured his dealers, resulting in an increased cash flow for the company. Thus, while Ford and the Ford Motor Company had been expected to be eventual failures, instead they were once again seen as the leaders of American industry. As a privately held company, rather than one with shares traded on a major stock exchange, Ford Motor Company differed from other major corporations. Partly because of this, Ford was even more admired by many Americans. It was at this point that Ford, with the assistance of

Crowther, decided to publish what was publicized as an autobiography, but which was in reality more of a philosophical statement. Read not only in America but translated into numerous languages, *My Life and Work* impacted political and economic thought around the world.

Author Biography

Henry Ford (1863–1947) was an American industrial leader of the early twentieth century. Growing up on a farm, he demonstrated an early mechanical aptitude. After being a machinist's apprentice in Detroit, he left to work on portable steam engines, eventually ending up as an engineer for Thomas Edison. In the 1890s, he began developing a quadricycle (automobile). After two failed attempts, in 1902, he, with several partners, formed what became the Ford Motor Company. His most successful car, the Model T, began production in 1908. An excellent engineer and shrewd businessman, he established the moving assembly line, set the forty-hour work week as the norm, and supported a living wage for workers, although he was sternly anti-union. Although Ford was inclusive in his business dealings and treatment of his workforce, he supported an anti-Semitic publication in the 1920s. However, when asked in 1924, he refused to support Germany's Nazi Party.

Samuel Crowther (1880–1947) was a journalist and author. In addition to articles in numerous publications, Crowther wrote, or co-wrote, fifteen books, mainly on business. He collaborated with Henry Ford on four books, this being the first.

HISTORICAL DOCUMENT: From *My Life and Work*

When we talk about improvements usually we have in mind some change in a product. An "improved" product is one that has been changed. That is not my idea. I do not believe in starting to make until I have discovered the best possible thing. This, of course, does not mean that a product should never be changed, but I think that it will be found more economical in the end not even to try to produce an article until you have fully satisfied yourself that utility, design, and material are the best. If your researches do not give you that confidence, then keep right on searching until you find confidence. The place to start manufacturing is with the article. The factory, the organization, the selling, and the financial plans will shape themselves to the article. You will have a cutting edge on your business chisel and in the end you will save time. Rushing into manufacturing without being certain of the product is the unrecognized cause of many business failures. People seem to think that the big thing is the factory or the store or the financial backing or the management. The big thing is the product, and any hurry in getting into fabrication before designs are completed is just so much waste time. I spent twelve years before I had a Model T—which is what is known today as the Ford car—that suited me. We did not attempt to go into real production until we had a real product. That product has not been essentially changed.

We are constantly experimenting with new ideas. If you travel the roads in the neighbourhood of Dearborn you can find all sorts of models of Ford cars. They are experimental cars—they are not new models. I do not believe in letting any good idea get by me, but I will not quickly decide whether an idea is good or bad. If an idea seems good or seems even to have possibilities, I believe in doing whatever is necessary to test out the idea from every angle. But testing out the idea is something very different from making a change in the car. Where most manufacturers find themselves quicker to make a change in the product than in the method of manufacturing—we follow exactly the opposite course.

Our big changes have been in methods of manufacturing. They never stand still. I believe that there is hardly a single operation in the making of our car that is the same as when we made our first car of the present model. That is why we make them so cheaply. The few changes that have been made in the car have been in the direction of convenience in use or where we found that a change in design might give added strength. The materials in the car change as we learn more and more about materials. Also we do not want to be held up in production or have the expense of production increased by any possible shortage in a particular material, so we have for most parts worked out substitute materials. Vanadium steel, for instance, is our principal steel. With it we can get the greatest strength with the least weight, but it would not be good business to let our whole future depend upon being able to get vanadium steel. We have worked out a substitute. All our steels are special, but for every one of them we have at least one, and sometimes several, fully proved and tested substitutes. And so on through all of our materials and likewise with our parts. In the beginning we made very few of our parts and none of our motors. Now we make all our motors and most of our parts because we find it cheaper to do so. But also we aim to make some of every part so that we cannot be caught in any market emergency or be crippled by some outside manufacturer being unable to fill his orders. The prices on glass were run up outrageously high during the war; we are among the largest users of glass in the country. Now we are putting up our own glass factory. If we had devoted all of this energy to making changes in the product we should be nowhere; but by not changing the product we are able to give our energy to the improvement of the making.

The principal part of a chisel is the cutting edge. If there is a single principle on which our business rests it is that. It makes no difference how finely made a chisel is or what splendid steel it has in it or how well it is forged—if it has no cutting edge it is not a chisel. It is just a piece of metal. All of which being translated means that it is what a thing does—not what it is supposed to do—that matters. What is the use of putting a tremendous force behind a blunt chisel if a light blow on a sharp chisel will do the work? The chisel is there to cut, not to be hammered. The hammering is only incidental to the job. So if we want to work why not concentrate on the work and do it in the quickest possible fashion? The cutting edge of merchandising is the point where the product touches the consumer. An unsatisfactory product is one that has a dull cutting edge. A lot of waste effort is needed to put it through. The cutting edge of a factory is the man and the machine on the job. If the man is not right the machine cannot be; if the machine is not right the man cannot be. For any one to be required to use more force than is absolutely necessary for the job in hand is waste.

The essence of my idea then is that waste and greed block the delivery of true service. Both waste and greed are unnecessary. Waste is due largely to not understanding what one does, or being careless in doing of it. Greed is merely a species of nearsightedness. I have striven toward manufacturing with a minimum of waste, both of materials and of human effort, and then toward distribution at a minimum of profit, depending for the total profit upon the volume of distribution. In the process of manufacturing I want to distribute the maximum of wage—that is, the maximum of buying power. Since also this makes for a minimum cost and we sell at a minimum profit, we can distribute a product in consonance with buying power. Thus everyone who is connected with us—either as a manager, worker, or purchaser—is the better for our existence. The institution that we have erected is performing a service. That is the only reason I have for talking about it. The principles of that service are these:

1. An absence of fear of the future and of veneration for the past. One who fears the future, who fears failure, limits his activities. Failure is only the opportunity more intelligently to begin again. There is no disgrace in honest failure; there is disgrace in fearing to fail. What is past is useful only as it suggests ways and means for progress.

2. A disregard of competition. Whoever does a thing best ought to be the one to do it. It is criminal to try to get business away from another man—criminal because one is then trying to lower for personal gain the condition of one's fellow man—to rule by force instead of by intelligence.

3. The putting of service before profit. Without a profit, business cannot extend. There is nothing inherently wrong about making a profit. Well-conducted business enterprise cannot fail to return a profit, but profit must and inevitably will come as a reward for good service. It cannot be the basis—it must be the result of service.

4. Manufacturing is not buying low and selling high. It is the process of buying materials fairly and, with the smallest possible addition of cost, transforming those materials into a consumable product and giving it to the consumer. Gambling, speculating, and sharp dealing, tend only to clog this progression.

GLOSSARY

Dearborn: a city in Michigan, near Detroit, that was Henry Ford's home and his company's headquarters

vanadium steel: steel with the element vanadium added, providing greatly increased strength

Document Analysis

Henry Ford understood that his approach to business was different from that of most other people. Early in the introduction to this book, he stated that his theory of business was really, "a theory that looks toward making this world a better place in which to live." Although Ford did not object to all the money his approach made for him, he claimed that this should not be the sole focus of business. He used the word "service" to encapsulate the essence of what should be one's life's goal. The section of the introduction to *My Life and Work*, which is reprinted above, is the last four pages. After outlining his principles in the introduction, nineteen chapters followed, with each focusing on a different aspect of Ford's business and personal philosophy. Because Ford was not an accomplished writer, Crowther was the one who put the words on paper. While the philosophy of the text was clearly Ford's, much of the phrasing represented Crowther's contribution to the text.

Although an engineer by inclination, Ford was a manufacturer by profession. Thus, he began this passage by focusing on the central aspect of what he did. This was to provide a service to the public, by manufacturing a reliable automobile at a reasonable price. This was the Model T, in production for twenty years, which he had developed twelve years after his first car, the quadricycle. From 1903 to 1908, Ford Motor Company produced eight models prior to the Model T's debut; during most of that period, Ford was not the major shareholder in the company. While these were successful products, none of them met his goal of a car that would be affordable to everyone. Although in the late 1920s, Ford was forced to follow the pattern of slightly changing car designs every model year, he was convinced that this was a wasteful exercise. In his mind, making the manufacturing process more efficient was a better change than slight changes in the product. When this book was written, the Ford Motor Company produced about forty percent of the cars sold in the United States. This allowed it to develop the multiple suppliers necessary to reliably provide essential components to its manufacturing plants.

Given his focus on the manufacturing process, rather than on continually redesigning cars, it is understandable why Ford considered waste a major problem. His adaptation of the assembly line, learned from meat packing plants, was an example of reducing waste in the human effort required, resulting in a lower manufacturing cost. While such efficiency added to his profits, he saw it as a byproduct of good service to the customer. He truly believed that his efforts to streamline the manufacturing process made all people "the better for our existence." While not everyone saw the steps he took to control the manufacturing process as positive for the nation, Ford believed that it allowed him to reduce waste and control costs. Similarly, some thought it was easy for Ford to say that greed was a bad thing, while at the same time, making more money than most people in the country (or any country). While ignoring that aspect of his success, Ford asserts elsewhere in the introduction that it takes strong individual leadership to direct a company; he uses the failing Soviet experiment in running factories by committee as a counter-example.

Four principles, which essentially close the introduction, illustrate some of what set Ford apart from most other businessmen. He advocates pushing for progress, being the best, serving the public, and seeking only a fair return for one's efforts—not extraordinary profits. This is a different mindset from that of most of his contemporaries in industry. While his views distinguished Ford from his competitors, it also allowed him to become a dominant force in the American economic system.

Essential Themes

As with many great men, Henry Ford was a contradiction: a man of his times as well as one far ahead of his times. This book, and related material, was a widely studied treatise on how to conduct business. While Ford could use his economic muscle to force suppliers to do things his way, he could also pay factory workers more than some of his competitors, while selling quality cars at a lower price. Two of the ideas he advocated, and which have had a big impact, were: 1) achieving efficiency by eliminating waste, and 2) what is now known as a "just-in-time" system of manufacturing, or making the next part in the line only when it is needed (as opposed to building up an inventory). By the end of the twentieth century, many did not associate key portions of these innovations with Henry Ford; rather, they were associated with Japanese business practices, especially with Toyota. After World War II, Japanese business leaders were searching for a model that would help them rebound from the war. Toyota executives studied Ford's approach to business and developed their model based partly on his, albeit without as much pressure on their suppliers. Thus, through a circuitous route, what was Ford's unique approach to business in the United States during the early twentieth century has continued to influence American business leaders into the twenty-first.

Ford's focus on an efficient manufacturing system, whether by using the assembly line or by not having a large inventory of components sitting idle in a warehouse, was his major contribution. When *My Life and Work* was written, not only was the United States coming out of an economic recession, but there was great turmoil in the larger world. Both extreme right-wing (i.e., Nazi) and left-wing (i.e., Communist) groups were not only challenging the political structure, they were advocating different economic systems. Ford's response was to promote an economic system he believed served the needs of society as well as his fellow industrialists. For him, this was possible only if wasteful and greedy practices were abandoned. Thus, "service," to use his term, was the key not only to producing a quality product, but to creating a stable foundation for society.

—*Donald A. Watt, PhD*

Bibliography and Additional Reading

Brinkley, Douglas. *Wheels for the World: Henry Ford, His Company, and a Century of Progress*. New York: Viking Adult, 2003. Print.

Ford, Henry, with Samuel Crowther. *My Life and Work*. New York: Garden City Pub. Co., 1922. Google eBook, 14 Sept. 2006. Web. 20 July 2014.

"Henry Ford." *American Experience*. Narr. Oliver Platt. PBS. WGBH, Boston, 15 July 2014. Television.

"The Life of Henry Ford." *The Henry Ford Museum*. Dearborn, MI: The Henry Ford, 2013. Web. 17 Jul. 2014.

Watts, Stephen. *The People's Tycoon: Henry Ford and the American Century*. New York: Vintage Books, 2009. Print.

Stafford Library
Columbia College
1001 Rogers Street
Columbia, MO 65216